Heresy and Inquisition in the Middle Ages
Volume 10

INQUISITION AND KNOWLEDGE
1200–1700

YORK MEDIEVAL PRESS

York Medieval Press is published by the University of York's Centre for Medieval Studies in association with Boydell & Brewer Limited. Our objective is the promotion of innovative scholarship and fresh criticism on medieval culture. We have a special commitment to interdisciplinary study, in line with the Centre's belief that the future of Medieval Studies lies in those areas in which its major constituent disciplines at once inform and challenge each other.

Editorial Board (2022)

Professor Peter Biller, Emeritus (Dept of History): General Editor
Professor T. Ayers (Dept of History of Art): Co-Director, Centre for Medieval Studies
Dr Henry Bainton: Private Scholar
Dr J. W. Binns: Honorary Fellow, Centre for Medieval Studies
Dr K. P. Clarke (Dept of English and Related Literature)
Dr K. F. Giles (Dept of Archaeology)
Dr Shazia Jagot (Dept of English and Related Literature)
Dr Holly James-Maddocks (Dept of English and Related Literature)
Dr Harry Munt (Dept of History)
† Professor W. Mark Ormrod, Emeritus (Dept of History)
Dr L. J. Sackville (Dept of History)
Professor Elizabeth M. Tyler (Dept of English and Related Literature): Co-Director, Centre for Medieval Studies
Dr Hanna Vorholt (Dept of History of Art)
Professor J. G. Wogan-Browne (English Faculty, Fordham University)
Dr Stephanie Wynne-Jones (Dept of Archaeology)

All enquiries of an editorial kind, including suggestions for monographs and essay collections, should be addressed to: The Academic Editor, York Medieval Press, Department of History, University of York, Heslington, York, YO10 5DD (E-mail: pete.biller@york.ac.uk)

Heresy and Inquisition in the Middle Ages

ISSN 2046–8938

Series editors

John H. Arnold, Faculty of History, University of Cambridge
Peter Biller, Department of History, University of York
L. J. Sackville, Department of History, University of York

Heresy had social, cultural and political implications in the middle ages, and countering heresy was often a central component in the development of orthodoxy. This series publishes work on heresy, and the repression of heresy, from late antiquity to the Reformation, including monographs, collections of essays, and editions of texts.

Previous volumes in the series are listed at the back of this volume.

Inquisition and Knowledge
1200–1700

Edited by
Peter Biller and L. J. Sackville

YORK MEDIEVAL PRESS

© Contributors 2022

All rights reserved. Except as permitted under current legislation
no part of this work may be photocopied, stored in a retrieval system,
published, performed in public, adapted, broadcast,
transmitted, recorded or reproduced in any form or by any means,
without the prior permission of the copyright owner

First published 2022
Paperback edition 2024

A York Medieval Press publication
in association with The Boydell Press
an imprint of Boydell & Brewer Ltd
PO Box 9, Woodbridge, Suffolk IP12 3DF, UK
and of Boydell & Brewer Inc.
668 Mt Hope Avenue, Rochester, NY 14620–2731, USA
website: www.boydellandbrewer.com
and with the
Centre for Medieval Studies, University of York
www.york.ac.uk/medieval-studies

ISBN 978-1-914049-03-3 Hardback
ISBN 978-1-914049-25-5 Paperback

A CIP catalogue record for this book is available
from the British Library

The publisher has no responsibility for the continued existence or accuracy of
URLs for external or third-party internet websites referred to in this book, and
does not guarantee that any content on such websites is, or will remain, accurate or
appropriate

Contents

List of Illustrations	vii
List of Contributors	x
Acknowledgements	xi

Introduction   1
Peter Biller and L. J. Sackville

PART I: MEDIEVAL

1   Inquisitorial identity and authority in thirteenth-century exegesis
and sermons: Jean Halgrin d'Abbeville, Jacques de Vitry and
Humbert of Romans   37
Jessalynn Lea Bird

2   Shaping the image of the heretics: The *narratio* in Gregory IX's
letters   57
Alessandro Sala

3   Nepos of Montauban, assistant to inquisition and defender of the
accused   72
Jörg Feuchter

4   The hunt for the Heresy of the Free Spirit: the 1332 enquiry into
the 'Cowled Nuns' of Świdnica   110
Paweł Kras

5   Late medieval heresiography and the categorisation of Eastern
Christianity   135
Irene Bueno

6   The portrayal of the Waldensian Brethren in the *De vita et
conversacione* (c. 1391–3)   157
Appendix: *De vita et conversacione*: edition and translation of the
Weimar Ms   173
Reima Välimäki

7   Means of persuasion in medieval anti-heretical texts: the case of
Petrus Zwicker's *Cum dormirent homines*   178
Adam Poznański

8   Constructing narratives of witchcraft   195
Richard Kieckhefer

Contents

PART II: EARLY MODERN

9   'Ut ex vetustis membranis cognosco': Matthias Flacius Illyricus
and his use of inquisition registers and manuals   211
Harald Bollbuck

10   The 'Cathars as Protestant' myth and the formation of heterodox
identity in the French Wars of Religion   238
Luc Racaut

11   The seventeenth-century introductions to medieval inquisition
records in Bibliothèque nationale de France, Collection Doat
Mss 21–26   255
Shelagh Sneddon

12   History in the Dominican Convent in Toulouse in 1666 and 1668:
Antonin Réginald and Jean de Doat   273
Appendix: Antonin Réginald, *Chronicon inquisitorum*, edition and
translation of excerpts, 1240–1340   295
Peter Biller

13   The Roman Inquisition: between reality and myth   317
Michaela Valente

Index   335

Illustrations

Biller and Sackville, 'Introduction'

Figure 0.1. Philip van Limborch, engraved by Pieter van Gunst from a portrait painted by David van der Plas when Limborch was 61 (*c.* 1694). Private collection.   3

Figure 0.2. The title page of the first edition of John Locke's letter on toleration, *Epistola de Tolerantia* (Gouda, 1689), with the names of the dedicatee, Philip van Limborch, and the author encrypted on the sixth and eighth lines. By permission of the Provost and Scholars of King's College, Cambridge.   4

Figure 0.3. Philip van Limborch, *Historia inquisitionis, cui subjungitur Liber sententiarum Inquisitionis Tholosanæ, ab anno Christi MCCCVII ad annum MCCCXXIII* (Amsterdam, 1692), title page. Private collection.   5

Figure 0.4. Jacques Bénigne Bossuet, bishop of Meaux, engraved by Gérard Edelinck after portrait by Hyacinthe Rigaud. Private collection.   21

Figure 0.5. Jacques Bénigne Bossuet, *Histoire des variations des églises protestantes*, 2 vols. (Paris, 1730), vol. 1, title page. Book 11 in vol. 2 contains his short history of Albigensians, Waldensians, Wycliffites and Hussites, whose 208 marginal notes attest remarkable knowledge of medieval sources. Private collection.   22

Figure 0.6. Bossuet, *Histoire des variations*, vol. 2, p. 113, showing succinct but precise marginal annotation of the account of the origins of the Waldensians. Private collection.   23

Figure 0.7. Peter Allix, *Remarks upon the Ecclesiastical History of the Antient Churches of the Albigenses* (London, 1692), title page. Private collection.   32

Figure 0.8. Allix, *Remarks*, p. 169, with conclusion of a translation of the deposition of William of Marnhac and extracts from a letter written by François Graverol to Pierre Jurieu on the character of the Albigensians. Private collection.   33

Feuchter, 'Nepos of Montauban, assistant to inquisition and defender of the accused'

Figure 3.1. *Liber fugitivus* (Lyon, 1536), title page; Österreichische Nationalbibliothek, Sammlung von Handschriften und alten Drucken, 74.W.161.(3). Once thought to be by Nepos of Montauban, this was written (probably *c.* 1240) by Bagarotus de Coradis and redacted by Nepos *c.* 1268. By permission, Österreichische Nationalbibliothek.   75

Illustrations

Figures 3.2a & 3.2b. Passage from Bagarotus's *Liber fugitivus* together with Nepos's elaborated version of it. Bagarotus: Staatsbibliothek zu Berlin, Ms Lat. Fol., fol. 399r, column a. By permission, Staatsbibliothek zu Berlin, Preußischer Kulturbesitz, Handschriftenabteilung. Nepos: *Liber fugitivus* (Lyon, 1536), fol. XXXVv, column a. By permission, Österreichische Nationalbibliothek. 102

Bueno, 'Late medieval heresiography and the categorisation of Eastern Christianity'

Figure 5.1. Nicholas Eymerich, *Directorium inquisitorum* (Venice, 1607), title page. The pagination is the same as in the Rome 1587 edition used in the chapter. Private collection. 151

Figures 5.2 & 5.3. Eymerich, *Directorium inquisitorum*, pp. 303–4, containing Eymerich's *De erroribus Græcorum* and Francisco Peña's commentary. Private collection. 152–3

Poznański, 'Means of persuasion in medieval anti-heretical texts: the case of Petrus Zwicker's Cum dormirent homines*'*

Figure 7.1. Jakob Gretser, *Lucæ Tudensis episcopi, scriptores aliquot succedanei contra sectam Waldensium* (Ingolstadt, 1613), title page. The major texts edited by Grester were the Anonymous of Passau of *c.*1260–6 and Peter Zwicker's *Cum dormirent homines* of 1395. Private collection. 183

Figure 7.2. Gretser, *Scriptores aliquot succedanei contra sectam Waldensium*, p. 208: Peter Zwicker, *Cum dormirent homines*, chapter 5. Here the treatise was wrongly attributed to Peter of Pillichsdorf. Private collection. 184

Bollbuck, 'Matthias Flacius Illyricus and his use of inquisition registers and manuals'

Figure 9.1. Portrait of Matthias Flacius Illyricus, copper engraving by Theodor de Bry after Tobias Stimmer. Private collection. 210

Figure 9.2. Matthias Flacius Illyricus, *Catalogus testium veritatis* (Basle, 1556), title page, with Flacius's hand-written dedication to his patron Joachim von Alvensleben. ULB Halle [Universitäts-und Landesbibliothek Sachsen-Anhalt, Halle], S: Alv. V 598, formerly in Herzog August Bibliothek, Wolfenbüttel. Reproduced by permission, Herzog August Bibliothek, Wolfenbüttel. http://diglib.hab.de 210

Figure 9.3. *Catalogus testium veritatis* (Basle, 1556), p. 711, which makes use of passages which Flacius marked for use in the manuscript reproduced in figs. 19–20. Reproduced by permission, Herzog August Bibliothek, Wolfenbüttel. http://diglib.hab.de 227

Illustrations

Figures 9.4 & 9.5. Herzog August Bibliothek, Wolfenbüttel, Cod Guelf Helmst 315, fols. 228v and 233v, both showing passages in a manuscript once in Flacius's library, marked by him for use in the *Catalogus*. Reproduced by permission, Herzog August Bibliothek, Wolfenbüttel. http://diglib.hab.de   228–9

Biller, 'History in the Dominican Convent in Toulouse in 1666 and 1668: Antonin Réginald and Jean de Doat'

Figure 12.1. Guillaume Catel, *Histoire des Comtes de Tolose* (Toulouse, 1623), title page. The appendix contained editions of works by Bernard Gui and William of Puylaurens. Private collection.   278

Figure 12.2. Jean-Jacques Percin, *Monumenta Conventus Tolosani* (Toulouse, 1693), title page. Private collection.   285

Figure 12.3. Jean-Jacques Percin, *Monumenta Conventus Tolosani* (Toulouse, 1693), p. 52b. Percin's first extract from Antonin Réginald's *Chronicon*. Private collection.   296

Valente, 'The Roman Inquisition: between reality and myth'

Figure 13.1. Silvestro Mazzolini, *Modus solennis et autenticus, ad inquirendum et inveniendum et convincendum Lutheranos* (Rome, 1553), title page. York Minster Library IX.K.24(2). This was a parody of an inquisitor's manual of procedure, and in reality it was written by Girolamo Massari and printed in Basle. Reproduced by permission of the Chapter of York.   328

The editors, contributors and publisher are grateful to all the institutions and persons listed for permission to reproduce the materials in which they hold copyright. Every effort has been made to trace the copyright holders; apologies are offered for any omission, and the publisher will be pleased to add any necessary acknowledgement in subsequent editions.

Contributors

Peter Biller – University of York
Jessalynn Lea Bird – St Mary's College, Notre Dame
Harald Bollbuck – Akademie der Wissenschaften zu Göttingen
Irene Bueno – Alma Mater Studiorum, Università di Bologna
Jörg Feuchter – Berlin-Brandenburgische Akademie der Wissenschaften
Richard Kieckhefer – Northwestern University, Evanston
Paweł Kras – John Paul II Catholic University of Lublin
Adam Poznański – Wrocław University Library
Luc Racaut – Newcastle University
L. J. Sackville – University of York
Alessandro Sala – Private Scholar, Milan
Shelagh Sneddon – University of York
Michaela Valente – Sapienza Università di Roma
Reima Välimäki – Turku Institute for Advanced Studies, University of Turku

Acknowledgements

This book originates in the Doat Project conference 'Inquisition and Knowledge', which was held at King's Manor, University of York on 9–10 April 2018. It brings together papers delivered on that occasion by Peter Biller, Jessalynn Bird, Irene Bueno, Jörg Feuchter, Richard Kieckhefer, Paweł Kras and Shelagh Sneddon, together with those of Harald Bollbuck and Reima Välimäki, who were not able to attend, and also papers by scholars subsequently invited to contribute, Adam Poznański, Luc Racaut, Alessandro Sala and Michaela Valente.

Gratitude is due to Simon Ditchfield, Andrew Roach, Claire Taylor and Julien Théry-Astruc, and all the other scholars and students who spent those two days in April discussing inquisition, heresy and knowledge; to the Centre for Medieval Studies at King's Manor for hosting the conference and to the Department of History at York for its support; and to the Arts and Humanities Research Council for funding the Doat Project and its conferences. Gratitude is also due to Peter Jones and Anna Cook at the library of King's College, Cambridge, Sarah Griffin and Steven Newman at York Minster Library and Gertrud Oswald at the Österreichische Nationalbibliothek for their help in obtaining photographs; to Christine Gadrat-Ouerfelli and Patrick Ferté for making available copies of their work; to John Arnold, Malcolm Barber, Kate Biller, Stuart Carroll, John Green, Shelagh Sneddon and Rob Wyke for their support and reading of papers; to Nick Bingham, Elizabeth McDonald, Caroline Palmer and others in the team at Boydell & Brewer, and to the copy-editor Sarah Thomas for their help in the production of this book; and finally to the contributors to this volume, for their enthusiasm, patience and scholarship.

P. B. and L. J. S.
York, April 2021

Introduction

Peter Biller and L. J. Sackville

Overture

In the late 1950s a London University student, Margaret Nickson, embarked on postgraduate research on a thirteenth-century Austrian inquisitor's treatise.[1] After completion of her doctorate she got a job in the British Library, which was then located in the British Museum in Great Russell Street. One day she was leafing through one of the library's eighteenth-century catalogues and came across an astonishing entry. As she knew from her postgraduate days, one of the most important of all records of medieval heresy and inquisition was the massive *Liber* (*Book*) containing the sentences delivered in Toulouse between 1308 and 1323 by the inquisitor Bernard Gui. And one of the most famous stories was its fate. Although the manuscript had long since been lost its contents at least had been preserved, thanks to an edition printed in 1692. But what Nickson was reading contradicted the first part of this. The catalogue said the manuscript was in the British Library. She recounted what followed in the British Museum café in the late 1960s.[2] She had run to the Manuscripts Room, quickly filled out an order slip and then counted the minutes. And then there it was, in front of her.

In the article she wrote on the manuscript's history she made particular use of John Locke's correspondence and journal in an account of the book's progress through the 1670s–90s. The protagonists were the Dutch Protestant theologian Philip van Limborch and Locke himself, two good friends who played crucial roles in the production of each other's work. Limborch helped Locke to get the first edition of his *Letter on Toleration* printed in Gouda in 1689. In turn Locke dedicated the *Letter* to Limborch and helped him with

---

[1] Her supervisor was an expert on Eastern European history, with an interest in Jan Hus: R. R. Betts (1903–61); on him, see H. Seton-Watson and J. Hurstfield, 'Professor R. R. Betts', *Slavonic and Eastern European Review* 40 (1961), 1–6. The PhD led to M. A. E. Nickson, 'The "Pseudo-Reinerius" treatise, the final stage of a thirteenth-century work on heresy from the diocese of Passau', *Archives d'histoire doctrinale et littéraire du moyen âge* 34 (1967), 255–314; see n. 58 below.

[2] Conversation with Peter Biller; M. A. E. Nickson, 'Locke and the Inquisitions of Toulouse', *The British Museum Quarterly* 36 (1972), 81–93. Cf. the rediscovery of a manuscript thought lost in L. J. Sackville, 'The *Ordo Processus Narbonensis*: The Earliest Inquisitor's Manual, Lost and Refound', *Aevum* 93 (2019), 363–95.

Gui's manuscript.[3] Locke had known of it for many years and he played a leading role in bringing about what happened: the edition of Gui's *Liber* as an appendix to Limborch's *Historia inquisitionis* in 1692.

The concerns of this book are encapsulated here. In the early fourteenth century Gui's sentences had contained and constructed a certain sort of knowledge about people the Church labelled and persecuted as heretics. Early modern scholarship discovered a text and through printing transmitted it, while also putting it to polemical use in the demonstration of the iniquity of inquisition. One charge was the creation of false knowledge: in his *Historia* Limborch devoted a chapter to detailed analysis of inquisitors' questions which, together with long detention in prison, led to people 'confessing everything, even those things that had never occurred to them in their minds'.[4] Contained in the story of this book there is medieval production of knowledge in texts; early modern transmission of text; and further *re*working and *re*discovery in modern work, which included a new edition in 2002.[5]

York

These concerns are shared widely, as this book shows. Its chapters are written by American, British, Finnish, German, Italian and Polish scholars, working in universities round the world where these topics are studied, written about and taught. At the same time the shape of this book owes something to just one of these locations: York.[6]

In 1976 the Department of History at York bought microfilms of six manuscripts of medieval inquisition records. Comprising six volumes of the so-called Doat collection (described in chapter 11 below) and held in the French national library, these manuscripts were copies made in the 1660s of thirteenth-century records of interrogations from Languedoc.[7] The object was

---

[3] J. Locke, *Epistola de Tolerantia. A Letter on Toleration*, ed. R. Klibansky and J. W. Gough (Oxford, 1968), xvii–xix. Figure 0.2 (on page 4) shows the title page of the first edition, with the names of both Locke and Limborch given in cryptograms.

[4] P. van Limborch, *Historia inquisitionis* (Amsterdam, 1692), p. 276: omnia, etiam quae nunquam ipsis in mentem venerunt.

[5] *Le livre des sentences de l'inquisiteur Bernard Gui, 1308–1323*, ed. A. Pales-Gobilliard, Sources de l'Histoire Médiévale Publiées par l'Institut de Recherche et de l'Histoire des Textes 30, 2 vols. (Paris, 2002).

[6] In Britain many universities became centres through the career of a specialist, such as Malcolm Lambert at Bristol and Bob Moore at Newcastle (and earlier at Sheffield). In some universities there has been a larger cluster or a longer line of specialists: at Nottingham, Bernard Hamilton, Claire Taylor, Rob Lutton and Peter Darby; at Reading, Malcolm Lambert (briefly), Malcolm Barber and Rebecca Rist; and at York, Gordon Leff, Peter Biller, Caterina Bruschi, Shelagh Sneddon and Lucy Sackville. We are grateful to Malcolm Barber, Bob Moore and Claire Taylor for help with this list.

[7] Bibliothèque nationale de France, MSS Collection Doat 21–26.

Figure 0.1 Philip van Limborch, engraved by Pieter van Gunst from a portrait painted by David van der Plas when Limborch was 61 (c. 1694). A friend of John Locke, Limborch helped bring about the printing of the first edition of Locke's letter on toleration in Gouda in 1689. See fig. 0.2. Private collection.

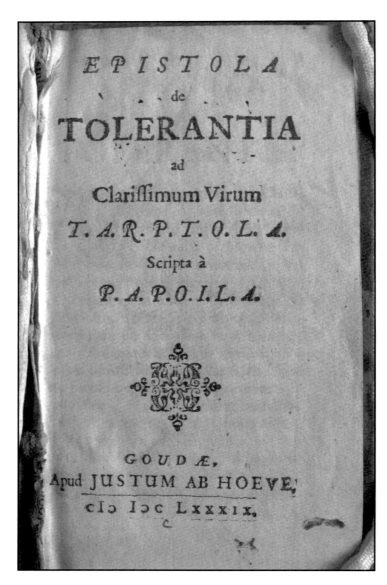

Figure 0.2 The title page of the first edition of John Locke's letter on toleration, *Epistola de Tolerantia* (Gouda, 1689), with the names of the dedicatee, Philip van Limborch, and the author encrypted on the sixth and eighth lines. By permission of the Provost and Scholars of King's College, Cambridge.

Figure 0.3 Philip van Limborch, *Historia inquisitionis, cui subjungitur Liber sententiarum Inquisitionis Tholosanæ, ab anno Christi MCCCVII ad annum MCCCXXIII* (Amsterdam, 1692), title page. John Locke helped his friend Limborch gain access to the manuscript of the book of the sentences delivered by the inquisitor Bernard Gui in Toulouse (1307–1323). Limborch used it in his *History of the Inquisition*, to which he appended an immaculate 414 page edition of the manuscript. Private collection.

to have ready availability of documents to be transcribed for use in an under-graduate Special Subject on heresy and inquisition.[8] Their use eventually led to two research projects at York in 2000–2 and 2014–19, funded by the AHRB and AHRC. These were for editions and translations of the bulk of these records. The work of the first project was published in 2011, while the second is still under way.[9] Collaborative work had led to an earlier conference held in York in 2000, whose papers were published by York Medieval Press.[10] This Press came to realise the need for a dedicated series, which was inaugurated in 2011 with the title 'Heresy and Inquisition in the Middle Ages'.[11] More recently there have been two conferences at York, arising out of the 2014–19 project, 'Origins of Inquisition' in 2016 and 'Inquisition and Knowledge' in 2018.

York's concern throughout these years with both thirteenth-century history and seventeenth-century scholarship and its editing projects have shaped two things in this book, its combination of medieval and early modern, and its allocation of two chapters to the Doat manuscripts.

The theme

It should be said at the outset that the title 'Inquisition and Knowledge' was preferred over the more precise 'Heresy, Inquisition and Knowledge' simply because the latter is a bit of a mouthful. What did we have in mind? Keeping epistemology gagged for the moment, let us use simple terms and take knowledge under two headings. The first is knowledge in a traditional sense: knowledge of heresy and inquisition and, in addition to this, knowledge through editions of evidence and empirical historical research.

The second heading appears as soon as we remove the gag. Here knowledge is on a spectrum. At one end of it there is concern with the angles from which heresy and inquisition were seen and at the other end the proposition that things were fabricated: and many positions in between. The disputed materials include the Church's theological and canon-legal texts and the ways

---

[8] Students who took this course included John Arnold and Chris Sparks, and a much-changed version of it is now taught at York by Lucy Sackville.

[9] *Inquisitors and Heretics in Thirteenth-Century Languedoc: Edition and Translation of Toulouse Inquisition Depositions, 1273–1282*, ed. P. Biller, C. Bruschi and S. Sneddon, Studies in the History of the Christian Traditions 147 (Leiden and Boston, 2011); *The Genesis of Inquisition in Languedoc: Edition and Translation of the Earliest Inquisition Records, 1235–1244*, ed. P. Biller, L. J. Sackville and S. Sneddon (forthcoming).

[10] *Texts and the Repression of Medieval Heresy*, ed. C. Bruschi and P. Biller, York Studies in Medieval Theology 4 (York, 2003). Bruschi's monograph *The Wandering Heretics of Languedoc*, Cambridge Studies in Medieval Life and Thought, 4th series (Cambridge, 2009), was based on Doat Mss 21–26; see on these ch. 11.

[11] L. J. Sackville, *Heresy and Heretics in the Thirteenth Century: The Textual Constructions*, Heresy and Inquisition in the Middle Ages 1 (York, 2011).

Introduction

in which they contain biblical language and imagery for talking about heretics and sects, and construct an archetype of the heretic; and the effects of the use of question-formulae by inquisitors and the character of the knowledge contained in written depositions. Two areas of construction of knowledge dominate consideration of the sixteenth and seventeenth centuries: knowledge of the history of medieval heresy and inquisition, principally to serve confessional and polemical purposes, and the construction of polemical images of contemporary faiths and the Roman inquisition. This is not the place for an account of the modern scholarship on heresy and inquisition that has raised these epistemological questions, but the survey of the book's chapters later in this introduction takes leave every now and again to signal pertinent discussion to be found elsewhere.[12]

The loudest debate in recent years has been about the claim that the Church fabricated the Cathars. Two conferences have been devoted to this and two volumes of papers have been published.[13] This volume raises different questions, and although the controversy provides a frame to

---

[12] The principal milestones are these: articles by H. Grundmann on the topos of heresy and its treatment in biblical exegesis and the problems of interrogation records, published between 1927 and 1965 and translated in *Herbert Grundmann (1902–1970. Essays on Heresy, Inquisition and Literacy*, ed. J. K. Deane, Heresy and Inquisition in the Middle Ages 9 (York, 2019), chs. 1 and 4–5; A. Borst, *Die Katharer*, Schriften der Monumenta Germaniae Historica 12 (Stuttgart, 1953), Part 1 'Die Katharer im Spiegel von Quellen und Forschungen', pp. 1–58; R. E. Lerner, *The Heresy of the Free Spirit in the Later Middle Ages* (Berkeley, Los Angeles and London, 1972); *The Concept of Heresy in the Middle Ages (11th–13th C.)*, ed. W. Lourdaux and D. Verhelst, Mediaevalia Lovaniensia, Studia 4 (Louvain and The Hague, 1976); G. G. Merlo, *Eretici e inquisitori nella società piemontese del trecento* (Turin, 1977), pp. 10–15; *Historiographie du Catharisme*, Cahiers de Fanjeaux 14 (Toulouse, 1979); R. I. Moore, *The Formation of a Persecuting Society: Power and Deviance in Western Europe 950–1250* (Oxford, 1987; 2nd edn, 2007); E. Peters, *Inquisition* (Berkeley and Los Angeles, 1989); *La parola all'accusato*, ed. J.-C. Maire Vigueur and A. Paravicini Bagliani (Palermo, 1991); *Inventer l'hérésie? Discours polémiques et pouvoirs avant l'inquisition*, ed. M. Zerner, Collection du Centre d'Études Médiévales de Nice 2 (Nice, 1998); J. H. Arnold, *Inquisition and Power: Catharism and the Confessing Subject in Medieval Languedoc* (Philadelphia PA, 2001); C. Bruschi, '"Magna diligentia est habenda per inquisitorem": Precautions before Reading Doat 21–26', in *Texts and the Repression of Medieval Heresy*, ed. Bruschi and Biller; K. U. Tremp, *Von der Häresie zur Hexerei: "Wirkliche" und imaginäre Sekten im Spätmittelalter*, Schriften der Monumenta Germaniae Historica 59 (Hannover, 2008); Sackville, *Heresy and Heretics in the Thirteenth Century*; R. I. Moore, *The War on Heresy. Faith and Power in Medieval Europe* (London, 2012) – the translation, *Hérétiques: Résistances et répression dans l'occident médiéval* (Paris, 2017), pp. 515–57, provides endnotes that were not in the English edn; I. Bueno, *Defining Heresy. Inquisition, Theology and Papal Policy in the Time of Jacques Fournier*, Studies in Medieval and Reformation Traditions 192 (Leiden and Boston, 2015), part 2.

[13] *Cathars in Question*, ed. A. Sennis, Heresy and Inquisition in the Middle Ages 4 (York, 2016); *Le "catharisme" en questions*, ed. J.-L. Biget, S. Caucanas, M. Fournié and D. Le Blévec, Cahiers de Fanjeaux 55 (Fanjeaux, 2020).

Peter Biller and L. J. Sackville

chapter 10, by Luc Racaut, it is otherwise generally absent from this collection.[14] Here, we pursue issues such as how medieval bishops, preachers and inquisitors formed networks, asking how this influenced both the knowledge they produced and that which they disseminated; we enquire into the practicalities of inquisition as process and the knowledge contained in its records; try to understand the broader intellectual contexts within which anti-heresy works were produced, disseminated, and understood; and look to the Reformation and beyond, to see how 'knowledge' of medieval heresy and inquisition was constructed and used by later scholars, polemicists and enthusiasts.

The chapters

Gregory IX's entrusting of inquisition to Dominicans in the early 1230s has often been seen as the pivotal moment in traditional histories, which treated earlier years as just a prologue.[15] Jessalynn Bird's has been the most powerful voice in redressing this, especially in the long study she published in 2008 of Paris masters and the repression of heresy from *c.*1198–*c.* 1235.[16] Here in chapter 1 she turns to 1228–30, the years of the legateship in Iberia of the Paris master and cardinal Jean Halgrin d'Abbeville. His actions there and use of synods and sermons to reform the clergy parallel what was being done in Languedoc, but are less widely known.[17] Bird studies his sermons, especially those delivered during the liturgical year on 'I am the good shepherd' (John 10. 11–18) and 'Beware of wolves who come to you in sheep's clothing' (Matthew 7. 15), which dealt often and extensively with heretics. She delicately delineates the fine line he had to tread when trying to persuade his audiences to trust orthodox but not heretical preachers, notwithstanding the moral frailty of some of the former and the seeming goodness of the latter. The sheer density of such anti-heretical preaching in these years is striking, as is the saturation of d'Abbeville's sermons with biblical language and imagery and the frequency of such preaching. Bird introduces a story about another preacher, Fulk (bishop of Toulouse, 1205–31). 'A heretic whom Simon de Montfort had viciously mutilated

[14] But see below, ch. 3, nn. 33–4.

[15] Note emphasis on the earlier period and bishops in L. J. Sackville, 'The Church's Institutional Response to Heresy', *A Companion to Heresy Inquisitions*, ed. D. S. Prudlo, Brill's Companions to the Christian Tradition 85 (Leiden and Boston, 2019), pp. 108–140 (pp. 111–131).

[16] J. Bird, '"The wheat and the tares": Peter the Chanter's Circle and the *fama*-based inquest against heresy and criminal sins, c.1198–c.1235', *Proceedings of the Twelfth International Congress of Medieval Canon Law*, ed. U.-R. Blumenthal, K. Pennington and A. A. Larson (Vatican City, 2008), pp. 763–856.

[17] The principal Anglophone exceptions are Peter Linehan and Damian Smith.

Introduction

promptly interrupted Fulk's sermon with: "You hear what the bishop said, that we are wolves and you sheep, but have you ever seen a sheep bite a wolf this way?"' Here in the early thirteenth-century preaching was making a world of shared knowledge and understanding of this language, one with a long future.[18]

Important in the historiographical background are John Baldwin and his *Masters, Princes and Merchants: The Social Views of Peter the Chanter and His Circle*.[19] With painstaking brilliance this masterpiece investigated the Paris masters of the late twelfth and early thirteenth centuries, their critical views on many pressing contemporary issues (including heresy) and the ideas for reform they produced, preparing the way for the Fourth Lateran Council of 1215. While building on Baldwin Bird covers a longer period, makes more use of sermons and her prosopography – a *pointilliste* picture in which the coloured dots are lit up – is more mobile than Baldwin's. She describes a network: d'Abbeville had in his entourage the Dominican canon lawyer Raymond of Peñafort, and contact with an Iberian writer on heresy, Lucas of Tuy, the archbishop of Tarragona Peter of Albalat, and many other important people in the Church. They knew each other, talked, met and collaborated over many years. Bird's is a persuasive and recognisable picture of how an establishment usually works. And in particular it is a demonstration of the important role played by these Paris masters in the fight against heresy both before and after the institution of the mendicant inquisition.

An image of Gregory IX receiving the *Five Books of the Decretals* from Raymond of Peñafort in 1234 graces the cover of this book, and it is the historical Gregory IX whose letters are the subject of chapter 2.[20] The years of the pontificate, 1227–41, saw crucial developments in the Church's dealing with heresy, and naturally historians in this area have raided papal letters for nuggets of data. Alessandro Sala demonstrates the need for historians to do two things before coming to a view of the sort of truth these letters contain. The first is to analyse and look at the roles of different parts of the letter: the preamble (*arenga*), expressing its theological and legal grounds; the statement of facts (*narratio*); the papal order or instruction (*dispositio*). The second is to look at the place of the papal letter within a sequence of letters. The simplest sequence is the exchange of just two letters, the first from a local figure, let us say an archbishop, writing to the pope and reporting the spread of heresy in his province. In the second letter, which is Pope Gregory's reply to the archbishop, the *narratio* virtually repeats the archbishop's report of heresy. Thus far, this seems just circular: but in fact it is more. The preamble to the papal letter is likely to be suffused with the theologico-legal language and imagery of heresy and its repression;

---

[18] On the language and imagery, see Sackville, *Heresy and Heretics*, ch. 5.
[19] John Baldwin, *Masters, Princes and Merchants: The Social Views of Peter the Chanter and His Circle*, 2 vols. (Princeton NJ, 1970).
[20] See below and n. 70 on the painting of Gregory IX.

9

the *narratio* is now the official narrative; and the letter ends with papal orders. The letter is now the papal view of the truth. At a later stage a few of the papal letters were selected to enter compilations of canon law. In this way the stereotypes and accounts of facts in papal letters became the Church's official version of reality: authoritative, long-lived and widely disseminated.

Sala presents a few samples of such letters relating to Germany, Italy, northern France and Bosnia, showing the extraordinary flow of data back and forth between pope and local agents. There is remarkable variation from region to region in the meaning of 'heresy', applied to Luciferans and reluctant tax-payers in Germany, for instance, and in Italy to political opponents of the pope. When there is a sequence of letters relating to the same area, change in the local ecclesiastic's report or the papal view of what is politic can bring dramatic about-turns in the 'truth' reported by letters. The most striking example is provided by three years of letters relating to the inquisitor Robert Le Bougre and the question of heresy in La Charité-sur-Loire: is heresy there? Or not? In 1233 there is heresy there; in 1234 it is not; in 1235 it is.[21] The abuses of this notorious inquisitor concerned both contemporary chroniclers and in the sixteenth century the Protestant historian John Bale. Matthew Paris said he condemned the innocent along with the guilty and executed fifty, and when he was repeated by Bale (as we shall see in Luc Racaut's chapter 10) the fifty was expanded to thousands. But these were not Gregory IX's preoccupation when suspending Robert, simply archiepiscopal insistence that there was no heresy. Here in chapter 2 a combination of diplomatics and empirical history provides a model of how such letters should be read and a brilliant demonstration of the subtly varying shades of papal truth in them.

The largest inquisition of the middle ages was the one conducted by the Dominicans Bernard of Caux and John of Saint-Pierre, who questioned over 5000 inhabitants from the Lauragais in 1245–6. Access to the depositions has been getting easier, and now they are being edited by Jean-Paul Rehr.[22] Recent studies of inquisitors' assistants have been showing how useful this route is

---

[21] Some of the papal letters relating to either or both La Charité and Robert are translated in *Heresy and Inquisition in France, 1200–1300*, ed. J. H. Arnold and P. Biller, Manchester Medieval Sources (Manchester, 2016): Innocent III, no. 20 a, b, pp. 151–6; Gregory IX, no. 22 a-d, pp. 159–67; Urban IV, no. 23, pp. 165–7.

[22] See J.-P. Rehr, 'Le catharisme et le manuscrit 609 de la Bibliothèque municipale de Toulouse', in *Le "catharisme" en questions*, pp. 373–93; translations in *Heresy and Inquisition*, ed. Arnold and Biller, pp. 380–440. Ms. 609 was efficiently filleted by C. Douais in his *Les hérétiques du comté de Toulouse dans la première moitié du xiiie siècle, d'après l'enquête de 1245* (Paris, 1891), and the manuscript and inquisition were given a magisterial study by Y. Dossat, in his *Les crises de l'inquisition Toulousaine au XIIIIe siècle (1233–1273)* (Bordeaux, 1959). A striking and colourful interpretation of the records was provided by M. G. Pegg, *The Corruption of the Angels. The Great Inquisition of 1245–1246* (Princeton and Oxford, 2001).

Introduction

for the understanding of how inquisition worked,[23] and now in chapter 3 Jörg Feuchter provides a major addition to them. He reconstructs the life and career of one of the leading figures in Bernard of Caux and John of Saint-Pierre's team, the lawyer Master Nepos (ob. *c.*1283).[24] Mentioned in Montauban charters from 1253 and several times consul towards the end of his life, Nepos seems to have made his way into the elite through talent rather than birth, fortunately for him doing this in a town where law and lawyers were held in very high regard. Nepos was a judge in the Albigeois in the 1260s, and around 1268 he produced the revision of a legal treatise. The population of Montauban had contained adherents of three faiths, Catholic, Waldensian and 'heretic', meaning 'Cathar'.[25] Though Nepos's own orthodoxy is in no doubt and from 1256 he was a donat of a Benedictine abbey just outside the town walls, he will have been familiar with many fellow-Montalbanais who had supported Waldensians or heretics or both, as also many who availed themselves of Waldensian medical assistance. He will also have known about the deal that had been done in April 1236, whereby the inhabitants of Montauban came forward willingly to confess to the inquisitors and received non-severe penances, and the similar deal – paving the way for this – that had been accorded to the seneschal of Quercy in the previous month.[26] The man, therefore, who was recruited to the team of inquisitors' assistants in 1245 offered legal expertise, and deep familiarity with people who supported Waldensians and heretics. At first sight his life and work offer a contradiction. On the one hand, he worked hard in a massive inquisition campaign. On the other hand, he carefully edited a legal treatise, the *Liber fugitivus*, that offered advice on legal ploys helping people who were accused to 'flee' – in other words, to get off scot free. Feuchter notes an interesting first. The earliest known (so far) record of a person being offered an opportunity of defence occurs in a deposition that was witnessed by Nepos in 1245.

There is a remarkable bringing together here of scraps of evidence to reconstruct Nepos and his long career, to depict him as someone woven into the various institutional fabrics of his home town as both a private person and as a legal mind, and lastly as part of that body of expertise that we see collected around inquisition, as Riccardo Parmeggiani has recently outlined for inquisition in Florence.[27]

---

[23] See for example C. Bruschi, '*Familia inquisitionis*: A study on the inquisitor's entourage (XIII-XIX centuries)', *Cittadinanza e disuguaglianze economiche: le origini storiche di un problema europeo (XIII-XVI secolo)*, Mélanges de l'École française de Rome. Moyen Âge 125.2 (Rome, 2013); J. Moore, *Inquisition and its Organisation in Italy, 1250–1350*, Heresy and Inquisition in the Middle Ages 8 (York, 2019), chs. 3 and 5.

[24] This replaces J. Feuchter, *Ketzer, Konsuln und Büßer. Die städtischen Eliten von Montauban vor dem Inquisitor Petrus Cellani (1236/1241)*, Spätmittelalter, Humanismus, Reformation 40 (Tübingen, 2007), pp. 402–7.

[25] See Feuchter below on these words, ch. 3 n. 34.

[26] See Feuchter, *Ketzer, Konsuln und Büßer*, pp. 297–305.

[27] R. Parmeggiani, *L'inquisizione a Firenze nell'età di Dante* (Bologna, 2018), ch. III.3.

Peter Biller and L. J. Sackville

The witnesses used by inquisitors, whose names were listed at the end of depositions, fell into several categories. One was of men like Nepos, used often by the inquisitors, members of their team and like Nepos sometimes equipped with special expertise. Feuchter refers to another frequently seen but under-studied category: parish priests. Parish priests were frequently present at the interrogations of those from their parish. In Languedoc from 1227 there was conciliar legislation which required parish priests to keep written record of those confessing and taking communion, and there is plenty of anecdotal evidence in inquisition records of parish priests involved in all sort of ways: hearing confessions of heresy; debating with heretics; having them to dinner and – in one famous case – habitually playing chess with them; and persecuting them. Along with experts like Nepos, their 'living experience' constitutes an important sector of the 'knowledge of heresy' in thirteenth-century Languedoc.[28]

Inquisitors sought and made use of knowledge, and their proceedings and records in some – disputed – senses created knowledge. A famous story encapsulating the latter was told by the Benedictine monk Richer of Senones in the middle years of the thirteenth century. The inquisitor Robert Le Bougre, he wrote, would put a little charter on the top of the head of a person and he was thereby able to make them confess whatever he wanted them to. Magic![29] The most famous example of such confessions and their dismantling in modern scholarship is recapitulated here. The *Ad nostrum* decree of the Council of Vienne (1311–12) denounced the heretical doctrines held in Germany by men called Beghards and women called Beguines (not the differently spelled Béguins of southern Europe), and called for bishops and inquisitors to act.[30] At the heart of the eight propositions listed in the decree was the notion that one could attain such a degree of perfection that one could not sin, and one could freely grant to the body whatever pleased it. These propositions were used in interrogations, and the records of these became the evidence used in the chapters on 'The Heresy of the Free Spirit' in modern histories of medieval sects. Then there was an about-turn, in two stages. Writing about the problems of interpreting inquisition depositions in 1964, Herbert Grundmann used these Free Spirit records as his examples, showing how the Free Spirit propositions listed in *Ad nostrum* re-appeared

---

[28] M.-H. Vicaire listed 'l'expérience vivante' alongside the 'dossier' of the Cistercians and the expertise of southern prelates and legates as three areas and sources of knowledge of heresy, in his 'Les cathares vus par les polémistes', in *Cathares en Languedoc*, Cahiers de Fanjeaux 3 (Toulouse, 1968), pp. 107–28 (110–12). This is discussed in *The Genesis of Inquisition in Languedoc*, ed. Biller, Sackville and Sneddon, ch. 2 (forthcoming).

[29] See 'Introduction', in *Texts and the Repression of Medieval Heresy*, ed. Bruschi and Biller, pp. 9–12; the text is translated again in *Inquisition and Heresy*, ed. Arnold and Biller, pp. 57–8.

[30] *Decrees of the Ecumenical Councils*, ed. N. Tanner, 2 vols. (London and Washington, 1990), I, 374 and 383–4, nos. 16 and 28.

Introduction

almost verbatim in the records of confessions.[31] This paved the way for the demolition of the sect by Robert Lerner in his 1972 monograph, *The Heresy of the Free Spirit in the Later Middle Ages.*[32]

An older account of the Free Spirit, by Gordon Leff in 1967, gave pride of place to the interrogations of Beguines in Świdnica (German Schweidnitz) in 1322, and their analysis was also an important section in Lerner's book.[33] The light they shone on the life of Beguine communities, the questionable character of the records and the sometimes lurid nature of the things that the Beguines confessed made these records of particular interest. Now in chapter 4 Paweł Kras provides the definitive modern summary of the affair. After outlining the enquiry, the history of the records which emerged from it and the modern scholarship that has been devoted to it, he describes the community of the cowled sisters of Świdnica, and then its investigation. The inquisitor, John of Schwenkenfeld, was a Dominican, a learned theologian and a subscriber to the existence of the Heresy of the Free Spirit. He was out to prove the heresy was there among the Beguines, he was equipped with a question-list and the records of his interrogations were filtered in various ways, including translation from German to Latin and simple omission. So far, so simple; but as Kras shows – in the model that he provides of critical reading of interrogations records – not so simple. Kras carefully distinguishes between the younger and older sisters' different experience and knowledge, and the impact of these on their testimonies: the younger ones freely attested their suffering and resentment, the older ones were reluctant to say anything, though they knew more. As in this volume's other example of reading such materials, Richard Kieckhefer's in chapter 8, Kras picks up 'voices' in the records. Especially interesting here is that this metaphor is also applied to the inquisitor Schwenkenfeld, whose questions stray outside the question-list and articulate his own interests. His is also a 'voice' that is audible.

While chapters 2 and 4 lead us towards the kind of knowledge contained within and constructed by papal letters and records of interrogation, chapters 5–7 deal with accounts of heretics' beliefs found in polemical treatises (chapters 5 and 7) and inquisitors' manuals (chapter 6). Mid-twentieth-century discoveries by Antoine Dondaine increased the known number of polemical treatises, and their use became easier with the production of road-map studies by

---

[31] Translated in *Herbert Grundmann Essays*, ed. Deane, ch. 4.

[32] (Berkeley, Los Angeles and London). Dustwrapper and title page put the sect name in italics, reversed inside the italics required in a title, a nuance which is usually lost in bibliographies: The Heresy *of the* Free Spirit *in the Later Middle Ages.*

[33] G. Leff, *Heresy in the Later Middle Ages*, 2 vols. (Manchester and New York, 1967), I, 308–407 (386–92); text of the interrogations, ibid., II, 721–40; Lerner, *Heresy of the Free Spirit*, pp. 112–19.

Peter Biller and L. J. Sackville

Walter Wakefield, Sackville's general account[34] and a spate of new editions.[35] Contrasting regional chronologies became clear. In southern France the earliest and simplest texts were short *Summae of Authorities*, lists of heretical doctrines and scriptural passages which can be used to refute them. These were followed by more elaborate treatises, two written by Durand of Huesca (the second in the 1220s) and one in Iberia, by Lucas of Tuy, in the mid-1230s.[36] In Italy the heyday was later, mainly between 1235 and the 1250s. The longest treatise, produced in Lombardy in the 1240s by the Dominican Moneta of Cremona, runs to nearly half a million words, its core is simple: the brief statement of Cathar or Waldensian doctrines, followed by citations from scripture and arguments that refute them.[37] A treatise against Waldensians written in 1395 by a German inquisitor had an essentially similar structure (see chapter 7).

Doubt is sometimes expressed about whether such treatises addressed any real heresy.[38] One might suggest a spectrum and place treatises at various points on it. At the realist end of the spectrum there is the minimum critical

---

[34] A. Dondaine, *Les hérésies et l'Inquisition, XIIe-XIIIe siècles. Documents et études*, Variorum CS 134 (Aldershot, 1990); W. L. Wakefield, 'Notes on some anti-heretical wrings of the thirteenth century', *Franciscan Studies* ns. 27 (1967), 285–321; 'A list of polemical sources', in *Heresies of the High Middle Ages*, ed. W. L. Wakefield and A.P. Evans (New York, 1969), pp. 633–8; Sackville, *Heresy and Heretics*, pp. 13–40.

[35] Anselm of Alessandria, *Tractatus de hereticis*, ed. A. Dondaine, *Archivum Fratrum Praedicatorum* 20 (1950), 234–324; Alvarus Pelagius, *Collyrium fidei adversus haereses* (*Colírio da fé contra as heresias*), ed. M. Pinto de Meneses, Instituto de Alta Cultura, 2 vols. (Lisbon, 1954); *Une somme anti-cathare: Le* Liber contra Manicheos *de Durand de Huesca*, ed. C. Thouzellier, Spicilegium Sacrum Lovaniense 32 (Louvain, 1964); Durand of Huesca, *Liber antiheresis*, ed. K.-V. Selge in his *Die ersten Waldenser*, 2 vols., Arbeiten zur Kirchengeshichte 37 (Berlin, 1967), II; Peter the Venerable, *Contra Petrobrusianos hereticos*, ed. J. Fearns, Corpus Christianorum Continuatio Mediaevalis 10 (Turnhout, 1968); F. Šanjek, 'Raynerius Sacconi O.P, Summa de Catharis', *Archivum Fratrum Praedicatorum* 44 (1974), 31–60; *Disputatio inter Catholicum et Paterinum Hereticum*, ed. C. Hoécker, Edizione Nazionale dei Testi Mediolatini 4, ser. 1, 3 (Tavarnuzze, 2001); Salvo Burci, *Liber suprastella*, ed. C. Bruschi, Istituto Storico Italian per il Medio Evo, Fonti per la Storia dell'Italia Medievale, Antiquitates 15 (Rome, 2002); Andreas Florentinus, *Summa contra hereticos*, ed. G. Rottenwöher, MGH Quellen zur Gesistesgeschichte des Mittelalters 23 (Hannover , 2008); Lucas de Tuy, *De altera vita*, ed. E. F. Rey, Corpus Christanorum Continuatio Mediaevalis 75A (Turnhout, 2009); William the Monk, *Contra Henricum scismaticum et hereticum*, and Anonymous, *Contra hereticos et schismaticos*, ed. M. Zerner, Sources Chrétiennes 541 (Paris, 2011); Pseudo Giacomo de Capellis, *Summa contra hereticos*, ed. P. Romagnoli, Ordines. Studi su Istituzioni e Società nel Medioevo Europeo 7 (Milan, 2018); Peter the Martyr (attributed), *Summa contra hereticos*, ed. D. S. Prudlo, Medium Aevum Monographs 38 (Oxford, 2020).

[36] Sackville, *Heresy and Heretics*, pp. 42–53; *Inquisition and Heresy*, ed. Arnold and Biller, docs. 11 and 14, pp. 92–7, 104–10.

[37] L. J. Sackville, 'The Textbook Heretic: Moneta of Cremona's Cathars', in *Cathars in Question*, pp. 208–28; P. Biller, 'Moneta's *Confutation of Heresies* and the Valdenses', in *Identità Valdesi tra passato e presente*, ed. S. P. Rambaldi (Turin, 2016), pp. 27–41.

[38] E.g. Moore, *War on Heresy*, p. 314, on Moneta.

Introduction

'take': that these showed real heretics and their propositions, but from a certain angle; at the other end, the maximum critical line, that these treatises fabricated the propositions they put into the mouths of heretics. While the extremes outline an intelligible approach, it is limited, resembling a study of presidential press-conferences that confined itself to 'true' or 'a lie' and ignored the complex layering of White House officials, media and popular credulity. More understanding is gained by stepping back from or postponing use of the epistemological spectrum, and examining the texts and their contexts more patiently.

Here in this collection of studies, it is useful to distinguish two sorts of context or objectives – one of them debates with people, the other book-learning. We can put in the first group the anti-Waldensian writings discussed in chapters 6–7; these were closely related to confessions recorded in deposi-tions, and they were used in preaching. Alongside them in the same group are many of the earlier polemical works from Languedoc and Lombardy. These were connected to direct exchanges between Catholics, heretics and Waldensians, who met in person for debate.

We can put into the second group an early treatise that has recently been illuminated in a study by John Arnold.[39] This is Benedict of Alignan's *Treatise against various errors*, written by 1261. Over 200,000 words, this was a long commentary on the *Firmiter credimus* (We firmly believe) opening creed of the Fourth Lateran Council of 1215. Via his gloss Benedict listed errors encyclo-paedically. He drew in heretics past and present, Eastern Christians, Jews, Muslims and others, and he copied: a lot from St Augustine and, in his own times, William of Auvergne and Moneta of Cremona. The twenty-six still extant manuscripts indicate its popularity. Clearly this sort of encyclopaedic book-learning about faiths and sects had a wide readership.

Alignan's treatise is an ancestor, Irene Bueno suggests, of the three major treatises of the fourteenth century that she surveys in chapter 5. These are Guido Terreni's *Summa de haeresibus et earum confutationibus* (c. 1338–42), Alvarus Pelagius's *Collyrium fidei contra haereses* (after 1344) and the *Directorium inquisitorum* (1376) of the Dominican inquisitor Nicholas Eymerich (see figs. 11–13). Bueno's describes and discusses the accounts provided in these works of the errors of Eastern Christians; very extensive in the case of Guido, who looks at Greeks, Armenians, Georgians and Jacobites. The issue for Bueno is contemporary interest in the Christians of the Levant and the setting of these works within the intellectual currents of the papal court at Avignon and the patronage of cardinals and popes; the setting of writings against heresy within the intellectual hub of Avignon is broadly comparable with the connection made by Bird in chapter 1 between actions against heresy and

---

[39] 'Benedict of Alignan's *Tractatus fidei contra diversos errores*: a neglected anti-heresy treatise', *Journal of Medieval History* 45 (2019), 20–64.

the masters of Paris. Bueno's authors were very learned men. Guido was a Paris theologian and Alvarus a Bologna canonist, and both participated in the intellectual controversies of their day, such as spiritual poverty, the ideas of William of Ockham and Marsilio of Padua and the nature of papal authority; Nicholas's long list of treatises show learning in many areas of logic and theology, which have not yet been integrated into a general account of him as an intellectual.[40] Bueno shows that a particular feature of the culture of the papal court was its association with the production of universal compilations in various sectors of knowledge, which included these three heresy treatises.[41] In line with Benedict of Alignan, Bueno's three authors brought together ancient and medieval heresiography, and dealt with many sorts of faiths and sects. In the case of Eymerich's treatise of course, the omnium-gatherum of errors was contained within a vast encyclopaedia of inquisition legislation and consultations. Their universality meant that these treatises were not practical guides for inquisitors. They provided, in Bueno's words, 'the Church elite with the necessary theological and juridical weapons'.

In 1953 the great German historian Arno Borst, then only twenty-eight years old, published his *Die Katharer*. The first part was a survey of how heretics had been depicted in various textual genres, faiths and schools of thought from the eleventh century to 1950. This was clearly a game-changer, establishing the variety and malleability of the masks worn by heretics, from early Protestants to social protesters and Occitan separatists. When we look more closely, however, at the account of polemical treatises, we see him directing his attention to those works that might be directly useful for the history of heretical movements; he only remarks in passing the names of such writers as Guido Terreni and Alvarus.[42] Bueno herself is a game-changer, as she showed when bringing together Jacques Fournier as theologian and as inquisitor.[43] She is now contributing to another shift in scholarship, along with Arnold, establishing the character and importance of the encyclopaedic genre of medieval heresiography. And in pointing to the importance of that larger project of systematisation and reception of knowledge of heresy, she erodes notions of discontinuity between late medieval and reformation polemic.

---

[40] C. Heimann, *Nicolaus Eymerich (vor 1320–1399) praedicator veridicus, inquisitor intrepidus, doctor egregius: Leben und Werk eines Inquisitors*, Spanische Forschungen der Görresgesellschaft 37 (Münster, 2001), pp. 168–206.

[41] Compare Alvarus's *De statu et planctu ecclesiae* (three versions, 1332–40), whose massive second part listing sins by estate is a sort of socio-graphic encyclopaedia; N. Iung, *Un Franciscain, théologien du pouvoir pontifical au XIVe siècle: Alvaro Pelayo, évêque et pénitencier de Jean XXII*, L'Église et L'État au Moyen Age 3 (Paris, 1931), pp. 52–5; P. Biller, *Measure of Multitude. Population in Medieval Thought*, rev. edn (Oxford, 2003), pp. 209–11.

[42] Borst, *Die Katharer*, p. 26.

[43] Bueno, *Defining Heresy.*

Introduction

A recent monograph by Reima Välimäki established the inquisitor Peter Zwicker as a major figure in the history of the Church in the years from around 1390 to the early 1400s.[44] Zwicker conducted a remarkable and massive campaign against Waldensians, interrogating Waldensians in Germanophone regions, ranging from Szczecin (Stettin) in the north to Austria and western Hungary in the south.[45] Zwicker was also notable as a writer, producing two treatises of theological polemic and inquisitor's manual materials; these are at issue in chapters 6 and 7. His authorship of one treatise against Waldensians from 1395, known from its opening words, *Cum dormirent homines* ('While men slept', Matthew 13. 25), had already been established, but Välimäki discovered that he was also the author of another and shorter one , known as the *Refutatio errorum* (*Refutation of Errors*); see figs. 14–15. Together with Adam Poznański, Välimäki is preparing an edition of both treatises.

Poznański examines the longer treatise, *Cum dormirent homines*, in chapter 7.[46] It has much in common with some of the thirteenth-century polemical texts of southern Europe. Zwicker had access to Moneta of Cremona's treatise in the library of the monastery of Garsten, near Steyr in upper Austria, and reading Moneta influenced him. Most of the chapters in *Cum dormirent homines* begin by attributing a proposition to Waldensians heretics. This is followed by the citation of authorities – almost entirely from the bible – that ran counter to them. Zwicker carefully took much of his account of the origins of the Waldensians from a Waldensian historical text, the *Liber electorum* (*Book of the Elect*). Likewise, the main difference between the articulation of Waldensian propositions in the chapters of *Cum dormirent homines* and in records of depositions is that the former are ideal-types, whereas the formulations in the depositions are more variable; often audible through the variations in wording is the voice of the individual deponent.

Zwicker's 'authorities' were accompanied by arguments, and these are Poznański's theme. He unpacks them to see how they worked. Using modern manuals of logic, he presents a typology of the arguments Zwicker used, their various logical cores. Zwicker used a wide variety. They were rarely deductive. He chose ones that were easy to follow. He avoided sophisms, 'dishonest' arguments, perhaps in order to avoid a charge that was sometimes levelled at heretics, that 'they argue sophistically'.[47] He cast slurs against

---

[44] R. Välimäki, *Heresy in Late Medieval Germany. The Inquisitor Petrus Zwicker and the Waldensians*, Heresy and Inquisition in the Middle Ages 6 (York, 2019).

[45] The report in a letter to Flacius Illyricus of three volumes of heresy trials preserved in upper-Austria – recounted by Harold Bollbuck in ch. 9 – reminds us that if these had survived and they were Zwicker's, we would have been comparing the size of Zwicker's inquisitions to that of the Lauragais in 1245–6; Välimäki, *Heresy in Late Medieval Germany*, p. 153 n. 204.

[46] See n. 52 below.

[47] See B. Gui, *Practica inquisitionis* v.II.8, ed. C. Douais (Toulouse, 1886), pp. 255–6; translated, *Heresies of the High Middle Ages*, ed. Wakefield and E vans, pp. 400–2.

Waldensian preachers, but not against their followers, for his target audience was simple Catholics and simple believers in heretics.

Poznański's is an original and illuminating approach, and it supports a view of Zwicker as someone who was really and realistically making efforts to persuade. It is fifty years since Raoul Manselli published his resumé of the change in the Church's treatment of heresy, distilled into a title of masterly economy: 'De la "persuasio" à la "coercitio"' ('From "persuasion" to "coercion"').[48] While the key-words are those that were used by the theologians, what happened was more complex than these binaries, and it is useful to have persuasion brought back into the discussion of action against heresy in the later middle ages.[49]

The fifth part of Bernard Gui's early fourteenth-century treatise on the practice of inquisition is famous for its accounts of individual sects, treated and described as ensembles of organisation, way of life, beliefs and in some cases history. A precedent for Gui's approach and also one of his sources was the *On the way of Life and Doings (De vita et actibus)* of the Waldensians, a sober and systematic account of the sect that was based on the confessions of a very well informed deponent.[50] The broader context of this is a sea-change in medieval writers' conceptualisation of such phenomena, evinced, for example, in Franciscan travellers' accounts of the Mongols' 'religion', while a narrower and more immediate one is simply the usefulness of sect-information to inquisitors and catering for this in compilations for inquisitors. In chapter 6 Reima Välimäki turns to a sect-description that is comparable to both Gui's and to Gui's anonymous source, but written later. This is *On the Customs and Way of Life (De vita et conversatione)*, one of the writings associated with the inquisitorial activities of Peter Zwicker. Hitherto confusion about this text has limited historians' understanding and use of it, but Välimäki has now clarified its origins in the conversion of a number of Waldensian preachers in 1391. He carefully delineates the various versions of the text and in an appendix provides an edition and translation of one of them. These versions are Jekyll and Hyde. One of them is sober and accurate, presenting an orthodox and morally positive view of the Waldensians. Other versions have been tinkered with; the *topoi* of hypocrisy and illiteracy have been introduced in order to darken the picture. Välimäki holds up for our reflection both inquisitors' need for accurate information and also their interest in denigratory propaganda.

In the last of its medieval chapters, 8, this volume returns to the questions adumbrated in chapter 4 – how to read trial records. It deals with the most

---

[48] In *Le Crédo, la Morale et l'Inquisition*, Cahiers de Fanjeaux 6 (Toulouse, 1971), pp. 175–97.

[49] Sackville, 'The Church's Institutional Response to Heresy', pp. 110–11; Välimäki, *Heresy in Late Medieval Germany*, ch. 4 'Communicating Faith'.

[50] P. Biller, 'Fingerprinting an Anonymous Description of the Waldensians', in *Texts and the Repression of Medieval Heresy*, ed. Bruschi and Biller, pp. 163–207; *Heresy and Inquisition*, ed. Arnold and Biller, docs. 53 and 56, pp. 469–75, 497–500.

Introduction

difficult of all: those in which suspects are recorded confessing the practice of sorcery and diabolism. The chapter presents two ages of Richard Kieckhefer: one from 2018 having a conversation with the earlier one who in 1976 wrote and published *European Witch Trials*.[51] That work rested on a distinction between popular culture (and belief there in malevolent sorcery) and learned or elite culture (containing theology, pacts with the devil, Sabbaths and so on). The two strands came together in trials. Today's Kieckhefer sees the need to take more things into consideration. These include a distinction (applicable to both people and the elite) between what they believed in and what they actually expected to happen; the phenomenon of the person who is accused and then becomes an accuser; regional differences; false confessions (or in Robert Lerner's terms 'the confessing personality'). Kieckhefer says that these need to be brought into 'narrative convergence', and he provides a typology of the narratives that can be discerned in the trials. These are 'discontinuous', 'subsuming', 're-contextualising' and 'pre-confessional'. We can use as an example the first and simplest of these, the 'discontinuous' narrative. In this narrative the question-list plays a strong role. The narrative starts with *maleficia* (accusations of acts of maleficent sorcery). These accusations recede quickly into the background as they are displaced by charges of diabolism. After outlining his current approach, Kieckhefer presents readings of trials that seem to fit one or other archetypal narrative, and he goes on to look at several which reject a narrative or go in a reverse direction. In addition to a master-class in the reading of such texts we are given an invitation to ruminate on intellectual fashions. Who uses 'elite and popular cultures' now? Although forty years on Kieckhefer is using subtler modelling of the trial narratives, the categories he put forward in 1976 still seem the most useful we have. They still shine light in a dark wood.

Post-medieval: the sixteenth and seventeenth centuries

In 1554 Flacius Illyricus recommended finding and asking old people about their ancestors who had supported heretics: oral history, as Harald Bollbuck comments when citing this detail. It reminds us of recentness. One group of older heretics were still there: the Waldensians in the Dauphiné and Piedmont. Correspondence with Swiss Protestants around 1530 stimulated one late Waldensian, called Georges Morel, to write a formal description of the group for their benefit.[52] This was from their side of the fence, and one irony is how much it shares with the

---

[51] R. Kieckhefer, *European Witch Trials. Their Foundations in Popular and Learned Culture, 1300–1500* (London and Henley, 1976).

[52] Ed. V. Vinay in his *Le confessione di fide dei Valdesi riformati, con i documenti del dialogo fra la "prima" e la "seconda" Riforma*, Collana della Facoltà Valdese di Teologia 12

fourteenth-century descriptions of Waldensians produced by inquisitors that were discussed in chapter 6. Meanwhile the libraries of monasteries and cathedral chapters provided another sort of continuity, through their volumes of compilations of canon law and the treatises discussed in the earlier chapters in this collection. Particularly numerous were the manuscripts of Peter Zwicker and Nicholas Eymerich's treatises, and these were further amplified as they came to be printed.[53]

We turn to the texts of the confessional historiography of this period. The deep bass note in the background was the rise of scientific scholarship: developments in the science of criticising documents and editing texts, the compilation of aids such as du Fresne du Cange's glossary of medieval Latin and the use of the layout of the learned book to provide references to sources, the *preuves*, the proof texts, in appendixes. Look at two late examples, one the *Histoire des variations des eglises protestantes* (*History of the Variations of the Protestant Churches*) written Jacques Bénigne Bossuet and published in Paris in 1688, the other of course the *Historia inquisitionis* (*History of the Inquisition*) written by Philip van Limborch and published in Amsterdam in 1692. For a moment let us forget the purposes, serving arguments about faiths and tolerance, and just contemplate the scholarship. Limborch's *History* was equipped with a bibliography, references to consulted works in the margins and an errata list. As the title page said, 'subjoined to this' (cui subiungitur), was the appendix of its proofs, an immaculate transcription of Bernard Gui's sentences; see fig. 3.[54] Book 11 in Bossuet's *Histoire des variations* contains a 131-page *Short History of the Albigensians, Waldensians, Wycliffites and Hussites* (*Histoire abrégée des Albigeois, des Vaudois, des Viclefistes , & des Hussites*); see figs. 5–6.[55] Comparison with a modern 800 page omnium-gatherum of texts on medieval heresy shows that Bossuet already knew a very high proportion of the texts translated in 1969, which he used in (for him) modern editions and sometimes in manuscript.[56] Placed in the margins of the pages are his 208 precise references to them.

(Turin, 1975), doc. 1, pp. 36–51; E. Cameron, *Waldenses. Rejections of Holy Church in Medieval Europe* (Oxford, 2000), pp. 212–16, 233–40.

[53] On the mss. of Zwicker's *Cum dormirent homines*, see Välimäki, *Heresy in Late Medieval Germany*, pp. 262–83, and, on the printed edition, n. 59 below. On the mss. of the *Directorium* see T. Kaeppeli and E. Panella, *Scriptores Ordinis Praedicatorum*, 4 vols. (Rome, 1970–83), III, 158–9 no. 3062, IV, 206–7, and Heimann, *Nicolaus Eymerich*, pp. 162–8, 175–82. On printed editions see E. Van der Vekene, 'Die gedruckten Ausgaben des "Directorum inquisitorum" des Nicolaus Eymeric', *Gutenberg Jahrbuch 1973* (Mainz, 1973), pp. 286–97.

[54] Setting aside punctuation and the use of ampersand for 'et', comparison of a sample of 1500 words with the manuscript in the British Library failed to find a single error.

[55] *Heresies of the High Middle Ages*, ed. Wakefield and Evans.

[56] Alfred Rébelliau produced a masterly analysis of Bossuet's scholarship in his *Bossuet, historien du Protestantisme. Étude sur l'"Histoire des Variations" et sur la controverse au dix-septième siècle*, 3rd edn (Paris, 1909). Jean-Louis Quantin has

Introduction

Figure 0.4   Jacques Bénigne Bossuet, bishop of
Meaux, engraved by Gérard Edelinck after portrait by
Hyacinthe Rigaud. Private collection.

Protestant and Catholic historians and state servants added to knowledge through hunting out texts, and preserving, copying or editing them. This volume contains a general account of the patriarch of Protestant historiography, Matthias Flacius Illyricus. While it contains nothing on his Catholic counterpart Cesare Baronio (Baronius), the efforts of two Jesuits who

---

demolished Rébelliau's claim that Bossuet was a modern scientific historian; 'Bossuet et l'érudition de son temps', in *Bossuet. Le Verbe et l'Hisoire (1704–2004). Actes du colloque international de Paris et de Meaux pour le troisième centenaire de la mort de Bossuet*, ed. G. Ferreyrolles (Paris, 2006), pp. 65–103. Quantin shows that history and patient scholarship were never ends in themselves, and erudition was always the servant of theology, while the broader claims made by Rébelliau say more about him and the nationalism of his time than they do about Bossuet. Since Quantin is clearly right, there is a danger that we forget that most of Rébelliau's demonstration of Bossuet's remarkable erudition is also right.

Figure 0.5 Jacques Bénigne Bossuet, *Histoire des variations des églises protestantes*, 2 vols. (Paris, 1730), vol. 1, title-page. Book 11 in vol. 2 contains his short history of Albigensians, Waldensians, Wycliffites and Hussites, whose 208 marginal notes attest remarkable knowledge of medieval sources. Though with different pagination, the 1730 edition is in the format of the first edition (Paris, 1688) and the location and contents of the notes in the section illustrated in fig. 0.6 are identical. Private collection.

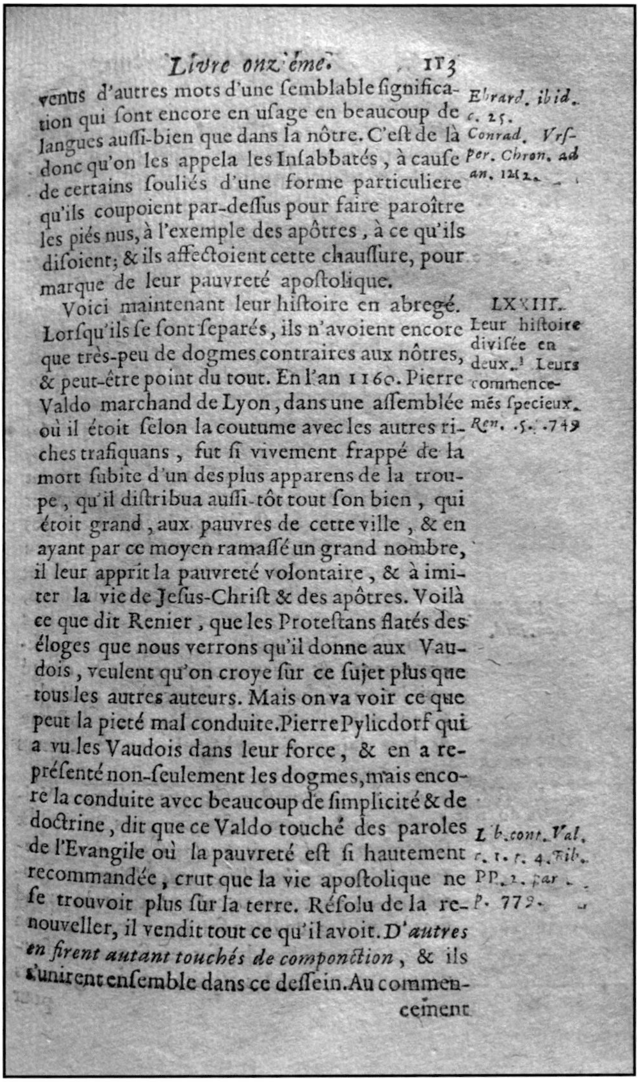

Livre onz'éme. 113

venus d'autres mots d'une semblable significa- *E¹brard, ibid.*
tion qui sont encore en usage en beaucoup de *c. 15.*
langues aussi-bien que dans la nôtre. C'est de là *Conrad. Vrs-*
donc qu'on les appela les Insabbatés, à cause *Per. Chron. ad*
de certains souliés d'une forme particuliere *an. 1212.*
qu'ils coupoient par-dessus pour faire paroître
les piés nus, à l'exemple des apôtres, à ce qu'ils
disoient; & ils affectoient cette chaussure, pour
marque de leur pauvreté apostolique.

Voici maintenant leur histoire en abregé. *LXXIII.*
Lorsqu'ils se sont separés, ils n'avoient encore *Leur histoire*
que très-peu de dogmes contraires aux nôtres, *divisée en*
& peut-être point du tout. En l'an 1160. Pierre *deux.¹ Leurs*
Valdo marchand de Lyon, dans une assemblée *més specieux.*
où il étoit selon la coutume avec les autres ri- *Ren. 5. .749*
ches trafiquans, fut si vivement frappé de la
mort subite d'un des plus apparens de la trou-
pe, qu'il distribua aussi-tôt tout son bien, qui
étoit grand, aux pauvres de cette ville, & en
ayant par ce moyen ramassé un grand nombre,
il leur apprit la pauvreté volontaire, & à imi-
ter la vie de Jesus-Christ & des apôtres. Voilà
ce que dit Renier, que les Protestans flatés des
éloges que nous verrons qu'il donne aux Vaudois, veulent qu'on croye sur ce sujet plus que
tous les autres auteurs. Mais on va voir que
peut la pieté mal conduite. Pierre Pylicdorf qui
a vu les Vaudois dans leur force, & en a re-
présenté non-seulement les dogmes, mais encore la conduite avec beaucoup de simplicité & de
doctrine, dit que ce Valdo touché des paroles *L¹ b.cont. Val.*
de l'Evangile où la pauvreté est si hautement *c. 1. r. 4.Tib.*
recommandée, crut que la vie apostolique ne *PP.2. par*
se trouvoit plus sur la terre. Résolu de la re- *P. 772.*
nouveller, il vendit tout ce qu'il avoit. *D'autres*
en firent autant touchés de componction, & ils
s'unirent ensemble dans ce dessein. Au commen-
                                                    cement

Figure 0.6   Bossuet, *Histoire des variations*, vol. 2, p. 113.
Bossuet based his account of the origins of the Waldensians
on two treatises which he cites in his marginal note LXXIII,
the first beginning 'Ren.' and the second 'Lib. cont. Vald.'
The two works had been edited by Jakob Gretser in 1613
(see figs. 8.1 and 8.2), and Bossuet's economical but precise
references are to their reprint in *Magna Bibliotheca Veterum
Patrum*, vol. 4 part 2 (Paris, 1644), pp. 749 and 779.
Private collection.

published texts in Ingolstadt in 1612 and 1613 provide the foundations for some of the points that crop up at various points in this book. They are Juan de Mariana (1536–1624) and Jakob Gretser (1562–1625). The medieval treatises they edited included one written in the mid-1230s in Spain by Lucas of Tuy, who appears as one of d'Abbeville's contacts in chapter 1; this seventeenth-century edition was only replaced in 2009.[57] A second treatise was an anonymous Austrian inquisitor's or inquisition assistant' compilation from c. 1260–6, which has never received a full modern edition.[58] A third was of the two polemical treatises written by Peter Zwicker, mentioned above – the longer one the object of discussion in chapter 7; again, there has been no other edition.[59] A French 'state' enterprise devoted to the preservation of documents through their copying is in the frame in chapters 11 and 12. Among the labourers off the stage of this book are James Ussher (1581–1665), scholar, Protestant minister and later archbishop of Armagh, and Samuel Morland, scholar, diplomat and envoy of Oliver Cromwell. Their labours secured the transportation of the manuscripts of the books of the Waldensians of the valleys, alongside many records of their trials dating from around 1500, and the safe preservation of these materials in Cambridge and Dublin.[60]

The drivers were the usual suspects: Protestant concern with the past of the true Church; counter-polemic from Catholics, arguing the novelty and variety (and hence falsity) of Protestantism; the iniquity or religious necessity of inquisition; and, within France, the Albigensian crusade as a precedent for contemporary use of force against Protestants and the latter's Albigensian

---

[57] Lucæ Tudensis episcopi, *De altera vita*, ed. Juan de Mariana (Ingolstadt, 1612), with the second dedicatory letter addressed to Jakob Gretser. See the modern edition in n. 35 above.

[58] Reineri Ordinis Prædicatorum, *Liber contra Waldenses hæreticos*, in *Lucæ Tudensis episcopi, scriptores aliquot succedanei contra sectam Waldensium*, ed. Jakob Gretser (Ingolstadt, 1613), pp. 46–99. This is one of the redactions of compilation of c. 1260–66 known as the Anonymous of Pasau and in one of the later redactions as the Pseudo-Reinerius treatise. Some extracts have been edited: Nickson, 'The "Pseudo-Reinerius" treatise', 291–311; *Quellen zur Geschichte der Waldenser*, ed. A. Patschovsky and K.-V. Selge, Texte zur Kirchen- und Theologiegeschichte 18 (Gütersloh, 1973), pp. 70–103. Flacius's edition of another version of this treatise in discussed below in ch. 9.

[59] *Tractatus Petri de Pilichdorf contra hæresin Waldensium* (= Zwicker, *Cum dormirent homines*) and *Refutatio errorum*, in *Lucæ Tudensis episcopi, scriptores aliquot succedanei*, ed. Gretser, pp. 201–90 and 291–308. Peter of Pillichsdorf features in early modern historiography – and until the late twentieth century – as the author of the *Cum dormirent* treatise. Because of the rarity of the 1613 edition, use of its reprint in 1677 has become usual in modern scholarship. Poznański's research has shown the dangers of this, because it has errors and omissions; see ch. 7 n. 5.

[60] M. Benedetti, *Il "santo bottino". Circolazione di manoscritti valdesi nell' Europa del Seicento*, Collana della Società di Studi Valdesi 24 (Turin, 2006), pp. 43–59 (Ussher) and 73–90 (Morland).

Introduction

ancestry. The French 'state' enterprise mentioned above, the production of the Collection Doat now held in the Bibliothèque nationale de France, was an outlier: its interest in royal rights was accompanied by a more Olympian concern with History.

Let us now turn to the chapters. The post-medieval section starts in chapter 9 with Harald Bollbuck's fundamental account of the most important of all the Protestant historians.[61] What Flacius set out to do is encapsulated in the longer title of his *Catalogue of witnesses to the truth, who before our age cried out against the Pope* (*Catalogus testium veritatis qui ante nostram aetatem reclamarunt papae*), which was first printed in Basle in 1556. Bollbuck outlines Flacius's combination of a dialectical view of the history of Church and his use of Kings 18. 21, with its 7,000 righteous people who would not have bowed the knee to Baal; this was the basis in scripture for the concept of a minority church. Bollbuck goes on to look at the logistics: the people and tools Flacius had to hand for the large enterprise of finding the witnesses to this minority.[62] There was a team of co-workers. There was a network of correspondents dotted around Europe who supplied Flacius with information.[63] They also helped in the finding and acquisition of the texts which were sent to Flacius and formed his own research library. Its remnants are now located and can be studied in the Herzog-August Library in Wolfenbuttel; they include the two manuscripts which are the basis for modern study of Peter Zwicker's inquisitions in Sczcecin (Stettin) in 1392–4. There was one very important preliminary point of methodology. This was that 'testimony' could also be received from members of the opposition: medieval inquisitors and Catholic polemicists also could also come to the stand to give evidence for a Protestant historian.

The longest and most systematic part of the *Catalogue* is the section devoted to the Waldensians, and it is this that Bollbuck chooses for deeper analysis. Immediately striking is the space – thirty-four pages – give to the edition of an inquisitors' manual of *c*. 1266, the one we mentioned earlier that was later edited again (from a different version) by Jakob Gretser. The anonymous author not only listed the beliefs of the Waldensians, he also attested their good character and inserted a no-holds-barred account of vices among the Catholic clergy into a chapter entitled *De causis heresum* (*On the causes of heresies*). A useful text! Bollbuck discusses Flacius's editing and

---

[61] M. Hartmann, *Humanismus und Kirchenkritik. Matthias Flacius Illyricus als Erforscher des Mittelalters*, Beiträge zur Geschichte und Quellenkunde des Mittelalters 19 (Stuttgart, 2001).

[62] Cf. the detailed account of the logistics of the Magdeburg Centuries in H. Bollbuck's *Wahrheitszeugnis, Gottes Auftrag und Zeitkritik. Die Kirchengeschichte der Magdeburger Zenturien und ihre Arbeitstechniken*, Wolfenbütteler Forschungen 138 (Wiesbaden, 2014).

[63] See n. 45 above.

putting to good use extracts from a rather positive inquisitor's description of the Waldensians from the 1390s; this is the one addressed by Välimäki in chapter 6 and (in another version) edited and translated by him. The *Catalogue* is illuminated: a foundation text. Its revisions and enlargements continued until the Frankfurt edition of 1672 and for centuries it dominated Protestant historiography.

Some book titles are both memorable and provide a brilliant distillation of their subject. One such is *Hatred in Print*, the monograph Luc Racaut published in 2002, with a subtitle that did the details: *Catholic Propaganda and Protestant Identity during the French Wars of Religion*.[64] Here, in chapter 10, Racaut looks at the notion of Cathars as ancestors of the Protestants, and asks, how did this myth emerge?[65] There are two preliminary points, the first that Catholic polemic had not only seen Protestants as heirs to earlier heretics. It had also tended to bundle together Cathars and many other earlier heretics. The second was that there was a tendency for both sides to harness the other's historiography and put it to its own uses. Racaut goes on to examine the chronology and geography of the adoption of heretics as ancestors. The process was slow, beginning with the Waldensians, who were not taken on as precursors before the 1550s. The adoption of the Cathars (in this section we use 'Cathars' and 'Albigensians' indiscriminately) shows an interesting geographical pattern. Through the figures of John Bale (1545, 1548) and John Foxe (from 1563), England was in the vanguard, quicker than the continent to welcome the Cathars for their opposition to the papacy; it was this that had had led to the imputation to them of false doctrine. Racaut then presents three themes, the first of them the incident of the rue St Jacques in 1557, when 400 Protestants were seized. The secrecy of the meeting was exploited to mount against them charges of various hideous practices. The slurs enabled Protestants to claim kinship with the early Christians and medieval heretics through the very fact that similar things had been said against them. Secondly, the crusade against Albigensian heretics (1209–29) came to be seen as directly comparable to religious war in mid-sixteenth century France. The contingencies of French politics provide the context for the writing of several histories of the crusade written in the early 1560s, as also editions and translations of Peter of les Vaux-de-Cernay's *Historia Albigensis* (*Albigensian History*), originally written between 1212 and 1218.[66] Finally, Racaut tells the story of the preoccupation of the reformed synods with

---

[64] L. Racaut, *Hatred in Print: Catholic Propaganda and Protestant Identity during the French Wars of Religion*, St Andrews Studies in Reformation History (Aldershot, 2002).

[65] An early milestone was provided by M.-H. Vicaire, 'Les Albigeois ancêtres de protestants: assimilations catholiques', and G. Bedouelle, 'Les Albigeois témoins du veritable Evangile: l'Historiographie protestante', in *Historiographie du Catharisme*, pp. 23–46 and 47–70.

[66] On the thirteenth–sixteenth century translations, see also *Petri Vallium Sarnai monachi, Hystoria Albigensis*, ed. P. Guébin and E. Lyon, 3 vols. (Paris, 1926–39), III, lxvi–xc; on Arnaud Sorbin's version, lxxxiii–xc.

Introduction

history, beginning with Nîmes in 1572 and the resolution adopted there to get an Occitan history of the Albigensians translated into French and printed. Racaut suggests a connection between the repetition of this commission at the synod of Montauban in 1594 and the appearance in the following year of the *Histoire des Albigeois* of Jean Chassanion. Chassanion had in his hands and used two old manuscripts of histories of the Albigensian crusades, one very favourable and one very hostile to the heretics.[67] His theologico-historical conclusion was clear and emphatic: Protestants were 'the harvest of the seed sown by the Albigensians'. With a stylish flourish, Racaut frames his chapter with allusions to the modern proposition that the heretics known hitherto as Cathars (see Feuchter, ch. 3 n. 34) were invented by the Church. The suggestion is of affinity between two myths: Cathar origins of Protestants as myth and the medieval Cathars as myth.

This collection moves forward to the 1660s in chapters 11–12. Written by Shelagh Sneddon and Peter Biller, these are devoted to Jean de Doat (*c*.1600–83). His employment by Jean-Baptiste Colbert to copy documents in southern France resulted in 258 volumes that are now in the French national library. After introducing Doat and the project, Sneddon turns to a subset of these volumes, nos. 21–26, containing copies of thirteenth-century inquisition records, mainly depositions. She describes how the copies are laid out. Their contents are two-fold and in two languages. On the one hand, there are the copies in Latin of the texts contained in the old registers. On the other hand, these Latin depositions are preceded by resumés of their contents. These summaries are in French and they were composed by the scribes. They were written in a larger hand and the mise-en-page was well thought out. It boldly and clearly signalled the alternation, and readers flicking through the leaves could see this in an instant and alight on what they wanted.

Since the scribes employed by Doat had to be able to transcribe Latin and to know broadly what it meant, they needed some education. The impression given by Doat's memoranda, however, is that they were a rough and ready lot who had just sufficient knowledge to do the job. Sneddon has seen an opportunity here. Their summary introductions provide rare access to one stratum of culture, that of men who were far removed from the polished literary humanists and erudite scholars of the period. Sneddon compares the summaries and the depositions, to see how these scribes understood the originals and what this shows about their own outlook and knowledge. And she adds a comparison between the Doat scribes' summaries and the descriptions provided by a near contemporary in the catalogue he produced of medieval inquisition manuscripts in Carcassonne. An ingenious method provides glimpses of the minds of a non-elite group.

---

[67] See *La Chanson de la Croisade Albigeoise*, ed. E. Martin-Chabot, 3 vols., 3rd edn (Paris, 1972–6), I, xxv, where it is suggested that Chassanion had at his disposal a prose version of the *Chanson*.

Sneddon states the importance of Doat's mission: it copied a vast number of documents from southern France whose originals have been lost. Its copies have therefore come to occupy a large role in the construction of our knowledge of earlier southern French history. Crucial, then, are how materials to be transcribed were chosen and, then, how faithfully they were copied. Here and there the survival of other manuscripts of some of the texts copied enables answers to the second question, but the first is less tractable. Memoranda about the project written by Doat and his immediate boss, Pierre de Carcavy (Colbert's librarian) provide many details, but do not open windows into Doat's mind.[68] This problem suggested the approach taken by Peter Biller in chapter 12. Doat visited the Dominican convent in Toulouse and chose three inquisition registers out of a dozen. If we cannot get inside his mind, can we at least look at the people he met, even the buildings in which he worked, to draw nearer to him as he was looking at the old manuscripts? The investigation led Biller to one Dominican who was at hand, a famous theologian and part-time historian called Antonin Réginald. Biller edits part of Réginald's *Chronicle of Inquisitors*. Biller sets Doat in the company of this erudite scholar and within the ambience of the convent, even the paintings of Dominican inquisitors and martyrs that Doat could see in the chapter-house: these are what surrounded him when he made his choice. The chapter presents a vignette, just a moment in Doat's life: contrasting with the large subjects and panoramic views of most of the other chapters in this collection.

Now long taken for granted is the distinction brilliantly described by Edward Peters in 1989 in his *Inquisition*: between the historical reality of inquisition on the one hand and the myth of The Inquisition on the other.[69] Michaela Valente's subject in the collection's final piece, chapter13, is the Inquisition in the sixteenth century. The main stage is Italy, but a wider European cast of commentators also play their roles. Her theme is not its reality, but its myth or images, and how these were constructed by its defenders and detractors. The increasing extremism of the institution was attributed to Gian Pietro Carafa (pope as Paul IV, 1555–9). He had already written in 1532 that history showed that great heresies were only destroyed by blood, and the tone is set for Valente's remarkable account by the infamous statement attributed to him in 1557: 'If our father were a heretic, we would carry the bundles of sticks to burn him'. Though much criticism of the Inquisition was kept private it

---

[68] See the detailed account by L. Albaret, 'La collection Doat, une collection moderne, témoignage de l'histoire religieuse méridionale des XIIIe et XIVe siècles', in *Historiens modernes et Moyen Âge méridional*, ed. M. Fournié, D. O. Hurel and D. Le Blevec, Cahiers de Fanjeaux 49 (Toulouse, 2014), pp. 57–93.

[69] For general views see F. Bethencourt, *The Inquisition. A Global History, 1478–1834* (Cambridge, 2009), ch. 9 'Representations'; M. Valente, *Contro l'inquisizione. Il dibattito europeo secc. XVI-XVIII*, Collana della Società di Studi Valdesi 29 (Turin, 2009).

Introduction

also found open expression. On Carafa's death in 1559 there was a violent attack on the palace of Inquisition in Rome. Various textual genres articulated criticism. They ranged from the popular satires of *pasquinate* to the recherché pleasures of an erudite Latin parody of an inquisitors' manual of procedure. This parody was published in Basle, but it was after all a spoof, a joke: so the title page bore Rome as the place of publication; see fig. 24. Images also played a role. Driven to rage by the way inquisitors had frustrated his career, the patriarch of Aquileia commissioned frescoes in his palace containing a representation of his conflict with them. Valente also cites as an example of 'the battle of images' the illustrations in Richard Verstegan's *Theatre of Cruelties of Heretics of Our Time* of 1587.

Defenders insisting on the legitimacy of the Inquisition claimed various degrees of antiquity: it went back to expulsion from the garden of Eden; to Christ and the apostles; to classical times; and to early fathers of the Church, Augustine and Tertullian, who were precursors, early fighters against heresies. Constant themes for those attacking the Inquisition were the charges of abuse, greed, ambition and mercilessness. Though much was endlessly and unchangingly repeated, Valente also discerns some fertile ground among these detractors for new things: the ultimate emergence of thought about the rejection of all persecution, and the development of an historical approach to inquisition. These lie in the future, as does also the extraordinary place which would come to be held by inquisition in the Gothic novel and modern popular culture.

Coda

On the front cover of this book is a reproduction of a fresco in the Stanza della Segnatura in the Vatican painted by Raphael. The editors chose it not only because of its elegance but because of its affinity with the book's chronology. Gregory IX is depicted receiving the *Five Books of the Decretals* from Raymond of Peñaforte in 1234. Its fifth book, title 7, 'On heretics', was a legislative milestone. A painting of 1511 represents an event of 1234, and there is a counterpart in the face of the pope. Raphael uses the features of his patron, Pope Julius II, for the face of the earlier pope. The image is a complex counterpart to early modern historians making their own use of medieval heresy and inquisition.

Modern history of art puts forward a strong case for seeing the iconographical schema painted by Raphael in these rooms as the product of the mind of Julius II's librarian, the humanist scholar Tommaso Inghirami.[70]

---

[70] C. L. Joost-Gaugier, *Raphael's Stanza della Segnatura: Meaning and Invention* (Cambridge, 2002), chs. 3 and 9; B. Talvacchia, *Raphael* (London and New York, 2007), ch. 3.

The schema is the coherent and unified product of one mind. Not so this book, nor any collection of essays originating in a conference and written by different scholars. 'Knowledge' is understood variously in this collection, and a scant dozen chapters can only give a selection of jigsaw pieces, not a whole picture. The point is the crackle and stimulus that comes from the different outlooks of the historians gathered here, the alternation between panorama and close-up as one goes from chapter to chapter, and serendipity. This or that heretic or inquisitor turns up unexpectedly in different chapters: Bernard Gui pops up as an author in Flacius's library in chapter 9 and in a painting on a convent wall in chapter 12. And there is a thread of dark humour. In chapter 1 there is the bitter witticism attributed to a mutilated heretic (cited above); in chapter 12 Jean-Jacques Percin getting something funny out of the story of decapitated friars marching back to their convent carrying their heads; and in the last chapter a *Private Eye* exercise, the spoof of an inquisition manual.

We end with a story. A recent manuscript discovery has brought into view a case which combines many of this volume's themes: inquisition records, their loss and at the same also preservation in part through copying in the seventeenth century, and their use in religious polemic. It is also bound up with personal tragedy, and we present it here as our *envoi*.[71]

There once existed an inquisition register of 159 parchment folios. It contained the depositions of 285 people who were interrogated between 1282 and 1319, and it probably came from Toulouse. In the late seventeenth century it was in private hands, but it has never been found. Its owner, however, had transcribed some extracts from it, amounting probably to about 13% of the original. This was spotted in 2017 in a library and it has just been published.[72] How significant are the extracts? Several inquisitors about whom some but not much is known were at work, and there is a reference to a text used by the 'Cathars', the *Vision of Isaiah*, which crops up sporadically but rarely in medieval evidence. This is a discovery and in a modest way it adds to our knowledge of medieval heresy and inquisition.

It also adds to our picture of erudition, polemic and the twisting of history in the late seventeenth century. The register's owner, François Graverol (1636–94), had been born into a Protestant family in Nîmes, where he was active as a lawyer, scholar and book-collector. He allowed his precious manuscript to be used by a Dominican historian, Jean Benoist, who was preparing a

---

[71] The following is based on D. Toti, 'François Graverol e un manoscritto perduto de l'Inquisizione di Tolosa', *Riforma e Movimenti Religiosi* 8 (2020), 215–89.

[72] The text was noticed by an anonymous reader in the Bibliothèque de la Société de l'Histoire de Protestantisme in Paris, who alerted the Protestant pastor and historian Michel Jas, who in turn alerted Daniel Toti. Michel Jas is cited by Luc Racaut as one of the Protestant pastors of today who still maintain the idea of Cathar ancestry; below, ch. 10 n. 6.

Introduction

history of medieval heresy (Benoist features in chapter 12). The revocation of the Edict of Nantes shaped Graverol's later years. In 1685 he tried to flee the country but was caught and put in prison. Six months of this persuaded him to abjure his faith and swear to live and die as a Catholic – though an eighteenth-century historian of Nîmes states that he continued to practise the reformed faith in secret. This chronology appears to explain the uses to which he put the register. Earlier, in 1684 – and therefore before his forced conversion – Graverol wrote to a reformed theologian, Pierre Jurieu, sending him the transcript of the interrogation of someone called William of Marnhac. William seems to have been a courageous man with plain and straight beliefs. In front of the inquisitor he maintained that taking an oath was forbidden in the Gospels, and he rejected the papacy and the Catholic hierarchy. William was a good figure to claim as an ancestor, and his deposition duly appeared in both Latin and English translation in the Huguenot Peter Allix's *Remarks upon the Ecclesiastical History of the Antient Churches of the Albigenses*, published in London in 1692; see figs. 0.7–0.8.[73]

Ten years later Graverol made the transcriptions that have just been published. Marnhac's deposition was included, but it was the exception. All the others seem to have been deliberately chosen to illustrate the opposite. They were depositions showing dualist and other very radically unorthodox beliefs. Graverol copies what he had written in French, in January 1694, to the unknown 'Monseigneur' who had asked for the copies. Here they are, 'and in many places you will find the Albigensians had the doctrines of the Manichaeans or the Anabaptists'. The 'Monseigneur' cannot be identified with certainty; it could be the bishop of Meaux, Bossuet, who had enquired about the manuscript, but he is not the only possibility.[74] But what of Graverol himself? He had been broken. In these last months before his death he was cherry-picking his text to help the enemy.

[73] pp. 165–9. On Allix see Benedetti, *Il "santo bottino"*, pp. 91–101.
[74] Toti, 'François Graverol e un manoscritto perduto', 226–7.

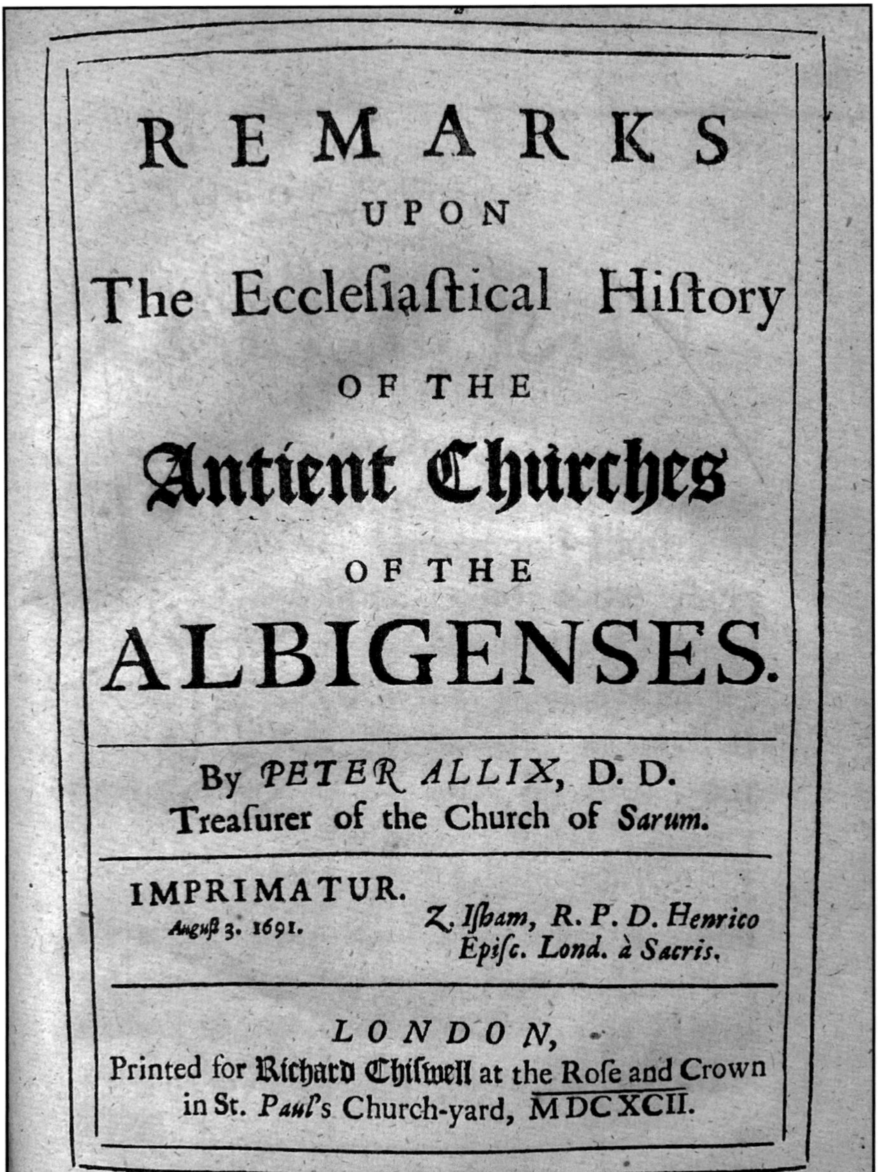

REMARKS

UPON

The Ecclefiaftical Hiftory

OF THE

𝕬𝖓𝖙𝖎𝖊𝖓𝖙 𝕮𝖍𝖚𝖗𝖈𝖍𝖊𝖘

OF THE

ALBIGENSES.

By *PETER ALLIX*, D. D.
Treafurer of the Church of *Sarum*.

IMPRIMATUR.
Auguſt 3. 1691.   *Z. Iſham, R. P. D. Henrico*
Epiſc. Lond. à Sacris.

L O N D O N,
Printed for 𝕽𝖎𝖈𝖍𝖆𝖗𝖉 𝕮𝖍𝖎𝖘𝖜𝖊𝖑𝖑 at the Roſe and Crown
in St. *Paul*'s Church-yard, MDCXCII.

Figure 0.7   Peter Allix, *Remarks upon the Ecclesiastical History of the Antient Churches of the Albigenses* (London, 1692), title page. Private collection.

Ancient Churches of the Albigenses.

169

" the Order of Friars Preachers ; and of *Julian Vascon*, pub-
" lick Notary of *Tholouse*, who wrote this.
The Letter which Mr. *G.* writ to my Friend, concluded with
these Words. " I muſt not forget to tell you, that accord-
" ing to my Copy, the *Albigenſes* ſaid of themſelves, that
" they were *de illis qui non reddebant malum pro malo, of thoſe*
" *who did not render Evil for Evil* ; that *boni homines, good Men*
" were their Miniſters. The Formality they obſerved when
" they made a Proſelyte, was this, *Hæreticaverunt eum ponentes*
" *librum & manus ſuper caput ejus, & interrogantes eum ſi volebat*
" *ſe reddere Deo & Evangelio. They made him a Heretick by lay-*
" *ing a Book, and their Hands upon his Head, and asking him, whe-*
" *ther he were willing to ſurrender himſelf to God and the Goſpel?*
" I have obſerved from ſeveral Paſſages, that on this occa-
" ſion they were uſed to read more particularly the Goſpel
" according to St. *John*, and that after theſe Solemnities the
" Proſelytes *adorabant dictos bonos homines, flexis ter genibus, di-*
" *cendo, Benedicite; Hæreticis reſpondentibus, Deus vos benedicat* ;
" Paid their Reverence to theſe good Men, by thrice bend-
" ing of the Knee, ſaying, *Give us your Bleſſing*: the Here-
" ticks anſwering, *God bleſs you.* The Inquiſitors call the
" Proſelytes and thoſe that are born *Albigenſes, Hereticks.*
It is eaſy to judg by this Specimen, that it is almoſt impoſſi-
ble to give any Credit to the Depoſition of Inquiſitors, concerning the Matters, which they ſay, they have made the
Albigenſes confeſs ; and that therefore this pretended Conviction of the *Albigenſes*, by the Regiſters of the Inquiſitors, is
abſolutely null.
The ſecond thing that I am to repreſent to the Reader, is,
that the Teſtimony of the Inquiſitors cannot be ſet againſt the
contrary Confeſſions of the *Albigenſes*, which thoſe who have
read, find very conformable to the Faith of the Proteſtants.
This is that which *Paradin* affirms in his Annals of *Burgundy*,
where he confeſſes that he has read ſome Hiſtories, which ex-
cuſe the *Albigenſes*, with their Princes and Lords, of all thoſe
Crimes which many have caſt upon them, affirming them to
be wholly innocent, as having never done any thing elſe, but reprove

Z

Figure 0.8   Allix, *Remarks*, p. 169. Allix received from a 'Friend' of 'Mr. G. Advocate of N.' – references to Pierre Jurieu and François Graverol – the deposition of William of Marnhac, printing it together with an English translation in his *Remarks*, pp. 165-9. It ends on the first two lines of p. 169 and is followed by an extract from Graverol's letter to Jurieu. Private Collection.

Part I: Medieval

1

Inquisitorial identity and authority in thirteenth-century exegesis and sermons: Jean Halgrin d'Abbeville, Jacques de Vitry and Humbert of Romans

Jessalynn Lea Bird

Contemporaneous with the foundation of the university of Toulouse (partly staffed by Paris-trained masters) and anti-heretical preaching, episcopal inquests, and synodal legislation in Narbonne (1227) and Toulouse (1229),[1] the Paris master and cardinal Jean Halgrin d'Abbeville was dispatched to the Iberian peninsula with full legatine powers (1228–30).[2] The spectrum of reactions to Jean's reforming legation mirrored responses to the legatine tour of Jean's former colleague Robert Courson in northern France, Flanders-Brabant and the Midi (1213–15). Both men combined powerful preaching in support of the Albigensian crusade and against heresy with holding reforming inquests, diocesan synods and provincial councils that attempted to entice or force local clergy into conformity with the Paris-based reform program that had influenced the very substance of the Fourth Lateran Council's decrees (1215) Jean was tasked to implement in Iberia: the education of clergy and the laity in the faith; combatting heresy through preaching, confession and inquest; an emphasis on preaching and confession; the differentiation of ecclesiastics from seculars in dress and conduct; curbing absenteeism, pluralism,

---

[1] See J. H. Arnold and P. Biller, ed. and trans., *Heresy and Inquisition in France, 1200–1300*, Manchester Medieval Sources (Manchester, 2016), pp. 190–7; B. M. Kienzle, *Cistercians, Heresy and Crusade in Occitania, 1145–1229: Preaching in the Lord's Vineyard* (York, 2001), pp. 174–201.

[2] J. Ribaillier, 'Jean d'Abbeville', *Dictionnaire de spiritualité*, VIII, 249–56; P. J. Cole, *The Preaching of the Crusades to the Holy Land, 1095–1270* (Cambridge MA, 1991), pp. 150–6; P. Linehan, *The Spanish Church and the Papacy in the Thirteenth Century*, Cambridge Studies in Medieval Life and Thought, 3rd s., 4 (Cambridge, 1971), pp. 20–82; P. Linehan, 'A Papal Legation and its Aftermath. Cardinal John of Abbeville in Spain and Portugal, 1228–1229', in *Historical Memory and Clerical Activity in Medieval Spain and Portugal*, ed. P. Linehan, Variorum Collected Studies Series 1011 (London, 2012), I, 236–56; and the discussion below.

Jessalynn Lea Bird

simony, and clerical concubinage. Despite inevitable criticism and resistance, Jean d'Abbeville found supporters in the curia (including Jacques de Vitry, Honorius III, and Gregory IX) and on the Iberian peninsula, including Jaime I, king of Aragon, Guillem, bishop of Vic, Pedro de Albalat, archbishop of Tarragona, and their associate Raymon de Peñafort, future Dominican master general (1238–41) and writer of tremendously influential works on canon law, penance, and compassionate guidelines for conducting blended episcopal-mendicant inquisitions. Raymon assisted Jean (1228–9) in reforming the very dioceses which would shortly become test-cases for the implementation of royally backed episcopal inquests in Iberia – Barcelona (1241) and Tarragona (1232, 1237, 1242) – before being lured to Rome at a period when important papal letters governing the treatment of heresy were being issued (1230–2).[3] While the Paris-educated Rodrigo Jiménez de Rada, archbishop of Toledo, possessed more ambivalent feelings about outside intrusion into Iberian affairs, Rodrigo's sometime associate Lucas of Tuy corresponded with Jacques de Vitry, wrote an anti-heretical treatise, and may have been taken by Jean d'Abbeville to Rome.[4] Pedro de Albalat remained in amicable contact with Jean d'Abbeville and Raymon de Peñafort in the early 1230s; Pedro's provincial council at Tarragona (1242) joined Jean's Parisian reform program to a declaration of a

---

[3] Although indebted to Peter Linehan's careful studies of Jean's legation, I do not share his assessment of Jean as lacking 'the common touch', and his sermons as laden with 'a stifling scholarly apparatus'. See Linehan, *Spanish Church*, esp. pp. 48–9, 55–62, 66, 69, 71–7; Peter Linehan, 'Pedro de Albalat, Arzobispo de Tarragona y su "Summa Septem Sacramentorum"', in *Spanish Church and Society, 1150–1300*, ed. P. Linehan, Variorum Collected Studies Series 184 (London, 1983), III, 9–30; D. J. Smith, *Crusade, Heresy, and Inquisition in the Lands of the Crown of Aragon (c. 1167 – 1276)*, The Medieval and Early Modern Iberian World 39 (Leiden and Boston, 2010), pp. 4–5, 104, 106, 113–17, 126–7, 188–209; D. J. Smith, 'Raymond de Penyafort and His Influence', in *The Friars and their Influence in Medieval Spain*, ed. F. García-Serrano, Church, Faith and Culture in the Medieval West (Amsterdam, 2018), pp. 45–60; C. C. Ames, *Righteous Persecution: Inquisition, Dominicans, and Christianity in the Middle Ages* (Philadelphia, 2009), pp. 148–52, 164, 169; A. García y García, ed., *Constitutiones Concilii quarti Lateranensis una cum commentariis glossatorum* , Monumenta Iuris Canonici. Series A: Corpus glossatorum 2 (Vatican, 1981).

[4] Both Rodrigo and Lucas had been in Paris, but each were selective in applying what they learned there to conditions in Iberia. See Smith, *Crusade, Heresy, and Inquisition*, pp. 133–7; R. Lerner and C. Morerode, 'The Vision of "John, Hermit of Asturias": Lucas of Tuy, Apostolic Religion, and Eschatological Expectation', *Traditio* 61 (2006), 195–225; P. Linehan, 'Dates and Doubts about Don Lucas', in *Historical Memory*, II, 201–17; Lucas of Tuy, *De altera vita*, ed. E. Falque Rey, Corpus Christianorum Continuatio Mediaevalis 74A (Turnhout, 2009); L. K. Pick, *Conflict and Coexistence: Archbishop Rodrigo and the Muslims and Jews in Medieval Spain*, History, Languages and Cultures of the Portugese and Spanish Worlds (Ann Arbor, 2004), pp. 81, 122–26, 172–81; T. Rojo Orcajo, 'La biblioteca del arzobispo don Rodrigo Jiménez de Rada y los manuscritos del monasterio de Santa Maria de Huerta', *Revista Eclesiástica* 1 (1929), 196–219 (pp. 198, 206–8, 218).

Inquisitorial identity and authority in thirteenth-century exegesis and sermons

'war against heresy' and planned unannounced episcopal visitations with the assistance of local mendicants. Pedro's *Summa septem sacramentorum* (which urged priests to make inquiries about heretics) and the inquisitor's manual generally attributed to Raymon de Peñafort were both indebted to the statutes of the Paris bishop Eudes de Sully introduced into Iberia by Jean d'Abbeville.[5] We ought perhaps also to consider Jean de Abbeville's sermons as another potential source for 'Parisian' influence on early anti-heretical inquests in Iberia. Careful tracing of networks, papal correspondence, synodal legislation, and John's surviving sermon collections (delivered at multiple points in his career but almost certainly compiled and retouched at later dates) provides crucial evidence for the transmission of pre-mendicant notions of clerical reform and how best to suppress heresy from Paris-trained masters to Rome, Iberian bishops, and the mendicant orders.

However, in order to understand the self-identity of the inquisitor, we must also examine how inquisitors explained to themselves and to their audiences the combination of pastoral and judicial offices inquisitors exercised as preacher, confessor, disputer, and judge. How did orthodox preachers explain that the 'good men' and their teaching were not as holy as they seemed and counter critiques of the ministers of the Latin Church while still demonstrating that they were aware of the fallibility of orthodox ministers and were taking measures to 'clean house'? This task was knotty enough for local bishops and their secular clerical or regular religious delegates conducting anti-heretical preaching and inquests (for example, Cistercians and Paris masters). Further complications ensued when these tasks were delegated to the mendicant orders, whose involvement, first in conjunction with episcopal inquests and later in other forms of inquests, raised questions of authority, credibility and the degree of poverty, asceticism, and learning required of orthodox ministers and their relationship to the local clergy and populace.[6]

Many of these questions are not new, but this chapter will outline fresh avenues for research into inquisitorial identities and mentalities. In addition to the traditionally utilized narrative sources on anti-heretical preaching and early inquisitors' manuals, there were many other sources used by the inquisitors and their supporters to justify and rationalize their activities. These included sermons typically preached by bishops or guest preachers during episcopal visitations and synods (occasions for the earliest prosecutions of heresy). Such sermons focused on reforming local orthodox clergy (considered essential to counteract heretical critiques), on establishing the identity and authority of the orthodox pastor, and on conveying the basics

---

[5] See notes 3 above and 37 below.

[6] For outstanding recent surveys, see Ames, *Righteous Persecution*; J. K. Dean, *A History of Medieval Heresy and Inquisition* (Lanham MD, 2011); L. J. Sackville, *Heresy and Heretics in the Thirteenth Century: The Textual Representations*, Heresy and Inquisition in the Middle Ages 1 (York, 2011); note 1 above.

of the faith to lay attendees either during or immediately after synods. Visitation and legatine sermons also outlined the responsibility of the bishop and/or legate to clean house and prosecute those of *mala fama* (evil repute).[7] Moreover, biblical commentaries intertwined discussions of the dangers of heresy with the duties of orthodox ministers.[8] This paper will instead largely focus on another mainstay for most congregations' knowledge of heresy: sermons for the liturgical year that outlined the duties of orthodox pastors to guide their flock through an exemplary life, preaching, confession, and discipline, as well as the dangers posed by corrupt and/or unorthodox ministers to the faithful.

While writing this chapter, I consulted a wide range of liturgical sermon collections, including those compiled by Popes Innocent III and Honorius III;[9] by the well-informed Cistercian Caesarius of Heisterbach; by secular or canon-regular Paris masters involved in anti-heretical work including Philip the Chancellor, Jean d'Abbeville and Jacques de Vitry; and by the first generation of masters to join the mendicant orders in Paris and some of later generations, including John of la Rochelle, Alexander of Hales, Odo of Châteauroux, Robert of Sorbonne, and Humbert of Romans.[10] I did

---

[7] For the complex resonances and legal consequences of the term *mala fama*, see J. Bird, 'The Wheat and the Tares: Peter the Chanter's Circle and the *Fama*-Based Inquest Against Heresy and Criminal Sins, c.1198-c.1235', in *Proceedings of the Twelfth International Congress of Medieval Canon Law, Washington, D.C., 1–7 August, 2004*, ed. U.-R. Blumenthal, K. Pennington and A. A. Larson, Monumenta Iuris Canonici, Series C: Subsidia 13 (Vatican, 2008), pp. 763–856, at pp. 780–94; J. Théry, 'Fama: l'opinion publique comme preuve. Aperçu sur la révolution médiévale de l'inquisitoire (XIIe-XIVe siècles)', in *La preuve en justice de l'Antiquité à nos jours*, ed. B. Lemesle, Collection "Histoire" (Rennes, 2003), pp. 119–47; H. A. Kelly, 'The Fourth Lateran Ordo of Inquisition Adapted to the Prosecution of Heresy', in *A Companion to Heresy Inquisitions*, ed. D. S. Prudlo, Brill Companions to the Christian Tradition 85 (Leiden and Boston, 2019), pp. 75–107.

[8] For sermons, see J. Bird, 'Before the Time of Grace?: Peter the Chanter's Circle, Philip the Chancellor, and Pre-Mendicant Sermons Against Heresy and in Support of Inquests', in *The Origins of Inquisition*, ed. L. J. Sackville (forthcoming); J. Bird, 'Synodal Sermons as Vectors for Reform and the Fourth Lateran Council (1215)', in *Teacher as Shepherd: Theology and Care of Souls at the time of Lateran IV*, ed. C. Monagle and N. Senoçak (forthcoming). For biblical commentaries, see P. Buc, '*Vox Clamantis in Deserto*? Pierre le Chantre et la Prédication Laïque', *Revue Mabillon* n.s. 4 (1993), 5–47; and the discussion below.

[9] See C. Grasso, 'La problématique de l'hérésie dans les sermons d'Innocent III', in *Innocent III et le Midi*, ed. M. Fournié, *et al.*, Cahiers de Fanjeaux 50 (Toulouse, 2015), pp. 231–53; I. Fonnesberg-Schmidt, 'The Sermons of Pope Honorius III', in *Papacy, Crusade, and Christian-Muslim Relations*, ed. J. Bird, Church, Faith and Culture in the Medieval West (Amsterdam, 2018), pp. 45–61.

[10] I am writing a monograph on the treatment of heresy in sermon collections in the thirteenth century. For useful summaries of existing literature on the individuals named, see notes 8–9 above; F. Morenzoni, 'Les sermons *Contra haereticos* du cardinal Eudes de Châteauroux (d. 1273)', *Sacris Erudiri* 54 (2015), 265–408; N.

Inquisitorial identity and authority in thirteenth-century exegesis and sermons

so in order to try to track changes in the justification of the right to preach against and prosecute heretics as a good pastor or as one of his assisting 'dogs'. Preachers and audiences would have been familiar with certain set times of the year when sermons tackled the identity and authority of the preacher and pastor and the need to distinguish between heretical and orthodox beliefs. Those preaching on these topics would have turned to a sermon collection or to the biblical authorities glossed in lectures (preserved in bible commentaries) to construct sermons around the verses embedded in the liturgical readings for the feast day. Because of the way in which the Bible was taught and glossed in Paris, certain chains of mental association were forged between biblical passages believed to describe heresy, such that a predictable association of metaphors and assumptions are found in, for example, commentaries on Matthew 7 and sermons on wolves in sheep's clothing.[11]

Both heterodox and orthodox preachers utilized a complex metaphorical discourse and expected their audiences to be familiar with it from synodal sermons and set-occasion *sermones dominicales* (Sunday sermons). One well-known reported or imagined instance of this is an anonymously authored *exemplum* about Fulk, bishop of Toulouse included in Albert Lecoy de la Marche's compilation of *exempla* from the Dominican inquisitor Stephen of Bourbon's treatise on the gifts of the Holy Spirit. While preaching to his flock on the verse 'Beware false prophets' (Matthew 7. 15), Fulk supposedly dutifully explained that the wolves in sheep's clothing were heretics and the true sheep were Christians. A heretic whom Simon de Montfort had viciously mutilated promptly interrupted Fulk's sermon with: 'You hear what the bishop said, that we are wolves and you sheep, but have you ever seen a sheep bite a wolf this way?' Fulk answered that just as Cistercian abbots do not keep all their livestock at the abbey but have granges where the sheep are defended from wolves by dogs, so the Church keeps Christians in many other sheepfolds besides Rome. Here the Church has sent a strong and good dog to guard her sheep, that is, the count of Montfort, who bit this wolf because he was devouring Christians.[12] The discourse is drawn directly from papal letters in support of anti-heretical preaching and crusading and Innocent III's and Honorius III's sermons on the good pastor, copies of

---

Bériou, *L'avénement des maîtres de la parole: la prédication à Paris au XIIIe siècle*, Collection des Études Augustiniennes. Série Moyen Âge et Temps Modernes 2, 2 vols. (Paris, 1998).

[11] See I. Bueno, 'False Prophets and Ravening Wolves: Biblical Exegesis as a Tool against Heretics in Jacques Fournier's *Postilla* on Matthew', *Speculum* 89.1 (2014), 35–65; I. Bueno, *Defining Heresy: Inquisition, Theology and Papal Policy in the Time of Jacques Fournier*, Studies in Medieval and Reformation Traditions 192 (Leiden and Boston, 2015), pp. 151–244; and the discussion below.

[12] A. Lecoy de la Marche, *Anecdotes historiques, légendes et apologues, tirés du recueil inédit d'Étienne de Bourbon, Dominicain du XIIIe siècle* (Paris, 1877), pp. 23–4, n. 3.

Jessalynn Lea Bird

which were sent to Arnaud Amaury (legate for the anti-heretical mission in the Midi before becoming archbishop of Narbonne) and the Cistercian and Dominican orders respectively.[13]

Criticism such as this was every orthodox preacher's nightmare. How could he justify to mixed audiences the repression of heresy by violence and help listeners to distinguish between true and false pastors, guard dogs and wolves, when the same language was being utilized by hostile orthodox and heterodox opponents? To answer this question, we must turn to the major set piece occasions for preaching on these topics. These included 'I am the good shepherd' (John 10. 11–18) Sunday (the second after Pentecost); the septuagesimal Sunday which took as its theme verse: 'Beware the wolves who come in sheep's clothing' (Matthew 7. 15); and virtually any other occasion that a sermon touched on the duties of the orthodox pastor and his sheep and their corrupt or heretical counterparts: mercenaries, thieves, brigands, and wolves.

Sources and discourses:
sermons on ideal preachers and good and bad shepherds

When the highly regarded preacher, Paris master, and cardinal Jean d'Abbeville was entrusted with a reforming and anti-heretical legation to the Iberian peninsula, he quickly drafted into his *familia* the future anti-heretical writer and Dominican master general Raymon de Peñafort. Jean's expertise as a Paris-trained theologian in detecting heresy was invaluable, and when charges of heresy were later levied against Guillem, bishop of Vic, it was to Jean that the hearing of the case was entrusted at a time when both he and Jacques de Vitry were likely compiling and revising their sermon collections in Rome.[14] Jean must have delivered many sermons during his Iberian legation and multiple collections of Jean's sermons survive. Those for the liturgical year appear fairly uniform in their content, and we know that at least one compilation of Jean's sermons was treasured by a canon Jean appointed to the chapter in Vic. Heresy was much on the mind of Iberian prelates and kings during John's tour, and Jean's sermon collections bear eloquent witness to his attempts to reform the local clergy, reiterate the duties of orthodox prelates,

---

[13] Innocent III, 'Ego sum pastor bonus', *Patrologia Latina* 217, 405–10; Honorius III, 'Ego sum pastor bonus', in *Honorii III romani pontificis opera omnia quae exstant*, ed. C. Horoy, Medii ævi bibliotheca patristica, seu ejusdem temporis patrologia ab anno MCCXVI usque ad Concilii tridentini tempora, 5 vols. (Paris, 1879–82), I, 916–25. For context, see note 9 above; J. Bird, 'Paris Masters and the Justification of the Albigensian Crusade', *Crusades* 6 (2007), 117–55.

[14] Ironically, Guillem possessed copies of standard Parisian texts, including Peter Comestor's *Historia scolastica*, and biblical commentaries. See E. Junyent i Subirà, 'Un importante legado de libros en el siglo XII, *Hispania Sacra* 2 (1949), 425–9 (p. 428); Linehan, 'Papal Legations', pp. 243–8, 251–3; note 3 above.

Inquisitorial identity and authority in thirteenth-century exegesis and sermons

and help lay and clerical audiences alike distinguish between heterodox and orthodox preachers.[15] Jean's approach and the content of his sermons follow that of other contemporary preachers and reformers including Jean's former master, Stephen Langton, Odo of Cheriton, the Cistercian Caesarius of Heisterbach, Innocent III and Honorius III, and Jacques de Vitry, Philip the Chancellor, and Odo of Châteauroux. Jean's advice would have found audiences not only in Iberia, but in Gregory IX's curia (where both Jean [1227–37] and Jacques de Vitry [1229–40] served as cardinals) and through Raymon de Peñafort, in the Dominican order.[16]

As did his contemporaries, Jean used Adventine sermons on the preaching of Christ and John the Baptist to openly counter Christological heresies, including those of the 'Manichees', clearly contemporary dualists although lumped into an examination of patristic heresies. Aware of heretics' detestation of John the Baptist, Abbeville championed him as a prototypical orthodox penance preacher, whose rejection of riches, soft clothing, and human adulation put to shame corrupt prelates who were all too willing to preach peace to sinners and pervert ecclesiastical justice and the penitential process in return for bribes while devouring the innocent with harsh rebukes. The Baptist's abstemious diet and ascetic clothing of camel-skin enacted his rejection of worldly delights and sin and rebuked clergymen who, 'like women', dressed in luxurious clothing and used delicate foods. Abbeville was clearly treading a fine line here – anticipating heterodox attacks on the concubinary and dissolute orthodox clergymen he routinely excommunicated during a legatine tour punctuated by numerous synods. He therefore moved to quickly provide an alternative ideal in John the Baptist, who in the following sermon was presented as a penance preacher who attacked worldly vices. Abbeville's detailed explication of how even the remedy of marriage could be undermined through adultery or loving one's wife excessively indicates an attempt to explain the benefits of orthodox marriage while countering, without planting too many deviant ideas into his audience's minds, what were considered the overly libertine attitudes towards sexual relations attributed by orthodox writers to Cathars and Muslims.[17] Contemporaries

---

[15] For the canon, see note 14 above; for Jean's sermons, J. B. Schneyer, *Repertorium der Lateinischen Sermones des Mittelalters für die Zeit von 1150–1350*, 11 vols. (Münster, 1969–90), III, 510–66.

[16] A. Paravicini Bagliani, *Cardinali di curia e 'familiae' cardinalizie dal 1227 al 1254*, Italia Sacra. Studi e Documenti di Storia Ecclesiastica 18–19, 2 vols. (Padua, 1972), I, 19–31, 98–112; Iacobus de Vitriaco, *Sermones vulgares vel ad status*, ed. J. Longère, 2 vols., Corpus Christianorum Continuatio Mediaevalis 255 (Turnhout, 2013–), I, vii–xcviii.

[17] 'In principio erat Verbum', Paris, Bibliothèque nationale de France (henceforth BnF), MS Lat. 2909, fols. 17r–18v; 'Cum Christus praedicaret', BnF MS Lat. 2909, fols. 10r–11v (fols. 10v–11r); 'Miserunt judei a<b> Iherosolimis sacerdotes', BnF MS Lat. 2909, fols. 13v–15r (fol. 14v). Comparable Adventine series may be found in

including Caesarius of Heisterbach and Jacques de Vitry similarly used sermons on John the Baptist to tackle the problem of reserving the right to preach to officially commissioned preachers and were all too aware that some orthodox clergymen with the duty to preach did not emulate John's ascetic lifestyle or faced hostile audiences. Clearly preachers operating in a number of arenas were being forced to outline for their audiences what precisely distinguished unorthodox from orthodox preachers.

In another Adventine sermon, Jean focused on a seasonal chant, 'You who are seated above the Cherubim' (Psalm 79. 2), commonly used to discuss the duties of the doctor or preacher to instruct others through a model life, learning and eloquence. After wrestling with the limitations of the human intellect to grasp the incarnation and virgin birth through 'scientia naturalis vel positiva' (natural or positively acquired knowing), he vigorously defends both against 'heretical pravity'. Citing a verse from Peter typically used for sermons to priests, 'You who are a chosen people, a royal priesthood' (I Peter 2. 9), he urges prelates not to neglect preaching and teaching. For the definition of the faith, the material and spiritual sword must be wielded by thoughtful, discerning, and God-fearing men. As judges, prelates must not be immoderately ferocious, but combine mercy with discipline, rigor, and zeal.[18] Jean calls priests and clerics to acquire learning and rule themselves and others, uprooting what ought to be uprooted, correcting what ought to be corrected, and planting what ought to be planted (Jeremiah 1. 10), words straight from legatine commissions to reform and curb heresy, including Jean's own. He cites Augustine on approaching the vice-ridden like a physician with a cauterizing iron. As judges and prelates, ecclesiastics must distinguish the wicked from the pious and cut the rotten flesh from the sound or themselves be judged, as were the princes of the people hung by Moses for allowing the sons of Israel to fornicate with the daughters of Moab (Numbers 25. 1–4). If prelates are negligent in correcting their flocks, they will be damned for their subjects' sins. Ecclesiastics must imitate the poverty and humility of Christ who taught by word and life example, instead of, as Bernard of Clairvaux decried, building up palaces and seeking plural rents, benefices, and vicarages or oppressing the poor. True preachers must not be fruitless trees, but yield chastity, prayers, and mortification of the flesh. Clearly, as did many other preachers of his generation, John was seeking to address the critiques of reformers and heterodox of the gap between the lifestyle and preaching of orthodox clergymen while urging orthodox ecclesiastics to reform themselves and vigilantly police their flocks.[19]

Innocent III, *Homiliae, Patrologia Latina* 217, 529–44 and Honorius III, *Opera omnia*, ed. Horoy, I, 609–60.

[18] 'Qui sedes super Cherubim', BnF MS Lat. 2909, fols. 18v–21r (fols. 19v–20r).

[19] Ibid., fol. 20v.

Inquisitorial identity and authority in thirteenth-century exegesis and sermons

Similarly, John's sermon on 'I am the good shepherd' follows a host of other sermons for the same occasion written by contemporary preachers involved in combatting heresy in differentiating the true pastor from the thief and the mercenary. Although the mercenary may seem to preach the truth, he does so for temporal gain or his own benefit and refuses to verbally defend his flock against wolves (tyrants or the devil). The sheepfold is the Church, just as Fulk of Toulouse had argued, to which Christ adds other sheep, Jews, and gentiles who were or will be converted to the true faith. The good pastor enters through the door and leads by example rather than obtaining his office through simony, force or usurpation, blood relations or princely patronage. In contrast, thieves and brigands kill the sheep by fostering their vices instead of combatting them; like roaring lions seeking prey, they abuse preaching, penance, and justice to justify war against or persecute those who refuse to give them bribes. Like ravening wolves, evil prelates lust after blood and profit.[20]

It was these very orthodox critiques and imagery that the mutilated heretic used to subvert Fulk of Toulouse's sermon on the sheep and the wolves. What if the real ravening wolf were the prince working at the behest of the local pastor, as Simon de Montfort did for Fulk? Or the pastor himself? Such were the orthodox yet anticlerical critiques levelled by contemporary poets against anti-imperial and anti-heretical crusades. Troubadours, including Pons de Capdoill, proved perfectly capable of appropriating the rhetoric of reforming sermons to criticize local clergymen for abusing the power of crusade preaching and of the penitential keys to mulct the faithful for money and (falsely) accuse opponents of 'sin' (including perhaps heresy). A contemporary of Jean d'Abbeville, Huon de Saint-Quentin, repurposed the imagery of sheep and wolf to lambast clerical shepherds for selling their sheep to the wolves for money by fraudulently redeeming crusading vows. Peire Cardenal similarly accused the clergy of appearing as wolves in sheep's clothing. Like Sir Ysengrin from the *Roman de Renart*, ecclesiastics devour whom they please through robbery, hypocrisy, violence, and false preaching.[21]

Heretics and irate poets drew their complaints straight from orthodox reformers. Jean likewise attacks ignorant priests and prelates who will not teach by life example and do not break the bread of doctrine or holy scripture for the little ones (the laity): they are rainless clouds, sterile eunuchs, twice-dead fruitless trees, who slay themselves and their flock through mortal sin or negligence. Those who teach must ensure that their life example aligns with rather than contravenes their teaching or they will have no effect; food offered by leprous hands will be rejected. Wicked pastors muddy the waters of the

---

[20] 'Ego sum pastor bonus', BnF MS Lat. 2909, fols. 111v–12v; notes 8 and 13 above.
[21] M. Aurell, *Des Chrétiens contre les Croisades, XIIe–XIIIe siècle* (Paris, 2013), pp. 234–58; L. Paterson. *Singing the Crusades: French and Occitan Lyric Responses to the Crusading Movements, 1137–1336* (Cambridge, 2018), pp. 126–9 and 156–7.

holy scriptures and trample the flock's pasture underfoot; these stand for the parts of the scriptures which are easily understood and those where the sense is more profound. When corrupt prelates teach the people, their words, like water, are muddied by their filthy deeds. Prelates store up treasure for themselves and their households, acting more like brigands than dispensers of charity. Instead of feeding the sheep, consoling the infirm, healing the sick, binding up the broken, and leading back the wandering, they deliver their flock to rapacious wild beasts; after fleecing their sheep, they slay them. In contrast, righteous pastors teach by knowledge of the scriptures, eloquence, and exemplary lives. They equitably judge themselves and their flocks, offer clemency while detesting vices and threatening penalties in their preaching, and show themselves merciful to good parishioners and strong and harsh towards the stiff-necked.[22]

For the dutiful pastor takes prudent measures against the ambushes of wolves, placing himself like a wall against all attackers. In contrast, wicked prelates are desert wolves who secretly harm their subjects instead of surrendering money and life for their sheep (including the poor and widows) or, like Paul, giving up meat and money rather than cause scandal. This is clearly a nod to the critiques of heterodox and orthodox mendicant preachers who attacked meat-eating and money-carrying prelates. Jean urges prelates to make vigorous inquiries into the lives of their parishioners, unlike mercenary pastors, who, like a guard-dog muted by a toad, do not 'bark' at sinners for fear of losing rents, fields, offerings, or the friendship of the powerful. Other prelates feign mercy and compassion and abuse the sacrament of penance for material gain or remain silent lest their parishioners spot the discrepancy between their rebukes and their own wicked lives.[23] One can imagine such advice dispensed during Jean's tour in synodal sermons intended to chivvy local bishops and pastors into prosecuting heresy and their parishioners to cooperate with Jean's reforming and anti-heretical program.

For Jean's criticisms were echoed and expanded on by multiple generations of Paris masters, from Peter Lombard to Peter the Chanter, Stephen Langton to Philip the Chancellor and Jacques de Vitry. They, in conjunction with popes trained in Paris (Innocent III, Gregory IX) or who consulted masters trained in Paris (Honorius III), shifted the definition of episcopal duties to stress not only financial, administrative, and judicial/penitential care of the flock, but preaching and the suppression of heresy, if necessary with the aid of assistants – secular clergymen, canons regular, Cistercians, and the mendicant orders. Drawing on Peter the Chanter, Innocent III famously utilized the Parisian reforming slogan 'mute dog' (referencing the 'canes muti non valentes latrare' or 'mute dogs incapable of barking' of

---

[22] 'Ego sum pastor bonus', BnF MS Lat. 2909, fols. 111v–12v (fols. 112r–13r).
[23] Ibid., fol. 113v.

Inquisitorial identity and authority in thirteenth-century exegesis and sermons

Isaiah 56. 10) to characterize the otherwise politically and administratively efficient Berengar, archbishop of Narbonne, and to make the case for the deposition and replacement of Berengar and other bishops not deemed effective preachers against or repressors of heresy.[24] Charged with being a 'mute dog' himself for failing to implement the statutes of Fourth Lateran in his archdiocese prior to Jean d'Abbeville's legation, Archbishop Rodrigo of Toledo nonetheless owned a compilation of the sermons of Stephen Langton and was the dedicatee of Diego García's *Planeta*, a work which may well have armed Rodrigo with reforming rhetoric he directed against his neighboring rival, the bishop of Cuenca.[25] Langton's sermon on the duties of the good pastor was very similar to that of his disciple Jean d'Abbeville described above, and Langton famously adapted the synodal decrees of the reforming Eudes de Sully, bishop of Paris, for the archdiocese of Canterbury. Perhaps inspired by Langton, Jean d'Abbeville cut a swathe through Iberia through the excommunication and deposition of concubinary and remiss clergy during his legation. Jean also held numerous reforming synods whose decrees focused on remedying the deficiencies of the local clergy and combatting heresy. His synodal decrees were later adopted by Pedro de Albalat, archbishop of Tarragona, who had worked with Raymon de Peñafort and Jean (they had perhaps recommended Pedro as an archiepiscopal candidate to Gregory IX) and proved zealous in suppressing heresy in his diocese through inquests.[26]

[24] Envisaged as primarily a preaching order from their origins, the Dominicans quickly became known as the 'dogs of the Lord' (*Domini canes*). The verse on mute dogs was typically glossed as applying to lack of preaching in biblical commentaries and sermons on the good shepherd. See note 8 above; Innocent III, 'Ego sum pastor bonus', *Patrologia Latina* 217, 405–10 (cols. 407–8); E. Graham-Leigh, 'Hirelings and Shepherds: Archbishop Berenguer of Narbonne (1191–1211) and the Ideal Bishop', *English Historical Review* 116.469 (2001), 1083–1102; K. H. Kendall, '"Mute Dogs Unable to Bark": Innocent III and the Call to Combat Heresy', in *Medieval Church Law and the Origins of the Western Legal Tradition. A Tribute to Kenneth Pennington*, ed. W. P. Müller and M. E. Sommar (Washington DC, 2006), pp. 170–8.

[25] Linehan, *Spanish Church*, pp. 11–14, 16, 35; Linehan, 'Doubts and Dates', p. 213.

[26] Linehan, *Spanish Church*, pp. 54–82; Smith, *Crusade, Heresy, and Inquisition*, pp. 188–99; A. Reeves, *Religious Education in Thirteenth-Century England: The Creed and Articles of Faith*, Education and Society in the Middle Ages and Renaissance 50 (Leiden, 2015), pp. 27–56; Stephen Langton, 'Ego bonus sum pastor', in Paris, BnF MS Lat. 16463, fols. 149vb–51ra; P. B. Roberts, *Stephanus de Lingua-Tonante: Studies in the Sermons of Stephen Langton*, Pontifical Institute of Medieval Studies, Studies and Texts 16 (Toronto, 1968), p. 197.

Jessalynn Lea Bird

Discernment of shepherds, sheep, dogs, and wolves

But if prelates sometimes acted more like wolves than shepherds, how were the faithful to distinguish between orthodox and heterodox ministers, between Christian and heretic? How could laypersons be persuaded that seemingly holy heretics were in fact, diabolical agents worthy of temporal and spiritual punishment? Jean d'Abbeville's sermon on 'Beware false prophets' (Matthew 7. 15) follows contemporary biblical commentaries in interpreting the rapacious wolves in sheep's clothing as heretics who veil themselves with exterior simplicity in order to ambush their prey. Heretics deceive the simple with their teaching and 'perverse additions or detractions' ('pravis suggestionibus seu detractionibus'). If they obtain troops or resources, they persecute the faithful openly through manifest injustice or wrongdoing. Just as wolves are not satisfied with slaying one sheep but continue killing until the entire fold is wiped out, so heretics do not stop with one soul; by the contagion of their poison an infinite multitude are lost. But how is one to recognize a wolf if it is dressed like a sheep? By their fruits you will know them, Jean, Caesarius, and others of their generation claimed. Because heretics oppress the faithful, the heterodox can be recognized by their deeds even if they do not blaspheme with words. They can particularly be discerned through their inability to endure hardship (*impacientiam*). They lack spiritual love (*caritas*) and are easily angered by adversity; like thorns and thistles, heretics wound those who approach them. No one harvests grapes from thorns or figs from thistles; fruit follows the nature of the tree. God judges by intent; good deeds performed by those harboring evil in their hearts earn hypocrites and heretics no merit. A good tree cannot bear bad fruit unless indirectly. For example, something done with good intent might cause a horrific accident; someone trying to rescue his father from a lion may kill his father rather than the lion.[27]

However, Jean explains, the possibility of conversion from wicked Saul to apostle Paul exists; ultimately everyone is judged by intent. When the apostle says, 'By their fruits you will know them', he was addressing the problem of someone who seems to have the truth of doctrine but does not himself profit from it. To solve this dilemma, Jean follows contemporary biblical commentaries in glossing the verse, 'Not everyone who says "Lord, Lord" will enter the kingdom of heaven' (Matthew 7. 21). Dogma or belief must be confirmed by the proof of one's actions (*argumentum facte*). If someone acknowledges God in their heart, but not their works, he will not enter the kingdom of heaven. What his audience believes in their hearts, they must confess orally and put into deeds. If someone lacks any of these three, he denies God.[28]

---

[27] 'Attendite a falsis prophetis', BnF MS Lat. 2909, fols. 151r–52v (fol. 151r).
[28] Ibid., fol. 151r–v.

Inquisitorial identity and authority in thirteenth-century exegesis and sermons

In another sermon on the same theme, Jean applies the false prophet image to hypocrites and wicked Christians, including false ministers of the Church who are ravening wolves similar to those decried in his 'good shepherd' sermon. The audience is thus faced with multiple potential wolves: heretics, hypocrites, and false Christians.[29] Just as heretics may appear to do good works and yet do not receive the merit for them, so too do hypocrites who call themselves Christians, because their intent is wrong; they do their good works for the sake of profit, human favor, glory, and pride. They may preach God but harbor the devil in their hearts and so lack charity and a serene conscience. John interprets a verse from Hosea on burdock and thistles as standing for carnal desire (*luxuria*) and cupidity, which particularly characterize heretics. Heretics are like Jerusalem thorns; they entangle and wound those approaching them incautiously by corrupting their listeners with teaching (*doctrina*) and nourishing them in error. Yet because thorns bear no grapes, the heretic's perverse intent means his work has no merit although it may seem to. There is no real good in heretics, although some believe so. So too, in a just man there is no vice even though others may be scandalized by his actions; Jean here may be thinking of the critiques of his legation or of those prosecuting heretics. Moreover, the good work (*opus*) which appears in the heretic is not his own even though he administers it to others, God permitting. Every tree which does not bear fruit is cut down and thrown into the fire. However, in Luke (13. 6–9), a tree is given three years and fertilized with the dung of rebukes and exhortations to penance so that it might recognize its sin and bear fruit. Yet Christ cursed the fruitless tree in Matthew (21. 18–22). Many trees bear the vices of the flesh, and not all who say 'Lord, Lord' will enter the kingdom of heaven. So too heretics will not enter heaven because they do not acknowledge God in heart, word, and deed.[30] Following the advice of Peter the Chanter's generation, which viewed biblical lectures as preparation for preaching, Jean's sermon attempted to translate the sophisticated exegesis of Matthew 7 familiar from lectures in Paris (which often, as we will see, broke out into informal *questiones* on seemly contrary biblical passages) into practical advice for laypersons and ecclesiastics on how to unveil seemingly pious heretics.

As a cursory survey of contemporary biblical commentaries traditionally attributed to Stephen Langton, Peter Comestor, and Peter the Chanter will illustrate, Jean was following the standard Parisian exegesis of Matthew 7 in constructing his sermon. According to the foremost lecturers on the Bible in Paris while Jean was a student and master there, heretics do not have wisdom or understanding of the truth but ingratiate themselves to others through the appearance of piety and religiosity. They may understand and

[29] 'Attendite a falsis prophetis', BnF MS Lat. 2909, fols. 151v–2v.
[30] Ibid., fols. 151v–2v.

teach the scriptures correctly, but corrupt others by their wicked lives and thereby attack the Church. Heretics are ravening wolves who through their honeyed and enticing words seduce the hearts of the innocent, but by their fruits they may be detected. The biblical lecturers anticipate their student audiences asking how they may detect heretics; they urge future priests and prelates not to attend to heretics' appearance (*vultum*) or clothing (*vestitum*), as heretics try to appear like sheep in their fasting, prayer, and alms, but rather scrutinize their works (*opus/operibus*) and the quality or nature of their deceits (*figuram fallacie*). Heretics claim to be apostles but announce things contrary to the apostles and martyrs who were persecuted and endured insult rather than persecuting the faithful and blaspheming. Sheep can be distinguished from the wolves by their fruits and by their lack of longsuffering; under pressure, heretics defect and flee. As does Jean, the commentators probe the relationship between action and intent. Although some substitute the example of a person lifting a heavy stone to help construct a church and inadvertently dropping it on the head of a passerby below (!) for Jean's scenario of the father and the lion, all follow the same chain of reasoning: God judges actions by the intent motivating them. Because heretics are lovers of this world, they may pretend to do good and have appearance of charity, but they lack good intention. While some may say 'Lord, Lord', heart, word and deed must simultaneously acknowledge God for a person to be saved.[31]

Jean had a similarly Paris-educated contemporary also involved in promoting the crusade, combatting heresy (he wrote the life of Marie of Oignies for Fulk of Toulouse) and equally devoted to preaching, the reform of the clergy and the promotion of the mendicant orders as a co-cardinal in the curia of Gregory IX: Jacques de Vitry. Jacques would likely have encountered Raymon de Peñafort and Jean d'Abbeville in Rome and certainly corresponded with the heretic-obsessed Lucas of Tuy. In a much more wide-ranging sermon on 'Beware the false prophets', Jacques dealt with the problem of false pastors (following other 'I am the good shepherd' sermons), but also with false hermits, recluses, visionaries, and fundraisers (*quaestores*) who preach deceptively to obtain money.[32] The discernment of spirits is clearly no easy task. Jacques also turns to the problem of detecting heretics. Clothed in external humility, heretics are full of deceit. Like ravening wolves,

---

[31] Peter Comestor, *Postilla super Matheum*, in Paris, BnF Arsenal 87, fols. 1–59, (fols. 21ra–rb); Peter Comestor (Pseudo-Langton), *Postillae in Matthaeum*, Paris BnF MS Lat. 620, fols. 1–85 (fols. 38ra–rb); Peter Comestor, *Postilla super Matheum*, Paris BnF MS Lat. 14424, fols. 99–160 (fol. 127rb–vb); Peter the Chanter, *Glose super unum ex quatuor*, in Paris, BnF MS Lat. 15585, fols. 63ra–64ra.

[32] See note 16 above; Jacques de Vitry, 'Attendite a falsis prophetis', in *Sermones in epistolas et evangelia dominicalia totius anni*, ed. D. a Ligno (Antwerp, 1575), pp. 699–705 (pp. 699–701).

Inquisitorial identity and authority in thirteenth-century exegesis and sermons

they use the pretense of virtue and alluring words to lead gullible sheep astray and will not stop until they slaughter the entire fold. If heretics always spoke wicked things, they would be quickly detected. However, like poisoners or scorpions with harmless faces and stinging tails, heretics disguise their venom and adopt sheep's clothing when they interweave catholic authorities with their own teachings so that they might more easily deceive their prey (*catholicorum patrum sententias ut magis decipiant suae doctrine interserunt*). Like flightless ostriches or apes who seem human from the front only, they have a pretense of piety but deny its power. They are the bewitching demonesses (*lamiae*) of Lamentations, the alien woman of Proverbs (7. 5–27) who with her soft words leads the youth astray. Heretics are 'women', soft and malleable when seeking the praise of men, and 'alien' because they are outside the Church and attempt to estrange others from it through flattering words; they teach what they ought not for 'filthy profit's sake' (Titus 1. 11). Jacques urges his audience to avoid the heretic after two warnings, lest in touching pitch, they be stained by it. Heretics may be discerned by their perverse teaching and feigned religiosity. Like pirates who lure ships onto rocks with lights at night and untrustworthy tavern-keepers (*caupones*) who water down their drinks, so heretics and hypocrites transform themselves into angels of light.[33]

Detection and rehabilitation: the image of the heretic as leper

The issue of how to detect, reveal, and rehabilitate heretics appears in other sermons for the liturgical year as well. For 'Walk in the spirit' (Galatians 5. 16) Sunday, Jean d'Abbeville refers to the day's introit, 'Our Protector, look!' (Psalm 83. 10) to appeal to God to defend the Church against heretical perfidy. Just as Jean had used the works of the flesh in Galatians 5. 19–21 to ally the call for reform with anti-heretical preaching, so here he stresses that heresies and schisms belong in that list; the lepers healed by Christ also signify heretics. Lepers' flesh is partly healthy and partly ulcerous; so too heretics mix truth with falsehood. He sets up an elaborate opposition of the flesh to the spirit, something slightly surprising in a sermon ostensibly devoted to counteracting heresy, as some heretics were notorious for their rigid separation of the two. The bulk of Jean's sermon is devoted to an assault on the works of the flesh, corrupt prelates who are focused on luxury and avarice, princely courts, and secular power. However, he also draws on contemporary anti-heretical rhetoric and biblical commentaries to present those bent on rending the seamless tunic of the Church through undermining charity and fraternal concord as worse than the soldiers who

[33] Ibid., pp. 701–3.

crucified Christ. These are the heretics who are the little foxes of the Song of Songs who twist away the holy scriptures from the rectitude of truth and destroy the flowers of the Church, the Lord's vineyard.[34]

Similarly, Jean's sermon on Christ and the ten lepers (Luke 17. 11–19) interprets the lepers, often glossed in other sermons as various types of sinners, as heretics. Just as lepers have various colors on their bodies, so the diverse sects of heretics mingle truth and falsehood in their preaching; they announce the truth so that they might convince others that it is false. Heretics sin against the decalogue and love neither God nor their neighbor. They stand far off like lepers and should be avoided like them, as heretics are cut off from the unity of the Church. However, pointing to the lepers who called out 'Jesus, Master', Jean acknowledges possibilities for rehabilitation. Christ's command that lepers show themselves to a priest pertains to those 'leprous' from heretical pravity, Jewish 'perfidy', or schism. These individuals must come to the church and show themselves to be like the others (orthodox believers) in the color of their faith, as did the converted Saul/Paul. Those who go to the priests and demonstrate a whole and true doctrine are thus cured from the leprous variety of lies; his audience ought to rejoice when someone returns to the unity of the Church. The leper who falls before Christ symbolizes the penitent sinner who humbles himself, does not relapse and is reconciled to the Church through the ministry of the priesthood. Interpreting the same verses as applying to mortal sins, Jean gave detailed instructions on how to make a proper confession to one's priest. His audience would thus have been advised of the necessity of confession and demonstration of true faith for heretics to be reconciled to the Church and would have been given detailed instructions on how to make a proper and thorough confession.[35] Surely Jean's humane approach to the reconciliation of heretics must have colored the provisions of the influential anti-heretical council of Tarragona (1242), held by Jean's former collaborators Pedro de Albalat and Raymon de Peñafort, and Jean's sermon provides valuable evidence for how such provisions might have been explained to audiences through preaching.[36]

---

[34] 'Spiritu ambulate', BnF MS Lat. 2909, fols. 170v–1r; S. LaVere, *Out of the Cloister: Scholastic Exegesis of the Song of Songs, 1100–1250*, Commentaria. Sacred Texts and their Commentaries: Jewish, Christian and Islamic 6 (Leiden, 2016), pp. 33, 109, 124, 162; Morenzoni, 'Les sermons', pp. 403–8; Kienzle, *Cistercians, Heresy, and Crusade*; Sackville, *Heresy and Heretics*, pp. 155–61.

[35] 'Dum iret Jhesus Jerusalem', BnF MS Lat. 2909, fols. 172r–3v.

[36] Council of Tarragona (1242), in *Heresy and Inquisition in France*, ed. and trans. Arnold and Biller, pp. 218–29; note 3 above.

Inquisitorial identity and authority in thirteenth-century exegesis and sermons

Masters and mendicants: sermons and inquests against heresy

But how precisely did sermons such as these influence early inquests against heresy? I would argue that just as early Dominicans and Franciscans drew on the disputational literature of the twelfth and thirteenth centuries for their anti-heretical treatises, so too, they turned to earlier preachers' and confessors' manuals and biblical commentaries and sermon collections which glossed key verses used to support the identity and mission of the orthodox preacher and inquisitor. These authorities had already been utilized in biblical commentaries read by and sermons delivered (and compiled) by secular masters who supported the involvement of the mendicant orders in early inquests against heresy. These masters included Jean d'Abbeville, Odo of Châteauroux, Philip the Chancellor (who preached against heresy and in support of the Albigensian crusade and participated in the inquests held by Robert *le Bougre* in France); and Jacques de Vitry, a close friend of Fulk of Toulouse and cardinal and spiritual advisor of Gregory IX in Rome at the time that the influential papal letter *Ille humani generis* (1231) was issued and Raymon de Peñafort, having been introduced to the papal curia by John of Abbeville, was serving as a papal penitentier and drafting the *Liber Extra* (1234).[37]

Jacques' histories, letters, sermons and subscription to many of Gregory IX's letters reveal his support of the mendicant order as the solution to many of the issues which dogged Paris masters and Cistercians involved in the fight against heresy, including accusations that orthodox preachers were not leading a sufficiently apostolic, humble, poor, and peregrinatory lifestyle. Caesarius of Heisterbach, a Cistercian contemporary of Jacques, in sermons intended for Cistercians involved in the anti-heretical arena, noted the difficulty of reconciling the anti-heretical preaching mission with the Cistercian lifestyle and the misgivings which greeted the early Dominicans and Franciscans in Germany (some viewed the mendicants as potential heretical wolves in sheep's clothing). Caesarius also praised Jacques and his generation and the mendicant orders as potential solutions to the image problems vexing orthodox Cistercian and secular clerical preachers, including the use of mounts, vestments, and coin.[38]

Thomas of Cantimpré, Stephen of Bourbon and Humbert of Romans also praised preachers of Jacques's generation and drew on their works for mendicants engaged in a similar combination of pastoral work, anti-heretical, and

---

[37] See notes 2–3, 16 above.

[38] I am writing an article on heresy in Caesarius's and Jacques's sermons. See J. Bird, 'The Religious' Role in a Post-Fourth Lateran World: Jacques de Vitry's *Sermones ad status* and *Historia Occidentalis*', in *Medieval Monastic Preaching*, ed. C. A. Muessig, Brill's Studies in Intellectual History 90 (Leiden and Boston, 1998), pp. 209–29.

pro-crusade preaching.[39] Humbert of Romans had mined Jacques' histories and sermons for his own treatise on preaching the crusade and model sermons,[40] and Humbert's treatise on preaching, intended to train members of the Dominican order of which Humbert had been master general, is similarly indebted to Parisian sources. The skeletal outlines for sermons on visitation and inquisition mirror earlier surviving sermons, such as those of Philip the Chancellor, rationalizing the process of inquisition to those undergoing it and promoting it.[41] Similarly, Humbert's outlines for sermons to be delivered at various stages of inquests against heresy depend on the discourse established by the collections of sermons for the liturgical year outlined above.[42] Humbert draws on set verses used to discuss the discernment of false versus true holiness to stress that while heretics may appear the same as true Christians, they are false prophets, sheep in wolves' clothing. Full of sins, they mix truth with falsehood, creep like cancer, and ambush little women in their homes. Despite being presented with authorities, reasons, and examples, heretics obstinately refuse to acknowledge the truth, and so the foxes laying waste the Lord's vineyard must be captured. His model sermon urges audiences to help inquisitors find and capture heretics and offers incentives including indulgences and escaping excommunication.[43]

In another model sermon meant to be delivered at an inquest's conclusion, Humbert acknowledges that many are moved by heretics' false piety and consider the Church overly cruel in sentencing heretics. Inquisitors must gather the people and explain why the Church more diligently inquires about heretics than other sinners, why heretics are punished more gravely and why it is harder to accept them as penitents. Heretics attack the very foundations of faith; unlike thieves and brigands, they continually sin by attempting to seduce and poison others by false piety and poisonous words, images already familiar from the sermons described above. Heretics and their supporters are guilty and should be punished, without exception and harshly, as worse than the idolaters stoned in Deuteronomy (17. 2–5): some to carry signs (presumably cloth crosses), others to prison, some surrendered to secular justice. Writing from a considerably later point in time when inquisitions were well-established,

---

[39] J. Bird, 'Heresy, Crusade and Reform in the Circle of Peter the Chanter, *c.*1187 – *c.*1240' (Unpublished D.Phil. thesis, University of Oxford, 2001), pp. 283–96.

[40] Humbertus Romanis, *De Predicatione crucis*, ed. V. Portnykh and C. Vande Veire, Corpus Christianorum Continuatio Mediaevalis 279 (Turnhout, 2018), p. 194; C. T. Maier, *Crusade Propaganda and Ideology: Model Sermons for the Preaching of the Cross* (Cambridge, 2000).

[41] Humbert of Romans, *De eruditione predicatorum*, in *Maxima bibliotheca veterum patrum*, ed. M. de la Bigne, 28 vols. (Lyon and Geneva, 1677–1707), XXV, 420–567 (nos. 53–7, pp. 540–2).

[42] Humbert of Romans, *De eruditione predicatorum*, ibid., 543–55, nos. 58–61 (the pages are misnumbered in this edition).

[43] *De eruditione predicatorum*, ibid., XXV, 554–5, nos. 60–1.

Inquisitorial identity and authority in thirteenth-century exegesis and sermons

Humbert is far less optimistic than Jean; he invokes the verses discussed above on lepers and confession to note that it is *rare* that heretics convert sincerely – they easily relapse and contaminate the faithful. The inquisitor should explain that the heretics' infamy (*infamia*) and vehement suspicion have caused him to make inquiries according to lawful procedure, and he should ask his audience to endure any seemingly unjustly imposed penalties – these are imposed with grief so that the guilty may return to salvation.[44]

Humbert clearly imagined that inquisitors would be faced with explaining how the Church not only could but must arrest and punish individuals for heresy. Inquisitors and local bishops also had to deal with the problem of prosecuting ostensibly holy individuals. How could a simple layperson discern between orthodoxy and heresy in faith and in practice? Humbert turns to the precise authorities utilized in the sermons above to appeal for cooperation with those conducting the inquest: verses on false apostles (2 Corinthians 11. 13–14), faked piety (Acts 13. 6), the wheat and the tares, the sheep and wolves, and the depiction of heretics as foxes out to ambush orthodox souls. These, as we have seen, were standard fare in surviving sermon cycles written by individuals involved in early inquests against heresy and preaching the anti-heretical crusade: Jacques de Vitry, Philip the Chancellor, and Jean d'Abbeville. Similarly, Humbert's sermon explaining why the Church must ferret out and punish with severe penances even rehabilitated heretics (for their salvation and the safety of Christendom) cited images and authorities familiar from sermons for synods, visitation, inquest, and on the good shepherd.[45]

In conclusion, despite the once prevalent picture that pre-mendicant Paris masters did not preach on a regular basis to the general populace in general, much less on heresy, it is clear that preaching to the laity on the faith and against heresy was in fact central to the identity of Peter the Chanter's circle and the generation of secular masters who welcomed (or joined) the mendicant orders in Paris.[46] Preaching (*predicatio*), lecturing (*lectio*), and disputation (*disputatio*) were part and parcel of university training and viewed as mutually complementary; Jacques de Vitry portrays his ideal preacher Fulk of Neuilly as attempting to preach to the populace what he had heard in the Chanter's biblical lectures.[47] Surviving bible commentaries on the *Song of Songs* and the

---

[44] Ibid.

[45] Ibid.; Bird, 'The Wheat and the Tares'.

[46] Bird, 'Before the Time of Grace?' (forthcoming); S. E. Young, *Scholarly Community at the Early University of Paris: Theologians, Education and Society, 1215–1248*, Cambridge Studies in Medieval Life and Thought, 4th s., 94 (Cambridge, 2014); notes 10, 39 above.

[47] J. Baldwin, *Masters, Princes and Merchants: The Social Views of Peter the Chanter and His Circle*, 2 vols. (Princeton, 1970), I, 36–7; Petrus Cantor, *Verbum abbreviatum: Textus conflatus*, ed. M. Boutry, Corpus Christianorum Continuatio Mediaevalis 196 (Turnhout, 2004), I.6, pp. 34–42.

Apocalypse from the Chanter's circle obsessively gloss these books as a clarion call to preach against heresy and in support of reform.[48] Masters took these calls seriously and experimented with multiple forms of sermon cycles. The image of the orthodox penance preacher and diocesan ecclesiastic and advice on how to distinguish their preaching from that of heretical preachers were introduced in lectures which taught students the unadulterated interpretation of the scriptures. Grey areas implied by reforming concepts, contested metaphors, and potentially contradictory yet key scriptural authorities were probed in disputation in the schools and against heretics. Key scriptural passages were reiterated and interpreted in the prothemes of sermons and on set points throughout the liturgical year when verses glossed as confirming the duty and right of the orthodox preacher to instruct the faithful and as outlining the dangers of heresy were explicated for lay audiences. Orthodox preachers and audiences were thus introduced to images and concepts which would become crucial to the construction of inquisitorial identity and the war of authentic apostolicity waged between orthodox secular and mendicant preachers and their rivals.

---

[48] I am writing an article on Parisian and Cistercian Apocalypse commentaries and sermons. For the *Song of Songs*; see note 34 above.

2

Shaping the image of the heretics:
The *narratio* in Gregory IX's letters

Alessandro Sala

When a historian comes across a papal letter or any other document relating medieval heretics, one of the first questions that inevitably arises is 'Where does this information come from?' Of course, the pope did not know the intricacies of every heresy, nor had he met every heretic. The information he was able to garner was shared in a continuous stream of data between the higher echelons of the Church and the ecclesiastical men in the field: this led to the creation of a careful and distinct image of the heretics. The textual representations provided in papal letters were collected and reported both in contemporary and in later texts regarding heretics and inquisition – that is, in treatises and handbooks.[1] In order to understand the construction of knowledge and information about the heretics we should focus on the *narratio*: a distinct narrative part of a papal letter which set out the backgrounds and the reasons that led the pope to write that specific document. Starting from the few elements gathered from the people fighting the heretics at the forefront, the pope shaped a specific depiction of the heretics and their beliefs – which then became the Church's official image.

It is well known that the image of medieval heretics went through a long process of development, which reached its peak in the first half of the thirteenth century.[2] This process was linked to the concurrent and progressive criminalisation of heretics and, therefore, the development of more repressive judicial instruments to eradicate them. A turning point was the papacy of Gregory IX (1227–41), the period in which many historians set the birth of the medieval inquisition.[3] During this nascent phase, neither

---

[1] L. J. Sackville, *Heresy and Heretics in the Thirteenth Century: The Textual Representations*, Heresy and Inquisition in the Middle Ages 1 (York, 2011).

[2] *The Concept of Heresy in the Middle Ages (11th-13th C.)*, ed. W. Lourdaux and D. Verhelst, Mediaevalia Lovaniensia, Studia 4 (Louvain and The Hague, 1976).

[3] On the development of the *inquisitio haereticae pravitatis* (inquisition into heretical wickedness) during the Gregory IX's papacy, see G. G. Merlo, 'Le origini dell'inquisizione medievale', in *L'Inquisizione*, ed. A. Borromeo, Studi e Testi 417

the information about heretics nor the procedures for dealing with those found guilty of heretical behaviour were clearly defined.[4] Papal letters can therefore be seen as evidence providing a unique insight into the shaping of the *inquisitio haereticae pravitatis*.[5] Through these letters, Gregory IX could establish and develop the judicial practice of the men who were entrusted with anti-heretical tasks. Because no legal procedure had been formally established each assignment and its *modus operandi* were individualised,[6] dictated by each case's unique political and social context. The papal letters have a detailed and consistent format and have been the subject of analysis of dozens of scholars, especially German and Italian palaeographers and specialists in diplomatics.[7] Concerning the study of heresy and inquisition, historians have focused their attention on the *dispositio*, which comprises the judicial and legal content of the document. That means, it contains papal orders. Here is where we find first Gregory's anti-heretical appointments, such as Conrad of Marburg, Robert Le Bougre, as well as bishops and friars. Scholars have often

---

(Città del Vaticano, 2003), pp. 25–39; M. Benedetti, 'Gregorio IX: l'inquisizione, i frati e gli eretici', in *Gregorio IX e gli Ordini mendicanti*, Atti dei Convegni della Società internazionale di Studi Francescani e del Centro interuniversitario di Studi Francescani n.s. 21 (Spoleto, 2011), pp. 293–324. A clear analysis of this topic is in P. Segl, 'Einrichtung und Wirkungsweise der *inquisitio haereticae pravitatis* im mittelalterlichen Europa. Zur Einführung', in *Die Anfänge der Inquisition im Mittelalter. Mit einem Ausblick auf das 20. Jahrhundert und einem Beitrag uber religiose Intoleranz im nichtchristlichen Bereich*, ed. P. Segl, Bayreuther historische Kolloquien 7 (Cologne, 1993), pp. 1–38. For an accurate analysis of the pope's role in this development, see O. Capitani, 'Gregorio IX', in *Enciclopedia dei Papi*, 3 vols. (Rome, 2000), II, 363–80.

[4] On the development of legal procedures against heretics, see W. Trusen, 'Von den Anfängen des Inquisitionsprozesses zum Verfahren bei der *inquisitio haereticae pravitatis*', in *Die Anfänge der Inquisition*, pp. 39–76.

[5] During his almost fifteen years of papacy, Gregory IX wrote more than six thousand letters, reported in seven registers. Those are published in *Les registres de Grégoire IX*, ed. L. Auvray, 4 vols. (Paris 1896–1955). Furthermore, we should not forget hundreds of letters not reported in papal registers, stored in European archives - in original or copies - and edited in several collections of documents. Gregory IX wrote more than 300 letters concerning heresy and inquisition; see A. Sala, 'Lo sviluppo dell'*inquisitio heretice pravitatis* nelle lettere di Gregorio IX (1227–1241)', (unpublished doctoral dissertation, University of Milan, 2017).

[6] R. Kieckhefer, 'The Office of Inquisition and Medieval Heresy: The Transition from Personal to Institutional Jurisdiction', *The Journal of Ecclesiastical History* 46 (1995), 36–61.

[7] For a useful handbook to papal letters see T. Frenz, *I documenti pontifici nel Medioevo e nell'età moderna* (Città del Vaticano, 1989). A recent analysis of the papal chancery is in A. Meyer, 'The Curia: The Apostolic Chancery', in *A Companion to Medieval Papacy: Growth of an Ideology and Institution*, ed. K. D. Sisson and A. Larson (Leiden, 2016), pp. 239–58. For the debate on the production of letters, see P. N. R. Zutshi, 'The personal role of the pope in the production of papal letters in the thirteenth and fourteenth century', in *Vom Nutzen des Schreibens. Soziales Gedächtnis, Herrschaft und Besitz im Mittelalter*, ed. W. Pohl and P. Herold, Forschungen zur Geschichte des Mittelalters 5 (Vienna, 2002), pp. 225–36.

Shaping the image of the heretics

cherry-picked isolated parts, and only rarely examined the significance of the letters in their totality. In considering these documents, particular attention should be paid to the *arenga* and the *narratio*, in which we find a specific image of the heretic the pope intentionally attempted to convey.

The *arenga* (preamble) is the first rhetorical part of a papal letter – just after the *intitulatio* (the sender), the *inscriptio* (the addressee) and the *salutatio* (a formula of greeting) – providing the theological and moral bases for what follows. The *arenga* shows not only the ideological reasons for the letter, but also the biblical and theological grounds of the papacy's decision.[8] This is particularly significant for letters regarding heresy, as the pope provides theological, biblical and moral arguments to be used as proofs against the heretics he condemns. Further, this is why we see a recurrence of the same rhetorical imagery and biblical quotations throughout these types of Gregory's letters.[9] Nevertheless, it is usually overlooked by historians, who tend to concentrate on the *dispositio*.

The *narratio* is the narrative part of a letter. Here the pope outlines and summarises the circumstances that led him to write that specific document. While the *arenga* is the place for the moral and theological arguments, the *narratio* provides the concrete, pragmatic reasons for the papal decision. It can be a short or long report on what happened – the facts – and on the consequent ramifications. In letters concerning the fight against heresy, this part of the document shows the behaviour of one or several heretics. The events set out inside the *narratio* do not necessarily represent what we might term the 'truth', but rather the papal version of the facts. These two are not mutually exclusive, of course, but they are two distinct concepts. The information within the *narratio* relies on what the pope gets from the people on the ground: those ecclesiastical men he had entrusted. The *narratio* could be extensive and very detailed or concise and presenting very limited detail. The path by which 'history' is written in these documents is as follows. Reports are made by the ecclesiastical 'boots on the ground' to the pope, writing from what we might think of as the periphery. The pope, positioned at the centre,

---

[8] On the *arenga* see H. Fichtenau, *Arenga. Spätantike und Mittelalter im Spiegel von Urkundenformeln*, Mitteilungen des Instituts für Österreichische Geschichtsforschung Erganzungsband 18 (Graz, 1957).

[9] Some scholars have studied specific and frequent heretical images, see M. Giansante, 'I lupi e gli agnelli. Ideologia e storia di una metafora', *Nuova rivista storica* 83 (1999), 215–24; J. Bird, 'The Wheat and the Tares: Peter the Chanter's Circle and the Fama-based Inquest Against Heresy and Criminal Sins, c.1198-c.1235', in *Proceedings of the Twelfth International Congress of Medieval Canon Law*, ed. U. R. Blumenthal, Monumenta Iuris Canonici Series C, Subsidia 13 (Città del Vaticano, 2008), pp. 763–856; M. T. Dolso, 'La parabola della zizzania e il problema ereticale tra XII e XIII secolo', *Cristianesimo nella storia* 26 (2005), 225–63; R. Rist, '*Lupi rapaces in ovium vestimentis*: heretics and heresy in papal correspondence', in *Cathars in question*, ed. A. Sennis, Heresy and Inquisition in the Middle Ages 4 (York, 2016), pp. 229–41.

then reviews this information and sends it, through his letters, back to the periphery from which it had come. What is essential to note here is that the information inside the papal letter will become the Church's official narrative. This papal interpretation was then sent to the free-roaming papal agents who were supposedly fighting heresy at the frontlines, and this is how the official version of the heretical situation emerged and developed. This ongoing exchange of information led to a continuously growing knowledge of the heretics, and specifically their beliefs and habits. This will be clear through some specific examples.

In the spring 1233 Conrad of Marburg, the archbishop of Mainz and the bishop of Hildesheim were collaborating in their campaign against the heretics of western Germany, mainly in the ecclesiastical province of Mainz.[10] They sent a report – no longer extant – to Gregory IX in order to inform him of the troublesome situation there and to describe the vast and serious crimes of the heretics. We are informed about this report in the consequent papal letter addressed to Conrad of Marburg on 10 June 1233.[11] Inside the *O altitudo divitiarum* the pope explains that his knowledge of the situation comes from a letter written by the three papal agents, most likely in the first months of 1233:

> Sane venerabilium fratrum nostrorum .. archiepiscopi Maguntini et .. Hildesemensis episcopi ac tuis litteris, grandi merore plenis et immenso dolore non vacuis, super abhominationibus quorumdam hereticorum nobis exhibitis, solita benignitate receptis, cor nostrum elanguit pre stupore, turbata est anima nostra valde.

> (Indeed, when your letters and those of our venerable brothers, the archbishop of Mainz and the bishop of Hildesheim, full of great grief and not lacking in immense sorrow, concerning the abominations of certain heretics, were shown to us and received with our accustomed favour, our heart grew faint with shock, and our soul was greatly disturbed.)[12]

The report written by the three men provoked the pope's wrath and he declared war against the heretics. Gregory's immediate response was to write a series of letters between the 10 and 14 June. The *O altitudo divitiarum* is the first of these. Likening heretics to a diseased limb that should be cut off in order to preserve the health of the body, Gregory IX appointed Conrad of Marburg to eradicate heresy from these lands:

---

[10] A. Patschovsky, 'Zur Ketzerverfolgung Konrads von Marburg', *Deutsches Archiv für Erforschung des Mittelalters* 37 (1981), 641–93; D. Kurze, 'Anfänge der Inquisition in Deutschland', in *Die Anfänge der Inquisition im Mittelalter*, pp. 131–93.

[11] *Bullarium ordinis fratrum Praedicatorum*, ed. T. Ripoll, 8 vols. (Roma, 1729–39) I, no. 80; *Epistolae saeculi XIII e regestis pontificum romanorum selectae*, ed. C. Rodenberg, 3 vols., MGH Epistolae (Berlin, 1883–94), I, no. 533; *Les registres de Grégoire IX*, ed. Auvray, I, no. 1387.

[12] Ibid.

Shaping the image of the heretics

quia in tam grandi et gravi morbo recurrendum est ad validiora remedia, ubi medicamenta levia non proficiunt et apponendum ferrum et ignis vulneribus, que fomentorum non sentiunt medicinam, putridis carnibus ne partem sinceram attrahant, amputatis, advoces contra eos receptatores defensores et fautores ipsorum spiritualis et materialis gladii potestatem.

(Because in so great and serious a disease recourse must be had to more powerful remedies, where gentler medicines have no effect, and iron and fire must be put to wounds, which do not respond to treatment with poultices, when the rotten flesh has been amputated, so that it does not take the healthy part with it, you should summon against them, and those who shelter, defend and support them, the power of the spiritual and material sword.)[13]

The letter is filled with biblical references, metaphors and rhetorical questions, and there is no substantial description of the activities of the heretics, just the announcement of a crusade against them. A detailed description of heretics' behaviour and rituals is outlined in the following *Vox in Rama*, which is perhaps the most famous of Gregory IX's letters.[14] There were four examples of *Vox in Rama* in a few days in June 1233: the first one was addressed to the emperor Frederick II,[15] the second sent to his son Henry (VII), *rex Romanorum* (king of the Romans),[16] the third addressed to the archbishop of Mainz, the bishop of Hildesheim and Conrad of Marburg,[17] and the last one sent to the bishops of the ecclesiastical province of Mainz.[18]

The *arenga* is an evangelical quotation (Matthew 2. 18) which refers to the Massacre of the Innocents, in which King Herod of Judea ordered the death of all male children under the age of two in the vicinity of the town of Bethlehem.[19] This tale is cited in order to create an immediate parallel with the Church's current agony of losing her children to the devil. Soon after the *arenga*, the pope describes the behaviour of the heretics – whose heresy is the

---

[13] Ibid.

[14] For a precise and detailed analysis of *Vox in Rama*, see B. U. Hergemöller, *Krötenkuss und schwarzer Kater* (Warendorf, 1996), pp. 76–108.

[15] *Epistolae saeculi XIII*, I, no. 537 (III); *Les registres de Grégoire IX*, ed. Auvray, I, no. 1393.

[16] *Epistolae saeculi XIII*, I, no. 537 (IV); *Les registres de Grégoire IX*, ed. Auvray, I, no. 1394.

[17] *Bullarium Praedicatorum*, ed. T. Ripoll, I, no. 81; *Epistolae saeculi XIII*, I, no. 537 (I); *Les registres de Grégoire IX*, ed. Auvray, I, no. 1391.

[18] *Bullarium Praedicatorum*, ed. T. Ripoll, I, no. 82; *Epistolae saeculi XIII*, I, no. 537 (II); *Les registres de Grégoire IX*, ed. Auvray, I, no. 1392.

[19] '"Vox in Rama audita est ploratus multus et ululatus Rachel plorat" videlicet, pia mater Ecclesia filios quos diabolus mactat et perdit' ('A voice in Rama was heard, Rachel lamenting and greatly mourning' – that is to say, holy mother Church mourning her 'children', whom the devil slays and destroys), in *Epistolae saeculi XIII*, I, no. 537 (II); *Les registres de Grégoire IX*, ed. Auvray, I, no. 1392. The Gospel of Matthew quotes a verse of the Old Testament (Jeremiah 31. 15). For the choice of this specific *arenga* see Benedetti, 'Gregorio IX', pp. 318–19.

Alessandro Sala

worst and the most widespread in Germany[20] – relying on the previous letter sent by Conrad of Marburg and the two prelates:

> Sicut enim littere vestre grandi merore plene et immenso dolore non vacue nobis exhibite, continebant inter diversas heresum species, que peccatis exigentibus Alemanniam infecerunt, una sicut detestabilior ceteris sic et generalior universis, que non solum referentibus, sed etiam audientibus est horrori, in nobilibus membris Ecclesie ac valde potentibus iam erupit.

> (Just as your letters which were shown to us, full of great grief and not lacking in immense sorrow, included among the various kinds of heresy, which, for her sins, have infected Germany, one which is both more loathsome than the others and more universal to all, which is a horror not only to those who write about it but also to those who hear about it, has now burst forth in the noble and very powerful members of the Church.)[21]

The *Vox in Rama* presents the initiation ritual that every novice was required to perform to be accepted into the sect.[22] At the end of the letter, Gregory repeats the same words used in the *O altitudo divitiarum*, again comparing the presence of heretics to a limb weakening the body - concluding, therefore, that these papal agents should promote a military intervention against the heretics. To those who will join this conflict, the pope will grant the same privileges entrusted to the crusaders committed to the Holy Land.[23]

Meanwhile, in northern Germany, the archbishop of Bremen was fighting against the Stedinger, peasants living along the river Weser in the Bremen diocese.[24] The Stedinger were protesting against taxes imposed by the

---

[20] On the so-called 'Luciferans', see K. Utz Tremp, *Von der Häresie zur Hexerei. "Wirkliche" und imaginäre Sekten im Spätmittelalter*, MGH Schriften 59 (Hannover, 2008), pp. 327–37. On this topic see also G. G. Merlo, '*Membra diaboli*: demoni ed eretici medievali', *Nuova rivista storica* 72 (1988), 583–98.

[21] *Bullarium Praedicatorum*, ed. T. Ripoll, I, no. 81; *Epistolae saeculi XIII*, I, no. 537 (I); *Les registres de Grégoire IX*, ed. Auvray, I, no. 1391.

[22] The rituals performed by the novice and by the members are described in Hergemöller, *Krötenkuß*, pp. 112–81.

[23] 'universos Christi fideles monentes attentius et efficaciter inducentes ut exurgentes in adiutorium Christi sui contra eos viriliter se accingant' (earnestly counselling and strongly urging all the faithful in Christ to rise up to the aid of Christ and gird themselves manfully against them), in *Bullarium Praedicatorum*, ed. T. Ripoll, I, no. 81; *Epistolae saeculi XIII*, I, no. 537 (I); *Les registres de Grégoire IX*, ed. Auvray, I, no. 1391. On the crusades against heretics, see G. G. Merlo, '*Militia Christi* come impegno antiereticale (1179–1233)', in *Militia Christi e crociata nei secoli XI-XIII*, Miscellanea del Centro di Studi Medioevali 13 (Milan, 1992) pp. 355–84; C. Maier, *Preaching the Crusades: Mendicant Friars and the Cross in the Thirteenth Century* (Cambridge, 1994), pp. 52–7; R. Rist, *The Papacy and Crusading in Europe (1198 - 1245)* (London, 2009).

[24] For a comprehensive overview of this topic see H. A. Schumacher, *Die Stedinger. Beitrag zur Geschichte der Weser-Marschen* (Bremen, 1865). More recent studies, in

Shaping the image of the heretics

archbishop, who organised several military campaigns to put an end to their revolts.[25] Since the Stedinger had no intention of paying these taxes, the archbishop excommunicated their entire community in 1230, reasoning that their rebelling against ecclesiastical authority made them heretics. During the summer of 1233, the pope declared a crusade against these German peasants who had been declared heretics. These events occurred in northern Germany and should not be confused with the activity of Conrad of Marburg in the archdiocese of Mainz, an area corresponding to the states of Hessen and Rhineland-Palatinate. Conrad did not fight against the Stedinger. Thus, it is incorrect to assign those stereotypes and *topoi* – described in the *Vox in Rama* and targeted against the so-called Luciferans – to the Stedinger.

Why were these Bremen peasants considered heretics? What picture arises from Gregory IX's documentation? The 1230 excommunication, ordered by the archbishop of Bremen, was confirmed by the provost of Münster, commissioned by the pope, as it is reported in a letter written on July 1231: the first papal letter regarding this issue.[26] As a year had passed since the group's excommunication from the Church, the Stedinger were declared heretics by the archbishop of Bremen in a regional synod which produced a text containing eleven counts.[27] This text could be considered the basis of the following papal letters. In the *Si ea que*, written on 26 July 1231, the pope mentioned just a few of the accusations levelled against the Stedinger, which included the looting of ecclesiastical properties, violence against religious men, desecration of the Eucharist and demonic venerations. Gregory IX then went on describe the Stedinger as rebels, not yet heretics, and appointed the bishop of Lübeck and two Dominican friars to resolve the matter. These initiatives were not successful, however, and on 29 October 1232 Gregory IX decided to declare a crusade in the dioceses of Bremen, Paderborn, Hildesheim, Verden, Münster, Osnabrück and Minden: the whole of north-west Germany.[28] The pope included in the letter *Lucis eterne lumine* all the accusations produced by the Bremen synod:

German or in English, have focused on specific aspects: R. Köhn, 'Die Verketzerung der Stedinger durch die Bremer Fastensynode', *Bremisches Jahrbuch* 57 (1979), 15–85; R. Köhn, 'Die Teilnehmer an den Kreuzzügen gegen die Stedinger', *Niedersächsisches Jahrbuch für Landesgeschichte* 53 (1981), 139–206; M. Cassidy-Welch, 'The Stedinger Crusade. War, Remembrance, and Absence in Thirteenth-Century Germany', *Viator* 44 (2013), 159–63.

[25] The economic and social revolt of Stedinger is analyzed in H. Schmidt, 'Zur Geschichte der Stedinger. Studien über Bauernfreiheit, Herrschaft und Religion an der Unterweser im 13. Jahrhundert', *Bremisches Jahrbuch* 60–61 (1983), 27–94.

[26] *Bremisches Urkundenbuch*, ed. D. R. Ehmck, 6 vols. (Bremen, 1873–1943), I, no. 166; *Oldenburgisches Urkundenbuch*, ed. G. Rüthning, 7 vols. (Oldenburg, 1914–35), II, no. 62.

[27] The counts are analyzed one by one in Köhn, 'Die Verketzerung der Stedinger', pp. 29–75.

[28] *Epistolae saeculi XIII*, I, no. 489; *Les registres de Grégoire IX*, ed. Auvray, I, no. 940.

Alessandro Sala

nec Deum nec hominem reverentes, doctrinam sancte matris Ecclesie vilipendunt, eius libertatem impugnant et dediti crudelitatis officio, quasi de ferinis uberibus fuerint enutriti, nulli parcunt sexui vel etati. Quid ultra? Effundentes sanguinem sicut aquam, clericos et religiosos ferali more lacerant et quosdam ad instar crucis affigunt parieti in opprobrium crucifixi. Ipsi etiam, ut expressione maiori se perfidos indicent et divine potentie contemptores, salutis nostre viaticum, quo vita tribuitur et mors tollitur peccatorum, horribilius quam deceat exprimi pertractantes, querunt responsas demonum, simulachra cerea faciunt et in suis spurcitiis erroneas consulunt phitonissas, alia perversitatis opera perpetrantes.

(Without reverence for God or man, they despise the doctrine of Holy Mother Church, they attack her liberty and, given over to cruelty, as if they had been fed at the teats of wild animals, they spare no sex or age. What more? Pouring out blood like water, they lacerate clerics and religious like wild beasts, and fix some to walls in the form of a cross as an insult to the Crucified. Further, that they might declare themselves more clearly to be traitors and despisers of the divine power, they handle the viaticum of our salvation (that gives life and takes away death from sinners) in a manner more horrible than is fitting to express: they seek the responses of demons, they make wax images, and, in their filthiness, they consult false witches, and commit other acts of perversity.)[29]

The pope continued to announce the crusade in the following year, trying to persuade noblemen to join the military campaign.[30] In a letter written on 17 June 1233, just a few days after the *Vox in Rama* was written, Gregory IX argued that the Stedingers' terrible deeds had woken up other dormant groups of heretics all across Germany.[31] The reference to the heretics of Mainz diocese and to the activity of Conrad of Marburg is clear. Gregory IX did not himself know the Stedinger and the reasons underlying their protest, and what is therefore clear from these letters is that he reposed complete trust in the archbishop of Bremen. The papal letters corroborate the opinion of the local archbishop: the Stedinger were considered to be heretics. In

---

[29] Ibid.

[30] For more on the people who joined the crusade, see Köhn, 'Die Teilnehmer an den Kreuzzügen', pp. 139–206.

[31] 'propter quod tamen est in partibus Alamannie scandalum suscitatum quod non solum illi, verum etiam aliarum sectarum heretici, qui prius latebant in angulis, de huiusmodi gloriantes contra Dei Ecclesiam et fidem catholicam, publice invalescunt nomen Domini Iesu' (Yet, on account of this, a scandal has arisen in part of Germany: that not only they but also heretics of other sects, priding themselves in this sort of thing against the Church of God and the Catholic faith, are publicly detracting from the name of our Lord Jesus), in *Bullarium Praedicatorum*, ed. T. Ripoll, I, no. 83; *Bremisches Urkundenbuch*, ed. Ehmck, I, no. 176; *Epistolae saeculi XIII*, I, no. 539; *Les registres de Grégoire IX*, ed. Auvray, I, no. 1402.

Shaping the image of the heretics

other words, what had begun as a local instance of socio-economic protest had escalated into a charge of heresy and a crusade.

The label of 'heresy' during the papacy of Gregory IX is, however, used completely differently in Italy. Here, it is not only used in relation to heretical beliefs and rituals but is more commonly used as a political tool.[32] In central and northern Italy the words *heretici* (heretics) or *fautores hereticorum* (supporters of heretics) are used to identify political opponents, like those loyal to emperor Frederick II,[33] or individuals responsible for crimes against religious men and their property. For these reasons those who killed the bishop of Mantua in June 1235 are called 'viri nephandissimi et fautores heretice pravitatis' (most heinous men and supporters of heretical wickedness).[34] Likewise, in Naples some citizens who attacked the local Dominican priory and injured several friars, whilst trying to avoid the admission of a novice, are described as 'quidam filii Belial credentes hereticorum' (some sins of Belial, believers in heretics).[35] The most famous example of this specifically Italian feature – where political enemies were labelled heretics – is set in Piacenza in 1233. In October some citizens assaulted Rolando of Cremona and other clerics during a sermon by this well-known Dominican friar, and in the scuffle a monk was killed.[36] The investigations were entrusted to Gregorio de Romania, subdeacon and papal chaplain,[37] who produced a report of his

---

[32] On the repression of heresy in northern Italy as part of the struggle between popes and emperors in the first half of thirteenth century, see W. Helmut, 'Ziele und Mittel päpstlicher Ketzerpolitik in der Lombardei und im Kirchenstaat (1184–1252)', in *Die Anfänge der Inquisition im Mittelalter*, pp. 103–30. On the political use of the charge of heresy see A. Fischer, 'Herrscherliches Selbstverständnis und die Verwendung des Häresievorwurfs als politische Instrument. Friedrich II. und seiner Ketzeredikt von 1224', *Quellen und Forschungen aus italienischen Archiven und Bibliotheken* 87 (2007), 71–108; G. G. Merlo, *Inquisitori e inquisizione nel Medioevo* (Bologna, 2008).

[33] For the use of the term 'heretics' and 'ghibelline' during this period, see R. Orioli, 'Eresia e ghibellinismo', in *Federico II e le città italiane*, ed. P. Toubert and A. Paravicini Bagliani (Palermo, 1994), pp. 420–30.

[34] *Epistolae saeculi XIII*, I, no. 642; *Les registres de Grégoire IX*, ed. Auvray, II, no. 2607. On this episode see G. Gardoni, '"Pro fide et libertate Ecclesiae immolatus". Guidotto da Correggio vescovo di Mantova', in *Quaderni di storia religiosa* 7 (2000), 131–88.

[35] *Antistitum praeclarissimae Neapolitanae ecclesiae catalogus*, ed. B. Chioccarello (Naples, 1643), p. 158; *Bullarium Praedicatorum*, ed. T. Ripoll, I, n. 125; L. Parascandolo, *Memorie storico-critiche-diplomatiche della chiesa di Napoli*, 4 vols. (Naples, 1847–51), III, n. 24.

[36] On this episode, see G. Albini, 'Piacenza dal XII al XIV secolo: reclutamento ed esportazione dei podestà e capitani del popolo', in *I podestà dell'Italia comunale. Reclutamento e circolazione degli ufficiali forestieri (fine XII sec.-metà XIV sec.)*, ed. J. C. Maire Vigeur, 2 vols., Istituto Storico Italiano per il Medioevo, Nuovi Studi Storici 51 (Rome, 2000), I, 422–32. For a portrait of the friar with a focus on his anti-heretical activity, see R. Parmeggiani, 'Rolando da Cremona († 1259) e gli eretici: il ruolo dei frati Predicatori tra escatologismo e profezia', *Archivum fratrum Praedicatorum* 79 (2009), 23–84.

[37] M. P. Alberzoni, 'Gregorio de Romania (de Campagna)', *Dizionario Biografico degli Italiani* 59 (2002), 287–91.

Alessandro Sala

inquiries. This was attached to a letter, written by the pope, in which the bishops of Parma and Piacenza are appointed to determine the penalties of the attack. The text, written by Gregorio de Romania, was also included in the papal registers. This document consists of a list of people culpable for the assault: *Super infamatione de heresi contra quosdam cives Placentinos* (*On defamation for heresy: against some Piacentine citizens*).[38] Many citizens testified against those accused of heresy: 'Quod Iohannes Capellarius sit infamatus de heresi probatur per multos' (It is proved by [the testimony of many] that Giovanni Capellario is defamed of heresy).[39] In some cases, accusations of heresy were based on other elements: Guglielmo Fontana gave an unspecified amount of money to the *nuntio hereticorum* (heretics' messenger) as it is written in a certain *liber hereticorum* (heretics' book): Ansaldo de Allo confessed that he had written and sold books to the heretics.[40] The accusation of heresy came along after the subjects were accused of assaulting the clergy. These individuals reportedly encouraged the murder of the clergymen and personally threw rocks at them.[41] Here, a heretic is not only defined as those individuals responsible for the initial assault, but also those who joined in after it had begun. The label of 'heretic' is applied in the process of the investigation, and not from the pope in this instance. But is clear that Gregory IX used it for his personal political purposes. The report made by Gregorio de Romania reveals the heretics' identities: according to Pierre Racine, twelve men were aligned with the *populares* party and linked to Guglielmo Landi, leader of the imperial party in the city.[42] Furthermore, it means that any political opponent of the papacy might be labelled as heretic. The accusations of heresy and the investigations of Gregorio de Romania enabled the pope to take political advantage from this single episode and his intervention 'turned into subtle long-term diplomacy designed to bring Piacenza to the anti-imperial side'.[43]

[38] *Bullarium Franciscanum Romanorum Pontificum*, ed. J. H. Sbaraglia, 7 vols. (Rome, 1759), I, no. 137; *Les registres de Grégoire IX*, ed. Auvray, I, no. 2065, 2066.

[39] *Bullarium Franciscanum*, ed. Sbaraglia, I, no. 137.

[40] Ibid. 'Item quod scripserit et vendiderit libros hereticis et conversatus fuerit cum eis, confitetur de plano' (item, he confesses that he wrote for and sold books to the heretics, and consorted with them).

[41] Ibid. 'Item quod est fama publica quod percussit de fratribus probatur [...]. Item quod proiecerit lapides dicitur per unum [...]. Item quod cridaverit "moriantur moriantur latrones" dicitur per unum' (Item, it is proved that there is public repute that he hit the friars ... Item, it is said by one that he threw stones ... Item, it is said by one that he shouted, 'Let the thieves die, let them die').

[42] P. Racine, 'Il movimento ereticale', in *Storia di Piacenza*, 6 vols. (Piacenza, 1984), II, 373–90 (p. 388)

[43] 'si tradusse di fatto in una delicata manovra diplomatica pluriennale volta ad assicurare Piacenza al fronte antiimperiale'; Racine, 'Il movimento ereticale', p. 388. The relationships between papacy and Italian communes are analyzed in L. Baietto, *Il papa e le città. Papato e comuni in Italia centro-settentrionale durante la prima metà del*

Shaping the image of the heretics

Sometimes the information referred to the pope led to an investigation in order to confirm or deny the reports. Indeed, this is what happened in 1232, when Gregory IX ordered an inquiry into the bishop of Bosnia.[44] The bishop was accused of being a protector of the heretics: he furthermore supported and protected his brother, who was a well-known heresiarch, rather than trying to convert him.[45] The investigation should have confirmed these accusations. One year later, on 30 May in 1233, the pope ordered the legate in Hungary to appoint three or four new bishops for Bosnia, because the former one had been removed.[46] Through the inquiry led by the legate, the pope became aware that the bishop was a leader of the heretics and by the end of it even the bishop himself admitted to having sinned.[47] The papal letter sums up these accusations, the inquiry and the final decision and puts an end to the whole story regarding the former bishop of Bosnia. He has been removed from his diocese because he had relationships with heretics, as he finally admitted. This is the official version of the facts and the pope sent it to the legate in Hungary, the individual who represented papal power in the region.

One final example sheds more light on this idea of how much the truth is actually represented in these official papal documents. In April 1233, Gregory IX ordered Friar Robert, known as Le Bougre, to eradicate the heresy with

---

secolo XIII (Spoleto, 2007); A. Piazza, 'Paix et hérétiques dans l'Italie communale: les stratégies du langage dans les registres du pape Grégoire IX', in *Prêcher la paix, et discipliner la société. Italie, France, Angleterre*, ed. R. M Dessì, Collection d'Études Médiévales de Nice 5 (Turnhout, 2005), pp. 103–22.

[44] On the so-called 'Bosnian Church', see J. Fine, *The Bosnian Church: A New Interpretation. A Study of the Bosnian Church and its Place in State and Society from the Thirteenth to the Fifteenth Century* (New York, 1975); Y. Stoyanov, 'Between heresiology and political theology: the rise of the paradigm of the medieval heretical "Bosnian Church"', in *Teologie politiche: modelli a confronto*, ed. G. Filoramo (Brescia, 2005) pp. 163–80.

[45] 'hereticorum publicus defensator fratrem eius carnalem manifestum heresiarcam, quem deberet ab inicio ad viam rectitudinis revocare [...] in suo errore foveat dampnabiliter et defendat' (a public defender of heretics: he defends and damnably protects his own brother, a manifest heresiarch, whom from the start he ought to be bringing back to the path of righteousness), in *Codex diplomaticus Arpadianus continuatus*, ed. G. Wenzel, 8 vols. (Budapest, 1860–74), I, no. 181; *Codex diplomaticus regni Croatiae, Dalmatiae et Slavoniae*, ed. T. Smiciklas, 18 vols. (Zagreb 1874–1990), III, no. 315; *Acta Honori III (1216–1227) et Gregorii IX (1227–1241)*, ed. A. L. Tautu (Città del Vaticano, 1950), no. 177.

[46] 'eodem episcopo a regimine Bosnensis ecclesie prorsus amoto' (the same bishop having been removed from the rule of the Church of Bosnia), in *Codex diplomaticus regni Croatiae*, ed. Smiciklas, III, no. 327; *Acta Honori III et Gregorii IX*, ed. Tautu, no. 194.

[47] 'episcopus tamen de Bosnia, prout inquisitionis tue processu diligenter examinato didicimus, qui dux aliorum esse debuerat, dampnabiliter pervaricans legem Christi ad doctrine incidit amaritudinem insensate [...] autem idem episcopus ex simplicitate asserat se peccavisse' (for the bishop of Bosnia, as we have learnt through diligently examining the record of your inquisition, damnably contravening the law of Christ fell into the bitterness of mad doctrine ... the same bishop, however, claims that he sinned out of simplicity).

Alessandro Sala

the help of at least one colleague – friars from the convent of Besançon.[48] The pope decided to write this letter and to increase the powers of the friar because he received from him the news that the situation in La Charité was worse than they thought and that heresy spread throughout northern France and Flanders.[49] In the following days, the pope entrusted the provincial prior of the Dominicans with the task of selecting several friars to investigate this purported heresy.[50] Less than one year later, in February 1234, Gregory IX wrote the letter *Olim intellecto quod* to the archbishops of Reims and Sens, returning to this topic but with a completely different perspective.[51] He had received the archbishops' complaints about the activity of the Dominicans: the prelates had claimed that the friars' intervention was not required since there was no heresy in the region. In his letter, Gregory IX apologises and informs them that he had no intention to send friars into a region that was free of heretics:

> Porro nec fuit mandantis intentio nec scribentis voluntas hoc habuit ut super aliis provinciis preter quam de heresi infamatis, ad eos scripta huiusmodi emanarent, sed si forte contrarius fuerit subsecutus eventus, credimus quod hoc ignara occupatio fecerit vel dolosa surreptio procurarit ac ideo ea volumus effectu carere, quibus causa non fuit efficiens intentio mandatoris.

---

[48] *Bullarium Praedicatorum*, ed. T. Ripoll, I, no. 70; *Corpus documentorum inquisitionis haereticae pravitatis Neerlandicae*, ed. P. Fredericq, 5 vols. (Ghent and The Hague, 1889–1906), I, 90–3, no. 90; *Les registres de Grégoire IX*, ed. Auvray, I, no. 1253.

[49] 'sicut ex tuarum intelleximus continentia litterarum […] ministri Sathane scelerati messi dominice semen superseminaverunt iniquum per Bituricensem, Remensem, Rothomagensem, Turonensem et Senonesem provincias, per totam etiam Flandriam et alia multa loca' (as we have learnt from the content of your letters …the wicked ministers of Satan have 'oversowed' [see Matthew 13.25] wicked seed in the Lord's crop through the provinces of Bourges, Rheims, Rouen, Tours and Sens, also throughout the whole of Flanders and many other places), in *Bullarium Praedicatorum*, ed. T. Ripoll, I, no. 70; *Corpus documentorum inquisitionis*, ed. Fredericq, I, 92, no. 90; *Les registres de Grégoire IX*, ed. Auvray, I, no. 1253. The activity of Robert in La Charité is analyzed in E. Chénon, 'L'hérésie à La Charité-sur-Loire et les débuts de l'inquisition monastique dans la France du Nord au XIIIe siècle', *Nouvelle revue historique de droit français et étranger* 41 (1917), 299–345.

[50] *Corpus documentorum inquisitionis*, ed. Fredericq, I, 89–90, no. 89; Y. Dossat, *Les crises de l'inquisition toulousaine au XIII siècle (1233–1273)* (Bordeaux, 1959), Piéces justificatives no. 1, pp. 325–7; *Texte zur Inquisition*, ed. K. V. Selge, (Gütersloh, 1967), p. 47. On the first Dominican inquisitorial assignments see P. Segl, '*Quoniam abundavit iniquitas*. Zur Beauftragung der Dominikaner mit dem *negotium inquisitionis* durch Papst Gregor IX', *Rottenburger Jahrbuch für Kirchengeschichte* 17 (1998), 53–65;

[51] The letter to the archbishop of Sens is edited in *Bullarium Praedicatorum*, ed. T. Ripoll, I, no. 106; *Les registres de Grégoire IX*, ed. Auvray, I, no. 1763. The letter to the archbishop of Reims is edited in *Archives administratives de la ville de Reims*, ed. P. Varin, 3 vols. (Paris 1839–48), I, no. 133; *Corpus documentorum inquisitionis*, ed. Fredericq, I, 94–5, no. 93; *Texte zur Inquisition*, ed. Selge, pp. 48–9.

Shaping the image of the heretics

(Furthermore, it was not the intention of the one who gave the orders, nor was this the will of the scribe, that these writings should go out against other provinces than those defamed of heresy, but if by chance the contrary happened we believe that ignorant encroachment did this, or deceitful stealth brought it about, and therefore we wish those things to be without effect, whose cause was not the effective intention of the one who gave the commands.)[52]

Gregory IX then promptly withdrew from the provincial prior the power to choose and delegate friars in the inquisition of heresy. That meant that the pope suspended the friars' activity in those ecclesiastical provinces. It seems that Gregory IX wanted to believe and share the impression presented by the prelates, that there was no heretical threat in the area. It is exactly the opposite of what he had written ten months before in April 1233, at that point relying on what Friar Robert reported him. A year and a half later, Gregory IX once again backtracked on his opinion on the presence of the heretics in northern France. In August 1235 he wrote to Friar Robert and to the provincial prior of the Dominicans, claiming that the complaints of the two archbishops were ultimately wrong, and that heresy was indeed rife throughout France.[53] The pope decided to recommence the repression of heretics and to appoint some friars with inquisitorial tasks:

> Dudum ad aliquorum murmur, qui non patiebantur te aut fratres tuos in partibus gallicanis ad inquirendum super heretica pravitate procedere, que, ut aiebant, de heresi non fuerant infamate, scripsimus tibi et aliis fratribus tecum ad hoc negotium deputatis ut supersederetis cepto negotio, ne ubi non precesserat infamia heresis, nota perquireretur erroris. Verum quia postmodum, [...] tanta de universis regni Francie partibus ebullire dicitur venenatorum multitudo reptilium et heresum sanies scaturire.

> (Formerly, at the complaint of some who did not allow you or your brothers to proceed to inquire into heretical wickedness in France, which, they said, was not suspected of heresy, we wrote to you and to other brothers appointed with you to this business, to cease proceedings in the business you had begun, so that, where there had been no previous reputation of heresy, no sign of error was to be enquired into. But because afterwards … so great a multitude of poisonous reptiles is said to break out in all parts of the realm of France and so great a pus of heresies gush forth.)[54]

---

[52] *Bullarium Praedicatorum*, ed. T. Ripoll, I, no. 106; *Les registres de Grégoire IX*, ed. Auvray, I, no. 1763.

[53] The letter to Friar Robert is edited in *Bullarium Praedicatorum*, ed. T. Ripoll, I, no. 139; *Corpus documentorum inquisitionis*, ed. Fredericq, I, no. 101; *Les registres de Grégoire IX*, ed. Auvray, II, n. 2735. The letter to the provincial prior is edited in *Bullarium Praedicatorum*, ed. T. Ripoll, I, n. 137; *Corpus documentorum inquisitionis*, ed. Fredericq, I, 100–1, no. 100; *Les registres de Grégoire IX*, ed. Auvray, II, no. 2736.

[54] *Bullarium Praedicatorum*, ed. T. Ripoll, I, no. 139; *Corpus documentorum inquisitionis*, ed. Fredericq, I, 101–2, no. 101; *Les registres de Grégoire IX*, ed. Auvray, II, no. 2735.

At this point, there is one main question: what was the truth? Were the provinces of Sens and Reims full of heretics? Or free of them? The answer is that the pope did not provide the truth of the matter in his letters, only what was necessary to explain his decisions: partly what he had received and partly what his addressees wanted to be told. In February of 1234, Gregory IX thought that suspending the friars' anti-heretical activity was the right choice. We do not know whether he did it because he trusted the two prelates or if decision was rather based on ecclesiastical game playing – if, in other words, this was simply a way of pleasing them. Some sentences at the end of the *Olim intellecto quod* indeed suggest the latter as more likely. Gregory IX, who had just written that he did not mean to send friars to regions free of heretics, warned them to control the threat of heresy in their provinces and, if necessary, to act in cooperation with the Dominican.[55] The pope understood the importance of the friars' contribution in combatting heretics and did not want to minimise their efforts. Although he wrote that the provinces of Reims and Sens were not haunted by heretics, he was aware of the need to pursue anti-heretical activity. The apparent discrepancy between the presence or absence of heretics is susceptible of explanation. The religious situation of the provinces of Reims and Sens was outlined in the letters sent by the prelates. The answer of the pope, as always, was based on the information provided in this source, and was intended to present a picture in which the activity of the friar was not necessary. Some historians in the past have tried to present the suspension as a way to stop the abuses and violence of Friar Robert:[56] as it was written in contemporary monastic chroniclers with the aim to provide a hostile and part-fictitious picture of Friar Robert.[57] However, in papal letters there is no evidence that the suspension is linked to wrong procedures, malpractice or brutality in his activity. Indeed, it was more likely a matter of jurisdiction and about who

[55] 'singuli vestrum in diocesibus suis [...] contra hereticos huiusmodi studeatis sollicite debitum pastoralis officii exercere [...]. Ceterum, quia dicti fratres eo sunt ad confutandos hereticos aptiores [...] sicut expedire videretis, advocetis' (each one of you in your diocese should apply yourself zealously in carrying out the duty of the pastoral duty. ... Further, because the said friars are better suited to overcoming heretics in arguments, you should summon them [to help you], as seems to you expedient), in *Bullarium Praedicatorum*, ed. T. Ripoll, I, n. 106; *Les registres de Grégoire IX*, ed. Auvray, I, n. 1763.

[56] J. Frederichs, *Robert le Bougre, premier inquisiteur général en France (première moitié? du XIIIe siècle)* (Ghent, 1892); C. H. Haskins, 'Robert Le Bougre and the Beginnings of the Inquisition in Northern France', *The American Historical Review* 7 (1902), 437–57.

[57] *Matthaei Parisiensis, monachi Sancti Albani Chronica majora*, ed. H. R. Luard, 7 vols., Rerum Britannicarum medii aevi scriptores 57 (London, 1872–83), III, 520; *Chronica Alberici monachi Trium Fontium*, ed. P. Scheffer-Boichorst, MGH Scriptores 23 (Hannover, 1874), pp. 937, 940, 945; *Chronique rimée de Philippe Mouskes*, ed. F. A. F. T. baron de Reiffenberg, 2 vols., Collection de chroniques belges inédites et relatifs à l'histoire de la Belgique 4 (Bruxelles, 1836–45), II, 607–13.

Shaping the image of the heretics

should be in charge in the repression of heresy in northern France while the inquisition was in its early stages.[58] And this, as we have seen, has implications on the *narratio* and the way the pope describes the reality.

The papal letters, and above all the *narratio*, rely not only on the information provided by the people at the coal-face but also on misconceptions, accusations, prejudices and stereotypes. Once they were written inside the letter, they found official approval and were formally established as historical fact. The effects were large. There was the legacy of the imagery and phraseology in the canonical legal texts, anti-heretical treatises and inquisitorial handbooks that emerged in the following years.[59] There is evidence to show that the pope had the power to present an account of the situation that could be different from what actually happened: nevertheless, what was written by the pope became the truth. It was a progressive construction of knowledge, which could start from nothing or just a few fragments, and forge out of them dangerous sects. Our understanding of heresy and inquisition depends, in other words, on what the pope chose to write – or decided entirely to omit.

---

[58] G. Despy, 'Les débuts de l'Inquisition dans les anciens Pays-Bas au XIIe siècle', in *Hommages à Jean Hadot*, ed. G. Cambier, Problèmes d'Histoire du Christianisme 9 (Brussels, 1980), pp. 77–104.

[59] Sackville, *Heresy and Heretics in the Thirteenth Century*; R. Parmeggiani, Explicatio super officio inquisitionis. *Origini e sviluppi della manualistica inquisitoriale tra Due e Trecento*, Temi e Testi 112 (Rome, 2012).

3

Nepos of Montauban, assistant to inquisition and defender of the accused

Jörg Feuchter

Nepos (Latin for 'nephew') of Montauban was a thirteenth-century scholar and practitioner of law from southern France. Until recently just two things were known about him. One was that at the end of the 1260s he wrote a major work of jurisprudence, a treatise on defences in law. Its stated aim was 'to teach defendants how to flee', hence its colourful title, *Liber* (or *Libellus*) *fugitivus*, 'The Fleeing Book' or more loosely 'The Escape Book'.[1] The other is that he officiated at the same time, in the second half of the 1260s, as a judge in the lands of Alphonse of Poitiers, the Capetian count of Toulouse. But our knowledge is changing. First, in 2005 Giovanna Murano demonstrated that Nepos was not the primary author but only the redactor of the *Liber fugitivus*.[2] Secondly, though hardly anything has been known about Nepos's life,[3] this chapter will show that the archives of his hometown and inquisition

---

[1] I have used the first printed edition of the *Liber fugitivus*, Paris, 1510, in the copy preserved in Ghent, Universiteitsbibliotheek, Res. 1444, and also the edition printed by Iacobus Giuncti in Lyon, 1536, in the copy preserved in Vienna, Österreichische Nationalbibliothek, 74.W.161.(3), accessing both through the digitised online versions provided by google books and by the Österreichische Nationalbibliothek, respectively. 'Et hec pauca dixisse sufficiant super presenti libellulo et dicitur fugitivus quia decet [*recte*: docet, as in 1st edn (Paris, 1510), fol. LIIIIr] reos fugere'; *Liber Fugitivus. Tractatus perutilis a magistro Nepote de Monte Albano subtili et laborioso ingenio in lucem proditus, frequens & et quotidianus aulis ecclesiasticis et secularibus, noviter impressus & a multis erroribus extirpatus, summariis in hac novissima impressione numeratim appositis ...* (Lyon, 1536). Note that the title of the work throughout the late middle ages is 'Libellus', while in the printed versions it is 'Liber'.

[2] G. Murano, 'Ricerche sul "Libellus fugitivus"', *Aevum* 79 (2005), 417–60. I am grateful to Dr Murano for reading and commenting on an earlier draft of the present text. Of course all errors in this text are mine.

[3] 'On n'a aucun détail sur la vie de l'auteur': A. Tardif, *Histoire des sources du droit francais: Origines romaines* (Paris, 1890), p. 377. Until the second half of the twentieth century, knowledge about Nepos was entirely based on inference from the *Liber fugitivus*; on this see below. This had already enabled Friedrich Carl von Savigny to ascertain that 'de Montealbano' did not mean an Italian place, such as Albano, but Montauban;

records can be used to establish a surprising number of facts about him. The most important new biographical information is that our judge, scholar and 'teacher of legal defence' played a very active role in the inquisition of heresy. As a young man he was a leading collaborator of the Dominican Friars Bernard of Caux and John of St Pierre in their mass trials in the mid-1240s. The two inquisitors[4] directed their ecclesiastical court procedures against the inhabitants of the Lauragais, a fertile and densely populated rural region to the east of Toulouse. Although their inquisition activities count among the earliest in the middle ages, they are also the largest in scope, as they involved several thousand men and women. And for over a year Nepos was one of the most important assistants in this huge endeavour.

It may strike us as odd that a man who had given his assistance to such a large-scale prosecution of people for heresy went on to redact, roughly two decades later, a juridical treatise that was openly intended to 'help defendants to flee'. Is the contradiction real or only apparent? Whatever the answer, the case of Nepos appears interesting enough in the context of a discussion of 'inquisition and knowledge' to justify systematically establishing what we know of his life.

In the following, we shall first give a summary of recent research on the *Liber fugitivus* (section 1). Then we shall discuss biographical clues in the *Liber* (section 2) and Nepos's activity as a judge (section 3). After that we shall turn

---

F.C. von Savigny, *Geschichte des römischen Rechts im Mittelalter*, 7 vols. (Heidelberg, 1834–51), V, *Das dreizehnte Jahrhundert*, 443–5. Cf. G. Bousquet, 'Montealbano, Nepos de', in *Nouvelle biographie universelle depuis les temps les plus reculés jusqu'à nos jours, avec les renseignements bibliographiques et l'indication des sources à consulter*, ed. F. Hoefer, 46 vols. (Paris, 1858–71), XXXVI, col. 153. Despite this, Hermann Kantorowicz expressly rejected the authorship of a 'Provencal from Montauban', arguing for an Italian in his *Einführung in die Textkritik. Systematische Darstellung der textkritischen Grundsätze für Philologen und Juristen* (Leipzig, 1921), p. 30. All doubt vanished when Eduard Maurits Meijers and Henri Gilles found Nepos being mentioned as a judge in the Languedoc lands of Alphonse of Poitiers in the 1260s: E. M. Meijers, *Études d'histoire du droit*, ed. R. Feenstra and H. F. W. D. Fischer, 4 vols. (Leiden, 1956–73), III, 170, nn. 12 and 13; H. Gilles, 'L'enseignement du droit en Languedoc au XIIIe siècle', *Cahiers de Fanjeaux* 5 (1970), pp. 205–29, reprinted in H. Gilles, *Université de Toulouse et enseignement du droit, XIIIe et XIVe siècles* (Toulouse, 1992), pp. 59–76 (62–3, n. 11). Before the present chapter, the most comprehensive and up-to-date account of Nepos was J. Feuchter, *Ketzer, Konsuln und Büßer. Die städtischen Eliten von Montauban vor dem Inquisitor Petrus Cellani (1236–1241)*, Spätmittelalter, Humanismus and Reformation 40 (Tübingen, 2007), pp. 390–2 and 402–7. The present text takes this up but develops it further and supersedes it in the light of Murano's insights and of newly found evidence in inquisition records.

[4] On the history of inquisition law and procedure see L. Kolmer, *Ad capiendas vulpes. Die Ketzerbekämpfung in Südfrankreich in der ersten Hälfte des 13. Jahrhunderts und die Ausbildung des Inquisitionsverfahrens*, Pariser Historische Studien 19 (Bonn, 1982), and V. Bivolarov, *Inquisitoren-Handbücher. Papsturkunden und juristische Gutachten aus dem 13. Jahrhundert mit Edition des Consilium von Guido Fulcodii*, Monumenta Germanise Historica Studien und Texte 56 (Wiesbaden, 2014).

Jörg Feuchter

to Montauban in order to investigate the situation in the town Nepos was from and in which he lived, and assemble the traces of Nepos's presence that are to be found in the town's charters (section 4), before addressing his relationship to the adjacent Benedictine abbey of St Théodard (section 5). We shall then assess Nepos's role as assistant to inquisition (section 6) before synthesising our findings in a general sketch of Nepos's life (section 7). Finally we present Nepos's discussion of heresy in the *Liber fugitivus*, reading it in the light of his own experience, on the one hand as the son of a town containing a lot of dissidents, and on the other as a collaborator in inquisition (section 8).

1. Nepos and his part in the *Liber fugitivus*: redactor, not author

The *Liber fugitivus* is a juridical treatise consisting of a systematic presentation and discussion of exceptions ('exceptiones'), that is to say, defences to be made in court by the defendant in the system of Roman Law. These exceptions are organised according to around two dozen sorts of actions or actors against which or whom they are directed. The treatise is not written in a neutral spirit, to provide useful information to both sides, for both accusation and defence. Rather, its declared intention is to provide the accused with instruments to neutralise attacks. The prologue's forceful wording underlines this – the exceptions are the 'weapons of the defendants' (arma reorum).[5] The author presented himself as having written the book 'out of compassion for poor and powerless people' (pauperibus et minoribus compatiens), and presented them as people 'who are attacked by unprincipled accusers' (qui ab improbis petitoribus impugnantur). The general idea of the treatise finds succinct expression in a concluding remark: 'Therefore in this present short book I want to teach defendants how to flee' (Ideo in hoc presenti libello reos docere volo fugere). Translating 'fugere' as 'how to escape' or 'how to get away' gets even closer to the wit and audacity of this.

The *Liber* turned out to be a lasting success, as is evidenced by its survival in no fewer than sixty medieval manuscripts located today in libraries all over Europe, from Kaliningrad to Seville, and even in the USA (New York).[6] It was also printed in no fewer than twenty-five different editions before 1600.[7] And it attracted high praise from later legal scholars, from Giovanni d'Andrea (ob. 1348)[8] to Thomas Diplovatatius, who praised it as a short but highly useful work in his *Liber de claris iuris consultis* (Book of Famous Law Scholars),

---

[5] *Liber fugitivus* (1536 edn.), page before fol. Ir (corresponding to fol. 1r in the 1510 first printed edn.).
[6] See the exhaustive list in Murano, 'Ricerche', 417–30.
[7] Ibid., 430–5.
[8] Savigny, *Geschichte des römischen Rechts*, V, 443.

Figure 3.1 *Liber fugitivus* (Lyon, 1536), title page; Österreichische Nationalbibliothek, Sammlung von Handschriften und alten Drucken, 74.W.161.(3). Once thought to be by Nepos of Montauban, this was written (probably *c.* 1240) by Bagarotus de Coradis and redacted by Nepos *c.* 1268. By permission, Österreichische Nationalbibliothek.

Jörg Feuchter

written at the beginning of the sixteenth century.[9] He described its presumed author, Nepos, as an 'outstanding canonist, ardent defender of the accused and excellent doctor of the laws' (canonista precipuus et reorum defensor acerrimus et excellens doctor legum).[10]

For over 700 years Nepos of Montauban was generally regarded as the sole author of the *Liber fugitivus*. Then, in 2005, Giovanna Murano followed an earlier lead by Roberto Abbondanza,[11] and convincingly demonstrated that there are two distinctive versions of the *Liber*. One is the original work, the other a redaction.[12] The original was written by Bagarot(t)us de Coradis (Bagarotto dei Corradi), an Italian legal scholar from Piacenza,[13] probably around the year 1240. The text had circulated for the most part anonymously; Bagarotus had written in the first person in the prologue, but without mentioning his own name. Around 1268 Nepos of Montauban took the text, made some changes, corrections and additions, and inserted his own name as the author in the prologue.[14] From then on, Nepos was more or less universally seen as the original and sole author. As Murano remarks, in medieval terms the author claim by Nepos in his version of the prologue would not have been seen as plagiarism.[15] In modern terms however it is clear that Nepos can no longer be called 'the author' of the *Liber fugitivus*, but rather its redactor. Nonetheless it is evident that Nepos closely shared Bagarotus's interest and expertise in exceptions. And this was not all: Nepos took legal thought on exceptions a decisive step further, by conceiving of them no longer strictly as counter-measures against the *actio* (legal action) in Roman Law, but as general 'weapons' of the defendant. The explicit statement about the 'arma reorum' in the prologue is not there in Bagarotus's original – it was added by Nepos in his redaction. The difference between the two scholars has been clearly stated by Boris Bernabé, a leading expert in the history of pre-modern legal procedure.

---

[9] 'Est tractatus parvus sed utilis viginti cartarum' (It is a little treatise, but a useful twenty sheets *or* as useful as twenty sheets); Thomas Diplovatatius, *Liber de claris iuris consultis, pars posterior*, ed. F. Schulz, H. Kantorowicz and G. Rabotti, Studia Gratiana 10 (Bologna, 1968), p. 163.

[10] Diplovatatius, *Liber*, p. 163.

[11] R. Abbondanza, 'Bagarotto (Bagarotto dei Corradi)', in *Dizionario Biografico degli Italiani* 5 (1963), http://www.treccani.it/enciclopedia/bagarotto_(Dizionario-Biografico)/ [accessed 8 March 2018], pp. 170–4; Murano, 'Ricerche', 445. Abbondanza's idea about Bagarotus's authorship was not widely noticed. It is absent, for example, in B. Bernabé, 'Montauban, Neveu de (Nepos de Montalbano), XIIIe siècle', in *Dictionnaire historique des juristes français (XIIe-Xxe siècle)*, ed. P. Arabeyre, J.-L. Halperin and J. Krynen (Paris, 2007), pp. 571–2.

[12] Murano, 'Ricerche', 441: 'testo originale e testo rimaneggiato'.

[13] On him, see Abbondanza, 'Bagarotto'.

[14] See Murano, 'Ricerche', 452, on the date of redaction.

[15] Ibid.

Nepos of Montauban, assistant to inquisition and defender of the accused

Pour Bagarotus, les exceptions sont encore les objections liées formellement à l'action et permettant de faire avorter celle-ci, tandis que pour Neveu, elles sont devenues des *arma* indépendantes, c'est-à-dire de véritables moyens de défense: selon Neveu, toute défense pouvait être qualifiée d'exception, quand bien même elle ne répondait pas strictement à l'action.

(For Bagarotus exceptions are still objections formally linked to the action and allowing it to come to nothing [to fail], whereas for Nepos they have become independent weapons, that is to say, veritable measures of defence. For Nepos, any defence could be described as 'exception', even if it did not correspond strictly to the action.)[16]

Bernabé considers this an important advance, with further implications.[17] Yet for us it is even more important to note that Nepos, much more emphatically than Bagarotus, was siding with the defendants, those who were poor and powerless.

2. Biographical information in Nepos's redaction of the *Liber fugitivus*

A few biographical clues can be gleaned from the treatise itself, or more precisely, from Nepos's additions to it. In it he refers once to eyewitness experience: 'according to what I saw done by the great masters of the laws at Montpellier' (secundum quod apud Montempessulanum et [corr: a, JF] magnis domnis legum vidi fieri).[18] This led the legal historian André Gouron to the idea that Nepos was one of the first southern French jurists who might have studied at home rather than in Italy, which would have been very rare before 1270.[19] Eduard M. Meijers pointed out that these words

---

[16] B. Bernabé, 'Naissance d'une éthique judiciaire à travers la théorie de la récusation des juges (XIIIe-XIVe siècle)', *Les justices d'Église dans le Midi (Xie-Xve siècle)*, Cahiers de Fanjeaux 42 (2007), pp. 343–72 (345).

[17] Bernabé also sees Nepos playing an important role in the development of the theory of juridical ethics, more specifically the idea of the personal responsibility of the judge, mediated through the notion of the recusation of the judge. See Bernabé, 'Naissance'; B. Bernabé, 'La rhétorique de la guerre dans le procès médiéval', in *Penser la guerre* (Aix-en-Provence, 2007), pp. 31–46 (on Nepos, 37–8); B. Bernabé, *La récusation des juges. Étude médiévale, moderne et contemporaine* (Paris, 2009), pp. 90–7. I am grateful to Dr Bernabé for reading an earlier draft of the present text.

[18] *Liber fugitivus* (1536 edn.), fol. XXVIIIr (corresponding to fol. XXVIIIr in the 1510 first printed edn.). Note that the one manuscript that I have been able to see, Staatsbibliothek zu Berlin Ms. Lat. Fol. 862 fols. 377r–406r (on this see below footnote 136), on fol. 394v, also has 'et', not 'a'. Yet the 1510 first print edn. Has 'a' exchanged for 'et', as suggested in my correction above.

[19] A. Gouron, 'The training of Southern French Lawyers during the Thirteenth and Fourteenth Centuries', in *Post Scripta. Essays on Medieval Law and the Emergence of the European State in Honor of Gaines Post*, ed. J. R. Strayer and D. E. Queller, Studia Gratiana 15 (Rome, 1972), pp. 217–27, 220 and 222.

showed only that Nepos had practised at Montpellier, not necessarily that he studied there.[20] Scepticism here finds support in the point – also mentioned by Meijers – that the authorities cited by name in the *Liber* were all scholars teaching in Italy,[21] apart from one who taught at a French law school, Guido de Guinis/de Cumis – though at Orléans rather than Montpellier.[22] But it is still possible that Nepos studied in both Italy and Montpellier.

There are only two further local references in Nepos's redaction of the *Liber*, both of them closer to his home region. On one occasion the case put forward by Nepos as an example runs thus: 'whence, suppose first of all that Peter, a Toulousan citizen, has had a certain B., citizen of Cahors, cited by apostolic [papal] letters' (unde primo pone quod quidam Petrus ciuis Tholosanus fecit citari per literas apostolicas quendam B. ciuem Caturicensem).[23] In another instance he refers to the custom in the dioceses of Toulouse and Cahors.[24] Yet this adds only a little, for we were already aware that Nepos was from the region and that he sat as a judge there.

3. Nepos as judge of the Toulousan Albigeois

Until recently the only established hard biographical fact about Nepos was that he officiated as a judge in the Toulousain in the second half of the 1260s. He is mentioned once as 'Master Nepos, judge of Villelongue in the Toulousain' (magistri Nepotis, judicis Ville Longe in Tholosano) in 1266,[25] and then several times as judge of the Albigeois from 1267 to 1269. 'Villelongue' is a somewhat obscure place name: there is no certain town or village in the region to identify it with. Yet it is clear that there was, at least for a certain period in the thirteenth century, a bailiwick and a jurisdiction going by that name in the *sénéchaussée* (seneschalcy: administrative province) of Toulouse. Created probably only in the 1260s, this jurisdiction was situated in the north of the *sénéchaussée* and thus was immediately adjacent to Montauban. In some cases, it also included the bailiwick of the Tescou, which is an area on the southern border of Quercy with the Toulousain, lying literally under

---

[20] Meijers, *Études* III, 170.

[21] See ibid., Azo, Tancred und Accursius.

[22] Ibid., III, 30.

[23] *Liber fugitivus* (1536 edn.), fol. XIXr (corresponding to fol. XIXv in the 1510 first printed edn.).

[24] *Liber fugitivus* (1536 edn.), fol. XIIIIr (corresponding to fol. XVr in the 1510 first printed edn.).

[25] *Enquêtes administratives d'Alfonse de Poitiers. Arrêts de son parlement tenu à Toulouse et textes annexes 1249–1271*, ed. P.-F. Fournier and P. Guébin, Collection de documents inédits sur l'histoire de France (Paris 1959), no 79, p. 229 (5 November 1266); Gilles, 'Enseignement', pp. 208 and 226, n. 11.

Nepos of Montauban, assistant to inquisition and defender of the accused

the city walls of Montauban.[26] However unclear the exact dimension of the Villelongue jurisdiction, it is clear that it coincided with an ecclesiastical district of the same name in the diocese of Toulouse, the archdeanery of Villelongue and that it included the region of Castelsarrasin – a fact that will become important to us later when we get to Nepos's inquisitorial activities.

The 'Albigeois' of which Nepos was a judge from 1267 on also needs some explanation. It was not coterminous with the former viscounty of Albi, known as one of the territories held by the viscounts of Trencavel until the demise of the last of them, Raymond-Roger, in 1209. After the end of the Albigensian Wars in 1229,[27] the viscounty had been divided by the royal administration into two halves, and the northwestern part eventually became a *sénéchaussée* of the counts of Toulouse. From 1249 on, the *sénéchaussée* of the Albigeois, as well as those of the Toulousain, the Agenais, Quercy and Rouergue, were all ruled together by the Capetian prince Alphonse (1220–71), a younger brother of the French king Louis IX. First a count of Poitiers – hence known as 'Alphonse of Poitiers' – he would also become count of Toulouse by inheriting the lands of the former Raymondine dynasty of Toulouse, since he had married the daughter of the last count of that line, Raymond VII (ob. 1249). The marriage and the eventual transition of the Raymondine lands to the Capetian dynasty had been one of the terms of the peace of Paris (1229) ending the Albigensian wars.

In our sources, Nepos is named as 'magister Nepos of Montauban, Albigensian judge', in Latin and in Occitan (magistri Nepotis, de Monte Albano, judicis Albiensis; maestre Neps de Montalba, jutges d'Albeges).[28] The documents do not yield much more about him as an individual person, although one of them deals with the competence of the office he held at the time,[29] and another is about problems arising from heresy prosecutions in his

---

[26] See *Enquêtes administratives d'Alfonse de Poitiers*, p. cix n. 1, and *Saisimentum Comitatus Tholosani*, ed. Y. Dossat, Collection de documents inédits sur l'histoire de France, Série in-8° 1, (Paris, 1966), pp. 38 and 101. See also Y. Dossat, 'Limites du Toulousain et du Quercy et la bailie du Tescou (1273–1329)', *Annales du Midi* 59 (1947), pp. 193–209.

[27] On the Albigensian wars see J. Sumption, *The Albigensian Crusade* (London, 1999; 1st edn 1978), and J. Oberste, *Der "Kreuzzug" gegen die Albigenser. Ketzerei und Machtpolitik im Mittelalter* (Darmstadt, 2003).

[28] *Enquêtes administratives d'Alfonse de Poitiers*, no. 93, § 4, p. 240 (1267, 7 January 17); no. 101, § 4, p. 250; Gilles, 'Enseignement', p. 208 and 226–7 n. 11. See further examples of the Latin form in *Histoire générale de Languedoc*, ed. Cl. Devic and J. Vaissète, revised E. Roschach and A. Molinier, 16 vols. (Toulouse 1872–1904; henceforth *HGL*), VIII, 1596–7, no. 513, § 2–3 (both documents from 17 January 1267), and VIII, 1672, no. 359, § 1 (20 May 1269): always 'magistri Nepotis de Montealbano judicis Albiensis'.

[29] It is a text relating a decision by Count Alphonse, informed by an inquiry held by his inspectors, that his judge in the Albigeois should also be his judge in Gaillac. The question came up because although that town was the administrative capital of the

hometown;[30] we shall come back to the latter document below, in the context of our discussion of Montauban. Much more informative are the facts that we can garner from hitherto overlooked sources, that is to say the archives of Nepos's hometown and inquisition records.

4. Nepos of Montauban and his home town

The fact that Nepos was from the town of Montauban has not been thought about.[31] But it is important to reflect on this, especially in the light of our new knowledge about Nepos as an inquisitors' assistant, and the fact that Montauban was a hotbed of religious dissidence and a place of inquisitorial persecution.

Montauban is a town roughly thirty miles north of Toulouse. It was founded in the mid-twelfth century at a strategic location on the bank of the Tarn river, at the southern border between Quercy and the Toulousain. The planned settlement, a precursor of the late-medieval 'bastides' of southwest France, was planted by Alphonse-Jordan, count of Toulouse, immediately next to the old, but not very prosperous Benedictine abbey of St Théodard, a member of the congregation of the house of La Chaise-Dieu in the Auvergne. There was a period of very rapid growth in its first decades, and by the turn of the twelfth century Montauban had already developed into a major urban centre in the lands of the counts of Toulouse. During the Albigensian wars (1209–29) it turned out to be an important and very loyal base of the 'southern' case, that is to say, of the resistance against the anti-heretical crusade launched by pope Innocent III and led by the northern French count Simon of Montfort. The town also had a very substantial presence of religious dissidents,[32] both Waldensians and members of another group. The latter

---

sénéchaussée of the Albigeois, its dominion was a shared one, between the abbot of Gaillac and the count; *HGL*, VIII, 1595–6, no. 519, § 2.

[30] Livre Rouge, Montauban, Archives Municipales, AA 1 (henceforth LR), fol. 12v, and Livre des Sermens, Montauban, Archives Municipales AA 2 (henceforth LS), fol. 16rv, ed. *Enquêtes administratives d'Alfonse de Poitiers*, no. 101, pp. 249–50.

[31] In the local historiography only E. Forestié, *Notes historiques ou éphémérides montalbanaises et du Tarn-et-Garonne* (Montauban, 1882), vaguely tries to connect Nepos to Montauban. On p. 107 he claims with respect to him that there was a family by the name of Nepos whose members were consuls in the late thirteenth and early fourteenth centuries. However as far as I can see there was no family of that name in the thirteenth century, just one individual, our legal scholar.

[32] On Montauban, heresy and inquisition, see the detailed study by Feuchter, *Ketzer, Konsuln und Büßer*. There are short overviews in French and English: J. Feuchter, 'Le pouvoir de l'inquisition à travers ses peines. Le cas de Montauban (1241)', in *Inquisition et Pouvoir*, ed. G. Audisio (Aix-en-Provence, 2003), pp. 235–55, J. Feuchter, 'Histoire religieuse des élites montalbanaises au XIIIe siècle entre catharisme, valdéisme et catholicisme', in *700 ans du diocèse de Montauban (1317–2017)*, ed. C. Mengès-Le Pape (Montauban, forthcoming), and J. Feuchter, 'The first systematic

Nepos of Montauban, assistant to inquisition and defender of the accused

were named *haeretici / heretici* in Languedoc inquisition documents. It is important to note that this designation was not used in a generic sense, that is to say, it did not mean 'dissidents from Roman Catholicism'. Rather it was a specific name for a group of dissidents that was clearly differentiated from others, as the Waldensians were. Contemporary historiographical sources from the region call them *haeretici* or *albigenses*.[33] Later medieval churchmen and early modern scholars opted for 'Albigensians', but modern scholarship since the nineteenth century usually flags them as 'Cathars'.[34]

A major inquisition document for the region of Quercy records more than 250 people in Montauban who received a sanction for involvement in one or both of the heretical groups. Peter Sellan, a Dominican friar, set up the document. One of the earliest medieval inquisitors and the first to conduct

---

mass inquisition: Peter Sellan in the Quercy, 1234–1236', in *The Origins of Inquisition*, ed. L. J. Sackville (York, forthcoming).

[33] It is clear that 'Albigensians' was a pars-pro-toto name. The inhabitants of the city and region of Albi were never understood to be the only or the original region where this dissidence flourished. On the rather arbitrary invention of the designation, see J.-L. Biget, 'Les "Albigeois". Remarques sur une dénomination', in *Inventer l'hérésie? Discours polémiques et pouvoirs avant l'inquisition*, ed. M. Zerner, Collection du Centre d'Études Médiévales de Nice 2 (Nice, 1998), pp. 219–55; Feuchter, *Ketzer, Konsuln und Büßer*, pp. 425–6; J. Feuchter, 'The Albigensian Crusade, the Dominicans, and the Antiheretical Dispositions of the Council', in *The Fourth Lateran Council. Institutional Reform and Spiritual Renewal*, ed. J. Helmrath and G. Melville (Affalterbach, 2017), pp. 225–41, here p. 225 footnote 1.

[34] The use of the term 'Cathars' is heavily contested in today's scholarship. It occurs in medieval sources from other western, southern and central European regions for dualist dissident groups similar to the *heretici* of Languedoc, even as a self-designation, but not in relation to dualist heretical groups in Occitania. Scholars have been long aware of this problem, usually giving cautionary remarks on the use of term. However given the lack of a distinctive name used by the Languedoc dissidents for themselves other than *heretici*, many historians (the present author among them) maintain the use of 'Cathars'. Others however deny even the existence of an organized, religiously dissident group in Languedoc or at least that it was a part of a larger, interconnected 'Cathar' movement in medieval Europe. For a broad spectrum of opinions on the legitimacy of the use of the term and the reality of the group in question: J. Thèry, 'L'hérésie des bons hommes. Comment nommer la dissidence religieuse non vaudoise ni béguine en Languedoc (XIIe-début du XIVe siècle)?', *Heresis* 36/37 (2002), 75–117; M. G. Pegg, 'The Paradigm of Catharism; or, the Historian's illusion', in *Cathars in Question*, ed. A. Sennis, Heresy and Inquisition in the Middle Ages 4 (York, 2016), pp. 21–52; C. Taylor, 'Looking for the 'Good Men' in the Languedoc: An Alternative to Cathars?', ibid., pp. 242–56; P. Biller, 'Goodbye to Catharism?', ibid., pp. 274–304, and J. Feuchter, 'The 'heretici' of Languedoc: Local Holy Men and Women or Organized Religious Group? New Evidence from Inquisitorial, Notarial and Historiographical Sources', ibid., pp. 112–30. The problem whether the Cathars really existed will not be touched upon further in the present contribution, as it goes without question that in the perception of contemporary churchmen the group and the threat it posed did exist.

a mass trial, he toured the Quercy no fewer than three times between 1234 and 1236. After initial early set-backs he successfully took depositions from hundreds of witnesses in many places, in fact covering all the parts of Quercy that were under the administration of the count of Toulouse. Montauban was the last town Sellan entered, together with his colleague William Arnaud. This was at the beginning of April 1236, and here the question arises, why so late? As I have laid out elsewhere,[35] the answer seems to be connected to what had immediately preceded this, in March 1236. The inquisitor William Arnaud[36] had dealt with a number of citizens of Castelsarrasin, a town very close to Montauban, but belonging to the diocese of Toulouse. One of the Castelsarrasin defendants is particularly significant. He was not only a wealthy international merchant[37] but also the seneschal (chief officer) for Quercy[38] and in Thomas

---

[35] See n. 31 above.

[36] As Castelsarrasin lay in the bishopric of Toulouse, in this instance Arnaud did not work together with Sellan who was technically suspended from this diocese on the request of Count Raymond VII.

[37] He had traded with England and had enjoyed the protection of king Henry III as his 'homo noster'. See *Patent Rolls of the Reign of Henry III Preserved in the Public Record Office*, 6 vols. (London, 1901–13), II, 193 (25 June 1228, Westminster): 'Pontius Grimewardi de Castro Sarraceno habet litteras de protectione sine termino, quod dominus rex recepit ipsum in protectionem et defensionem suam' (Pons Grimeward of Castelsarrasin has letters of protection, with no fixed term, because the king has taken him under his protection and defence); and 194–5 (13 July 1228, Westminster): 'Rex omnibus ad quos presentes littere pervenerint, salutem. Sciatis quod Pontius Grimeward homo noster est, et ipsum pro negociis nostris ad dilectum et fidelem nostrum Henricum de Trublevill, senescallum nostrum Wasconie, misimus' (The king to all those to whom the present letters come, greetings. Know that Pons Grimeward is our man, and we have sent him on our business to our beloved and faithful Henry de Trubleville, our seneschal of Gascony). See also ibid., III, 319 (1 September 1242, Bordeaux): 'Safe-conduct until one year after Michelmas for William Arnaldi de Villa Dei and Gerard Ispano, serjeants of Pons Grimaudi, to trade in the king's power with the goods of the said Pons'. On Pons Grimoardi and the group of deponents from Castelsarrasin, see also C. Taylor, *Heresy, Crusade and Inquisition in Medieval Quercy*, Heresy and Inquisition in the Middle Ages 2 (York, 2011), esp. pp. 144–7, 186–7, 217–19 and 235.

[38] According to his deposition from 25 January 1245 he held this office after the treaty of Paris/Meaux (1229), Ms Bibliothèque nationale de France, Fonds Languedoc-Doat, henceforth Doat, vol. 22, fols. 40v–2r (42r): 'tempore quo erat senescallus pro domino comite tholososano in caturcensi diocesi post factam pacem inter dominum comitem et ecclesiam' (at the time when he was seneschal for the Toulousan Count in the diocese of Cahors after peace had been made between the Lord Count and the Church). This will appear, as all the content of Doat vols. 22–24, in *The Genesis of Inquisition in anguedoc. Edition and Translation of the Earliest Inquisition Records*, ed. P. Biller, L. J. Sackville and S. Sneddon (forthcoming). According to J. Vaissete, 'Sur les grands officiers de la maison des comtes de Toulouse', in *HGL*, VII, pp. 128–31 (131), note 45, he was the seneschal of Quercy around 1234. See also Kolmer, *Ad capiendas vulpes*, p. 140, and Taylor, *Heresy, Crusade and Inquisition*, p. 217.

Nepos of Montauban, assistant to inquisition and defender of the accused

Bisson's words one of the 'leading members of an inner circle of councillors'[39] of Raymond VII. This man, a certain Pons Grimoardi, was that count's first high officer to confess to the inquisitors. On 29 March 1236 a penitential letter to Pons was issued by Friar William Arnaud, in Castelsarrasin.[40] We shall see below that a few years later Nepos would appear in close proximity to Pons and Peter Sellan, in an inquisitorial context.

We stay for the moment in 1236. After issuing the letter for Pons in Castelsarrasin at the end of March, William Arnaud went directly from there to nearby Montauban. He was there together with Peter Sellan at the beginning of April 1236, as his fellow Dominican William Pelhisson indicates in his inquisition chronicle.[41] What did the penance for Pons Grimoardi in Castelsarrasin have to do with the entry of the inquisitors to Montauban? A strong case can be made that the Quercy town had arrived at a collective political decision to come forward towards the inquisitors, that is to say, to cooperate with them and for everybody to make a full confession, but on the basis of a deal for relative leniency within the framework of the 'period of grace' (tempus gratiae). Such a deal had been offered by Sellan to people in many other places in Quercy in the two years before 1236. Actually the inquisitors had been forced to do so by a papal legate, for their initial hard-line policies had had little or no success. Yet although Sellan travelled 'through many towns and villages' of Quercy in 1235, as was related by Pelhisson, who was himself a companion on these inquisitorial travels, it was only in 1236 that Sellan was able to gather depositions in Montauban. It is thus highly probable that the town's citizens followed the individual example of Pons Grimoardi, their former (and maybe even current) seneschal, who had also received a penance under these mild conditions just a few days earlier. As can be demonstrated, the appeasement of the inquisitor proved to be a very effective general strategy for the whole town, and especially for its elites. They survived the inquisition trial without major consequences. And after 1236 there were few cases of heresy prosecution in Montauban.

---

[39] T. N. Bisson, 'The General Assemblies of Philip the Fair. Their Character reconsidered', *Studia Gratiana* 15, 1972, 537–64 (p. 64); reprinted in *Medieval France and Her Pyrenean Neighbours. Studies in Early Institutional History*, ed. T. N. Bisson (London, 1989), pp. 97–124.

[40] Doat vol. 22, fols. 38v–40r.

[41] 'Et postquam fuerunt aliquandiu [sic] Fratres in conventu Tholosano, dictus prior cum Fratre Guillelmo Arnaldi collega suo ivit apud Montem Albanum in dyocesi Caturcensi, ut ibi contra hereticos facerent inquisitionem' (And when the friars had been in the Toulousan convent for some time, the said prior together with Friar William Arnold, his colleague, went to Montauban in the diocese of Cahors, in order to carry out inquisition there against heretics); *Guillaume Pelhisson, Chronique (1229–1244) suivie du récit des troubles d'Albi (1234)*, ed. J. Duvernoy (Paris, 1994), pp. 90, 92.

Jörg Feuchter

It was in this hotbed of religious dissidence that our legal scholar and inquis-itors' assistant, Nepos, grew up. He also lived there as an adult for at least part of his life. For we can find him more than a dozen times in the charters collected by the town's administration in its cartularies, the *Livre rouge* and the *Livre des Sermens*:

1253 August (without day): 'Neps'[42]

Between 1260–1285 (undated): 'magister Nepos'[43]

[1267 June 27: 'maestre Neps de Montalba, jutges d'Albeges'[44]]

1273 November 9: 'magister Nepos'[45]

1273 November 13: 'maestre Neps de la Davinia'[46]

1275 (without day or month): 'maestre Nepos'[47]

1277 (without day or month): 'mestre Nepos'[48]

1277 December 14: 'maestre Neps'[49]

1278 April 14: 'maestre Neps de la Davenia'[50]

1278 April 15: 'maestre Neps de la Davenia'[51]

1278 April 16: 'maestre Neps'[52]

1282 September 26: 'magistro Nepoti'[53]

1282 May 31: 'maestre Neps'[54]

1284 (without day or month): Maestre Neps[55]

It is striking that in every instance apart from the first his name is given as 'master Nepos', and that in three instances a byname is added, 'de la Davinia' or 'de la Davenia'; its significance is unclear, but we shall see it again in the inquisition documents.[56] And in one instance, his name is given

---

[42] LR, fol. 11rv, and LS, fols. 14v–15v.

[43] LR fol. 40r, LS fol. 53r; dated between 1260 and 1285 on the basis of the names of the people mentioned in the document and their occurrence in other documents in this range of years; see Feuchter, *Ketzer, Konsuln und Büßer*, p. 516.

[44] LR fol. 12v, LS, fol. 16r–v. This document was edited in *Enquêtes administratives d'Alfonse de Poitiers*, no. 101, pp. 249–50, and is parenthesised here because it was mentioned in our discussion of Nepos's office as a judge.

[45] LR fol. 18r.

[46] LR fol. 19r, LS fols. 22v–3r.

[47] LR fols. 20v–1r, LS fols. 24r–5v.

[48] LR fol. 22v.

[49] LR fol. 22r.

[50] LR fol. 22v.

[51] LR fol. 23r.

[52] LR fols. 54v–5r

[53] LR fol. 32v.

[54] LR fols. 40v–1v and 101v–2r.

[55] LR fol. 37r–v.

[56] In those documents the name form is also present in the obviously vernacular, i.e. Occitan, forms 'Daurnia' and 'Daurina'; Ms. 609, fols. 4v, and 36r, ed. Jean-Paul

Nepos of Montauban, assistant to inquisition and defender of the accused

as 'magister Nepos of Montauban, judge of the Albigeois'. This is the only charter in the urban cartularies carrying Nepos's name that was not issued by the town's but by the count's administration. Since it dealt with a case from Montauban, it was transcribed into the town's cartulary.[57] In all the other charters in the Montauban cartularies where Nepos is mentioned it is as a consul, that is to say a member of the town government, or as a witness. As in Toulouse and many other southern French communities, Montauban appointed every year a body of consuls chosen from the so-called *probi homines* – or *prohomes* in Occitan: a group of 'honourable men'.[58] The urban charters provide us with their names, for they contain not only the consuls, but long witness lists, taken from the group of the *probi homines*. Most of those witnesses were past and / or future consuls. In the case of Nepos he is listed as a witness in many documents between 1274 until 1284, and as consul in the years 1273, 1277, 1278 and 1282. The fact that he was four times a consul evidences his intense involvement in the running of the town at the time. Given the frequency of the mentions until 1284 and their sudden cessation, we may assume that Nepos died in that year or shortly thereafter. As he is not present in urban charters dated before 1273, except for one isolated instance in 1253, we may also conclude that Nepos rose to the status of a permanent member of the urban elites only at the beginning of the 1270s, after his retirement as a judge and that he was probably propelled by his former office – which may well also have provided him with a considerable fortune – rather than by birth, as was the case with many other men of the town. In fact there is no mention at all of other carriers of his byname 'de la Davinia' – in the Montauban urban charters. It is therefore highly unlikely that he was by birth a member of the town's elites.[59]

Rehr, 'The Registry of the Great Inquisition at Toulouse, 1245–46: Edition and Translation of Bibliothèque municipale de Toulouse MS 609; documents nos. MS609-0077 (henceforth Rehr, 'Registry 609'), http://medieval-inquisition.huma-num.fr/doc/MS609-0077, and MS609-0518, http://medieval-inquisition.huma-num.fr/doc/MS609-0518, accessed 2020-01-12. We could speculate about an identification with the place name of Dourgne, a village in the département Tarn; in Occitan, the name is 'Dornha', pronounced almost or totally identical to 'Daurnia'. But note that Dourgne lies relatively far away from Montauban, about 100 kilometres to the southeast. Yet another etymology we might consider is 'd'Avinha" (Occitan for 'of Avignon"). However this is to be excluded because of the 'de' before Davinha. A double 'de' would make no sense. Also note that Rehr seems to identify Daurnia with a certain – not yet identified place – perhaps Dourgne (?), as he uses 'Nepos de Dournia' in his translations and as the standardized name form in his database. However that name form is nowhere to be found in the sources.

[57] LR fol. 12v, LS fol. 16r–v. See note 44 above.

[58] On the very special and complicated semantics of the term in Montauban and the region, see discussion in Feuchter, *Ketzer, Konsuln und Büßer*, pp. 143–50.

[59] See Feuchter, *Ketzer, Konsuln und Büßer*, pp. 164–203 on the political and economic elites of Montauban and their anthroponyms, esp. p. 170 on Nepos.

Jörg Feuchter

Interestingly, both in the consular and witness lists, Nepos is always among the first persons to be named, together with some others who are qualified as a magister (*maestre*). There are at least ten different men with that title in Montauban in the second half of the thirteenth century. The position of their names at the beginning of consular and witness lists indicates the high status conferred by an academic degree. Although we cannot exclude the possibility that some of the 'masters' may have pursued studies other than law, or even that some bore the title for other reasons,[60] it is safe to assume that most of them were legal scholars. For Montauban, although not itself a centre of administration, produced an astonishing number of experts in law.[61] For example, in the late 1260s people originating from Montauban filled all three positions of judges of the northern territories of the count of Toulouse. Beneath Nepos as judge of the Albigeois, there were magister Bartholomew de la Posaca as judge of the Agenais, and magister Peter Raimond Folcaut in the same position in Quercy. Both colleagues of Nepos are frequently present in the urban charters and among the consular elite, just like Nepos. But there was also a major difference with our legal scholar. Both Bartholomew de la Posaca and Peter Raimond Folcaut had received penances from the inquisitor Peter Sellan.[62] Nonetheless, all three were named together as witnesses to a document of the count's administration regarding heresy in Montauban. It was the publication of a decision of 1267 concerning a complaint by the town's consuls about assets of local heretics confiscated by the count's officers. Count Alphonse, informed by his *enquêteurs* (enquirers), decided that third parties who had legitimate claims on those goods – such as creditors' repayments and wives' marriage portions – should be recompensed by his officers.[63] Unfortunately the document does not provide any hint on when the confiscations and condemnations had happened.

How can the extraordinary flourishing of legal scholars in Montauban be explained? Certainly not simply by the fact that there was a university in nearby Toulouse. Although that institution was founded immediately after the end of the Albigensian war, it was largely ineffective. It was only in the last third of the thirteenth century, after the expulsion of scholars from the capital of law teaching, Bologna, that the metropolis on the Garonne river became a centre of legal studies.[64] Yet the first mention of a 'magister' among the consuls and *probi homines* of Montauban occurs already in 1255. Two of the

---

[60] Leaders of religious houses could, in some instances, carry the title as well. Yet we would not expect them to be members of the urban elites.

[61] On jurists in or from Montauban, see Feuchter, *Ketzer, Konsuln und Büßer*, pp. 390–2.

[62] Ibid., pp. 390–2.

[63] LR fol. 12v and LS fol. 16r–v, ed. *Enquêtes administratives d'Alfonse de Poitiers*, no. 101, pp. 249–50. See also no. 98, pp. 245–8, esp. p. 247.

[64] See Gouron, 'Training', pp. 221–2, following Meijers, 'Etudes'. Henri Gilles is ready to accept the possibility of a real law school in Toulouse even earlier; Gilles, 'Enseignement', pp. 64–5.

Nepos of Montauban, assistant to inquisition and defender of the accused

years' consuls are qualified with that title: *maestre Francx* (Frank) and *maestre Ugues* (Hugh). The importance jurists had in the town already by the middle of the thirteenth century is evidenced also by a very remarkable clause from the same year, 1255. It is part of a settlement between the traditional urban elites and another socio-political faction vying for participation in power – and for a fairer mode of taxation. In the settlement on taxes, both parties agreed among other points on fiscal exemption for the jurists' books. The reason given for this is very interesting. 'Item, they ordained that the books of the jurists, which they possess and in which they study in public service to the town, should not come under taxation' (Item ordinaverunt quod libri jurisperitorum, quos habent et in quibus student ad commune servitium ville, non veniant in collectam).[65] What is said here, therefore, is that the studying in books by the legal scholars who owned them was considered a contribution to the 'common good'[66] of Montauban. We may also infer from this that the group of jurists in town was already rather numerous – if not, there would have been no need for this special clause. A further indication of the importance of the jurists is to be found in a charter dated from 1266. There it is noted that the consuls, before taking a decision, had consulted not only the *prohomes*, that is to say, the other members of the urban elites, but also the 'savis de la vila' (the learned people of the town), 'savis' being the Occitan word for Latin 'periti'.[67] Nepos himself was mentioned very early on as one of those 'learned people'. For this, however, we do not look in the town charters, but elsewhere.

5. Nepos as *donatus* of the abbey of St Théodard

Nepos is not only present in the urban charters of Montauban. We also find him in documents referring to the Benedictine abbey of St Théodard, situated just outside the town walls. He figures twice as a witness. In the first instance, from the year 1256, we are provided with an important piece of information. Nepos is qualified here not only as a 'magister (maestre Neps), but also as a

---

[65] *Enquêtes administratives d'Alfonse de Poitiers*, p. 73. On the context see Feuchter, *Ketzer, Konsuln und Büßer*, pp. 145–6 and 370–7. Jurists usually bought their books as students; Gouron, 'Training', p. 221. Gouron names the Digest and the Codex Iustinianus with the gloss from Accursius as examples of the books southern French jurists brought with them from university.

[66] On the politically highly important concept of common good as a 'communal', that is to say urban, value, see P. Blickle, 'Der Gemeine Nutzen. Ein kommunaler Wert und seine politische Karriere', in *Gemeinwohl und Gemeinsinn. Historische Semantiken politischer Leitbegriffe*, ed. H. Münkler and H. Bluhm, Forschungsberichte der interdisziplinären Arbeitsgruppe 'Gemeinwohl und Gemeinsinn' der Berlin-Brandenburgischen Akademie der Wissenschaften 1 (Berlin, 2001), pp. 85–107.

[67] LR fols. 64v–5r, 9 March 1266.

donatus of St Théodard. A *donata* or *donatus* – in English, donat – is a lay person who 'gave' herself or himself and usually also some or all of their possessions to a religious house. Yet this act of self-donation did not make the person a proper nun or monk. Instead it secured her or him the right to be received into this status on the deathbed, in a *professio in extremis* (profession when dying). In the meantime, the donat could remain a lay person leading an existence in the world. Yet there are also other donats living more like lay brothers or sisters, closely tied to or even staying with the religious community. In the case of St Théodard, both groups existed. We have a document from 1231 in which the twofold character of donats is explained. It is a settlement between the abbot and the count of Toulouse in the aftermath of the Albigensian wars. Among other issues it defines respective rights in Montauban, for the town was officially under their dual dominion. In the two decades of the Albigensian wars the abbot had played a very minor role, a position he wanted to change in 1231. One point he claimed at the outset of negotiations were the judicial rights over the persons pertaining to the abbey:

> justicias [...] monachorum et clericorum et donatorum suorum et spetialis familie sue, videlicet illorum donatorum qui in capitulo Sancti Theodardi donant se et sua eidem monasterio et promittunt hobedientiam abbati et successoribus suis, et victum percipiunt a dicta ecclesia.

> (the judicial rights ... over the monks and clerics and his donats and his particular household, that is to say, over the donats who – at a chapter in St Théodard - give themselves and their possessions to the monastery and promise obedience to the abbot and his successors, and receive their sustenance from the said church.)[68]

In the final settlement this point is taken up and regulated as follows. The abbot has the full judicial rights over monks, clerics 'et spetialis familie sue et donatorum suorum, videlicet illorum donatorum qui sunt recepti, ut supradictum est' (and his particular household and his donats, that is to say, of those donats who have been received, as said above).[69] Thus it emerges from the document that there is one group of donati who have been 'received', have pledged obedience to the abbot and whose livelihood is provided by the abbey, and there is another group of donati who are still living in the world. It is obvious that Nepos did not belong to the first but to the second group, if he was able to officiate as a judge and act as a town consul. Although we

---

[68] 1231 October 13, AN J 310, 49 (also in J 309, 9 (minute)), partially edited in *Layettes du Trésor des Chartes*, ed. A. Teulet et al., 5 vols. (Paris, 1863–1909), II, 221–3, no. 2159. The transcription in Doat is edited in *Gallia Christiana*, 16 vols. (Paris, 1715–1865), XIII, 188–91, Instrumenta Ecclesiae Montalbanensis no. 10, and J.-U. Devals, *Histoire de Montauban* (Montauban, 1855; only vol 1 published), I, 429–34, pièce justificative no. 24. For context, see Feuchter, *Ketzer, Konsuln und Büßer*, pp. 161–3.

[69] Ibid.

Nepos of Montauban, assistant to inquisition and defender of the accused

are not able to establish more precisely the exact character of the bond to the abbey implied by his donation, we can safely assume that there was some kind of agreement about a later reception into the abbey in old age or at the point of death, given that that was generally the main thing guaranteed by being a donat.[70]

Interestingly, the 1256 document mentioning Nepos as a donat is itself about a dispute about the last will of another donat who was a citizen of Montauban, who had been received in the chapter of St Théodard and who had given all of his possessions to the abbey in his last will. Thus this man had been a donat in the same sense as Nepos himself, although it is possible he only 'gave himself' when on his deathbed. The abbot and the kin of the deceased disagreed on what exactly had been the individual possessions of the deceased himself, as opposed to those of his wife and children. Hence the litigation. What is important to us is that the settlement lists a considerable number of witnesses for both sides, for the abbey and for the family. Nepos is found among those on the abbey's side, together with two other men. All three together are described as 'donats of the house of St Théodard' (donat de la mayo de Sant Auzard).[71] Nepos himself is named 'magister' (Maestre Neps), as we have already seen. And it is intriguing to find next to him another man we have already encountered. This is Frank (Franx), one of the very early bearers of the title of magister in the consulate, in 1255, as we saw earlier. His leading role in town society went further back. Already in 1247 we find him as one of two arbiters in a settlement of a dispute between the abbey of St Théodard and the Templars of La Ville-Dieu.[72] The other arbiter was Bernard Capel, none other than the *vicarius* (viguier), the local officer of the count of Toulouse at Montauban. We can safely assume that the two men were chosen both for their expertise in legal and administrative business and also because they were close to one of the religious institutions involved in the dispute. Although Frank is not mentioned with the title in the 1247 document nor in the 1256 document concerning the abbey, nonetheless it remains a very remarkable fact that two of the earliest known law scholars from Montauban, Nepos and Frank, were both donats of the local abbey. And they have even more in common, as we shall realise when we come to inquisition records.

---

[70] On donats in general, see C. de Miramon, *Les 'Donnés' au Moyen Âge. Une forme de vie religieuse laïque (v. 1180-v. 1500)* (Paris, 1999), and, on the situation in southern France in particular, J. Oberste, 'Donaten zwischen Kloster und Welt. Das Donatenwesen der religiösen Ritterorden in Südfrankreich und die Entwicklung der städtischen Frömmigkeitspraxis im 13. Jahrhundert', *Zeitschrift für Historische Forschung* 29 (2002), 1–37.

[71] Archives Departementales de Tarn-et-Garonne (henceforth ADTG) G 239, fols. 291r–300r – quotation at fol. 294v (21 June 1256). For more context, Feuchter, *Ketzer, Konsuln und Büßer*, p. 163.

[72] 1247 July 31; Doat vol. 89 fols. 22r–6r.

Another document from St Théodard, dating from 1277, mentions Nepos. It does not qualify him as a donat. Yet again he is a witness to a settlement involving the abbey, this time between St Théodard and its motherhouse, La Chaise-Dieu in Auvergne, head of the eponymous congregation. At that point, there had been long and strenuous dispute about the rights of La Chaise-Dieu at St Théodard.[73] Nepos was not the only witness. There were four of them, each qualified as a 'magister' and all together called 'iurisperiti' (law scholars). Two of them we have encountered before – Bartholomew de la Posaca and Peter Raimond Folcaut, Nepos's former colleagues as judges for count Alphonse in the northern parts of the county of Toulouse. The presence of the three (ex-) judges indicates the standing they had gained through their office. At the same time at first sight the witnesses of a settlement between two abbeys look like an odd mixture: on the one hand two men who had been on the receiving end of inquisition, and on the other a former inquisition assistant! But it is simply an example of the point made above: the urban elites escaped unscathed from inquisitorial 'persecution' in Montauban.

6. Nepos as inquisitor's assistant and scribe in the 1240s

We have established that the scholar and judge Nepos of Montauban was a member of his hometown's governing urban elites, and also one of the earliest bearers of the title of 'magister', that is to say, a university-trained jurist. Furthermore he was a donat of the adjacent abbey St Théodard. Now we turn to look for him in inquisition records. As mentioned above, there had been a strong presence of religious dissidence in Montauban and there is a large document that sanctions with penances more than 250 of its inhabitants, many of them members of the urban elite. Nepos is not to be found among them. Rather he was involved in the persecution of dissidents elsewhere and on the opposite side, that is to say, with the inquisitors.

From May 1245 to August 1246,[74] the Dominicans Bernard of Caux and John of St Pierre conducted an inquisitorial campaign in the Lauragais region between Toulouse and Carcassonne. It is the largest mass inquisition we know of in the middle ages. Although the extant manuscript, Ms. 609 of the Bibliothèque municipale de Toulouse, transcribes only a fraction of

---

[73] ADTG G 239, fol. 610r (9 June 1277). For context, Feuchter, *Ketzer, Konsuln und Büßer*, pp. 396–7.

[74] Y. Dossat, *Les crises de l'inquisition toulousaine au XIIIe siècle (1233–1273)* (Bordeaux, 1959), pp. 156–7, gives as first and last dates 1 May 1245 and 1 August 1246. W. L. Wakefield, 'Inquisitors' Assistants. Witnesses to Confessions in Manuscript 609', *Heresis* 20 (1993), 57–65 (p. 59), mentions another day in December 1246. Henceforth Bibliothèque municipale de Toulouse Ms. 609 is referred to as Ms.609.

Nepos of Montauban, assistant to inquisition and defender of the accused

the written documentation of the interrogations,[75] it still contains depositions of more than 5600 individuals from the Lauragais communities. They
were interrogated on more than 200 business days of the inquisitorial court
in Toulouse, at the priory of St Sernin. The two Dominicans clearly lead
the investigation, but they did not attend all the interrogations.[76] The daily
work of the court was done by a team. Apart from the prior of St Sernin who
was present on most days, probably as honorary presider over proceedings,
there was a group of people who attended frequently. According to a
list compiled by Walter L. Wakefield for Ms. 609, this group consisted of
nineteen men who were recorded as witnesses to depositions on between
twelve and sixty-seven days.[77] They are clearly to be distinguished from a
large number of other people (more than 150) functioning as witnesses only
once or a few times, and also from the members of the parish clergy who
were present at the interrogations of their flock and apparently provided
the inquisitors with local knowledge about heretical activities.[78] Wakefield
calls these nineteen the 'assistants' of the inquisition. They not only bore
witness to the depositions and the abjurations, i.e. the oaths of renunciation
of heresy. Rather it is obvious – although never mentioned explicitly – that
they were also involved in the business of interrogating, at least when
neither of the two Dominican inquisitors was present.[79] They – or some
of them - were also responsible for writing down the depositions. In some
cases, this is explicitly stated. For example, 'et P. Ariberti, publicus notarius,
qui hec scripsit'[80] (and P. Ariberti, notary, who wrote this), or 'et P. Fresapa,

---

[75] About one fifth. Cf. J.-P. Rehr, 'Re-mapping the 'Great Inquisition' of 1245–46: The
Case of Mas-Saintes-Puelles and Saint-Martin-Lalande', *Open Library of Humanities*
5(1): 28 (2019), 1–52; https://doi.org/10.16995/olh.414, (p.76, n. 76), following
Dossat, *Crises*.

[76] Rehr, 'Re-mapping', pp. 40–1, following similar remarks by Dossat, *Crises*, and
Wakefield, 'Inquisitors' Assistants'.

[77] Wakefield, 'Inquisitors' Assistants', 62–3.

[78] Ibid., 60–1 gives some examples for incriminating information provided by accompanying local clergy. Dossat, *Crises*, p. 241, too observes the presence of the parish
clergy, but also the fact that it was not always the case. The phenomenon deserves
a more thorough examination.

[79] Wakefield, 'Inquisitors' Assistants', 65, and Rehr, 'Re-mapping', p. 41. There is an
indication on Ms. 609 fol. 253v, containing added texts from later inquisitors dating
from the years 1253 and 1254, that at least some of the witnesses of the 1245/6 were
considered as inquisitors themselves, as part of a group of colleagues ('sociis') of
inquisitors. One of them is a certain 'magister' Arnaldus, also called a chaplain
in the church of Toulouse and a 'cancellarius' (chancellor); e.g. fols. 31v and 136r.
See also G. Modestin and M. Ostorero, 'Le notaire, figure oubliée de l'Inquisition.
L'exemple du diocèse de Lausanne (XVe siècle)', in *Le notaire entre métier et espace
public en Europe VIIIe-XVIIIe siècle*, ed. L. Faggion, A. Maillou and L. Verdon (Aix-en-
Provence, 2008), pp. 29–41 (29–30) for some general observations on the importance
of scribes in the inquisitorial procedure and in the shaping of inquisitorial texts.

[80] Testes: Galhardus, prior de Manso; Willelmus, capellanus de Manso; et Petrus

publicus notarius, qui inde fecit publicum instrumentum'[81] (and P. Fresapa, notary, who made a notarial charter of this). Professional notaries, like these two, were accustomed to add their names at the end of the witness lists in charters they had drawn up, and to add such formulas. But in most cases a statement is lacking, probably because the respective scribes were not professional notaries. Nonetheless it is safe to assume, as a general rule, that the name positioned last[82] was that of the scribe of the deposition's or the abjuration's text. This is actually confirmed by two witness lists in the sentencing documents. There, a handful of assistants frequently occupying the last position in Ms. 609 are found grouped together and collectively labelled 'scriptores inquisitorum' (scribes of the inquisitors).[83] Apart from the already mentioned Peter Ariberti and Peter Fresapa, their names, combined from the two lists, are these: Bernard of Ladinhac, Bernard of Gaus, Peter of Montbiza and Nepos of Davinia.[84]

Ariberti, publicus notarius, qui hec scripsit; Ms. 609, fol. 42r, ed. J.-P. Rehr, 'The Registry of the Great Inquisition at Toulouse, 1245–46: Edition and Translation of Bibliothèque municipale de Toulouse MS 609 (document no. MS609-0616)', http://medieval-inquisition.huma-num.fr/doc/MS609-0616, accessed 6 August 2020.

[81] Testes: fratres Ordinis Predicatorum Willelmus Pellisso, Petrus Barrau; et Petrus Fresapa, publicus notarius, qui inde fecit publicum instrumentum'; Ms. 609, fol. 32r, ed. Rehr, 'Registry', ibid., accessed 6 August 2020.

[82] I.e. positioned last overall or last before the name of the inquisitor, which is sometimes added after all the other witnesses, but clearly distinguished from them with the label 'inquisitor'. It is unlikely that inquisitors themselves acted as scribes.

[83] 'in presentia […] Bernardi de Ladinhac et Nepotis de Davinia, Bernardi de Gaurs, Petri Frezapa, Petri Ariberti, scriptorum dictorum inquisitorum' (Jean-Paul Rehr, 'Sentences from the Inquisition at Toulouse: Edition and Translation of Bibliothèque nationale de France MS Latin 9992 (document no. MS9992-02)', http://medieval-inquisition.huma-num.fr/doc/MS9992-02, accessed 28 October 2020 (henceforth Rehr, 'Sentences'); previously edited C. Douais, *Documents pour servir à l'histoire de l'inquisition dans le Languedoc*, 2 vols. (Paris, 1900), II, 1–89 (p. 7–8)); 'Petri Ariberti, P. de Montbiza et Bernardi de Gaus, scriptorum inquisitorum' (the Ms. has 'scriptor inquisitorum') (Rehr, 'Sentences', document no. MS9992-03, accessed 28 October 2020; previously edited Douais, *Documents*, II, 10)

[84] This is however clearly not an exhaustive list of the regular scribes. E.g. a very frequent assistant (sixty times according to Wakefield, 'Inquisitors' Assistants', 62) who also appears in last position in some witness lists in Ms. 609 is Arnald Cerda. However he is never labelled a 'scriptor' in Ms. 609 (but neither is Nepos) and in the sentencing documents his name does not even appear. Note that there are also some other men who were explicitly mentioned as scribes in Ms. 609, but only appear once or twice, cf. Wakefield, 'Inquisitors' Assistants', 59, n. 6. Then there is also the case of John of Saint-Gaudens who is explicitly mentioned as a scribe in one of the sentencing documents, but does not appear in Ms. 609 ('et Johanne de Sancto Gaudencio, scriptore') (Rehr, 'Sentences', document no. MS9992-37, accessed 2020-06-8; previously edited Douais, *Documents*, II, 75).

Nepos of Montauban, assistant to inquisition and defender of the accused

Nepos of Davinia: this assistant's name rings in our ears. It is present very frequently both in the first sentencing documents (five times)[85] and in Ms. 609 (fifty-nine times).[86] Although mostly just given shortly as 'Nepos clericus', it is also to be found in the form 'Nepos de Davinia' (or Davina, Daurnia, Daurina), and as 'magister Nepos'.[87] In view of the congruity of the (very rare[88]) name 'Nepos', the (also very rare) byname 'de Davinia' and the title 'magister' both in the sentencing documents and the Ms. 609, it seems evident that this is the same person as our legal scholar, the judge and consul from Montauban. Here we find him as a core member of the team of assistants and as one of the scribes of the two most active inquisitors of the thirteenth century, overseeing the largest ever medieval inquisition trials.

Before exploring this further, we need to dwell on the frequent designation of Nepos as a 'clericus'. For if Nepos really was an ordained man of the church, as this seems to imply, how could he go on to officiate as a secular judge and as a member of his hometown's circle of consuls? There were strong limitations on clerics participating in secular occupations. Canon 16 of the Fourth Lateran council (1215) stated that clergy should not exercise secular offices. Already the Third Lateran council (1179) had explicitly forbidden them from acting as advocates in secular courts,[89] and Innocent III had done the same

---

[85] In five out of the thirteen first sentences, proclaimed between March and July 1246; see 'Index of People', entry 'Nepos de Dournia, notary', in J.-P. Rehr, *de Heresi: Documents of the Early Medieval Inquisition* (online resource, last accessed on 12 December 2019 through http://medieval-inquisition.huma-num.fr). In the previous edition by Douais, *Documents*, II, the notices of Nepos are on 7, 18, 31, 34 and 36. His name is given in three instances as 'Nepos de Davin(i)a clericus', once as 'Nepos de Davinia' and once as 'Nepos clericus'.

[86] Cf. Wakefield, 'Inquisitors' Assistants', 62.

[87] These data are based on the 'Index of People', entry 'Nepos de Dournia, notary', in Rehr, *de Heresi*). Note that *de Heresi* gives (at the date of last accession) only a partial edition of Ms. 609, containing fols. 1r–49r and 186r–8v of the manuscript (that is about one fifth). Among those pages, Nepos is mentioned in eighteen depositions of individuals. A digital search of a transcription made by J. Duvernoy of the whole document, albeit with many errors (J. Duvernoy, *Catharisme, hérésies médiévales & inédits*, online resource, last accessed on 12 December 2019 through jean.duvernoy. free.fr/text/pdf/ms609_a.pdf; jean.duvernoy.free.fr/text/pdf/ms609_b.pdf; jean. duvernoy.free.fr/text/pdf/ms609_c.pdf) shows no significant diversion from these forms, with the exception of the form 'magister Nepos' (fols. 129r and 189v), which is not present in the folios edited so far by Rehr.

[88] There is no other person of that name either in the many twelfth- and thirteenth-century documents from Montauban I looked through for my book Feuchter, *Ketzer, Konsuln und Büßer* or in the Ms. 609, certainly one of the biggest single sources for contemporary Languedoc anthroponyms. The same goes for 'Davinia' or other variations of the name.

[89] On laws barring clerics from secular offices in the twelfth and thirteenth centuries see J. Barrow, 'Clergy and the IV Lateran', in *Fourth Lateran Council*, ed. Helmrath and Melville, pp. 125–36 (33); H. Gilles, 'Le clergé méridional entre le roi et l'église',

with regard to notaries.[90] Medieval city councils generally did not tolerate clerics among their members, for the sake of their autonomy. Furthermore it is well known that men of the church hardly ever returned to lay status. Are we therefore dealing with two persons, one a cleric assisting inquisitors in Toulouse, the other a lay person from Montauban, officiating as a judge and a consul?

This is highly unlikely, not only because – as we shall see below – the assistant Nepos was first recruited by the Dominican inquisitors in the region of Montauban: there would need to have been two men of the same name, byname and academic title in a small town in the same period.[91] Further, the contradiction is only an apparent one. There are several possible explanations. First we have to remember that many exceptions were made from prohibitions regarding exercising secular offices for clerics, and this held particularly in Languedoc.[92] There, numerous clerics worked in the secular administrations of the Capetians, and Count Alphonse of Poitiers actually seems to have preferred them to lay persons.[93] Even leaving clerical status seems to have been more common in Languedoc than elsewhere.[94] There is another and simpler explanation for Nepos being a cleric as well as a judge in a secular court and a consul. It might just be that he had only progressed to the minor orders. For the limitations against clerics mingling in secular business were not necessarily applied to those who had not progressed to the major orders – in other words, not become a subdeacon, deacon or priest. And indeed many clerics delayed such progression in order to remain flexible.[95]

There is even another possibility, to be added to this list even if less likely: that Nepos's status as a donat or as a scholar made him count as a cleric.[96]

Furthermore, a closer look at the documents of the inquisition of 1245/6 and their usage of the term 'clericus' supports the notion that being labelled a 'clericus' and exercising a secular office is not at odds. For Nepos is not the only assistant to inquisition carrying the label, even though he was the most prominent one. One example is the already mentioned Peter Fresapa, present

---

in *Les évêques, les clercs et le roi (1250–1300)*, Cahiers de Fanjeaux 7 (Toulouse, 1972), pp. 393–417 (406–7).

[90] Ibid., p. 406.

[91] In this case we would expect to find the two men differentiated by additions like 'son of X' v 'son of Y' or 'the younger' v 'the older', as was the rule in Montauban. On that system see Feuchter, *Ketzer, Konsuln und Büßer*, pp. 166–8.

[92] Gilles, 'Le clergé meridional', pp. 407–9.

[93] Y. Dossat, 'Alphonse de Poitiers et les clercs', in *Les évêques, les clercs et le roi (1250– 1300)*, Cahiers de Fanjeaux 7 (Toulouse, 1972), pp. 361–91.

[94] Gilles, 'Le clergé meridional', p. 410.

[95] Ibid., pp. 407–9 for Languedoc, and Barrow, 'Clergy and the IV Lateran', p. 130 in general.

[96] Gilles, 'Le clergé meridional', p. 407, on universities: 'Maîtres et étudiants sont des clercs'.

Nepos of Montauban, assistant to inquisition and defender of the accused

in Ms. 609 almost as often as Nepos, fifty-four times.[97] Although in most cases called a 'publicus notarius', Peter appears twice as a 'clericus' too![98] It is evident that at least in that region at that time, a 'clericus' could also officiate in a lay profession. Incidentally we find in Ms. 609 a chaplain, i.e. someone who was in major orders, as a public notary.[99] And although that man is in some instances only labelled a 'notarius', without the addition 'publicus', we may exclude a confusion with someone who, while being a cleric, just functioned as notary for the inquisitors, as there is a special label for that function in Ms. 609 too: Bernard of Gaus is called a 'notarius inquisitorum'.[100] Another interesting cleric in Ms. 609 – an infrequent assistant and only once a witness – is a 'magister Egidius clericus domini comitis Tholosani'[101] (master Egidius cleric of the count of Toulouse). As the date is 1250, the count in question is Alphonse of Poitiers, and the case either exemplifies a secular ruler's propensity to employ clerics in his administration[102] or usage of 'clericus' for a learned lay person.[103]

Moreover, what springs to mind from the examples in Ms. 609 is that 'clericus' is only used there when a witness to inquisition is not labelled in any other way, i.e. with any function in the church (like chaplain, prior, canon, provost, archpresbyter, archdeacon etc.),[104] or as a public notary. In other words: apparently this is the label for a member of the clergy without office,

---

[97] Wakefield, 'Inquisitors' Assistants', 63.

[98] Ibid.

[99] Ms. 609, fols. 108r: testis P. capellanus Drulie nottarius [sic] qui hec scripsit (witness P., chaplain of Dreuilhe, notary, who wrote these things); 140v: et P. ca[pellanus] Drulie publicus notarius qui hec scripsit (and P., chaplain of Dreuilhe, public notary, who wrote these things); 142r: testis P. capellanus Drulie notarius qui hec scripsit (witness P., chaplain of Dreuilhe, notary, who wrote these things); 191r: testis P. capellanus Drulie notarius publicus qui hec scripsit (witness P., chaplain of Dreuilhe, notary public, who wrote these things); 207v: testis P. capellanus Drulie notarius qui hec scripsit (witness, P., chaplain of Dreuilhe, who wrote these things).

[100] recitata [...] per B.[ernardum] Gaus notarium inquisitorum' (recited ... by Bernard of Gaus, notary of the inquisitors); Ms. 609, fol. 136r. Bernard of Gaus is also labelled a cleric; fol. 169v.

[101] Ms. 609, fol. 140v.

[102] Alphonse preferentially employed clerics as his 'inquirers' (French: enquêteurs), i.e. as supervisors or fact-finders about certain problems in his administration. The words 'clerici domini comitis' (clerks of the lord count) and 'inquisitores domini comitis' (inquisitors of the lord count) were interchangeable. See *Correspondance administrative d'Alfonse de Poitiers*, ed. A. Molinier, Collection de Documents inédits sur l'Histoire de France (Paris, 1894–1900), II, xxxiv; see also xxxvii. [Among the most important 'clerics' of Alphonse was a certain Egidius Camelini, a canon – see Dossat, 'Alphonse de Poitiers et les clercs', pp. 375–9 – but he only enters the service of the count in 1267. So this is probably not the same Egidius]. The mention of Egidius is part of an addition made by inquisitors John of St Pierre and Reginald of Chartres.

[103] Dossat, *Crises*, p. 241, considers him a lay person.

[104] See the list of parish and other clergy in Ms. 609 compiled by Wakefield, 'Inquisitors' Assistants', 60.

someone who is neither part of the parish clergy nor with the bishop nor in a monastery. Yet such a 'without' position is precisely what we would expect with people in minor orders.[105]

Apart from the use in respect to witnesses, 'clericus' in Ms. 609 is applied as a label to some of those interrogated and some of the individuals referred to in interrogations, and also as a generic term for 'men of the church', as opposed to lay people. There is also an interesting mention of a 'puer clericus' (a boy who was a cleric).[106] In fact, it was fairly typical for people in the thirteenth century to receive minor orders already as children or teenagers during education, and still to remain very much open for a career in a secular profession that needed education.[107] This might very well have been the case with Nepos, the law scholar. His university education is signalled clearly by the title 'magister'. The use of this title in the inquisition document is rare. Only a few of Nepos's fellow witnesses in Ms. 609 have this label. We may assume that their academic skills were highly appreciated, because some of these 'masters' clearly occupied important positions at the inquisitorial court.[108]

Apart from him being a very frequent assistant and one of the scribes almost from the beginning to the end of the interrogation period of this 'great' inquisition, from June 1245 to July 1246, the full pattern of Nepos's attendance and role in the court remains to be established. Yet according to the most detailed study of the procedure, focussing on only two localities, certain sets of assistants were dedicated to interrogating the inhabitants of certain localities on the direction of the leading inquisitors who wanted to gather evidence against certain groups of people.[109] In the case of these two localities, it was a trio of scribes, and Nepos was one of them. The author, Jean-Paul Rehr, notes

---

[105] There is however at least one assistant to inquisition who is never labelled in any way. This is the very frequently present Arnald Cerda (see note 86 above). Dossat, *Crises*, p. 241, considers him a lay person.

[106] et quidam puer clericus qui vocatur Rotger; Ms. 609, fol. 155r.

[107] Barrow states with respect to the thirteenth century: 'Most clerics in minor orders were probably schoolboys being supported by their parents, and while many doubtless intended to progress to major orders, a growing number did not expect to do so but instead hoped to use their clerical training as freelance scribes and clerks in an administrative rather than a sacramental sense: job opportunities in these areas were expanding'; 'Clergy and the IV Lateran', p. 130.

[108] Two of them, the chancellor Arnaldus (on him see footnote 79), and Bernard of Ladignac (on him see below), are occasionally described as colleagues among inquisitors.

[109] Rehr, 'Re-mapping', p. 41: 'The investigations focused on specific people, and once inquisitors turned up a story that could indict those they targeted, it could be easily followed up by the small staff of notaries who provided the day to day continuity at Saint-Sernin'. See also n. 73 on pp. 41–2: 'The key story for every chain of corroborative stories was identified by friars Bernard or John. There were three principal notaries who provided continuity for depositions of le Mas and Saint-Martin: Peire Fresapa, Nepos de Dournia, and Peire Aribert'. Rehr notes that the assistants of the interrogations were also present at the sentencings.

Nepos of Montauban, assistant to inquisition and defender of the accused

that the assistants of the interrogations were also present at the sentencings. Yet Nepos's mentions as a witness to sentencing are limited to its starting period, from March to July 1246. This coincides with the final period of his work with the depositions. After that time, Nepos seems to have left the inquisition team.[110] His name is missing when the two friars resumed their work in the Lauragais for another year-long period, 1247–48, mostly sentencing. Nor did he accompany them to their in-between mission in Pamiers, autumn 1246 and spring to summer 1247. Yet while we do not find Nepos involved with Bernard of Caux and Jean of St Pierre after July 1246, he was with them even before their great inquisition in the Lauragais, during another campaign the two inquisitors led. This campaign took place in the Agenais, Quercy and the northern parts of the Toulousain, from November 1243 until 1245.[111]

---

[110] One of his last presences ('Nepos clericus') is on the witness list of a deposition from 9 July 1246, together with Bernard of Caux, John of St Pierre, and even the prior of Saint-Sernin. It is not recorded in Ms. 609, but in Doat vol. 22, fol. 85r.

[111] It took from 30 November 1243 until 17 March 1245, cf. Y. Dossat, 'L'inquisiteur Bernard de Caux et l'Agenais', *Annales du midi* 63 (1951), 75–9. Readers should take careful note of chronological mistakes in this area. The year given in the manuscript, i.e. the Doat transcriptions from the seventeenth century, is '1244'. But in our modern dating system this must be converted to '1245'. The complex problem of ascertaining the style of the beginning of the year in inquisition records was solved by Yves Dossat, in his 'Du début de l'année en Languedoc au Moyen Age', *Annales du Midi* 54–5 (1942–3), 520–29. The most important result was this. Bernard of Caux followed the Easter Style, meaning that all dates from 1 January 1245 until 15 April 1245 (Saturday before Easter Sunday) are given by him with the year '1244'. Unfortunately, Dossat himself did not apply this insight to the dates of the inquisition campaign of Bernard of Caux in the northern Toulousain of which Pons's deposition was a part - he dated that campaign '1243–1244' rather than '1243–1245'; Dossat, *Crises*, p. 38. Although Jean Duvernoy was aware of the correct way of resolving the date established by Dossat, he created even more confusion by suggesting that '1244' in Pons's deposition was an error by the scribes of the 'Collection Doat' and should be amended to '1243', thus yielding – when converted! – a modern date of 1244; in his typescript edition with French translation, available online as a pdf file: http://jean.duvernoy.free.fr/text/pdf/bdecaux.pdf, last accessed on 12 August 2020, page 52. In his edition of the Peter Sellan's inquisition texts, he even indicated that Bernard's inquisition campaign in the northern Toulousain ended in 1244; *L'inquisition en Quercy. Le registre des pénitences de Pierre Cellan 1241–1242*, ed. J. Duvernoy (Castelnaud-la-Chapelle, 2001, p. 29). Another expert on inquisition in the region, Taylor, was, like Duvernoy, in principle aware that the campaign lasted until March 1245 – see her *Heresy, Crusade and Inquisition in Medieval Quercy*, p. 24 – but like Duvernoy dates Pons's above-mentioned deposition, and others, to 1244. I have also used contradictory dates. In general I followed Dossat, *Crises*, p. 38, therefore erroneously dating Pons's deposition to 1244 and the period of the campaign it was part of to 1243–1244; Feuchter, *Ketzer, Konsuln und Büßer*, pp. 10, n. 28, 74, n. 178, 225, n. 138, 298, n 168, 300, nn. 172, 173, 178, and 306. However I did correctly resolve another date of a deposition from that campaign into '1245'; Feuchter, *Ketzer, Konsuln und Büßer*, p. 404, n. 219, following Dossat, 'Du début de l'année'.

The names of the places where the two Dominicans held their trials are not mentioned in the documents, but Yves Dossat has deduced from the names of the witnesses that they stayed first at Agen, and then from May 1244 at Cahors.[112] The witnesses were mostly from the clergy of those two episcopal seats or the localities nearby.[113] The people however who were interrogated at Agen and Cahors were not from the Agenais or Quercy, but from the northern Toulousain – although some of the events that were recorded by the inquisitors had taken place in the dioceses of Agen and Cahors. There were mainly two groups of people, one from Castelsarrasin, one from Villemur. As mentioned, the inquisitors also exercised jurisdiction in the northern parts of the Toulousain, namely the archdeaconry of Villelongue, covering the town Castelsarrasin and its surroundings, and the adjacent archdeaconry of Villemur.[114] That is to say that Nepos then worked with an ecclesiastical court in the very same jurisdiction which he would preside over as a secular judge for a prince two decades later, in 1266, as 'judge of Villelongue'.

It is during the final period of this campaign, in the early months of 1245, that we first encounter Nepos among the witnesses to interrogations. He is present two times, first on 26 January 1245, then again on 17 March 1245. In the first instance, he is one of only two witnesses, together with 'B. de Ladinhac'.[115] This man, Bernard of Ladinhac, we have already encountered above when discussing Ms. 609, the document of the great Lauragais inquisition, as an assistant and scribe. He had already been a frequent witness in the Agen / Cahors campaign. In Ms. 609 he is often labelled a *magister*, like Nepos, but once also as *archipresbiter* (archpriest),[116] and several times

---

[112] Dossat, *Crises*, p. 156.

[113] It is remarkable that the bishop of Agen seems to have been opposed to the inquisition by the two friars, thus aligning himself with the count of Toulouse. Raymond VII contested the inquisitorial authority of the Friars Preacher in this diocese (and also in that of Cahors, Rodez, and Albi) and declared that he would only tolerate their business if they acted as assistants to episcopal inquisition. See Dossat, 'L'inquisiteur Bernard', 75.

[114] This is evidenced by a sentence issued 26 August 1244 at Cahors against an inhabitant of Castelsarrasin: 'Nos, fratres Ordinis Predicatorum Bernardus de Caucio et Johannes de Sancto Petro, inquisitores heretice pravitatis in Agennensi et Caturcensi dyocesi, de Villamuro et de Villa Longa archidiaconationbus [*recte*: archidiaconatibus] dyecesis [sic] Tholosane auctoritate apostolica deputati' (We, friars of the Order of Preachers Bernard of Caux and John of St Pierre, deputed by apostolic authority inquisitors of heretical wickedness in the diocese of Agen and Cahors, [and] the archdeaneries of Villemur and Villelongue of the Toulousan diocese); Rehr, 'Sentences', document no. MS9992-16, last accessed 24 June 2019; previously edited Douais, *Documents*, II, 40.

[115] Doat vol. 22, fol. 44r.

[116] Testes: dominus A., episcopus Agennensis, Sancius capellanus Sancti Caprasii, R. capellanus Sanctæ Fidis, magister B. de Ladinhac archipresbiter, Arnaldus Serda (lord A., bishop of Agen, Sans, chaplain of Saint-Caprais, R., chaplain of Sainte-Foy, master B. of Ladignac, archpriest, Arnold Serda); Doat vol. 22, fol. 9r–v.

Nepos of Montauban, assistant to inquisition and defender of the accused

as a *capellanus* (chaplain or parish priest) of Ladinhac.[117] The place name 'Ladinhac' is probably best identified with Ladignac, the small but well-known parish, not far from Agen, located in the *bailie* of Penne d'Agenais, rather than the more distant and less prominent places called Ladignac in the Lot, Aveyron and Dordogne.[118] Among the scribes and assistants of the two Dominicans, Bernard was of a special importance. He is one of their steadiest collaborators, as he is be found with them throughout from 1243 until 1248, and is even called their *socius* (colleague).[119] In the second witness list, Nepos still figures together with Bernard of Ladinhac, yet two more names are added: 'testes W. de Concous, Francus de Monte Albano iurisperitus, B. de Ladinhac, Nepos clericus'.[120] William of Concots was a chaplain of Cahors[121] of whom we know little else. 'Frank of Montauban' is of course already a familiar name to us. This is Nepos's fellow donat and jurist from Montauban. Frank's status as a legal scholar is emphasised by the designation *iurisperitus*, a rare or maybe even unique title in inquisition documents of those years. It is astonishing to find Nepos and Frank, the two Montauban legal scholars and donats, together here. It is also the only time we find Frank's name in the inquisition records. Nepos, however, went on to become a core member of Bernard of Caux and John of St Pierre's team, like Bernard of Ladinhac and also like another man from the Agenais/Quercy campaign, Arnald Cerda.[122] Yet a further core member, the public notary Peter Aribert, was with them in that campaign too. Earlier on he had already served another inquisitor, Ferrier, in August 1243.[123] But apart from him, it seems that the two Dominicans collected their essential staff on the Agenais / Quercy campaign of 1243–45 and then kept them on for their larger campaign in the Lauragais. It is evident now that Nepos was just one of several Quercy men recruited by the two Dominicans. This does not mean that he was a random choice. It is intriguing to observe which testimonies Nepos witnessed when he is first mentioned in inquisition documents, in January and March 1245. The deponents were all high-ranking inhabitants of Castelsarrasin. Their

---

[117] In several instances in the sentences; see for example Rehr, 'Sentences', documents no. MS9992-08 and MS9992-35, last accessed 17 December 2019; previously edited, Douais, *Documents*, II, 26 and 73.

[118] See Dossat, 'L'inquisiteur Bernard', 76, for identification of Ladignac, and other place-names near Agen attached to the names of persons, together with a function ('chaplain of …').

[119] magister Bernardus de Ladinhac socius inquisitorum; Ms. 609, fol. 130r. On this see note 108 above.

[120] witnesses W. of Concots, Frank of Montauban, jurist, B. of Ladignac, Nepos, clerk; Doat vol. 22, fol. 46r.

[121] W. de Concoutz, capellani Caturci; Rehr, 'Sentences', document no. MS9992-14, last accessed 24 December 2019; previously edited, Douais, *Documents*, II, 37–8.

[122] On him, see notes 84 and 105.

[123] August 1244; Doat vol 21, fol. 323v.

names are 'Arnalda uxor Poncii Grimoardi, domina de Baretges' (Arnalda, wife of Pons Grimoard, lady of Baret) and 'Otho de Baretges'. All three were closely connected to each other and to Pons Grimoardi, the former seneschal (governor) of Quercy, whom we have already encountered in our discussion of events in springtime of 1236, when inquisition finally came to Montauban. As we see, Arnalda was Pons's wife. The woman called 'lady of Baret' was a close relative, probably the mother or stepmother of Pons.[124] Otho of Baret was also a relative, and in addition the *baillivus* – 'bailli', bayle: that is to say, the count's officer in the district of Moissac.

We should also note that the records of the depositions of Arnalda, the lady of Baret and Otho of Baret all state that they were asked if they wished to defend themselves against the things that were found against them in the inquisition.[125] Providing a deponent with such an opportunity of defence was part of the guidance to inquisitors provided a year later by the Council of Béziers (1246), held by the archbishop of Narbonne and his suffragans.[126] Shortly after this there is another specific example, in a sentence (itself delivered in February 1248) relating to depositions received against the wealthy Toulouse citizen Peter Garcia (August–December 1248). Here an additional detail is given, that a written record of what had been found against Peter had been handed over to him.[127] A classic account of defence in inquisition procedure found many examples in a notary's register from the inquisition in Carcassonne in the 1250s.[128] It is difficult to find other examples in the inquisition records of the 1240s. A word-search has not revealed any in the digitised versions of Ms Toulouse 609 or the register FFF of the inquisitor

---

[124] She is named as 'uxor Petri Grimoart senioris' (wife of Pons Grimoard the elder); Doat vol. 22, fol. 43v. Petrus Grimoardi senior probably was Pons Grimoardi's father; Feuchter, *Ketzer, Konsuln und Büßer*, p. 300.

[125] Doat vol. 22, fols. 44r, 46r. Otho: Requisitus si vult se defendere de his quæ inventa sunt in inquisitione.

[126] Edited by R. Parmeggiani, *I consilia procedurali per l'inquisizione medievale (1236–1330)* (Bologna, 2011), p. 39, no. viii. Already at the very beginning of inquisition in Languedoc, in 1234, there had been setbacks because inquisitors tried to curtail the rights of defendants. In several cases trials were annulled. See Feuchter, *Ketzer, Konsuln und Büßer*, p. 284 and n. 124.

[127] Rehr, 'Sentences', document no. MS9992-36, accessed 06 November 2020. Note that the manuscript reads 'Quia per illa que in inquisitione invenimus' (Because through those things we have found), not 'invertimus' (we have inverted *or* turned over) as in Rehr's edition. It is given correctly in Douais, *Documents*, II, 74.

[128] L. Tanon, *Histoire de tribuneaux de l'inquisition en France* (Paris, 1993), pp. 396–400. For 1250–53, see Douais, *Documents*, II, 1250: 123–4 no. xviii, 132–3 no. xxx, 136 n. xxxvii, 136–7 no. xxxviii, 138–9 no. xlii, 139–40 no. xliii; 1251: 155 no. lxix, 163 nos, lxxxix–xc, 162 nos. lxxxvi–lxxxvii; 1252: 172–3 no. cxi, 178 no. cxxii, 180–1 no. cxxix, 183–5 no, 189–90 no. cl, 194–6 no. clv. Common to all those documents which conclude with a list of witnesses and the scribe is the name of the notary Peter Aribert, who, as we have seen, worked alongside Nepos in the inquisitorial campaign of 1245–6.

Nepos of Montauban, assistant to inquisition and defender of the accused

Ferrier contained in Bibliothèque nationale de France Mss Collection Doat 22–4. Notable is that in the four cases of the 1240s mentioned here the opportunity of defence is spelled out in the cases of people of high rank and wealth.[129] Notable also is the presence of our Montauban legal experts in the earliest cases cited here.

We return to Otho of Baret. Administratively he had come under Pons. Now this Pons Grimoardi himself had also recently appeared – in fact, re-appeared – before the inquisition, at the beginning of the year 1245. On the 22 and 25 January he had been interrogated, just a day before Nepos of Montauban first officiated as an inquisition witness, on 26 January. Pons had not been questioned by the leading inquisitors, Bernard of Caux and John of St Pierre, but by none other than Peter Sellan himself.[130] The original inquisitor of the Quercy, now in extreme old age, had been reactivated! There is no question that Sellan acted in the context of the inquisition of Bernard of Caux and John of St Pierre, for among the witnesses of Pons's deposition to Sellan we encounter Bernard of Ladinhac, the inquisition assistant with whom Nepos would be listed together as witnesses on the very next day. There is thus a direct connection between Nepos and inquisitorial activities in his home region of southern Quercy and the neighbouring zones of the Toulousain, and an almost direct one with the inquisitor who had dealt with Montauban, in 1236. From the information at our disposal it seems that Nepos first became involved with inquisition, when people from the greater Montauban region were interrogated. There is more. In his 1245 testimony, Pons Grimoardi implicated people from Montauban, Nepos's hometown. And this may well have been a major reason for taking on witnesses like Nepos and Frank – not only that they were both experienced in legal procedure, but also that they were highly knowledgeable about locals in Montauban. After all, in Ms. 609 we find the same principle, when parish priests are accompanying their flock to the inquisitors in Toulouse, in order to help the inquisitors elicit truthful confessions. In striking contrast to Frank, however, Nepos did not occur just once in the inquisition records but went on to become a permanent member of the Lauragais inquisition team for more than a year. He also remained involved in the repression of heresy in his hometown. One of the documents from 1246 he witnessed was a life sentence on a man from Montauban, who was sanctioned for relapsing into support of the 'heretics'.[131] This was the only person convicted for heresy in Montauban in the first decades after Sellan's 1236 inquisition, as far as

---

[129] Note the contrast with the poor and powerless envisaged by the author of the *Liber fugitivus*; section 1 above and n. 5.

[130] Doat vol. 22, fol. 42r.

[131] Sentence from 8 July 1246; ed. Rehr, 'Sentences', document no. MS9992-12, accessed 24 December 2019; previously edited, Douais, *Documents*, II, 31–4. On this case see Feuchter, *Ketzer, Konsuln und Büßer*, pp. 43, 321 n. 63, 399 and 405.

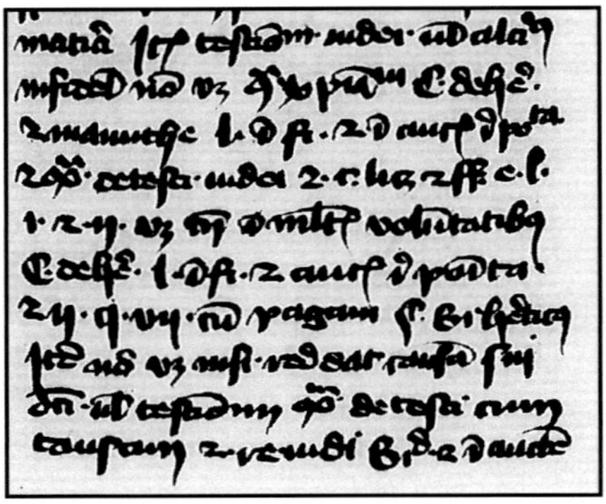

Figure 3.2
Passage from Bagarotus's *Liber fugitivus*
on the left-hand side, with Nepos's
elaborated version of it on the right.

3.2a (above)
Bagarotus: Staatsbibliothek zu Berlin,
Ms Lat. Fol., fol. 399r, column a.
By permission, Staatsbibliothek zu
Berlin, Preußischer Kulturbesitz,
Handschriftenabteilung

3.2b (right)
Nepos: *Liber fugitivus* (Lyon, 1536), fol.
XXXVv, column a.
By permission, Österreichische
Nationalbibliothek.

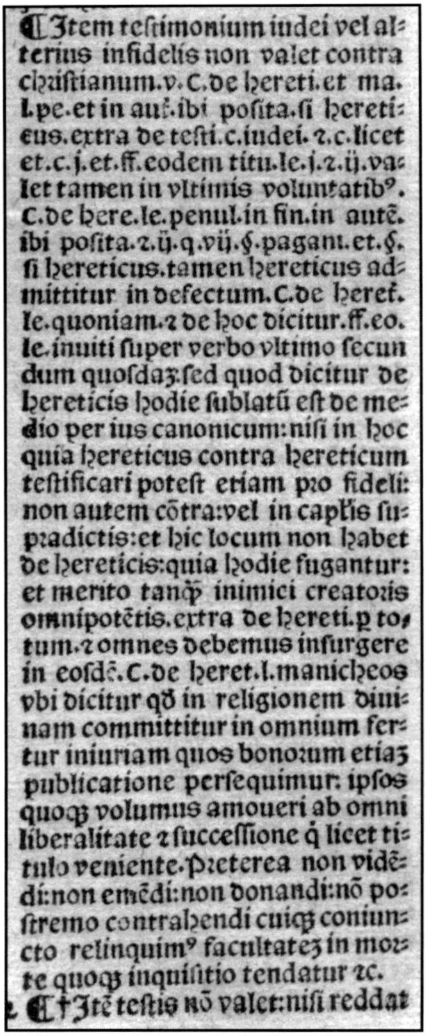

¶ Item teſtimonium iudei vel alterius infidelis non valet contra chriſtianum.v.C.de hereti.et ma. l.pe.et in auť.ibi poſita.ſi hereticus.extra de teſti.c.indei.z.c.licet et.c.j.et.ff.eodem titu.le.j.z.ij.valet tamen in vltimis voluntatib⁹. C.de here.le.penul.in fin.in autē. ibi poſita.z.ij.q.vij.ſ.pagant.et.ſ. ſi hereticus.tamen hereticus ad-mittitur in defectum.C.de heref. le.quoniam.z de hoc dicitur.ff.eo. le.inuiti ſuper verbo vltimo ſecun dum quoſdaz:ſed quod dicitur de hereticis hodie ſublatū eſt de medio per ius canonicum:niſi in hoc quia hereticus contra hereticum teſtificari poteſt etiam pro fideli: non autem cōtra:vel in captis ſupradictis:et hic locum non habet de hereticis:quia hodie fugantur: et merito tanꝗ inimici creatoris omnipotētis.extra de hereti.p totum.z omnes debemus inſurgere in eoſdē.C.de heret.l.manicheos vbi dicitur qð in religionem diuinam committitur in omnium fertur iniuriam quos bonorum etiaz publicatione perſequimur. ipſos quocꝗ volumus amoueri ab omni liberalitate z ſucceſſione ꝗ licet titulo veniente.preterea non vidē-di:non emēdi:non donandi:nō poſtremo contrahendi cuicꝗ coniuncto relinquim⁹ facultatez in morte quocꝗ inquiſitio tendatur ꝛc.
¶ † Ité teſtis nō valet:niſi reddat

we know from the records that survive.[132] Also remarkable is the fact that in another sentence that Nepos witnessed in the same year, the first name in the series of witnesses is Alphonse, the abbot of St Théodard. He is one of only a few representatives of religious houses (abbots, priors) in the region to function as a witness to these sentences. This points to a relationship between Bernard of Caux and Jean of St Pierre with the Benedictine abbey near Montauban which could well have played a part in Nepos, a donat of the abbey, becoming their assistant.[133]

7. A sketch of Nepos's life

It is now time to turn what we have established into a rough biographical sketch. Our protagonist must have been born before or at the latest around the year 1220, for he is mentioned as a university-trained legal scholar, a 'magister', already in 1245. His name was Nepos, sometimes with the byname 'de la Davinia', of unclear significance. He lived his life mostly in Montauban, a young and prosperous town ruled by an oligarchy of consular families. Yet although studying law certainly required an economically stable background, Nepos de la Davinia cannot be connected to one of the town's leading families, nor is his byname 'de la Davinia' mentioned in any Montauban document before Nepos or during his life. It is thus highly likely that Nepos was a 'homo novus' (new man), a social climber who came from outside the urban oligarchy and gained his later positions through the study of law, which he probably pursued in Italy rather than France, although he had, at some point in his career, had the opportunity to learn from law masters at Montpellier. Montauban was also marked by the strong presence of Waldensians and the 'heretics', otherwise known as the Cathars – the latter enjoyed particular popularity among the town's elites. But Nepos did not share either leaning. He had probably obtained minor orders in his youth, for he was named a 'cleric' in 1245/6, and he was one of the donats of the nearby Benedictine abbey of St Théodard. While the town was very open to dissident religious tendencies and strongly supportive of the southern cause in the Albigensian wars, Nepos kept to the abbey's side.

---

[132] In the 1270s there was the case of Bernardus of Solhac from Montauban, a very individualistic dissident compared to the organized followers of 'heretics' ('Cathars') and Waldensians. See Feuchter, *Ketzer, Konsuln und Büßer*, pp. 407–4088 and 493–7.

[133] in presentia Aldofossi, abbatis Montis Albani (in the presence of Alfonse, abbot of Montauban); sentence from 17 May 1246, ed. Rehr, 'Sentences', document no. MS9992-05, accessed 24 December 2019; previously edited, Douais, *Documents*, II, 16–20. Note that there is also a witness 'W. capellani de Monte Albano' (W., chaplain of Montauban) in one of the sentences; Rehr, 'Sentences', document no. MS9992-50, accessed 15 June 2020; previously edited, Douais, *Documents*, II, 88.

Jörg Feuchter

It was not allied to the counts of Toulouse. One of its abbots had even been held captive by Count Raymond VI. [134]

Montauban finally experienced the coming of inquisition in 1236, but this was not the terrible scourge that is usually imagined. A high number of Montauban citizens, many of them from the urban elites, gave full depositions to the inquisitor Sellan and received relatively lenient sentences under the conditions of the 'period of grace'. It looks as though a bargain had been reached, probably prompted by a similar deal made by an individual, a major officer of the count of Toulouse and a leading figure in the Montauban region. This was Pons Grimoardi, from nearby Castelsarrasin, a wealthy international merchant and the count's seneschal in Quercy. Curiously it is also with this man and his relatives that we find Nepos first involved in inquisition, in the beginning of the year 1245. In January and March of that year, Nepos is witness to depositions from three persons very closely connected to Pons Grimoardi. The day before Pons himself had been interrogated, and with the ancient inquisitor Sellan as a witness. That 1243–5 campaign, spanning the territories of the Agenais, Quercy and the northern part of the Toulousain, was led by two inquisitors, Bernard of Caux and John of St Pierre. Nepos was not the only citizen of Montauban who figured as a witness on this occasion. He appears once together with another townsman, Frank, who shared important traits with Nepos: both were legal scholars and lay associates of St Théodard. Their education, Catholic credentials and local knowledge were ideal qualifications for assisting inquisitorial interrogations of people from the region. Nepos however did not remain just a local expert on heretical connections. Together with a few other men from his home region north of Toulouse who had been assistants to this earlier inquisition he went with the two inquisitors when they began a new campaign, the famous 'great inquisition' in the Toulosain, involving thousands of inhabitants of that region. Our scholar became one of the scribes and a very frequent assistant to the inquisitorial court sitting at Toulouse at the abbey of St Sernin. Present for more than a year at interrogations and also at sentencings, he then disappears from the entourage of Bernard and John after July 1246.

Next we find him in Montauban in 1253 again, this time as a witness to a consular charter. This is evidence that he had already achieved some modest social status in his hometown, which – as we have seen – already treasured the work of legal experts like him. After that he occurs in 1256 in a charter of the abbey of St Théodard as a donat. We may deduce from the notices in these two charters that Nepos was living in Montauban in the mid-1250s. A decade later, in 1266, we find him as a secular judge of the district of Villelongue (adjacent to Montauban but a part of the *sénéchaussée* of Toulouse), the very same region where he had started his 'career' as inquisitorial staff member. In both ecclesiastical and secular jurisdictions his areas of territorial competence coincided. He

---

[134] See Feuchter, *Ketzer, Konsuln und Büßer*, p. 158

Nepos of Montauban, assistant to inquisition and defender of the accused

then rose in the ranks of the Capetian administration, for from 1267 on he was the judge of an entire *sénéchaussée*, the Albigeois. In that office he is last mentioned in 1269, but it is very possible that he officiated for longer. It seems therefore highly probable that he redacted his version of the *Liber fugitivus* – which has been dated to around 1268 – while still in office. After 1273, however, Nepos seems to have retired from his court function, for from that year on he was very much present in his home town's consular government. After frequent notices as a consul and as a witness to consular charters for more than a decade after 1273, from 1284 Nepos's name disappears from the urban charters. We may thus assume that he died that year or soon after, at the age of at least sixty.

8. Discussion of heretics and heresy in Nepos's version of the *Liber fugitivus*

The issue of religious dissidence and its juridical persecution was present throughout in Nepos's life. Not only was he himself active for more than a year in an enormous inquisition campaign, he also grew up and lived in a town where many men and women had been implicated with dissidents and had been sanctioned for this by an inquisitor. Even in his position as a secular judge in the Capetian administration, he had direct colleagues who were both fellow townsmen of Montauban and receivers of an inquisitorial penance. Despite all this, he went on to redact a pre-existing juridical treatise whose explicit aim was to 'help defendants to flee'. There seems to be a huge biographical contradiction in this siding with defendants after playing such an important role in the largest persecution of people accused of heresy in the middle ages. Or is this only a problem to the modern eye, as medieval men could also feel very 'righteous' in persecuting heretics? On the other hand, it is quite evident that inquisition, especially in its primordial stage, was far from unanimously accepted in medieval society and the church.[135]

With this question in mind, let us at last turn to the *Liber fugitivus* and ask if and how heresy is treated there. As far as I can see only once does the work touch on heresy for more than a fleeting mention. The paragraph in question already appears in Bagarotus's original version, but Nepos makes a remarkable addition to it. The passage appears in the context of exceptions to be made against certain types of witnesses. In the original, Bagarotus notes that not only is the testimony of a Jew invalid, but also that of a heretic. In his

---

[135] For the viewpoint of prosecutors of medieval heresy on the justification of their activities, see C. Caldwell Ames, *Righteous Persecution: Inquisition, Dominicans, and Christianity in the Middle Ages* (Philadelphia, 2009), and the review by J. Feuchter, in H-Soz-Kult, 23.06.2010, www.hsozkult.de/publicationreview/id/reb-13516.

Jörg Feuchter

redaction, Nepos keeps Bagarotus's text, but elaborates it substantially. In the following, the additions in his version are underlined.[136]

Item[137] testimonium iudei vel alterius infidelis non valet contra christianum; v(ide) C. de hereti(cis) et ma(nicheis) I. pe(nultima)[138] et in aut(entica) ibi posita,[139] Si hereticus; extra de testi(bus) c. Iudei[140] et c. Licet[141] et c. I[142] et. ff. eodem titu(lo) le(ge) I et II.[143] Valet et tamen in ultimis voluntatibus; C. de here(ticis) le(ge) penul(tima) in fin(e) in aut(entica) ibi posita[144] et II q.

---

[136] In Murano's account, all printed versions are based on Nepos's redaction and Bagarotus's original survives only in manuscripts. Given this, I took a manuscript to compare with the printed version: Staatsbibliothek zu Berlin Ms. lat. fol. 862 fols. 377r–406r (the passage is on fol. 399r, column a). Note: According to Murano ('Richerche', 435–6), this manuscript belongs clearly to group A, representing Bagarotus's original, and not to the small group of contaminated manuscripts (441), although it does give Nepos's name in the prologue. But in my inspection of the Berlin manuscript I found more contamination than just Nepos's name. Thus on fol. 388v col. a, the case in question contains examples referring to citizens of Toulouse and Cahors, as in Nepos's redaction. On fol. 394v col. b, there is the mention of 'the great masters of the law' that the author claims to have seen in Montpellier, as in the redaction. On fol. 395r col. a, specific year dates are given in a formulary, as in the redaction, though somewhat scrambled. And finally the explicit in the manuscript (fol. 407r, col. a) is followed by the first words of the addendum typical in the redaction. Despite these contaminations, in the section about heresy the Berlin manuscript clearly does represent the text of Bagarotus's original. The text of the printed version is given according to *the Liber fugitivus* (1536 edn.), fol. XXXVv, corresponding to fol. XXXVIv in the 1510 first printed edn.

[137] I am deeply obliged to my colleague Dr Thomas Woelki (Humboldt Universität zu Berlin) for reading a draft of my manuscript, for decoding the citations and references in the passage of the *Liber fugitivus* and for counselling me with his expertise in medieval law.

[138] C. 1.5.21pr: Quoniam multi iudices in dirimendis litigiis nos interpellaverunt, indigentes nostro oraculo, ut eis reseretur, quid de testibus haereticis statuendum sit, utrumne accipiantur eorum testimonia an respuantur, sancimus contra orthodoxos quidem litigantes nemini haeretico vel etiam his qui Iudaicam superstitionem colunt esse in testimonia communionem, sive utraque pars orthodoxa sit sive altera. Translated, *The Codex of Justinian. A New Annotated Translation with Parallel Latin and Greek Text*, ed. B.W. Frier et al., 3 vols. (Cambridge, 2016), I, 220: Since many judges, in resolving cases, have consulted Us, requiring that Our oracle be opened unto them as to how they should proceed concerning heretical witnesses, whether they and their testimony should be admitted or rejected, We decree that no heretic or even those who follow the Jewish superstition may have any part in the testimony against orthodox litigants, whether both parties are orthodox or just one.

[139] Nov. before C. 1.5.21 = Frid. 1.5, ed. E. Osenbrüggen, *Corpus Juris Civilis*, 3 vols. (Leipzig, 1856), III, 885.

[140] X 2.20.21, ed. Friedberg II, col. 322.

[141] X 2.20.23, ed. Friedberg II, col. 322–3.

[142] X 2.20.1, ed. Friedberg II, col. 315.

[143] Dig. 22.5.1 and 2.

[144] See n. 134.

Nepos of Montauban, assistant to inquisition and defender of the accused

VII § Pagani[145] et § Si hereticus.[146] Tamen hereticus admittitur in defectum; C. de heret(icis) le(ge) Quoniam.[147] Et de hoc dicitur ff. eo(dem titulo) le(ge) Inviti super verbo ultimo[148] secundum quosdam. Sed quod dicitur de hereticis, hodie sublatum est de medio per ius canonicum: nisi in hoc, quia hereticus contra hereticum testificari potest etiam pro fideli, non autem contra; vide[149] in capitulis supradictis. Et hic locum non habet de hereticis, quia hodie fugantur et merito tanquam inimici creatoris omnipotentis; extra de hereti(cis) per totum,[150] et omnes debemus insurgere in eosdem; C. de heret(icis) I. Manicheos,[151] ubi dicitur: *Quod in religionem divinam committitur, in omnium fertur iniuriam. Quos bonorum etiam publicatione persequimur.*[152] *Ipsos quoque volumus amoveri ab omni liberalitate et successione quolibet titulo veniente.*[153] *Preterea non vendendi*[154] *non emendi, non donandi non*

---

[145] C. 2 q. 7 c. 25, ed. Friedberg I, col. 489: Pagani, uel heretici, siue Iudei non possunt Christianos accusare, aut uocem infamationis eis inferre (Pagans or heretics or Jews cannot accuse Christians, or bring to bear against them the voicing of defamation) [spoken accusation that they are of ill-repute].

[146] C. 2 q. 7 c. 26, ed. Friedberg I, p. 489.

[147] C. 1.5.21pr (see above).

[148] Gloss or commentary to Dig. 22.5.8 s.v. Licet: Inviti testimonium dicere non coguntur senes valetudinarii vel milites vel qui cum magistratu rei publicae causa absunt vel quibus venire non licet (Old men, the sick, invalids, soldiers, those holding office who are absent on public business, and people who are forbidden to appear, cannot be compelled to testify, if they are unwilling to do so).

[149] Correction from 'vel".

[150] X 5.7, ed. Friedberg II, col. 778–90.

[151] C. 1.5.4pr: Manichaeos seu Manichaeas vel Donatistas meritissima severitate persequimur. Translated, *Codex of Justinian*, I, 191: We persecute the Manichaeans and Donatists, whether men or women, with perfectly warranted severity.

[152] C. 1.5.4.1: Ac primum quidem volumus esse publicum crimen, quia, quod in religione divina committitur, in omnium fertur iniuriam. quos bonorum etiam publicatione persequimur: quae tamen cedere iubemus proximis quibusque personis, ita ut ascendentium vel descendentium vel venientium ex latere cognatorum usque ad secundum gradum velut in successionibus ordo servetur. quibus ita demum ad capiendas facultates esse ius patimur, si non et ipsi pari conscientia polluuntur. Translated, *Codex of Justinian*, I, 191: And first of all, We want it (adherence to the Manichaeans or Donatists) to be a public crime, because wrongs committed with respect to divine religion are to the detriment of all. We persecute them indeed by the confiscation of their property, but We order that it go to their nearest relatives. Thus the order of heirs in the ascending, descending or collateral line of cognates up to the second degree shall be observed as in testamentary succession; and We grant the heirs the right to seize their property only if they themselves are not polluted by equal guilt.

[153] C. 1.5.4.2.

[154] Correction from 'videndi'.

Jörg Feuchter

postremo contrahendi cuiquam convicto[155] *relinquimus facultatem.*[156] *In morte quoque inquisitio tendatur*[157] et cetera. Item testis non valet nisi reddat causas.

The important passage is clearly the one between 'Sed quod dicitur' and 'tanquam inimici creatoris omnipotentis'. It is remarkably different not only from the rest of the paragraph but also from the whole *Liber*. For here, the otherwise steady and fast rhythm of citation chasing citation slows down for a few lines of writing in an almost narrative style. We may translate as follows:

> but what is said about heretics, is nowadays suspended by canon law, except in this, that a heretic may testify against a heretic and also for a [catholic] believer, but not against him; see the sources quoted above. But this does not apply to heretics for today they are driven away, and rightfully so, as enemies of the almighty creator.

What is most remarkable here is that Nepos writes that 'nowadays' heretics are expelled (or chased away, driven away). Nepos could easily have intended *fugantur* as the 'historic present' (= 'heretics have been expelled'), and indeed the statement seems like an update to what Bagarotus had said. So: is this a reflection of what had happened in the course of roughly three decades between Bagarotus writing the original version and Nepos redacting it? In other words, is this Nepos's personal summary of developments since inquisition fully kicked in and drove out religious dissidents from Languedoc, a process in whose beginnings he had been personally very much involved? That heretics had been effectively driven out?

If we consider that Nepos was a citizen of Montauban – a town which had once had a very strong presence of dissidence, had heresy removed with almost no social repercussions in the 1230s and was thereafter heresy-free – his statement does not seem odd. The older Nepos lived in an urban society which one might label 'post-heretic'. Remarkable also is the emphasis in Nepos's justification of the driving out of dissidents – rightly so, for they are God's enemies. Finally there is Nepos's choice when naming God: the 'almighty creator'. The wording runs directly counter to the fundamental

---

[155] Correction from 'coniuncto'.

[156] C. 1.5.4.3: Praeterea non donandi, non emendi, non vendendi, non postremo contrahendi cuiquam convicto relinquimus facultatem. Translated, *Codex of Justinian*, I, 191: Furthermore, We leave no one who has been convicted the power to give, buy, sell, or even make a contract.

[157] C. 1.5.4.4: In mortem quoque inquisitio tendatur. nam si in criminibus maiestatis licet memoriam accusare defuncti, non immerito et hic debet subire iudicium. Translated, *Codex of Justinian*, I, 191: The inquisition shall be extended against death (i.e. against the dead). For if it is possible to impeach the memory of the deceased with accusations of treason, one shall not undeservedly undergo judgement in this case too.

Nepos of Montauban, assistant to inquisition and defender of the accused

belief of the heretics, the 'Cathars': that the visible creation is not from God. The sharp nuance in Nepos's formulation may well reflect the mind of a man who had once lived alongside 'heretics' in Montauban who believed the exact opposite.

4

The hunt for the Heresy of the Free Spirit: the 1332 enquiry into the 'Cowled Nuns' of Świdnica*

Paweł Kras

On 7–12 September 1332, the refectory of the priory of the Friars Preachers in Świdnica (German Schweidnitz) in Lower Silesia witnessed the interrogations of sixteen women about the life and *mores* of a Beguine community whose members called themselves 'the cowled nuns' (moniales Capuciatae) and 'the Daughters of Odelind' (filiae Udilindis). The investigation was carried out by John of Schwenkenfeld, a Dominican friar and the papal inquisitor in the Dioceses of Wrocław (German Breslau) and Lubusz (German Lebus). Its purpose was to examine the beliefs of the Świdnica Beguines and learn whether they had anything in common with the heretical doctrine of the Free Spirit. The testimonies of all deponents were translated from German into Latin and written down by an assistant notary, revised by Schwenkenfeld, and recorded in the notarial instrument, which is currently preserved in the Vatican Library under the catalogue number Vat. Lat. 13119a.[1]

---

* The paper is published with financial support from the National Programme for the Development of the Humanities, operated by the Polish Ministry of Education and Science, Grant Agreement No 0156/NPRH8/H21/87/2019 (2019–22).

[1] The findings presented in this paper are based on the research carried out in 2015–17 and published in the study by Paweł Kras, Tomasz Gałuszka and Adam Poznański, *Proces beginek świdnickich w 1332 roku: Studia historyczne i edycja łacińsko-polska* (The Trial of the Beguines from Świdnica in 1332: Historical Studies and the Latin-Polish Edition), 2nd edn (Lublin, 2018). All references to the testimonies recorded in the 1332 register of John of Schwenkenfeld are made to its Latin edition published in this book, the *Examinatio testium Capuciatarum monialium in Swydnicz*, edited by T. Gałuszka and annotated by P. Kras. It is cited as *Examinatio testium*. In addition, an abbreviated system of references in brackets is also used within the text. The first Roman numeral indicates the first (I) or second (II) part of the 1332 records; the second figure refers to the deposition of witnesses questioned in a specific sequence (I–XI) or the 'cowled nuns' (I–V); and the third Arabic numeral indicates the consecutive paragraphs of the testimony (1–42).

The 1332 enquiry into the 'Cowled Nuns' of Świdnica

The 1332 inquisitorial records and past research

The inquisitorial proceedings on the Świdnica 'cowled nuns' conformed to the provisions of the Council of Vienne (1311–12), published by Pope John XXII in November 1317. Two of the conciliar constitutions, *Cum de quibusdam mulieribus* and *Ad nostrum*, directly addressed the cases of lay women calling themselves Beguines and undertaking a quasi-monastic lifestyle.[2] The former constitution accused Beguines of pretending to be cloistered congregations and wearing a religious habit referred to as the Beguines' dress. It also accused the Beguines of becoming engrossed in discussions on the doctrine of the Church, especially deliberations over the dogma of the Trinity. As a result, numerous errors arose and led to scandals among the faithful. The constitution *Cum de quibusdam mulieribus* ordered the dissolution of Beguine communities.[3] This provision did not concern only pious women who wanted to continue to live in chastity and poverty on an individual basis. The constitution *Ad nostrum* accused Beguines and Beghards of subscribing to the Free Spirit heresy whose followers disdained the teaching of the Church and believed that they themselves were able to achieve a state of mystical union with God, without recourse to the sacraments and the ministry of the clergy. *Ad nostrum* listed the heretical beliefs of the Free Spirit in eight articles, commissioning bishops and papal inquisitors to carry out investigations against its followers.[4]

In Silesia, Bishop Henry of Wierzbna (died 1319) started to implement these constitutional provisions and bring them into practice soon after his return from Vienne. In 1315 he entrusted to Franciscan and Dominican lectors the inquisition against heresy suspects in the diocese of Wrocław.[5] This resulted in the trials of the Waldensians in Wrocław, Nysa (German Neisse), and Świdnica which put to death a few dozen individuals.[6] At the same time,

---

[2] R.E. Lerner, *The Heresy of the Free Spirit in the Later Middle Ages* (Berkeley, Los Angeles and London, 1972), pp. 78–84; W. Simons, *The Cities of Ladies. Beguine Communities in the Medieval Low Countries, 1200–1565* (Philadelphia PA, 2001), pp. 133–5; J. Voigt, *Beginen im Spätmittelalter. Frauenfrömmigkeit in Thüringen und im Reich* (Cologne, Weimar and Vienna, 2012), pp. 183–92; P. Kras, 'Sobór w Vienne i herezja wolnego ducha' (The Council of Vienne and the Heresy of the Free Spirit), in Kras, Gałuszka and Poznański, *Proces beginek*, pp. 60–4.

[3] N. Tanner, ed., *Decrees of the Ecumenical Councils*, 2 vols. (Ann Arbor, 1990), I, 374.

[4] Ibid., I, 383–4.

[5] T. Silnicki, *Dzieje i ustrój Kościoła na Śląsku* (The History and Organisation of the Church in Silesia) (Kraków, 1939), pp. 200–4; *Polski Słownik Biograficzny* (Polish Biographical Dictionary), ix, pp. 424–5; J. Maciejowski, *Episkopat Polski dzielnicowej 1180–1320* (The Bishops in the Period of Poland's Fragmentation, 1180–1320) (Kraków and Bydgoszcz, 2003), pp. 477–9.

[6] A. Patschovsky, 'Waldenserverfolgung in Schweidnitz 1315', *Deutsches Archiv für Erforschung des Mittelalters* 36 (1980), 137–76; J. Szymański, *Ruchy heretyckie na Śląsku w XIII i XIV wieku* (Heretical Movements in Silesia in the Thirteenth and Fourteenth Century) (Katowice, 2007), pp. 25–50.

Paweł Kras

Henry of Wierzbna ordered inspections of Beguine communities across his diocese.[7] The formulary book drafted by Arnold of Protzan, the Wrocław canon and his close collaborator, contains three documents on Beguines, modelled on the constitution *Cum de quibusdam mulieribus*. They draw attention to the 'serious and contemptible vice of certain women, commonly known as Beguines who should be cut off from the Church'. Implementing the conciliar constitution, Bishop Henry of Wierzbna ordered the dissolution of all Beguine communities, threatening anyone who continued this way of life with excommunication.[8]

His sudden death in 1319, followed by the seven-year vacancy in the bishopric, distracted the process of implementing this order. It was only after 1326 and the installation of Bishop Nanker (*c.* 1265/1270–1341), transferred from Kraków to Wrocław, that the process could be resumed.[9] The 1332 trial of the 'cowled nuns' of Świdnica is the first inquisitorial operation against Silesian Beguines evidenced in the sources during the term of Bishop Nanker. It was supervised by the papal inquisitor John of Schwenkenfeld and authorised by Nanker. During the investigation John of Schwenkenfeld, a Dominican friar and lector in the Holy Cross convent in Świdnica, interrogated the sisters of the Świdnica community and witnesses who either had been once its members or possessed valuable information about this group. Schwenkenfeld was descended from a knightly family settled in Schwenkenfeld (today Makowice) near Świdnica.[10] It was probably in Świdnica that he joined the Order of Preachers and started his theological training. In unknown circumstances he earned a bachelor's degree in theology which boosted his later career within the Dominican Order. Probably in 1327 he was appointed lector in the Dominican convent of Świdnica, and kept this office until 1339 when he became the prior.[11] His appointment to the position of papal inquisitor in the diocese of Wrocław testifies to his theological skills and pastoral experience

---

[7] P. Kras, 'Inkwizycja papieska w średniowiecznej Polsce. Zarys problematyki badawczej' (The Papal Inquisition in Medieval Poland. An Overview of Research Problems), *Almanach Historyczny* 5 (2003), pp. 33–4; idem, 'Dominican Inquisitors in Mediaeval Poland', in A. Palacios Bernal, ed., *Praedicatores, Inquisitores*, vol. 1: *The Dominicans and the Mediaeval Inquisition. Acts of the 1st International Seminar on the Dominicans and the Inquisition. Rome, 23–25 February 2002* (Rome, 2004), pp. 260–1.

[8] W. Wattenbach, ed., 'Das Formelbuch des Arnold von Protzan', in *Codex diplomaticus Silesiae* 5 (Wrocław, 1862), pp. 59–62.

[9] *Polski Słownik Biograficzny*, xxii, pp. 514–7; T. Silnicki, *Dzieje i ustrój Kościoła*, pp. 215–22; idem, *Biskup Nanker* (Bishop Nanker) (Warsaw, 1953), pp. 95–8; J. Swastek, 'Biskup Nanker jako ordynariusz diecezji wrocławskiej' (Bishop Nanker as the Pastor of the Wrocław Diocese), in K. Matwijowski, ed., *Ludzie śląskiego Kościoła katolickiego* (Wrocław, 1992), pp. 7–14.

[10] Kras, 'Dominican Inquisitors', pp. 260–1 and *Annex*, no 15, pp. 301–2; J. Szymański, 'Joannes Swenkenfeldt – inquisitor et martyr', *Śląski Kwartalnik Historyczny Sobótka* 58/1 (2003), pp. 1–17.

[11] *Polski Słownik Biograficzny*, x, p. 421; K. Kaczmarek, *Szkoły i studia polskich dominikanów*

The 1332 enquiry into the 'Cowled Nuns' of Świdnica

among Friars Preachers of Silesia. In 1330s Schwenkenfeld's status in the Order was further enhanced by his close cooperation with Bishop Nanker of Wrocław. On behalf of the Provincial of Polish Dominicans in 1334–6 John of Schwenkenfeld supervised the foundation of a new Dominican convent in Brzeg (German Brieg). He probably drafted the foundation charter of Duke Bolko III of Legnica (German Liegnitz) and Brzeg dated 9 January 1336, and six months later, on 29 July, together with Jan Sutorka, Dominican lector in the Wrocław convent, presented the plans for the establishment of the Brzeg convent with Bishop Nanker. Thanks to his position as Nanker's collaborator the foundation of the Dominican convent in Brzeg was successfully implemented with the bishop's blessing and support.[12]

The way he conducted the 1332 interrogations bears testimony to his high skills and good knowledge of current theological controversies. Schwenkenfeld was well-trained in the teachings of Thomas Aquinas and applied the arguments of the *Doctor Angelicus* in his dealings with the Świdnica sisters.[13] His theological background played a role in his appointment by the Dominican provincial as papal inquisitor for the Diocese of Wrocław. He took the office of papal inquisitor in succession to Peregrinus Polonus (Peregrinus of Opole), a prolific preacher and author of a popular sermon collection *de tempore* (Sunday sermons) and *de sanctis* (saints), and a three-times provincial minister of the Polish Dominicans.[14] Schwenkenfeld's appointment took place sometime between 1327 and 1330. On 23 November 1330, Bishop Nanker of Wrocław endorsed his inquisitorial operations in Silesia in a document requiring all parish priests to render the inquisitor any necessary assistance.[15] Actually, this is the first document confirming Schwenkenfeld's position as papal inquisitor. The proceedings against the Świdnica 'cowled nuns' in 1332 was the first inquisitorial assignment of Schwenkenfeld recorded in historical sources.

The Dominican inquisitor's assistant was Nicholas, the son of Henry *de Pencwynsdorph* (today Panków near Świdnica), a notary public *ex auctoritate imperiali* (by imperial authority) who was closely associated with the Wrocław

---

w okresie średniowiecza (Schools and Studies of the Polish Dominicans in the Middle Ages) (Poznań, 2005), pp. 139, 149, and 412.

[12] Tomasz Gałuszka, Krzysztof Kaczmarek, *Fratres apud Sanctam Crucem. Z badań nad dziejami dominikanów w Brzegu* (Studies on the History of the Friars Preachers in Brzeg), (Poznań, 2018), pp. 28–34 and 54–6.

[13] T. Gałuszka, 'Jan ze Schwenkenfeldu – tomista inkwizytorem' (John of Schwenkenfeld – a Thomist Inquisitor), in Kras, Gałuszka and Poznański, *Proces beginek*, pp. 139–41.

[14] Kras, 'Dominican Inquisitors', p. 159, and *Annex*, no xxix, p. 306.

[15] The original document is preserved in the State Archive in Wrocław, City records of Wrocław, Dominican Friars, Rep. 57, no 64; G. Grünhagen and K. Wutke, ed., *Regesten zur schlesischen Geschichte (1327–1333)*, Codex diplomaticus Silesiae 22 (Wrocław, 1903), no. 4982, p. 108.

Paweł Kras

curia and the consistory tribunal.[16] Notary Nicholas produced the report of the 1332 investigation shortly after the interrogations had been completed. It covers the inquisitorial proceedings and other actions taken by the inquisitor. All deponents were Germans and the questioning was held in German. During the work on the official register all depositions were translated from German into Latin. Only a few German words were left to describe items that – according to the notary's knowledge – had no proper equivalents in Latin. Exceptionally, the notary also recorded a contemptuous German statement of the older sisters against Hedwig of Wrocław, linked to her prolonged prayers at church: *du mynsth selbe* – 'you think only about yourself' (I.I.5).[17]

The written material collected by the assisting notary during the interrogations was put together as a draft to be used later for the production of the Latin register. The notary, in cooperation with the papal inquisitor, made a selection of the material and rendered it in the proper form. In the draft version of the testimonies, with a few exceptions, the inquisitor's questions were removed and the statements were edited based on Schwenkenfeld's interrogatory (*interrogatorium*) used during the interrogations. When drawing up the official record, the notary used the inquisitorial discourse suitable for recording interrogations. The notarial document of the 1332 interrogations, preserved in the Vatican Library under the catalogue number Vat. Lat. 13119a, was edited carefully and does not contain any deletions. It has the form of a roll, 195.5 cm in length and 37.5 cm in width, and consists of four parchment folios sewn together. In a later period, a paper insert was added between folio 3 and 4 of the roll with a description of the death of John of Schwenkenfeld. Its text, *Historia interfectionis fratris Iohannis Swenkenfelt* (History of the killing of brother John of Schwenkenfeld) comprises four pieces of *Kronika książąt polskich* (The Chronicle of the Polish Dukes), dated from the 1380s.[18]

The circumstances of the register's delivery to the Papal Curia remain unknown. John of Schwenkenfeld or more probably one of his fellow friars wished to demonstrate to the Holy See the eagerness with which the Dominican friar – or generally Dominicans – had been engaged in the combat against heresy. If this is the case, this material might have been used for a planned canonisation of Schwenkenfeld who had been killed in 1341 in Prague while performing his inquisitorial duties. As mentioned earlier, Nicholas *de Pencwynsdorph* was a notary currently employed at the chancellery of Bishop Nanker. In late 1320s and 1330s he produced a number

---

[16] F. Luschek, *Notariatsurkunde und Notariat in Schlesien von dem Anfangenbis zum Ende des 16. Jahrhundert*, Historisch-Diplomatische Forschungen 5 (Weimar, 1940), pp. 216–17; new information on his notarial activities is collected and discussed by Kras, 'Przesłuchania', p. 84.

[17] *Examinatio testium*, p. 182.

[18] T. Gałuszka and P. Kras, 'Opis rękopisów' (Description of Manuscripts), in Kras, Gałuszka and Poznański, *Proces beginek*, pp. 151–2.

The 1332 enquiry into the 'Cowled Nuns' of Świdnica

of documents for the bishop and his deputy judge Apeczko of Ząbkowice (German Frankenstein). His work in the service of John of Schwenkenfeld during the 1332 interrogations testifies to Bishop Nanker's engagement in the inquisitorial operations against the 'cowled nuns' from Świdnica. Whether Bishop Nanker himself incited Schwenkenfeld to carry out this investigation remains unclear. But there is no doubt that while dealing with heresy suspects Nanker and Schwenkenfeld collaborated closely with each other, consulted about their actions and shared information.[19]

Probably the second, almost identical instrument of the 1332 interrogations, drawn up by Notary Nicholas, had been handed over to Bishop Nanker, and was later deposited in the archives of the Wrocław Cathedral. It differs significantly from the notarial document now in the Vatican Library.[20] In the middle of the fifteenth century this second version of the interrogations was used to produce a copy for an unknown canon of Kraków Cathedral, which is now kept in the Archive of the Kraków Cathedral Chapter under the catalogue number LA 37.[21] At some point in time, it was joined by a collection of letters and documents, including some copies of letters of Popes Pius II and Paul II from the years 1463–7 relating a conflict between the municipal authorities of Wrocław and the Bohemian king, George of Poděbrad.[22]

In the 1880s the Kraków copy of the 1332 interrogations was found by Fr. Ignacy Polkowski, director of the Kraków Cathedral Archive, and handed over to Bolesław Ulanowski, professor of law at the Jagellonian University, who in 1889 published its edition in the fifth volume of *Archiwum Komisji Historycznej* (Archives of the Historical Commission).[23] This publication was titled *Examen testium super vita et moribus Beguinarum per inquisitorem hereticae pravitatis in Sweydnitz anno 1332 factum*.[24] In his short foreword, Ulanowski linked the 1332 interrogations with the persecution of Beguines after the

---

[19] In 1339–41 John of Schwenkenfeld supported Bishop Nanker in the conflict with the city council of Wrocław which ignored interdict and replaced parish priests loyal to the bishop with some 'vagabond priests'. Due to his involvement in this controversy Schwenkenfeld was summoned by King John of Luxembourg to Prague where he was killed shortly after his arrival on 6 October 1341. Patschovsky, *Die Anfänge*, pp. 62–3; Szymański, *Ruchy heretyckie*, pp. 122–31.

[20] Robert Lerner was the first to pay attention to the significant differences between these two versions of the 1332 records (*The Heresy of the Free Spirit*, p. 112, n. 15). A detailed philological analysis of these differences is offered by T. Gałuszka, 'Analiza krytyczna' (Critical Analysis), in Kras, Gałuszka and Poznański, *Proces beginek*, pp. 157–63.

[21] Gałuszka and Kras, 'Opis rękopisów' (Description of Manuscripts), pp. 153–6.

[22] Ibid., pp. 153–4.

[23] P. Kras, 'Wstęp' (Introduction), in Kras, Gałuszka, Poznański, *Proces beginek*, pp. 16–20.

[24] B. Ulanowski (ed.), *Examen testium super vita et moribus Beguinarum per inquisitorem hereticae pravitatis in Sweydnitz anno 1332 factum*, in *Archiwum Komisji Historyczne* 5, Scriptores rerum Polonicarum 13 (Kraków, 1889), pp. 239–55.

Paweł Kras

proclamation of the anti-Beguine constitutions of *Ad nostrum* and *Cum de quibusdam mulieribus*. Neither Bolesław Ulanowski nor any later researcher working on the 1332 inquisitorial records knew about the original notarial instrument kept in the Vatican. It was Vladimír Koudelka, a Dominican historian, who in 1955 made the fact of its existence public.[25] Two years later, a concise description of the notarial document of the 1332 investigation, placed under the catalogue number of 13119, was published in a new volume of the inventory of the Vaticana Latina manuscripts.[26] Still, only few researchers reached for the manuscript, and others kept on using Ulanowski's edition.

The 1332 interrogations of the Świdnica 'cowled nuns' are commonly regarded as one of the most valuable source materials for the study of the Beguines, their doctrine and organisation, in particular after the Council of Vienne had forbidden this form of female piety. They also provide first-hand information about the so-called heresy of the Free Spirit which was widely attributed to the beliefs of the Beguines. The publication of the records of the 1332 interrogations by Bolesław Ulanowski gave a strong impulse for Polish and international research on this valuable material. In 1903, a comprehensive *regestum* of the records was published in *Regesten zur schlesischen Geschichte*.[27] However, it was only thirty years later, in 1924, that the Polish scholar Kazimierz Dobrowolski made a short analysis of the content of the 1332 records. He argued that the Beguines of Świdnica belonged to a greater community of the Free Spirit heresy that promoted their ideas in Beguine and Beghard convents across Germany and 'represented a uniform system confirmed in the sources – in a form generally unchanged – even in the second half of the fifteenth century'.[28] Another Polish researcher, Jerzy Wyrozumski, was very interested in the involvement of the Beguines in a larger international community and in the internal structure of their group. In his 1971 article he stressed that 'Beguine houses pursued the idea of a common life, and the records of the Świdnica interrogations give insight into the organisation of their community'.[29]

In international literature, it was Herbert Grundmann who first took notice of the testimony of the *moniales Capuciatae* from Świdnica. In his magisterial summary account of medieval heresy of 1963, he found that the 1332 interrogations corroborated that the Free Spirit doctrine was disseminated among

[25] V.J. Koudelka, 'Zur Geschichte der böhmischen Dominikanerprovinz im Mittelalter', *Archivum Fratrum Praedicatorum* 25 (1955), p. 92.

[26] H. Laurent, *Inventario dei codici Vaticani Latini 12848–13735* (Città del Vaticano, 1957), p. 52 (typescript).

[27] Grünhagen and Wutke, *Regesten zur schlesischen Geschichte (1327–1333)*, no. 5146, pp. 161–2.

[28] K. Dobrowolski, 'Pierwsze sekty religijne na ziemiach polskich' [First Religious Sects in Poland], *Reformacja w Polsce* 3 (1924), pp. 196–201.

[29] J. Wyrozumski, 'Beginki i begardzi w Polsce' [Beguines and Begards in Poland], *Zeszyty Naukowe Uniwersytetu Jagiellońskiego*, 261 (1971), Prace Historyczne, no. 35, pp. 7–22.

The 1332 enquiry into the 'Cowled Nuns' of Świdnica

Beguine communities. For Grundmann, the 'cowled nuns' of Świdnica were – just after the Strasbourg Beguines – a community that shared the belief that spiritual perfection could be attained without the sacramental ministry of the Church.[30] In 1967, the British historian Gordon Leff used Ulanowski's edition of *Examen testium* as a primary source for the study of the Free Spirit heresy. In his two-volume book, *Heresy in the Later Middle Ages,* he devoted a dozen pages to the study of the Świdnica Beguines. He believed that thanks to the 1332 interrogations, 'some key questions can be asked for the first time' on the functioning of Beguine groups promoting the ideas of the Free Spirit.[31] Leff was convinced that the depositions of the women from the Świdnica community confirmed the reception of the Free Spirit doctrine among the Beguines.[32] While citing the extensive statements of the 'cowled nuns' in the 1332 register, Leff took no account of the interrogation technique that underpinned them and the technology of producing inquisitorial records.

Five years after Gordon Leff's work, Robert E. Lerner published a comprehensive study in which he proposed a new interpretation of the so-called heresy of the Free Spirit. Like Grundmann and Leff, he emphasised that the 1332 interrogations of Świdnica Beguines were a source of exceptional value for studying the Free Spirit heresy. However, unlike those historians, he doubted the very existence of a Free Spirit sect. In his analysis of the Świdnica records Lerner challenged the reliability of some information recorded in the testimonies. In particular he cast doubt on the most controversial statements about sexual promiscuity, regarding them as the product of the insane imagination of women who had been subject to physical and mental abuse while in the community of the 'cowled nuns'. In his view, the interrogations offer a valuable picture of inquisitorial technique and the dominating role of the papal inquisitor. In Lerner's opinion, John of Schwenkenfeld believed that the Beguines he investigated expressed views attributed to the Free Spirit and worked hard to prove this during the questioning. With this end in view, when asking questions, Schwenkenfeld referred to the constitutions of the Council of Vienne, *Cum de quibusdam mulieribus* and *Ad nostrum,* as the notary sometimes noted in the records.[33] Lerner's reinterpretation of the 1332 enquiry into the life of the Beguine community of Świdnica has been generally accepted by later scholarship.[34]

---

[30] H. Grundmann, *Ketzergeschichte des Mittelalters, Die Kirche in ihrer Geschichte. Ein Handbuch,* 2, issue G, 1st part (Göttingen, 1963), pp. 55–6.

[31] G. Leff, *Heresy in the Later Middle Ages: The Relation of Heterodoxy to Dissent c. 1250–1450,* 2 vols. (Manchester and New York, 1967), I, 386–95

[32] 'The value of the Sweydnitz evidence is that it makes the presence of the Free Spirit among the Beguines a reality, depicting their interaction and the forms it took'; ibid., I, 394.

[33] Lerner, *The Heresy of the Free Spirit,* pp. 112–19.

[34] An example is M. D. Lambert, *Medieval Heresy. Popular Movements from the Gregorian Reform to the Reformation,* 3rd edn (Oxford, 2002), p. 234: 'In an interesting case at

Recent years have seen a revival of studies on the Beguine community of Świdnica. In 2007 Jarosław Szymański published his doctoral dissertation on heretical movements in Silesia in the thirteenth and fourteenth centuries, devoting a whole chapter to this group. His study is focused on the life and devotion of the 'cowled nuns'.[35] Five years later, in his work on Beguines in the Empire, Jörg Voigt recognised the 1332 interrogations as the most valuable source for investigating Beguine communities in the first half of the fourteenth century. In his view, the recorded testimonies give a good insight into the organisational structure, spirituality and everyday life of a group of Beguines in the period after the promulgation of the anti-Beguine constitutions of the Council of Vienne.[36]

In 2017 three Polish researchers, Paweł Kras, Tomasz Gałuszka OP and Adam Poznański, published a critical edition of the 1332 Latin interrogations with the parallel Polish translation. The edition rests on the notarial instrument from the Vatical Library (Ms Vat. Lat. 13119a), however all differences in the Kraków copy (Ms AKKK LA 37) are also marked within the philological apparatus. The Latin-Polish edition is accompanied by a lengthy introduction which contains seven studies discussing the origins of the Beguine movement and its diffusion in Central and Eastern Europe, the rise of the 'cowled nuns' community in Świdnica, its organisation and beliefs, the activities of papal inquisitor John of Schwenkenfeld, the technology of interrogation during the 1332 trial and the production of records. The detailed analysis of the two manuscripts of the 1332 investigation and an overview of past research are also presented.[37]

The 'cowled nuns' of Świdnica

The records of the 1332 investigation refer to the women, whose life and *mores* were put to test by the papal inquisitor, as *moniales Capuciatae* or simply *Capuciatae*.[38] It looks like *moniales Capuciatae* was a sort of

---

Schweidnitz in Silesia the inhabitants of a beguinage were shown to be followers of a fiercely ascetic life, with much flagellation, fasting and hard work, believers in their superiority, despite outward humility, and despising church attendance for which they were inclined to substitute their own prayers. Free Spirit beliefs in union with God did exist among them, but not libertinism, though they were accused of it.' See also A. Patschovsky, *Die Anfänge einer ständigen Inquisition in Böhmen. Ein Prager Inquisitoren-Handbuch aus der ersten Hälfte des 14. Jahrhunderts*, Beiträge zur Geschichte und Quellenkunde des Mittelalters 3 (Berlin and New York, 1975), pp. 74–8.

[35] Szymański, *Ruchy heretyckie*, pp. 77–118.

[36] Voigt, *Beginen im Spätmittelalter*, pp. 315–20

[37] See note 1 above.

[38] The term *moniales Capuciatae* was deliberately used during the 1332 investigation (*Examinatio testium*, pp. 178 and 180). It occurs twice in the introductory formula

The 1332 enquiry into the 'Cowled Nuns' of Świdnica

official name for this small religious community from Świdnica. This Latin phrase is not recorded in any sources related to the Beguines; however *capuciatae* does appear in its German form of 'Kapuzen' as a name of two Beguines from Erfurt (*Eychlindis dicta Kapuzen, soror Cunegundis dicta Kapuzen*).[39] The first part of the name (*moniales*) typically denoted nuns belonging to cloistered congregations.[40] In Latin texts related to Beguines, it was used interchangeably with *sanctimoniales, sorores* or *religiosae*.[41] The choice of the word 'nuns' (*moniales*) may indicate that the Beguines of Świdnica intentionally imitated the members of cloistered congregations.[42] The 1332 interrogations provide numerous statements implying a certain rivalry between the community of 'cowled nuns' and established religious convents. The former were convinced of the superiority of their model of religious life and claimed to be better than other sisters (I.V.1; II.III.1).[43] Fourteenth-century Świdnica had no nunnery, so the local 'cowled nuns' may have been regarded as regular nuns. This explains the origin of the name of Sisters' Street (*platea monialium*) where the Beguines still dwelt in the second half of the fourteenth century. Interestingly, this street adjoined Cowl Lane (*Keppingasse*) which had a Franciscan friary and the church of the

---

of the 1332 records and reappears in the depositions with reference to the Beguine community of Świdnica. In the second part of the 1332 investigation each of present members of the Świdnica community is named *Capuciata. Examinatio testium*, pp. 236, 238, 242, 244, and 246.

[39] Voigt, *Beginen im Spätmittelalter*, p. 128.

[40] D. Degler-Spengler, 'Die religiöse Frauenbewegung des Mittelalter: Konversen – Nonnen – Beginen', *Rottenburger Jahrbuch für Kirchengeschiche* 3 (1984), 75–88; B. Delmaire, 'Les béguines dans le Nord de France au première siècle de leur histoire (vers 1230–vers 1350)', in M. Parisse, ed., *Les religieuses en France au XIIIe siècle* (Nancy, 1989), pp. 121–62; C. Neel, 'The Origins of the Beguines', in J.M. Bonnet and E.A. Clark, ed., *Sisters and Workers in the Middle Ages*, (Chicago and London, 1989), pp. 321–41.

[41] E. Makowski, '*Mulieres Religiosae*, Strictly Speaking: Some Fourteenth-Century Canonical Opinions', *The Catholic Historical Review* 85 (1999), pp. 1–14; W. Simons, 'Beginnings: Naming Beguines in the Southern Low Countries, 1200–1250', in L. Böhringer, J. Kolpacoff Deane, H. van Engen, ed., *Labels and Libels. Naming Beguines in Northern Medieval Europe* (Turnhout, 2014), pp. 9–52.

[42] P. Kras, '*Moniales Capuciatae, filiae Udyllindis*: pochodzenie i organizacja świdnickiej wspólnoty "sióstr w kapturach"' (*Moniales Capuciatae, filiae Udylindis*: the Origins and Organisation of the Świdnica Community of the 'cowled nuns'), in Kras, Gałuszka and Poznański, *Proces beginek*, pp. 86–91.

[43] '(...) cum quereret ab eis in Wratislauia, si essent aliis sororibus meliores, responderunt, quod sic, quia haberent durissimam uitam et plus aliis perfectam' (When those in Wroclaw were asked [literally this is 'when s/he asked] if they were better than other sisters, they answered yes, because they led a very harsh life, and one more perfect than others); *Examinatio testium*, p. 224; 'sic attraxerunt eam dicentes, quod earum uita esset melior, quam aliarum sororum' (They attracted her in this way, saying that their life was better than that of other sisters). Ibidem, p. 242.

Blessed Virgin Mary.[44] In this case, the street name in German alludes to the characteristic hood worn as part of the Franciscan garment.

The members of the Świdnica community called themselves 'sisters' (*sorores*) and addressed one another in this way. For example, in her testimony recorded in the 1332 report, Adelaide recalled different activities performed by Heilwig of Prague, the superior of the community, in the service of other 'sisters' (I.II.17).[45] According to Catherine of Leipzig, the older women claimed that working at home would benefit other 'sisters' better than going to church or to sermons (I.III.11).[46] A similar opinion with respect to the Świdnica 'sisters' surfaces in the testimony of Margaret the Embroideress (I.IV.1).[47] In the German-speaking Beguine community, the Latin word *sorores* corresponded to the German 'Swestere' or 'Swestrionen', well known from other sources.[48] In the Beguine communities of the Rhine region, the concept of 'sister' had the same meaning as 'Beguines', and both words were used interchangeably.[49] At the turn of the thirteenth century, the Beguine group in the Rhine region began to shift gradually away from using the word "Beguine" and towards 'Swestere'. The growing aversion to and impatience with mendicant and itinerant groups of Beguines and Beghards among the ecclesiastical authorities led to pejorative associations with the term "Beguine" and cast a shadow of suspicion on the activities of other established and organised communities of lay women. For this reason, from the end of the thirteenth century, Beguines began to refer to themselves increasingly as 'sisters'".[50]

The other component of the term *moniales Capuciatae* refers to the specific garment worn by Beguines. The wide cowl or hood covering the head *(caputium)* became an inseparable element of their habit. Already in the first half of the thirteenth century, Beguines tried to distinguish themselves from the 'crowd' by wearing distinctive, cowled clothing similar to a religious habit. It was intended to emphasise the poverty and non-demanding lifestyle of women pursuing the *vita apostolica*. In addition to taking vows of poverty, chastity and obedience in front of the superior, admission to the community also involved the change of the 'ordinary' clothing for the garment of the Beguines. The German synodal statutes from the years

---

[44] M. Goliński, *Wokół socjotopografii późnośredniowiecznej Świdnicy* (On the Socio-Topography of Late Medieval Świdnica), I (Wrocław, 2000, = Acta Universitatis Wratislaviensis, 2203), p. 100.

[45] *Examinatio testium*, p. 196.

[46] Ibidem, p. 206.

[47] Ibidem, p. 210.

[48] W. Simons, *The Cities of Ladies*, pp. 112–14; idem, 'Beginnings: Naming Beguines', p. 48.

[49] J. Voigt, *Beginen im Spätmittelalter*, pp. 23–5.

[50] L. Böhringer, 'Kölner Beginen im Spätmittelalter – Leben zwischen Kloster und Welt', *Geschichte in Köln*, 53 (2006), Dezember, pp. 20–1.

The 1332 enquiry into the 'Cowled Nuns' of Świdnica

1307–10 provide some descriptions of the garment that made Beguines similar to cloistered nuns.[51] The Council of Vienne was devoted in part to discussion of appropriate religious dress, and the constitution *Cum de quibusdam mulieribus* stressed that Beguines could not be regarded as nuns even though they wore the so-called Beguine habit.[52]

Another name used to denote the sisters of Świdnica is more baffling. In the testimonies some members of this community thought of themselves as 'Udilind's Daughters' *(filiae Udilindis)*. Such term appears four times in the 1332 record (I.II.7; I.IV.28; I.VI.2; II.V.1).[53] Anne, one of the oldest sisters in the group, and Ludgard of Leipzig, one of the younger sisters, testified that they belonged to the 'association of Udilind's Daughters' (II.V.1; I.VI.2).[54] The latter spent almost two years in the similar Beguine houses in Erfurt and Leipzig before joining the Świdnica community. Her knowledge about Udilind was very vague and asked by the inquisitor about that figure she could say only that 'Udilind was a good sister who led the others towards God' (I.VI.2).[55] It can be inferred that if the Świdnica Beguines regarded themselves as 'Udilind's Daughters', 'Udilind' must have been a remarkable figure. Research carried out in 2015–17 made it possible to identify 'Udilind' with Odelind of Pyrzyce *(Odelindis dicta de Piritz)*, who in 1291 founded a new Beguine community in Cologne.[56] Her beguinage was housed in Marzellenstraße, not far from the Dominican priory. Odelind was the superior of a new group which stood out among the other, quite numerous Beguine communities in Cologne. The religious life of the community was governed by the principle of absolute poverty and resembled that of cloistered congregations.[57] These Beguines

---

[51] P. Fredericq, ed., *Corpus documentorum inquisitionis haereticae pravitatis Neederlandicae*, 5 vols. (Ghent, 1889–1906), I, 153–4; see also comments by Voigt, *Beginen im Spätmittelalter*, pp. 194–5.

[52] Tanner, ed., *Decrees*, I, 374.

[53] *Examinatio testium*, pp. 192, 220, 226 and 246.

[54] 'titulus earum est in unione filie Vdillindis'; a literal translation would give singular daughter rather than plural daughters, e.g. 'their title is "in the union of the daughter of Udilind"'; ibid., p. 246.

[55] 'quod Vdyllindem bene audiuit commendare, quod esset bona soror, et teneret alias ad Deum' (that she certainly heard her commend Udilind: because she was a good sister, and kept the others obedient to God); ibid., p. 226.

[56] P. Kras, 'Moniales Capuciatae', pp. 93–9. The identification of 'Udillind' with the Cologne mistress Odelind of Pyrzyce was possible thanks to Dr. Letha Böhringer who drew my attention to this intriguing figure and supplied me with source materials and literature related to the Beguine communities in Cologne.

[57] 'dicta Odelindis assumet sibi ad inhabitandum cum ipsa undecim begginas quas esse noverit caste vite, bone fame et conversacionis honeste, ipsa Odelinde duodecima et magistra dicte domus super dictas beginas existente et permanente' (the said Odelind will take to live with her eleven beguines whom she knows to be of chaste life, good repute and honest habits, the same Odelind being and remaining over the said beguines as the twelfth, and the mistress of the said house); G. M. Löhr, *Beiträge zur Geschichte des Kölner Dominikanerklosters Dominikanerklosters im*

called themselves 'sisters' (*Swesteren, Swestrisse, Swestriones*).[58] Odelind was a highly respected personality in her community, whose members referred to it as 'Lady Odelind's'.[59] The community was never suspected of heresy and was not exposed to any persecution after the provisions of the Council of Vienne came into effect. Thus, the 1332 testimonies of the 'cowled nuns' of Świdnica confirm the tremendous impact of the Cologne community of Odelind over other groups of German-speaking Beguines in the first quarter of the fourteenth century.[60]

The 'association of the Daughters of Odelind' to which the Świdnica house belonged, did not have a fixed rule, but merely certain rules of community life (*statuta*) that the older sisters taught to the younger members (I.II.7).[61] The community followed a relatively regular daily schedule which comprised the making of cloth, teaching/study, and mortification. The key role in the Świdnica community was held by the superior known as the mistress (*magistra*). Following the model of other Beguine groups in Flanders, Brabant and the Rhine region, the mistress of this Silesian community wielded total power over all the sisters.[62] She approved new candidates and accepted their vows of loyalty and obedience. The mistress controlled all the community's activities and instructed sisters on the rules of community life. Every Friday, she presided over a meeting called a 'chapter' (*capitulum*), during which the sisters knelt before her, confessed their sins and received a penalty of flogging. Only when the mistress had levied a penalty for transgression, were

---

Mittelalter, Quellen und Forschungen zur Geschichte des Dominikanerordens in Deutschland 15–17 (Leipzig, 1920–22), II, 51–2, no. 96.

[58] 'Et si dictam Odelindem decedere vel adeo debilem effici contigerit ita, quod sibi ipsi videtur quod ad magisterium non sufficiat, tunc alie sorores inibi existentes aliam magistram [this read 'magisram', surely a mistake] inter ipsas sibi constituent et assument quam ipsis noverint expedire. Et si concordare in constitucione talis magistre non poterint, tunc prior fratrum Predicatorum domus in Colonia qui pro tempore fuerit ipsas concordabit, eisdem inter ipsas unam magistram ... conferendo' (And if it should happen that the said Odelind should die or become so weak that it seems to her that she is not capable of exercising the mistressship, then the other sisters living there should appoint and admit another mistress from among themselves, who seems suitable to them. And if they cannot agree on the appointment of such a mistress, then the Prior of the house of the Brothers Preacher in Cologne, for the time being, will bring them to agreement, ... conferring on them a mistress from among themselves); ibid., II, 52.

[59] In the last will of Cunegund *de Nova Ianua* dated 7 March 1333 there is a donation of one pound to the community of 'Frau Oda', which can be safely identified with the Beguine house founded by Odelind of Pyrzyce. Ibidem, no. 359, p. 145. I owe this precious piece of information to Dr. Letha Böhringer.

[60] J. Asen, 'Die Beginen in Köln (Forsetzung)', *Annalen Historischen Vereins für den Niederrhein*, 112 (1928), 145–7.

[61] *Examinatio testium*, p. 192; see comments by Kras, '*Moniales Capuciatae*', pp. 104–5.

[62] W. Simons, *The Cities of Ladies*, pp. 50–60; idem, 'Beginnings: Naming Beguines', pp. 49–50.

The 1332 enquiry into the 'Cowled Nuns' of Świdnica

the sisters free to confess their sins to a parish priest (II.III.2).[63] The mistress also approved the sisters' contacts with the outside world (I.VI.5).[64] In the absence of the mistress, her deputy was charged with the responsibility of taking care of the community. During the 1332 trial, the mistress of the 'cowled nuns' from Świdnica was Heilwig of Prague and her deputy was Gertrude of Oleśnica.[65]

The Beguine community in Świdnica was established at least at the outset of the fourteenth century. The oldest of the sisters testifying in 1332, Gertrude of Świdnica, had belonged to the group for 28 years (I.II), i.e. since 1304.[66] Blind Anne had joined the Beguines about two years later (II.V).[67] Testimony also revealed the figure of a former community mistress, Geza, later replaced by Heilwig of Prague. Geza was probably the first superior of the Świdnica community, and only the oldest sisters had met her in person. The younger women knew her only from accounts.[68] The Beguine community of Świdnica came about in parallel or shortly after a similar group formed in Wrocław; the two communities maintained close contacts. The number of sisters in the Świdnica 'convent' was not fixed but, most probably, did not exceed twelve women.[69]

The 'cowled nuns' were not part of any established order nor did they have any written rule to obey. Regardless of that they developed a strong religious identity which made them believe that they were living a perfect Christian life, even better than that of the Friars Mendicant. The strictly organised life and tough discipline made the Świdnica beguinage similar to a regular convent. The Beguines wore distinct habits and referred to one another as

---

[63] 'Audiuit ab Anna ceca et a Gertrude de Olsna, quod Heilwig alias etiam esset magistra, sed Gertrudis de Olsna modo [tenet uices] loco Heilwig, que tenet eis capitulum sexta feria, in quo uerberat eas cum corrigiis, flectuntque genua coram magistra et dicunt culpam suam, tunc magistra parcit eis et tamen postea confitentur sacerdotibus' (She heard from blind Anna and from Gertrude of Oleśnica that Heilwig had also previously been mistress, but that Gertrude of Oleśnica is now [the deputy] in the place of Heilwig; she holds a chapter for them on Fridays, in which she flogs them with a scourge, they genuflect before the mistress and confess their sin, then the mistress forgives them, and yet they confess to priests afterwards); *Examinatio testium*, p. 242.

[64] 'ipsaque Cunegundis cum esset inter eas oportuit, si quandoque uoluit extra domum aliqua necessitate ire, licentiam accipere a magistra semperque metsecundam incedere' (when she was among them, if at any time the same Cunegund wished to go outside the house for some need, she was obliged to receive permission from the mistress and always to go with a companion); ibid., p. 226.

[65] Kras, '*Moniales Capuciatae*', pp. 104–5.

[66] *Examinatio testium*, p. 240.

[67] Ibid., p. 246.

[68] Ibid.

[69] Kras, '*Moniales Capuciatae*', p. 104. Similar Beguine communities were established in the towns of the Rhine region. They numbered 10–12 women who lived together in a single house; Böhringer, *Kölner Beginen*, p. 18.

sisters. Though there was no rule the Świdnica community developed its own system of values and power relations. It maintained a strict hierarchy by dividing the members into senior and junior sisters. The former, who resided in the community from a few to over twenty years, enjoyed a privileged position. They were served better food, drinks and clothing. In contrast to junior sisters the senior were not exposed to severe discipline and corporeal mortifications. On the contrary, in liaison with the mistress they administered the house, instructed the younger sisters on the principles of life in the community, and also decided and supervised various chores within the house.[70] As the 1332 interrogations reveal, only the older sisters realised that they were part of a more extensive organisational structure though they were rather unaware of its territorial reach.[71]

The junior sisters were subject to the authority of the mistress and senior sisters. Upon admission to the community they took vows of obedience and poverty in the presence of the mistress and were deprived of any personal belongings (I.V.5).[72] In the eyes of the older sisters, being admitted to their community was a great honour. Through partaking in community life, each woman was given a unique chance to 'cleanse her body and soul' (I.VII.3).[73] Mortification, flogging and fasts were intended to combat carnal desires and make the members perfect. According to some witnesses, the older sisters believed that younger members must be 'broken' by strict discipline, absolute obedience and total poverty (I.I.3).[74]

The ultimate pursuit of the sisters of Świdnica was spiritual perfection. To achieve such a condition, the soul had to be liberated from the control of the sinful body by stifling physical needs and desires. To this end, they undertook strict fasts and various mortifications; these were enforced especially among the younger sisters. Elizabeth of Strzegom, one of the younger sisters, who spent only eleven weeks among the 'cowled nuns', testified before the papal inquisitor that she had joined the community to be healed in her body

---

[70] Kras, 'Moniales Capuciatae', pp. 108–10.

[71] Szymański, Ruchy heretyckie, pp. 90–7; Kras, 'Moniales Capuciatae', pp. 102–3.

[72] 'Et quidquid proprii habent uenientes ad eas ab earum proprietate et possessione et potestate deponunt, recedentibus ab eis non reddunt. Unde sicut in potestate prioris uel Guardiani sunt res subditorum, ita est inter eas (And whatever they have of their own when they come to them, they remove it from their ownership and possession and power; and they do not return it when they leave them. So, just as the belongings of those subject to them are in the power of the Prior or Warden, so it is among them)'; Examinatio testium, p. 226; P. Kras, 'W poszukiwaniu duchowej doskonałości' (In Search of Spiritual Perfection), in Kras, Gałuszka, Poznański, Proces beginek, p. 122.

[73] Examinatio testium, p. 228.

[74] 'dixit eas obedientiam habere inter se, cum non sint alicuius ordinis approbati dicuntque ad subdictas sibi "Oportet uos flecti uel frangi"' (She said that they had obedience among themselves, since they are not of any approved order, and that they say to those subject to them 'You must be bent or broken'); ibid., p. 182.

The 1332 enquiry into the 'Cowled Nuns' of Świdnica

and soul. Contrary to her expectations she had been so much tortured by permanent fasting, vigils and other mortifications that her health was totally ruined and she lost her former beauty (I.VII.3).[75]

The state of perfection was expected to free souls from worldly compulsion and to promise sinlessness.[76] Adelaide, the second witness interrogated by John of Schwenkenfeld, in effect said that those who reached the state of perfection were free from any worldly obedience (I.II.28).[77] She also added that the 'cowled nuns' held the view that 'only the imperfect had to look after the acts of virtue; the perfect soul did not care for virtues any longer' (I.II.29).[78] This opinion was regarded as central to the spirituality of the Świdnica Beguines, and as such was repeated by other deponents.[79] Hedwig of Wrocław testified that the 'cowled nuns' believed that those who achieved the ultimate state of perfection and the freedom of spirit did not have to obey anyone (I.I.11).[80] This approach in the form recorded in the 1332 report resembles Article 3 of the constitution *Ad nostrum*.[81] In the

---

[75] 'extenuauerent eam ieiuniis, uigiliis ac aliis exerciciis tam irrationabiliter, quod cum prius esset puella speciosa, paruo tempore fuit in tantum destructa, quod uix nunquam recuperabit, nec de pane dando ei ad saturitatem et carnes nominatas per eas (They weakened her with fasting, vigils and other exercises so unreasonably, that although she was a beautiful girl before, in a short time she had been ruined to such an extent that she will hardly ever recover, even through giving her bread to the point of satiety and meats specified by her): *Gotirslagen fleyz* (carrion); ibid., p. 228.

[76] E. McLaughlin, 'The Heresy of the Free Spirit and Late Medieval Mysticism', *Medievalia Humanistica. Studies in Medieval and Early Renaissance Culture. New Series*, 4 (1973), pp. 42–53.

[77] 'iste, que sunt in perfectione, non sunt humane subiecte obediencie, et deffendunt offertoria et dicunt, quod transcenderunt omnem obedientiam; hee sunt, que ab eis ueniunt ad spiritum libertatis' (these women, who are in a state of perfection, are not subject to human obedience, and they forbid offerings and say that they have transcended all obedience; these are [the ones] who from them come to the spirit of liberty); *Examinatio testium*, p. 200.

[78] 'Capuciate dicunt, quod se exercere in actibus uirtutis est hominis imperfecti, perfecta autem anima licenciat a se omnes uirtutes' (The hooded [sisters] say that practising acts of virtue is for imperfect people, but the perfected soul dismisses from itself all virtues); ibid., p. 200.

[79] Kras, 'W poszukiwaniu duchowej doskonałości', pp. 115–18.

[80] 'Audiuit etiam ab ipsis quod dixerunt: homo hic tantum posset profici, quod esset perfectus, et ille, que sunt in tali statu perfectionis et spiritu libertatis non tenentur alicui obedire' (She also heard from them that they said: here [in this world] a man could be improved so much that he became perfected, and they, who are in such a state of perfection and spirit of liberty are not obliged to obey anyone); *Examinatio testium*, pp. 184–5.

[81] 'quod illi, qui sunt in praedicto gradu perfectionis et spiritu libertatis, non sunt humanae subiecti oboedientiae, nec aliqua praecepta ecclesiae obligantur' (that those who have reached the said degree of perfection and spirit of liberty, are not subject to human obedience nor obliged to any commandments of the Church); Tanner, ed., *Decrees*, I, 383.

view of some testifying sisters, this sense of sinlessness would lead to promiscuity and conduct contrary to Christian moral standards. For example, Adelaide testifying as the second witness spoke extensively about abominable sexual practices between the older sisters and visiting Beghards. In her view, the sisters were convinced of their sinlessness, and kissed the Beghards and allowed them to touch their private parts (I.II.10).[82] Adelaide's account of the indecent conduct of the older sisters was corroborated only by Margaret the Embroideress (I.IV.30).[83] At this point Robert Lerner has noted that in both cases the testimonies came from younger sisters who had not witnessed the scandalous conduct of their elders, and only possessed second-hand information.[84] Their suspicions about the nature of the reunions between other sisters and Beghards can be explained by the fact that none of them had actually participated in those meetings. Adelaide even recalled that she had once been forced to leave such a meeting (I.II.11).[85] Presumably, the imagination of Adelaide, a woman whose deposition suggests someone with mental problems, fuelled her suspicions about the perverse relations between the Beguines and Beghards, which the papal inquisitor explored eagerly.

The 'cowled nuns' believed that by means of hard work, intensive fasting and flagellation they might restrain the sinful desires of their bodies and achieve a status of spiritual perfection. They held the view that such perfection could be attained regardless of traditional forms of piety and without the ministry of the clergy. Though they attended masses on Sundays and other feast days, and went to Easter confession in the parish church, they found such practices of little significance.[86] One of the younger sisters was told by the older members that although she had spent much time in church,

---

[82] 'eademque iurata dicit, quod inter tales Beghardos et huiusmodi mulieres portantes imaginem sanctitatis maxime et artissime paupertatis committuntur opportunitate nacta quasi omnia genera peccatorum sodomiticorum et inmundiciarum, hec dicit de certa sciencia, quia audivit ab illa, cui talia acciderunt, et etiam de certo ab aliis est experta, quod abutuntur se mutuo lateraliter et in anum tangentes se mutuo inpudice et lingwas suas in ora sua ad inuicem pre delectacione mittentes' (the same woman says, on oath, that between such Beghards and these women bearing the image of the greatest holiness and strictest poverty are committed, as the opportunity arises, almost all kinds of sins, sodomies and filthinesses. She says this from certain knowledge, because she heard it from her to whom such things happened; and she has also learned for certain from others that they abuse one another mutually, touching one another from the side and on the anus in an unchaste manner, and putting their tongues in one another's mouths for pleasure); *Examinatio testium*, p. 194.

[83] Ibid., p. 222.

[84] Lerner, *The Heresy of the Free Spirit*, p. 117.

[85] *Examinatio testium*, p. 194.

[86] Kras, 'W poszukiwaniu duchowej doskonałości', p. 120.

The 1332 enquiry into the 'Cowled Nuns' of Świdnica

she attained no perfection (I.II.2).[87] These and similar words of criticism probably referred to the earlier status of Adelaide who had spent a part of her life as a recluse. Prayer in church was considered to be contrary to the model of life followed in the Świdnica house and working for the benefit of the entire community. By their standards, ultimate poverty, hard work and mortification were of superior value. In other words, it would have been better to stay at home during holiday periods and work for the community than go to church.[88] Such an attitude was commonplace among the older sisters who avoided going to church and forced the younger ones to work on holidays. Hedwig of Wrocław said that the sisters had worked on Sundays and Church holidays in their house, and they had found such work good (I.I.2).[89] Another former member of the Świdnica community, Adelaide, confirmed Hedwig's words. She also added that one of the sisters acted as a guardian who kept their work secret from anyone from outside (I.II.2).[90] Work was of a utilitarian nature and secured upkeep for the whole community as well as helping the spiritual growth and attainment of perfection of the sisters. The older sisters argued that by not shying away from hard work they followed the Virgin Mary who 'cleaned the temple and performed a variety of menial activities' as a child. As follows from the testimony of Catherine of Leipzig, they believed that 'if she had not done that, she would not have become the mother of Christ' (I.3.18).[91]

---

[87] 'Et cum super hoc reprehenderentur per ipsam Adylheydim, utpote quia contra ordinationem facerent ecclesie, stumachando responderunt "Miramur multum, quod ecclesia est ydolum tuum effectum, et quod tot annis non meruisti aput Deum, quod haberes esse perfectam, ut sederes domi et operareris opera caritatis"' (And when they were rebuked about this by the same Adelaide, because they acted against the ordinance of the church, they replied, angrily, 'We are greatly amazed that the church has become your idol, and that for so many years you have not found merit with God to manage to become perfect, when you sat at home and performed works of charity'); *Examinatio testium*, p. 188.

[88] Ibid., pp. 186 and 196.

[89] 'isto anno feria quarta in ebdomada Penthecestes incluse in earum cameris laborauerunt, in diebus quoque dominicis disp[onunt] lanas suas ad operandum per ebdomadam et in diebus apostolorum suerunt post prandium et hoc dicunt esse bona opera' (this year on the Wednesday in the week of Pentecost they worked enclosed in their chambers, and also on Sundays they set out their wools for working during the week, and they sewed on the days of the apostles after lunch: and they say that this is good works); ibid., p. 180.

[90] 'quod est communis modus inter seniores earum, quod diebus dominicis et festiuis operantur opera similia nerendo, suendo et alia opera similia faciendo, incluse tamen et custodem ponendo, ut si quis uenerit et pro eis sciscitatus fuerit, respondeant eas esse in ecclesia uel alibi' (that it is the common custom among their seniors to work similar works on Sundays and holidays, spinning, sewing and doing other similar works – but enclosed and posting a guard, so that if anyone should come and ask for them, she might reply that they were in church or elsewhere); ibid., p. 188.

[91] 'si hoc non fecisset, nunquam mater Christi effecta fuisset'; ibid., p. 208.

Paweł Kras

John of Schwenkenfeld and his 1332 investigation

The controversial doctrine and quasi-monastic life of the 'cowled nuns' alerted the Church seniors of the diocese of Wrocław. Some opinions held by the Świdnica sisters resembled the doctrine of the Free Spirit which had been described and condemned by the Council of Vienne. The view that spiritual perfection might be attained by virtue of his or someone's own efforts and outside the ministry of the clergy sounded identical to the key element of the Free Spirit doctrine listed in the constitution *Ad nostrum*. The nuanced treatment of Church sacraments and reserve towards traditional forms of lay piety might have also cast a shadow of suspicion on the Świdnica Beguines. The circumstances of the 1332 investigation carried out by John of Schwenkenfeld remain unknown. It is hard to determine why it was launched in that year and what was the direct impulse behind Schwenkenfeld's enquiry. Neither the 1332 records nor other documents mentioned any inquisitorial operations related to the Świdnica Beguines before 1332. It may look odd that a quasi-monastic community of lay women, living at the heart of a busy Silesian town and violating the provisions of the Council of Vienne, was tolerated by the ecclesiastical authorities for so long. Probably, the long vacancy of the Wrocław See after the death of Bishop Henry of Wierzbna in 1319 and the subsequent conflict between his successor, Bishop Nanker, and the Wrocław Cathedral Chapter obstructed the enforcement of the anti-Beguine legislation of the Council of Vienne and delayed investigation into the life of Beguine communities such as that of the 'cowled nuns' of Świdnica.[92]

The 1332 records document the opening part of the inquisitorial investigation into the life and *mores* of the Świdnica Beguines. The trial was held before a specially appointed tribunal headed by the papal inquisitor John of Schwenkenfeld. It was composed of nine other members including Henry Schammonis, the parish priest from Mościsko, Arnold, the rector of the leper-house in the suburbs of Świdnica, and three Dominicans and three Franciscans (among them the lector Peter Swarczmann) from local friaries.[93] During the opening phase of the trial, between 7 and 11 September 1332, eleven women, most of them former Beguines from Świdnica and Wrocław, were interrogated. They testified as witnesses speaking freely about their experiences concerning the 'cowled nuns'. In the first part of the proceedings, eight women testified: Hedwig of Wrocław, Adelaide the former recluse, Catherine of Leipzig, Margaret the Embroideress, Cunegund of Ziębice, Ludgard of Leipzig, Elizabeth of Strzegom and Iliana. On the first day, 7 September, two

---

[92] See above.

[93] *Examinatio testium*, pp. 179–81; for the identification of the court members see P. Kras, 'Przesłuchania w sprawie beginek świdnickich i ich dokumentacja' (The Inquisition of the Beguines of Świdnica and the Interrogation Records), in Kras, Gałuszka and Poznański, *Proces beginek*, pp. 71–2.

The 1332 enquiry into the 'Cowled Nuns' of Świdnica

women were questioned: Hedwig of Wrocław and Adelaide. On 8 September, the feast of the Nativity of the Blessed Virgin Mary, two other women were interrogated: Catherine of Leipzig and Margaret the Embroideress. On the third day of the trial, 9 September, four women testified: Cunegund of Ziębice, Ludgard of Leipzig, Elizabeth of Strzegom and Iliana, as was noted by the notary after writing down the oath of the eighth witness, Iliana. After a one-day break on 10 September, the inquisition tribunal resumed the proceedings and interrogated three other women on 11 September: Margaret of Środa Śląska, Elizabeth of Ząbkowice and Gertrude of Mościsko.[94]

In the second part of the trial, on 11 and 12 September, testimonies were collected only from members of the 'cowled nuns' community.[95] The opening formula contained in the records underlined the different status of the women interrogated as *moniales Capuciatae*. It reveals that nine women were summoned before the tribunal. However, the record of the enquiry contains only five testimonies. It remains unknown what happened to the other four sisters who apparently did not appear before the inquisitorial court. Among these were Gertrude of Oleśnica, who acted as locum for Heilwig of Prague, mistress of the Świdnica community, and three other senior sisters.[96] The notary failed to give any explanation of the absence of their testimonies.

The questionnaire employed during the interrogations by John of Schwenkenfeld revolved around several key issues. They were intended to determine how the Beguine community operated and whether their activities had anything to do with heresy or violation of ecclesiastical laws. The Dominican inquisitor attempted to learn the circumstances surrounding the admission of each of the present and former sisters to the community. He was interested in the ceremony of initiation of new members: the procedure and text of the oath they swore. Almost all of the questioned women were asked about their status and the position of the 'cowled nuns' in the structure of the Church. John of Schwenkenfeld inquired extensively about the mistress, her authority and role in the administration of the community.[97] He was very inquisitive about sisters' religious life, their views on the Church, attitude to religious practices and participation in parish life. Particularly interesting are the statements of the older sisters on theological matters, often referred to by the younger women. As a well-educated theologian the inquisitor easily picked out any controversies and tried to get to their gist and origin.[98] The

---

[94] *Examinatio testium*, pp. 180–237.

[95] Ibid., pp. 236–49.

[96] Ibid., p. 236.

[97] A thorough analysis of the inquisitorial procedure is offered by Kras, 'Przesłuchania', pp. 72–82.

[98] Three important theological statements discussed by the Świdnica Beguines and reported during the 1332 interrogations were related to Christ's Incarnation, the double nature of Christ and the problem whether Christ took His cross to Heaven;

Paweł Kras

interrogatorium also contained questions about physical labour performed by the women on Sundays and Church holidays. The papal inquisitor kept asking why the sisters had worked on prohibited days. He was also interested in the management of their common property. During the questioning John of Schwenkenfeld did not rely exclusively on the ready-made questionnaire, but was eager to ask additional questions to explore some areas of his own interest. The 1332 records demonstrate that the Dominican inquisitor fully controlled the course of the interrogation and skilfully framed his questions to elicit new information.[99] Only in the case of the older sisters, Gertrude of Świdnica and Blind Anne, did his attempts to obtain additional explanation of disputable theological statements prove to be in vain.[100]

The records of the inquisition on the life and *mores* of the 'cowled nuns' offer a revealing insight into both the inquisitor's modus operandi and the procedure of producing inquisitorial records. During subsequent interrogations, the Dominican inquisitor relied on the draft record of previously submitted testimonies, as the notary recorded properly in the report. The women's statements were written down immediately and numbered. Each statement consisted of several, or more than a dozen or even several dozen paragraphs, each of which closed with the answer to the inquisitor's questions. Such an arrangement of the written material facilitated references to previous statements and allowed the inquisitor to quote any passage he desired during subsequent interrogations. Sometimes Schwenkenfeld quoted a statement and awaited the woman's answer; at the same time, the notary noted down which testimony the statement came from. For example, in the records of the second testimony of Adelaide, in paragraph 20, the notary recorded that 'where flogging is concerned, she, on oath and interrogated, speaks like Hedwig' (I.II.20).[101] On the other hand, Catherine of Leipzig, who testified third, was confronted with the testimony of the two women who had made statements before her, Hedwig and Adelaide. In item 6 of her testimony, the notary noted that 'like Adelaide' (*ut Adylheydis*), they say that she heard repeatedly how *Capuciatae* said "If it was permitted for us to preach, we would know better than many priests or doctors, because they see [what is written] on cows' skins, but we see from the inside"' (I.III.6).[102] And in item 9 concerning the lessons taught to the junior sisters, the notary noted that

---

T. Gałuszka, 'Jan ze Schwenkenfeldu', in Kras, Gałuszka and Poznański, *Proces beginek*, pp. 122–41.

[99] On the dominant role of the inquisitor during the heresy trial, see J.H. Arnold, *Inquisition and Power. Catharism and the Confessing Subject in Medieval Languedoc* (Philadelphia, 2001), pp. 74–115.

[100] Kras, 'Przesłuchania', pp. 76–8.

[101] 'De flagellis uero dicit iurata et interrogata, ut Hedwigis'; *Examinatio testium*, pp. 198.

[102] 'Item Katherina iurata et interrogata dicit, ut Adylheydis, se multociens audisse, quod Capuciate dixerunt "Si fas esset nos predicare, melius sciremus, quam multi

The 1332 enquiry into the 'Cowled Nuns' of Świdnica

she had spoken like the other two sisters, Hedwig and Adelaide (I.III.9).[103] Another time, the notary, perhaps to save some space, only noted which items in the testimony the inquisitor referred to in his questioning. In the testimony of Margaret interrogated on 8 September as the fourth witness, the notary failed to write down the questions referring to Adelaide's statements but provided those items of her testimony to which the questions alluded (I.IV.23–25). Under item 23, Margaret was asked about Adelaide's statement recorded in her testimony as item 3 (*super articulo IIIo per Adylheydim confesso*). As preserved in the record her statement is an almost verbatim reiteration of Adelaide's testimony.[104] When asked in item 24 about Adelaide's statement recorded in item 4 of her testimony, Margaret said that 'it is entirely true' (*totus sit verus*). Still she added information about some recommendations given to the younger sisters by the older ones in which they argued that the failing in the obligation to attend mass was not a matter that required confession (I.IV.24).[105]

The questions asked by Schwenkenfeld and the rendering of the depositions say a lot about the way the Dominican inquisitor perceived the doctrine of the Free Spirit. As a trained theologian and an experienced Dominican friar, he did not doubt the existence of the Free Spirit sect. Schwenkenfeld knew which ideas formed its doctrine, and how they were disseminated among Beguines and Beghards. As an inquisitor his task was to prove that the 'cowled nuns' of Świdnica were exponents of the Free Spirit heresy. The 1332 inquisition report reveals that he worked hard to gather information and put together distorted pieces of evidence to demonstrate that the community of Świdnica Beguines was a hotbed of heresy. His knowledge about the Beguines and the Free Spirit heresy rested first of all on the constitutions of the Council of Vienne. Schwenkenfeld was a diligent reader of *Ad nostrum* and extensively used the list of eight articles ascribed to the Free Spirit during his interrogations.[106] Having the text of *Ad nostrum* right on his table, he frequently quoted extracts from this document and expected deponents to comment on them. Sometimes, being aware of the complex theological discourse of *Ad nostrum* Schwenkenfeld rendered some articles in a simpler form. Frequently he asked leading questions and suggested possible links between the condemned tenets of the Free Spirit doctrine and particular beliefs of the Świdnica Beguines. The notary Nicholas omitted most of these

---

 sacerdotes uel doctores, quia ipsi uident in cutibus faccarum, sed nos uidemus ab intus"'; ibid., p. 204.

[103] Ibid., p. 206.

[104] Ibid., p. 218.

[105] Ibid.

[106] 'the Dominican Inquisitor wanted to show that the women were exponents of errors condemned by the pope and therefore confronted them with the decree *Ad nostrum*. But the notary only occasionally indicated this fact'; Kras, 'W poszukiwaniu duchowej doskonałości', p. 116, translated.

Paweł Kras

questions, but recording the depositions sometimes he made references to particular articles of *Ad nostrum*, as is well demonstrated by the testimony of Margaret the Embroideress (I.IV. 11, 16, 18).[107]

To get to the 'truth' about the doctrine of the 'cowled nuns' John of Schwenkenfeld used various techniques of interrogation. He found it much easier to elicit information from former sisters who were disappointed with their life in the community. Embittered and disillusioned with their past experience, the former sisters spoke openly and willingly about their suffering and humiliation. They also provided most details about the controversial views and suspicious behaviour of the Świdnica Beguines. The Dominican inquisitor exploited their willingness to cooperate and asked them a number of questions related to the beliefs and religious life of the 'cowled nuns'. The most detailed testimonies come from Margaret the Embroideress and Adelaide. The former spent a little more than half a year in the Świdnica community, the latter less than a year.[108] Though their experience among the Świdnica community was relatively short, they provided lengthy answers to the inquisitor's questions and offered unique information about the religious ideas and everyday life of the Świdnica community. The recorded testimony of Margaret is the longest and contains forty-one articles.[109] The testimony of Adelaide is a bit shorter and contains thirty-four articles.[110]

As noted above, the recorded testimonies consistently lack the inquisitor's questions. The notary left some only in a few places of his report. Four of them are found in the record of the testimony of Gertrude of Świdnica, one of the older sisters, who, apparently, attempted to dodge the inquisitor's probing questions.[111] Her statements were vague and evasive; probably for this reason the notary decided also to note down Schwenkenfeld's questions. Some more questions were recorded within the testimony of Margaret the Embroideress. The questions were rather 'technical', exposing the method of interrogation, during which the inquisitor referred to the constitutions *Ad nostrum* and *Cum de quibusdam mulieribus*.[112]

---

[107] 'Item iurata, utrum assererent secundum articulum, qui ponitur in *Clementinis*, uel aliquid ei simile de hereticis, *Ad nostrum*, dixit se non audiuisse ab eis ita expresse uerba illa, sicut in illo articulo continentur, sed similia uerba et appropinquancia huic sensui audiuit, ut dixit' (Item, on oath, whether they affirmed the article which is put in the *Clementines*, or anything similar to it concerning heretics, in *Ad nostrum*, she said that she had not heard those precise words from them, as contained in that article, but she heard similar words and ones approximating to this sense, as she says); *Examinatio testium*, p. 214. For further comment, see Kras, 'Przesłuchania', pp. 79–81.

[108] *Examinatio testium*, p. 188.

[109] Ibid., pp. 210–55.

[110] Ibid., pp. 188–203.

[111] Ibid., p. 240.

[112] Ibid., pp. 214–19.

The 1332 enquiry into the 'Cowled Nuns' of Świdnica

The statements of the women written down by the notary Nicholas *de Pencwynsdorph* have reached our time in a distorted form as a result of a process of several layers – copying, translating and editing. Recent studies of the structure and language of the inquisitorial records have highlighted that they 'fail to provide the "authentic voices"' of the interrogated individuals, but only statements recorded in a specific inquisitional discourse and heavily cropped and manipulated in the course of further processing. Yet, the interrogation reports on the life and *mores* of the Świdnica Beguines do not entirely support this view. Most statements in the 1332 records contain the third-person singular characteristic of such documentation (*dicit, dixit, respondit, scit, subiunxit, audivit* etc.), and any quoted words are usually given in reported speech, However, there are also many statements by the women that were recorded in direct speech – for example, 'Katherine said that they say, "Our prayers are worthier than those of priests"'. The reader is left with the impression that these statements really were made before the inquisitional tribunal. It seems that the inquisitor or notary wished to obtain as faithful a record of some of the statements as possible.

Conclusion

The records of the 1332 interrogation of the 'cowled nuns' of Świdnica offer a unique insight into the life of a small religious community which was part of the broader network of German-speaking Beguines. The statements of the women interrogated by the papal inquisitor John of Schwenkenfeld and recorded in the Latin register provide a multi-faceted picture of the piety and organisation of this group. While analysing the records, there are three different 'voices' to be considered. The former members of the community, generally younger sisters, recalled their stay among the 'cowled nuns' as a period of mental and physical anguish. They expressed their resentment and anger towards the older sisters who resorted to violent methods to accommodate them to life in the Świdnica community. Neither did they embrace the ideals of community spirituality nor did they comprehend the purpose of severe discipline inflicted by senior sisters. These women openly spoke to the inquisitor about their past experience and provided him with the most detailed accounts about the life of the Świdnica group, though the most shocking details came second-hand and frequently they were based on hearsay.

Another, much weaker 'voice' is that of the older sisters who, along with the mistress, administered the Świdnica community and inducted the younger members into the rules of community life. Only two older sisters – Gertrude of Świdnica and Blind Anne – faced the inquisitorial tribunal and were interrogated by John of Schwenkenfeld. In contrast to the younger sisters, Gertrude and Anne were unwilling to share confidences with the inquisitor and attempted to conceal details of the community life. They were aware that their group was not approved by the ecclesiastical authorities, but still they claimed that it was good. Their 'voice' reflects the views of older sisters who believed their community was living the pious life which would bring salvation to all its members. The two older sisters felt disturbed by the inquisitorial trial and intimidated by the accusations of the former members of their community. Only Gertrude was confident enough to engage in a dispute with the inquisitor and attempt to put straight some controversial opinions attributed to her during the interrogations.

The third 'voice' surfacing in the 1332 records is that of the papal inquisitor John of Schwenkenfeld who conducted the interrogations and, subsequently, together with the assisting notary, drew up the Latin documentation of the testimonies. As an experienced religious and a theologian he perceived the 'cowled nuns' as a community whose activity violated ecclesiastical laws and verged on heresy. The Dominican inquisitor was convinced that the Świdnica Beguines, in particular the older sisters, adhered to some views of the heretical doctrine of the Free Spirit, condemned by the Council of Vienne in 1312. In September 1332 he carried out the interrogations to prove this assumption. Schwenkenfeld was much puzzled by the religiosity of the Świdnica Beguines. Curious about and attentive to detail, he had his notary write down all the intriguing statements of the women who were testifying.

The voice of the papal inquisitor seems to prevail in the written record, even though most of his questions were not written down in the 1332 records. The women's statements, often recorded in reported speech, reveal many facts about the views and mentality of the younger sisters, most of whom were no longer with the Świdnica Beguines at the time of their interrogation. Many of these statements seem to be 'authentic voices'[113] that were translated faithfully from German into Latin and consigned to the notarial document. Unfortunately, we learn the least from the older sisters who, because of their age and long period of seniority in the community, had the most extensive knowledge about the life of the *moniales Capuciatae*. Their refusal to talk during the questioning can be regarded as a 'silent cry of despair' in the face of the dissolution of the community in which they had spent more than twenty years.

---

[113] On the 'voices' recorded within the inquisitorial records, see J.H. Arnold, 'The Historian as Inquisitor: The Ethics of Interrogating Subaltern Voices', *Rethinking History. The Journal of Theory and Practice* 2 (1998), 379–86; idem, *Inquisition and Power*, pp. 164–226.

5

Late medieval heresiography and the categorisation of Eastern Christianity

Irene Bueno

Only rarely do medieval anti-heresy writings contain discussions about Christian communities in the East. Greeks, Armenians, Jacobites, Georgians or Nubians are usually absent from Western anti-heresy treatises, even when these are concerned with the Oriental sects from late antiquity drawn from Augustine and their subsequent updates. Indeed, the pragmatic concern to defeat those sects which seemed to be threats to the Latin West was the obvious mission inspiring the authors of most anti-heretical polemic.[1]

Yet we do have a few treatises, directed against a great variety of errors, which also contain refutations of the errors of various Eastern Christian groups. The mid-thirteenth century *Tractatus fidei contra diversos errores* (*Treatise of faith against various errors*) by Benedict of Alignan, for example, engages with the errors of Greeks and Armenians, while also including discussions of Muslim beliefs and Jewish practices.[2] Similarly, various anti-heresy treatises compiled in the fourteenth century include lists of errors of the Eastern Christians: they comprise Guido Terreni's *Summa de haeresibus et earum confutationibus* (*Summa of Heresies and their Refutations*), Alvarus Pelagius's *Collyrium fidei contra haereses* (*Eye-salve of Faith against Heresies*) and the renowned *Directorium inquisitorum* (*Directive for Inquisitors*) by the Dominican inquisitor Nicholas Eymerich. The two latter works include rebuttals of the

---

[1] A list of anti-heresy polemics is given in *Heresies of the High Middle Ages*, ed. W. L. Wakefield and A. P. Evans (New York, 1969), pp. 633–8. On these sources see also L. J. Sackville, *Heresy and Heretics in the Thirteenth Century. The Textual Representations*, Heresy and Inquisition in the Middle Ages 1 (York, 2011), pp. 190–200, especially pp. 13–40.

[2] On this work, see especially J. H. Arnold, 'Benedict of Alignan's *Tractatus fidei contra diversos errores*: A Neglected Anti-Heresy Treatise', *Journal of Medieval History* 45 (2019), 20–54. I am grateful to the author for sharing with me the manuscript before publication along with related materials. For a discussion of Benedict's account of Eastern Christians, see J. Rubin, 'Benoit d'Alignan and Thomas Agni: Two Western Intellectuals and the Study of Oriental Christianity in Thirteenth-Century Kingdom of Jerusalem', *Viator* 44 (2013), 189–200.

Greeks only, whereas Guido's *Summa* contains lengthy descriptions and refutations of the errors of Greeks, Armenians, Georgians and Jacobites, with a special focus on the Greeks and Armenians.[3] In addition, Guido engages in polemical argumentation against the doctrines and practices of the Jews, while one copy of the *Summa*[4] contains a further fragment referring to twenty-five *errores Sarracenorum*, whose attribution to the same author has however been disputed.[5]

How did Eastern Christians' errors fit into anti-heresy treatises? And what do discussions about these groups reveal about learned approaches to heresy in the later Middle Ages? This essay focuses on what Guido Terreni and Alvarus Pelagius had to say against heresy in two comprehensive *summae* that were produced in the intellectual milieu of the Avignon court. I shall consider these treatises and look comparatively at the treatises by Benedict of Alignan and Nicholas Eymerich, in order to examine the place occupied by Eastern Christianity in the construction of a universal knowledge of heresy in the later Middle Ages. I shall first of all try to illustrate the continuity of arguments and methods employed against Eastern Christians in Western anti-heresy writings, pointing to the blurred distinction between the medieval notions of heresy and schism. The convergence established between Christian errors in every space and time surfaces in the aim and structure of these texts, in their lexical choices and in the production of textual aids, such as comparative indexes and internal cross-references. These considerations will shed new light on the role of the papal court of Avignon as a key intellectual hub fostering universalistic approaches to the systematisation of knowledge. Finally, I shall also look at the long-term reception of medieval discussions of Eastern Christianity. Far from marking a clear-cut distinction with the past, Counter-Reformation polemicists rest upon the shoulders of medieval heresiology.

---

[3] I rely on the following editions: Guido Terreni, *Summa de haeresibus et earum confutationibus* (Paris, 1528), fols. 19r–42v; Alvarus Pelagius, *Colírio da fé contra as heresias*, ed. Miguel Pinto de Meneses, 2 vols. (Lisbon, 1954–6), II, 80–189; and Nicholas Eymerich, *Directorium inquisitorum*, ed. F. Peña (Rome, 1587), pp. 303–4.

[4] Vatican City, Vatican Library, MS Vat. lat. 988, fols. 9v–69v. On the Jews see Terreni, *Summa*, fols. 11r–19r.

[5] On this problematic attribution, see C. Ferrero-Hernández, 'Los 25 errores de los musulmanes, segun el ms. Vat. lat. 988. Notas sobre su atribucion a Guido Terrena', in *Guido Terreni, O. Carm. († 1342): Studies and Texts*, ed. A. Fidora, Textes et études du Moyen Âge 78 (Barcelona and Madrid, 2015), pp. 269–80. See also J. Tolan, 'Guido Terrena de Perpignan', in *Christian-Muslim Relations. A Bibliographical History*, ed. D. Thomas (Leiden, 2009–), IV, 928–31.

Late medieval heresiography and the categorisation of Eastern Christianity

Anti-heresy writing and the reception of Greeks and Armenians

Despite their differences, the chief anti-heresy works by Guido Terreni and Alvarus Pelagius are the product of similar intellectual environments and they share common ambitions and textual features. Both authors had personal links and profound intellectual connections with the papal court of Avignon, and both took part in various theological discussions leading to new delimitations of the bounds of orthodoxy. Moreover, their textual outputs fit into a wider 'encyclopedic' attitude, which seems to have flourished in the atmosphere of the curia at Avignon.

As a prominent advisor to John XXII, Guido repeatedly offered the pope his theological counsel, taking part in crucial debates of the time regarding burning issues such as evangelical poverty and papal infallibility, and evaluating the works of William of Ockham, Peter John Olivi and Marsilius of Padua.[6] The Carmelite compiled the *Summa de haeresibus* at the end of his life whilst in Avignon (*c.* 1338–42), addressing it to Cardinal Pierre Roger, future pope Clement VI. His anti-heresy commitment was not only the outcome of his theological background, which followed his education in Paris and culminated in his distinguished role at the papal court. It also manifested itself in the inquisitorial campaigns he had conducted when bishop of Majorca and Elne, which demonstrates how intimate the relation was between judicial and intellectual anti-heresy endeavours.

Close individual connections with the papal court were also at the core of Alvarus Pelagius's own trajectory. A Franciscan from Galicia, he spent a long time in Italy, most notably in Bologna, where he studied law. Then, in 1329, he was appointed papal penitentiary by John XXII. Later on the pope nominated him bishop of Coron, Morea (1332), and then of Silves, Portugal (1333). From the late 1320s onwards, the Franciscan canonist repeatedly took the floor as an advocate of papal positions in the current controversies regarding matters like the *plenitudo potestatis* (plenitude of power) of the pope, the relation between temporal and spiritual power, and the ownership

---

[6] The bibliography on these matters includes B. Xiberta, *Guiu Terrena. Carmelita de Perpinyà* (Barcelona, 1932); idem, *Guidonis Terreni quaestio de magisterio infallibili Romani pontificis* (Münster, 1926); Guiu Terrena, *Confutatio errorum quorundam magistrorum*, ed. A. Fidora (Santa Coloma de Queralt, 2014); T. Turley, 'Infallibilists in the Curia of Pope John XXII', *Journal of Medieval History* 1 (1975), 71–101; B. Tierney, *Origins of Papal Infallibility 1150–1350: A Study on the Concepts of Infallibility, Sovereignty and Tradition in the Middle Ages* (Leiden, 1988), pp. 238–72; T. Shogimen, 'William of Ockham and Guido Terreni', *History of Political Thought* 19/4 (1998), 517–30; T. Turley, 'The Impact of Marsilius: Papalist Responses to the *Defensor Pacis*', in *The World of Marsilius of Padua*, ed. G. Moreno-Riaño (Turnhout, 2006), pp. 47–64; J. Meirinhos, 'Alvarus Pelagius and Guiu Terrena against Marsilius of Padua on the *temporalia Ecclesiae*', in *Guido Terreni*, ed. Fidora, pp. 153–85.

Irene Bueno

of temporal goods by the Church, engaging – just like Guido – in various refutations of Marsilius of Padua.[7]

Although completed in Spain after 1344, the *Collyrium fidei contra haereses* can be ascribed to Alvarus's activity in the pontifical milieu. The work is directed 'against new and old heresies and errors, which sprout in some parts of Spain and elsewhere to the detriment, danger, and damage of the faith and the faithful'.[8] As a true physician of souls, the author claims to be willing to cleanse the infidels' eyes, blinded by the devil, by providing them with the appropriate medicament.[9] The resulting treatise thus addresses a large number of errors and heresies, discussing them from the perspective of an eminent canon lawyer and counsellor to the pope. It is organised into six parts focusing, respectively, on the following: various errors against the notion of papal primacy; Augustine's sects, examined via Gratian; another seventeen heresies derived from Gratian; a series of propositions taken from the collections of decretals; various recent heresies, including those of Marsilius of Padua and Thomas Scoto; and, finally, forty-one errors of the Greeks. While Augustine is an essential point of reference, Alvarus's aim of comprehensiveness impels him to dig into legal sources and commentaries in search of further information on more recent heresies, with a special focus on the contexts he was more familiar with: Italy, Iberia and the papal court. Rather than a systematic treatise, the resulting text offers accurate lists of biblical, patristic and – most importantly – canon-legal references for each error.

Similarly, Guido Terreni's *Summa de haeresibus* is conceived as a monumental treatise against all heresy. The objectives of this work are stated in the preface. Guido aims to update and integrate Augustine's *De haeresibus*: first, by offering a comprehensive and updated inventory of all heresies, past and present, with reference to every error in doctrine and in religious practice; and second, by providing a refutation of each error, which Augustine had omitted

---

[7] N. Iung, *Un franciscain, théologien du pouvoir pontifical au XIVe siècle. Alvaro Pelayo, évêque et pénitencier de Jean XXII* (Paris, 1931); M. Damiata, *Alvaro Pelagio. Teocratico scontento* (Florence, 1984); W. Kölmel, 'Paupertas und Potestas. Kirche in der Sicht des Alvarus Pelagius', *Franziskanische Studien* 46 (1964), 57–101; L. Handelman, 'Ecclesia primitiva. Alvarus Pelagius and Marsilius of Padua', *Medioevo* 6 (1980), 431–48; J. M. Barbosa, 'A problemática das relações entre o poder espiritual e o poder temporal na obra de Álvaro Pais', *Anais da Academia Portuguesa de História* 31 (1986), 343–9; J. A. C. R. Souza, *As relações de poder na Idade Média Tardia. Marsílio de Pádua, Álvaro Pais e Guilherme de Ockam* (Oporto, 2010), pp. 73–94; J. Miethke, *Ai confini del potere. Il dibattito sulla potestas papale da Tommaso d'Aquino a Occam* (Padua, 2005), pp. 196–203.

[8] 'Opusculum composui hoc contra haereses et errores novos et veteres, quae in quibusdam partibus Hispaniae et alibi pestifere pullularunt in fidei et fidelium detrimentum, periculum et iacturam'; Pelagio, *Colírio*, I, 34, 36.

[9] Ibid., I, 38, II, 188.

Late medieval heresiography and the categorisation of Eastern Christianity

from his treatise by reasons of brevity.[10] The result is a veritable encyclopedia of religious dissent. It includes lengthy discussions and rebuttals concerning Jews, Eastern Christians and heretics from late antiquity and derived from Augustine and Isidore, as well as materials on modern sects (dualist heretics, Waldensians, Pseudo-Apostles, Béguins) and various 'heretics' like Joachim of Fiore and Peter John Olivi. As for Christians in the East, Guido concisely focuses on Jacobites and Georgians, discussing four errors of the former, and making a brief remark about the latter.[11] Conversely, he allocates much more space to Greeks and Armenians, organising his arguments in a detailed list of twenty-six and thirty errors respectively.[12]

Overall, the attention devoted to Levantine doctrines and practices appears remarkable in both treatises, resulting in a spectrum of religious dissent that enlarges and rectifies the one usually considered by medieval heresiography. What Guido and Alvarus intended to do was to draft wide-ranging tracts about heresy, that were meant to provide the Church elite with the necessary theological and juridical weapons, rather than to offer practical tools for the use of inquisitors.

In this perspective, both works were particularly in tune with the intellectual ambience of the papal court during a period of intensive discussions and new theorisations about unorthodox belief.[13] In Avignon, this entailed not only involvement in crucial controversies of the time, including the evaluation of Eastern Christian groups. It also meant responsiveness to past and current stimuli to the production of 'universal' compilations aimed at collecting, reorganising and systematising essential knowledge in a given field.[14] Paolino of Venice's universal chronicles, Pierre Bersuire's repertories

---

[10] 'Augustinus vero in suis libris copiose quidem haereticorum multorum errores reprobavit, sed causa brevitatis in recitatione haeresum eas reprobare non curavit ut vitaret tedium prolixitatis. Idcirco has haereses per beatum Augustinum sic signatas non ex praesumptione, sed ex humili devotione et fidei zelo, et ut particeps mercedis efficiar quae Dei sapientiam elucidantibus promittitur reprobare studui, necnon et alias quas post sancti Augustini decessum exortas potui reperire' ('In fact, in the books he wrote [against individual heretics and heresies] Augustine provided copious refutations of the errors of many heretics, but in his summary of heresies [viz. the brief list provided in his *On Heresies*] he did not deal with their refutation, in order to avoid tedious longwindedness. This is why I have been at pains to refute the heresies pointed out by blessed Augustine, doing this not out of presumption, but out of humble devotion, zeal for the faith and in order to share the reward that is promised to those who elucidate the wisdom of God. I was also at pains to refute other heresies I could find that had sprung up after St Augustine's death'); Terreni, *Summa*, fol. 1r.

[11] Ibid., fols. 28v–9r (on Jacobites), 29v (on Georgians).

[12] Ibid., fols. 19r–28r (on Greeks), 29v–42v (on Armenians).

[13] A survey of these debates under John XXII is given by S. Piron, 'Avignon sous Jean XXII, l'Eldorado des théologiens', in *Jean XXII et le Midi*, Cahiers de Fanjeaux 45 (Toulouse, 2012), pp. 357–91.

[14] M. Picone, *L'enciclopedismo medievale* (Ravenna, 1994); B. Roest, 'Compilation as Theme and Praxis in Franciscan Universal Chronicles', in *Pre-modern Encyclopaedic*

Irene Bueno

of moral theology and various summaries of Thomas Aquinas's works appeared in the same milieu. As these examples illustrate, the production of comprehensive *summae*, abridged compendia, *florilegia* and repertoires aimed to assemble the information available in specific domains, which developed especially in the thirteenth century, seems to have received renewed encouragement at the court of Avignon, most notably under the reign of John XXII.[15] Heresiography was not immune to or isolated from these things, and Avignon's role as a theological centre and the current enhancement of the pontifical library were further elements in the receptive environment that was provided for Guido and Alvarus's works against heresy.

Various surviving codices and ancient catalogues of the pontifical library demonstrate that these texts were available at the papal court. An elegantly decorated copy of the *Summa*, realised and illuminated in Avignon and today preserved in Wolfenbüttel, was to be part of Clement VI's personal library;[16] moreover, various catalogues attest that a copy of the *Collyrium* was extant in the papal collections at least from 1369, appropriately appearing among the *libri heresum*.[17] Interestingly, these inventories also attest the presence of other comprehensive anti-heresy treatises in the library of the popes: a copy of Benedict of Alignan's *Tractatus fidei* was part of the papal collections at least from 1369,[18] whereas Eymerich's *Directorium inquisitorum* appears various times in the catalogues drafted from 1405 until 1429.[19]

Guido's and Alvarus's refutations of Eastern Christianity deserve special attention. How were Greeks and Armenians included among the many heretical sects discussed in the two treatises? The authors' introductory remarks and lexical choices might offer a more nuanced understanding of their underlying motivations and methods.

Texts, ed. P. Binkley (Leiden, 1997), pp. 213–25 (213). See also A. J. Minnis, 'Late Medieval Discussions of *compilatio* and the Role of the *compilator*', in *Beiträge zur Geschichte der deutschen Sprache und Literatur* 101 (1979), 385–421.

[15] See especially I. Heullant-Donat, 'L'encyclopédisme sous le pontificat de Jean XXII, entre savoir et propagande. L'exemple de Paolino da Venezia', in *La vie culturelle, intellectuelle et scientifique à la cour des papes d'Avignon*, ed. J. Hamesse (Turnhout, 2006), pp. 255–76; M.-H. Tesnière, 'Le *Reductorium morale* de Pierre Bersuire', in Picone, *L'enciclopedismo*, pp. 229–49.

[16] Wolfenbüttel, Herzog August Bibliothek, MS Cod. guelf. 5.1 Gud.lat. See I. Bueno, 'Guido Terreni at Avignon and the "Heresies" of the Armenians', *Medieval Encounters*, 21/2–3 (2015), 169–89 (184–5); E. Anheim, 'La bibliothèque personnelle de Pierre Roger/Clément VI', in *La vie culturelle*, ed. Hamesse, pp. 1–48 (43).

[17] F. Ehrle, *Historia bibliothecae romanorum pontificum, tum Bonifatianae tum Avenionensis* (Rome, 1890), p. 558, n. 1637; M.-H. Jullien de Pommerol and J. Monfrin, *La bibliothèque pontificale à Avignon et à Peñiscola pendant le grand schisme d'Occident et sa dispersion. Inventaires et concordances*, 2 vols. (Rome, 1991), I, xxvi.

[18] Ehrle, *Historia bibliothecae*, n. 1493, p. 397.

[19] Jullien de Pommerol and Monfrin, *La bibliothèque pontificale*: Pb 865; Pc 304; Cv 3; Bal 86, Pa 725, Fa 142.

140

Late medieval heresiography and the categorisation of Eastern Christianity

In the preface, Guido announces how he intends to proceed: 'And I will prove everything which is contained in that heresy through the Sacred Scripture, since heretics despise the words of the saints and of the Church ... And, since heretics place little weight on the words of the saints [patristic theologians] and the Church, I shall disprove every bit of a particular heresy through holy Scripture'.[20] The truth of the Bible alone (the New Testament especially) is thus the source, which inspires and sustains most of his arguments: 'indeed that opinion is heretical, which explicitly and plainly contradicts holy Scripture'.[21] Accordingly, Guido often remarks that heretics are described as such because of the clear discrepancy between them and particular passages in the Bible. Greeks and Armenians therefore prove to be heretics just like Cathars and Waldensians, since in many ways they 'err against the faith and the Scriptures'.[22]

Divergence from the unity of the Roman Church obviously appears as another fundamental mark of heresy. Following Isidore, Guido's preface goes on as follows, listing what is required for someone to be a heretic:

> fourthly, it is required that this heretic should be divided from the truth of faith and the unity of the Church through error. Therefore, he is said to be a 'heretic' because of the sect and division by which he cuts and divides [himself] from the truth of faith and from the unity of the Catholic Church[23] – here the play of words between *secta* and *secat* (cuts) cannot be reproduced in translation.

As demonstrated by the case of Christians in the East, holding different views from the determinations of the Apostolic See often involves falling into heretical error. In this way, when discussing the Greeks' opinions about *Filioque*, Guido claims that they prove to be 'malevolent, ignorant – not catholics but heretics', because they reject the truth of the Apostolic See and

---

[20] 'Et unumquodque contentorum in ipsa haeresi improbabo per Scripturam Sacram, quia haeretici dicta sanctorum et Ecclesiae parvipendunt', Terreni, *Summa*, fol. 1v.

[21] 'Opinio etenim illa est heretica que expresse et evidenter Scripture sacre adversatur', ibid., fol. 4v.

[22] 'Graeci in hoc errant contra fidem et Scripturam sanctam' (In this the Greeks err against faith and holy scripture); ibid., fol. 22v. 'Patenter ergo contra Scripturam sacram errant Graeci' (Therefore the Greeks clearly err against holy scripture); fol. 25v. 'Hic error patenter continet heresim contra sacram Scripturam' (This error plainly contains heresy against holy scripture); fol. 26v. 'Unde isti Armeni errant quia sacra Scriptura non mentitur, ut ipsi mendose imponuntur' (Whence these Armenians err, because holy scripture does not lie, as they mendaciously imply); fol. 42v. 'hoc enim est hereticum et contra evangelium' (for this is heretical and against the gospel); fol. 31r.

[23] 'Quarto requiritur quod talis hereticus a veritate fidei et unitate Ecclesie per errorem dividatur, unde hereticus a secta et divisione dicitur qua se secat et dividit a fidei veritate et ab ecclesie catholice unitate'; ibid., fol. 3v.

of the Roman Church.[24] With respect to various sacramental practices, he similarly reports that the Greeks 'err against the determination of the Church, indeed they are heretics'.[25] Likewise, Armenian fasting practice – eating meat on Fridays – appears erroneous because it contradicts the orders of the Roman Church.[26] Reference to the Bible thus sustains the core architecture of Guido's *Summa*. At the same time it is hardly surprising that the author, a prominent advisor to the pope, also emphasises divergence from the determinations of the Holy See as a fundamental mark of unorthodox belief and behaviour.

Unlike Guido, Alvarus essentially bases his anti-Greek arguments on a thorough legal expertise. Canon law thereby stands as the fundamental source and interpretative frame, which inspires his anti-heresy discourse. It is via Gratian's *Decretum* (c. 24 q. 3) that Alvarus approaches the late antique sects described by Augustine, as well as other more recent heresies.[27] Similarly, the collections of decretals stand as the main source of information about the errors dealt with in the fourth part of the treatise.[28] Along this line, Alvarus's legal background also informs his refutations of the Greeks, which rely on frequent citations from Gratian's *Decretum*, the collections of decretals, and the glosses of various medieval canonists, in addition to references from the Scriptures and patristic writings (including the Greek doctors).

Alvarus's lexical choices, however, reveal an attitude towards the Greeks that differs from his way of dealing with late antique or more recent sects. Compared to Guido, when referring to the Greeks Alvarus appears to be more reluctant to use terms such as *haeresis* or *haereticus*, preferring the milder word *error*. Conversely, he does not hesitate to mobilise terms like heresy, heretic or heresiarch in the previous five sections of the *Collyrium*. Accordingly, each doctrine or religious practice of the Greeks is presented in his work as *primus error*, *secundus error* and so on, instead of *alia haeresis*, *alii haeretici* or other such formulas recurring elsewhere in the treatise.

---

[24] 'Item quia confessionem huius veritatis, scilicet quod Spiritus sanctus procedit a patre et filio, Sedes apostolica et ecclesia Romana approbat et docet tenendam, patet Grecos qui in hoc nos culpant se probant (*recte*: probare) malivolos, imperitos, non catholicos, sed hereticos' (Item, because the Apostolic See and Roman Church approves and teaches that one should hold to profession of this truth – that is, that the Holy Spirit proceeded from the Father and the Son – it is clear that the Greeks, who hold us at fault on this, prove themselves to be malevolent, ignorant – not catholics but heretics); fol. 19v. 'Hic error expresse adversatur determinationi Sedis apostolicae et sanctae Romanae Ecclesiae quae in his quae fidei sunt non errat' ('This error openly contradicts the determination of the Apostolic See and of the saint Roman Church, which does not err in matters of faith'); ibid., fol. 19r.

[25] '...in quo errant contra Ecclesiae determinationem immo sunt heretici'; ibid., fol. 25r.

[26] 'Errant contra ordinationem Ecclesiae catholicae carnes aliquibus sextis feriis comedendo'; ibid., fol. 29v.

[27] Pelagio, *Colírio*, part 2, I, 232–73.

[28] Ibid., part 4, II, 10–23.

Late medieval heresiography and the categorisation of Eastern Christianity

Even if the qualification 'heresy' sometimes appears, there seems to be a preference for indirectness, through its use in sentences that are conditional. For example, when dealing with the primacy of Rome, Alvarus writes as follows: 'If the Greeks said that the above mentioned law was instituted by the Roman Church for its own advantage, this should not be believed, for it is heretical to say that the Roman Church lies and writes false things'.[29] Likewise, when discussing simony he states: 'If these Greeks believe that they can buy and sell spiritual things (*spiritualia*) without sin, then they are heretics, since such simony is a heresy (…). If however someone does not believe this, but commits simony, then he is not a heretic…'.[30] In line with broader medieval anti-Greek polemic, the Franciscan canonist thus underscores the role of divergent belief, rather than erroneous behaviour, in identifying manifestations of heresy.

Like Guido, Alvarus also concentrates in particular on the themes of disobedience to the pope and divergence from the Roman Church. A chief advocate of papal primacy, which he defends in various works, he proves well equipped on these matters, pointing to the Greeks' separation from the Roman shelter as a fundamental reason for their falling into error. Their standing outside Roman obedience and denial of papal primacy are recurring themes throughout the treatise, but Alvarus also dedicates to them four specific articles.[31] Overall, he appears reluctant to mobilise the language of 'heresy' when discussing these issues. Greeks are rather qualified as *acephali* (leaderless or headless) due to their denial of the authority of the pope, and *sc[h]ismatici* (schismatics) for their separation from Peter's Church. Moreover, they are said to have fallen into the sins of paganism (*peccatum paganitatis*), divination and idolatry (*peccata ariolandi et idolatriae*) for their disobedience to the Holy See.[32]

After all, theology and canon law had not provided a clear-cut distinction between the notions of heresy and schism. Drawing from Jerome, Gratian's *Decretum* and the following canonistic tradition, they regarded heresy as a dogmatic error, but intended schism to mean a separation from the religious community.[33] Yet, at the same time, canon lawyers demonstrated that no

---

[29] 'Si dicant Graeci quod iura superius allegata pro se statuit Romana Ecclesia nec ei credendum est, quod hoc dicere haereticum est quod Romana Ecclesia mentiatur et falsa scribat'; ibid., II, 86.

[30] 'Si isti Graeci credunt possunt emere et vendere spiritualia sine peccato, haeretici sunt, quia talis simonia haeresis est (…). Si autem non credit, sed simoniam facit, haereticus non est'; ibid., p. 136.

[31] Articles 2 (on the primacy of the Roman Church), 3 (on the obedience to the Roman Church), 4 (on papal primacy), and 40 (on the observance of papal sentences and decrees); ibid., pp. 82–96.

[32] Article 3, ibid., pp. 92–4.

[33] 'Inter heresim et scisma hoc esse arbitror, quod heresis perversum dogma habeat, scisma post episcopalem discessionem ab ecclesia pariter separat' ('I claim that

long-lasting schism was possible without heresy, for the obstinacy of the schismatic within separation became ipso facto heresy.[34]

Guido Terreni himself contributed to shedding light on the continuity between the notions of heresy and schism in his commentary on Gratian's *Decretum*. When discussing the *scismatis et heresis differentia* (difference between schism and heresy; c. 24 q. 1), he states that one becomes a schismatic in two main ways: first, when he separates from the Church by rejecting the faith; and second, when he rejects the unity of and obedience to the Church.[35] Both cases result in a characterisation of the schismatic as heretic, revealing the centrality of the Roman Church as a reference point for the evaluation of the trajectory of those who separate from orthodoxy, both in terms of detachment from the true faith and disobedience. Heresy and schism thus become easily associated, a shift which derives especially from the affirmation of Peter's primacy over the universal Church, and from the related idea that those who abandon communion with Rome fall into error and cannot partake of God's spiritual gifts. If the Roman Church is defined as the standard against which others are measured, then those who abandon it are easily identifiable as heretics.

These considerations, however, were especially concerned with the idea of schism *within* the Latin Church, including cases of rebellion against the papacy, or similar instances of division occurring in Western contexts, rather than the

---

this is the difference between heresy and schism: that heresy has a perverted dogma; schism is a separation from the Church following episcopal separation'); *Decretum*, c. 24 q. 3 c. 26, ed. Friedberg, I, col. 997. See especially O. Hageneder, 'Der Häresiebegriff bei den Juristen des 12. Und 13. Jahrhunderts', in *The Concept of Heresy in the Middle Ages*, Mediaevalia Lovaniensia, series 1, studia 4 (Louvain, 1976), pp. 42–103; republished in Italian as 'Il concetto di eresia nei giuristi del XII e XIII secolo', in *Il sole e la luna. Papato, Impero e regni nella teoria e nella prassi dei secoli XII e XIII*, ed. and trans. M. P. Alberzoni (Milan, 2000), pp. 69–130 (79–80). For a recent discussion of the inquisitorial understanding of schism in the early modern period see also V. Lavenia, '*Quasi haereticus*. Lo scisma nella riflessione degli inquisitori dell'età moderna', *Mélanges de l'École française de Rome. Italie et Méditerranée modernes et contemporaines* 126/2 (2014), on-line: http://journals.openedition.org/mefrim/1838 (accessed 01/02/2019).

[34] Hageneder, 'Il concetto di eresia', p. 80.

[35] 'Potest aliquis esse in scismate uno modo, quia se separat ab Ecclesia quo ad fidem, ut infidelis et hereticus, et taliter extra Ecclesia sic est, quod non habet veram fidem [...]. Secundo modo est schismaticus qui recedit ab unitate et obediencia Ecclesie, non tamen a fide, et isto modo scismaticus cito [...] fit hereticus' ('One can be a schismatic in a first way: as he separates from the Church by rejecting the faith, like the infidel and the heretic, and in this way he is outside the Church, as he does not have the true faith. [...] Secondly, schismatic the one who separates from the unity and obedience of the Church, but not from the faith, and in this way the schismatic soon [...] becomes a heretic'; Guido Terreni, *Commentarium super Decretum Gratiani*, MS Vatican City, Vatican Library, Vat. lat. 1453, fol. 154vb. On Guido's commentary on Gratian see T. Turley, 'Guido Terreni and the *Decretum*', *Bulletin of Medieval Canon Law* 8 (1978), 29–34.

Late medieval heresiography and the categorisation of Eastern Christianity

separation of the Eastern Churches from Rome. Further hints about the quali-fication of Oriental Christians as heretics are given in Guido's preface to the *Summa*, where the author, drawing from patristic writings, defines what heresy is: an erroneous opinion held with pertinacity against the Scripture, the truth of faith and the determinations of the Church.[36] Yet, as he points out, not every such opinion can be qualified as heresy. Indeed, one has to make a distinction between fundamental matters regarding the faith, the moral conduct and what is necessary to salvation, whose rejection involves heresy; and secondary articles, which are only held by the Church as probable, and whose rejection does not involve condemnation by the Church. Interestingly, in both matters Guido offers typical examples related to the Greek Christianity. He thus refers to the *Filioque* as an indubitable article of faith; and to the use of unleavened bread in the Eucharist as an example of probable opinion.[37]

Despite these distinctions offered in the preface, when turning to the main body of the text we often find heresy appearing as a more inclusive category. The architecture of the *Summa* further demonstrates Guido's uncertain distinction between heresy and schism and the attitude he takes towards exacerbating the convergence between heretics of all kind. His engagement against various Oriental Churches is attested by many cross-references, with the Greeks appearing as fundamental benchmarks. For example, when dealing with the Armenians' account of eternal salvation, Guido refers to the seventh article of the Greeks, and when focusing on the Armenians' denial of purgatory and criticism of prayers for the dead he invites the reader to check what he has already written about the Greeks' fifth and sixth errors.[38] But Guido does not limit himself to drafting compar-isons between different Eastern Christian communities. Thus, he often links the errors of Greeks and Armenians to those of other heretics: for example, the *Pelagiani* (for their opinion that children are immune to Original Sin);[39] or *Serdonitae* (because of monophysitism).[40]

Although more rarely, such internal references appear in the *Collyrium* too. For example, when arguing against the Greeks' proposition that the pope has no more powers than their Patriarch, Alvarus has no hesitation in juxtaposing their proposition – that there are 'multa capita' (many heads) in the Church – to what the Manichees say. 'They also propose many principles (*principia*), like the Manichaean heretics', he writes, thereby extending his charge towards theological dualism.[41] Likewise, the Greeks prove to belong to that 'sect of

---

[36] Terreni, *Summa*, fols. 3r–3v.
[37] Ibid., fols. 8v–9r.
[38] Ibid., fols. 31r, 32r.
[39] Ibid., fol. 30v.
[40] Ibid., fol. 30r.
[41] 'Ponunt etiam multa principia, sicut manichaei haeretici'; Pelagio, *Colírio*, II, 94 (article 4).

Irene Bueno

heretics, who are called "Cathars"' because of their common condemnation of second and later marriages.[42]

In a few manuscripts, the consultation aids further complement the internal cross-references given in the main text. For example, a late fourteenth-century copy of the *Summa* preserved in Paris enumerates the common beliefs of Armenians, Maronites, Saracens, Cathars, Waldensians and Pseudo-Apostles. For example, Armenians and Pseudo-Apostles are compared because of their similar opinions regarding the primacy of the pope. Armenians and Waldensians appear to have in common the conviction that laymen can administer the Eucharist and their denial of the saints' feasts, while the Cathars seem to share with the Armenians, Jacobites and Nestorians their opinions regarding baptism, purgatory, Eucharist, prayers and confession.[43] The criteria of reorganisation used in such tables illustrate how the categories of Western heresiology affected the reception of Oriental Christianity through the conceptual and technical features of the progressive systematisation of knowledge. The general aim was to facilitate the identification of all errors and all heretics. To this end Guido, Alvarus and their later copyists employed two methods in tandem. On the one hand, they showed the specificity of each sect by means of accurate lists of errors, and on the other hand, through comparison they emphasised the similarity of all sects, regardless of any distinction between past and present, East and West, heresy and schism. Within this approach a variety of sources could be combined with each other: not only earlier lists of heresies, such as the fundamental ones produced by Augustine and Isidore, but also evidence from the most recent debates promoted by the popes of Avignon, which involved the direct participation of Guido and Alvarus.

Other manuscripts demonstrate that the rebuttals of Greeks and Armenians sometimes circulated independently from the rest of the treatise, as they were copied into collections aimed to sustain dialogue with the Eastern Churches. Such is the case of a fourteenth-century miscellany containing a section of Guido's *Summa*, now preserved in the Bibliothèque nationale de France, that Clement VI addressed to Armenian Church representatives in order to foster reunion.[44] In this case, Guido's refutations of Greeks and Armenians were complemented by a number of lengthy indexes that aimed to summarise the material and rearrange it in various ways. Once again, indexes and summaries enable the reorganisation of the available information according to changing objectives.

Overall, the two heresiologists' acquaintance with the Oriental Churches proves to be rather limited. It is difficult to reconstruct the key points of reference, which inspired their refutations, since both of them seem to disregard

---

[42] 'Contempnant secundas et ulteriores numptias dicentes natos ex talibus nuptiis non esse legitimos. In hoc isti graeci sunt de secta haereticorum, qui dicuntur catharre'; ibid., p. 128.

[43] Paris, Bibliothèque Mazarine, MS 891, fols. 79r–86r.

[44] Paris, BnF, MS lat. 3365.

Late medieval heresiography and the categorisation of Eastern Christianity

the usual anti-Greek controversialists. But it may still be worthwhile making a few observations about their sources and the relationship between them. As for the Armenians, Guido's knowledge was the product of his direct engagement in a consultation held in Avignon at the turn of the 1330s.[45] He was charged with the evaluation of a booklet of errors attributed to the Armenians, which was circulating at the papal court at the time, attracting great attention and eliciting papal preoccupation with the orthodoxy of the Armenian Church – which was by then formally united to Rome.[46] Guido's discussion of Armenian Christianity proves to be essentially based on this polemical source, which he closely follows in the *Summa*. He does not seem to have been aware that other Armenian texts were circulating at the papal court at the time, including an apologetic response to the same list, drafted in Latin by the Armenian unionist Daniel of Tabriz.[47] Guido examines the accusatory booklet through the lens of a Western theologian and inquisitor, interested in emphasising the Armenians' divergence from Rome. This filter produces a transformation of the original list of errors into a list of actual heresies, which deserves inclusion within a universal anti-heresy treatise. As discussed above, the new framework of inter-pretation is confirmed by Guido's lexical choices, characterised by the recurring use of terms such as 'heretic', 'heresy', 'sect' and so on.

As far as the Greeks are concerned, the works by Guido and Alvarus reveal a remarkable convergence, the list of errors offered in the *Summa* being very close to the one drafted in the *Collyrium*. As I have shown elsewhere, a comparative reading of the two works indeed reveals that the single themes listed by the two heresiologists, their relative position within the text and even the terms employed to address them are all extremely similar.[48] Despite their different approaches to the very notion of heresy, and despite the different nature of the sources and arguments mobilised against the Greeks, the two authors clearly influenced each other. Indeed, textual analysis suggests either that Guido was dependent of Alvarus, or, that both of them referred to a common, yet still unidentified, source.[49] The proximity of the two anti-Greek sub-treatises is very understandable considering the common

---

[45] On the theological consultation on the Armenians, see F. Tournebize, 'Les cent dix-sept accusations présentées à Benoît XII contre les Arméniens', *Revue de l'Orient Chrétien* 9 (1906), 163–81, 274–300, 352–70. On Guido's role in these debates, see Bueno, 'Guido Terreni', and I. Bueno, 'Avignon, the Armenians, and the Primacy of the Pope', *Archa Verbi* 12 (2015), 108–29.

[46] P. Halfter, *Das Papsttum und die Armenier im frühen und Hohen Mittelalter. Von den ersten Kontakten bis zur Fixierung der Kirchenunion im Jahre 1198* (Cologne, 1996), especially pp. 221–32.

[47] Daniel of Tabriz, *Responsio fratris Danielis ad errores impositos Hermenis*, in *Recueil des historiens des croisades. Documents arméniens*, ed. É. Dulaurier, 2 vols. (Paris, 1869–1906), II, 559–650.

[48] Bueno, 'Les erreurs des orientaux', pp. 260–4.

[49] Ibid., pp. 265–7.

Irene Bueno

intellectual milieu in which Guido and Alvarus were active. Moreover, the infrequent inclusion of Oriental Christianity in medieval anti-heresy polemic must have further encouraged the sharing of information. Therefore, it should not be surprising to find overt connections between these works. In various ways the *summae* by Guido and Alvarus complement each other, as they provide, respectively, a theological and juridical repertoire of arguments against all heretical error, centred on the key notion of the separation from the Roman faith, unity and obedience. As such, they demonstrate at the same time the proximity of sources and inspiration and the occasional divergence of methods, which inspired late medieval 'encyclopedic' heresiography.

Generally, Christians in the East occupied limited space in anti-heresy writing, preventing modern scholars from gaining an overall view of the shifting reception of their beliefs and religious practices. Indeed, comprehensive polemical works were occasionally concerned with Jews and Muslims, but usually neglected Oriental Christianity. As was mentioned above, there are two significant exceptions – the *Tractatus fidei contra diversos errores* of the bishop of Marseille, Benedict of Alignan (*c.* 1190–1268), and the *Directorium inquisitorum* of the Dominican inquisitor Nicholas Eymerich (*c.* 1316–99) – two widely-circulating works which, like the ones analysed above, aimed at the description and rebuttal of virtually *all* heretical error.

As shown by John Arnold, Benedict's *Tractatus* is conceived as a kind of gloss to the creed *Firmiter credimus* of the Fourth Lateran Council and discusses many aspects of faith along with related errors. The resulting text engages with the beliefs and practices of a number of heretical groups as well as Jews, Muslims and Eastern Christians.[50] Benedict was likely to have confronted the latter personally both during his two sojourns in the East (where he seems to have completed the treatise)[51] and during the Council of Lyon, while gaining further knowledge from those texts that were circulating overseas.[52]

Benedict takes into account various Eastern communities, including Greeks, Armenians, Jacobites and Nestorians. Unlike Guido and Alvarus, however, he does not organise his work through addressing individual groups. As pointed out by John Arnold, he rather proceeds thematically, focusing on each form of divergence from the Lateran creed and engaging with the arguments and authorities mobilised by heretics and infidels by means of 'reasons, authorities and examples'.[53] The outcome is not a theological summa, but rather a comprehensive collection of tools aimed at supporting clerics and pastors of souls in the defence of the orthodox faith.[54]

---

[50] Arnold, 'Benedict of Alignan's *Tractatus fidei*'.
[51] On Benedict's sojourns in the East see Rubin, 'Benoit d'Alignan', n. 59, p. 198.
[52] Ibid., p. 193.
[53] Ibid., n. 8, p. 190; Arnold, 'Benedict of Alignan's *Tractatus fidei*', pp. 37, 44.
[54] Arnold, 'Benedict of Alignan's *Tractatus fidei*', pp. 43–4.

Late medieval heresiography and the categorisation of Eastern Christianity

In his treatise, then, Benedict engages with the Oriental Christians sporadically, discussing their specific errors whilst focusing on matters like the nature of God and the Trinity (book 1), purgatory (book 2) and the sacraments (book 3). For example, the celebration of the Eucharist provides the opportunity for lengthy and detailed discussions of the Greek use of fermented, instead of unleavened bread[55] and of the Armenian use of pure, instead of mixed wine.[56] In neither case does the awareness of these differences in sacramental practice result in a plain accusation of heresy. Benedict rather identifies them as 'errors', occasionally emphasising the 'absurdity' of the confronted arguments. An example: 'Moreover, that they [the Greeks] oppose the idea that Christ anticipated [the celebration of] Easter seems absurd'.[57] Indeed, like Guido and Alvarus, Benedict embraces the traditional conviction that if the Greeks had fallen into heresy regarding the use of leavened bread in the Eucharist, this did not derive from their sacramental practice, but from their denial of the legitimacy of the Western practice: 'And therefore we judge the Greeks as heretics not because they confer the Eucharist with fermented bread, but because they condemn what is legitimate, and reject our sacrament'.[58] Likewise, Benedict avoids the accusation of heresy when focusing on the Armenian's use of pure wine in the Eucharist, leaving space for rapprochement: 'Even though different people feel differently, it is certain that if one does not intend to introduce or contemplate heresy, but omits water for oblivion or ignorance, this does not make the sacrament invalid'.[59]

Similarly, when commenting on the Orientals' rejection of purgatory, Benedict's polemic is grounded upon the quotation of the *rationes* of both parties, rather than invective. The bishop knows that several Eastern Christian groups deny the existence of purgatory and he is well aware of the authorities they use to support their position. In particular, he rejects the conviction that each one is responsible for his own deeds and that someone else's prayers cannot facilitate final salvation. The identity of those who claim that after death the soul is immediately saved or damned, prayers and services for the

---

[55] I quote from Rome, Biblioteca Alessandrina, MS Cod. 141, fols. 264vb–7vb.

[56] Ibid., fols. 267vb–9va.

[57] 'Item quod obiciunt [Greci] Christum anticipare pascha, absurdum videtur'; ibid., fol. 265vb.

[58] 'Et ideo Grecos iudicamus de heresi nec quia de fermentato conficiunt, sed quia quod licitum est dampnant, et quia nostrum reprobant sacramentum'; ibid., fols. 267va–7vb. Cfr. Pelagio, *Colírio*, error 5, pp. 96–8; and Terreni, *Summa*, error 2, fols. 20r–20v: 'Nec [Romana Ecclesia] Graecos damnat in hoc, immo concedit eis ex pane fermentato corpus Christi conficere' ('And the Roman Church does not condemn the Greeks on this, but it allows them to confer the body of Christ from fermented bread').

[59] 'Licet diversi diversa sentiant, illud tenendum pro certo, quod si non intendit heresim introducere vel tueri, set oblivione set ignorantia pretermisit aquam, non est propter hoc irritum sacramentum'; Alessandrina, MS Cod. 141, fol. 269va.

Irene Bueno

dead notwithstanding, is patent: 'in this error lie the Greeks, the Armenians, and almost all the other overseas nations'.[60] But once again the *Tractatus fidei* avoids those polemical notes that are such a feature of Guido's *Summa*. Indeed, Guido turns the Greeks' rejection of purgatory into the prospect of damnation: 'The Greeks thus deny purgatory, and will be deprived of the purifying purgation, unless they repent in this life of their sins and of this heresy'.[61]

Benedict's attitude towards other forms of Christianity, and especially the Eastern Christians, generally proves more indulgent than the one adopted by Guido and Alvarus.[62] At the same time, his knowledge of the Orientals appears to be more exhaustive and accurate. Sustained both by his direct experience and by reference to the Scriptures and authorities, including the ones mobilised by 'those situated overseas', Benedict is capable of and willing to develop more profound discussion than the fourteenth-century heresiologists I have taken into account.

Nicholas Eymerich's ambition is essentially different. The *Directorium inquisitorum* stands as one of the most complete handbooks for inquisitors compiled in the Middle Ages and as a fundamental point of reference for later polemicists.[63] This work was completed in Avignon in 1376, when the general inquisitor of Aragon was exiled following his conflict with King Peter IV.[64] It comprises three sections, which focus respectively on patristic, conciliar, and pontifical definitions of the orthodox faith; on the notion of heresy and on a large survey of past and recent heresies; and on inquisitorial procedures. The scope of the treatise is essentially practical: to guide inquisitors in their daily activities, providing them with the necessary theological and normative references and offering indications for any possible difficulty arising during their work. In this perspective, when focusing on sects and heretics, Eymerich aims at comprehensiveness rather than analytical depth. With the noticeable exception of Ramon Llull and the Llullists, who were Eymerich's main targets, his account of individual heresies is usually very synthetic.

---

[60] 'In hoc errore sunt Greci, Armeni et fere omnes alie nationes transmarine'; ibid., fol. 227ra.

[61] 'Negant igitur et male Greci purgatorium, quibus negabitur purgationis emundatio, nisi de suis peccatis in hac vita poenituerint, et de heresi presenti'; Terreni, *Summa*, fol. 22r.

[62] Conversely, according to Jonathan Rubin, Benedict 'seems to have perceived them to be simply heretics'; Rubin, 'Benoit d'Alignan', p. 195.

[63] Eymerich, *Directorium*.

[64] The fundamental modern account is C. Heimann, *Nicolaus Eymerich (vor 1320–1399) – praedicator veridicus, inquisitor intrepidus, doctor egregius. Leben und Werk eines Inquisitors* (Münster, 2001). Recent bibliography includes D. Hill, *Inquisition in the Fourteenth Century. The Manuals of Bernard Gui and Nicholas Eymerich*, Heresy and Inquisition in the Middle Ages 7 (York, 2019), which regrettably I have been unable to consult.

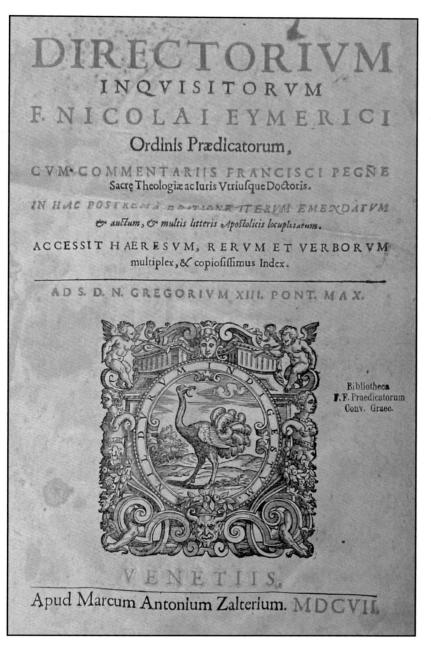

Figure 5.1 Nicholas Eymerich, *Directorium inquisitorum* (Venice, 1607), title page. The pagination is the same as in the Rome 1587 edition used in the chapter. Private collection.

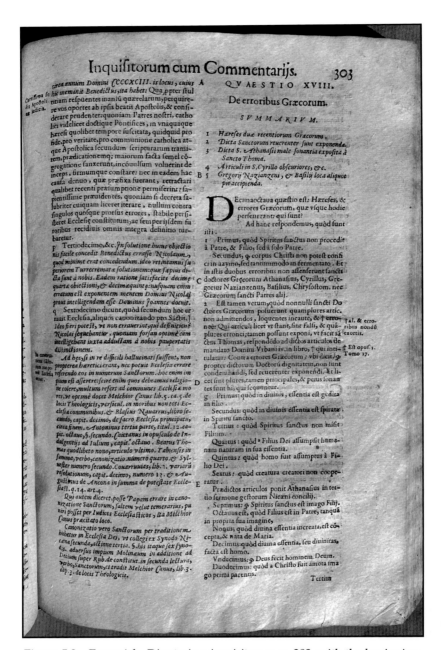

Figure 5.2 Eymerich, *Directorium inquisitorum*, p. 303, with the beginning of *De erroribus Græcorum*, a summary, and nos. 1–12 of the errors. Private collection.

Secunda pars Directorij

304

Tertiusdecimus: quòd qui semel blasphema-
uit, impossibile est non blasphemare.

Quartusdecimus: quòd iudæ non est nobis mi
nistrata per Angelos.

Hos articulos ponit Athanasius in Epistol. ad
Serapionem.

4 Quinquædecimus: quòd Iesus Christus filius
dicitur paternæ essentiæ.

Sextusdecimus: quòd quæ sunt naturaliter propria Dei patris, sunt propria Dei filij.

Decimusseptimus: quòd nomine Christi intelligitur Spiritus sanctus.

Decimusoctauus: quòd docente Paulo, Sera-
phim addiscunt.

Decimusnonus: φ quãdo Moyses dixit de ho
minis formatione, φ Deus inspirauit in faciem
eius spiraculum vitæ, & factus est homo in aiam
viuentem, quòd istud spiramen, seu spiraculum,
non suit anima rationalis; quia tunc fuisset anima de Dei essetia; sed intelligitur, quòd suit Spi
ritus sanctus homini inspiratus.

Hos artic. possut Cyrillus in lib. thesaurorũ.

5 Vigesimus: quòd Spiritus sanctus est in medio Patris, & Filij.

Hunc articulum ponit Gregotius Nazianz.
in sermone de Epiphania.

Vigesimusprimus, quòd Spiritus sanctus est
verbum Filij.

Hûc articulum ponit Basilius in sermone de
Spiritu sancto.

Vigesimus secundus: φ Spiritus sanctus per
Filium operatur.

Vigesimustertius: φ in Angelis, quo ad naturam non dicimus secundum, nec tertium.

Hos artic. ponit Basilius contra Eunomium.

COMMENT. XLIII.

Græcorum ar-
rogãtia, & in
Ecclesiam la-
tinã, inuidia.
GRæci tametsi initio nascentis Ecclesiæ catho.
fuerint amplexi fidem, & viros quamplures
sanctitate, et doctrina clarissimos habuerint: tamen
labentib. saculis itá eorum arrogantia creuit, vt Ec
clesia Latina inuidentes, summo Romano Pontifici obedire recusarint; & Schismate facto ab Ecclesia Latina desciuerint, multasque in eam iniurias in
tulerint; quas recenset Leo Papa Nouus Epis. quadam contra inauditas præsumptiones Michaelis, et
Acridani Episcoporum, c.19. & eiusdem Epistolæ,
cap.8. dicit, Græcos diuersis temporibus, diuerso errore, ad corrumpendam catholicæ matris Ecclesiæ
virginitatem nonaginta, & eo amplius hæreses
peperisse.

Ecclesiæ Ro-
mæ in Græ-
cos singula-
ris benigni-
tas.
Hos sæpe Ecclesia Rom. conata est in viam veritatis reuocare, vt abunde legitur in Concil. Flore.
sub Eugenio IV. Sess. 3. Eisdem reducendis ad Ecclesiæ vnitatem incubuerunt diuersi Romani Pon-
tifices, Innocentius III. Gregorius x. & Eugenius
IV. Hi tempore Eugenij Quarti circa annos Domini
MCCCCXXXII. in Concilio Florent. Ecclesia La-
tinæ voluntas, vt sessione vltima vius Concilij scri-
ptum est; idque post Eymerici, & B. Thomæ tempo
ra, cæterum ea vnio non diu auit.

Quanta vero animi acerbitate essent Græci con-

A tra Latinos; tametsi ex multis perspicere licet; maxime tamé constat ex Concil. Later. sub Innoc. iij.
capitu. 4. nam si quandoque sacerdotes Latini super
eorum altaria celebrassent, non prius ipsi sacrificare
volebant in ipsis, quàm ea tanquam per hoc inqui-
nata lauissent. Quin & baptizatos à Latinis iterū
ausa temerario rebaptizare præsumebant. quod refertur in capitul. licet Græcis. extra de baptismo, &
eius effectu.

Iam quantù attinet ad errores Græcorum, quos
hic cõmemorat Eymer. eos copiose refert, & in sen-
sa catholico explicat B. Thomas opusc. quodam contra errores Græcorum inscripto, quod est primú to-
B mi 17. inter opera S. Thomæ, cuius hic quoque men-
tionem facit auctor. ac multi quidem ex his decla-
rati, sicut docet S. Thomas errores non sunt.

Cæterù iidé Græci, præsertim nostris saculis pro-
ximiores, multos alios grauissimos errores pepere-
runt, quos bene interpretari non licet; cum ex purga
torium negent, et secundas nuptias dãnent, & sim-
plicem fornicatione non esse peccatum, & alios mul
tos impie profiteantur, quos refert, et confutat Guido Carmelita in summa de hæresibus, titulo de hære
sibus Græcorum. commemorat etiam Græcorum errores Beatus Antoninus in 3. par. histor. tit.12.4.
11.§.12. Arnaldus Albertinus in Rubrica de hæ-
C ret. lib.6. quæst. 12 circa finem. Bernardus Lutze-
burgu. in catalogo hæreticorum, lib.2. verbo; Græci. Augustin. de Ancona in summa de potestate Ec-
clesiast. q.25. art. 5. & 6. & Prateolus lib.7. de vi-
tis, & sectis hæret. cap.15.

a Quartus quòd filius Dei assumpsit humanã
naturam in sua essentia.] Hic articulus duplicem
sensum habere potest. Unus est, quòd Filius Dei assumpsit naturam humanam in sua essentia, idest, per
fectam ex corpore, & anima constantem: et hoc est
verum, catholicum, ac secundum fidé tenendum iux
ta illud Athanasij in regula suæ confessionis. Perfectus Deus, perfectus homo, ex anima rationali
D & humana carne subsistens. traduntque copiose
Theologi scholastici, lib. 3. senten. dist.2.

Alter sensus esse pũt, quem hic crederem damna
ri; scilicet, Filius Dei assumpsit humanam naturam
in sua essentia, quasi vnio naturæ humanæ, & diui
næ facta sit in essentia ad tertiam quandam naturã
constituendam; quod est falsum, vt scribunt Theolo
gi, lib. 3. sent. dist. 4. natura enim humana persona
Fili Dei vnita fuit primo, & per se, non naturæ,
& essentiæ diuinæ; inde natura diuina humana naturæ in filio vnita fuit; vt veré, & subtilius explicat Magister præcitato loco. §. non autem.

QVAESTIO XIX.

De erroribus Tartarorum.

SVMMARIVM.

1 Tartari multifariam distincti.

2 Ex eis quidam patriæ adeundæ desiderio se ipsos necant.

3 Alij litteras etiam, quas defunctis perferant,
ab amicis accipiunt.

Decima

Figure 5.3 Eymerich, *Directorium inquisitorum*, p. 304, with the
nos. 13–23 of the errors of the Greeks, followed by Francisco Peña's
commentary printed in italics and the beginning of *De erroribus
Tartarorum*. The following pp. 305–8 contain *De Turcorum erroribus*, *De
erroribus Saracenorum* and *De Iudæorum erroribus*.
Private collection.

Irene Bueno

As for the Eastern Christians, only the Greeks are taken into account, while sections dealing with Turks, Saracens and Tartars are also present in the treatise.[65] The author limits himself to providing a concise list of 'heresies and errors' of the Greeks, devoid of any commentary, explanation or refutation. He first mentions two articles maintained by the Greeks *usque hodie* (until now) – the rejection of *Filioque* and of the use of unleavened bread in the Eucharist – noticing however that they had not been received by a number of Greek fathers. Conversely, various Greek doctors (Athanasius, Cyril, Gregory of Nazianzus and Basil) retained other errors, which Eymerich essentially derives from Thomas Aquinas's *Contra Graecos* and summarises within a list of thirty-three. Interestingly, the inquisitor agrees with Aquinas that because of the Greek doctors' dignity these errors 'should be respectfully exposed' rather than condemned.[66] Facing the Eastern Christian groups, even a severe inquisitor like Eymerich appears to be cautious when setting up the boundary lines of heresy.

While Eymerich had limited himself to quoting from Aquinas with regard to the Greeks, further references appear in Francisco Peña's edition of the *Directorium inquisitorum*, published in 1578, 1585 and 1587 and then reprinted in 1595 and 1607. The Iberian canonist was involved in a thorough reflection on the history and jurisprudence of the inquisitorial tribunals and on the differences between ancient and modern, Roman and Spanish Inquisition. This was the intellectual context within which he revised and commented extensively upon Eymerich's *Directorium inquisitorum*, supplying a collection of recent papal documents and paying particular attention to legal and procedural matters.[67] With respect to the Greeks, Peña first mentions a few papal and conciliar documents concerning the schism or pointing to their many heresies. Afterwards, he comments upon these errors and in this context he explicitly refers to Guido Terreni. In particular, Peña mentions several *gravissimi errores* (extremely serious errors) of the Greeks, such as the denial of purgatory, the refusal of second marriages and the toleration of simple fornication that he notes that he drew from Guido's discussions in *De haeresibus Graecorum*.[68] Although active in Avignon, Eymerich did not rely upon Guido Terreni, but his sixteenth-century editor did. Just like his late medieval predecessors, Francisco Peña aimed to complement preceding anti-heresy treatises in order to offer a most comprehensive dissertation on the jurisprudence and

---

[65] Eymerich, *Directorium*, pp. 303–4 (about Greeks), 304–5 (Tartars), 305–6 (Turks), 306–7 (Saracens).

[66] Ibid., p. 303.

[67] On the wider context of Francisco Peña's activity and on his edition of the *Directorium inquisitorum*, see V. Lavenia, 'Peña, Francisco', in *Dizionario storico dell'inquisizione*, III, 1186–9, along with bibliography.

[68] Eymerich, *Directorium*, p. 304.

Late medieval heresiography and the categorisation of Eastern Christianity

legal practice of the Inquisition. Via his commentaries, Terreni's account of the Greeks, neglected by Eymerich, was able to reach wider audiences.

Unlike Francisco Peña, however, other heresiologists raised criticisms of the Carmelite, occasionally concentrating on his discussions of Greeks and Armenians. A few years after the *Summa*'s first printed edition, which appeared in 1528, the Iberian Franciscan Alfonso de Castro, a representative of Charles V at the Council of Trent and author of a summa *Adversus omnes haereses*, engaged critically with Guido's treatment of the Eastern Christians.[69] First, he criticises Guido's methods, claiming that he should have provided more detailed descriptions of heresies instead of useless refutations. Alfonso complains, moreover, about Guido's confusion of different sects, which he ascribes to a superficial knowledge of their various errors, as was clear in the case of the Armenians.[70] As noted by Vincenzo Lavenia, Alfonso seems to be willing to adopt a more nuanced distinction between heresy and schism, claiming that 'schism cannot be called heresy unless an error of the intellect is added'.[71]

Overall, the anti-heresy treatises by Guido Terreni and Alvarus Pelagius appear to have had a modest circulation, nowadays attested by a limited number of surviving manuscripts, two early modern printed editions of the *Summa* and one recent edition of the *Collyrium*. Nonetheless, Guido's *Summa* proves to have had a long-lasting impact on later heresiology, especially in Spain, which suggests the worthwhileness of further exploration of the continuity of methods, arguments and textual typologies used by late medieval and early modern controversialists. Several manuscripts show that Guido's compilation was still in use in the fifteenth century. Just like other anti-heresy texts, it was sometimes updated in the light of the most recent heresies of John Wyclif and Jan Hus.[72] The reason for Guido's impact on later heresiology was his omni-comprehensive ambition, combined with his effort to provide a full repertory of biblical references. The similar universally comprehensive drive of the earlier treatise by Benedict of Alignan and the later handbook by Nicholas Eymerich led to their vast popularity, attested respectively by forty-six and thirty-five extant manuscripts and further enhanced, in the case of Eymerich, by Francisco Peña's edition.

---

[69] I refer to the following edition: Alfonso de Castro, *Adversus omnes haereses* (Cologne, 1543); see also the related entry in *Dizionario storico dell'Inquisizione*, I, 301–2; and S. Pastore, *Il vangelo e la spada. L'inquisizione di Castiglia e i suoi critici, (1460–1598)*, (Rome, 2003).

[70] Alfonso de Castro, *Adversus omnes haereses*, preface.

[71] Cfr. Lavenia, 'Quasi haereticus'.

[72] This happens in particular in Caen, Bibliothèque municipale, MS 27. On similar connections of Benedict of Alignan's work with anti-Hussite polemics, see Arnold, 'Benedict of Alignan's *Tractatus fidei*', p. 42 and Appendices, pp. 52–4.

Irene Bueno

Conclusions

The place occupied by Greeks and Armenians within the *Summa* and the *Collyrium* testifies to the continuity of categories and arguments used in the fight against all enemies of the Roman Church. The convergence between Eastern Christians and Western heretics appears to have been encouraged by the uncertain boundaries between schism and heresy in the elaborations of medieval theologians and canon lawyers. Through the lens of an inquisitor, theologian and advisor of the pope, such as Guido Terreni, and of a canonist and papal penitentiary, such as Alvarus Pelagius, the memory of late antique heresies is thus combined not only with patristic and medieval anti-heresy writing, but also with the ongoing debates of the Avignon court about the Christian communities in the East.

What the works analysed in this chapter have in common is a universalistic approach to the polemical fight against heterodoxy. Despite their different organisation, they share the ambition of offering comprehensive rebuttals of all errors of the past and present, aiming to support the anti-heresy endeavours of modern inquisitors, theologians, canon lawyers, preachers and pastors of souls. These treatises were shaped, I would argue, by the convergence of the ways of reasoning, categories and textual organisation of two distinct traditions: medieval heresiography and its long legacy, dating back to the late antiquity; and late medieval 'encyclopedism', in particular its distinct approach to the summarisation of the essential knowledge of a given field. Both traditions enjoyed a particularly fertile season at Avignon, encouraged by the emergence of the Provençal city as a key intellectual hub and the massive growth of the pontifical library.

But the production of updated and comprehensive inventories of religious dissent was to last for centuries. And the persistent and long-lasting circulation of the works produced by Guido Terreni, Benedict of Alignan and Nicholas Eymerich points to and prepares the way for future lines of research: exploration of the continuities of heresiology and anti-heresy writing before and after the Council of Trent.

6

The portrayal of the Waldensian Brethren in the *De vita et conversacione* (*c.* 1391–3)

Reima Välimäki

Among medieval descriptions of the Waldensians, the short tract *De vita et conversacione* is among the few that attempt to give a relatively coherent picture of Waldensian practices.[1] It is particularly important with regards to the lay confessors and spiritual leaders of the movement, the Brethren. It describes their ascetic way of life, from strict fasting practices to vile or humble clothing. The text also explains how a new Brother was ordained in a meeting of Brethren, and their commitment to seven articles of faith and obedience to senior Brethren. Rather than providing outright condemnation of the Brethren, the tract hovers between a description of holy men and defamation of dangerous heresiarchs. The probable reason for this is that the text itself comes from multiple sources, parts of it being information that converted Brethren passed on, with other parts arising from inquisitors' intervention in the text. From the perspective of a modern scholar, it is an elusive and unstable work: besides two redactions that have a relatively wide circulation with other anti-heretical texts and inquisitorial formularies, there is an early version of the work with considerable variation between different manuscripts.

The *De vita et conversacione* belongs to the significant body of anti-heretical literature written during the persecution of German Waldensians in the last years of the fourteenth century.[2] Some of these texts were careful polemical

---

[1] P. Biller, 'Fingerprinting an Anonymous Description of the Waldensians', in *Texts and the Repression of Medieval Heresy*, ed. P. Biller and C. Bruschi, York Studies in Medieval Theology 4 (York, 2003), pp. 163–207 (p. 163).

[2] For overviews of the persecution of German Waldensians, see especially R. Kieckhefer, *Repression of Heresy in Medieval Germany* (Liverpool, 1979), pp. 53–73; J. M. Kolpacoff, 'Papal schism, Archiepiscopal Politics and Waldensian Persecution (1378–1396): The Ecclesio-Political Landscape of Late Fourteenth-Century Mainz' (unpublished Ph.D. dissertation, Northwestern University, 2000), pp. 247–61; G. Modestin, *Ketzer in der Stadt: der Prozess gegen die Strassburger Waldenser von 1400*, MGH Studien und Texte 41 (Hanover, 2007), pp. 1–12; R. Välimäki, *Heresy in Late Medieval Germany: The Inquisitor Petrus Zwicker and the Waldensians*, Heresy and Inquisition in the Middle Ages 6 (York, 2019), pp. 31–7.

Reima Välimäki

compositions, such as Petrus Zwicker's *Cum dormirent homines*, others were rudimentary lists of heretics' errors, and yet others formularies and guidelines for the interrogation of these heretics. A vast majority of these works relate to the Celestine inquisitor Petrus Zwicker, quite likely the most active prosecutor of Waldensians at the time and certainly the writer most eager to warn his fellow Catholics about the danger they posed.[3] The *De vita et conversacione*'s most likely date of composition is immediately after the conversion of several Waldensian brethren in 1391, and the text reached its most common form by 1393. It thus represents an intellectual engagement of inquisitors and other repressors of heresy with new knowledge on the Waldensians, gained from the recent converts.

In this article, I begin by briefly presenting the known manuscript tradition and versions of the *De vita et conversacione*, with some remarks on its probable dating. I then discuss the image the tract gives of the Waldensian Brethren, as well as the specific differences between different versions pointing towards inquisitors' intervention in the text. These interventions show how Waldensian Brethren were framed as heresiarchs instead of holy ascetics, and how a potentially dangerous description of dissident confessors was turned into a text that was safe to circulate as a tract against heretics.

Manuscripts and versions

There are twenty-four known manuscripts of the *De vita et conversacione*.[4] The most common version, preserved in thirteen manuscripts, is the one that circulates with the *Processus Petri*, that is different inquisitorial compilations that are based on Petrus Zwicker's inquisitor's manual.[5] In addition, five Bohemian, Silesian or German compilations of inquisition formularies

---

[3] On Zwicker as an anti-heretical author, see Välimäki, *Heresy in Late Medieval Germany*, pp. 38–170; G. Modestin, 'The Anti-Waldensian Treatise *Cum dormirent homines*: Historical Context, Polemical Strategy, and Manuscript Tradition', in *Religious Controversy in Europe, 1378–1536*, ed. M. Van Dussen and P. Soukup (Turnhout, 2013), pp. 211–29; P. Biller, *The Waldenses, 1170–1530: Between a Religious Order and a Church*, Variorum CS 676 (Aldershot, 2001), pp. 237–91.

[4] Most of these have been already listed in P. Biller, 'Aspects of the Waldenses in the fourteenth century, including an edition of their correspondence' (unpublished Ph.D. dissertation, University of Oxford, 1974), pp. 366–7; for the additional discovery of the Weimar manuscript, see Välimäki, *Heresy in Late Medieval Germany*, pp. 121–3.

[5] Augsburg, Staats- und Stadtbibliothek (StaSB), MS 2° Cod 338, fols. 153r–4r; Göttweig, Stiftsbibliothek, MS XV 250, fol. 287rb–vb; Salzburg, Erzabtei St Peter, MS b V 1, fols. 33v–4r; Seitenstetten, Stift Seitenstetten, MS 188, fols. 60r–1r; ibid., MS 252, fol. 170ra–va; St Florian, Stift St Florian, MS XI 234, fols. 84va–5ra; Vatican City, Biblioteca Apostolica Vaticana (BAV), MS Pal. lat. 677, fols. 47v–8v; Würzburg, Universitätsbibliothek (UB), MS M. ch. f. 51, fols. 34v–5r.

The Waldensian Brethren in the De vita et conversacione *(c. 1391–3)*

have the same version.[6] This version has been edited several times, the best being Ernst Werner's edition from an Olomouc manuscript.[7] In the collation of Petrus Zwicker's inquisitor's manual and its parts, I labelled it with the abbreviation (vcc),[8] and Peter Biller has called it C2.[9] It forms a unit with three other texts describing the Waldensians and their interrogation. In the *Processus Petri* manuscripts, it is always preceded by a list of eleven converted Waldensian Brethren, dated 4 September 1391, and followed by a list of Waldensians' errors (*Articuli Waldensium*) as well as the so-called long question list used by Petrus Zwicker and Martinus of Prague.[10] The same conglomerate appears in the Olomouc manuscript edited by Werner.[11] In four compilations of Bohemian, Silesian and German provenance, the (vcc) version circulated with the *Articuli Waldensium* and the long question list, but without the list of the converted Brethren.[12]

This version is the only one that can be dated with relative certainty: the earliest manuscript, Wrocław, BU MS Mil. II 58, is a compilation that once belonged to the Franciscans in Zgorzelec in Silesia, dated to 1393. There the *De vita et conversacione*, the *Articuli Waldensium* and the long question list, together with a formulary for the inquisition of heresy, form a unit added by a later hand to an existing collection of anti-heretical texts. Although the manuscript does not bear any explicit reference to Petrus Zwicker, it comes

---

[6] Olomouc, Státní archive, MS 69 (edited by E. Werner, see below); Wrocław, Biblioteka Uniwersytecka (BU), MS Mil. II 58, fols. 229va–vb; ibid., MS I F 230, fols. 231va–2ra; Berlin, Staatsbibliothek, MS Theol. Lat. fol. 704, pp. 22a–3a; Prague, Knihovna Metropolitní kapituly (KMK), MS D LI, fols. 136v–7v. I wish to thank Dr Adam Poznański for checking the correct folio numbers for MS Mil. II 58. The folio numbers in this article should be preferred over the ones in Välimäki, *Heresy in Late Medieval Germany*, which were based on an old folio numbering in a microfilm reproduction of the manuscript.

[7] E. Werner, 'Nachrichten über spätmittelalterliche Ketzer aus tschechoslowakischen Archiven und Bibliotheken', *Wissenschaftliche Zeitschrift der Karl-Marx-Universität Leipzig. Gesellschafts- und sprachwissenschaftliche Reihe* 12 (1963), 215–84 (pp. 265–7). For other editions, see G. Friess, 'Patarener, Begharden und Waldenser in Österreich während des Mittelalters', *Österreichische Vierteljahresschrift für katholische Theologie* 11 (1872), 209–72 (pp. 257–59); J. J. I. von Döllinger, *Beiträge zur Sektengeschichte des Mittelalters. Zweiter theil. Dokumente vornehmlich zur Geschichte der Valdesier und Katharer* (Munich, 1890), pp. 367–9; G. Friess, 'Die Häretiker des 14. Jahrhunderts im Erzherzogthume Österreich', *Hippolytus: theologische Quartalschrift der Diöcese St. Pölten* 5 (1862), 45–59, 129–46 (pp. 135, 145–6).

[8] Välimäki, *Heresy in Late Medieval Germany*, pp. 110, 120.

[9] Biller, 'Aspects', pp. 366–7.

[10] See the collation of the manuscripts, Välimäki, *Heresy in Late Medieval Germany*, pp. 114, 292. E. Werner called this combination of texts the 'Austrian-German type'; see Werner, 'Nachrichten', p. 222.

[11] Werner, 'Nachrichten', pp. 265–74.

[12] Wrocław, BU MS Mil. II 58, fols. 229va–31va; ibid., MS I F 230, fols. 231va–3vb; Berlin, Staatsbibliothek, MS Theol. Lat. fol. 704, pp. 22a–8a; Prague, KMK MS D LI, fols. 136v–9v.

from his geographical vicinity: Zgorzelec is situated only fifty kilometres from Zwicker's home monastery at Oybin.[13] Both the contents and the earliest manuscript circulation of these texts point to their origin: the conversion of the Waldensian Brethren in 1391 and the early involvement of inquisitors Petrus Zwicker and Martinus of Prague in their prosecution. The composition of this version took place almost certainly between late 1391 and 1393. The final form of this small compilation in the *Processus Petri*, including the list of converts, is a remarkably concise but informative exposition of Waldensian heretics: these are the heresiarchs who converted, this is their way of living, these are their errors, this is how you should interrogate them. It is almost a small inquisitor's manual in itself, albeit one concentrated on describing the heretics, not on the finer points of legal procedure.[14]

Although the earliest manuscripts of the *De vita et conversacione* have the version (vcc), it is not the first redaction of this text. It seems probable that Petrus Zwicker, Martinus of Prague, or both of them reworked the version (vcc) from an earlier text, dismissing certain parts that described the brethren as too pious and orthodox and adding some explanatory clauses to make them more heretical. These are discussed in more detail below, but one example illustrates this revision work. The Weimar manuscript Fol 20 describes the fasting practices of the Waldensian Brethren as follows:

> Firstly, that they fast four days in a week, namely Monday, Wednesday, Friday and Saturday, and one of them on water and bread, namely Friday, unless they are travelling or working hard or prevented by a reasonable cause.[15]

The version with the *Processus Petri* (vcc) has fewer details about the days that the Brethren used to fast, but instead, it represents their fasting regimen as hypocritical:

> Firstly, they fast three or four days in a week, one on water and bread unless they are set to hard travel or work, and this they do among their followers in order to appear holier in front of them.[16]

---

[13] J. Szymański, '"Articuli secte Waldensium" na tle antyheretyckich zbiorów rekopismiennych Biblioteki Uniwersytetu Wroclawskiego', *Studia zródloznawcze* 42 (2004), 85–96 (pp. 90, 93); Välimäki, *Heresy in Late Medieval Germany*, p. 119. Another Wrocław manuscript, MS I F 230, is also an early copy, composed in 1399.

[14] An emphasis on the doctrine of the heretics instead of legalities of inquisition is characteristic of almost all copies deriving from Zwicker's manual; see Välimäki, *Heresy in Late Medieval Germany*, pp. 169–70.

[15] Weimar, Herzogin Anna Amalia Bibliothek (HAAB), MS Fol 20, fol. 320vb: 'Primo quod quatuor dies in ebdomada ieiunant; videlicet feriam secundam, quartam, sextam et sabbatum; et vnum illorum in aqua et pane scilicet feriam sextam; nisi in itinere uel aliquo graui labore siue casu rationabili impediantur.' Cf. C. Schmidt, 'Actenstücke besonders zur Geschichte der Waldenser', *Zeitschrift für die historische Theologie* 22 (1852), 238–62 (p. 243).

[16] Werner, 'Nachrichten', p. 265: 'Primo ieiunant tres uel quatuor dies in ebdomada,

The Waldensian Brethren in the De vita et conversacione *(c. 1391–3)*

The direction and intention of revisions are clear: a less detailed description, but one that is clearly contextualised as heretical.

This less-polemical version is best known from C. Schmidt's 1852 edition of a since-lost Strasbourg manuscript, dated to 1404.[17] I marked it with the abbreviation (vca),[18] and Biller with C1.[19] Three characteristics set this version apart from the two others. Firstly, its manuscript tradition is independent of Petrus Zwicker's polemical treatises or inquisitorial formularies. In addition to the lost Strasbourg manuscript, five others are known,[20] and the bishop of Brandenburg, Stephan Bodecker, incorporated this version in his *Continuatio cimboli apostolorum* (*Continuation of the Apostles' Creed*) in the 1440s.[21] Secondly, the manuscript tradition is very inconsistent. The different manuscripts contain the same or similar parts, but their order of composition varies. For example, the Strasbourg manuscript opens with a list of Waldensians errors, as does the Augsburg manuscript.[22] However, they have a clearly different set of Waldensian errors. The Weimar manuscript opens with the description of Waldensian Brethren's way of living (including the fasting regimen quoted above), followed by the same list of errors as the Strasbourg manuscript, but this Strasbourg manuscript has the way of living only after the errors.[23] The Augsburg manuscript has the same description of the way of living, but only at the very end.[24] Thirdly, these manuscripts have certain sections that distinguish them from the two other versions. They go with short lists of Waldensian errors, whereas two other versions are usually accompanied by the long *Articuli Waldensium*. Apparently, the versions with the *Articuli* had no need for another, less comprehensive list of errors. All versions of the *De vita et conversacione* include a description of a new Brother's ordination, but the details vary. Chastity is always required from a candidate, but the

---

unam in aqua et pane nisi sint in graui itinere uel labore constituti et hoc faciunt inter suos subditos, ut coram eis appareant sanctiores.' The wording appears already in the oldest manuscript; see Wrocław, BU MS Mil. II 58, fol. 229va: 'Nam ieiunant iii uel iiii dies in ebdomada vna[m] in aqua et pane nisi sint in graui itinere uel labore constituti, et hoc faciunt inter subditos ut coram eis appareant sancciores.' The version (vcb) has the same claim; see e.g. Trier, Stadtbibliothek, MS 680/879, fol. 88r.

[17] Schmidt, 'Actenstücke', pp. 243–5.
[18] Välimäki, *Heresy in Late Medieval Germany*, p. 110.
[19] Biller, 'Aspects', p. 366.
[20] Augsburg, UB MS II. 1.2° 78, fols. 245va–6rb; Prague, KMK MS D 54, fols. 51r–3r; ibid., MS O 29, fols. 137v–8r; Vienna, Österreichische Nationalbibliothek (ÖNB), MS 4761, fols. 194r–5v; Weimar, HAAB MS Fol 20, fols. 320vb–1rb.
[21] *Quellen zur Ketzergeschichte Brandenburgs und Pommerns*, ed. D. Kurze (Berlin, 1975), pp. 280–1.
[22] Schmidt, 'Actenstücke', p. 243. Cf. Augsburg, UB MS II. 1.2° 78, fol. 245va.
[23] Weimar, HAAB MS Fol 20, fols. 320vb–1rb, cf. Schmidt, 'Actenstücke', pp. 243–4.
[24] Augsburg, UB MS II. 1.2° 78, fol. 246ra–rb.

version (vca) is the only one underlining that a candidate must be 'chaste and free from all consort of women with respect to carnal deeds'.[25] Even more importantly, the version (vca) lists the seven articles of faith, to which the Waldensian Brethren subscribed. These were omitted from the version (vcc). This omission is far from insignificant and unintentional, and it is discussed below.

Finally, there is a version that circulates with another anti-Waldensian treatise by Zwicker, the *Refutatio errorum*,[26] the version (vcb),[27] or Biller's C3.[28] It has been edited twice.[29] All five known manuscripts of this version are compilations having Zwicker's *Refutatio errorum* and the *De vita et conversacione* with the *Articuli Waldensium,* the long question list as well as a short treatise against the Beghards and Beguines. Of these five, the Michelstadt, two Trier and Wiesbaden manuscripts resemble each other very closely and probably share a common exemplar.[30] The version (vcb) is a hybrid, sharing common characteristics with the two other versions. The ordination of a new Brother is described twice, first at the beginning of the text in a way similar but not identical to the version (vca): a candidate is to take six vows (*vota*), resembling monastic vows: obedience to senior Brethren, chastity, voluntary poverty, not to live from his own hands' work, not to save his life with lies or perjury, and not to have greater confidence in his family than in other people. These are followed by the seven articles of faith: (1) God created the heaven and the earth, (2) Father, Son and the Holy Ghost are one God, (3) God gave the law to Moses at the Mount Sinai, (4) Christ was born of the Virgin, (5) Christ ascended to the heaven, (6) resurrection of the

---

[25] Schmidt, 'Actenstücke', p. 244. 'Quia alias nullus suscipitur nisi sit castus et ab omni consortio mulierum immunis, quoad opera carnalia'. Cf. Weimar, HAAB MS Fol 20, fol. 321rb; Augsburg, UB MS II. 1.2° 78, fol. 245vb.

[26] On Zwicker's authorship and the different redactions of the *Refutatio errorum*, see Välimäki, *Heresy in Late Medieval Germany*, pp. 39–64.

[27] Välimäki, *Heresy in Late Medieval Germany*, pp. 110, 114, 120, 124.

[28] Biller, 'Aspects', p. 367.

[29] A. Molnár, 'La Valdensium regula du manuscrit de Prague', *Bollettino della Società di Studi Valdesi* 123 (1968), 3–6; H. Haupt, 'Waldensia', *Zeitschrift für Kirchengeschichte* 10 (1889), 311–29 (pp. 328–9).

[30] Michelstadt, Kirchenbibliothek, MS I. Db. 685, fols. 211ra–28vb (vcb, fols. 211ra–13va); Prague, NKCR MS XIII. E. 7, fols. 175r–87r, 191r–v (vcb, fols. 175r, 191r–v); Trier, Stadtbibliothek, MS 680/879, fols. 87v–104v (vcb, fols. 87v–8v); Trier, Bibliothek des Bischöflichen Priesterseminars (Priesterseminar), MS 81, fols. 147r–65r (vcb, fols. 147r–8r); Wiesbaden, Hessische Landesbibliothek, MS 35, fols. 113r–32v (vcb, fols. 113r–14r). See the collation of manuscripts at Välimäki, *Heresy in Late Medieval Germany*, p. 114. This collation does not take into account the Trier, Priesterseminar MS 81, which I thought to hold only the *De vita et conversacione*. In fact, it has the same compilation as the other Trier manuscript and Wiesbaden and Michelstadt manuscripts, including a so far unknown copy of the *Refutatio errorum* (Redaction 1).

The Waldensian Brethren in the De vita et conversacione *(c. 1391–3)*

dead, (7) the Last Judgement of the living and the dead.[31] These are followed by the candidate's genuflection and ordination by imposition of hands. The text continues to describe the way of living of the Brethren, which is common to all versions. However, then comes another version of a Brother's ordination, repeating the vows, genuflection and imposition of hands in a form that comes from the version (vcc).[32]

How did this hybrid come about? Werner called this version the *Prager typus*, based on the Prague manuscript known to him through H. Haupt's and R. Holinka's work.[33] Werner was also aware of the differences between this version and the one edited by Schmidt (vca) and the one circulating in Austrian and German manuscripts as well as in the Olomouc manuscript he had discovered (vcc).[34] Werner is not entirely clear in his analysis, but he seems to have attributed both what he called the *Prager typus* (vcb) and the version (vcc) of the Olomouc manuscript to Martinus of Prague, together with the *Articuli* and the long question list, and he dated these texts between 1394–1404. He proposed that either Martinus worked from a different exemplar than the Strasbourg manuscript (vca), or himself added details he had acquired from the converts of 1391.[35] Werner's dating and the attribution to Martinus do not stand up against the accumulated evidence of the works' transmission. As we have already seen, the earliest manuscript of the (vca) version demonstrates that the *De vita et conversacione*, the *Articuli Waldensium*, and the long question list were all composed by 1393. By this time Petrus Zwicker and Martinus of Prague used some versions of these texts in the inquisitions of Würzburg and Stettin.[36] Werner was right, however, in that the version (vcb) was probably composed in Bohemia, as the long question list accompanying it has references to the archbishop of Prague, even in the exemplars from Trier and Rhine-Main area.[37] The Prague manuscript (NKCR MS XIII. E. 7) probably dates to the early fifteenth century, but it has a different redaction of the *Refutatio errorum*, and it cannot have been

---

[31] Trier, Stadtbibliothek, MS 680/879, fol. 87v; cf. Molnár, 'La Valdensium regula', pp. 4–5.

[32] Trier, Stadtbibliothek, MS 680/879, fols. 87v–8v; cf. Molnár, 'La Valdensium regula', pp. 5–6; for the corresponding text in (vcc), see Werner, 'Nachrichten', pp. 266–7.

[33] Werner, 'Nachrichten', pp. 215–20; cf. Haupt, 'Waldensia', pp. 328–9; R. Holinka, 'Sektářství v Čechách před revolucí husitskou', *Sborník filosofické fakulty university Komenského v Bratislavě*, 52 (1929), 125–312 (pp. 130, 176–9).

[34] Werner, 'Nachrichten', pp. 215–17, 220–5.

[35] Werner, 'Nachrichten', pp. 219–20, 222, 225.

[36] Välimäki, Heresy in Late Medieval *Germany*, pp. 119, 126–29.

[37] Werner, 'Nachrichten', p. 216. See the oath formula, Trier, Priesterseminar MS 81, fol. 149v: 'Ich N swer eyn yet Gat dem almetigen; mynem herren von prage vnd den gegenwerdigen herren An synet stat' (I N swear an oath to God the Almighty, my lord [Archbishop] of Prague and the present lord acting on behalf of him). See also Trier, Stadtbibliothek, MS 680/879, fol. 90v; Wiesbaden, Hessische Landesbibliothek, MS 35, fol. 116r.

the direct exemplar of the western German manuscripts, which have much more in common and form a relatively coherent manuscript tradition.[38] Of these, the earliest datable copy is Trier, Priesterseminar MS 81, written in 1407 by a certain Johannes of Trier.[39]

Consequently, rather than being an early, unfinished form between the two other redactions, or composition of Martinus of Prague, it is more likely that the version (vcb) originates from the hand of an unknown compiler working in the archdiocese of Prague in the late 1390s or early 1400s. The compiler had in front of him exemplars of both (vca) and (vcc) and noticing that they contained complementary information, compiled the version (vcb). By 1407 an exemplar ended up in Trier or vicinity, starting the main transmission of the work in western Germany.

The manuscript transmission history of the *De vita et conversacione* may be tedious for some readers, but it is essential for the theme of this book, inquisition and knowledge. Tracking the versions of the work reveals how inquisitors dealt with a sudden influx of valuable but potentially dangerous information about heresy. The conversion of several Waldensian Brethren in 1391 provided details about the movement previously inaccessible to inquisitors and polemicist. Even the well-informed confessant (probably a priest called John Philiberti who confessed to Bernard Gui in 1319) whose confession served as the basis for another coherent and sober-toned description of medieval Waldensianism, the *De vita et actibus*, was ignorant about how new Brethren were ordained.[40] This was revealed when the leading members of the German Waldensians converted. In the circle of two involved inquisitors, Petrus Zwicker and Martinus of Prague, the description was quickly reworked and above all placed safely within guidelines to interrogating Waldensians, resulting in the most common redaction (vcc). However, 'wild' copies of the unrevised text (vca) remained in circulation surfacing here and there independent of Zwicker's and Martinus's inquisitorial version. If

---

[38] See the manuscript collation and the manuscript descriptions, Välimäki, *Heresy in Late Medieval Germany*, pp. 114, 265, 267–9. Trier, Priesterseminar MS 81, not described there, has the following texts: *De vita et conversacione* (vcb), fols. 147r–8r; *Articuli Waldensium*, fols. 148r–9v; the long question list, fols. 149v–51r; *Errores beghardorum et beginarum*, fols. 151r–2v; *Refutatio errorum* (Redaction 1), fols. 152v–65r; a manual of confession (copied without a break or title directly after the *Refutatio*), fols. 165r–9r.

[39] Trier, Priesterseminar MS 81, fol. 114r: 'Explicit tractatus de peccato originali editus a fratre Egidio Romano ordinis sancti Augustini deo gratias scriptus et finitus per me Io[annes] de Treueris Anno domini M. ccccvii [1407] tertia die mensis Junii.' The hand is the same that copied the *Refutatio errorum* and other texts on Waldensians, and they belong to the same fascicule manuscript, likely produced at one time.

[40] He explicitly said that 'he does not know how they ordain as 'sandalled' (Qualiter autem in sandaliatos ordinent ignorat); edition and translation in Biller, 'Fingerprinting an Anonymous Description of the Waldensians', pp. 202–3. On the probable attribution of John Philiberti as the informant, see pp. 182–9.

The Waldensian Brethren in the De vita et conversacione *(c. 1391–3)*

my interpretation is correct, a few years later, someone got into his hands both the inquisitorial version and some of the 'wild' copies in circulation. Seeing that they contained complementary information, he added details about ordination and articles of faith from (vca) to the revised text (vcc), thus creating the hybrid version (vcb).

The slippery slope from holy men to heresiarchs

What was the picture painted by the *De vita et conversacione* of the Waldensian brethren? Although the text has been occasionally referred to in studies on late medieval German Waldensianism,[41] its value has not been fully recognised, perhaps because its dating and version history have been uncertain. It is, therefore, worthwhile to summarise the redaction a medieval reader was most likely to face, the version (vcc) incorporated into the *Processus Petri*.

Brethren fasted three or four days a week, one of them on bread and water unless engaged in heavy labour or travel. They did this when they were among their followers in order to appear holier in front of them. They prayed seven times a day, led in prayer by a senior Brother. They moved from place to place in pairs, a senior with a junior brother, using modest or vile clothing, were cautious in their words and avoided all lies and oaths. They likewise instructed their followers to follow the same conduct. For the most part, they were unlearned and ignorant.

When the seniors among the Brethren considered that some young man was chaste and of good conduct, they were not concerned about his birth or occupation but placed him into the custody of a senior Brother, with whom the candidate spent a year or two moving around from place to place. After that, he was led to their council or chapter ('Concilium seu capitulum ipsorum'), which was held in larger cities where the Brethren could hide in the crowd. The young man was led to the Brethren, and if he wanted to become one of them, he was led to a room where all masters were assembled with 'associates of the sect' (socii eiusdem secte), probably younger Brethren not yet authorised to hear confessions. The candidate confessed all his sins to one of the masters. He was questioned about the sacraments and the seven articles

---

[41] J. Gonnet and A. Molnár, *Les Vaudois au Moyen Âge* (Torino, 1974), p. 192; *Quellen zur böhmischen Inquisition im 14. Jahrhundert*, ed. A. Patschovsky. MGH Quellen zur Geistesgeschichte des Mittelalters 11 (Weimar, 1979), p. 29, n. 55; E. Cameron, *Waldenses: Rejections of Holy Church in Medieval Europe* (Oxford, 2000), p. 127; Biller, *Waldenses*, pp. 71–2, 182; P. Biller, 'Heretics Doing Things Secretly', in *Secrets and Discovery in the Middle Ages: proceedings of the 5th European Congress of the Fédération Internationale des Instituts d'Études Médiévales (Porto, 25th to 29th June 2013)*, ed. J. Meirinhos, C. López Alcalde and J. Rebalde, (Barcelona, 2017), pp. 15–26 (pp. 18–19); particularly comprehensive is Biller's discussion about the ordination of a Brother. It is unfortunately unpublished, see Biller, 'Aspects', pp. 47–52, 55–6.

of faith, and if he answered that he believed in them, he was then asked to give the following vows to be kept until he died: to remain chaste to the extent he was able and human fragility permitted; that he would not live off the work of his hands but from alms; that he would obey the Brethren and go wherever he was sent; that he would not trust more in his parents or relatives than in other people; and that he would not redeem himself from the peril of death by false oath. If he consented to the vows, he knelt and a senior Brother ordained him through the laying on of hands. When the newly ordained Brother rose, he embraced his senior Brethren. Each of them said to him: 'Welcome, good brother, now you are ordained in our faith in the way of the apostles'. After the ordination, the young Brother was again sent to accompany a senior for six to ten years and to refrain from hearing confessions except from his senior Brethren when necessity demanded. These confessors changed their routes almost yearly so that no one served in one place or route for more than one or two years, in order to remain unnoticed by Christians.

The description paints a picture of an organised group with its leaders and yearly chapters where new Brethren were ordained and new routes and destinations assigned. The group had established rituals of ordination and rules for advancement from a junior to a senior Brother, not unlike monastic or mendicant rules. Although the German Waldensians had to be even more clandestine and careful than their Francophone predecessors described in the *De vita et actibus* some eighty years earlier, who still had houses for both men and women to live under quasi-monastic discipline, the *De vita et conversacione* demonstrates continuity and organisation within the Waldensian movement.[42] Certain pieces of information get corroboration from earlier or contemporary accounts of German and Bohemian Waldensians. The absolute chastity required from Brethren as well as their long training period as junior companions of actual 'masters' was attested by a certain Henricus Librarius to the Dominican inquisitor Gallus of Jindřichův Hradec (Neuhaus) in 1337. Henricus's brother Rudlinus had been made the disciple (*discipulus*) of Waldensians thirty-eight years earlier. He had been a virgin, which according to Henricus was the condition: 'because one can never be a master unless one is a virgin, nor can one be accepted as disciple unless one is a virgin'. Rudlinus was made master after being a disciple for twelve years.[43] In Strasbourg trials (1400–1) the key witnesses, including Kuningund Struss Senior, who had been born in Nördlingen and had escaped the Waldensian

---

[42] On the *De vita et actibus*, see Biller, 'Fingerprinting an Anonymous Description of the Waldensians', pp. 192–3; on continuity and the role of these descriptions in general, see P. Biller, 'Goodbye to Waldensianism?', *Past and Present* 192 (2006), 3–33 (pp. 22–3).

[43] *Quellen*, ed. Patschovsky, p. 250: 'numquam potest magister esse nisi virgo nec recipitur nisi virgo in discipulum; et mansit discipulus XII annis, et post hoc magistratus fuit.'

The Waldensian Brethren in the De vita et conversacione *(c. 1391–3)*

trials in Augsburg in 1393, described the ordination of Waldensian Brethren (*meister*) – and remarkably, Sisters (*meisterin*) – in a way similar to the *De vita et conversacione:* complete chastity was again required, as was living from alms instead of their own labour, a candidate was ordained in a meeting of masters, and they were required not to betray their faith with a false oath.[44]

Unlike many other medieval accounts of heresies, the *De vita et conversacione* was not fear-mongering, and its aim was not to convince readers about a satanic counter-church, but to provide accurate information about the little-known ways of dissident confessors. Obviously, it was not a text intended for the general public but inquisitors, prelates and preachers. As such, it demonstrates their thirst of solid and sober information alongside polemical refutations of heretics' errors.

However sober in tone, the *De vita et conversacione* is not a neutral description. What I have here called the inquisitorial version (vcc) has subtle ways of downplaying the piety of the Brethren. We have already seen the example of how the strict fasting regimen was explained as a hypocritical act whose purpose was not to *be* holy but to *appear* to be holy in front of their followers. Another revision that was textually inconspicuous but significant with regards to the context took place in the sentence about Brethren's learning. Manuscripts of the version (vca) portray Brethren as unlearned men who knew the Bible by heart and in the vernacular: 'the majority of them are unlearned men, and they keep the Scripture in their heart and express it in their mother tongue'.[45] The inquisitorial version has instead a blunt statement: 'the majority of them are unlearned and ignorant ('ydeote')'.[46] It does not mention that they know the Scriptures and it stresses the old *topos* of heretics as *illitterati et idiote*, unlearned and ignorant, not knowing Latin.[47] Comparison

---

[44] *Quellen zur Geschichte der Waldenser von Strassburg (1400–1401)*, ed. G. Modestin, MGH Quellen zur Geistesgeschichte des Mittelalters 22 (Hanover, 2007), pp. 93–4, 114–15, 175–6. The ordination of the masters is discussed, but without taking into account the *De vita et conversacione*, in Modestin, *Ketzer in der Stadt*, pp. 141–5. On the Waldensian Sisters, see also Biller, *Waldenses*, pp. 125–58; J. Feuchter, 'Waldenserinnen im Mittelalter', in *Fragmenta Melanchthoniana Bd. 1. Zur Geistesgeschichte des Mittelalters und der frühen Neuzeit*, ed. G. Frank and S. Lalla, (Heidelberg, 2003), pp. 47–68.

[45] Schmidt, 'Actenstücke', p. 244: 'Item pro maiori parte sunt illiterati, et scripturam lingua materna in corde retinentes et exprimentes'. Cf. Weimar, HAAB MS Fol 20, fol. 320vb: 'Item pro maiori parte sunt illiterati in scriptura in corde retinentes'; Augsburg, UB MS II. 1.2° 78, fol. 246va: 'Pro maiori autem parte sunt illiterati, et scripturam in corde retinentes'.

[46] Werner, 'Nachrichten', p. 266: 'Item pro maiori parte sunt illiterati et ydeote'. The version (vcb) has traces from the two other versions, cf. Trier, Stadtbibliothek, MS 680/879, fol. 88r: 'Item pro maiori parte sint illiterati et ydeote, scripturam in theutonico discentes et in corde retinentes'.

[47] Biller has remarked that the choice of words reflects the *topos*, but he has not

Reima Välimäki

of these two versions confirms Biller's reading of this sentence as one containing different layers: from a genuine contemporary observation of the Brethren's education to a reflection of the *topos* of illiterate heretics. Closer scrutiny of the manuscripts reveals that the layers of the *De vita et conversacione* are not only layers of possible interpretation (medieval or modern) but concrete textual layers due to revision and intervention.

In general, the *De vita et conversacione* uses Waldensian or neutral terminology of the Brethren and their followers. In the compilations where the list of converted Brethren precedes the *De vita et conversacione*, they are bound with an explanatory clause: 'those mentioned above are called among them apostles, masters and brethren'.[48] Consequently, in the ordination of a new Brother, the senior Brethren are called 'masters' (*magistri*) and younger 'associates' (*socii*). The followers (laypeople who had not vowed to the lifestyle of the Brethren) are *subditi* (servants, subjects or laymen). Occasionally, however, the language in the inquisitorial version (vcc) betrays the interference of someone used to the terminology in contemporary inquisitions. When the masters chose some chaste, young man as a candidate, he could have been either 'born in or seduced into the sect'.[49] 'Born in the sect' ('natus/nata in secta') is the standard formulation used in Zwicker's Stettin depositions 1392–4 to describe someone whose parents were Waldensians.[50] Although the notaries in Stettin preferred the verb *induco* (introduce) and its derivates to describe the introduction of a follower to Waldensian practices, above all confession to the Brethren,[51] the terms *seductor* and *seductus* in this sense appear in marginalia, written by the hand who numerated the depositions.[52] Moreover, Martinus of Prague used the term 'seducer' in a rather more general sense in his response (1396) to the officials of the bishop of Regensburg concerning the trial of Konrad Huter, his wife Elizabeth and niece Margareta. Martinus asserted that according to his knowledge 'they have been innocent and free [of heresy] after the first abjuration and after that shunned the company of the seducers'.[53] The

---

discussed the variation between different manuscript versions at this point; see Biller, *Waldenses*, p. 182.

[48] Werner, 'Nachrichten', p. 265: 'Praedicti nominantur inter eos apostoli, magistri et fratres'.

[49] Werner, 'Nachrichten', p. 266: 'Aliquem iuvenem sive in secta natum, sive seductum'.

[50] *Quellen*, ed. Kurze, pp. 79, 100, 112, 119, 148, 175, 209, 213, 259. The list is not comprehensive.

[51] For example, Grete Beyer told Zwicker on 14 February 1394 that 'she was first introduced to the sect by the wife of Coppe Zyue in Moryn, [who said] so that one heresiarch is more benign than priests of the Church.' (Et primo eam induxit ad sectam uxor Coppe Zyue in Moryn, taliter quod benignior quam sacerdos ecclesie esset heresiarcha unus); *Quellen*, ed. Kurze, p. 223.

[52] *Quellen*, ed. Kurze, pp. 98–9, 101.

[53] Vienna, ÖNB MS 3748, fol 150r: 'ipsos esse post primam abiuracionem innocentes et immunes et vitasse deinceps talium consorcia seductorum'.

The Waldensian Brethren in the De vita et conversacione (c. 1391–3)

introduction of terms 'sect' and 'seduced' was thus a subtle way to change the tone of the text: they made it clear that the masters and brothers were members of a heretical sect, not an order of the Church.

The most significant revision for the inquisitorial version (vcc) was the omission of the articles of faith, on which a candidate Brother was questioned in his ordination. The inquisitorial version has a laconic sentence: 'then one of the more knowledgeable of them [the Brethren] proposes to him [the new Brother] something about the sacraments and the seven articles of faith in which they notwithstanding believe'.[54] This is all that is said about the articles, and the reason becomes apparent when compared to other versions. The articles of faith are entirely orthodox and contain nothing that the medieval Church would not have approved.[55] The articles of the interpolated version (vcb) have been already listed above. The version (vca) has slightly different articles:

1. There is one God who has a trinity of persons and a unity of essence.
2. The same God is the creator of all things visible and invisible.
3. He gave the Law to Moses at Mount Sinai.
4. He sent his son to be incarnated from an uncorrupted virgin.
5. He chose an immaculate church for himself.
6. The resurrection of the body.
7. He is to come to judge the living and the dead.[56]

Apparently, such an orthodox profession of faith was not to remain in the description of Waldensian heresiarchs.

The revisions in the inquisitorial version (vcc) were subtle and almost imperceptible yet effective in maintaining the desired heretical picture of the Waldensian Brethren. However, the compilers and scribes of the least polemical version (vca) also faced the same problem, namely that the text gave a too pious representation of the Waldensians. The Strasbourg manuscript has a concluding remark that attempts to convey the message that these ascetics were indeed heretical:

---

[54] St Florian, MS XI 234, fol. 84vb: 'tunc sciencior ex ipsis proponit sibi aliquid de sacramentis et de vii articulis fidei quos tamen credunt.' Cf. Werner, 'Nachrichten', p. 266, 'tantum' instead of 'tamen'.

[55] Välimäki, *Heresy in Late Medieval Germany*, pp. 123–4.

[56] Weimar, HAAB MS Fol 20, fol 321rb: 'interrogantur de septem articulis fidei, scilicet vtrum credat vnum deum in trinitate personarum et vnitatem essencie; Secundo quod idem deus sit creator omnium visibilium et invisibilium; Tertio quod tradidit legem moysi in monte synay; Quarto quod misit filium suum incarnandum de virgine incorrupta; Quinto quod elegit sibi ecclesiam immaculatam; sexto carnis resurrectionem; Septimo quod venturus est iudicare viuos et mortuos et sic de aliis articulis fidei nullam faciunt mencionem.' Cf. Schmidt, 'Actenstücke', p. 244; Augsburg, UB MS II. 1.2° 78, fols. 245vb–6ra.

Reima Välimäki

Item, note that the above-mentioned sect often flees men who are erudite in the sacred scriptures, and as much as they can, they lead their own to the hatred of the Catholic Church's pastors and prelates, collecting all evil that they know or can speak of them, in order to defame them among the people. And if they should hear any good about them, they do not believe it nor preserve it in memory, but always interpret it as evil. In addition, whoever should leave their error, they tell many lies about him. And if such a person would like to introduce others to the truth, as [someone therefore now regarded as] a morally corrupt person he is no longer believed. And this how they are able to keep other people in their most dangerous error.[57]

The Weimar manuscript lacked such a polemical exclamation. It is perhaps the most neutral in tone of all the manuscripts of the *De vita et conversacione*, to the extent that a later reader had to correct it. The original scribe had introduced the short list of Waldensian beliefs with the words: here 'follow the articles of faith'. Later, somebody replaced this dangerously bland introduction to the denial of Purgatory, the intercession of the saints, and the Church's property among other things, with 'the errors of this heresy', striking through the original words.[58]

Conclusion

The *De vita et conversacione* in all its variations demonstrates two elements of inquisitors' knowledge and truth-production. The first is the need for accurate and authentic information, and the second is the will to locate this information safely within the inquisitorial discourse. I am consciously turning to Foucauldian terminology since the process is comparable to the knowledge production John H. Arnold has analysed in the depositions of inquisition: there is the need for details and spontaneity combined with the need to control random elements.[59] The inquisitor's truth was best achieved in the version (vcc), probably revised in the circle of Petrus Zwicker and Martinus of Prague: too orthodox sections were suppressed, and inquisitorial language

---

[57] Schmidt, 'Actenstücke', pp. 244–5: 'Item nota quod predicta secta ut frequenter fugit viros sacris literis eruditos, et inquantum possunt inducunt suos ad odium pastorum et ecclesie katholice prelatorum, colligentes omnia mala que sciunt vel possunt de eis loqui, ut ex hoc in in populo infamentur; et si que bona de eis audierint, non credunt nec retinent in memoria, sed semper in malum interpretantur. Insuper qu cunque [sic] recesserit ab eorum errore, de illo multa mentiuntur; et si vellet talis alios ad veritatem inducere, ei de cetero tamquam perverso non creditur; et sic possunt suos in errore periculosissimo detinere.'

[58] Weimar, HAAB MS Fol. 20, fol. 320vb: 'Secuntur articuli fidei [later hand:] errores huius heresis'. See also Välimäki, *Heresy in Late Medieval Germany*, p. 122.

[59] J. H. Arnold, 'Inquisition, Texts and Discourse', in *Texts and the Repression of Medieval Heresy*, ed. Bruschi and Biller, pp. 63–80.

The Waldensian Brethren in the De vita et conversacione *(c. 1391–3)*

was introduced into the text, and finally the tract was combined with a list of converted heresiarchs, an exhaustive list of their errors and guidelines for their interrogation. One should not, however, exaggerate these revisions: the core of the text, originating probably from the converted Waldensian Brethren, remained. Luckily, the messy and uncontrollable transmission of late medieval manuscripts has preserved other, more extreme copies of the text, allowing us to trace places where the inquisitors intervened. To do justice to this short but rich description of Waldensians, a critical edition with parallel text versions is in preparation. However, in order to pave the way for the critical edition, and in order to give the reader a better impression of the least polemical text version of the *De vita et conversacione*, the Appendix provides a preliminary edition and translation of the Weimar manuscript. By necessity, it is not a very elaborate edition, and variant readings are provided only to make sense of some probably corrupted passages.

Appendix

Edition and translation of *De vita et conversacione* (*On Customs and Manner of Life*; abbreviated as vca), Weimar, Herzogin Anna Amalia Bibliothek, MS Fol 20, fols. 320vb–321rb.
Translation by Shelagh Sneddon

Abbreviations are expanded and modern word separation has been introduced. Otherwise the original orthography has been preserved, as is the original division of sentences. For sake of space, the original manuscript lines have not been preserved. In text passages that have been likely corrupted, a variant reading is given from C. Schmidt, 'Actenstücke besonders zur Geschichte der Waldenser', *Zeitschrift für die historische Theologie* 22 (1852), 243–5.

Reima Välimäki

[fol 320vb:]
Sequitur heresis secte qui vocantur Waldenses.[1]

Notandum quod Rectores huiusmodi secte waldensium talem habent modum et conuersacionem; Primo quod quatuor dies in ebdomada ieiunant videlicet feriam secundam, quartam, sextam et sabbatum; et vnum illorum in aqua et pane scilicet feriam sextam; nisi in itinere uel aliquo graui labore siue casu rationabili[2] impediantur.

Item sepcies in die orant et non orant aliud nisi pater noster; sed simbolum et Aue mariam non orant. Item in orando non habent numerum deteriatum[3] [sic] sed senior inter eos incipit oracionem et facit eam prolixam uel breuem secundum quod sibi videtur expedire.

Item pro maiori parte sunt illiterati in scriptura in corde retinentes[4] in verbis sunt sibi cauti mendacia voluntaria et verba turpia solent euitare; vestimentis vilibus vtuntur; diligenter subditos suos informant ad exercendum virtutes, ad cauendum a viciis; et quia ut sic eorum conuersacio apparet subditis commendabilis ideo subditi eorum ex hoc multum confortantur fidem eis in omnibus exhibendo.

Secuntur articuli ~~fidei~~[5] [later hand:] errores huius heres[is]

Secuntur articuli fidei. Primo purgatorium et mortuorum suffragia non credunt. Item veneracionem sanctorum dicunt esse ydolatriam. Item nec concedunt sanctos posse intercedere pro nobis siue pro viuis siue pro mortuis. Item

[321ra:]
omne iuramentum prohibent indifferenter. Item nullum morte puniendum affirmant. Item dicunt quod Apostoli, Episcopi, Religiosi et clerici non debent habere proprium siue possessiones. Item indulgencias ecclesie non aduertunt nec peregrinacionem curant. Item dicunt papam non habere Iurisdictionem in temporalibus nec posse quemquam excommunicare. Item dicunt quod ipse papa et omnes clerici propter malam vitam quam ducunt auctoritate ordinaria priuentur; et per consequens non possunt subditis conferre ecclesiastica sacramenta. Item quod omnes clerici ordinati sunt equalis potestatis siue auctoritatis in absoluendo peccata hominum confitencium scilicet quod papa non habet in hoc et in aliis sacramentis maiorem auctoritatem conferendi

---

[1] A rubric by a later hand follows: 'Heresis Waldensium'.
[2] Schmidt, 'Actenstücke', p. 243: 'alia causa rationabili'.
[3] Ibid.: 'determinatum'.
[4] Ibid., p. 244: 'et scripturam lingua materna in corde retinentes et exprimentes'.
[5] Rubricated.

Appendix

[fol 320vb:]
There follows *The Heresy of the Sect [of those] who are called Waldensians.*

It is to be noted that the leaders of this sect of Waldensians have the following customs and manner of life.

Firstly, they fast four days in the week: namely Monday, Wednesday, Friday and Saturday; and one of those, namely Friday, on bread and water: unless they are on a journey or are prevented by some heavy labour or reasonable cause.

Item: they pray seven times a day, and they do not pray any prayer except the Our Father; but they do not say the Creed or the Hail Mary.

Item: in praying they do not have a set number, but the senior among them begins the prayer, and makes it long or short as seems appropriate to him.

Item: for the greater part they are illiterate in scripture, retaining [it] in their hearts. In their words they are cautious with themselves; they tend to avoid deliberate lies and foul words; they wear clothes of little value; they diligently teach those subject to them to exercise virtues, to guard against vices; and because in this way their manner of life appears commendable to those subject to them, they – those subject to them - are therefore greatly comforted by this, showing trust in them in all things.

There follow the articles ~~of faith~~ [later hand:] the errors of this heresy

There follow the articles of faith.

Firstly, they do not believe in purgatory or prayers for the dead.

Item: they say that the veneration of the saints is idolatry.

Item: they do not grant that the saints can intercede for us – either for the living or for the dead. Item:

[321ra:] they prohibit all oaths without distinction.

Item: they state that no-one should be punished by death.

Item: they say that apostles, bishops, religious and clerics should not have any property or possessions.

Item: they pay no attention to the indulgences of the church, and they have no interest in pilgrimage.

Item: they say that the pope has no jurisdiction in temporal matters, and cannot excommunicate anyone.

Item: they say that the pope himself and all the clergy are deprived of ordinary authority because of the bad lives that they lead; and consequently they cannot confer the sacraments of the church on those subject to them.

Item: that all ordained clergy are of equal power or authority in absolving the sins of people who confess – that is, that the pope does not have, in this or in other sacraments, a greater authority in conferring that the simplest cleric or priest.

quam simplicissimus clericus siue presbiter. Item dies festiuos non celebrant nec honorant ut puta festum beate marie, omnium apostolorum excepto die dominico [sic]. Item ipsi docent in occulto. Item ipsi reputant sacerdotes siue ecclesie ministros esse deceptores et ypocritas propter horarum canonicarum lectiones. Item dicunt quod in qualibet missa quilibet sacerdos plura quam xxxª mortalia peccata facit, ex eo quod in canone facit mencionem de sanctis. Item dicunt quod boni layci possunt absoluere peccata melius quam mali sacerdotes. Item diuidunt vnitatem ecclesie, credentes hominem virtuose viuentem solum in eorum fide;

[321rb:]
non credunt sanctum gregorium, Nycolaum, Martinum, Katherinam et ceteros esse sanctos.
Nota quando volunt assumere ad eorum habitum aliquem prius per aliquod tempus examinant eum a[6] tempore ordinacionis faciunt eum confiteri omnia peccata que potest habere in memoria a iuuentute sua quia nullus suscipitur alias nisi sit castus et ab omni consortio mulierum immunis quo ad carnalia. Item tempore ordinacionis examinantur et interrogantur de septem articulis fidei scilicet vtrum credat vnum deum in trinitate personarum et vnitatem essencie. Secundo quod idem deus sit creator omnium visibilium et invisibilium. Tertio quod tradidit[7] legem moysi in monte synay. Quarto quod misit filium suum incarnandum[8] de virgine incorrupta. Quinto quod elegit sibi ecclesiam immaculatam. Sexto carnis resurrectionem. Septimo quod venturus est iudicare viuos et mortuos et sic de aliis articulis fidei nullam faciunt mencionem. Item interrogantur de septem sacramentis, scilicet baptismo, ordinacione presbiterorum, et sic per imposicionem manuum semel non plus ordinantur huius secte.

Explicit heresis secte waldensium.

---

[6] Schmidt, 'Actenstücke', p. 244: 'et'.
[7] Ibid.: 'condidit'.
[8] Ibid.: 'ad incarnandum'.

Appendix

Item: they do not celebrate or honour feast days, such as the feast of the Blessed Mary, or of any of[9] the apostles – except for Sunday.

Item: they teach in secret.

Item: they think that the priests or ministers of the church are deceivers and hypocrites because of their readings of the canonical hours.

Item: they say that in each mass each priest commits more than thirty mortal sins, because in the canon mention is made of the saints.

Item: they say that good lay people can forgive sins better than bad priests.

Item: they split the unity of the church, believing that people live a virtuous life only in their faith.

[321rb:]

They do not believe that saints Gregory, Nicholas, Martin, Catherine and the others are saints.

Note that when they want to accept someone into their habit, they first examine him for some time. And at the time of his ordination they make him confess all the sins that he can remember, from his youth – because no-one is received, unless he is chaste and without any carnal dealings with women.

Item: at the time of ordination they are examined and questioned about the seven articles of faith – that is, whether he believes in one God in a trinity of persons and unity of essence.

Secondly, that the same God is the creator of everything visible and invisible.

Thirdly, that he gave the law to Moses on Mount Sinai.

Fourthly, that he sent his son to become incarnate of the incorrupt Virgin.

Fifthly, that he chose the immaculate church for himself.

Sixthly, the resurrection of the flesh.

Seventhly, that he will come to judge the quick and the dead – and thus they make no mention of other articles of faith. Item: they are questioned about the seven sacraments – that is, baptism, the ordination of priests. And thus by the imposition of hands once and not more the leaders of this sect are ordained.

Here ends *The Heresy of the Sect of the Waldensians*.

[9] Literally 'of all of the apostles'.

7

Means of persuasion in medieval anti-heretical texts: the case of Petrus Zwicker's *Cum dormirent homines*[1]

Adam Poznański

In modern times the topic of medieval heresy has always aroused special interest among scholars and to some degree the general public. One reason may be that heretics were a minority and they were persecuted. The other reason is probably that the phenomenon of heresy still remains mysterious to us. Although we know more and more about heretics, many aspects of their life remain unclear. This is caused by the character of the sources that have come down to us. Heretics had to live in hiding, and they had to protect their own texts. On the other hand, the Catholic Church had its own purposes and was not particularly concerned with portraying its enemies in an unbiased way. Like it or not, we have to rely mostly on the sources written by Catholic priests to refute heterodox teachings.

The reading of anti-heretical treatises plays therefore a crucial role in apprehending heresy. Usually our approach is based on historical methods – in the texts we search for all the facts about the doctrine in question and historical events related to the particular religious movement. However, in my opinion, we should focus not only on the contents, but also on the medium that was used to convey them – the language. I think that the language of such literature reveals the attitude to the topic, although not always explicitly. And not only is that the attitude of an author, but also, to some extent, the attitude of a society. In the context of anti-heretical discourse it has a special meaning, because all the authors belonged to one institution, the Catholic Church, and represented its interests. What is more, that group had considerable control over that society, and since the Church

---

[1] This article is derived from my unpublished PhD Thesis 'Środki perswazji w pismach antyheretyckich na przykładzie traktatu Piotra Zwickera *Cum dormirent homines*', defended at the University of Wrocław in 2011. I would like to express my sincere gratitude to Fr. Tomasz Gałuszka OP, who advised me to choose Zwicker's treatise as the focus of my research on anti-heretical argumentation.

Means of persuasion in medieval anti-heretical texts

was operating across Europe with a highly organised administration, its texts could spread widely and easily. Hence all the ideas or approaches supported by the Church could reach and influence wide masses of the faithful in a relatively short time.[2] And the main language of the Church, Latin, was the one universal language in Europe at the time.

Latin in the middle ages had some special features. It was the second language for all its users. Moreover, it was closely related to the scholastic way of teaching based on *lectio* and *disputatio*. At a higher level, how someone wrote in Latin depended on what he read. Of course, all clergymen were well acquainted with the Bible and liturgical texts. However, for some, classical literature was more influential and as a result they adopted a classical style, while others were not and did not. Some preferred the rather rough and logical style of university disputations, as displayed for example in the prose of Aquinas's *Summa Theologiae*, others not.[3] As a result, even within one genre of medieval texts, we have to deal with the range of nuances offered by a great variety of prose styles that, in my experience, should not be neglected when it comes to the interpretation of a given work.

There are many aspects to the language of medieval anti-heretical texts,[4] but to me the most interesting are the means of persuasion and the ways of structuring arguments. The controversy between Catholics and those labelled as dissidents was of incomparable seriousness: at stake was eternal life. What choices should one make in order to merit it? Also at stake was the social order – heretics were unwilling to obey the hierarchy of the Church. Of course, this second problem was dealt with by violence, the exercise of the so-called *brachium saeculare* (the 'secular arm', in execution). But in the treatises the only weapons were words. To persuade someone just with words, one needs to get their free assent. And to achieve this, one has to use these words in a very skilled way.

For the purposes of this chapter, I shall analyse just one work that has a special place in this area. It was written by Petrus Zwicker (died in or after 1404), a Celestine monk who became an inquisitor and was very efficient in battling against Waldensians in Central Europe. Not only did he interrogate

---

[2] On the transmission of the texts in the middle ages, see for example M. B. Parkes, *Scribes, Scripts, and Readers: Studies in the Communication, Presentation, and Dissemination of Medieval Texts* (London and Rio Grande OH, 1991).

[3] On the style of medieval disputations, see O. Weijers, *In the Search of the Truth: a History of Disputation Techniques from Antiquity to Early Modern Times* (Turnhout, 2013), pp. 119–47.

[4] For example, specific vocabulary used to describe a heretic was analysed by H. Grundmann, 'Der Typus des Ketzers in mittelalterlicher Anschauung', in *Ausgewählte Aufsätze*, 3 vols. (Stuttgart, 1976), I, 313–27; English translation in *Herbert Grundmann (1902–1970). Essays on Heresy, Inquisition and Literacy*, ed. J. K. Deane, Heresy and Inquisition in the Middle Ages 9 (York, 2019), pp. 16–29.

the suspects and condemn the guilty, but also wrote a polemical treatise[5] against their heresy in 1395. It does not have a real title, but in recent scholarship it is called *Cum dormirent homines* from the biblical quotation at the very beginning (*verba thematis* – 'words of the theme' which will be taken up and developed).[6] The treatise is not very long, compared for example to Moneta of Cremona's monumental work *Adversus Catharos et Waldensians*. It comprises approximately fifty modern pages and in manuscripts it is usually divided into thirty-six chapters of differing length. Each chapter is supposed to refute, more or less, a single error of the Waldensians. What I find remarkable in this treatise is the sheer variety of techniques of persuasion that it exhibits. Further, there is the fact that it was composed one century after the heyday of anti-heretical literature.[7] Zwicker was able to look at the problem of heresy from a broader perspective and evaluate the measures taken by earlier authors. In general, the treatise is based on *ratio et auctoritas* (reason and authority). In other words, the two main techniques of persuasion are the use of logical arguments and reference to authorities. Such a method of dealing with heresy had already been adopted by Peter the Venerable in his *Epistola sive tractatus adversus Petrobrusianos haereticos*, written in the early 1130s.[8] However, those two terms are not enough to describe the means of persuasion

[5] Zwicker's treatise lacks a modern critical edition. The first printed edition was prepared by Jacob Gretser: [Pseudo-] *Petri de Pilichdorf contra Haeresin Waldensium Tractatus*, in *Lucae tvdensis episcopi, Scriptores aliqvot svccedanei contra sectam waldensivm*, ed J. Gretser (Ingolstadt, 1613), pp. 203–90. This is most commonly read and cited in its reprint in *Maxima bibliotheca veterum patrum et antiquorum scriptorum ecclesiasticorum*, ed. M. de La Bigne, 27 vols. (Lyon, 1677), XXV, 277F–99G. I use and refer to the 1613 edition, while also providing references to the equivalent page numbers in the 1677 reprint. The reader should be warned that the 1677 reprint occasionally omits a few words from the 1613 edition, or represents them erroneously.

[6] In recent years much has been written about Zwicker and his work. First on the correct attribution: P. Biller, 'The Anti-Waldensian Treatise *Cum Dormirent Homines* of 1395 and Its Author', in P. Biller, *The Waldensians, 1170–1530: Between a Religious Order and a Church*, Variorum Collected Studies Series 676 (Aldershot, 2001), pp. 237–69. On his life and work: G. Modestin, 'Peter Zwicker (gest. nach dem 7. Juni 1404)', in *Schlesische Lebensbilder* 10, ed. F. Andreae (Wrocław, 2010), pp. 25–34; G. Modestin, 'The Anti–Waldensian Treatise *Cum dormirent homines*: Historical Context, Polemical Strategy, and Manuscript Tradition', in *Religious Controversy in Europe, 1378–1536*, ed. M. Van Dussen and P. Soukup (Turnhout, 2013), pp. 211–29; R. Välimäki, *Heresy in Late Medieval Germany. The Inquisitor Petrus Zwicker and the Waldensians*, Heresy and Inquisition in the Middle Ages 6 (York, 2019). The last work in particular discusses the content and manuscript tradition of the treatise.

[7] On the anti-heretical literature in the thirteenth century, see W. L. Wakefield and A. P. Evans, ed., *Heresies of the High Middle Ages* (New York, 1969, repr. 1991), pp. 633–8; L. J. Sackville, *Heresy and Heretics in the Thirteenth Century: The Textual Representations*, Heresy and Inquisition in the Middle Ages 1 (York, 2011).

[8] Petrus Venerabilis, *Contra Petrobrusianos haereticos*, ed. J. Fearns, CCCM 10 (Turnhout 1968). For more on *ratio et auctoritas* see H. Fichtenau, *Ketzer und Professoren. Häresie und Vernunftglaube im Hochmittelalter* (Munich, 1992), pp. 199–211.

Means of persuasion in medieval anti-heretical texts

used by Zwicker, as I shall show below.[9] In addition, *Cum dormirent homines* was clearly a very popular text at the time when it was written: forty-six manuscript copies are extant and given the textual variants, we may assume there were many more. So, this text met the expectations of readers in its own time: all the more reason for treating it in our times as a significant work.

In the dissertation upon which this chapter is based, I used argumentation theory in my investigation of the methods used by Zwicker to refute Waldensian heresy. Although it has a long tradition going back to Greek Antiquity, I referred to argumentation theory as it is viewed by contemporary scholars.[10] Rather than looking for Zwicker's sources or inspiration, I wanted to analyse his forms of argument and to investigate how he thought and reasoned. The result of this enquiry was a division of his means of persuasion into three groups: deductive, inductive and eristic, and this is what I am now presenting in this chapter. Below I shall give examples of different types of Zwicker's arguments within each of those groups.[11] Since different scholars use different names for arguments, I have decided to use traditional Latin ones in order not to be confined to the language of a particular school or theory.

Deductive reasoning is an inference that gives absolute certainty that the conclusion is true if the premises are true. An argument is called deductively correct, if it is not possible that true premises lead to untrue conclusion. Aristotle called such arguments syllogisms.

An **enthymeme** is a deductive argument devoid of one or several premises that can be guessed. Aristotle called it a rhetorical syllogism and considered it as a basic tool of rhetoric, e.g.:

> Ecce manifesta confusio tua Waldensis Hæretice. CHRISTVS dicit, aurum templi, et donum altaris, esse sanctum quae sunt res inanimatæ, et per consequens, irrationales, et tu non credis, quod dicit Christus; ergo tu es hæreticus.

---

[9] Some other attempts to describe anti-heretical persuasion are G. Vallée, *A Study in Anti-Gnostic Polemics. Irenaeus, Hippolytus, and Epiphanius* (Waterloo Ontario, 1981), and D. Iogna-Prat, *Order and Exclusion: Cluny and Christendom Face Heresy, Judaism, and Islam, 1000–1150* (Ithaca, 2002), pp. 120–47.

[10] On general aspects of argumentation theory, see T. A. Govier, *A Practical Study of Argument*, (Belmont CA, 1988); F.H. van Eemeren, et al., *Fundamentals of Argumentation Theory. A Handbook of Historical Backgrounds and Contemporary Developments* (Mahwah NJ, 1996); F. Besnard and A. Hunter, *Elements of Argumentation* (Cambridge MA and London, 2008). In this article, to distinguish different argumentation schemes, I used mainly D. Walton, C. Reed and F. Macagno, *Argumentation Schemes* (Cambridge and New York, 2008), and S. Rubinelli, *Ars Topica: The Classical Technique of Constructing Arguments from Aristotle to Cicero* (Dordrecht, 2009).

[11] Some preliminary remarks on Zwicker's argumentation can be found in an earlier article I published in Polish: A. Poznański, 'Reakcja Kościoła na kryzys ortodoksji w średniowieczu Piotra Zwickera traktat *Cum dormirent homines*' (The Reaction of the Church to the Crisis of Orthodoxy in the Middle Ages: Peter Zwicker's treatise *Cum dormirent homines*), in *Ecclesia semper reformanda: Kryzysy i reformy średniowiecznego Kościoła*, ed. T. Gałuszka, T. Graff and G. Ryś (Kraków, 2013), pp. 195–210.

(Your confusion is manifest, you Waldensian heretic! Christ said that the gold of the temple and the gift of the altar are holy, which are inanimate things and, consequently, irrational, and you do not believe what Christ said, so you are a heretic!).

Zwicker, *Cum dormirent homines* xxxvi, p. 274 (1677: p. 298G).

Zwicker maintained that Waldensians did not respect the words of Christ concerning swearing and the errors of Pharisees (Matthew 23. 16–22). Waldensians believed that nothing but God could be called holy, especially the Holy Virgin, whereas the inquisitor shows that Jesus did not refrain from calling holy simple objects like gold or gifts in the temple. The assertion that rejection of Christ's words leads to heresy was implicit. This argument can be presented as follows:

Anyone who does not believe in the word of Christ is a heretic. (unstated premise)

The Waldensians do not believe in the word of Christ.

---

therefore: Waldensians are heretics.

Argumentum ad absurdum is an argument in which it is indicated that one of the opponent's statements contradicts another, e.g.:

Respondeas ergo Waldensis hæretice, si sacerdotium Apostolicum ablatum est tempore Papae Siluestri, sicut mentitur tibi iniquitas tua; quis ergo ordinauit primum Waldensem in sacerdotem, cum nullum fuerit aliud sacerdotium in mundo verum, nisi illud Christi secundum ordinem Melchisedech? Vel ergo dices, quod te ordinauerit sacerdos Iudæus, vel Paganus, vel Christianus; vel, DEVS, vel Diabolus; vel, tu teipsum elegeris? Si Iudæus vel Paganus, vnde tibi ergo nomen Christiani; cum nemo nihil det, quod non habet? Si Christianus, et quis potuit fuisse, cum tu mentiaris sublatum fuisse sacerdotium? Si DEVS: ostende per signa. Sed non credis hodie in Ecclesia fieri signa. Ergo non poteris ostendere per signa; quia nemo approbat se per hoc, quod impugnat.

(Answer, Waldensian heretic: if the apostolic priesthood lost its validity at the time of Pope Sylvester – as in your wickedness you lie to yourself – who ordained the first Waldensian as a priest, since there was no other true priesthood in the world, but the one of Christ according to the order of Melchizedek? Will you say that you were ordained as a priest by a Jew, pagan, Christian, God or devil, or did you choose yourself? If a Jew or a pagan, why do you call yourself a Christian, since no one can give anything that he does not have? If a Christian, who could it have been, since – according to your lie – the priesthood has been abolished? If God, show me signs! But you do not believe that there are signs in the church today. So

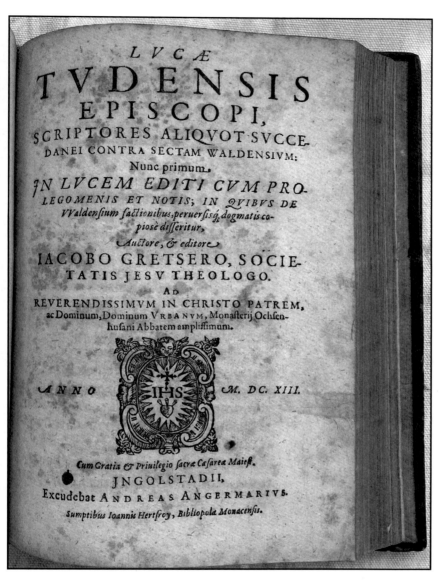

Figure 7.1   Jakob Gretser, *Lucæ Tudensis episcopi, scriptores aliquot succedanei contra sectam Waldensium* (Ingolstadt, 1613), title page. The first of the two major treatises edited here were Reinerius's *Liber contra Waldenses*, now dated c.1260–6 and referred to as the Anonymous of Passau and, in a slightly later version, the Pseudo-Reinerius treatise. The second was a treatise of 1395 written by Peter of Pillichsdorf, now known as the *Cum dormirent* treatise and ascribed to the inquisitor Peter Zwicker. These are the two works used by Bossuet for his account of the origins of the Waldensians; see fig. 0.6. Private collection.

PILICHDORFFIVS

CAPVT V.

Vnde prius VValdensis ordinatus fuerit?

ESPONDEAS ergò Waldensis hæretice, si sacerdotium Apostolicum ablatum est tempore Papæ Siluestri, sicut mentitur tibi iniquitas tua; quis ergò ordinauit primum Waldensem in sacerdotem, cum nullum fuerit aliud sacerdotium in mundo verum, nisi illud Christi secundum ordinem Melchisedech? Vel ergò dices, quòd te ordinauerit sacerdos Iudæus, vel Paganus, vel Christianus; vel, DEVS, vel Diabolus; vel, tu te ipsum elegeris? Si Iudæus vel Paganus, vnde tibi ergò nomen Christiani; cum nemo nihil det, quod non habet? Si Christianus, & quis potuit fuisse, cum tu mentiaris sublatum fuisse sacerdotium? Si DEVS: ostende per signa. Sed non credis hodie in Ecclesia fieri signa. Ergò non poteris ostendere per signa; quia nemo approbat se per hoc, quod impugnat.

Quod autem oporteat te probare per signa, probatur; quia, tu credis te vices gerere Apostolorum; Et illis dedit Saluator, signa facere. Nec quidem voluit hoc esse donum illi magno suo Baptistæ Ioanni. Ioan. 10. *Quia Ioannes quidem signum fecit nullum.* Signa ergò facere, fuit euidens signum Apostolorum: imò etiam Iudæ pessimi: quem etiam Dominus non excepit, cum discipulis dixit Matth. 10. *Infirmos curate, mortuos suscitate, leprosos mundate, dæmones eijcite.* Relinquitur ergò quod sis ordinatus & missus à diabolo. *Vos ex patre Diabolo estis,* Ioan. 8. Mendaces, homicidis peiores, fures: qui non venitis nisi vt furemini, mactetis, & perdatis. Ioan. 10. *Quotquot venerunt,* scilicet non legitimè missi, *fures sunt & latrones.* Non estis pastores boni, qui relinquitis credentes vestros, & fugitis ab eis, & non paretis, quia Ioan. 3. dicitur; *Qui malè agit, odit lucem.* Si verò tu temetipsum elegisti; hoc sine Diabolo non fecisti. Hebr. 5. *Nec quisquam sibi sumit honorem, sed qui vocatur à DEO, tanquam Aaron.* Ergò percussus es lepra, vt Ozias, qui accepto thuribulo, voluit adolere incensum Domino. 2, Paral. 26. Deglutit te terra, id est, infernus, vt Dathan & Abyron, Num. 26.

CAPVT

Means of persuasion in medieval anti-heretical texts

you cannot show by signs, because no one approves their viewpoint using statements that they fight.)

Zwicker, *Cum dormirent homines* v, p. 208 (1677: p. 279B–C).

Zwicker found a contradiction in the Waldensian doctrine. They asserted that since the time of Constantine's donation, ordinations of priests were not valid, ergo there were no real priests in the Catholic Church. Therefore, as Zwicker points out, there was also nobody to ordain Waldensian priests. This reasoning can be presented in the following way:

If since the donation of Constantine priesthood is not valid, there are no more priests now.

Waldensians regard themselves as priests.

therefore: the Waldensian doctrine is false.

It should be mentioned here that probably Waldensians did not understand their priesthood in the same way as Zwicker did. Rather, they claimed that their faith came from Christ and existed continuously. Zwicker also added irony to his reasoning by asking whether their ordination into the priesthood came from Jews, pagans, Christians, God or the devil. He then showed, one by one, that none of these possibilities could have taken place, because each of them contradicts what Waldensians say about themselves. In the conclusion we could also find another *argumentum ad absurdum*: since Waldensians reject all the signs or miracles taking place after Christ, they were not able to receive priesthood from God.

Inductive reasoning is one in which the true premises do not necessarily entail the true conclusion, but only make it more or less probable. Thus, in the case of inductive arguments, we do not talk about correctness, but only about greater or lesser effectiveness in terms of persuasion.

Argumentum ex auctoritate – this is accepting a given statement as true, because a person or a group of people of great authority agrees with it, e.g.:

Ipse tempore recessus, et separationis ab eis, dixit Luc. 22. *Quando misi vos sine sacculo et pera, et calciamentis, nunquid aliquid defuit vobis?* Et cum discipuli respondissent; nihil, Dominus adiunxit: *Sed nunc, qui habet sacculum tollat, similiter et peram.* Quod prius prohibuit, postea concessit. Ideo licet Prælatis Ecclesiasticis habere proprium, ad defendendam Ecclesiam contra hæreticos, et alios iniuriosos inuasores.

(He himself [Christ], when in isolation and away from them, said: *When I sent you without purse, and scrip, and shoes, did you want anything?* They answered: Nothing. But he continued: *But now he that hath a purse, let him take it, and likewise a scrip* [Luke 22. 35–36]. What he forbade earlier, he allowed later. That is why the prelates of the Church are allowed to possess things to defend the Church against heretics and other wicked attackers.)

Zwicker, *Cum dormirent homines* i, p. 204 (1677: p. 278B).

Waldensians believed that the Catholic Church lost its mission when, under Pope Sylvester I, it received many goods and privileges from the Emperor Constantine. That was supposed to be against the command given by Christ to the apostles: *Do not possess gold, nor silver, nor money in your purses* (Matthew 10. 9). According to the Waldensian doctrine, all priests, as advocates of the apostles, should practise absolute poverty and not possess anything. Zwicker responded to this plea in the following way: although the renunciation of temporal goods was ordered by Christ, there is an exception – the situation when the Church is in danger. According to Zwicker's interpretation any means may be taken to defend the Church against heresy. Therefore, when the prelates take up possessions, they are following the words of Christ, who is the greatest authority.

Argumentum a simili – this is recognising a given statement as true, because another, a similar one, is true; inference by analogy.

Rosa rubens æqualiter rubet in manu Imperatoris, et alterius fœtidæ mulieris. Similiter carbunculus in manu regis et rustici, Et famulus meus ita bene mundat stabulum cum furca ferrea, et rubiginosa, sicut cum aurea, et lapidibus preciosis adornata. Nemo dubitat, Heliæ temporibus multos fuisse cygnos in sæculo; nec tamen Dominus per cygnos, sed per corvum nigrum Prophetam cibavit. 3. Reg. 17. Licet forte iucundius fuisset per cygnum; tamen æque saturatus (fuit) per corvum. Et licet iucundius bibatur nectar de scypho aureo, quam de vase luteo; tamen non minus inebriat undecunque potatum. Etsi acceptior et gratior sit, si rex per summum eius militem donat mihi annulum aureum, æque tamen nobilis est annulus, si portat ipsum ad me rusticus.

(The red rose has the same colour in the hand of an emperor as of a foul smelling woman. Similarly a ruby in the hands of a king and a peasant. Also, my servant cleans the stable equally well with an iron fork, which is rusty, or with a golden one ornamented with precious stones. No one doubts that in Elijah's time there were many swans in the world, but the Lord did not send them to feed the prophet, but the black raven. 3 Kings 17. Although it would have been more pleasant being fed by a swan, the [prophet] was equally well fed by the raven. And although it would have been more pleasant to drink nectar from a golden chalice than a clay pot, it makes one equally drunk, whatever the vessel. Although it is more

Means of persuasion in medieval anti-heretical texts

honorable and more enjoyable when the king presents me with a gold ring via his highest knight, the ring is equally noble if a peasant brings it to me.)

Zwicker, *Cum dormirent homines* xvii, p. 218 (1677: p. 282A–B).

Through a series of analogies, Zwicker tried to show that the essence of the sacraments is completely independent of priests as people. The beauty and colour of the rose or ruby are immutable and independent of the qualities of people who possess them. In turn, the tools that serve to clean the stable fulfil their functions regardless of the appearance and the material from which they were made. The prophet Elijah was fed by the black raven, and thus by a bird which is not the most beautiful and does not have particularly good associations. Drinking wine leads to intoxication no matter what one drinks from, and a golden ring loses nothing in value through being handed over by a person of low estate. In the same way, the power and importance of the sacraments come from God and they are not affected by the attitudes or the sins or the opinions of the priests who give them. If, therefore, a priest has been validly convicted of some crime or is in a state of sin, he still has the power to administer the sacraments and the faithful should not judge his power on the basis of his deeds. They should, however, be convinced that the sacraments are signs of grace coming directly from God. These *argumenta a simili* are an example of inductive reasoning. Their power to persuade, depends on readers' views of the plausibility and realistic nature of the comparisons that are presented.

Argumentum a fortiori – this is accepting a statement as true, because another statement which is similar is true. The comparison is based on a feature or features that in the latter statement are stronger, or are even more conclusive, e.g.:

Quis enim dubitat sacerdotes Hierosolymitanos temporibus Christi fuisse, vt plurimum, impios et iniquos: qui tot conuiciis, tot improperiis Dominum IESVM Christum, et eius discipulos infestabant? Eosdem tamen Dominus propter sacerdotij dignitatem plurimum honorauit. Vnde Matth. 8. postquam iam leprosum Dominus mundasset, dixit; *Vade, et ostende te sacerdotibus.*

(Who doubts that the Jerusalem priests at the time of Christ were for the most part abominable and wicked, since they were attacking the Lord Jesus Christ and his disciples with so many affronts and insults? But for the sake of the dignity of the priesthood, the Lord paid them special respect. Whence – Matthew 8. 4 – after the Lord healed the leper, he said: *go, shew thyself to the priests*).

Zwicker, *Cum dormirent homines* xviii, pp. 218–9 (1677: p. 282B–C).

One of the duties that the Catholic Church required from its faithful, and which Waldensians could not accept, was obedience to priests and ecclesiastical superiors. According to Waldensian doctrine, if they acted wickedly, they completely lost their power and no one was obliged to obey them. In the Gospel, we read that Christ and the apostles received a lot of hatred from the priests of the Jerusalem temple. Nevertheless, Jesus did not detract from their priestly dignity. In this way Zwicker tried to show that the priesthood, and not only that given by Christ at the time of the Last Supper, but also in the Old Testament, should be seen as a supernatural gift, granted by God and independent of any man's actions. This is an example of *argumentum a fortiori*: since Jesus respected the wicked Jerusalem priests, how much more should all Catholic priests be respected by the faithful. This reasoning has the following scheme:

The Jerusalem priests were respected by Christ.

Catholic priests are the successors of the Jerusalem priests.

---

therefore: Catholic priests should be respected by all the faithful.

In addition to deduction and induction, there are also other ways of persuading, the **eristic** ones. Their aim is above all to undermine the credibility of the opponent and discredit him before the public. They are not always arguments in the formal sense, because they do not have to contain inference. Nevertheless, they have a large impact on the audience and are very effective means of persuasion. Zwicker used techniques of this type in his treatise quite often, although they are usually considered to be dishonest. The fact that human nature is more prone to succumb to eristic tricks than to the analysis of categorical syllogisms was mentioned by the philosopher John Locke in his famous work on human reason published in 1690. He distinguished four types of eristic arguments as frequently used in everyday conversations.[12] A more complete list of such devices can be found in a booklet by Artur Schopenhauer, published in 1831, *Eristische Dialektik: Die Kunst, Recht zu behalten* (*Eristic Dialectic: The Art of Winning an Argument*). Although it may be seen as facetious, it contains relevant observations on effective persuasion. In anti-heretical literature different types of eristic methods had been around since Antiquity,[13] and Zwicker did not ignore the tradition.

Argumentum ad hominem – this is referring directly to the opponent as a person (usually with insults) instead of the disputed matter, e.g.

Mendaces, homicidis peiores, fures: qui non venitis nisi ut furemini, mactetis, et perdatis.

(Liars, worse than killers, thieves who only come to steal, kill and destroy!)

Zwicker, *Cum dormirent homines* v, p. 208 (1677: p. 279C–D).

---

[12] J. Locke, *An Essay Concerning Human Understanding* (Amherst NY, 1995), pp. 567–83.
[13] A list of invectives against ancient heretics can be found in I. Opelt, *Die Polemik in der christlichen lateinischen Literatur von Tertullian bis Augustin* (Heidelberg, 1980), pp. 229–68.

Means of persuasion in medieval anti-heretical texts

This invective alluded to John 10. 10: *The thief cometh not, but for to steal, and to kill, and to destroy.* So, according to Zwicker, Waldensians were liars who acted like thieves with the intention of harming the faithful.

Argumentum ad baculum – this is using fear to strengthen arguments, e.g.

> Sic tu Waldensis Heretice, offendas imaginem sanctæ Crucis, aut B. Virginis Mariæ, aut alterius sancti, ultrices flammæ Christiane iustitiæ devorabunt te: cum nec rex aliquis terreneus pateretur suam galeam, vel clenodium deturpari.

> (So, Waldensian heretic, you offend the image of the Holy Cross, the Blessed Virgin Mary, or another saint: in revenge the flames of Christian justice will devour you, because no king on earth would allow his insignia or jewel to be dishonoured.)

> Zwicker, *Cum dormirent homines* xxxiii, pp. 266–7 (1677: pp. 296E).

Zwicker tried to influence the audience by arousing fear of God's vengeance – perhaps also by reminding them of death by burning. God would not let the heretics reject images of the cross, Mary or the saints, and would punish them for lack of respect.

Argumentum ad iudicium – this is reference to the knowledge and experience of the listeners, presenting as true what seems certain or at least probable, e.g.:

> An putas nos Catholicos in tantam delapsos esse dementiam; ut, non intelligamus impendendæ Deo et sanctis eius servitutis esse differentiam?

> (Do you think that we Catholics have fallen into such madness that we do not understand that there is a difference between serving God and his saints?)

> Zwicker, *Cum dormirent homines* xx, p. 226 (1677: p. 284E).

Zwicker appealed to common sense, stating that it is impossible that all the Catholics have become insane and cannot understand whom they worship.

Having looked at the types of arguments used by Zwicker, we can attempt to find out which of them he considered more effective than others and which he might have considered his favourites. First, we must recognise the unevenness of the treatment of individual doctrinal issues. Of course the division into chapters is different in different manuscripts, and the author's intentions are hard to assess. Nevertheless, a basic contrast is clear: sometimes Zwicker's deliberations are long and exhaustive, and sometimes very laconic.[14]

Zwicker's most common ploy is to take a quotation from the Bible and use it to build an *argumentum ex auctoritate* (argument from authority). Usually, this argument has a simple structure and the biblical quotation itself has no

---

[14] Compare for instance chapter iii on the continuity of the faith (one short paragraph) and chapter xxi on purgatory (several pages).

additional comment or explanation. In some cases, to make such an argument stronger, Zwicker referred to the very words of Christ or to some evangelical event in which he participated. Second in frequency is the *argumentum a simili*, which is often based in biblical stories, although some present everyday situations – as we have seen in the analogies used to refute the significance for the sacraments of the sinfulness of priests. Zwicker also valued *argumentum a fortiori*, which in ordinary conversation is seen as very convincing. Thus, we see that inductive arguments form the core of Zwicker's means of persuasion. Deductive arguments are quite rare, and, when he does employ them, they are usually in the form of an enthymeme (an argument in which one premise is not explicitly stated) that is sometimes difficult to distinguish from an *argumentum ex auctoritate*. There are also several distinctive *argumenta ad absurdum*. It seems that by using them the author tried to emphasise the dishonest attitude of Waldensians towards their listeners and lack of consistency in the Waldensian doctrine. Finally, apart from real arguments, there are eristic ones. Notably invectives (*argumenta ad hominem*) played an important role in Zwicker's treatise. The Waldensian preacher is described as evil (*nequam*), stupid or uneducated (*asinus, idiota, illiteratus, stolidus*), with dull senses (*surdus, mutus*, deaf, dumb), thief (*fur*), liar (*mendax*), student of Satan (*sicut Magister et Pater tuus Diabolus*), worse than killers (*homicidis peior*), night animal (*vespertilio, noctua caeca*, bat, blind night-owl), rodent (*glis*, dormouse), poisonous animal (*venenosa rana*, venomous frog). All of these are designed to evoke specific feelings, in this case fear, disgust and contempt for Waldensians. And as a result, they convey the message that the Waldensians should be avoided and not helped, and it is better not to have any exchanges with them. Frequent reproaches, occurring within the *argumenta ex auctoritate*, that Waldensians misunderstood the message of biblical quotations were intended to have a similar function.

Generally, Zwicker avoided arguments with complex structures, and he did not rely on authorities other than the Bible, such as the Church fathers or canon law.[15] He followed the rule that an argument should be easy to follow. Consequently he kept away from the sort of complicated dialectical explanations that were common in the *quaestiones* of the medieval university. It is clear from this, first of all, that Zwicker wanted to reach a wide audience, not just those who were learned in theology, and, secondly that he was aware what type of arguments were more likely to convince readers. It is also significant that he did not use the unfair arguments known as sophisms or fallacies. He treated his audience seriously, with some respect, and did not try to lead them astray with trickery. He very often accused the heretics of dishonesty – perhaps he did not want to be tarred with the same brush?

---

[15] There are very few references outside this frame: just one quotation from Boethius's *De consolatione philosophiae* and one popular Latin proverb.

Means of persuasion in medieval anti-heretical texts

Now that we have outlined the different types of arguments used by Zwicker, we can stand back and take another look, now trying to evaluate his attempts to persuade more thoroughly and at a deeper level. In order to do this, I shall bring into the discussion two theories of argumentation that became very influential in the twentieth century. The first one is called *New Rhetoric* and was developed by Chaïm Perelman and Lucie Olbrechts-Tyteca; the second one was invented by Stephen Toulmin.[16] Despite the fact that they differ in many respects, they both take the *Organon* and *Rhetoric* of Aristotle as a starting point for analysing arguments. They see three crucial elements in effective persuasion: the feelings of the audience towards the speaker (*ethos*), the feelings that the speaker arouses in the audience (*pathos*) and sound arguments (*logos*). Both theories agree that in order to evaluate persuasion, we should first determine all the circumstances of a given controversy. This means that it is crucial to define the subject matter of the dispute and the audience. Only then can we get clearly into our sights the effectiveness of the strategy of the person who tries to persuade others.

As far as Zwicker's persuasion is concerned, two issues need to be addressed. First, against whom was the treatise written? Who was the opponent? Secondly, who was the audience? Who were supposed to be persuaded? The general view is that Catholics and Waldensians were the two sides of the dispute. But the *Cum dormirent homines* case can be described more precisely. In the prologue to the treatise, Zwicker stated that:

> Maxime vero inimici sunt, qui omnium virtutum fundamentum; quod est fides Christiana, impugnare conantur, sicut sunt hæresiarchæ; qui Prælatis Ecclesiae, velut hominibus rationabiliter et humane viuere debentibus, in corpore neglegentiæ dormientibus, illas pauculas, et vtinam non multas ouiculas rapiunt, inficiunt et furantur.

> (Most of all, in truth, the enemies are those who try to impugn the foundation of all virtues, which is the Christian faith, such as the heresiarchs who kidnap, spoil and steal those small sheep, hopefully not many, from the prelates of the Church — people [the prelates] who ought to be living in a rational and human way but are sleeping in the body of negligence.)

> Zwicker, *Cum dormirent homines*, p. 203 (1677: p. 277F).

Among the Waldensians, as in other medieval sects, there were two groups: the masters and the faithful (*credentes*).[17] The former were itinerant preachers who taught the doctrine, the latter were simple believers, supposed to host

---

[16] On those theories, see C. Perelman, *The Realm of Rhetoric*, trans. W. Kluback (Notre Dame IN and London, 1982); S. E. Toulmin, *The Uses of Argument: Updated Edition* (Cambridge, 2003).

[17] See G. Audisio, G., *The Waldensian Dissent: Persecution and Survival, c. 1170–c. 1570*, trans. C. Davison (Cambridge, 1999), pp. 114–15.

and support the masters. Zwicker's words can therefore be interpreted in this way: careless prelates allowed the enemies (the Waldensian masters called heresiarchs) to attack and harm the helpless sheep (the faithful of the Church) and then to make them the faithful of their sect. Quite often Zwicker addressed the Waldensians directly, sometimes introducing a form of dialogue. He used the singular or the plural form (*Waldensis heretice* or *Waldenses*), but the way he did this indicates that the addressees of his accusations were primarily the masters. Zwicker also strived to present them in a very bad light. He underlined that their intention was to attack simple people who did not expect danger: 'Tu vero fur, et latro, lupe, glis et vespertilio, noctua caeca nocte ad simplices volitas, cursitans circuis quaerens quem deuores' (You, thief and villain, wolf, rat and bat, blind owl, fly to simple people at night-time, running and wandering around, hunting for someone to devour).[18] Once they have recruited them to their sect, they do not explain their doctrine to them and thus they condemn the poor souls to damnation: 'Si intelligis, et tuis credentibus non exponis, traditor es pauperum animarum; quos quidem sapere non docet' (If you understand and do not explain it to your faithful, you are a betrayer of poor souls, whom you certainly do not teach wisdom).[19] Finally, when the sect was threatened, they left their flock without worrying about their fate:

> Quare non perstitisti cum ouibus in Turingia, Marchia, Bohemia, Morauia, vbi ex DEI gratia, iam infra spatium duorum annorum, citra mille personas, hæretici Waldenses, ad fidem Catholicam sunt conuersi?

> (Why didn't you persist with the sheep in Thuringia, March, Bohemia and Moravia, where by God's grace, within two years, about a thousand people, Waldensian heretics, have been converted to the Catholic faith?)

> Zwicker, *Cum dormirent homines* xv, p. 218 (1677: p. 281E).

In my view, the audience Zwicker was trying to persuade with his treatise can be recognised as all simple believers: not just Catholics but also the members of the sect. In other words, he had in mind both those who already followed the Waldensian masters, and those who could potentially meet them and be convinced. Importantly, Zwicker did not condemn those who were deceived by the heresiarchs. Instead, he tried to explain how the heresiarchs deceived their listeners. The responsibility of the Waldensian masters is clearly separated from that of *credentes*. While the former were condemned, the latter still had a choice. I believe that Zwicker had this deliberate intention: he wanted to give them the room to take up their position after hearing the arguments. His strategy was to show the masters in the

[18] Zwicker, *Cum dormirent homines* viii, p. 210 (1677: p. 279G).
[19] Zwicker, *Cum dormirent homines* xxxv, p. 272 (1677: p. 298B).

Means of persuasion in medieval anti-heretical texts

worst possible light and make them lose all credibility. Potential adepts were supposed to decide not to get involved in any meetings or conversations with a Waldensian preacher, because he would deliberately misrepresent the Bible in order to harm those who came to believe in his teachings. In accordance with Aristotle, this would be a matter of *ethos*: in this case, the feelings of the audience towards the heresiarchs, who were being discredited. The audience is willing to reject even the best arguments of a person whose morality is questionable. In addition to allegations of lack of morality, Zwicker constantly emphasised the low intellectual level of the Waldensians and accused them of lacking academic education.[20] By doing so, he sought to further emphasise their lack of competence in the interpretation of the Bible and to expose the false wisdom of the masters.

On the other hand, Zwicker defended the *credentes*. He even sympathised with them. He repeatedly compared them to innocent lambs who are attacked by a cunning wolf. Interestingly, under other circumstances, Zwicker as inquisitor interrogated and condemned those 'innocent lambs' to severe punishments.[21] In the treatise, however, he may have used these gentle comparisons in an attempt to please an audience that had contact with Waldensianism, to prepare better ground for his argumentation.[22] So he also appealed to the *ethos* in his own favour. He wanted to show that he and other inquisitors were the ones who defended and cared for the weakest and defenceless.

Could the persuasion techniques used by Zwicker be effective in the eyes of the medieval readers of his treatise? Any answer to this question is of course conjecture. But having looked at the strategy of the whole work and the structure of individual arguments, we can conclude that the *Cum dormirent homines* was composed skilfully and that the author's intention was to maximise the effectiveness of argumentation. The work consists of various elements – along with a large number of biblical quotations there are also sophisticated invectives. Consequently, it is not just a monotonous compilation of facts about the Waldensians. Not without significance was Zwicker's extensive experience as an inquisitor: in the area of practical struggle against heresy he was a very experienced professional. It is also worth remembering that the large number of still extant copies demonstrates the favour the text enjoyed among contemporaries. The reason for this, I believe, is that the treatise was supposed to be primarily practical and not theoretical. It contains a set of ready and understandable arguments that could easily be used in discussions. These arguments are rarely deductive and they lack the formality

---

[20] See P. Biller, 'The *Topos* and reality of the heretic as *illiteratus*', in P. Biller, *Waldenses*, pp. 169–90.

[21] On Zwicker's career as inquisitor see Välimäki, *Heresy*, pp. 22–37.

[22] This was a technique called *captatio benevolentiae*, recommended already in ancient treatises on rhetoric.

that was the order of the day in university texts. But they were user-friendly for people with a more ordinary knowledge of the world. The *Cum dormirent homines* itself seems to have been aimed at preachers rather than university lecturers. Finally, persuasion in this treatise underlines the lure of the word. It reminds us that, at a time when violence was present and available as the way to solve doctrinal disputes, rhetorical measures had not completely lost their meaning and power.

8

Constructing narratives of witchcraft

Richard Kieckhefer

In 1976, in a book on late medieval witch trials, I argued for a distinction between popular and élite or learned conceptions of witchcraft.[1] The documents most likely to reveal popular notions of witchcraft differ markedly, I proposed, from those most susceptible to the bias of judges familiar with current demonological theories. In a significant subset of trial records the original testimony of the accusers is preserved, and these documents refer only to sorcery or maleficent magic, not to the diabolism of the witches' Sabbath and related notions. Furthermore, the charge of diabolism arises far more often in ecclesiastical than in secular courts, and more often when the records are in Latin than when they are in the vernacular. All of this I took as evidence that sorcery was a datum of popular belief, while diabolism was introduced by learned élites, particularly inquisitors. Accusers and other witnesses believed in sorceresses who bewitched children and cattle, compelled men to love them and rendered people lame. Inquisitors and others who knew the current theological notions about witchcraft and the devil believed in witches who flew through the air to the Sabbath, entered into pacts with the devil, had sexual intercourse with him, and performed *maleficia* at his behest. If ordinary people did not even believe in diabolism, it is highly unlikely that it was actually practiced.

After more than thirty years, I remain persuaded of the general validity of this argument, but I would phrase it a bit differently and would admit some qualifications. Not long after that book emerged, it became unfashionable thanks to Peter Brown and others to speak in terms of a two-tier culture, to distinguish between popular and élite cultural levels. Yet it still seems to me that when we attend to accusations from the neighbors of the accused we are hearing one set of voices, while the confessions extracted under judicial coercion (most obviously torture) come from a different set of voices. Even in a confession, the voices we are actually hearing are those of the theologian and the inquisitor.

---

[1] R. Kieckhefer, *European Witch Trials: Their Foundations in Popular and Learned Culture, 1300–1500* (London, 1976).

Richard Kieckhefer

That does not necessarily mean, however, that the accusers and others in society did not believe in the Sabbath. If there are distinct perspectives voiced in the trial records, they may differ less in belief than in expectation. By way of comparison, the educated clergy at a modern pilgrimage shrine may in principle believe in miracles but not expect to experience them often, while the pious pilgrims may have higher expectations. Both believe in the possibility of miracles, but the lay devout may expect them more than the sophisticated clergy.[2] Somewhat similarly, the people who accused their neighbors of bewitching cows and cursing men to impotence may have believed in the mythology of the Sabbath but may not have expected that to be among their neighbors' transgressions. In the cases I have given, the modern pilgrim may be more credulous than the clergy, while in late medieval witch trials it was arguably the clergy who were more credulous. Whether that is precisely the right formulation, the patterns that emerge in the trial records may show differences in expectation more than in belief. If so, that would account for the late medieval records that claim the Sabbath is something widely believed among the populace,[3] a claim that need not be wrong, even if the trial records themselves do not give evidence for it.

A further qualification that I would now pay closer attention to is the phenomenon of the accused who becomes an accuser. Famously, the inquisitors who had extracted confessions of diabolism then turned to the question who else had been at the Sabbath. The harvest of prosecution was rich largely because it was self-enriching: a person who had broken down and confessed her own presence at the Sabbath would seldom have the nerve to resist the demand for names. These incriminations may have been coerced, but they were not necessarily random or fleeting. Those who accused were at times quite insistent on their own accusations, and in at least some cases seem to have internalized the mythology of diabolism sufficiently to believe they actually had seen others at the Sabbath.[4]

---

[2] The official literature distributed at Holy Hill in Wisconsin acknowledges the reality of physical miracles but places them in the context of sacramental and moral life, as seen in C. Rosario, *Inside Holy Hill: Basilica of the National Shrine of Mary, Help of Christians* (Hubertus WI, 2009), 54: 'A visitor once asked a friar when the last miracle had taken place at the Shrine. The friar looked at his watch and said, "About five minutes ago, I imagine. They are celebrating Mass and hearing confessions right now."' The unofficial compendium of T. R. Lindvis, *Healing at the Hill, Being a True and Concise Account of the Miraculous Healings at Holy Hill, National Shrine of Mary, Help of Christians; Hubertus, Wisconsin* (Milwaukee, 1998), is more in the classic tradition of miracle collections.

[3] See, for example, *Hazards of the Dark Arts: Advice for Medieval Princes on Witchcraft and Magic*, trans. R. Kieckhefer, Magic in History Sourcebooks (University Park PA, 2017), 117.

[4] For a particularly poignant case see S. Strobino, *Françoise sauvée des flammes? Une Valaisanne accusée de sorcellerie au XVe siècle*, Cahiers Lausannois d'Histoire Médiévale 18 (Lausanne, 1996).

Constructing narratives of witchcraft

A third factor that I would now take into account is that of regional difference. The mythology of witchcraft was not everywhere the same: the pattern that emerged in western Switzerland in the second quarter of the fifteenth century and then spread to parts of France was not widely adopted in either Germany or England until later, and it differed from the mythologies of witchcraft found in central and northern Italy.[5] Nor were the judicial forms used in witch trials everywhere the same. In French-speaking regions it was far more common for ecclesiastical proceedings to be followed by secular trials, which could take cognizance of what had been determined in the earlier proceedings but could be quite independent in their own formulation of the charges.[6] And yet there was movement across cultural boundaries: at times we find charges in France that we might have expected in Italy, and the paradigm of western Switzerland sometimes blends with that of northern Italy.

The fourth factor I would now emphasize is the proliferation of literature in recent decades on false confession under police interrogation.[7] Legal scholars and psychologists have written extensively on this issue, which gained public attention in the 1980s when trials for Satanic ritual abuse were very much in the public eye.[8] Investigators tell the accused that it is common not to remember crimes one has committed. They feed their suspects 'misleading specialized knowledge' that only a guilty party would have, then they persuade jurors that this knowledge actually came from the accused. False confessions are sometimes referred to as voluntary, coerced-internalized, and coerced-compliant: people will volunteer false confession to gain attention or out of delusional psychopathology, they will come in the course of interrogation to believe what the interrogators are telling them, or they will break down and confess in the hope of gaining mercy or respite. All three patterns are likely to have occurred in the historic witch trials, although

---

[5] R. Kieckhefer, 'Mythologies of witchcraft in the fifteenth century', *Magic, Ritual, and Witchcraft* 1 (2006), 79–107.

[6] R. Kieckhefer, 'The role of secular authorities in the early witch-trials', in *Hexenprozess und Staatsbildung / Witch-Trials and State-Building*, ed. J. Dillinger, J. M. Schmidt and D. R. Bauer (Bielefeld, 2008), pp. 25–39.

[7] The literature is extensive, but see *True Stories of False Confessions*, ed. R. Warden and S. A. Drizin (Evanston IL, 2009); S. Larmour et al., 'Behind the confession: relating false confession, interrogative compliance, personality traits, and psychopathy', *Journal of Police and Criminal Psychology* 30 (2015), 94–102; R. A. Leo and D. Davis, 'From false confession to wrongful conviction: seven psychological processes', *Journal of Psychiatry and Law* 38 (2010), 9–56. For reflection on the nature of confessions in the historical witch trials, Keith Thomas, *Religion and the Decline of Magic* (New York, 1971), pp. 512–69, remains worth consulting.

[8] L. Wright, *Remembering Satan: A Tragic Case of Recovered Memory* (New York, 1994); R. Ofshe and E. Watters, *Making Monsters: False Memories, Psychotherapy, and Sexual Hysteria* (New York, 1994); and the set of articles in *Psychology, Public Policy, and Law* 4, no. 4 (1998), 933–1225.

the actual dynamics in any particular case may remain unclear. In any case, one cannot now write about false confession in the premodern period without being aware of this recent literature on modern cases. If nothing else, this literature confirms what historians have long suspected: that the promise of lighter treatment or cessation of torture can lead people to confess to crimes they did not commit, that those subjected to brutal interrogation can come to believe false charges against them, and that in some cases people will step forward voluntarily to accuse themselves when they are innocent.

If we want to tie together these various factors, recognizing that there were differences, geographical differences and otherwise, but that the judicial records bring together different strands in varying pattern, the category that may prove most useful is *narrative convergence*. Each witch trial, like trials of other sorts, sets out to produce a narrative, and the ways different elements become integrated into a sometimes more and sometimes less coherent narrative are worth investigating and may give a more nuanced understanding than any simple distinction between popular and élite input. It no doubt often happened that neighbors brought neighbors to court with narratives of personal transgression to tell, and that the mechanisms of judicial coercion, especially the use of torture and interrogatories, brought a shift to a largely unrelated narrative of diabolical conspiracy. No doubt all this was crucial – but I hope to approach the process with a finer sense of nuance, and the framework of narrative convergence allows for nuance and complexity. The model of accumulation (associated with Joseph Hansen) does not do justice to the fluidity of the process. The model of archaic foundation (developed by Carlo Ginzburg) ascribes too central and universal a role to a peripheral element.[9] But even a simple model of cultural overlay (which my own early work might seem to suggest) misses the complexity of the narrative convergence. Let us look, then, at some revealing cases.

One way to formulate this convergence is in terms of three patterns firmly grounded in biblical texts and recurrent in Christian thinking: the fixation on 'my enemies', 'our enemies', and 'God's enemies'. No book of the Bible contains the word 'enemy' more than the Psalms. But there it is overwhelmingly 'inimicus meus' (my enemy), or 'inimici mei' (my enemies), that provoke an outburst of agonized prayer, not 'inimici nostri' (our enemies). If a text like the Dead Sea War Scroll insists that our political enemies are God's enemies, the Psalms are equally certain that my personal enemies must be God's enemies. Yet a third narrative is of course also a perennial favorite: that which tells how God's spiritual enemies, the demons, are enemies also to humankind, both in general and in particular. Our enemies are God's, my enemies are God's, and God's enemies are both ours and mine.

---

[9] J. Hansen, *Zauberwahn, Inquisition und Hexenprozeß im Mittelalter, und die Entstehung der großen Hexenverfolgung* (Munich, 1900; reprint, Aalen, 1964); C. Ginzburg, *Ecstasies: Deciphering the Witches' Sabbath*, trans. R. Rosenthal (Chicago, 1991).

Constructing narratives of witchcraft

No doubt these narratives have converged in many ways, but never more fully than in the late medieval mythology and trial records for witchcraft. Heretics, Jews, lepers, and others might be enemies of God and Christian society, but they were not also routinely enemies lurking in one's neighborhood, bewitching cows and children, disrupting family relations. To an exceptional degree, late medieval witchcraft brought full convergence of all three narrative themes. Narratives of nocturnal assemblies that had been developed in anti-heretical literature, legends of necromancers forming pacts with demons, and reports of bewitchment that affected individuals and smaller or larger communities were the most important elements in the mélange. The writer who perhaps most forcefully creates the specter of witchcraft as a conspiracy is Hans Fründ, the Lucerne chronicler who around 1429 warned that there were so many hundreds of witches that they threatened to set up a king and become so strong they would fear no other ruler, but would set up their own court and bring Christendom under their power.[10] In the witchcraft literature this convergence of private, public, and spiritual peril is relatively clear and straightforward.

Turning to a closer look at the texts that tell how people were prosecuted for witchcraft, we find more than one pattern. In some cases what we find is a discontinuous narrative, in others a subsuming narrative, and in yet others a recontextualizing narrative. There is also, on some occasions, what we could call a pre-confessional narrative.

In what I am calling the discontinuous narrative, the trial begins with testimony about *maleficia*, and at some point, under torture or other judicial coercion, the accused confesses to demonic magic, attendance at the Sabbath, and all the forms of conspiratorial witchcraft associated with the Sabbath, but with no further mention of the original bewitchments. Perrissone Gappit, tried in the diocese of Lausanne in 1464, was accused of poisoning people with food that was evidently bewitched, threatening her husband in the course of a quarrel and causing him to lose his power of speech, and causing young children to fall ill or even die. When she began making a confession, however, all these *maleficia* were set aside in favor of the standard confession extracted from other suspects: attending the witches' assembly, eating the flesh of infants, having sex with the devil, trampling on a host, and the like.[11]

Discontinuous narrative of this sort suggests strong use of an interrogatory. The judges (usually in these cases inquisitors) had clearly defined notions of what the sect of witches was about, and they were interested more in the 'heresy' of witchcraft than in the crimes that could be just as well prosecuted by secular courts. What results is a strong emphasis on enmity between the individual and

---

[10] In *L'imaginaire du sabbat: Edition critique des textes les plus anciens (1430 c.–1440 c.)*, ed. M. Ostorero, A. Paravicini Bagliani and K. U. Tremp, in collaboration with C. Chène, Cahiers Lausannois d'Histoire Médiévale 26 (Lausanne, 1999), pp. 63–97.

[11] G. Modestin, *Le diable chez l'évêque: Chasse aux sorciers dans le diocèse de Lausanne (vers 1460)*, Cahiers Lausannois d'Histoire Médiévale 25 (Lausanne, 1999), pp. 276–317.

the broader community, and not a great deal of interest in those quarrels among neighbors that so often brought the accused to court in the first place.

Distinct from these discontinuous narratives are what I will refer to as subsuming narratives, in which the focus shifts from *maleficia* to conspiratorial and demonic witchcraft, but the *maleficia* rather than disappearing from the record become subsumed into the new narrative. The judges in these cases may or may not be using an interrogatory, but in any case they make more flexible use of a narrative paradigm. They are interested in the particulars of bewitchment, and in the ways demon masters make the bewitchment possible. The emphasis here is on enmity both with the community and particular members: the witch is both 'my enemy' and 'our enemy', and the demonic element makes all the more clear that she is simultaneously God's enemy.

Giovanna Motossa was one of three women tried as *masche* or witches at Rifreddo, near Saluzzo, in 1495, by the Dominican inquisitor Vito Beggiami. The trial record begins with testimony from witnesses, four of whom told how she had killed the eighteen-year-old serving maid of a local nunnery. The servant had caught her stealing herbs from the garden; in retaliation, Giovanna had attacked her at night in bed, causing a sudden and severe infirmity. The next we hear in the trial record is Giovanna's confession, which focuses on her entry into and activities in the witches' sect: her association with a demon named Martin (who came to her as a man dressed in black, with a white beret), her denying God and trampling on a cross, her having sex with a demon, and so forth. But the same stories told by witnesses reappear in the confession with a different slant, integrated as they are into her tale of membership in the sect. It was true that she had bewitched and killed the servant girl at the local nunnery, but Giovanna explained how it was a demon who had made the bewitchment possible: the demon had led her to the nunnery and opened the portal, and when she touched the girl on her ribs and head the demon pressed her hands down, causing the girl to grow sick and die. The demon wanted her also to kill some of the nunnery's livestock, which she was reluctant at first to do, but the demon dragged her by the hair up to a rooftop, from which they killed three of the cattle, and on another occasion pigs. She and the other witches could enter closed houses because their demons squeezed through small holes and then opened the doors from inside. The demon also wanted her to harm the abbess of the nunnery, whom he hated because she did so much good, but on this occasion the demon could not open the door. Another of these *masche* at Rifreddo, Caterina Bonivarda, confessed that she had bewitched many people and animals to please her demon, who thirsted cruelly for human blood.[12]

---

[12] *"Lucea Talvolta la Luna": I processi alle "masche" di Rifreddo e Gambasca del 1495*, ed. G. G. Merlo, R. Comba and A. Nicolini, Società per gli studi storici, archeologici ed artistici della Provincia di Cuneo (Cuneo, 2004). On the term 'masca' and its variants, see the discussion by J. Franck in J. Hansen, ed., *Quellen und*

Constructing narratives of witchcraft

In these trials there seems to be a direct correlation between local reputation for sorcery and willingness to confess demonic witchcraft. Giovanna Motossa was accused by several neighbors of practicing bewitchment against several victims. She was a marked woman. Nothing in the initial depositions pointed in the direction of demonic witchcraft, but still she was the one to capitulate immediately. Caterina Bonivarda represents here the opposite extreme: only one of her neighbors spoke of her *fama* (repute) as a witch, with no specific details of her bewitchments, and she was the one who held out longest before finally confessing.

A subsuming narrative can work in more than one way. The *maleficia* may become incidental to confessions swirling about the Sabbath, but the focus may just as well be the other way around, as in the trial of Martiale Espaze at Boucoiran in 1491. In this case rumors abounded. Martiale and her mother had come to Boucoiran thirteen or fourteen years earlier, when she was pregnant. She turned out to be notoriously promiscuous, and adulterously so. It was said that her mother had been suspect of sorcery, and a relative of theirs had been burned as a witch. Indeed, it was bruited about that Martiale and her mother had come to Boucoiran in the first place to evade suspicion of sorcery. Now there was widespread mortality of animals and young children in the vicinity, and from all sides fingers pointed to Martiale, causing her to flee. Her husband said he did not think she was a witch, but she fled for fear of that allegation. All this preliminary investigation took place in late April of 1491. By June, Martiale had been found and arrested. A lacuna in the manuscript leaves us to imagine the circumstances under which she began confessing, but at the outset she seems to have admitted attending the Sabbath, paying homage to a devil, having sex with him, and so forth. The devil had forbidden her to attend church, say her prayers, or make the sign of the cross at a roadside crucifix. Asked if she placed faith in what the devil said to her, she said sometimes yes, sometimes no. While these admissions come only at the beginning of her confession, they provide a narrative backdrop to everything that follows, which centers on administering powders and potions to the children and livestock of named victims, and in one case using image magic against a child. The relevance of the demonic master is threefold: he provided the means for performing *maleficia*, he opened people's doors for her, and at least sometimes her only motive for bewitchment was that her diabolical master had ordered her to do it, although on other occasions Martiale herself or some relative or companion had quarreled with the victim's family. Martiale was kept in prison at least four months, and by late October there were more witnesses testifying to her bewitchments, but now without reference to the narrative of demonic association.[13]

Untersuchungen zur Geschichte des Hexenwahns und der Hexenverfolgung im Mittelalter (Bonn, 1901), pp. 663–5.

[13] É. Bligny-Bondurand, 'Procédure contre une sorcière de Boucoiran (Gard), 1491',

Richard Kieckhefer

Similar to the subsuming narrative yet in in some ways different is what I will call the recontextualizing narrative, in which the main elements remain the same but their context becomes transformed. The trial of Else of Meersburg before the court of Lucerne, around 1450, took place in two stages. In the first phase the focus was mainly on cursing personal enemies and causing hail and lightning to fall on them with the aid of demons. Else could perform a water ritual to cause this foul weather. She had learned the art forty years ago, as a child, from a great hail-raiser at Meersburg named Else Schiesserin, who had instructed her how to invoke a devil during Ember Weeks and cause hail. Recently she had done this to avenge an affront from a beggar. Many years previously, when the people of Constance had done some offense to her and her family, she had brought on a hailstorm to harm them. In the second phase the confessions became fundamentally different in their overall framing, but with key continuities. She had assembled with twelve witches on Ember Thursday to hold Ginzburgesque tournaments with hemp-stalks. The group had a beautiful woman from Schaffhausen as its mistress. Members of the group rode on dogs or wolves, or applied salve to sticks as a means of flight. The enmity was now broader in scope: the Swiss Confederation had somehow caused her harm. Bewitchment was still carried out with the aid of devils, but the opposition to Christianity was more explicit: if members of the group turned back to God and his Mother, they could no longer perform witchcraft. Still, the second phase of the trial is recognizably an extension of the first. In both, the *maleficium* practiced is chiefly hail-raising, and the theme of flight through the air is consonant with a tendency to cause disruptions of the air. If there is a transition, it is not from *maleficium* to invoking devils; the latter element is there all along. But now it is fused with a narrative absent from the earlier phase, that of the presumably nocturnal flight and assemblies, in a form well familiar from northern Italy especially.[14]

The narrative patterns I have suggested provide for the main outlines of many, perhaps most, of the trials in which narrative complexity developed. But there are subplots worth noting, and one of these we might call the pre-confessional narrative. Even before breaking down and confessing fully developed demonic witchcraft, the suspect shows signs of a guilty conscience, which probably makes it easier for the judge to wear down resistance.

Catherine Quicquat was tried by the Dominican inquisitor Pierre d'Aulnay and a representative of the bishop of Lausanne in 1448 at Vevey. The priest of a nearby village told of rumors that had been circulating for some years about

---

Bulletin philologique et historique du Comité des travaux historiques et scientifiques (1907), 380–405.

[14] E. Hoffmann-Krayer, 'Luzerner Akten zum Hexen- und Zauberwesen', *Schweizerisches Archiv für Volkskunde* 3 (1899), 25–9.

Constructing narratives of witchcraft

her sorcery. When another witch was being taken through the streets of Vevey, she had seen Catherine and another woman and pointed them out as equally deserving of prosecution. Not surprisingly, when Catherine herself was being interrogated she admitted the rumors, saying she had often been accused of 'heresy' or sorcery by various persons. She admitted also, before torture, that a woman who had been burned for witchcraft had taught her to give her husband three drops of her blood to make him love and not abuse her. But the most telling evidence was her admission to a guilty conscience. One day when she was alone with the village priest she put her hand on his shoulder and said, 'I have done such horrible evils, I don't know what will become of me'. The day after a session of torture, she called for the inquisitor and offered to tell all her crimes. But she began by recalling how eleven or so years ago she had been coming from church and met her associate in sorcery, who was later burned. The woman said to her that they should confess to each other; Catherine refused, saying she was not a priest, but she did not deny that she had sins to confess. Later in the trial, when she was giving details of her activities as a member of the witches' sect, one of her transgressions was having sex with a certain Pierre Mugnier and others at the witches' assembly. She later denied that he had been at the assembly, but still she had had sex with him, presumably while married to the man who had been abusing her.[15]

The guilty conscience of the accused may actually be unrelated to charges of witchcraft, but still may make it easier to coerce a confession according to script. When Jordana de Baulmes was brought before an inquisitor in the diocese of Lausanne in 1477, she insisted on telling her past experience of giving birth to an illegitimate baby and leaving it exposed. With some difficulty she had found a priest who gave her absolution for this sin, but it still weighed on her conscience. It was not what the inquisitor wanted to hear, but it was what she wanted to tell, and it may have predisposed her to think of herself as morally reprehensible and prone to other sins, leading perhaps to her confession of witchcraft.[16]

All the cases I have sketched so far show how over the course of a trial more than one narrative is told, and the narrative strands become in one way or another linked. There are, however, cases in which multiple narratives are made available and in the end all rejected.

One of the most revealing cases, exceptionally of interest for what did *not* develop as it unfolded, is that of Catherine David and Monnet Sinhon, who were tried at Draguignan in Provence in 1439 by the Franciscan inquisitor Guillaume de Malavielle.[17] Two circumstances were particularly important.

---

[15] M. Ostorero, *"Folâtrer avec les démons": Sabbat et chasse aux sorciers à Vevey (1448)*, Cahiers Lausannois d'Histoire Médiévale 15 (Lausanne, 1995), pp. 236–57.

[16] E. Maier, *Trente ans avec le Diable: Une nouvelle chasse aux sorciers sur la Riviera lémanique (1477–1484)* (Lausanne, 1996), pp. 333–61.

[17] R. Aubenas, *La sorcière et l'inquisiteur: Épisode de l'inquisition en Provence (1439)* (Aix-en-Provence, 1956).

First, Catherine had an elderly father and three sisters. On her telling, she was more attentive to her father than any of her sisters, and for that reason he wrote a will shortly before his death in which he left all his property to her alone. But the disinheritance of the three sisters quickly became a local scandal, and rumor had it that she had manipulated her father's affections with a magic potion containing sacred chrism, blessed salt, herbs, and her own menstrual blood. At the most fundamental level, the trial was a competition between these competing narratives. Secondly, however, there was a local healer, Monnet Sinhon, who had already been tried by an ecclesiastical court for heresy, idolatry, and apostasy, but had made solemn abjuration. Catherine patronized him for his healing remedies, which she found effective. They addressed each other as godfather and godmother because years ago she had agreed hypothetically that he could serve as godfather for a child she in fact never conceived. Now the finger of suspicion pointed to him as the source of the magic potion she is supposed to have given her father, while a local priest was said to have supplied the chrism and blessed salt. Evidence was collected not by the inquisitor but by another Franciscan who served as fiscal procurator for the inquisitorial tribunal.

Under interrogation, Monnet confessed that he had provided the potion for Catherine at her request, although he denied that the potion was really magical. The fiscal procurator proposed bringing forth three witnesses, and before long three individuals were brought in to give testimony, including one of Catherine's disinherited sisters and one of her brothers-in-law. It was the brother-in-law who gave the most detailed and most damaging report. He and Monnet had been traveling back from Aix one day, and in the course of their conversation Monnet had apologized profusely for his role in the father's bewitchment. He had not really wanted to provide the potion, but Catherine had constrained him with her own sorcery. Under that pressure, Monnet agreed but said he did not have the recipe at hand and would have to give it to her the next day. In the meantime he invoked his demon master, Barrabas, from whom he obtained the formula. This shocking revelation led to vigorous and repeated reproaches, which the trial record reproduces in vivid detail. The second witness, the sister, repeated what she had heard from the brother-in-law, and more importantly challenged Catherine's account of the father's inclinations: until the potion was administered, said this sister, the father had been well disposed toward all his daughters and intended to divide his property equally among them. The third witness served mainly to confirm that the village was buzzing with gossip about Catherine's sorcery.

Catherine herself was then interrogated, and from the outset it was clear that she meant to defend herself and purge the record of all suspicion; at one point she declared that she would defend herself *viriliter* (vigorously, manfully). Her consistent line of defense was that there had never been a magic potion, that she had never requested one, and that the allegation was simply a fabrication. The inquisitor probed systematically to learn all he could about the dysfunctional

Constructing narratives of witchcraft

family. He called attention to the gossip that was circulating, and asked Catherine if she understood what that meant, even posing to her the question *Quid est fama?* (What is *fama* [repute]?) to which she gave a reply that was put into the record in the form, *fama est gentium locutio, sive in bonum sive in malum* ('repute' is what people say, for good or ill). Repeatedly she asked the inquisitor for a full record of the proceedings, with which she intended to defend herself from her enemies and repay them for their malice. Recognizing the justice of her cause, the inquisitor acceded to this request, wryly commenting at one point that even the devil is allowed to defend himself. Another Franciscan, now playing the role of fiscal procurator, insisted that she be transferred to a royal prison and tortured, but the inquisitor saw neither vehement nor urgent grounds for suspicion, and thus no reason for torture. After a recess for reflection and potentially consultation, the inquisitor decided that the trial should proceed with renewed interrogation of Monnet, this time in Catherine's own presence, as she had requested.

When the day came for the renewed interrogation, Monnet was duly sworn in, then fell to his knees and retracted his previous depositions. He had falsely accused Catherine of giving her father the potion. It was all a lie. But Monnet could not stop talking. Not only had he perjured himself; he had done so at the urging of his demon master Barrabas, who had appeared to him sometimes in the form of a black cat. Indeed, the demon had come several times even while Monnet was in prison. He claimed never to have conjured the demon, although on that point he vacillated. He had been inconsistent on other matters, reflecting the shifting counsel of the demon, and the demon's ploy was to make Monnet seem inconsistent so that he would be tortured, knowing that he could not endure torture and would thus become all the more reliant on the demon. Monnet had been reluctant at first to accuse Catherine falsely, but the demon had indicated that if Monnet was going to disobey him he could not expect the demon's aid in getting out of prison. He threw himself on the mercy of God and of Catherine. Clearly flummoxed by this unexpected turn in the narrative, Catherine made a gesture toward forgiveness. Yet more astonishing was the inquisitor's decision to absolve Monnet of his offenses, with the stipulation that he should daily lament his sins and ask God's pardon.

Seeing that the inquisitor was proposing to release both Catherine and Monnet, two individuals who had previously not played a role now raised vigorous protest: a representative from the diocese of Fréjus, and an official from the royal court of Draguignan. Threatening appeal to higher authority, they wanted the accused to be tortured under the authority of the royal judge Pierre Durand, who was also present in the tribunal. But Durand refused to cooperate, saying the matter was under the sole competence of the inquisitor. The Franciscan acting as fiscal procurator also protested. But the inquisitor remained firm, granted Catherine full exculpation, and ordered that a transcript of the proceedings be prepared for her, as she had requested.

205

Richard Kieckhefer

It would be pleasant to record that the inquisitor, Guillaume de Malavielle, emerges from the record as a force for justice and rationality – that he was essentially a fifteenth-century Alonso de Salazar Frías. Six years later, however, in 1445, he presided over a trial for a group of five witches in the Dauphiné, from Val de Prés, Saint-Chaffrey, and Pont de Cervières. In this case, while we are not well informed about the circumstances, the prosecution ended in conviction and sentencing. It is perhaps not coincidental that here the inquisitor acted in association with the secular judge Claude Tholosan, who around 1436 had summarized his own experience as a witch-hunter in a treatise with the incipit *Ut magorum et maleficiorum errores*, one of a series of works from the 1430s that had seminal influence on the development of witchcraft theories. Was the inquisitor here overruled by a more seasoned and persuasive voice? Or did the inquisitor himself come to recognize Tholosan's narrative as convincing? We are speaking about the early years of prosecution for conspiratorial witchcraft, a time when many needed to be persuaded about that narrative, and many – not all – did soon find it compelling to think of themselves as surrounded everywhere by witches who were personal enemies, enemies of society, and enemies of God.

In another complicated case the sequence of accusations in the trial record was the opposite of what we might expect: from diabolical witchcraft to maleficent magic to magical healing. This was a trial at Clarensac, also in Provence, in 1496, in which the main defendant was an elderly woman named Paulette Julien.[18] The records begin with interrogation in November of 1496 in the court of the lord of Clarensac. Already, however, Julien had been tried by an inquisitor and denounced as a 'heretic'. Another woman, Frénouze Pradoune of Saint-Côme, who had been burned as a witch, had accused Julien of being an accomplice: she had used sorcery to prevent childbirth; her family was notorious, and some members had fled to avoid prosecution; she had bewitched olive trees, animals, persons; she had renounced Catholic faith and given herself to a devil named Barbanson, to whom she paid homage and a tribute of five beans; she had gone to the Sabbath and had sex with Barbanson. When the secular hearings began on 13 November, three alleged accomplices testified. Each of them had a demon master, as did Julien, and they told how she had joined them at the Sabbath and had used sorcery against humans and animals and the harm the trees of the region. But then immediately a second phase of interrogation ensued, from the 13th to the 18th of November, in which twelve people gave detailed testimony about how Julien and another woman had killed people, rendered a young boy paralyzed, and impeded childbirth. A majority of the witnesses were family members of the victims. Amid the sustained testimony about bewitchment, the charge of diabolism was set aside.

---

[18] P. Casado, *Un procès de sorcellerie dans la Vaunage (Calvisson, Clarensac) à la fin du XVe siècle* (Nîmes, 2005).

Constructing narratives of witchcraft

And a third phase of inquiry on the 18th, with one witness from the second phase and five new ones, led in again a different direction. There was some testimony about bewitchment by Paulette Julien and one of her accomplices: magical poisoning, killing of goats and children. There was reference to the notoriety or *fama* of the accomplices as witches (*masc* or *masca*), but not Julien. But the greater emphasis now lay on the healing practices of the accused: Paulette Julien and a male accomplice, Antoine Jonquier, were said to have healed people and occasionally also animals with 'conjurations' (which here would mean charms) and medicines. One witness also told about encountering Julien on the road from Saint-Côme and seeing her behave strangely: she had paid him no attention, but she had a strange expression on her face, and had her arms out and her mouth wide open and bent over a bush as if to embrace and eat it; she had a distorted face, and when he asked what she was doing she said something of no obvious relevance. On the whole, what we see is a process of stripping down: the secular court inherited from the ecclesiastical court allegations of diabolical witchcraft, but these were overshadowed first by charges of bewitchment and then by reports of healing magic.

What was going on in this trial? How can we best explain its unexpected transitions? It is important to note that Paulette Julien had the support of her two sons, who secured a legal defender for her, although she insisted she did not want to be defended but rather placed herself at the mercy of the lord of Clarensac. Despite her own inclination, her legal defender protested irregularities in the trial and lodged an appeal. Furthermore, there was tension between the bailiff and lieutenant active in the trial, who seem to have been sympathetic to the accused, and the procurators who were pressing charges. The bailiff and lieutenant took the initiative of appointing an advocate as caretaker and defender of Julien and another defendant, distinct from the one engaged by Julien's sons. Both Julien and her alleged female accomplice were sentenced as sorceresses, and a command was issued that the sentence against the accomplice be carried out, but Julien's sons intervened on her behalf by presenting letters of appeal by the sergeant of Nîmes, meaning the case was moved to a higher court. Julien had clearly not only confessed to the worst of the charges made against her but had thoroughly internalized the narrative to which she confessed. Not everything she told was under torture or threat of torture: after she had been interrogated by the inquisitor she told her guard that she had forgotten to tell the inquisitor about someone else who was also a witch and had brought two women to the Sabbath, so the inquisitor should be summoned to hear that information, and a messenger was dispatched to fetch the inquisitor. The story of her strange behavior on the road from Saint-Côme is consonant with the suggestion that she needed not just a defender but a caretaker. She was eighty-five years old, and evidently had seen better days. The narrative to which she herself assented remained open to challenge, and because her sons reinforced the doubts of the bailiff and lieutenant the convergence of the demonological narrative with that of healing and cursing could be pried apart. The sequence of interrogation can be read as itself a narrative, in which some of the actors in the prosecution hear the allegations of diabolical witchcraft, are skeptical, bring in witnesses to show that within the local population more ordinary bewitchment was the concern, and then brought in further witnesses to suggest that even the charge of *maleficia* grew out of longstanding reputation for magical healing. Step by step, the building up of charges was reversed. And the result was an appeal – whether in the end successful or not we do not know – for one of the accused but not all.

We may still wish to say that it was people familiar with the latest demonological theories who were most likely to introduce charges of diabolical witchcraft into the prosecution, and that the neighbors who bore testimony were more likely to focus on other matters, but to say that is merely the first step in tracing how judicial narratives came to be formulated. Constructing a narrative of witchcraft was a process of convergence in which different elements could be brought into rough harmony, but they could remain rival narratives, and the convergence might be undone, all depending on circumstances to which we sometimes – but seldom – have documentary access.

Part II: Early Modern

Figure 9.1 (left) Portrait of Matthias Flacius Illyricus, copper engraving by Theodor de Bry after Tobias Stimmer. Private collection.

Figure 9.2 (right) Matthias Flacius Illyricus, *Catalogus testium veritatis* (Basle, 1556), title-page, with Flacius's hand-written dedication to his patron Joachim von Alvensleben. Universitäts- und Landesbibliothek Sachsen-Anhalt, Halle, S: Alv. V 598, formerly in Herzog August Bibliothek, Wolfenbüttel <http://diglib.hab.de/drucke/alv-v-598/max/00005.jpg>. Reproduced by permission, Herzog August Bibliothek, Wolfenbüttel.

9

'Ut ex vetustis membranis cognosco': Matthias Flacius Illyricus and his use of inquisition registers and manuals[1]

Harald Bollbuck

1. The formation of a Lutheran concept of history

From the very beginning, the Reformation movement in Germany faced the problem of its historical legitimation. Just before Martin Luther's interrogation in Augsburg in October 1518, Cardinal Thomas de Vio Cajetan levelled the accusations. Luther's doctrine of grace and sacraments was an innovation, an outpouring of human imagination and a deviation from church tradition.[2] Luther replied that only that is true which is according to the bible. Everything else, including church tradition, is only human words and thus subject to the historical transience.[3] The Reformer cultivated a dialectical conception of church history. There are times of the revival of the faithful and the proclamation of the gospel, in which the Word of God would travel among the people like a 'downpour'. These alternated with times of decay and apostasy.[4] When the Word of God is at its highest, the diabolic seed of doubt is formed. When the Emperor Constantine raised Christianity to the status of a state religion, the heresies that would lead to the reign of the Papal Antichrist were formed.

---

[1] 'Ut ex vetustis membranis cognosco' (As I know from old parchment leaves): Flacius's foundation for his statement that Valdes was 'homo doctus', an educated man; *Catalogus Testium Veritatis* (Basle, 1556), p. 706.

[2] Cf. G. Hennig, *Cajetan und Luther: Ein historischer Beitrag zur Begegnung von Thomismus und Reformation* (Stuttgart, 1966), pp. 49, 58, 70; K.V. Selge, *Die Augsburger Begegnung von Luther und Kardinal Cajetan im Oktober 1518. Ein erster Wendepunkt auf dem Weg zur Reformation*, Jahrbuch der hessischen Kirchengeschichtlichen Vereinigung 20 (1969), pp. 37–54 (49); B. Lohse, *Luthers Theologie in ihrer historischen Entwicklung und in ihrem systematischen Zusammenhang* (Göttingen, 1995), p. 128.

[3] WA, II, 108–19. WA is used here and in the following notes to denote the Weimar edition (Weimarer Ausgabe) of Luther's works: *D. Martin Luthers Werke: kritische Gesammtausgabe* (Weimar, 1883–).

[4] WA, XV, 32, 37. Cf. H. Dörries, *Neuheit und Zusammenhang: Zu Luthers Geschichtsverständnis*, Lutherjahrbuch (Göttingen, 1961), pp. 86–103 (100).

Harald Bollbuck

Luther did not see himself as an apostle or inspired prophet, but as a teacher sent by God in the tradition of Giovanni Pico della Mirandola, Johann von Wesel, Johannes Reuchlin and Jan Hus.[5] After all, he had even called himself a Hussite.[6] In the exegesis of the Apocalypse of John, published in 1530, he recognized in the revelation an interpretation of both past and future history.[7] The rebuilding of the Holy City was the victory of the Reformation. But apart from this figurative interpretation of history, there is no return to a blessed original state. Luther's view of history is progressive; not linear, but dialectical. The present is not a restoration of the Early Church, but an epoch in its own right. In the last years of his life Luther sees the end of history coming. According to the preface to the book of Daniel of 1541,[8] all the signs proclaimed by Christ and the apostles were being fulfilled in history.

Luther's interpretations shaped the historical picture of Lutheran theologians of the sixteenth century. This was dominated by a figurative interpretation of the past, a dialectical, forward-looking concept with an apocalyptic undertone and eschatological expectation, and it was based on a Reformation tradition of reference to proscribed heretics such as Jan Hus.

2. Matthias Flacius and his concept of truth witnesses

Just one year after Luther's death the Schmalkaldic War (1546) between the Imperial and Lutheran parties ended with the deposition of Elector Johann Friedrich of Saxony and led to a split in the Lutheran camp. Philipp Melanchthon (1497–1560) was the new spokesman for Lutheran theology. Initially he had fled from the victorious imperial troops, but he soon came to terms with the new circumstances and gathered his followers again in the small university town of Wittenberg, which was now under the rule of the new Elector Moritz of Saxony, who had joined the imperial party. In order to save the theology of grace, the distribution of the Lord's Supper in both forms, and the abolition of celibacy, Melanchthon submitted to some compromises ordered by the emperor. He declared some components of the liturgy as 'adiaphora', that is to say subordinate, less important matters.[9] Against this position, a radical opposition formed around Nicolaus von Amsdorf and Matthias Flacius Illyricus (1520–75).

---

[5] WA, VI, 183–4, I, 574.

[6] WA, XXX.3, 387; VII, 612; II, 404; VI, 454; VII, 431; XVIII, 651; XLIV, 744.

[7] Cf. H. Bornkamm, *Luthers Vorreden zur Bibel* (Göttingen, 3rd edn, 1989), p. 221.

[8] Ibid., p. 121. Luther's exegesis of Daniel in WA.DB (= Weimarer Ausgabe. Die deutsche Bibel), XI.2, 50,1–124, 20.

[9] Cf. J. Mehlhausen, 'Interim', *Theologische Realenzyklopädie*, 36 vols. (Berlin and New York, 1977–2007), XVI, cols. 230–1; *Das Interim 1548/50: Herrschaftskrise und Glaubenskonflikt*, ed. L. Schorn-Schütte (Gütersloh, 2005); *Politik und Bekenntnis: Die Reaktionen auf das Interim von 1548*, ed. I. Dingel and G. Wartenberg (Leipzig, 2006).

Matthias Flacius Illyricus and his use of inquisition registers and manuals

It regarded every abandonment of liturgical positions as Satan's gateway into the Lutheran theology of grace. Around 1548 this circle gathered in Magdeburg, later also at the newly founded University of Jena in the Duchy of Saxony, which had now become the dominion of the deposed former electoral dynasty.

Flacius was born in Labin (Albona, Istria). Melanchthon's model student before the war in Wittenberg, he became the most important opponent of his former teacher. On the one hand, he wanted to historically refute Melanchthon's concept that there are adiaphores in the liturgy which are indifferent in a sense of salvation.[10] At the same time, he countered the renewed accusation by papal theologians that Lutheran doctrine was an innovation, while Catholic doctrine was based on the old doctrine.[11] Flacius reversed this accusation by presenting the customs of the old doctrine as deviations from the biblically based original Christianity, to which, on the other hand, the Lutheran doctrine returned. While it was manifest that the Lutheran confession was in complete accord with that of the Apostles, it was still necessary to subject the whole history of the Church to a test. At any given period, what doctrinal commonality did it have with the church of the apostles? The test demanded the seeking out and display of testimonies to the truth.[12]

A key text for witnesses to the truth was 1 Kings 18. 21, with its 7,000 righteous people who would not have bowed the knee to Baal:[13] the basis for the concept of a minority church of just a few righteous. Flacius adhered to Luther's association of church reformers with those same 7,000 righteous,[14]

---

[10] On the dispute about *adiaphora* cf. J. Mehlhausen, 'Der Streit um die Adiaphora', in *Vestigia Verbi: Aufsätze zur Geschichte der evangelischen Theologie*, ed. J. Mehlhausen (Berlin and New York, 1999), pp. 64–92; *Der Adiaphoristische Streit (1548–1560)*, ed. I. Dingel, Theologische Kontroversen 1548–1577/80, Kritische Auswahledition 2 (Göttingen, 2012); most recent, W. Johnston, *The Devil behind the Surplice: Matthias Flacius and John Hooper on Adiaphora* (Eugene OR, 2018).

[11] Thus the titular bishop of Mainz, Michael Helding (1506–61), had asserted the constancy and immutability of the Roman canon in sermons at the Reichstag in Augsburg in 1547. Cf. E. Feifel, *Grundzüge einer Theologie des Gottesdienstes: Motive und Konzeption der Glaubensverkündigung Michael Heldings (1506–1561) als Ausdruck einer katholischen 'Reformation'* (Freiburg, 1960), p. 165; H. Bollbuck, *Wahrheitszeugnis, Gottes Auftrag und Zeitkritik: Die Kirchengeschichte der Magdeburger Zenturien und ihre Arbeitstechniken* (Wiesbaden, 2014), pp. 67–8.

[12] Cf. M. Becht, *Pium consensum tueri. Studien zum Begriff consensus im Werk von Erasmus von Rotterdam, Philipp Melanchthon und Johannes Calvin* (Münster, 2000), pp. 326–45; Bollbuck, *Wahrheitszeugnis*, pp. 320, 327.

[13] The first time in his tract *Etliche greiffliche unnd gewisse scheinbarliche warzeichen* (Magdeburg, 1549), sigs. D7v–D8r; later in a letter to Nidbruck (10 November 1552), Vienna, Österreichische Nationalbibliothek (henceforth ÖNB), Cod. Pal. Vind. 9737b, fol. 1v.

[14] M. Luther, *Vom Mißbrauch der Messen*, in WA, VIII, 555. For this see V. von der Osten-Sacken, 'Die kleine Herde der 7000: die aufrechten Bekenner in M. Flacius Illyricus konzeptionellen Beiträgen zur Neuformulierung der

Harald Bollbuck

and this was the basis for the compilation of his *Catalogus testium veritatis* (*Catalogue of Witnesses to the Truth*). A first handwritten version was available around 1552,[15] and an expanded version was first printed in 1556.[16] The memorialisation of ancient and now new martyrs and confessors of the Reformation churches was in full swing, as is shown by all the catalogues of John Foxe, Jean Crespin, Ludwig Rabus and (somewhat later) Adrian Cornelis van Haemstede.[17] Flacius differed from them at one point. Confessors of the truth were not necessarily confined to their own martyrs and church teachers. Those in opposing party could often involuntarily and unwittingly provide witness to divine truth.

3. Networking: the collection of inquisition manuals and registers

Flacius put together an extensive collection of church-historical sources for his historically based arguments. For this purpose he recruited a team of up to fifteen co-workers. There were eight to ten students who worked as excerptors, one or two writers who put the excerpts into a narrative form, and one or two so-called *rectores* (leaders) who did the entire editorial work, the correspondence for the collection of sources and the administration and the external presentation.[18] Flacius and his pupil in Wittenberg, Caspar von Nidbruck[19] (1525–57), an Imperial court councillor in Vienna, used a Europe-wide network of correspondents from Canterbury and Paris to the

---

Kirchengeschichtsschreibung aus protestantischer Sicht', in *Matija Vlačić Ilirik III: Proceedings of the 3rd International Conference on Matthias Flacius Illyricus*, ed. M. Miladinov (Labin, 2012), pp. 184–212 (194–5).

[15] Vienna, ÖNB, Cod. Pal. Vind. 11591.

[16] See the statement on the 7,000 righteous people in M. Flacius, *Catalogus testium veritatis* (Basel, 1556), sigs. α5v–α6r. There is a different interpretation, which recognises a more philological basis of his concept of witness, in W. F. Schäufele, 'Matthias Flacius Illyricus und die Konzeption der Zeugenschaft im Catalogus testium veritatis', in *Matthias Flacius Illyricus: biographische Kontexte, theologische Wirkungen, historische Rezeption*. ed. I. Dingel, J. Hund, and L. Ilić (Göttingen, 2019), pp. 159–74. On the *Catalogus*, see C.B.M. Frank, *Untersuchungen zum Catalogus testium veritatis des Matthias Flacius Illyricus* (diss. Tübingen 1990); M. Hartmann, *Humanismus und Kirchenkritik: Matthias Flacius Illyricus als Erforscher des Mittelalters* (Stuttgart, 2001); T. Haye, *Der 'Catalogus testium veritatis' des Matthias Flacius Illyricus: Zur Auswahl, Verarbeitung und kritischen Bewertung seiner Quellen* (Göttingen, 1990).

[17] Cf. M. Pohlig, *Zwischen Gelehrsamkeit und konfessioneller Identitätsstiftung: Lutherische Kirchen- und Universalgeschichtsschreibung 1546–1617* (Tübingen, 2007), pp. 348–61.

[18] Most recently on this, Bollbuck, *Wahrheitszeugnis*, pp. 106–23; cf. earlier H. Scheible, *Der Plan der Magdeburger Zenturien und ihre ungedruckte Reformationsgeschichte* (diss. Heidelberg, 1960), p. 61; R. E. Diener, *The Magdeburg Centuries: A Bibliothecal and historiographical analysis* (diss. Harvard, 1978), pp. 64–6, 167–70.

[19] Cf. *Allgemeine Deutsche Biographie*, 56 vols. (Leipzig, 1875–1912), LII, cols. 621– 9; G.C. Knod, *Deutsche Studenten in Bologna (1289–1562)* (Berlin, 1899), pp. 375–6;

Matthias Flacius Illyricus and his use of inquisition registers and manuals

Rhineland, Frankfurt, Regensburg and Venice to identify and compile source texts.[20] The result of this research was, in addition to the already mentioned *Catalogus testium veritatis*, the so-called *Magdeburg Centuries*, the most comprehensive Protestant church history to date, thirteen volumes of which were printed between 1559 and 1574.

In his search for witnesses of truth throughout church history, Flacius used any source that provided evidence of statements about opponents of the papal Church or about the papal Church's deviations from apostolic doctrine. The Waldensians played a central role as truth witnesses and forerunners of the Lutheran Church. In his March 1554 *Consultatio de conscribenda accurata historia ecclesiae* (*Consultation on Writing Accurate Church History*), Flacius argued that this religious group had a purer faith which was closer to that of the apostles and Lutheran doctrine. It was especially in France, their country of origin, that one should search for Waldensian writings. In looking to interview older people who still had knowledge of the Waldensian past from their ancestors, he was even engaging in a form of oral history.[21]

The German version of this *Consultatio*, which was written at the same time, cites already known aspects of a Waldensian confession, presumably also in order to provide the staff of the church history project with a ready reference handbook to use when they were looking through sources. The Waldensians, who had been spreading in France, Italy, Germany, Bohemia and Poland for 400 years, had rejected the supremacy of the pope, Church traditions, purgatory, mass, invocation of saints, celibacy and indulgence, and they had supported communion in both kinds and accepted only two

---

Les livres des procurateurs de la nation germanique de l'ancienne Université d'Orléans 1444–1602, 4 vols. (Leiden, 1971–2015), I, 395–7 no. 1144.

[20] Cf. Bollbuck, *Wahrheitszeugnis*, pp. 150–95; J.W. Schulte, 'Beiträge zur Entstehungsgeschichte der Magdeburger Centurien', in *Bericht der Philomatie in Neisse* 19 (1877), 50–148 (100–01), 224–9; H. Schneider, 'Die Bibliotheksreisen des Marcus Wagner', *Zentralblatt für Bibliothekswesen* 50 (1993), 678–82 (679).

[21] Cod. Guelf. here and henceforth denotes a manuscript in Wolfenbüttel, Herzog August Bibliothek. Cod Guelf. Cod. Guelf. 11.20 Aug. 2°, fol. 8v: Octavo conquirenda essent ante omnia Valdensium scripta. Nam illi soli ferme hisce 400 annis puriorem religionem habuerunt. Credo autem plurima potissimum in Gallia inveniri posse. Nam illis partibus in primis hoc dogma ortum est & viguit. Denique explorandum e senibus esset, an meminerint se audisse alicubi olim aliquem recte sentientem aut docentem, vel in tota religione vel in aliquibus eius partibus fuisse. (Eighthly, before everything else the writings of the Waldensians must be sought out. For during these 400 years, they alone firmly had the purer religion. I believe many could be found, most of all in Gaul. For it was first of all in these regions that the dogma originated and flourished. Then it should be sought out from old people, whether they remember that they have heard some right-thinking or right-teaching person anywhere once upon a time and that they either lived throughout in a religious community [= of Waldensians] or in some of its parts.)

sacraments.[22] For Flacius and his project, it was important to have this formulation of the Waldensian confessions of faith as in accordance with Lutheran doctrine.

Flacius was aware that Waldensian confessions of faith were hardly to be found in their original form and had instead to be extracted and put together from the writings of their opponents, primarily inquisition records and inquisition manuals. He therefore placed particular emphasis on the search for those sorts of texts. In a letter to Nidbruck in Vienna, dated 10 November 1552, he requested the sending to him of Nicholas Eymerich's inquisition manual (*Directorium inquisitorum, Directory for Inquisitors*), along with other writings, especially those about Waldensians: all of them texts that showed traces of the 7,000 righteous in history.[23] He confessed that he already

---

[22] Munich, Bayerische Staatsbibliothek, Cgm 4110b, fol. 141v: Zum Achten müste man sonderlich vnd fur allen dingen die schrifften der Waldenser tzusammen suchen, den sie fast alleine diese 400 jhar anhero die reine Religion haben gehabt vnd verteidingt, den sie seindt (wie ich des gewisse tzeugnus aus alten geschrieben büchern habe) die 400 jar her mitt tzimlicher antzal gewesen in Franckreich, Welschlandt, Deudtschlandt, Behmen vnd Polen, vnd haben disse nachfolgende Artickel gegleubet vnd geleret, Das man allein der heiligenn schrifft in Religionssache sol gleuben, Das der Bapst nicht hoher ist den ein ander Bischoff, Das man nach der menschen satzungen gahr nichtes sol fragen noch etwas darauff geben, Das kein Fegfeur sei, Das die Messe ein abgotterei sei, Das man die heiligen nicht soll anruffen, Das die priester ihre eheweiber haben sollen, Das man unter beider gestalt sol communiciren, Das nur tzwei Sacrament in der Kirchen seindt, Jtem das die ablas breiffe nichts gelten, vnd dergleichen mehr. Vnd sehr viel, welches alles mitt vnser Religion ja mitt der warheit selbst vberein stimmet (Eighthly, one should especially and above all collect the writings of the Waldensians, because they alone had had and defended pure religion for these 400 years, because they were (as I have reliable evidence from old manuscripts) in large numbers in France, Italy, Germany, Bohemia and Poland during these 400 years. They have believed and taught these articles: that one should believe only the Holy Scriptures in matters of religion; that the Pope is not higher than any other bishop; that one should not give anything to human ordinances [in matters of religion]; that there is no purgatory; that Mass is an idolatry; that one should not call upon the saints; that priests should have wives; that the Lord's Supper should be communicated under both kinds; that there are only two sacraments in the Church; that the letters of indulgence are not valid and so on. And much more, that all this is in accordance with our religion and therefore with the truth itself.)

[23] Vienna, ÖNB, Cod. Pal. Vind. 9737k, fol. 317v: Hos vero autores nominatim habere cupio: Inquisitiones Nicolai Emerici impressas, Monarchiam Dantis, Caesarii de haereticis, libros theologicos Johannis de Vesalia, Johannis de Janduno, Arnoldi de nova Villa; denique omnia ea, quae quoquo modo vestigia aliqua illorum 7000 piorum monstrare possent, praesertim autem quaecunque antiquiora de Waldensibus habere possunt (I want to have these authors, [listed here] by name: the printed Inquisitions of Nicholas Eymerich, Dante's Monarchy, Caesarius [of Heisterbach] On Heretics, the theological books of John of Wesel, John of Ghent, Arnold of Villanova; lastly, all those that in whatever way can show some traces of those pious 7000, especially whatever texts can contain older things about the

Matthias Flacius Illyricus and his use of inquisition registers and manuals

possessed some – supposedly – 400-year-old writings on Waldensians by Catholic authors, which he intended to publish.[24]

On 7 March 1553 he asked the Superintendent of Frankfurt am Main, Hartmann Beyer, for inquisition registers.[25] Flacius chose Beyer to write to, because he lived at the location of the most important book fair of his time. Later he reminded him to ask merchants from Lyon about Waldensian writings.[26] In early summer of 1554 he found two more manuscripts of Eymerich's inquisition manual in the Council Library and the library of the monastery of St Aegidien in Nuremberg, and took them away with him.[27] The Dutch humanist and theologian Cornelis Wouters (Cornelius Gualterus), who was involved in the project as a collector of sources, informed Nidbruck on 16 June 1554 that he had records of Cologne inquisitors which he could copy.[28] If these were the inquiries into the newly established Order of the Brothers of Common Life held in Cologne in 1398, it is possible that another manuscript has been identified that can be attributed to Flacius's library.[29] This manuscript, which was

---

Waldensians). The sheets are an enclosure to the letter of the same day, written by Flacius' secretary Marcus Wagner. They are in a different manuscript volume.

[24] Vienna, ÖNB, Cod. Pal. Vind. 9737b, fol. 1v: Habeo praeterea quaedam historica iam olim a papistis de Waldensibus scripta, quae simul coniuncta aedam. Video enim illos potissimum fuisse hisce 400 annis illa 7000 piorum, qui pure Christum adorantes Romanum Baal detestati sunt. (Further, I now some historical [texts] written about the Waldensians a long time ago by the Papists, which I shall publish collected together. For I see that for these 400 years they have been above all those 7000 pious, who worshipped Christ purely and detested the Roman Baal.)

[25] Frankfurt am Main, UB, Ms. Ff. H. Beyer A, Nr. 200a, fol. 236r: Ad hanc porro rem praeter alios impressos libros hi potissimum quaerendi essent: [...] Deinde inquisitiones et processus contra pios homines ante haec tempora facti. (Further to this matter, apart from other printed books these above all should be looked for ... Thereafter, inquisitions and proceedings carried out in earlier times against pious men.)

[26] Frankfurt am Main, Universitätsbibliothek (henceforth UB), Ms. Ff. H. Beyer A, Nr. 202, fol. 239r.

[27] Cod. Guelf. 680 Helmst. and Cod. Guelf. 279 Helmst. See Hartmann, *Humanismus*, pp. 108–9. On 28 June 1554 Flacius reports to Nidbruck about the findings in a letter (Vienna, ÖNB, Cod. Pal. Vind. 9737b, fol. 21r–2v). Flacius had discovered and brought back even more manuscripts to Nuremberg. On 6 September 1554 he sent a letter to the preacher Wolfgang Waldner, who was there, to return three manuscripts from the library of the Ägidienkirche to Nuremberg (Gotha, Forschungsbibliothek, Chart. A 127, fol. 4r).

[28] Vienna, ÖNB, Cod. Pal. Vind. 9737i, fol. 112v: Responsiones ad artic<ulos> inquisit<orum> Coloniensium ubi recognitae fuerint, et quod adhuc deest additum fuerit, describentur uti petis. (As soon as the responses to the articles of the Cologne inquisitors have been examined and what is currently lacking has been added, they may be copied, at your request.)

[29] Cod. Guelf. 315 Helmst., fol. 214r—17v: Responsa et observationes iurisperitorum Coloniensium de fratribus vitae communis in Daventria. (The responses and observations of the Cologne legal experts about the brothers of the common life in Deventer.)

217

written in northern Germany, also contains another copy of Eymerich's manual.[30] Nidbruck offered Flacius yet another manuscript of this work on 23 August 1554.[31] Flacius replied on 6 October that he already had two manuscripts of Eymerich's work – the ones from Nuremberg mentioned above.[32] The sending of the manuscript is not documented, but given library's contents it must have happened eventually.[33] Flacius first hints at possessing another important volume of manuscripts of inquisition records on 14 October 1555, in a letter to the Bohemian Brothers.[34] This volume is now divided into two manuscripts.[35] It contains the records of the inquisition of the Celestine prior Petrus Zwicker (died after 1403) in Stettin (modern Szczecin) from 1392–4, as well as inquisitions in Berlin and Kerkow near Angermünde in 1458.[36]

---

[30] Cod. Guelf. 315 Helmst., fol. 1r–173v. On this manuscript in Flacius's possession, see Hartmann, *Humanismus*, pp. 186–9, 228–9.

[31] Vienna, ÖNB, Cod. Pal. Vind. 9737i, fol. 122r: Nicolai de Clemangiis epistolas, item librum inquisitionum Emerici num desideres, mature indica, nam alioquin restituendi sunt. (The letters of Nicholas of Clémanges, item the book of inquisitions of Eymerich – should you actually want it – indicate quickly, otherwise they should be sent back.)

[32] Vienna, ÖNB, Cod. Pal. Vind. 9737b, fol. 27r: Nicolai Emerici inquisitiones bis habeo et non pauca inde selegi in meum catalogum, sed epistolas N. Clemangiis tuo exemplari adiunctas videre valde cupio. (I have the inquisitions twice and I have chosen quite a few things from them for my Catalogue, but I very much want to see the letters of N. Clémanges that are united with them in your copy.)

[33] Flacius must also have owned a copy of the letters of Nicholas of Clémanges, as they were used by him. See Flacius, *Catalogus* (1556), pp. 937–44. Cf. K. Strecker, 'Quellen des Flacius Illyricus', *Zeitschrift für deutsches Altertum und deutsche Literatur* 66 (1929), 65–7.

[34] Cf. *Quellen zur Geschichte der Böhmischen Brüder*, ed. A. Gindely, Fontes Rerum Austriacarum, Oesterreichische Geschichts-Quellen, Abt. 2, Diplomataria et Acta 19 (Vienna, 1859), p. 275. See also D. Kurze (ed.), *Quellen zur Ketzergeschichte Brandenburgs und Pommerns*, Veröffentlichungen der historischen Kommission zu Berlin 45, Quellenwerke 6 (Berlin, 1975), p. 29 n. 9. The letter was among the manuscripts from Lissa in Herrnhut and has not yet been identified.

[35] Cod Guelf. 403 Helmst. and Cod. Guelf. 348 Novi. On the division of the manuscript volume see Kurze, *Quellen*, pp. 18–22.

[36] The manuscript was handed over to the Dominican monastery in Prenzlau; Kurze, *Quellen*, p. 28. It is unknown how it came into Flacius's possession. On the deposition records, see Kurze, *Quellen*, pp. 18–31 (no. 8), and their edition pp. 77–261 (no. XIII); pp. 39–40 (no. 16), and their edition pp. 288–306 (no. XXV); W. Preger, *Beiträge zur Geschichte der Waldesier im Mittelalter*, Abhandlungen der historischen Classe der Kgl. Bayerischen Akademie der Wissenschaften zu München 13/1 (1875), pp. 50–1; W. Wattenbach, *Über die Inquisition gegen die Waldenser in Pommern und der Mark Brandenburg*, Abhandlungen der Kgl. Preussischen Akademie der Wissenschaften zu Berlin. Sitzungsberichte der Phil.-hist. Classe 4 (1886), pp. 3–4. On Zwicker, see now R. Välimäki, *Heresy in Late Medieval Germany. The Inquisitor Peter Zwicker and the Waldensians*, Heresy and Inquisition in the Middle Ages 6 (York, 2019).

Matthias Flacius Illyricus and his use of inquisition registers and manuals

During his stay in Speyer in 1554, Caspar von Nidbruck searched through the manuscripts of the collector and lawyer Job Vener (*c.* 1370–1447), and among these he again found Eymerich's manual and took it with him to Vienna.[37] Finally, Flacius had learned from the preacher Michael Stieffel (1487–1567), who had stayed in Steyermark between 1525 and 1527, that three large volumes of inquisitional files were to be found in a monastery there.[38] These must have been the records of interrogations by the inquisitor Peter Zwicker in the diocese of Passau, which were once in the Benedictine monastery of Garsten and are lost today.[39]

Beyond the inquisition manuals and protocols, there were already compilations of heretical doctrine. On 26 July 1555 Nidbruck pointed Flacius to a volume of a Waldensian confession printed by Melchior Lotter in Leipzig in 1512.[40] A copy of this publication can be found in Flacius's library.[41] In September 1555 Flacius was still looking for further Waldensian confessions in Leipzig, but he was already saying that he possessed some more recent writings on this subject.[42] He could refer to a codex in his possession that contained various tracts on Waldensians.[43] Moreover, Flacius even included archaeological findings in his research, using these to underline the importance and distribution of Waldensian groups in the past. In his letters Flacius referred to the remains of a Waldensian prayer house and

---

[37] Vienna, ÖNB, Cod. Pal. Vind. 5099. Cf. H. Heimpel, *Die Vener von Gmünd und Strassburg 1162 – 1447: Studien und Texte zur Geschichte einer Familie sowie des gelehrten Beamtentums in der Zeit der abendländischen Kirchenspaltung und der Konzilien von Pisa, Konstanz und Basel*, 3 vols. (Göttingen, 1982), II, 969.

[38] In the article *Stier* ('Steyrmark') in Flacius, *Catalogus* (1562), p. 583.

[39] See G.E. Friess, 'Patarener, Begharden und Waldenser in Österreich während des Mittelalters', *Österreichische Vierteljahresschrift für katholische Theologie* 11 (1872), 209–72 (244 n. 4). In the library of the Abbey in Seitenstetten there are still some interrogation protocols, inquisition reports, *formae juramenti* and a *forma absolutionis*, ibid., pp. 267–71; better in Kurze, *Quellen*, 74–6, and now Välimäki, *Heresy*, pp. 275–6, 282–3.

[40] Vienna, ÖNB, Cod. Pal. Vind. 9737i, fol. 338v: Duplicem confessionem Waldensium Lipsiae impressit Lother anno 1512 in folio crassa littera. (In the year1512 Lotter printed at Leipzig a double confession of Waldensians, in folio [and] in bold print.)

[41] J. Ziegler, *In hoc volumine haec continentur Duplex Confessio Valdensium ad Regem Vngarie missa* (Leipzig: Lotter, 1512). The copy in Flacius's possession: Wolfenbüttel, HAB, H: A 98.2° Helmst. (2).

[42] Vienna, ÖNB, Cod. Pal. Vind. 9737b, fol. 15r: De Waldensium confessione quaeram Lipsiae. Quasdam recentiores habeo.

[43] Cod. Guelf. 431 Helmst. The volume was number '7' in the Flacian library. The title entry *De erroribus Waldensium* on fol. 1r is most likely made by Nidbruck's hand. According to this the volume was sent to Flacius from Vienna.

Harald Bollbuck

their cemetery in the Austrian towns of Steyr[44] and Neustadt.[45] It is possible that he had obtained this information either from Michael Stieffel as well, or from his correspondent Wolfgang Waldner (*c.* 1530–91), who lived in Styria before becoming a preacher in Nuremberg.[46] However, this material was not included in the *Catalogus*.

4. Inquisition records and manuals in the library of Flacius: an overview

The book collection of Matthias Flacius was sold by his widow to Duke Heinrich-Julius of Braunschweig-Wolfenbüttel on 20 April 1597. In 1618 the collection moved to the University of Helmstedt. Some of the books were added to the collection of the historian and Helmstedt Professor Hermann von der Hardt (1660–1746) and sold by his heirs. In 1806/7 the Napoleonic army brought selected books of the Flacius Collection to the National Library in Paris. But despite all this, the collection was essentially preserved and re-united in the Herzog August Bibliothek in 1817.[47] The librarian Liborius Otho (tenure 1612–18) made a list of the holdings of the Flacius book collection.[48] His text provides the basis for a listing of the inquisition

---

[44] Vienna, ÖNB, Cod. Pal. Vind. 9737b, fol. 27v: Die Waldenser haben gleichwol für jharen eine meile weges von Steyr gewonet unnd ein eigen kirchen gehabt, Davon das gemeur noch stehet. Aber endlich vertrieben unnd ihr viel gerichtet worden, davon noch ein coemiterium vorhanden, welcher der Ketzer Fridthoff genennet wirdt (Years ago, the Waldensians had lived a mile from Steyr and had their own church, of which the walls still remain. However, eventually they were driven out and many of them were executed. There is still a cemetery left, which is called the cemetery of the heretics.)

[45] Vienna, ÖNB, Cod. Pal. Vind. 9737i, fol. 217v: Vide et alibi circumquaque multi fuerunt Waldenses in Austria ante 200 annos, extat alicubi dirutum templum non procul a Newstade, quod der ketzer kirchoff appellari audio (Look – and elsewhere two hundred years ago there were many Waldensians all around in Austria, [and] there is still a dilapidated temple, somewhere not far from Neustadt, which I hear is called 'the heretic graveyard').

[46] See R. Dollinger, *Das Evangelium in Regensburg: Eine evangelische Kirchengeschichte* (Regensburg, 1959), pp. 285–6, 311–15. See also 'Waldner, Wolfgang', in *Controversia et Confessio Digital*, ed. I. Dingel <http://www.controversia-et-confessio.de/id/b4efd7ee-b5d9-4866-84a6-3dd2d9088a26> (accessed 17 September 2020).

[47] On the history of the book collection, see O. von Heinemann, *Die Handschriften der herzoglichen Bibliothek zu Wolfenbüttel*, 9 parts [Die alte Reihe = old series] (Wolfenbüttel, 1884–1913; reprinted within Die neue Reihe = new series, Frankfurt am Main, 1963), part 1, *Die Helmstedter Handschriften*, pp. IX, 16ff, 50–1, 210–11; H. Schneider, *Beiträge zur Geschichte der Universitätsbibliothek Helmstedt* (Helmstedt, 1924), pp. 29–36; B. Savoy, *Kunstraub: Napoleons Konfiszierungen in Deutschland und die europäischen Folgen* (Wien, 2011), pp. 132–4.

[48] Cod. Guelf. A Extrav., esp. fol. 298 (293)–305 (300).

Matthias Flacius Illyricus and his use of inquisition registers and manuals

manuals and records in Flacius's possession. Among the so called *Missalia Papalia* (*Papal missals*) there are seven manuscript volumes on the subject of inquisition. The old signature is placed in front, while the current follows, after a hyphen:

– Y 14 Liber inquisitionis haereticae pravitatis. Epistolae quaedam Pontificis et Episcoporum. Ibidem Bulla Caroli 4ti. Ibidem Iohannes Lignanus de pace. (Book of inquisition of heretical wickedness. Certain letters of the Pontiff and Bishops. In the same place, Bull of Charles the Fourth. In the same place, John of Legnano, On Peace) – Cod. Guelf. 279 Helmst.

– Y 24 Jus Inquisitorum haereticae pravitatis (Law of the Inquisitors of Heretical Wickedness). – Cod. Guelf. 315 Helmst.

– Y 28 Modus procedendi in Inquisitione manuscr. [...] Et de Beginis Constitutiones quorundam paparum (Mode of proceeding in Inquisition, manuscript [...] And certain popes' Constitutions about the Beguines). – Cod. Guelf. 311 Helmst.

– Y 33 Mutilatum Registrum quarundam Mulierum et personarum offerentium se et sua ad citationes Inquisitionis anno 1393. In eodem libro etiam reperitur processus totus Inquisitionis contra Matthæum Hagen credentem cum Husso in Diocesi Brandenburgica anno 1458 (Register, damaged [*or* truncated], of some Women and persons presenting themselves and their things [possessions] in response to summonses of Inquisition in the year 1393. Also found in the same book is the complete process of Inquisition against Matthew Hagen, a believer with Hus, in the Diocese of Brandenburg in the year 1458). – Cod. Guelf. 403 Helmst. + Cod. Guelf. 348 Novi.[49]

– Z 15 Fragmentum Inquisitionis haereticae pravitatis [...] Tractatus Inquisitionis contra Biklefistas et Hussitas (A fragment of Inquisition of heretical wickedness ... Treatise of Inquisition against Wycliffites and Hussites). – Cod. Guelf. 473 Helmst.

– Z 70 Unum folium articulorum inquisitorum haereticae pravitatis super Hussitas vel Wiclefistas (One folio of articles of inquisitors of heretical wickedness on Hussites and Wycliffites). – Karlsruhe, BLB, Cod. K 349.

– Z 100 Fragmentum inquisitorum haereticae pravitatis. – Karlsruhe, BLB, Cod. K 364.

– A.a 19 Processus contra Johannem Gudulchi et Franciscum de Archita haereticos tempore Innocentii Septimi papae (Process against the heretics

---

[49] Today what survives of this volume is split and found in these two manuscripts. See above n. 35.

Harald Bollbuck

John Gudulchi and Francis of Arquata during the time of pope Innocent the Seventh). – Cod. Guelf. 1006 Helmst.

The manuscript volumes upon which Flacius concentrated most for his historical research studies contain the following pieces which are relevant to our theme:

– Cod. Guelf. 279 Helmst.:[50]

fols. IIv–261r Nicolaus Eymerici: Directorium inquisitorum variis documentis auctum (Nicholas Eymerich: Directory for inquisitors, augmented with various texts).

fols. 278v–286v Otto episcopus Herbipolensis: Documenta ad inquisitionem haereticae pravitatis in diocesi Herbipolensi spectantia (Otto bishop of Würzburg: Documents pertaining to the inquisition of heretical wickedness in the diocese of Würzburg).

fols. 287r–288v Rabanus episcopus Spirensis: Sententia definitiva contra Petrum Turnouwe (Raban bishop of Speyer: Definitive Sentence against Peter Turnau).[51]

– Cod. Guelf. 311 Helmst.:[52]

fols. 1r–42va Manuale inquisitionis haereticae pravitatis (Manual of inquisition of heretical wickedness); this is the manual of a Prague inquisitor.[53]

– Cod. Guelf. 315 Helmst.:[54]

fols. 1ra–173vb Nicolaus Eymerici: Directorium inquisitorum variis documentis auctum.
therein: fol. 26v Henricus Schoenvelt: Articuli haeretici flagellatorum in Thuringia; fols. 27ra–28ra Henricus Schoenvelt: Sermo de traditione relapsi haeretici (Nicholas Eymerich: Directory for inquisitors, augmented with various texts. Henry Schoenvelt: Heretical articles of flagellants in

---

[50] See http://diglib.hab.de/?db=mss&list=ms&id=279-helmst&catalog=Lesser

[51] Cf. H. Heimpel, *Drei Inquisitions-Verfahren aus dem Jahre 1425: Akten der Prozesse gegen die deutschen Hussiten Johannes Drändorf und Peter Turnau sowie gegen Drändorfs Diener Martin Borchard* , Veröffentlichungen des Max-Planck-Instituts für Geschichte 24 (Göttingen 1969), pp. 138–40.

[52] See http://diglib.hab.de/?db=mss&list=ms&id=311-helmst&catalog=Lesser and A. Patschovsky, *Die Anfänge einer ständigen Inquisition in Böhmen. Ein Prager Inquisitoren-Handbuch aus der ersten Hälfte des 14. Jahrhunderts*, Beiträge zur Geschichte und Quellenkunde des Mittelalters 3 (Berlin and New York, 1974), pp. 4–7.

[53] Patschovsky, *Anfänge*, pp. 96–231 (text), 232–46 (contents list with commentary).

[54] See http://diglib.hab.de/?db=mss&list=ms&id=315-helmst&catalog=Lesser

Matthias Flacius Illyricus and his use of inquisition registers and manuals

Thuringia. Henry Schoenvelt: Address on the handing over of a relapsed heretic [viz. to the secular arm for execution]).[55]

fols. 174ra–195va Bernardus Guidonis: Practica inquisitionis haereticae pravitatis (The Practice of inquisition of heretical wickedness).

fols. 196ra–198ra Guido Fulcodi: Consilium de quibusdam dubita-bilibus inquisitionis haereticae pravitatis (Guy Foulques [Clement IV]: Consultation about some problematic [questions] in the inquisition of heretical wickedness).

fols. 214v–217r Responsa et observationes iurisperitorum Coloniensium de fratribus vitae communis in Daventria (Responses and observations by legal experts from Cologne on the brothers of the common life in Deventer).

fols. 218ra–247rb Manuale inquisitionis haereticae pravitatis (Manual of inquisition of heretical wickedness).
included: fols. 223rb–228va Guido Fulcodi: Consilium de quibusdam dubitabilibus inquisitionis haereticae pravitatis; fols. 228va–230va Consilia de inquisitione haereticae pravitatis; fols. 230va–233ra Statuta concilii Narbonensis (Guy Foulques: Consultation about some problematic [questions] in the inquisition of heretical wickedness. Consultations on inquisition of heretical wickedness. Statutes of the Council of Narbonne).

– Cod. Guelf. 403 Helmst.[56] and Cod. Guelf. 348 Novi: inquisition deposi-tions of the Celestine Prior Petrus Zwicker from Stettin (1392–94), and further records of inquisition proceedings against Matthaeus Hagen in Berlin (1458) and against inhabitants of the village Kerkow near Angermünde (1458).[57]

– Cod. Guelf. 431 Helmst.:[58]

fols. 1ra–2va Petrus Zwicker: Relatio de erroribus Waldensium in Austria (Peter Zwicker: Report about the errors of Waldensians in Austria).

fols. 2vb Index rectorum sectae Waldensium. Anno domini MCCCLXXXXI [...] (List of leaders of the sect of Waldensians. AD 1391).

fols. 3ra–6va Petrus Zwicker: Formulae quibus processu inquisitionis

---

[55] Edition in A. Patschovsky, 'Zeugnisse des Inquisitors Heinrich Schoenvelt in einer Nicolaus-Eymericus-Handschrift', in *Vera lex historiae: Studien zu mittelalterlichen Quellen für Dietrich Kurze zu seinem 65. Geburtstag am 1. Januar 1993*, ed. S. Jenks et al. (Cologne, 1993), pp. 264–8.
[56] See http://diglib.hab.de/?db=mss&list=ms&id=403-helmst&catalog=Lesser
[57] See above n. 36.
[58] On this manuscript see http://diglib.hab.de/?db=mss&list=ms&id=431-helmst&catalog=Lesser and Välimäki, *Heresy*, pp. 277–8.

223

Harald Bollbuck

haereticae [pravitatis] contra Waldenses utentur (Peter Zwicker: Formulae which are used in the proceedings of inquisition wickedness against Waldensians).

fols. 7ra–8rb, 10ra–14rb Petrus Zwicker: Tractatus contra haeresim Waldensium (Peter Zwicker: Treatise against the heresy of the Waldensians).

fols. 9ra–vb, 15ra–vb Ps.-Reinerus Sacconi: Tractatus de haereticis (Pseudo-Reinerius Sacconi: Treatise on heretics).

fols. 26ra–48vb: Petrus Zwicker: Tractatus contra haeresim Waldensium (Peter Zwicker: Treatise against the heresy of the Waldensians).

– Cod. Guelf. 473 Helmst.:[59]

fols. 1ra–7vb Johannes Gerson: De necessaria communione laicorum sub utraque specie (Jean Gerson: On the necessary communion of lay people in both kinds [= bread and wine]).

fols. 7ra–8va Johannes Maurosii: Allegationes contra communicantes sub utraque specie in concilio Constantiensi (Jean Mauroux: Arguments at the council of Constance against communion in both kinds).

fols. 9ra–36rb Petrus de Pulka: Tractatus contra IV articulos Hussitarum (Peter of Pulkau: Treatise against the four articles of the Hussites).

fols. 36va–86vb Petrus de Pulka: Tractatus universitatis Viennensis de communione sub utraque specie contra Hussitas (Peter of Pulkau: Treatise of Vienna University on communion in both kinds against the Hussites).

In addition, Flacius possessed some manuscripts which are no longer found in the collection of his books as it is today. Of great importance for his information about Waldensians was the *Passau Anonymus*, a collection of texts by a Dominican from the diocese of Passau. Flacius was the first person to publish extracts from it.[60] The contents of this anthology fluctuate in the many extant manuscripts, whose tradition is therefore very difficult to elucidate. The definitive modern study identifies five redactions, with Flacius's manuscript belonging to redaction B.[61] The Jesuit Jakob Gretser

---

[59] See http://diglib.hab.de/?db=mss&list=ms&id=473-helmst&catalog=Lesser

[60] Flacius, *Catalogus* (1556), pp. 723–57; Flacius, *Catalogus* (1562), pp. 431–45. Cf. Hartmann, *Humanismus*, p. 183; A. Patschovsky, *Der Passauer Anonymus. Ein Sammelwerk über Ketzer, Juden, Antichrist aus der Mitte des 13. Jahrhunderts*, Schriften der Monumenta Germaniae Historica 22 (Stuttgart, 1968), p. 3.

[61] See Patschovsky, *Anonymus*, pp. 3–4, 19–21. A fold-out table on p. 201 facilitates

Matthias Flacius Illyricus and his use of inquisition registers and manuals

accused Flacius of 'counterfeiting', for Flacius had published passages in the *Catalogus* which were unknown to him.[62] Flacius's copy seems to have been lost.

Flacius did not obtain information about the proceedings against Ulrich Grünsleder and Heinrich Ratgeb (he called them 'Henricus Grunfelder' and 'Henricus Radtgeber'),[63] which ended with their burning, from trial records, but from the unprinted *Chronica Husitarum* of Andreas of Regensburg (around 1380–1438).[64] This manuscript is also not to be found among Flacius's books.

The records of the proceedings of Johannes Rucherath from Wesel in 1479 were taken by Flacius from Caspar Hedio's supplements (*paraleipomena*) to the Chronicle of Ursberg and editions published additionally to Aeneas Silvius Piccolomini's work on the Council of Basel.[65] Flacius took over the German doctrinal sentences almost literally and paraphrased the Latin ones on the basis of the records of Rucherath's interrogations.[66] While researching the edition, he also came across Rucherath's treatise against indulgences, *De indulgentiis*, whose manuscript he also possessed.[67]

---

comparison between the contents of Flacius's manuscript and those of other manuscripts within the redaction B group, and between the five redactions overall.

[62] Ibid., pp. 4–5.

[63] Flacius, *Catalogus* (1556), p. 853.

[64] Hartmann, *Humanismus*, pp. 171, 189.

[65] Cf. Flacius, *Catalogus* (1556), p. 976–8. Sources are *Paradoxa D. Ioannis de Wesalia [...] mox damnata per Magistros Nostros haereticae pravitatis inquisitores* and *Examen magistrale ac theologicale Doctoris Ioannis de Wesalia*, both published in C. Hedio and P. Melanchthon, *Chronicum abbatis Urspergensis [...] Paraleipomina rerum memorabilium a Friderico II. usque ad Carolum V. Augustum* (Straßburg, 1539), pp. 442–5 and in Aeneas Silvius, *Commentariorum [...] De Concilio Basileae celebrato libri duo* (Basel, 1523), pp. 335–44. The publisher of the last book was Jacobus Sobius, who announces in the preface that he edited some additional tracts found in the manuscript volume of Aeneas' commentary. Ibid., fol. A1v. For Sobius see *Allgemeine Deutsche Biographie*, XXXIV, p. 529–30. Hedio/ Melanchthon, *Chronicum*, pp. 457–8 with an additional small account *De Ioanne Wessalo*. On these sources cf. Hartmann, *Humanismus*, pp. 191–2. On the trial of Johannes Rucherath see *Theologische Realenzyklopädie*, XVII, cols. 150–3.

[66] The German sentences in Aeneas Silvius, *Commentariorum*, p. 336 and Flacius, Catalogus (1556), p. 977. They are missing in Hedio/Melanchthon, *Chronicum*, 443.

[67] Cf. Flacius, *Catalogus* (1556), p. 978, based on Aeneas Silvius, *Commentariorum*, p. 341. The manuscript of *De indulgentiis* is now held in the Badische Landesbibliothek Karlsruhe, Sign. 370. Cf. Hartmann, *Humanismus*, pp. 192.

Harald Bollbuck

5. Techniques and aims of the use of inquisition protocols and manuals by Flacius

In the investigation of how Flacius edited and worked with inquisition records and manuals, the analysis of the extensive Waldensian article in the *Catalogus* proves to be very useful. At fifty-six pages[68] it is the longest and most comprehensive article dedicated to one topic in the whole of the *Catalogus*. It contains a short history of the origin of the sect, including the biography of Peter Valdes, a list of articles of faith, a description of the sect's spread to Italy, Bohemia and Germany, a presentation of some of its trial proceedings, a list of its teachers in Austria and a broad description of its doctrine. Finally, there is information from various inquisitorial sources, each with its own heading, e.g. *Ex alio inquisitorio libello* (*From another inquisitorial booklet*). It is obvious that Flacius wanted to impose order on the materials, but kept on being distracted from his plan by the heterogeneity of the sources.

Flacius describes the emergence of the Waldensian community in terms of dialectical, Lutheran historical thought as a reaction to the 'four satanic apostles': the *Decretum* of Gratian, the *Sentences* of Peter Lombard and the teachings of St Francis and St Dominic.[69] Peter Valdes was sent by Christ to restore Christian truth from the darkness of the Antichrist. Faced with the death of a council member in Lyon, Valdes had begun to reflect on repentance – an awakening similar to that of Luther. By translating the Bible into French and discovering a number of errors in the papal Church,[70] he became a forerunner of Luther, who however is highlighted by his fight against indulgences. When Valdes in turn collected the writings of the Church Fathers to arm himself against the arguments of his opponents,[71] Flacius becomes his successor.

In connection with the first list of Waldensian confessional articles, Flacius states his method that their doctrine must be reconstructed from the writings of their opponents, the inquisitors.[72] For the narrative of the Waldensians' spread to Narbonne and Lombardy, Flacius gives his sources. These are legal

---

[68] Flacius, *Catalogus* (1556), pp. 704–60.

[69] Ibid., p. 705.

[70] Ibid., pp. 706–7.

[71] Ibid., p. 707.

[72] Ibid., pp. 709–10. Interestingly, Flacius does not state on what basis he had collected these confessional articles. The inquisition depositions from Pomerania (Cod. Guelf. 403 Helmst.; 348 Novi) report a lot of principles of Waldensian faith which are consistent with the articles cited by Flacius, but never completely or even in that given order. Most of the confessions drawn up by inquisitors have in the first place the Waldensians' self-designation as lay confessors (*confessores*). Flacius, however, starts with their primacy of the Bible, in this way suggesting proximity to Lutheran doctrine.

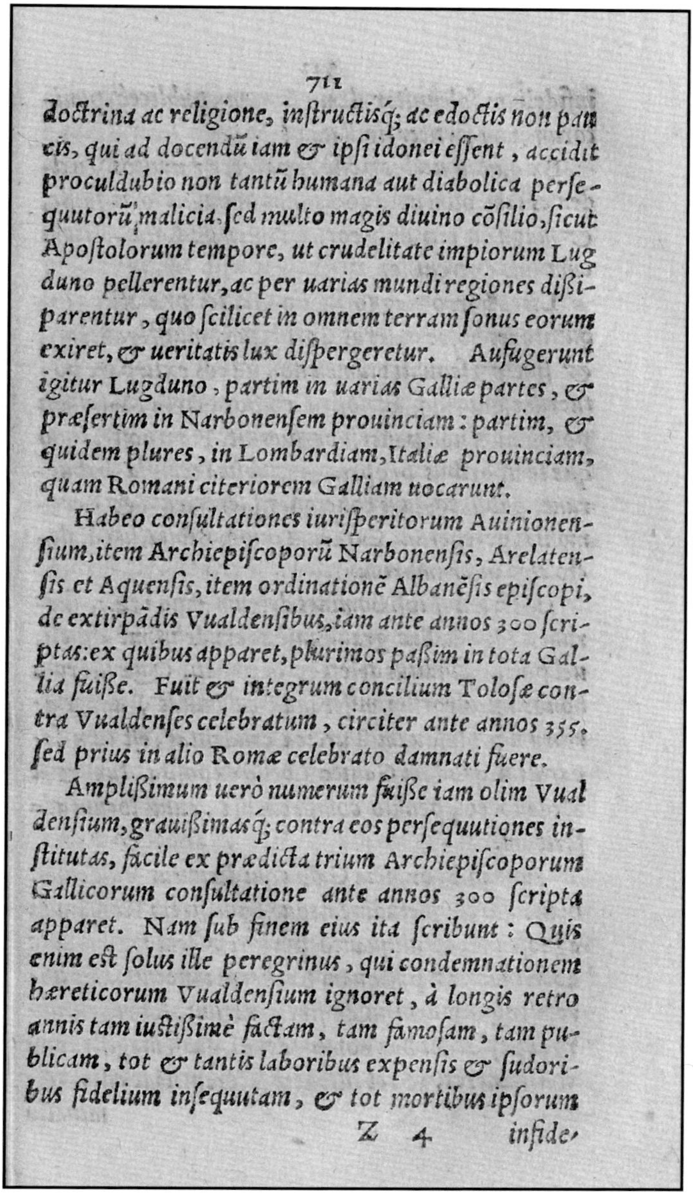

711

doctrina ac religione, instructisq; ac edoctis non paucis, qui ad docendū iam & ipsi idonei essent , accidit proculdubio non tantū humana aut diabolica persequutorū malicia. sed multo magis diuino cōsilio, sicut Apostolorum tempore, ut crudelitate impiorum Lugduno pellerentur, ac per uarias mundi regiones dissiparentur , quo scilicet in omnem terram sonus eorum exiret, & ueritatis lux dispergeretur. Aufugerunt igitur Lugduno , partim in uarias Galliæ partes , & præsertim in Narbonensem prouinciam: partim, & quidem plures , in Lombardiam, Italiæ prouinciam, quam Romani citeriorem Galliam uocarunt.

Habeo consultationes iurisperitorum Auinionensium, item Archiepiscoporū Narbonensis, Arelatensis et Aquensis, item ordinatiōnē Albanēsis episcopi, de extirpādis Vualdensibus, iam ante annos 300 scriptas: ex quibus apparet, plurimos passim in tota Gallia fuisse. Fuit & integrum concilium Tolosæ contra Vualdenses celebratum , circiter ante annos 355, sed prius in alio Romæ celebrato damnati fuere.

Amplissimum uerò numerum fuisse iam olim Vualdensium, grauissimasq; contra eos persequutiones institutas, facile ex prædicta trium Archiepiscoporum Gallicorum consultatione ante annos 300 scripta apparet. Nam sub finem eius ita scribunt : Quis enim est solus ille peregrinus , qui condemnationem hæreticorum Vualdensium ignoret, à longis retro annis tam iustissimè factam, tam famosam, tam publicam, tot & tantis laboribus expensis & sudoribus fidelium insequutam, & tot mortibus ipsorum

Z 4   insidei

Figure 9.3 *Catalogus testium veritatis* (Basle, 1556), p. 711, which makes use of passages which Flacius marked for use in the manuscript reproduced in figs. 19–20 <http://diglib.hab.de/drucke/alv-v-598/max/00747.jpg>. Reproduced by permission, Herzog August Bibliothek, Wolfenbüttel.

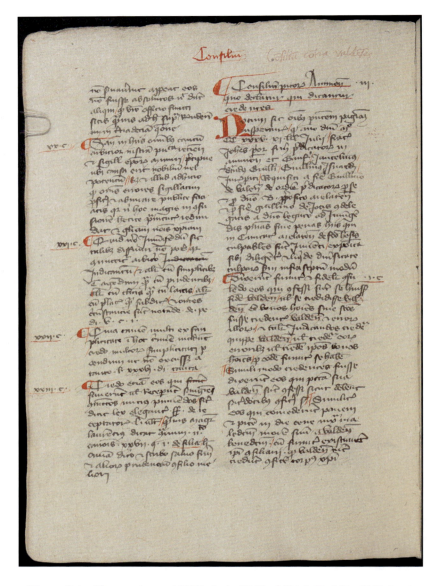

Figure 9.4   Herzog August Bibliothek, Wolfenbüttel, Cod Guelf Helmst 315, fol. 228v. The manuscript was in Flacius's library. In Flacius's hand are the heading above the right-hand column, Consilia contra valdenses, and the cross made out of dots in the margin to the right of line 6, both written in the original in red ink. See note 73 on these consultations and conciliar texts from southern France in the 1230s–40s. Reproduced by permission, Herzog August Bibliothek, Wolfenbüttel. http://diglib.hab.de

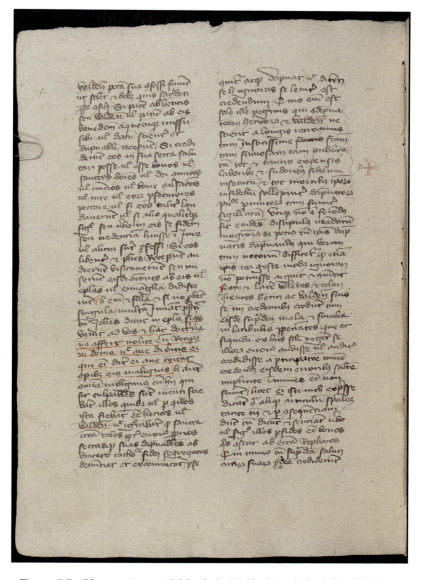

Figure 9.5 Herzog August Bibliothek, Wolfenbüttel, Cod Guelf Helmst 315, fol. 233v. In Flacius's hand is the squiggly line against lines 4–14 in the right-hand column, as also the cross in the margin to the right of lines 9–10, both in the original in red ink. See note 74 on the passage which begins on line 3, 'Quis enim est'. Reproduced by permission, Herzog August Bibliothek, Wolfenbüttel. http://diglib.hab.de

Harald Bollbuck

consultations and ordinances of the archbishops of Narbonne, Arles and Aix, as well as expert opinions from legal scholars in Avignon.[73] In the corresponding manuscript Flacius has marked with red pencil those parts relevant to the printing.[74] In contrast, Flacius did not perceive the movement of the flagellants as a sect of its own right, although he had a list of sixteen articles from a trial against flagellants in Sangershausen (Thuringia) in 1414, drawn up by the inquisitor Heinrich Schoenvelt.[75] For the report on the spread of the

---

[73] Flacius, *Catalogus* (1556), p. 711: Habeo consultationes iurisperitorum Avinionensium, item Archiepiscoporum Narbonensis, Arelatensis et Aquensis, item ordinationem Albanensis episcopi, de extirpandis Waldensibus, iam ante annos 300 scriptas: ex quibus apparet, plurimos paßim in tota Gallia fuiße. (I have the consultations written 300 years ago of Avignon legal experts, item those of the Archbishops of Narbonne, Arles and Aix, the ordinance of the bishop of Albano, on the rooting out of Waldensians: from which it is clear there were many of them, scattered throughout Gaul.). He refers first to the *Consilium peritorum Avenionensium* of 1235 (edn: *Quellen zur Geschichte der Waldenser*, ed A. Patschovsky and K.-V. Selge (Gütersloh, 1973), pp. 50–4), secondly to these archbishops' directives, established at the Council of Narbonne in 1243 (ed n: *Texte zur Inquisition*, ed. K.-V. Selge (Gütersloh, 1967), pp. 60–9) and thirdly the ordinance of 1245/6 of Peter of Collemieu, a Frenchman whose cardinalate gave him an Italian episcopal title (edn: Y. Dossat, *Les crises de l'inquisition Toulousaine au XIIIe siècle (1233–1273)* (Toulouse , 1969), pp. 348–9). These texts are to be found in Cod. Guelf. 315 Helmst., fols. 228vb–34ra.

[74] Cf. the following passage in Flacius, *Catalogus* (1556), p. 711–12: Nam sub finem eius ita scribunt: Quis enim est solus ille peregrinus, qui condemnationem haereticorum Waldensium ignoret, a longis retro annis tam iustißime factam, tam famosam, tam publicam, tot et tantis laboribus expensis et sudoribus fidelium insequutam, et tot mortibus ipsorum [712] infidelium solenniter damnatorum publiceque punitorum, tam fortiter sigillatam? (For at its end they write thus (= the three French Archbishops, at the end of their consultation): Who is the lonely traveller, who is unaware of the condemnation of the Waldensian heretics, carried out so many years ago [and] so justly? So famous, so public? Followed by so much expenditure and sweat [and toil] of the faithful? So firmly sealed by so many deaths of those [712] infidels, who have been solemnly condemned and publicly punished?). The text is based on the following passage marked with a red pencil and a cross by Flacius: Cod. Guelf. 315 Helmst, fol. 233v: Quis enim est solus ille peregrinus qui condempnationem hereticorum Waldensium nescierit a longis retro annis tam iustissime factam, tam famosam, tam publicatam, tot et tantis expensis laboribus et sudoribus fidelium insecutam et tot mortibus ipsorum infidelium solempniter dampnatorum publice punitorum tam firmiter sigillatam. (Who is the lonely traveller, who does not know of the condemnation of the Waldensian heretics, carried out so many years ago [and] so justly? So famous, so public? Followed by such a matter, so much expenditure and sweat [and toil] of the faithful? So firmly sealed by so many deaths of those infidels, who have been solemnly condemned and publicly punished?) Modern edn: *Texte zur Inquisition*, ed. Selge, p. 68.

[75] Cod. Guelf. 315 Helmst., fol. 26v. Cf. Patschovsky, 'Zeugnisse', 264–5. Together with some autograph inquisition manuals and forms (Cod. Guelf. 315 Helmst., fols. 27ra–8ra, 102ra–6rb), the list (which is likewise autograph) shapes the *codex unicus* of Schoenvelt's tracts.

230

Matthias Flacius Illyricus and his use of inquisition registers and manuals

Waldensians in Italy to Sicily, he used a mandate from Emperor Frederick II against the sect.[76]

The assertion that there was a close relationship between the Lombard Waldensians and Bohemian heretics, and that they were even trained in academies in northern Italy,[77] is based on the use of a Prague Inquisitor's manual from the first half of the fourteenth century.[78] However, all the information in this manual comes from older French and Austrian manuals based on Waldensian inquisitions.[79] Flacius's updated handbook for Bohemian inquisitors used this information and compiled it to trace heresies better and more accurately. However, it does not tell us whether the heretics in Bohemia were Waldensians or whether they had contact with French or Italian brethren in faith.[80]

In the article on Nikolaus Rutze[81] (*c.* 1460 – before 1520), which was to remain the most important source for this Rostock theologian for a long time, Flacius implies direct contact between Bohemian Waldensians and Rostock.[82]

---

[76] Flacius, *Catalogus* (1556), p. 719, referring to Cod. Guelf. 315 Helmst., fols. 220vb–3rb ('Fridericus II. Imperator: Statuta contra haereticos').

[77] Cf. Flacius, *Catalogus* (1556), p. 720: Habeo inquisitionem in Boemia et Polonia contra Valdenes sub rege Ioanne, circa 1330 Domini annum factam, ubi inter alia diserte fit mentio collectarum, quas fratribus et praeceptoribus suis in Lombardiam soliti sunt mittere; et in alia inquisitione invenio, eos esse solitos ex Boemia causa discendi Theologiam ad suos praeceptores Valdenses in Lombardiam proficisci, veluti ad scholam seu Academiam quandam. (I have an inquisition carried out in Bohemia and Poland under king John, around AD 1330, where among other things there is mention – distinctly – of the collections [of money] which they were in the habit of sending to their brethren and teachers in Lombardy. And in another inquisition I find that they were in the habit of travelling from Bohemia to their teachers in Lombardy, as though to a school or some academy.)

[78] Cod. Guelf. 311 Helmst., fols. 1r–42va (*Manuale inquisitionis haereticae pravitatis*). Fol. 1r has a possession entry of Flacius; on fol. 8v Johann is mentioned as king of Poland and Bohemia; this is underlined by Flacius. Fol. 2v mentions Waldensians in relation to the inquisitional question – 'an [heretici] umquam collectam fecerunt ad mittendum fratribus in Lombardiam' (Whether [the heretics] ever made a collection to send to their brethren in Lombardy) – and Flacius took over this wording. Cf. Hartmann, *Humanismus*, p. 183. The question on sending money to brothers in Lombardy came from the Passau Anonymous; see Patschovsky, *Anfänge*, pp. 1–3, 67 and 102, and his *Passauer Anonymus*, pp. 27, 66–7 and 115 n. 10.

[79] Ibid.

[80] Ibid., pp. 2–3 and 67.

[81] On Rutze, see J.B. Krey, 'Nikolaus Rutze', in *Beiträge zur mecklenburgischen Kirchen- und Gelehrtengeschichte*, 2 vols. (Rostock, 1818–21), II, 58–9, 174–86; id., 'Nikolaus Rutze', in *Andenken an hiesige Gelehrte aus dem 16., 17. und der ersten Hälfte des 18. Jahrhunderts*, 4 parts (Rostock, 1812–14), III, 1–5; S. Hoyer, *Nicolaus Rutze und die Verbreitung hussitischer Gedanken im Ostseeraum*, Neue Hansische Studien 17 (1970), pp. 157–70; C. Stöllinger-Löser, 'Nikolaus Rutze', in *Die deutsche Literatur des Mittelalters. Verfasserlexikon*, 2nd edn, 14 vols. (Berlin and New York, 1978–2008), VIII, 433–6.

[82] Flacius, *Catalogus* (1556), pp. 1014–16.

Harald Bollbuck

Flacius, who possessed a manuscript of the Low German translation of one of Jan Hus's writings,[83] thought that Rutze could be identified as the translator.[84] But in fact Magister Johann von Lübeck (about 1430–1502) translated the writings.[85] According to Flacius, Rutze rejected abuses such as indulgences and the veneration of saints and relics, which is why he had to go into exile in Wismar and Livonia. Ultimately, however, it is not only the connection between Rostock and Bohemia that must be questioned,[86] but also the fact itself of Rutze's heresy, given that he probably remained a member of the University of Rostock until the end of his life and did not have to go into exile.[87]

In this article, Flacius also provides, based on Rutze, an etymology of the *poßkeller*, that is *putzkeller* or *bußkeller* (cleaning, kissing or penance-cellars) which was discovered by the inquisition in Pomerania.[88] These were secret places of gathering of believers, presumably Waldensians. Flacius's reference is, apart from Thomas Kantzow's Pomeranian Chronicle, the only source for this name of these meeting places.[89]

---

[83] Cod. Guelf. 760.7 Helmst. It is a manuscript copy of an incunabulum which is titled *Dat Bôkeken van deme Rêpe*.

[84] Rutze only possessed the manuscript. It is not known if he permitted its printing. His book box came via the Rostock merchant Hans Kaffmeister to Andreas Reinhardt in Jena, who printed from the box the Four Prague Articles 1524; cf. S. Hoyer, *Rutze*, pp. 157–70; id., 'Martin Reinhart und der erste Druck der Prager Artikel in Deutschland', *Zeitschrift für Geschichte* 18 (1970), 1597–1615.

[85] Cf. Hoyer, *Rutze*, pp. 157–8; *Deutsches Literatur-Lexikon. Deutsches Literatur des Mittelalters*, ed. W. Achnitz, 8 vols. (Berlin and New York, 2011–16), II, *Das geistliche Schrifttum des Spätmittelalters*, cols. 1005–6.

[86] See Hoyer, *Rutze*, pp. 162–3, who, while referring to the delegation of the Brethren Unity from Bohemia to the Mark 1480–2, emphasises the vanishing influence of the Waldensians in Bohemia in view of their absorption into the Brethren community. Cf. H. Kaminsky, *A History of the Hussite Revolution* (Berkeley, 1967), pp. 171–80, 354–5; id., 'The Religion of Hussite Tabor', in *The Czechoslovak Contribution to World Culture*, ed. M. Rechcigel (The Hague, 1964), pp. 215–18.; W. Eberhard, 'Die hussitische Revolution in Böhmen: Ursachen – Ziele und Gruppen – Verlauf – Ergebnisse', in *Europa im 15. Jahrhundert: Herbst des Mittelalters – Frühling der Neuzeit?*, ed. K. Herbers and F. Schuller (Regensburg, 2012), pp. 136–60; T.A. Fudge, *The Magnificent Ride: The First Reformation in Hussite Bohemia* (Aldershot, 1998); F. Šmahel, *Die Hussitische Revolution*, 3 vols. (Hannover, 2002).

[87] Cf. Hoyer, *Rutze*, 164–5.

[88] Flacius, *Catalogus* (1556), p. 1015. Cf. D. Kurze, 'Zur Ketzergeschichte der Mark Brandenburg und Pommerns vornehmlich im 14. Jahrhundert. Luziferianer, Putzkeller und Waldenser', *Jahrbuch für die Geschichte Mittel- und Ostdeutschlands* 16–17 (1968), 50–94 (63–6); Kurze, *Quellen*, pp. 9 n. 17, 270–2; Hartmann, *Humanismus*, pp. 187–8. The German word *Buß[e]* means penance, and the Waldensians heard confessions and imposed penances in covert places, including cellars, hence *Bußkeller*, 'penance-cellars'. For this etymology and also its misunderstanding, see H. Heimpel, *Zwei Wormser Inquisitionen aus den Jahren 1421 und 1422*, Abhandlungen der Akademie der Wissenschaften in Göttingen, Phil.-hist Kl., 3rd ser. 75 (Göttingen, 1969), p. 80.

[89] Flacius mentions the slanderous etymology of some inquisitors that fornication was being committed in these secret places, but he did not reproduce it, since he

Matthias Flacius Illyricus and his use of inquisition registers and manuals

Back to the article on Waldensians. From the already mentioned process files against Waldensians in Pomerania and Brandenburg,[90] Flacius states that 443 Waldensians were examined and listed by name.[91] The files showed that many of them had been in the sect for twenty or even thirty years, or that their parents had already been members. Their teachers also came from Saxony, Thuringia, Hungary, Poland, Vienna and Switzerland.[92] In the context of the Inquisition in Berlin in 1458, Flacius recognised a strong influence of Bohemian Waldensians.[93] He concluded that Waldensianism had spread widely in Bohemia and prepared the way for Hussitism, and that both had existed at the same time.[94]

To describe the Waldensian teachings, Flacius relied on the Passau Anonymous, which – according to the source – he attributed to Reiner Sacconi.[95] His quotations from this is the most extensive of any in his article

---

emphasised its character of counterfeiting. See Flacius, *Catalogus* (1556), p. 1015: Nam praeter alia, etiam illud contra eos commenti sunt, solere illos noctu convenire, et in illis suis conventiculis promiscuas libidines exercere. Quare vulgo dictitatum est, convenire eos in poßkeller, id est osculorum cellario (For among other things also this was forged against them that they used to meet at night and practice collective debauchery at these meetings. Therefore, it was generally claimed that they meet in *poßkellern*, that is, in a kissing cellar). Flacius could find a lot of proofs of secret meeting places and rumours such like those of practiced debauchery in his sources, for instance in Peter Zwicker's treatise *Cum dormirent homines* in Cod. Guelf 431 Helmst., fol. 8rb (Quando mulierculas audis confitentes in cellariis et cavernulis et domorum angulis [...]) or in the records in Cod. Guelf. 403, fols. 38r–v, 70v, 108r, 112v, 114r, 127v (ed. Kurze, *Quellen*, pp. 123, 160, 211, 218, 221, 223).

[90] The item in Flacius, *Catalogus* (1556), pp. 709–10 comes from Cod. Guelf. 403 Helmst.; 348 Novi.

[91] Flacius, *Catalogus* (1556), p. 721, but with the misprint '44'. The later edition, Flacius, *Catalogus* (1562), p. 430, has the correct number.

[92] See note 102. Flacius had knowledge of the wide spread of the Waldensians in Thuringia, Brandenburg, Bohemia, Moravia, Austria and Hungary among other sources from Peter Zwicker's treatise *Cum dormirent homines*, Cod. Guelf. 431 Helmst., fol. 36r (see the passage edited by Kurze, *Quellen*, pp. 261–2, using a different ms).

[93] Probably a reference to Cod. Guelf. 403 Helmst., fol. 9v: videlicet Friderico Ryß, pretenso episcopo antedicto in Bohemia. A. Molnár, *Die Waldenser: Geschichte und europäisches Ausmaß einer Ketzerbewegung* (Göttingen 1980), p. 387, showed that Flacius probably possessed two sermons of the Waldensian bishop Friedrich Reiser, but attributed them to 'Petrus Waldus cardinalis Romanus' (Peter Waldo Roman cardinal). Cod. Guelf. 306 Helmst., fol. 2r–v; without traces of use; see Hartmann, *Humanismus*, p. 228. On Reiser, see Molnár, *Waldenser*, pp. 269–71, 274–8 280–98, 387; *Friedrich Reiser und die 'waldensisch-hussitische Internationale*, ed. A. de Lange and K.U. Tremp (Heidelberg, Ubstadt-Weiher and Basel, 2006), chs. 1–4.

[94] Flacius, *Catalogus* (1556), pp. 722–3. Here he mentions that he possesses a Taborite confession of 1431, adding that Aeneas Silvius Piccolomini attests that Waldensian doctrine held sway among the Taborites.

[95] Flacius, *Catalogus* (1556), pp. 723–55. Cf. Frank, *Untersuchungen*, p. 121; Hartmann, *Humanismus*, pp. 183–4, 253. On the erroneous attribution, see Patschovsky, *Anonymus*, p. 3 n. 2.

Harald Bollbuck

on Waldensians. It adheres very closely to the source, with few significant deviations, or shifts in and interruptions to the text.[96] Flacius quotes about 100 rules and doctrines of the Waldensians, but conceals the fact that they knew the sacrament of Penance and considered good works to be meritorious.[97] This would have distanced them too much from Lutheran doctrine. His interest in the Passau Anonymous lies precisely in the fact that this treatise recognises errors, deviations and abuses in the Catholic Church as the causes of the sect's emergence.[98] The way the Waldensians prayed was taken from another, unspecified volume of inquisition trials (ex alio inquisitorio libello).[99] This was a mostly literal copy from Bernardo Gui's *Practica inquisitionis*.[100] Flacius possessed only a manuscript of the fourth book of this manual,[101] but his quote is taken from book 5. It is unknown where he obtained that information from.

He then provides a list of Waldensian teachers, which was again based 'on another very old inquisitorial booklet' (ex alio inquisitorio libello perveteri). This had been originally a catalogue drawn up in 1391 by inquisitors of Waldensian leaders who had been converted,[102] and in its long and short versions it had circulated among the texts associated with the inquisitions of Peter Zwicker. It is a roughly accurate reading.[103] At one point the order of the persons mentioned got mixed up. It is followed by a short text on the way of life and customs of the teachers, originally written between 1391 and 1393 and often following the 1391 list in the medieval manuscripts.[104]

---

[96] Cod. Guelf. 431 Helmst., fol. 9ra–vb, 15ra–vb with the title: Reineri [scil. Sacconi] ordinis Praedicatorum liber contra Waldenses'. Cf. its edition in Patschovsky, *Quellen*, pp. 19–20, 70–103. Flacius, *Catalogus* (1556), p. 724: 'exemplum de malo exemplo quorundam' as the fourth cause for the rise of the heresy. At the same place the Passau Anonymous says: 'Quarta causa haeresum, est scandalum de malo exemplo quorundam.'

[97] Cf. Frank, *Untersuchungen*, p. 122.

[98] Cf. Patschovsky, *Anonymus*, p. 4 with n. 7.

[99] Flacius, *Catalogus* (1556), 757–9.

[100] Cf. B. Guidonis, *Practica Inquisitionis heretice pravitatis*, v.II.5, ed. C. Douais (Paris, 1886), pp. 249–50.

[101] Cod. Guelf. 315 Helmst., fols. 174ra–95va.

[102] Flacius, *Catalogus* (1556), p. 759, from Cod. Guelf. 431 Helmst., fol. 2vb. Edited in Kurze, 'Ketzergeschichte', 94; see ibid., 78–9; P. Biller, 'The 1391 lists of Waldensian magistri. Three further manuscripts', *Bollettino della Società di Studi Valdesi* 153 (1983), 51–55; id., *The Waldenses, 1170–1530. Between a religious order and a church* (Aldershot, 2001), pp. 233–6. These are now superseded by Välimäki, *Heresy*, pp. 30, 109, 112, 116–18, 164–5, 169.

[103] The *Catalogus* says 'Conradus de Saxonia de villa dicta Dubun prope Weysseburg' instead of 'Conradus de saxonia de villa dicta Dorbran prope Witteberg'; 'Walricus de Hardech' instead of 'Ulricus de Haydekk'; 'Simon de Salig Ungarus' instead of 'Symon de Galicz de Ungaria'.

[104] Flacius, *Catalogus* (1556), pp. 759–60: Habent autem talem vitam et conversationem. Primo ieiunant tres aut quatuor dies in hebdomada in pane et aqua, nisi fuerint in gravi continentia ad laborem constituti. Secundo faciunt inter suos subditos, ut coram eis appareant superiores. Item septies in die orant. sentior incipit orationem,

Matthias Flacius Illyricus and his use of inquisition registers and manuals

From a manuscript containing the *Sententia diffinitiva* against the Hussite Peter Turnau, Flacius reconstructed the life and work of Turnau and his brother in faith Johann von Drändorf.[105] Both had written a manifesto against the secular rule of the clergy. They were executed in 1425 and already remembered as witnesses of faith by Luther and Melanchthon.[106] However, there are some errors in Flacius. He wrote that Drändorf was executed in Worms in 1424, instead of Heidelberg in 1425, and Turnau in Speyer in 1426, though in fact he died in Udenheim in 1425.[107] In this context he mentions a tailor named 'Hager', who was also condemned.[108] This is Matthaeus Hagen, who was sentenced in Berlin in 1458.[109] Flacius's knowledge was based on the volume of process records of various inquisitions which has already been mentioned several times.[110]

In one manuscript volume with texts about Waldensians Flacius found a record of a process at the papal court against Heinrich Totting of Oyta (1330–97).[111] Totting, who had acquired the degree of Master of Arts in Prague in 1335 and was within a sphere of influence of Milič von Kremsier (*c.* 1320–74),[112]

---

et faciteam prolixam vel brevem, secundum quod sibi videtur expedire: et alii sequuntur eum in oratione. Item in vestibus vilibus incedunt doctores: bini et bini ambulant, senior scilicet cum iuniore, quocunque pergunt. Item in verbis sunt cauti: mendacia, iuramenta, et quaelibet natura turpia [760] devitant. Item suos subditos ad eadem diligenter informant. (They have the following way of life and customs. First, they fast three or four days a week on bread and water, unless they are already under severe strain at work. Secondly, they do this [fasting] among those subject to them, in order to appear superior among them. Item, they pray seven times a day. A senior one begins the prayer, and makes it prolix or brief, as seems expedient to him: and the others follow him in the prayer. Item, the preachers go around in shabby clothes; wherever they travel, they walk in pairs, that is to say, senior with junior. Item, they are careful in their speech: they avoid lies and oaths and anything of a shameful nature. Item, they are diligent in instructing those subject to them to act likewise.) See chapter 6 in this volume, Reima Välimäki's study of this text, followed by the edition and translation of one of its redactions.

[105] Flacius, *Catalogus* (1556), p. 853, from Cod. Guelf. 279 Helmst., fol. 287–8. On this cf. Heimpel, *Inquisitions-Verfahren*, p. 13–14.

[106] Ibid., pp. 11–12; K.V. Selge, 'Heidelberger Ketzerprozesse in der frühen Neuzeit der hussitischen Revolution', *Zeitschrift für Kirchengeschichte* 82 (1971), 167–202; Molnár, *Waldenser*, pp. 254–7.

[107] Cf. Hartmann, *Humanismus*, p. 189 n. 323.

[108] Flacius, *Catalogus* (1556), p. 853.

[109] On this, cf. D. Kurze, 'Märkische Waldenser und Böhmische Brüder. Zur brandenburgischen Ketzergeschichte und ihrer Nachwirkung im 15. und 16. Jahrhundert', in *Festschrift für Walter Schlesinger*, ed. H. Beumann, Mitteldeutsche Forschungen 74, 2 vols. (Cologne and Vienna, 1973–4), II, 471–81.

[110] Cod. Guelf. 403 Helmst., fols. 1r–18v. Edited in Kurze, *Quellen*, pp. 288–302. See n. 35 above.

[111] Flacius, *Catalogus* (1556), p. 923, based on Cod. Guelf. 431 Helmst., fols. 22av–5vb. Cf. Hartmann, *Humanismus*, pp. 190–1; edited in G. Sommerfeldt, 'Zu Heinrich Totting von Oyta (Gest. 20. Mai 1397 in Wien)', *Mitteilungen des Instituts für Österreichische Geschichtsforschung* 25 (1904), 576–604, edition 585–96.

[112] Flacius was interested in material which proved predecessors of Hus in Bohemia.

Harald Bollbuck

was called to Prague by Emperor Charles IV, and later, together with Heinrich von Langenstein, he played a decisive role in the establishment of the University of Vienna. In 1371, Totting wrote six theses in a dispute with the cathedral *scholasticus* (master of the school) Adalbert Ranconis de Ericinio (1320–88), which were condemned at a process in Avignon in 1373.[113] According to Flacius the theses of Totting – whom he called 'Henricus de Iota' (or 'Heuta') – were these, and he reported the first five of them. 1. All people living in mortal sin or outside grace, even though they act in the best way, sin mortally. 2. God, not a priest, remits sin. The priest just announces, by the word of God, whom God has bound and whom he has loosed. It is not the priest himself who binds and loosens. 3. It is better to confess to a learned priest who does not have the right to absolve than to an ignorant one who does. 4. The reservation of cases [= system of referring complex sins away from the priest and upwards to episcopal or papal penitentiaries], used now by Popes and Bishops, is a matter of human law, not divine. For all priests have an equal power of the keys [= the keys of binding and loosing]. 5. All 'counsels', as they are called by the Papists, are precepts [= not voluntary but obligatory]: as is taught by our people today and as is the truth of the matter. It is striking that Flacius does not quote Totting's theses, but paraphrases and modernises them by adapting them to the current ecclesiastical situation of his readers. Thus he inserts into the first thesis 'extra gratiam' (outside grace) which does not belong to the source, but points to the Reformation's discourse of grace. And he immediately adds 'quod et Lutherus affirmavit', that Luther also supported this position. Where Totting had dealt with the question of the role of priests in matters of salvation without even mentioning the pope and bishops, Flacius introduces them, and he inserts the fifth thesis into the frame of opposition between the vocabulary of the 'Papists' and what 'our' people teach. The deliberate presentation and interpretation of Totting's theses in an anti-Roman direction is transparent, as is also their adjustment for contemporary readers.

Conclusion

In the struggles against Rome, the Catholic Church and different Lutheran parties of his time, Matthias Flacius Illyricus advocated an ideology of truth witnesses that would historically legitimise the correctness of his own

---

Milič was regarded as such. Flacius's library contained a volume of 'sermones Magistri Milicii' (Cod. Guelf. 826 Helmst.). Flacius, *Catalogus* (1556), pp. 908–10, 912–14, has articles on Milič and Mahias Janov (before 1355–93). The text about Milič' is based on the bull of Pope Gregory XI to the archbishop of Prague, which excommunicated Milič. It is preserved in a manuscript in Flacius's library; Cod. Guelf. 367 Helmst., fols. 14r–15v under the title 'Bulla contra Militzium' (Bull against Milič), and with handwritten markings. Cf. Hartmann, *Humanismus*, p. 139.

[113] Cf. Sommerfeldt, 'Totting', 576–85. The list of theses is given ibid., 586.

Matthias Flacius Illyricus and his use of inquisition registers and manuals

theology. The truth of his doctrine was to be proved by its agreement with the *consensus Apostolicus*. At the same time within the history of the Church a number of forerunners were to be identified, people who had been defamed as heretics by the Catholic Church and whose identity as forerunners was to be established on the basis of significant doctrinal commonalities. In this way a kind of 'counter-church history' was formed. To construct this history Flacius had a team working throughout Europe to gather sources. Inquisition records and manuals played an essential role. They were read critically in order to compile the history of the counter-movement, its geographical diffusion, its teachings, its rites and its undergoing persecution. Of particular interest were Waldensians and Hussites as the postulated predecessors of the Lutheran churches. Truth witnesses were not only the forerunners themselves, that is to say martyrs or heretics, as they were listed and presented in the contemporary catalogues of martyrs. They were also inquisition reports, manuals, Church edicts against heretics, and suchlike. These also 'testified' to both the abuses and doctrinal errors of the Papal Church and to the teachings of the heretics. The proof for the confessional truth of the historical witnesses was based on *topoi* of the right Church doctrine. They shaped the view on church history which was primarily examined in terms of papal abuses and appearance of true doctrine of grace and sacraments.

Although there are long quotations from his sources, Flacius often adapts the sources linguistically to contemporary readers. Waldensians, Jan Hus, Lutheranism: in accordance with a dialectical view of history, influenced by Luther, they all appeared in times when the power of the Papal Antichrist seemed to spread.[114] They all have a similar function in the plan of salvation, especially since factionalism and doctrinal falsifications began to appear soon after the expansion of a sect or after the death of teachers such as Hus or Luther. In this way, Flacius sets a tone against the theological group around Melanchthon in Wittenberg, which in his view would have opened the door to the Antichrist with their adiaphora doctrine. For Flacius, persecution is a proof of the truth of his teachings: whether in past history by Rome, or in the present day through banishment and expulsion arising from internal Lutheran doctrinal disputes. The violence of persecution is always attributed to the opponent.[115] The persecuted form a small group of just 7,000 righteous people in world history. Flacius's view of history is an attempt to historically legitimise a minority church.

---

[114] See the article on Jan Hus in Flacius, *Catalogus* (1556), pp. 849–52. Cf. Pohlig, *Gelehrsamkeit*, p. 316.

[115] On the Hussite warlord Jan Žižka as defender of the Bohemian Church against the Antichrist of Rome and as avenger against the greed of the clergy, see Flacius, *Catalogus* (1556), p. 854. The violence of Fra Dolcino's followers is not mentioned, only their persecution and murder; see Flacius, *Catalogus* (1556), pp. 867–8. On this topic, see Frank, *Untersuchungen*, pp. 123–4.

10

The 'Cathars as Protestant' myth and the formation of heterodox identity in the French Wars of Religion[1]

Luc Racaut

An exhibition entitled *Les Cathares: une idée reçue?* that suggested that the Cathars were invented travelled around France in 2018–19 and reignited the controversy over the existence of a unified Cathar Church.[2] The academic debate can be provocatively reduced to the title of Monique Zerner's edited collection, *Inventer l'hérésie*, which suggested that twelfth-century heresy

---

[1] Author's note: early modern books are described following the conventions used by early modern historians, featuring the name of the author and the title as it appears on the title page. The abbreviation 's. n.' (*sin nomem*) indicate that the author's name is missing from the original title page, 's. d.' (*sin datum*), the date, and 's. l.' (*sin locus*) the place of publication. If the author's name, location or date is known it is indicated in between square brackets []. In some cases, instead of indicating folio numbers, recto (r) and verso (v), or the page number, the convention of indicating the page signature (sig.) is sometimes used in case the page or the folio has been mis-numbered which was common in early-modern books. The signature refers to the letter and number that featured on the bottom right-hand corner at the beginning of each folio and is followed sequentially depending on the format (usually a1–a8 for *in-octavos*, a1–a4 for *in-quartos* then b1, B1, Bb1 and so on) and was used by the printers to fold and bind the folios in order, and is therefore more reliable. References in the body of the text are to the first edition, and in the footnotes to the actual edition consulted.

[2] 'Les Cathares: une idée reçue?', exhibition organized by Alessia Trivellone (University of Montpellier) in October 2018. The exhibition travelled to various cities in France until November 2019; S. Bardy, 'Les Cathares ont-ils vraiment existé ? Une exposition relance ce débat d'historiens', *La Dépêche du Midi*, 23 October 2018: https://www.ladepeche.fr/article/2018/10/23/2893868-les-cathares-ont-ils-vraiment-existe.html consulted on 22/06/2021; C. O'Brien, 'For 800 years, they were celebrated as martyrs to their faith. Just one problem: The Cathars may never have existed', *Los Angeles Times*, 31 December 2018: https://www.latimes.com/world/europe/la-fg-france-cathars-20181231-story.html consulted on 22/06/2021; V. Coste, 'Les Cathares, "une invention" pour une universitaire montpelliéraine', *Midi Libre*, 19 January 2019: https://www.midilibre.fr/2019/01/19/les-cathares-une-invention-pour-une-universitaire-montpellieraine,7962321.php consulted on 22/06/2021.

The 'Cathars as Protestant' myth and the formation of heterodox identity

could not have given rise to a unified Cathar Church.[3] The exhibition compressed scholarly arguments into bite-size chunks that could be better absorbed by the general public and simplified the message without the context and nuance. The reduction of a complex controversy to two standpoints that can be boiled down to a chicken-and-egg problem (was it heresy that caused persecution or the other way around?) is indicative of the way public history operates. Nevertheless, such simple binaries are redolent of the dualism that the Cathars were accused of and the 'all or nothing' aspect of the medieval controversies.[4] For the early modernist it also echoes the cosmic war between good and evil that characterised so much of the printed polemic and propaganda of the French Wars of the Religion.

The formation of a Protestant identity as a response to the enforcement of Catholic orthodoxy evokes the medieval past constantly in a way that not only invites a comparison but suggests striking continuities with the Cathars. Catharism was never so historically significant than when it was revived by the Protestants and their enemies in a way that was crucial to the formation of confessional identities. Catholics seized upon the medieval concept of a Cathar Church in order to draw a parallel with Protestants who then turned it to their advantage, arguing that the Cathars had been True Christians like themselves. I should like to argue that the 'Cathars as Protestant' myth is at the origin of the Cathar identity that is a source of regional pride amongst the people of the Midi to the present day. The events of the French Wars of Religion that led to the invention of this identity will be considered here as well as other Protestant identities that emerged in parallel and contributed to this myth. Attempts to debunk the myth, such as Bishop Bossuet's *Histoire des Variations des Églises Protestantes*, written in the wake of the Revocation of the Edict of Nantes, only served to strengthen it as they were interpreted as Catholic propaganda.[5] Since then Protestants have routinely recycled the myth to argue that Albigensians had been martyrs of the True Church at the hands of the Papal Antichrist just as they were. In 1901, for instance, the Albigensians were brought up once more by the liberal pastor of Castres, Camille Rabaud, arguing that the separation of Church and State was the only way to bring an end to persecution.[6] The legacy of the 'Cathars as Protestants' myth is so enduring that there are still Protestant pastors today to defend it, building bridges across time between 1215, 1517, 1685 and the present.[7]

---

[3] M. Zerner ed., *Inventer l'hérésie ? Discours polémiques et pouvoirs avant l'Inquisition* (Nice, 1998).

[4] R. I. Moore, *War on Heresy: Faith and Power in Medieval Europe* (London, 2012).

[5] Jacques-Bénigne Bossuet, *Histoire des Variations des Églises Protestantes*, 2 vols. (Paris, 1688).

[6] C. Rabaud, *Ce que la France doit aux Protestants* (Paris, 1901).

[7] M. Jas, *Braises Cathares: Filiation secrète à l'heure de la Réforme* (Portet-sur-Garonne, 1992), p. 196.

It is at the Leipzig disputation of 1519 that Martin Luther first turned the Catholic comparison between Protestantism and earlier heresies to his advantage, arguing that the papacy had erred in previous Councils, notably at Constance in 1415 when it had condemned John Hus. The Catholic strategy of lumping all heresies together backfired in this instance as it allowed Luther to claim legitimacy from earlier critics of the papacy and argue for a community of belief with earlier evangelical movements.[8] From 1520 onwards, Luther referred to the Revelation of John's concept of an invisible Church to claim lineage with medieval heretics, arguing that they had been wrongfully persecuted by the Papal Antichrist.[9] This allowed Luther to claim spiritual continuity of belief with the Early Church while legitimising his position politically by denouncing the tyranny of the Popes at the expense of the Germanic Emperors. Luther's references to medieval persecutions were therefore only meaningful within the wider context of the condemnation of the papal monarchy, notably during the Investiture Contest. In 1532, John Carion, Philip Melanchthon and Gaspard Peucer published the *Cronica Carionis*, where the concept of the True Church featured prominently.[10] It built on Luther's references to medieval apocalypticism, arguing that the True Church had been eclipsed for a thousand years until the advent of Protestantism.[11] The chronicle focuses on the conflict between popes and emperors that culminated with the humiliation of Emperor Henry IV at the feet of Pope Gregory VII at Canossa in 1077. But if the *Cronica Carionis* evoked the invisible Church (notably Jan Hus) it steered clear of direct comparisons with medieval heretics, insisting instead on the conflict between temporal and spiritual power over investiture and denouncing the pope as Antichrist.

Prior to the beginning of the wars of religion, no heterodox group from the central middle ages featured in Lutheran material in spite of its insistence on the survival of the True Church during the reign of the Papal Antichrist. Only Genevan editions of Carion's *Chronicles*, under the editorship of Simon Goulard (1579), mention the 'poor of Lyon' in the context of the founding of the mendicant orders.[12] During the 1530s the Waldensians received far more attention from Catholic authors than the Albigensians with whom they

---

[8] E. Cameron, 'Medieval Heretics as Protestant Martyrs', *Studies in Church History* 30 (1993), 185–207.

[9] Unless otherwise stated biblical quotations are from the *New Revised Standard Version* (Nashville, 1993); Revelation 12. 1–7, 13–18; Martin Luther, 'On the Babylonian Captivity of the Church': *De captivitate Babylonica ecclesiae, praeludium Martini Lutheri* (Basel, 1520).

[10] Johannes Carion, *Chronica* (Wittenberg, 1532).

[11] For Protestant apocalypticism, see I. Backus, *Les Sept Visions et la Fin des Temps : les Commentaires Genevois de l'Apocalypse entre 1539 et 1584* (Geneva, 1997).

[12] Otherwise none of the editions prior to 1579 mention the Waldensians or the Albigensians; for instance Jean Carion, *Histoire ou Cronique des choses plus memorables depuis la creation du monde* (Lyon, 1577), p. 308.

The 'Cathars as Protestant' myth and the formation of heterodox identity

were often confused, because of their survival in Lubéron, Piedmont and Bohemia.[13] A tenacious tradition holds that the Waldensians were absorbed by the French Reformed Church in 1532 by Guillaume Farel at Chanforan (Piedmont) but Euan Cameron has shown that this synod was a myth and their adhesion to Calvinism came later.[14] Rather, it was the Bohemian Waldensians that were first approached by Lutheran theologians, notably Johannes Brenz, at a time when the Augsburg Confession looked like a likely candidate to unite all Protestant denominations under one banner.[15] Yet in spite of sympathy for the Waldensians, especially after the massacre that took place in Cabrières and Mérindol in 1545, Lutherans avoided a direct comparison with their twelfth-century counterparts. It was not until 1559 that Lutherans began to do so with the *Magdeburg Centuries* (Basel, 1559–74), at a time when Protestantism was gaining momentum all over Europe. One of its authors, Matthias Flacius Illyricus, was a Gnesio-Lutheran who disputed Luther's legacy with the phillippists (named after Philip Melanchthon) for favouring a rapprochement with the Emperor and Calvinism.[16]

The *Centuries* were a step up from Carion's *Chronicles*, drawing from Flacius's *Catalogue of the Witnesses of the Truth* (1556) that literally tracked all heterodox groups that had denounced the pope as the Antichrist and were persecuted for it.[17] It was in this work that the Waldensians were first mentioned in favourable terms, suggesting that they had been accused of false doctrines and persecuted precisely because they had been one of the first to accuse the pope of being the Antichrist: 'Nam alioqui Waldenses iam annis 400. Papam esse Antichristum docuerunt' (For already, 400 years ago, some Waldensians taught that the Pope was Antichrist).[18] But even so Flacius did not mention the Albigensians in such terms that encouraged a comparison with Protestantism: 'Anno Domini 1213, haeresis Albigensium dilatata, totam Provinciam coepit maculare' (AD 1213, having spread, the heresy of the Albigensians began to stain the whole of Languedoc).[19] It was in England

---

[13] Bernard of Luxemburg, *Catalogus haereticorum omnium* (Erfurt, 1522); Alfonso de Castro, *Adversus Omnes Haereses* (Paris, 1534), sigs o1v, o2v–o3r, p3r; Georg Witzel, *De moribus veterum haereticorum: et quibus cum illi hac aetate affinitatem habeant* (Leipzig, 1537).

[14] E. Cameron, *The Reformation of the Heretics: the Waldenses of the Alps 1480–1580* (Oxford, 1984), pp. 244–5.

[15] Stanislas Hosius, *Verae, Christianae, catholicaeque doctrinae solida propugnatio* (Cologne, 1558). The latter includes a reference to the Lutherans' attempt to rehabilitate the Bohemian Waldensians, notably by Johannes Brenz with whom Hosius entered in direct conflict in Poland.

[16] Matthias Flacius Illyricus, *Ecclesiastica Historia, integram Ecclesiae Christi ideam* (Basel, 1559). See the account of Flacius in this volume's chapter 9.

[17] Matthias Flacius Illyricus, *Catalogus Testium Veritatis, Qui Ante Nostram Aetatem Reclamarunt Papæ* (Basel, 1556).

[18] Ibid., p. 930

[19] Ibid., p. 599.

that the Albigensians were first favourably mentioned, in a commentary on the Revelation of John published by John Bale in 1545, where they feature alongside the Waldensians:

> Consequently ensued the Waldeans and Albigeans [sic] pretending the apostles' life and doctrine, men doubtless of a godly zeal and spirit; and of them the antichrists slew more than a hundred thousand, besides an hundred and fourscore whom they burnt because they would never abjure.[20]

In 1548, Bale had also published a commonplace book, using the *Chronica Majora* of Matthew Paris (*c.* 1200–59) on the persecution of heretics. In one striking passage he repeated both Matthew's denunciation of the frauds of the Dominican inquisitor Robert Le Bougre, who had had thousands of people burnt to death as heretics, and also Matthew's concluding comment, that the inquisitor had been 'deservedly' (meritis exigentibus) condemned to life imprisonment.[21] The Albigensians featured independently from the Waldensians in John Foxe's *Actes and Monuments* (1563) in a section drafted by Bale who redeemed them on their own merit.[22]

The idea that medieval heterodox groups had been ascribed with false doctrine and accused of sexual promiscuity by the Catholics simply because they had criticised the papacy gradually emerged in Protestant circles just as the same strategy was being applied to them. Protestant apologists turned this strategy on its head to claim kinship with medieval forebears, following in the footsteps of Flacius with the Waldensians, and John Foxe with the Albigensians: 'What these Albingensis wer, it cannot be wel gathered by the olde popish historie .... Otherwise it is to be thoughte ... that the opinions of the sayde Albigenses were sounde ynoughe'.[23] Catholic criticisms of Protestant martyrology, here by Thomas Stapleton against Foxe (1567), only served to reinforce the Protestants' conviction that Catholics had indeed lumped all heretics together irrespective of their beliefs: 'M. Foxe ... of hys holy martyrs ... howe manie ... have not mayntaeyned the sayd errours, of the Albigenses, Paterans, or Waldenses[?]'.[24] The Lutheran re-interpretation of medieval history in favour of monarchs whose spiritual authority, it was argued, had been usurped by the pope suited the situation

---

[20] John Bale, *The image of bothe churches after the moste wonderfull and heavenly Revelacion of Sainct John the evangelist* (Antwerp, 1545), sig. Gg7r; *Select Works of John Bale*, ed. H. Christmas (Cambridge, 1849), p. 563.

[21] John Bale, *Scriptorum illustrium maioris Brytanniae Catalogus*, 2 vols. (Basel, 1557–9), I, 282.

[22] John Foxe, *Actes and Monuments* (London, 1563), II, 188; Thomas Freeman, 'John Bale's "Book of Martyrs"? The Account of King John in the *Acts and Monuments*', *Reformation* 3 (1998), 175–223, p. 220.

[23] Foxe, *Actes and Monuments*, sig. *I3r-v, fol. 71ᵛ; Bale, *Catalogus*, pp. 234–5, 261–2.

[24] Thomas Stapleton, *A Counterblast to M. Hornes Vayne Blaste Against M. Fekenham* (Louvain, 1567), fols. 318v, 319r.

The 'Cathars as Protestant' myth and the formation of heterodox identity

in England where the Reformation had begun with the king breaking from Rome. Moreover, arguing for a quasi-Apostolic continuity with an historical True Church, via medieval groups such as the Lollards, was critical for the English Church in order to justify episcopacy in the face of its many critics. In France, however, the Lutheran and English Protestant arguments were neutered by the specificity of the French Gallican Church that was arguably as critical of the papacy's infringements on secular power as the Protestant churches.[25] The Pragmatic Sanction of Bourges (1438) had favourably ruled in favour of the Gallican Church's relative independence from the papacy while the Concordat of Bologna (1516) had strengthened the position of the king within it.

The freedoms of the Gallican Church may explain in part why the Lutheran and English Protestant arguments were not used in a French Reformed context until Simon Goulard's 1619 edition of Jean Crespin's *Livre des Martyres*.[26] Before the French Wars of Religion, if the Albigensians were mentioned at all it was merely as part of a long list of heresies that Protestants were assimilated to in Catholic propaganda. They were often confused with the Waldensians and ascribed with the same beliefs drawn from the first Christian heresies, especially from the Church Fathers' writings against the Manichaeans.[27] Accusations of sexual misconduct in particular were commonplace where the combination of secrecy and claims to high moral standards came up against biblical warnings against false prophets. Thus, for instance St Bernard of Clairvaux condemned those who claimed the Apostolic life *c.*1144: 'Ubi apostolica forma et vita, quam jactatis ? Illi clamant, vos susurratis ; illi in publico, vos in angulo ; illi ut nubes volant, vos in tenebris ac subterraneis domibus delitescitis'[28] (Where is the apostolic model and life of which you boast? They cry aloud, you whisper. They preach in public, you in corners. They 'fly as the clouds' [see Isaiah 60. 8], you lurk in your homes, in darkness and in cellars). Before the wars of religion, persecution had forced Protestants into hiding and the exact nature and spread of Calvinism was largely unknown to the Catholic authorities who were nonetheless aware that an underground Church led from Geneva was in operation. This led to a flurry of conspiracy theories that drew from a rich repertoire of anti-heretical commonplaces that can be traced back to the eleventh century and recycled

---

[25] L. Racaut, 'Anglicanism and Gallicanism: Between Rome and Geneva?', *Archive for Reformation History* 96 (2005), 198–220 (218).

[26] Jean Crespin, *Histoire des martyrs persécutez et mis à mort pour la vérité de l'Evangile depuis le temps des Apotres jusqu'à présent* (Geneva, 1619).

[27] Contra *Fortunatum*, in Augustine, *Six traités anti-Manichéens*, ed. J. Jolivet and M. Jourgeon, Bibliothèque Augustinienne 17 (Paris, 1961), p. 137.

[28] Bernard of Clairvaux, *Sermones in Cantica Canticorum* 65, §4, in *Opera omnia*, ed. J. Leclercq, C. H. Talbot and H. M. Rochais, 8 vols. (Rome, 1957–77), II, 172–7. Translated in *Heresies of the High Middle Ages*, ed. W. L. Wakefield and A. P. Evans (New York, 1969), pp. 132–8 no. 15b (at p. 135).

material from the Church Fathers.[29] Most of this material is unremarkable except for a particular story that emerged in 1557 and suggests the resurgence of a medieval persecutory mechanism.

In the night of 4 September 1557, a large group of some 400 Protestants was discovered in rue St Jacques where they had gathered in a house to sing psalms, just as Paris was preparing for a siege in the aftermath of the Imperial victory at St Quentin in August. The clandestine nature of the meeting invited a comparison with earlier heresies and the scriptural warnings against false prophets that had been mobilised against heretics in the eleventh and twelfth century, especially those who claimed to follow the Apostolic life.[30] After the Affair of the Rue St Jacques in 1557, even if Catholics did not directly accuse Protestants of Manicheanism, they ascribed to them sexual crimes that were directly lifted from Early Church Fathers' writings against 'gnostics'. This in turn allowed French Protestant authors to point out the similarity between these accusations and those levelled at the First Christians and to turn them into an argument in favour of an historical True Church. The accusation of sexual misconduct allowed Protestants to turn the table on the Catholics and not only claim kinship with the Early Christians but also with medieval heretics who had been accused of the same crimes. As I have shown elsewhere, the myth of a satanic eucharist was transposed from the pagan critics of Christianity to the first Christian heresies by the Church Fathers, and subsequently to other groups, notably Jews (the 'blood libel') and from the eleventh century to heretics.[31]

The first trace of this story that I could find, in fact, predates Christianity and goes back to the plunder of the Temple of Jerusalem by Antiochus Epiphanes (168 BCE) when it was rumoured that a gentile destined for sacrifice had been found there:

> ... they used to catch a Greek foreigner, and fatten him thus up every year, and then lead him to a certain wood, and kill him, and sacrifice with their accustomed solemnities, and taste of his entrails, and take an oath upon this sacrificing a Greek, that they would ever be at enmity with the Greeks.[32]

Various versions of this story were circulated by the Church Fathers in their struggle against the first Christian heresies and were recycled by medieval authors against various groups and finally employed in the anti-Protestant

---

[29] L. Racaut, *Hatred in Print: Catholic Propaganda and Protestant Identity during the French Wars of Religion* (Aldershot, 2002).

[30] *NRSV*: Matthew 7. 15, Revelation 19. 20.

[31] L. Racaut, 'Accusations of infanticide on the eve of the French Wars of Religion', in *Infanticide: Historical Perspectives on Child Murder and Concealment, 1550–2000*, ed. M. Jackson (Aldershot, 2002), pp. 18–34.

[32] Flavius Josephus, *Against Apion*, ii.8, ed. S. Mason, in Flavius Josephus, *Works. Translation and Commentary*, (Leiden, 2000-), X, 216–21; *NRSV*, 1 Maccabees 1. 10.

The 'Cathars as Protestant' myth and the formation of heterodox identity

polemic of the French Wars of Religion.[33] The similarity between the description of the Manichaeans' bacchanalia by the Church Fathers and stories that were circulated about medieval heretics was not a coincidence. The fact that this story emerges time and again in Adhémar de Chabannes (1018), Guibert of Nogent (1114), and against the Fraticelli in later medieval Italy suggests a well-oiled persecutory mechanism.[34]

The amalgamation of the Albigensians with the Manichaeans, on the one hand, and Protestants with Albigensians, on the other, worked on the assumption that false doctrine was linked to depravity. In the wake of the Reformation various versions of the story were circulated, notably by Desiderius Erasmus (1533) who followed in the footsteps of ancient and medieval authors:

> But these examples are all in the past. Surely much more to be deplored is that within recent memory there have been discovered nightly gatherings at which, after praise has been given to God, the lights are extinguished and the men and women consort in promiscuous love. Or the ceremonies in which mothers freely hand over their infants to be butchered, and even watch serenely the horrid crime, so persuaded are they that their children will thus find a high place in heaven. This madness seems to have taken its origin from the heresy καταφρυ'γας [Montanists], which would make the Eucharist from flour mixed with the blood of an infant. This blood they would draw from small pinpricks, and if in the process the child died, it was venerated as a martyr.[35]

When this story was dredged up in the wake of the Affair of the Rue St Jacques by Antoine de Mouchy, however, it was answered by pastor Nicolas des Gallars with a reference to the persecution of Christians, quoting Tertullian's apology against the pagans: 'N'est-ce point la mesme calomnie qui estoit anciennement dressée contre les Chrestiens, faisant à croire qu'ils tuoyent les petits enfans pour les manger?' (Is this not the same slander that was spread against the first Christians, claiming that they killed little children to eat them?).[36] In spite of Des Gallars' protestations the story was

---

[33] Racaut, *Hatred in Print*, pp. 52–67.

[34] Moore, *The War on Heresy*, p. 56; Guibert de Nogent, *Autobiographie* , ed. E. R. Labande (Paris, 1981), pp. 430–1; Jean de la Vacquerie, *Catholique remonstrance aux roys et princes chrestiens, a tous magistrats & gouverneurs de Repub. touchant l'abolition des heresies, troubles & scismes qui regnent aujourd'huy en la Chrestienté* (Paris, 1560), sigs E5v-E7v.

[35] Erasmus, 'On mending the Peace of the Church (*De Sarcienda Ecclesiae Concordia*) 1533', in *The Essential Erasmus*, ed. J.P. Dolan (London 1964), pp. 342–3.

[36] Antoine de Mouchy, *Responce a quelque apologie que les heretiques ces jours passés ont mis en avant sous ce titre: Apologie ou deffence des bons Chrestiens contre les ennemis de l'Eglise catholique* (Paris, 1558), sig. K1r ; Nicolas des Gallars, *Seconde apologie ou defense des vrais chrestiens, contre les calomnies impudentes des ennemis de l'Eglise catholique. Ou il est respondu aux diffames redoublez par un nommé Demochares* [Antoine

reproduced several times, by Jean de la Vacquerie for instance who linked the event directly to the Fraticelli in 1298 or Antoine du Val who made a direct reference to Erasmus's passage cited above.[37] Protestants were familiar with the same patristic sources that their Catholic adversaries were drawing from and made good use of them even in debates internal to Protestantism. Philippists and Gnesio-Lutherans quarrelled over the Interim of Augsburg (1548), and Calvinists were careful to make a distinction between themselves and 'Sacramentarians' (Zwinglians). Nor did these various denominations shy away from using the same weapons as the Catholics against the Anabaptists, whom they called Manichaean and accused of sexual promiscuity.

The accusation of sexual misconduct that went hand in hand with alleged Manicheanism was so common that it was even used by Zwingli against the Anabaptists in 1527 and by Carion against Müntzer in 1532.[38] To cite a Genevan edition of the *Cronica Carionis* (1579): 'Les rêveries des Anabaptistes ressemblent à celles des Manichéens' (The daydreams of the Anabaptists are like those of the Manichaeans), and the editor (Goulard) even added Michael Servetus to the list for good measure![39] The Protestant apologists' familiarity with the sources that were used by their Catholic detractors led them to see through the Catholic persecutory mechanism and dismiss what had been written about medieval heretics. But even if the indiscriminate use of the same crimes and beliefs, especially the 'blood libel', against all heretics was denounced, there was no specific reference to the Albigensians until the beginning of the wars of religion.

The comparison between the Albigensians and Protestants emerged in the course of the French Wars of Religion for contingent reasons, linked to specific events and the politicisation of the conflict, rather than from theology or apocalypticism. It is only after years of the Albigensians being mentioned in Catholic material that the Lutheran and English arguments mentioned above were finally used in French Reformed circles.[40] French references to the Albigensians derived from chronological, political and geographical coincidences (between Albigensian and Protestant strongholds in the Midi) and grew from strength to strength until they were favourably received by the French Reformed Church

---

de Mouchy] *docteur de la Sorbonne* (Geneva, 1559), p. 63; Tertullian, *Apologeticus*, ed. J. E. B. Mayor (Cambridge, 1917), p. 27.

[37] De la Vacquerie, *Catholique remonstrance*, sigs D3r, E5v ; Antoine du Val, *Mirouer des Calvinistes et armures des chrestiens pour rembarez le lutheriens & nouveaux evangelistes de Genève* (Paris, 1562), p. 9.

[38] Johannes Carion, *Chronica* (Wittenberg, 1532); R. Scribner, 'Practical Utopias: Pre-Modern Communism and the Reformation', *Comparative Studies in Society and History*, 36:4 (1994), 743–74, pp. 745–6, 750.

[39] Johann Carion, *Chronique et Histoire Universelle* (Geneva, 1579), pp. 293–5, 306–8, 328–9, 335–44.

[40] G. B. Lyon, 'Baudouin, Flacius, and the Plan for the Magdeburg Centuries', *Journal of the History of Ideas* 64 (2003), 253–72.

The 'Cathars as Protestant' myth and the formation of heterodox identity

in the seventeenth century. But the Albigensian Crusade was first brought up by French Catholics as a precedent in the wake of the events that led to the war, urging the crown to organise a crusade against Protestants rather than pass the Edicts of Pacification that made concessions towards them.

After the Affair of the Rue St Jacques, French Protestants made a show of force, in the open, at the Pré-aux-Clercs in May 1558, where they gathered in their thousands to sing psalms. The stock accusation of meeting in secret to take part in unspeakable practices could no longer be used, as prominent noble houses were represented – the nobles were armed and they demanded a relaxing of Henri II's heresy laws. It was not until the following year, however, that references to the Albigensian Crusade really began to flourish.[41] Henri II's accidental death in 1559 left a fourteen-year-old Francis II on the throne and a Queen Mother, Catherine de' Medici, torn between aristocratic factions that invited a comparison with the early reign of Louis IX. The Conspiracy of Amboise of March 1560, a failed Protestant coup to seize young Francis II and his mother, was compared to attempts by malcontents, led by Hugues de Lusignan, to kidnap the regent Blanche de Castille and Louis IX (1226–9). Francis II's death in December 1560 and the coming to the throne of the ten-year-old Charles IX turned him into a latter-day Louis IX (who was 12 in 1226) and the regent Catherine de' Medici into Blanche de Castille. This relatively short period of time between Henri II's death in 1559 and the beginning of Catherine de' Medici's regency saw the mobilisation of arguments in favour of the summoning of the Estates General on the part of the Protestants. In his *Histoire du Tumulte d'Amboise*, the Protestant apologist François Hotman defended the actions of the conspirators on the basis that the young Francis II was being manipulated by his uncles the Guise.[42] The Prince of Condé was imprisoned for the Conspiracy of Amboise and François second Duke of Guise was given the lieutenancy of the kingdom. His brother Charles Cardinal of Lorraine, moreover, was unpopular amongst the nobility for trying to recoup income lost during the Franco-Hapsburg war and delaying the payment of noblemen's expenses and wages.[43]

The accusation of wanting to usurp the throne was flung liberally on both sides, which spurred the royal archivist, Jean du Tillet, to defend the independence of the crown against the claims of both parties evoking a comparison between Saint Louis and Francis II.[44] The death of the latter

---

[41] For a more detailed account, see L. Racaut, 'The Polemical Use of the Albigensian Crusade during the French Wars of Religion', *French History* 13 (1999), 261–79.

[42] [François Hotman], *Responce au livre inscript, Pour la Majorité du Roy François Second* (Amboise, 1560), sig. B6r.

[43] S. Carroll, *Martyrs And Murderers: The Guise Family and the Making of Europe* (Oxford, 2011).

[44] Jean du Tillet, *Pour l'Entiere Majorite du Roy Treschrestien, Contre le Legitime Conseil Malicieusement Inventé par les Rebelles* (Paris, 1560), sig. e3r.

confirmed the regency of Catherine de' Medici, however, who proved just as incapable as Blanche de Castille in dealing with troublesome noble houses. There was an attempt at conciliation and policing of anti-Protestant opinions that were deemed to cause violence. For example, a history of the Albigensian Crusade by Jean Gay, a member of the Toulouse *Parlement*, was quashed for creating a diplomatic incident with England as Gay implied that having numerous wives was a sign of heresy.[45] Catherine released Condé from captivity and gave the lieutenancy of the kingdom to his brother Antoine de Bourbon while issuing the Edict of January 1562, which permitted public Protestant worship with restrictions.[46] Jean du Tillet, alongside many members of the Paris *Parlement*, refused to ratify the edict and drafted a complaint on their behalf to Charles IX, urging him to follow the example of Louis IX in his war against heresy.[47] In addition, Du Tillet penned a manuscript history of the Albigensian Crusade, which he presented to Catherine in April 1562, which coincided with the taking of Tours and Orléans by the troops of the Prince of Condé.[48] The beginning of the Wars of Religion, and the argument that the Reformation was a pretext for armed rebellion, gave the comparison with the Albigensian Crusade particular urgency.

In France, the Albigensians resurfaced in Catholic polemic to argue for a renewal of persecution every time a new Edict of Pacification punctuated the French Wars of Religion. The hope that Catholic battlefield success would mark the end of the policy of conciliation was quashed when the Edict of Amboise was issued in March 1563, confirming and in some areas extending Protestant rights. Both Catholic and Protestant authors from the South of France evoked the Albigensian Crusade and alluded to the geographical coincidence between hotbeds of Catharism and contemporary Protestantism.[49] On the Protestant side, a history of the 'war against heretics' was published by a lawyer of Toulouse who mentioned the siege of Montauban in 1562 and noted the geographical coincidence with the Albigensian Crusade.[50] A year

---

[45] Jean Gay, *Histoire des scismes et heresies des Albigeois conforme à celle du present: par laquelle appert que plusieurs grands princes, & seigneurs sont tombez en extremes desolations & ruynes, pour avoir favorisé aux heretiques* (Paris, 1561), p. 5; *Calendar of State Papers, Foreign series, of the reign of Elizabeth*, 23 vols. (London, 1863–1950), IV, *1561–1562*, ed. J. Stevenson, 503 no. 833.

[46] L. Racaut, 'The Cultural Obstacles to Religious Pluralism in the Polemic of the French Wars of Religion', in *The Adventure of Religious Pluralism in Early Modern France*, ed. K. Cameron, M. Greengrass and P. Roberts (Bern, 2000), pp. 115–27.

[47] Jean du Tillet, *Remonstrances faictes au Roy par Messieurs de la Court de Parlement de Paris, sur la publication de l'Edict du Moys de Janvier* (Cambrai, 1561).

[48] Jean du Tillet, *Sommaire de l'Histoire de la Guerre faicte contre les Heretiques Albigeois, extraicte du Tresor des Chartres du Roy par feu Jehan du Tillet* (Paris, 1590), sig. Ã7r.

[49] Esprit Rotier, *Antidotz et regimes contre la peste d'heresie* (Paris, 1558), pp. 40–3 ; M. G. Bosquet, *Sur les troubles advenus en la ville de Tolose l'an 1562* (Toulouse, 1572).

[50] Jean Fornier, *L'Histoire des Guerres faictes en plusieurs lieux de la France, tant en la Guienne & Languedoc contre les Heretiques* (Toulouse, 1562), sigs B3ᵛ, C4ʳ.

The 'Cathars as Protestant' myth and the formation of heterodox identity

later, a Toulouse Dominican, Esprit Rotier, published another account of the wars that contravened the terms of the edicts that explicitly forbade authors to engage in vitriolic polemic.[51] Printing 'privileges' were granted by the French *Parlements* that were on the whole hostile to the edicts, and, in this instance, the privilege for Rotier's book was signed by Jean du Tillet himself. To enumerate all the publications that referred to the Albigensian Crusade in this period would take up an entire monograph and certainly exceed the space given here. Suffice it to say that at every turn, the abatement of the hostilities between the crown and the Protestants and the issuing of a new Edict of Pacification was the occasion for yet another salvo of vitriolic polemic that criticised the crown for not embarking on a crusade. The Catholic party in France benefited from the sympathy of regulating bodies in spite of the crown attempting to gain control of censorship with the Edict of Moulins in 1564 as the Catholic printing presses were increasingly critical of the crown.

Of note is the year 1568 that saw the mobilisation of Catholic confraternities that took vows to protect the crown from heresy at all cost, which prefigured the emergence of the Catholic League in 1576.[52] Histories of the Albigensian Crusade began to extol the virtues of its champions rather than the king, for instance comparing Simon de Montfort with François, second Duke of Guise, after his assassination at the hand of a Protestant fanatic in 1562 had turned him into an Ultra-Catholic martyr. His son Henry, third Duke of Guise, was the figurehead of the Holy Catholic League during the Wars of Succession (1584–94) and became the new Simon of Montfort in the Catholic histories of the Albigensian Crusade. The Holy Catholic League was fascinated by the Crusade and many earlier histories were reprinted during this period: Arnaud Sorbin's edition of Peter of Les-Vaux-de-Cernay, first published in 1568, was reprinted in 1585 under the title *Histoire de la Ligue Sainte*.[53] Jean Gay's *Histoire des Schismes et Heresies des Albigeois*, which had been censored in 1561, was reprinted in Paris along with the history that Du Tillet had presented to the Queen Mother in 1562 while the city

---

[51] Esprit Rotier, *Response aux Blasphemateurs de la Saincte Messe: avec la confutation de la vaine & ridicule coene des Calvinistes* (Paris, 1563), sigs A7^{r-v}.

[52] Gabriel de Saconay, *De la providence de dieu sur les roys de france treschrestiens, par laquelle sa saincte religion Catholique ne defaudra en leur Royaume. Et comme les Gotz Arriens, & les Albigeois en ont esté par icelle dechassés* (Lyon, 1568), sig. X4^v; Jean du Tillet, *Advertissement a la Noblesse, tant du party du Roy, que des Rebelles & Conjurez* (Lyon, 1568), sig. C1^r.

[53] Pierre de Vaux-Cernay, trans. Arnaud Sorbin, *Histoire des Albigeois, et Gestes de Noble Simon de Monfort* (Paris, 1567), sig. A4^r; I. D. S. A., 'Similitude des Regnes du Roy Loys IX. par nous nomme S. Loys, et de celuy du Roy Charles à present regnant' in Sorbin, *Histoire des Albigeois* (1569), 186^v–9^r, fols. 187^v, 188^r, 189^r; Pierre de Vaux-Cernay, *Histoire de la ligue saincte faicte il y a 380 ans a la conduite de Simon de Montfort*, trans. Arnaud Sorbin (Paris, 1585).

was in the hands of the League in 1589–90.[54] In spite of the almost constant references to the Albigensian Crusade on the part of the Catholics, French Protestant apologists were reluctant to acknowledge a connection that would have reinforced the Catholic insinuation that religion was indeed a pretext for rebellion, notwithstanding the fact that across the channel an entire chapter entitled 'The historie of the Waldenses or Albigenses' featured in John Foxe's second edition of the *Actes and Monuments* (1570).[55]

The first acknowledgement of any kinship between French Protestants and Albigensians took place when the national synod of the French Reformed Church first moved south of the Loire to Nîmes in May 1572. It was presided over by Nicolas des Gallars, already mentioned, in the presence of Antoine de la Roche-Chandieu and Theodore Beza, all three having denounced the use of the 'blood libel' by the Catholics during the Affair of the Rue St Jacques.[56] This synod commissioned the pastors of Montauban to produce a French translation of an Occitan history of the Albigensian Crusade, although the revival of the fighting following the Massacre of St Bartholomew's Day in August 1572 probably cut these efforts short.[57] The existence of a Protestant desire to include medieval heretics in their martyrology, however, is confirmed by the denunciation it aroused in François de Belleforest in his history of France in 1579:

> Or les Albigeois ... se vautrèrent néanmoins en l'Athéisme des Ariens, & en l'abomination des Manichéens, & se souillèrent es folies de tous les hérétiques qui les avoient précédez. Et d'autant qu'il y eut lors (comme il y a maintenant) des temporisateurs & neutres au fait de la religion ... lesquels ... dirent que les Vaudois, & Albigeois n'estoient si mauvais garçons ... & qu'on les persecutoit, a cause qu'ils publioient les abus tant des ecclésiastiques que des Princes.[58]

> (It is known that the Albigensians nonetheless wallowed in the atheism of the Arians and the abomination of the Manichaeans, and soiled themselves with the follies of all the heretics that preceded them. Notwithstanding the fact that there were then (as there are now) temporisers and those indifferent to matters of faith who argue that the Waldensians and Albigensians

---

[54] Jean Gay, *Histoire des scismes et heresies des Albigeois* (Paris, 1589); Du Tillet, *Histoire de la Guerre* (Paris, 1590).

[55] Foxe, *Actes and Monuments* (London, 1570), fol. 295^r.

[56] Des Gallars, *Seconde apologie*, sig. D8r–v; Antoine de la Roche-Chandieu, *Histoire des persecutions, et martyrs de l'Eglise de Paris, depuis l'an 1557. Jusques au temps du Roy Charles neufviesme* (Lyon, 1563), sigs D1v, X7r–X8r; *Histoire Ecclésiastique des Eglises Réformées au Royaume de France*, ed. G. Baum and E. Cunitz, 3 vols. (Paris, 1883–9), I, 143–4, 237–8.

[57] J. Aymon, *Tous les Synodes Nationaux des Eglises Reformées de France*, 2 vols. (The Hague, 1710), I, part 2, 123.

[58] François de Belleforest, *Les Grandes Annales, et Histoire Générale de France* (Paris, 1579), fols. 593r–v, 594r.

The 'Cathars as Protestant' myth and the formation of heterodox identity

were not as bad as all that, and that they were only persecuted because they denounced the abuses of the Church as well as the Princes.)

Belleforest hints at the reason Protestants were able to use Catholic sources selectively while rejecting certain aspects such as the accusation of Manicheanism and ritual murder, a strategy used by historians until recently.[59] The first Reformed acknowledgement of any kinship with the Albigensians in print appears in Lancelot du Voisin de la Popelinière's *Histoire de France* (1581) although it was condemned by the synod of La Rochelle the same year for being 'too impartial'![60] Also of note was Peter Wesenbec, a Calvinist from Antwerp, who in 1585 argued for a continuity of belief from the end of the Albigensian Crusade to the massacres of Mérindol and Cabrières in 1545.[61] The second synod of the French Reformed Church held in the south, at Montauban in 1594, renewed the 1572 commission which was probably at the origin of Jean Chassanion's *History of the Albigensians* (1595) that used an Occitan source and criticised Sorbin's translation of Peter of Les-Vaux-de-Cernay.[62] Chassanion accused Catholic authors in general, and Arnaud Sorbin in particular, of adding the usual accusations of Manicheanism and ritual murder that were not found in his Occitan original, referring obliquely to the Affair of the Rue St Jacques:

Les Albigeois ont esté faussement chargés de plusieurs damnables opinions … On les a diffamés …. Ainsi il en est avenu ancienement aux Chrestiens …. De semblable vitupere nos premieres assemblées secretes ont esté chargées iniquemant, le bruit courant ça & la, que les chandeles esteintes on se mesloit sans aucune discretion & honnesteté.[63]

(The Albigensians were falsely accused of several damnable opinions. They were slandered just as the first Christians were in their time. The same reproach circulated about our first secret assemblies where it was rumoured that once the candles were put out we lay with each other without any shame or guilt.)

The thread that linked the Early Church with the Reformation, via the Albigensians, was identified by Chassanion as the false accusations that were circulated about the Christians, the Manichaeans, the medieval heresies and

---

[59] M. Tardieu, 'Brève chronique du dualisme', *L'Histoire* 430 (2016), 50–1.

[60] Lancelot du Voisin de la Popelinière, *L'Histoire de France enrichie des plus notables occurances survenues ez Provinces de l'Europe & pays voisins*, 2 vols. (Geneva, 1581), I, fol. 7ᵛ; G. Bédouelle, 'Les Albigeois, Témoins du Véritable Evangile: l'historiographie Protestante du XVIe et du début du XVIIe siècle', *Cahiers de Fanjeaux* 14 (1979), 47–70 (55).

[61] Peter Wesenbec, *Oratio de Vvaldensibus et Albigensibus christianis* (Jena, 1585), sigs B1r-v.

[62] Aymon, *Tous les Synodes Nationaux*, I, 186 ; Jean Chassanion, *Histoire des Albigeois: touchant leur doctrine & religion, contre les faux bruits qui ont esté semés d'eux, & les ecris dont on les a à tort diffamés* (Geneva, 1595), pp. 12–16.

[63] Chassanion, *Histoire des Albigeois*, pp. 12, 15, 51, 58.

Luc Racaut

finally the Reformation itself. Although Chassanion refuted these accusations and the assertion so often repeated in Catholic polemic that Protestants had descended from the Manichaeans, he accepted the filiation between Albigensians and Protestantism without any need for further evidence: 'Les Eglises réformées du Languedoc et autres païs circonvoisins sont comme la moisson de la semence jettée par les Albigeois'[64] (The Reformed Churches of Languedoc and other neighbouring regions are like the harvest of the seed sowed by the Albigensians). The foundation of the 'Cathars as Protestant' myth was laid down and remained unchallenged until recently.

The beginning of the seventeenth century saw a renewal of interest in the Albigensians, who were once more lumped together with the Waldensians, in a pan-European Protestant campaign to answer authors of the counter-Reformation. Robert Bellarmine, the Italian Jesuit and doctor of the faith, was a particular bugbear of the Protestants who employed a great deal of energy to refute his criticisms.[65] In their defence of the invisible Church in particular, Calvinists flaunted warnings that Calvin himself had issued against interpreting the Revelation of John.[66] These warnings were also printed in introductions to the Apocalypse in various editions of the Geneva Bible (notably 1577 and 1588), and they were repeated at the 1596 national synod of the French Reformed Church.[67] In 1599 Philippe de Marnix disregarded these warnings and made the Albigensians and the Waldensians 'the two olives or the two lamps, of which St John spoke, whose oil and light spread to the ends of the earth' (Revelations 11. 4).[68] The 'Pope as Antichrist' became an official article of the French Reformed Confession of Faith (the 31st) in 1603 and the synods of 1607, 1609 and 1612 mention the commission of a history of the Albigensians and Waldensians by Jean-Paul Perrin as well as a history of the Antichrist by Nicolas Vignier.[69] Nicolas Vignier produced several works in which he took Bellarmine to task, *L'Antechrist Romain* (1606), the *Legende Doree* (1608) and the *Theatre de l'Antechrist* (1610), in which the Mendicant Orders are linked to the persecution of the Albigensians and

[64] Ibid., pp. 250–1.

[65] Robert Bellarmine, *Disputationes de controversiis Christianae fidei adversus hujus temporis haereticos*, 3 vols. (Ingolstadt, 1586–93).

[66] On Calvin's reluctance to write a commentary on Revelation, see Backus, *Les Sept Visions et la Fin Des Temps*.

[67] François du Jon, *Apocalypse ou Revelation de S. Jean Apostre Evangeliste de nostre Seigneur Jesus Christ* (Geneva, 1592), p. 208; G. T. Sheppard, 'The Geneva Bible and English Commentary, 1600–1645', in *The Geneva Bible*, ed. G.T. Sheppard (New York, 1989), p. 1, fol. 129^v; *Le Nouveau Testament c'est à dire, la nouvelle alliance de nostre seigneur Jesus Christ* (Geneva, 1577), p. 682; *La Bible qui toute la saincte escriture du vieil & du nouveau testament* (Geneva, 1588), fol. 122^v; Aymon, *Tous les Synodes Nationaux*, I, p. 203.

[68] Cameron, *The Reformation of the Heretics*, p. 249.

[69] Aymon, *Tous les Synodes Nationaux*, I, 303, 313, 316, 331, 361, 404.

The 'Cathars as Protestant' myth and the formation of heterodox identity

Waldensians.[70] Jean-Paul Perrin published his history of the Waldensians in 1618 in which a section labelled 'Waldensians called Albigensians' was reproduced word for word in Goulard's definitive edition of the *Livre des Martyrs* in 1619 where the reign of Antichrist was precisely dated as having started in 1200 and ended in 1550.[71]

The inclusion of the Albigensians alongside the Waldensians in the Calvinist canons of martyrs concluded almost a century of controversy that had begun with Martin Luther. In spite of Bishop Bossuet's 1688 rebuttal – 'les Protestants, après avoir pris pour choses avouée que les Albigeois et les Vaudois n'étaient qu'une même secte, ont conclu que les Albigeois n'avaient été traites de Manichéens que par calomnie' (The Protestants, after having taken as read that the Albigensians and the Waldensians were one and the same, have concluded that calling the Albigensians Manichaean was just slander) – the myth endured.[72] The French Revolution, which turned the Sicilian Vespers, the Albigensian Crusade and the Massacre of St Bartholomew's Day into as many examples of the tyranny of the Catholic Church, did not dispel the myth and in fact added to Catholicism's black legend. In 1833 Jules Michelet could write in his history of France: 'A côté de l'Église s'élevait une autre Église, dont la Rome était à Toulouse' (Alongside the Church, another Church the Rome of which was in Toulouse had arisen), mentioning the apocryphal Council of St-Felix of 1167 and praising the Waldensians 'dont le rationalisme semble un fruit spontané de l'esprit humain'[73] (The rationalism of the Waldensians seems to have emerged spontaneously from the human spirit). Rationalism and free thinking had replaced Protestantism but the result was the same: the victims of the persecution of the Catholic Church were fellow travellers, as was argued by the liberal pastor Camille Rabaud in a history of Protestantism in the *Albigeois* (1898).[74]

Even if it could be argued that the 'Cathars as Protestant' myth was borrowed from the Protestants' opponents, it nonetheless became a potent symbol of defiance against the established order. The development of a Protestant identity in the sixteenth century was driven by violence and persecution and the need to find alternative sources of legitimacy and inspiration. This need to identify with mythical medieval forebears has not disappeared.

---

[70] [s.n.] *L'Antechrist Romain, Opposé à l'Antechrist Juif du Cardinal de Bellarmin, du Sieur de Remond & autres* (s.l., 1606), p. 159 ; Nicolas Vignier, *Legende Doree ou Sommaire de l'histoire des freres Mendians de l'Ordre de Dominique, & de François* (Leiden, 1608), p. 67 ; Nicolas Vignier, *Theatre de l'Antechrist* (Saumur, 1610).

[71] Crespin, *Histoire des Martyrs*, fol. 22r-v.

[72] Jacques-Bénigne Bossuet, *Histoire de Variations des Eglises Protestantes*, ed. O. Chalandre, *Œuvres Complètes de Bossuet*, 20 vols. (Paris, 1841), IV, 1–299 (197).

[73] J. Michelet, *Précis de l'histoire de France jusqu'à la Révolution Française* (Paris, 1833), p. 93.

[74] C. Rabaud, *Histoire du protestantisme dans l'Albigeois et le Lauragais, depuis la révocation de l'Edit de Nantes (1685) jusqu'à nos jours* (Paris, 1898).

Luc Racaut

Online comments to the 2019 exhibition mentioned above reveal an emotional attachment to a Cathar identity irrespective of religion or beliefs. Scholars should respect this identity as having real value for those who claim it, even if its origins can be considered apocryphal and indeed have little to do with the twelfth-century heretics or indeed Protestantism.

11

The seventeenth-century introductions to medieval inquisition records in Bibliothèque nationale de France, Collection Doat Mss 21–26

Shelagh Sneddon

Between 1665 and 1670, Jean de Doat, Président of the Chambre des Comptes of the Parlement of Pau, was commissioned by Jean-Baptiste Colbert, Louis XIV's minister, to copy documents held in various archives in Languedoc, 'for the conservation of the rights of our crown and to serve history' (pour la conservation des droicts de nostre couronne et pour servir à l'histoire). These fill 258 large volumes, now preserved in the Bibliothèque nationale de France in Paris as 'Collection Languedoc Doat'.[1] Among the materials selected for copying were a number of thirteenth-century inquisition documents, mostly depositions, produced in Toulouse and Carcassonne, the two main centres of inquisition in Languedoc, which now occupy volumes 21–26 in this collection. All the original documents are now lost, which makes their survival in the Doat collection doubly precious.

The documents copied are of very uneven length, from the giant volume 'FFF' from the Inquisition archives in Carcassonne, whose original contained 247 pages, and which now occupies Doat 23 and significant portions of Doat 22 and Doat 24, to the smaller inquisitions and collections of sentences found in Doat 21. Some appear to have been copied in their entirety – others are extracts. Some of the material in Doat 21, for example, comes from a register from which extracts have also been copied into other volumes.

Doat 21 contains a wide variety of material – short inquisitions, collections of sentences, safe-conducts and other documents. The remaining five volumes contain depositions before various inquisitors. The large volume FFF from Carcassonne, containing the inquisitions of Ferrier and his colleagues, as has been said, occupies Doat 22 from fol. 107r, Doat 23 and Doat 24 to fol. 238r. These date from the 1230s and 40s. At the beginning of Doat 22 is a collection

---

[1] H. Omont, 'La collection Doat à la Bibliothèque nationale. Documents sur les recherches de Doat dans les archives du sud-ouest de la France de 1663 à 1670', *Bibliothèque de l'École des chartes* 77 (1916), 286–336 (p. 286).

255

of roughly contemporary depositions before the inquisitors Bernard of Caux and John of Saint-Pierre, taken from a composite volume in the archives of the Dominicans of Toulouse; the remainder of Doat 24, from fol. 239r, contains a collection of depositions from Pamiers in front of the same inquisitors. The depositions in Doat 25 and 26 are from the later thirteenth century: in Doat 25 and folios 1r–78v of Doat 26 are depositions from Toulouse before Ranulph of Plassac, Pons of Parnac and their colleagues; from fol. 79r of Doat 26 there are slightly later depositions from Carcassonne, before John Galand and others.[2]

As can be seen, the material in the six volumes is copied in roughly chronological order, and no attempt has been made to tailor a Doat volume to fit one individual document – rather, they are copied as space permits, sometimes several to one volume, sometimes one spreading over several. That does not mean that the structure of the originals is not preserved. Each is followed by a postscript, in French, separate from the Latin text and in a smaller, distinctive hand, which describes the original manuscript and gives the date of copying. That for 'FFF' for example, on fols. 237v–238r of Doat 24, reads:

> Extrait et collationné dun livre en parchemin contenant deux cent quarante sept feuilles, cote des lettres F F F, trouvé aux archives de Linquisition de Carcassonne, par lordre et en la presence de Mossire Jean de Doat, conseiler du Roy en ses conseils, president en la Chambre de Comptes de Navarre, et Commissaire deputé par Sa Maiesté pour la recherche des titres concernant les droits de Sa Maiesté de la Couronne, et qui peuvent servir a lhistoire, dans toutes les archives de Sadit Maiesté des communautes eclesiasiastiques et seculieres de Languedoc et Guienne, et des archevesques, evesques, abes, prieures, et commandeurs qui en pourroient avoir de separees de celles de leurs chapitres, faire faire des extraits de ceux quil iugera necessaires, et leur envoyer au garde de la Biblioteque Royale par moy, Gratian Capot, un des deux grefiers prives en la dite commission, soubsigné. Fait a Alby le dix septisme octobre, mil six cent soixante neuf.
>
> Capot.[3]

---

[2] There have been four editions of this material: *L'inquisition en Quercy: Le registre des pénitences de Pierre Cellan, 1241–1242*, ed. and trans. J. Duvernoy (Paris, 2001) covers the penances of Peter Seila in Doat 21, fols. 185r–312v; *Cahiers de Bernard de Caux. Ms Doat XXII B.n. Paris* (1988), ed. and trans. J. Duvernoy, http://jean.duvernoy.free.fr/text/pdf/bdecaux.pdf and Registre de Bernard de Caux, Pamiers 1246–1247, ed. and trans. J. Duvernoy (Saint-Girons, 1990) contain the inquisitions of Bernard of Caux and John of Saint-Pierre from Doat 22 and Doat 24 respectively; *Inquisitors and Heretics in Thirteenth-Century Languedoc: Edition and Translation of Toulouse Inquisition Depositions 1273–1282*, ed. and trans. P. Biller, C. Bruschi, S. Sneddon, Studies in the History of Christian Traditions 147 (Leiden, 2011) is an edition of Doat 25 fol. 1r to Doat 26, fol. 78v. A full edition of Doat 22–24, with part of Doat 21, is being prepared by P. Biller, L. Sackville, and S. Sneddon. In what follows, I will be quoting from the original documents.

[3] 'Extracted and collated from a parchment book containing two hundred and forty-seven leaves, marked with the letters FFF, found in the archives of the Inquisition of

The seventeenth-century introductions to medieval inquisition records

This postscript follows a prescribed form, substantially the same in each case. It is stated clearly that the manuscript has been copied and collated on the orders and in the presence of Jean de Doat, who is given his full titles and honours, and his mission is described: then it is dated and signed by Gratian Capot, one of the chief *greffiers* employed by the Doat project. According to Laurent Albaret, in his article on Doat in *Cahiers de Fanjeaux* 49, this is a necessary legal formula – since one of the aims of the project was to copy manuscripts concerned with the rights of the crown, the copies had to be certified as correct to have legal status – and this provided this certification.[4]

The beginning of each medieval manuscript is also marked. Folio 1r of Doat 22, for example, starts with the following title:

> Interrogatoires et depositions de plusieurs heretiques Albigeois pardevant les inquisiteurs de la foy, dont la substance et les dattes sont marquéés dans les tiltres particuliers. Extraittes des cayers des archives de l'inquisition de Tholose.
>
> Depuis lannéé 1243, jusqu'en lannéé 1247.[5]

These dates have been changed several times by later hands. Again, these introductions seem to be written to a template. The heretics are always 'Albigeois', the inquisitors are not named, and the only variants are the dates (which tend to be rough and impressionistic, and are frequently corrected by readers) and whether the manuscript comes from Toulouse or Carcassonne. Usually this introduction marks the beginning of a medieval document, but that for 'FFF', is found on the first folio of Doat 23, rather than at the beginning of the extracts from that manuscript, on fol. 107r of Doat 22.

The template is substantially the same even when the documents are not depositions. Here is fol. 1r of Doat 21:

Carcassonne, on the order and in the presence of Monsieur John of Doat, councillor of the King in his councils, President of the Chamber of Accounts of Navarre, and Commissioner deputed by his Majesty to research into titles that concern His Majesty's rights of the Crown, and that can serve history, in all his said Majesty's archives of communities ecclesiastical and secular of Languedoc and Guienne, and of archbishops, bishops, abbots, priors and commanders who may have them separately from those of their chapters, to have extracts made of those that he will deem necessary, and to send them to the safe-keeping of the Royal Library via me, Gratian Capot, one of the two private registrars in the said commission, signed below. Done at Albi, the seventeenth of October, 1669. Capot.'

[4] L. Albaret, 'La collection Doat, une collection modern, témoignage de l'histoire religieuse méridionale des XIIIe et XIVe siècles', *Cahiers de Fanjeaux* 49 (2014), 57–93. Capot: pp. 70–1. There is also a full page photograph of a Capot authentication on p. 75.

[5] 'Interrogations and depositions of several Albigensian heretics before the inquisitors of the faith, of which the substance and the dates are indicated in the individual titles. Extracted from the notebooks [or quires] of the archives of the Toulouse inquisition. From the year 1243 to the year 1247.'

Shelagh Sneddon

Sentences de condamnation des inquisiteurs de la foy contre les heretiques Albigeois, et saufconduits donnez par lesditz Inquisiteurs a plusieurs des dits heretiques pour comparoistre pardevant eux, dont la substance et les dates sont marquéés dans les tiltres particuliers, Extraittes d'un livre des archives de l'Inquisition de Tholose.

Depuis l'annéé 1237 (changed to 1165 by a later hand)

Jusqu'en l'annéé 1244[6]

Thus the beginning and end of each medieval document is marked, and some very basic details are given about it. Between these headings are the documents, copied in the original Latin, although the spelling has been somewhat classicised in line with early modern practice. But, as fol. 1r of Doat 22 makes clear, each deposition has its 'tiltre particulier': a French introduction added by the seventeenth-century editors. Like the general introductions, this is in a slightly larger hand than the Latin text, and clearly separate from it. It gives the name of the deponent, the date, and a brief summary of its contents. Sometimes one introduction covers a number of related depositions – those of the friars and others who gave evidence against the heresies of Peter Garsias on folios 88r–106v of Doat 22, for example, or depositions from members of the same family, such as those of Raymond of Péreille and his son Jordan on folios 201r–232v of Doat 23. The connection can sometimes be rather tenuous: in Doat 25 a single introduction covers the depositions of Stephen Roger of Roumens and Guilabert of Saint-Michel of Touzeilles, which are quite unrelated – except that both mention the heretical activities of a Peter of Laurac.[7] In those cases the later depositions have only a brief introduction giving the name of the witness, or, in the case of Raymond and Jordan, merely saying 'Seconde audition' (Second hearing) or similar.

Who wrote these introductions? The most obvious scenario for these introductions would be that each copyist provided the introduction as he worked. However, from Doat's comments on them, it would seem doubtful if they would be up to the task: in one memorandum of expenses he complains 'On eut peine à trouver des personnes capables de ce travail: ceux qui lisoient les vieux titres en latin, en espagnol et en vulgaire, n'escrivoient pas assés bien, et ceux qui écrivoient bien, ne scavoient pas lire'.[8] Instead, as another

---

[6] 'Sentences of condemnation by the inquisitors of the faith against Albigensian heretics, and safe-conducts given by the said inquisitors to several of the said heretics to appear before them, of which the substance and the dates are indicated in the individual titles. Extracted from a book from the archives of the Toulouse inquisition. From the year 1237 to the year 1244.'

[7] Doat 25, fol. 26r.

[8] Omont, 'Collection Doat', p. 294, from a memorandum of Doat's expenses, Paris, Bibliothèque nationale de France, MS nouv. acq. fr. 22765, fols. 1–37. 'It was hard to find people capable of this work: those who read the old documents in Latin,

The seventeenth-century introductions to medieval inquisition records

memorandum of expenses reveals, two more senior scribes, Cabanès and Aurieres, were employed for this task: 'Les apointements de Cabanès et Aurieres, employés à la recherche et lecture des titres, et à faire les extraits pour en marquer la substance et les dates à la teste des copies, avoient esté comptés au precedent compte …'.[9] Further information from the memoranda of the project shows that Cabanès was employed in 1667 to correct texts: 'Le nommé Cabannès s'estant venu offrir audit s^r de Doat, le 14 dudit mois de may, en ladite ville de Vabres, il luy donna de l'employ et prit un prestre sur le lieu, nommé Ricart, pour les employer tous deux à la correction des copies'.[10] Aurieres, too, came on board at about this time: 'Pendant que le bureau estoit à Rodés, ledit s^r de Doat y receut les nommés Borjos, Cabanès et Aurieres, sçavoir ledit Borjos le 14 février, Cabanès le 24 may et Aurieres le 19 juin …'.[11] In the same document, we see Cabanès travelling with Doat and two other employees to seek for manuscripts in Tarascon and Ax.[12]

These, then (perhaps with others, like the priest Ricart, for example?), were the men who provided the documents in Doat 21–26 with these distinctive frames. In this article I would like to look at the introductions to the different registers, but especially the 'tiltres particuliers'. What aspects of the depositions do they mention? What can they tell us about how Cabanès and Aurieres, and by extension the Doat project, saw the thirteenth-century inquisition? What can they tell us about the seventeenth-century understanding of heresy? Do they reveal any sources of knowledge other than the depositions themselves? This will be more interesting as these men, although educated enough to read and understand Latin, were not experts on heresy – their introductions can therefore provide us with the perspective of a layman, rather than a specialist.

The first feature of the introductions is the names. The name of the deponent is usually taken from the first line of the deposition. The Christian name is normally translated into French – sometimes a surname is as well, sometimes that is left in Latin. Place of origin can also be given. Some place-names, like Mirepoix, are clearly familiar to the authors and are translated –

---

in Spanish and in the vernacular, did not write well enough, and those who could write well could not read.'

[9] 'The appointments of Cabanès and Aurieres, employed in the search for and reading of documents, and in making extracts in order to mark the substance and the dates at the head of the copies, have been accounted for in the previous account': Omont, 'Collection Doat', p. 321, from Paris, Bibliothèque nationale de France, MS nouv. acq. fr. 22765 fols. 50–52.

[10] 'The man named Cabannès came to offer to work for the said seigneur de Doat on the 14th of the said month of May, in the said town of Vabres; and he gave him work and hired a priest in the [same] place, named Ricart, to employ them both in the correction of copies': Omont, *Collection Doat*, p. 300, from the same document.

[11] 'While the office was at Rodés, the said seigneur de Doat took on the men named Borjos, Cabanès and Aurieres, that is, the said Borjos on 14th February, Cabanès on 24th May, and Aurieres on 19th June': Omont, 'Collection Doat', p. 301.

[12] Omont, 'Collection Doat', p. 303.

others are simply copied from the Latin text in the original language. So, for example, on fol. 2r of Doat 23, a deponent who in the Latin is Arnalda de Lamota de Monte Albano, becomes in the introduction Arnaude de Lamote de Montauban, while on fol. 57r, 'Dias, uxor quondam Pontii de Sancto Germerio, generosi de Caramainhes, diocesis Tholosanæ', becomes 'Dias, femme de Pons de S^{to} Germerio, dit le Genereux' (Dias, wife of Pons of Saint-Germier, called the Noble). Not only is the place of origin, Saint-Germier, not translated, but the author of this introduction seems to have mistaken the word 'generosus', describing Pons's noble birth, for a nickname. He has also missed the vital 'quondam' (formerly) which reveals that Dias is no longer a wife, but a widow. On fol. 3r of Doat 22, the deponent, William Faure of Pechermier, (Willelmus Faber de Podio Hermer), is reduced to 'Faber de Podio Hermer'. Minor mistakes in names, like these, are not uncommon.

A more serious mistake is found in Doat 25. On fol. 212 is an introduction to four depositions, headed 'Deposition d'Aldricus puer, fils de Raymond Saichii de Caraman ...' (The deposition of the boy Aldric, son of Raymond Saix of Caraman). Apart from the question of why such a common Latin word as 'puer' was not translated, this description is problematic. A closer reading of the text reveals that the first two are not by Aldric at all, but seem to be later depositions by someone whose name was only given in a first deposition, which is now missing, and have been mistakenly tacked onto the following one.

The other names in the introductions are more illuminating. It is not surprising that names feature strongly – a name might well decide for a reader whether the document will be of interest – and it is not surprising, either in this respect or given that one of the aims of the project was to collect documents concerning the king's rights, that the compiler of the introductions should particularly notice those of more eminent people. The count of Toulouse, the count of Foix, various papal legates are all prominent. This is especially notable in the introductions to the sentences in Doat 21, fols. 143r–185r, where there is often a long list of the churchmen assisting the inquisitors. Occasionally a mistake will be made in a name. The introduction to the evidence about Bernard Oth of Niort and his family in Doat 21. fols. 34r–50v, for example, speaks of the inquisition held by the archbishop of Toulouse, when Toulouse only became an archbishopric in 1319. In the text and in other introductions he is clearly a bishop.

This preference for the names of the socially important goes further down the social scale than counts and archbishops, however. The introduction to the depositions of Isarn of Tauriac and Finas his wife begins

> Deposition d'Isarn de Tauriac, chevalier, et de Finas sa femme, contenant que ledit Isarn, B. de Poalhac, P. de Turre, et Matfredus, chevaliers, avoient assisté aux predications des hæretiques, et les avoient adores.[13]

---

[13] 'The deposition of Isarn of Tauriac, knight, and of Finas his wife, containing that the

The seventeenth-century introductions to medieval inquisition records

The relevant passage is in Finas's deposition, listing those present at the preaching of the heretic Pons Guilabert and his companion:

> Et erant ibi Isarnus de Tauriaco et B. de Paolhac, milites, et P. de Turre et Matfredus, milites, et Arbrisa, filia eius quæ loquitur, et Mathalios, uxor modo Raimundi de Galhac, et Poncius Fabri, et Guillelma Fabrissa.[14]

Of the people listed here, the knights are mentioned in the introduction, the others are not. This is not the only time that this happens – it is common enough to suggest a pattern.

The inquisitor is only sometimes named, but again there seems to be a pattern to the cases where he is. In the depositions in Doat 22, fols. 1r–106v, taken from a collection of inquisitions held before Bernard of Caux and John of Saint-Pierre, later gathered together and preserved in the archives of the Dominicans of Toulouse,[15] the inquisitors are not mentioned, possibly because their names rarely feature in the text. But a new set of inquisitions starts on fol. 107r of Doat 22 – the great volume FFF, held before Ferrier and his team and preserved in Carcassonne – and, as has been said above, the introduction is found not here, but at the beginning of Doat 23. The 'tiltre particulier' for the first of these depositions starts 'Trois auditions d'Arnaud Roger, chevalier de Mirepoix, rendues pardevant Ferrarius et Pierre Duranti de l'ordre des freres precheurs, inquisiteurs'.[16] The next six depositions also mention the names of the inquisitors – then they are mentioned more rarely, dying out almost completely in Doat 23. The composers of the introductions are clearly keen to inform a reader of the new inquisitors. A similar thing is found in Doat 25: the first deposition is noted as being 'par devant Ranulphe, inquisiteur' (before Ranulph, inquisitor),[17] and the inquisitors continue to be named quite frequently in the early part of the book, and more rarely thereafter. In referring to Ranulph of Plassac as 'Ranulphe', the introductions are again following the texts, where his somewhat unusual Christian name is seen as sufficient to identify him, but he is once called 'Ranulphe de

---

said Isarn, B. of Paulhac, P. of La Tour, and Matfre, knights, had been present at the preachings of heretics, and had adored them': Doat 22, fol. 62r.

[14] 'And there were there Isarn of Tauriac and B. of Paulhac, knights, and P. of Latour and Matfre, knights, and Arbrisa, the speaker's daughter, and Mathelio, now the wife of Raymond of Gaillac, and Pons Faure, and Guillelma Fabrissa' Doat 22, fol. 67r.

[15] 'vingt caiers de parchemin atachées ensemble, dont la premiere est marquee n° 2 et la derniere clxviii, trouvé aux archives des freres prescheurs de Toulouse' ('twenty booklets/quires of parchment attached together, of which the first is marked n° 2 and the last clxviii, found in the archives of the Brothers Preacher of Toulouse'): Doat 22, fol. 106r. It is unclear to me whether this is one register, or a collection of documents bound together because they concern the same two inquisitors.

[16] 'Three hearings of Arnold Roger, knight of Mirepoix, made before Ferrier and Peter Durand of the Order of Brothers Preacher, inquisitors': Doat 22, fol. 107r.

[17] Doat 25, fol. 1v.

Shelagh Sneddon

Galiaco'.[18] It is difficult to see why, as this is not his name, and Gaillac is not mentioned anywhere in the following deposition.

More usually, where names appear in a form different to that which is found in the text it is a simple expansion of a name which is only an initial in the Latin – R., bishop of Toulouse, becoming Raimond, for example – but, if this is not simply a common-sense expansion, it could easily be explained as the result of reading elsewhere in the Doat manuscripts. Perhaps more suggestive is the fact that prominent heretics, like Aimery of Collet, Bernard Engilbert and Guilabert of Castres, are named without being identified as 'heretiques' – which suggests that the writer is familiar with these names, and, perhaps, that he thinks a reader will be too. Here again, however, it would be quite possible to acquire this familiarity simply through reading the Doat documents.

While the names in the introductions tell us little, there does seem to be evidence for outside information available to the writers in the date of the deposition with which each introduction ends. Usually, this is simply copied from the first line of the deposition; sometimes there is evidence of more careful reading and deduction. The first of the three depositions of William Faure of Pechermier, for example (Doat 22, fols. 3r–10r) begins 'Anno et die prædictis' (In the aforesaid year and on the aforesaid day), and the introduction states confidently 'La premiere est pridie kalendas Decembris' (The first is from the day before the kalends of December), giving the date of the previous deposition in the collection, that of Bernarda Targueira – apparently evidence that the writer of the introduction was using his brain.

But on some occasions a date is equally confidently given for which no rationale is apparent. The deposition of P. de Noye again starts 'Anno et die prædictis', which the introduction gives as four days before the ides of December 1243.[19] The preceding deposition is dated eight days before the kalends of February 1243, and there seems to be no reason for the December date. This is not an isolated case: the deposition of Na Bareges also starts 'Anno et die quo supra' (In the same year and on the same day as above), and is dated in the introduction to 14 days before the kalends of March, while that of Peirona of Claustre starts 'Anno et die prædictis' and is dated to the nones of February.[20] Several other depositions have equally precise dates volunteered on no textual basis at all. Did the manuscript Doat's team were copying contain an index or a calendar? Did they only make a partial copy, and did the depositions they omitted provide evidence for the dates? What information did Doat's team have, or think that they had, to assert these dates so confidently?

The most interesting matter, however, is the content of the introductions, what they say about heresy. The individual introductions tend to follow the depositions themselves by referring to the main group under investigation –

---

[18] Doat 25, fol. 15r.
[19] Doat 22, fol. 27v.
[20] Doat 22, fol. 43r and fol. 56v.

The seventeenth-century introductions to medieval inquisition records

those whom historians have sometimes called 'Cathars' or 'Albigensians' – as 'heretiques', while calling the secondary group, the Waldensians, 'Vaudois'. The general introductions, however, refer to the first group as 'heretiques Albigeois'.

What would they have understood by 'heretiques Albigeois'? Seventeenth-century scholars had access to William of Puylaurens, Peter of Les-Vaux-de-Cernay and others, including the main general and regional Church councils. And, as Malcolm Barber points out, there is a history of some Protestant writers seeing the Albigensians as proto-Protestant martyrs, and some Catholics seeing them as part of 'a continuous tradition of wicked dissent which reached back to the Manicheans but could be traced through the preceding centuries in the form of Waldensians, Albigensians, and Hussites, among others'.[21] Is there any evidence for where the writers of the introductions are getting their information from, or of any strong opinion about the heretics?

The full introduction to the depositions of Isarn of Tauriac and his wife is this:

> Deposition d'Isarn de Tauriac, chevalier, et de Finas sa femme, contenant que ledit Isarn, B. de Poalhac, P. de Turre, et Matfredus, chevaliers, avoient assisté aux predications des hæretiques, et les avoient adores; et qu'ils leur avoient ouy prescher que l'hostie n'estoit qu du pain, que le mariage et le baptesme estoient inutiles, et qu'il ni avoit point de resurection.[22]

Isarn denies hearing any preaching on these subjects,[23] and again the relevant passage comes from Finas's deposition: 'Et dicebant quod hostia sacrata erat panis purus, et quod matrimonium et baptismus non proficiunt, et quod illa quæ Deus fecit non præteribunt, et caro hominis mortua non resurget'.[24] It is very typical of the depositions of Bernard of Caux and John of Saint-Pierre, the inquisitors in this case, that they record whether the deponent heard heretics preaching that God did not make the world, that marriage and baptism were of no benefit, that the host was not the body of Christ, and that

---

[21] M. Barber, *The Cathars: Dualist Heretics in Languedoc in the High Middle Ages*, (Harlow, 2000), p. 213.

[22] 'The deposition of Isarn of Tauriac, knight, and of Finas his wife, containing that the said Isarn, B. of Paulhac, P. of La Tour, and Matfre, knights, had been present at the preachings of heretics, and had adored them; and that they had heard them preach that the host was only bread, that marriage and baptism were useless, and that there was no resurrection': Doat 22, fol. 62r.

[23] 'Dixit etiam quod non audivit hæreticos exprimentes errores suos de visibilibus, de hostia sacrata, de baptismo, nec de matrimonio' (He also said that he did not hear the heretics expressing their errors about visible things, about the consecrated host, about baptism or about matrimony): Doat 22, fol. 64v.

[24] 'And they said that the consecrated host was pure bread, and that marriage and baptism are of no benefit, and that the things that God made will not pass away, and the dead flesh of man will not rise again': Doat 22, fol. 66r.

263

there was no resurrection – seemingly the typical doctrines that established which sect they were dealing with. These questions were often included in the introductions. Here we have all five of these doctrines in the text, but only four in the introduction. Is it significant that it is the most 'Cathar' one, the one that wouldn't be said by Protestants or sceptics or anti-clerical Catholics – that the things that God created do not perish, and that therefore he could not have created the material world – that is left out? But it is included in other introductions, when it appears in the Latin text in its more usual form – 'quod Deus non fecerat visibilia' (that God had not made visible things), and I think that it is omitted here because of the form it is in – because the writer of the introduction did not fully grasp the significance of 'that the things that God made will not pass away'. As we shall see, the writers' understanding, or lack of it, of some of the Latin of the text creates problems in other areas.

The writers of the introductions do show interest in other heretical beliefs. This is typical:

> Deposition de R. Centolh, contenant qu'il avoit ouy dire a la femme d'Arnaud Bos de Gontaud, que le diable, ayant fait lhomme dargile, dit á Dieu d'y mettre l'ame, Dieu luy respondit qu'il seroit plus fort que luy, et que le diable - et alors le diable le fit du limon de la mer, et Dieu lanima.[25]

This is a story overheard by the deponent, which makes up the whole of this very short deposition. Strange or heretical beliefs – such as the man who said that if he died on a Friday he would be damned, or the woman who was suspected because she called on the Holy Spirit, rather than Jesus Christ or the Virgin Mary, in childbirth – are often recorded.[26] But other beliefs are passed over, and it is very hard to see anything in this other than the choice of an interesting or lively detail from the text. No so very different from this introduction:

> Deposition de B. de Podio de Pradis, contenant entre autres choses que Pierre Bertrand de Montesquieu, fils de Saxius, chevalier de Puy Laurens, avoit assiste aux predications des heretiques, et leur avoit fait present de deux anguilles salées.[27]

---

[25] 'The deposition of R. Centolh, containing that he had heard it said by Arnold Bos of Gontaud's wife that when the devil had made man from clay, he told God to put a soul into him, and God /32r/ answered him that he would be stronger than him, and than the devil – and then the devil made him from sea silt, and God animated him': Doat 22, fol. 31v

[26] Doat 25, fols. 166v, 61v.

[27] 'The deposition of Bernard of Puy of Prades, containing among other things that Peter Bertrand of Montesquieu, the son of Saix, knight of Puylaurens, had been present at the preachings of the heretics, and had made them a present of two salted eels': Doat 25, fol. 125r.

The seventeenth-century introductions to medieval inquisition records

Whether it is a heretical folk tale, or a present of two salted eels, the introductions seem to be written with an eye for the picturesque detail that might arouse a reader's curiosity, rather than a systematic examination of a belief system. There seems to be little evidence of any knowledge of heresy from outside the texts themselves.

Even the word 'Albigeois', so conspicuous in the general introductions, is found in the Latin text. A rare case where the heretics are given a name in a 'tiltre particulier' is found in the deposition of a Bernard of La Garrigue, which speaks of him having abjured 'la secte des heretiques qui se disoient l'eglise Albigeoise'.[28] This reflects the use of the word in the text: 'postquam ipse Bernardus de Lagarriga dimisit sectam hæreticorum et eam abiuravit, in qua, ut dixit, fuerat hæreticus consolatus, et filius maior inter illos hæreticos qui se dicunt ecclesiam Albiensem'.[29]

This introduction is unusual as one of a very view that seems to express an opinion about the text it precedes. It describes the deathbed heretication of a William Mate of Carcassonne, including many details of ritual taken from the text, but what does not reflect the text is the strongly moralistic tone:

> Deposition de Bernard de la Garrigue de Lados par devant B. eveque d'Alby faisant pour soy et pour Jean Galandi inquisiteur, contenant entre autres choses que, depuis quil avoit abiuré la secte des heretiques qui se disoient l'eglise Albigeoise, il avoit adore deux sectateurs de ceste religion qui pervertirent Guillaume Mate de Carcassonne en sa maladie, luy disant sil vouloit recevoir le don de Dieu que Jesus Christ avoit porté du ciel et laisse a ses apostres, lesquels lavoient laisse aux bonnes gens successivement iusqu'a eux, et a ceus de leur secte ...[30]

A similar tone is found in the introduction to another deposition from the same collection:

> Deposition de Barthelemy Cerdani de Pechnautier, contenant qu'Arnaud Morlana, recteur de Pechnautier, sestoit rendu heretique en presence de Sancius Morlana, archidiacre de Carcassonne, son frere, de Pierre d'Aragon

---

[28] 'The sect of heretics who called themselves the Albigensian church': Doat 26, fol. 244r.

[29] 'after the same Bernard of La Garrigue left the sect of the heretics and abjured it, in which, as he said, he had been a consoled heretic and elder son among those heretics who call themselves the church of Albi': Doat 26, fol. 246r.

[30] 'The deposition of Bernard of La Garrigue of La Doux before B., Bishop of Albi, acting for himself and for John Galand, inquisitor, containing among other things that, after he had abjured the sect of heretics who called themselves the Albigensian church, he had adored two sectaries of that religion who perverted William Mate of Carcassonne in his illness, asking him if he wished to receive the gift of God that Jesus Christ had brought from heaven and left to his apostles, who had left it successively to the good people, down to them and to those of their sect'.

265

de Carcassonne, et autres qui adorerent les heretiques qui pervertirent ledit recteur en sa maladie.[31]

Words like 'sectateurs' and 'pervertirent' are not generally found in these introductions: when reporting someone undergoing the ceremony known as the *consolamentum*, the introduction usually uses the much more neutral 'se rendre heretique' (to make oneself a heretic). Was this written by someone other than the two senior copyists, a priest perhaps, who might have wanted to condemn, rather than view the heretics with scholarly detachment? It is tempting to speculate, but all that can be said for sure is that these two introductions are the exception, not the rule.

The largest collection of depositions copied by Doat and his team was the book FFF from Carcassonne, containing depositions mostly from the 1240s before an inquisitor called Ferrier and his colleagues. They contain much less detail about belief, and the introductions are correspondingly lacking in amusing stories. Ferrier was much more interested in ritual – so, while Avignonet looms large, the stories and lists of heretical beliefs are replaced by careful descriptions of the adoration, of the *consolamentum*, of the prayers said over food – and these things are reflected in the introductions.

This, for example, is the introduction to the deposition of Arnalda of Lamothe:

> Deposition d'Arnaude de Lamote de Montauban, par devant Ferrarius, inquisiteur, contenant quelle a assisté aux predications de deux femmes heretiques, et aux adorations qu'on leur faisoit; que Raimond Aimeric, diacre, estant au chasteau de Villemur, avec plusieurs heretiques, fut obligé de sen retirer, craignant les croisés; que Longue, mere d'Arnaud Estienne de Taravello, et toute sa famille, et Guillaume de d'Eyme, chevalier, assistoient aux predications de Guillaume de Lamote, diacre; que ladite deposante, estant allee a Lantar dans la maison de Pons Saquet, chevalier de Lantar, ledit Pons et ceux de sa famille y nommés ladorerent; et que la femme de Guillaume Rubet, et celle de Hugues Rog, chevaliers de Lantar, et ceux de leur famille y nommés, la feitrent visiter et adorer.[32]

---

[31] 'The deposition of Bartholomew Cerdan of Pennautier, containing that Arnold Morlana, rector of Pennautier, became a heretic in the presence of Sans Morlana, archdeacon of Carcassonne, his brother, of Peter of Aragon of Carcassonne, and of others who adored the heretics who perverted the said rector in his illness': Doat 26, fol. 288v.

[32] 'The deposition of Arnalda of Lamothe of Montauban, before Ferrier, inquisitor, containing that she had been present at the preachings of two women heretics, and at the adorations that people made to them; that when Raymond Aimery, deacon, was at the castle of Villemur, with several heretics, he had to withdraw from there, fearing the crusaders; that Longa, mother of Arnold Stephen of Taravel, and all her family, and William d'Eyme, knight, were present at the preachings of William of Lamothe, deacon; that when the said deponent had gone to Lanta, into the house of Pons Saquet, knight of Lanta, the said Pons and those of his /2v/ family named here adored her; and that the wife of William Rubet, and that of Hugh Rog, knights

The seventeenth-century introductions to medieval inquisition records

At first sight it looks quite conventional, a succession of preachings and adorations – and of course the mention of the crusaders, which might naturally be expected to interest a reader. But Arnalda was a *conversa*, as is made clear in the first line of her deposition. What this introduction does not mention was that she was also at Villemur, brought there by Raymond Aimery, deacon of the heretics, and that she underwent the 'consolamentum' there – with the long and careful description of the ceremony that is the typical result of Ferrier's questioning. She was a girl at the time, and most of the rest of her long deposition – the first forty-nine folios of Doat 23 – is taken up with her wanderings as a heretic, firstly with her sister, Peirona, then, after her sister's death, with another companion, Jordana. None of this – not even the briefly told, but moving, death of Peirona – makes it into the introduction. This is such a striking omission that it suggests, to me at any rate, that the words 'et ibi consolaverunt ipsam testem et dictam Peironam, sororem ipsius testis' did not convey any important change in status, and neither did the frequent description of the deponent as a *haeretica*. Only the mention of people adoring her informs us that she was a *perfecta*,[33] a full member of the heretical church – and the introduction does not seem to make any kind of comment on this.

The problem, here, I think, is the language. The words 'consolamentum' and 'consolari' are used very frequently in the depositions of Ferrier and his colleagues for the process of becoming a heretical *perfectus* – but the writer or writers of these introductions do not seem to have grasped that this is what they mean. Instead, they are translated directly into the French as 'consolation' and 'consoler', and, as most people received the 'consolamentum' in a serious illness, they seem to be understood to refer to formal visits to condole with the afflicted person. This seems to be clear from this example, where the people doing the 'consoling' are all lay men and women:

> Deposition de Pierre de St Michel du chasteau de St Michel, contenant que Roger de Turre de Laurac, son oncle, estant atteint d'une maladie dont il mourut, dans sa maison de Laurac, se rendit heretique, et fut consolé par Pons Fort, Bernard de St Julien, et Guillaume de Insula, chevaliers, et par plusieurs personnes y nommeés …[34]

This describes this Latin text:

---

of Lanta, and those of their family named here, used to visit and adore her': Doat 23, fol. 1r.

[33] See L. J. Sackville, *Heresy and Heretics in the Thirteenth Century: The Textual Representations*, Heresy and Inquisition in the Middle Ages 1 (York, 2011), pp. 201–2, '*Perfecti* as a term to denote heretics'.

[34] 'The deposition of Peter of Saint-Michel from the castrum of Saint-Michel, containing that when Roger of Latour of Laurac, his uncle, was suffering from an illness of which he died, in his house at Laurac, he became a heretic, and was consoled by Pons Fort, Bernard of Saint-Julien, and William of La Hille, knights, and by several people named here': Doat 23, fol. 87v.

Shelagh Sneddon

Petrus de Sancto Michaele ... dixit quod cum Rogerius de Turre de Lauraco, avunculus ipsius testis, infirmaretur apud Lauracum in domo sua propria, ea infirmitate qua mortuus fuit, vidit ipse testis quod Arnaudus Faure de Lauraco adduxit in domum ipsius infirmi, duos hæreticos, quorum nomina ignorat, ad consolandum ipsum infirmum; et steterunt ibi præfati hæretici per duas, vel per tres, noctes, antequam consolarentur ipsum infirmum. Et, eis elapsis, cum ipse testis ivisset apud Castrum Novum de Arrio, interim, præfati hæretici consolaverunt ipsum infirmum. Et postquam fuit inde reversus, invenit ipsum infirmum consolatum, et factum hæreticum. Et erant ibi Poncius Fortis, et B. de Sancto Iuliano, milites, et Arnaldus Faure, et Guillelmus de Insula, miles, et Guillelmus de Balaguer, et Poncius de Sancto Michaele, frater ipsius testis, et Aladaicia, uxor Guillelmi Bernardi, et Ermessendis, uxor Bernardi Mir Arresat, sorores ipsius testis, et Aladaicia, uxor infirmi, et Poncius de Turre, filius infirmi.[35]

The words 'factum hæreticum' have shown the writer of the introduction what has happened, but he has quite misunderstood 'consolare'.

Similarly, this description of a consolamentum

dicit quod cum Alzeu de Massabrac infirmaretur ... ea infirmitate qua mortuus fuit, vidit ipse testis quod Iohannes Cambiaire et socius suus, hæreticus, venerunt in dictam domum ad consolandum ipsum infirmum. Et tunc præfati hæretici receperunt et consolaverunt eumdem infirmum, secundum modum et formam superius comprehensam.[36]

becomes this, in the introduction:

que Alseu de Massabrac atteint d'une maladie dont il mourut, fut visité et consolé par Raymond Bertrand, Bernard et Gaillard del Congost, par

---

[35] 'Peter of Saint-Michel ... said that when Roger of Latour of Laurac, the same witness's uncle, was ill at Laurac in his own house, with that illness of which he died, the same same witness saw that Arnold Faure of Laurac brought two heretics, whose names he does not know, into the same sick man's house, to console the same sick man; and the aforementioned heretics stayed there for two, or for three, nights, before they consoled the same sick man. And, when they had passed, when the same witness had gone to Castelnaudary, in the meantime, the aforementioned heretics consoled the same sick man. And after he had returned from there, he found the same sick man consoled and made a heretic. And present there were: Pons Fort, and B. of Saint-Julien, knights, and Arnold Faure, and William of La Hille, knight, and William of Balaguier, and Pons of Saint-Michel, the same witness's brother, and Aladaicia, the wife of William Bernard, and Ermessendis, the wife of Bernard Mir Arresat, the same witness's sisters, and Aladaicia, the sick man's wife, and Pons of Latour, the sick man's son': Doat 23, fol. 88r.

[36] 'He says that when Alzieu of Massabrac was ill ... with that illness of which he died, the same witness saw that John Cambiaire and his companion, [also a] heretic, came into the said house to console the same sick man. And then the aforementioned heretics received and consoled the same sick man, according to the manner and form described above': Doat 24, fol. 50v.

268

The seventeenth-century introductions to medieval inquisition records

Bernard Bataille de Ventenac, et par Raymond de Sales de Lordat, chevaliers, et par plusieurs autres chevaliers et dames y nommés.[37]

All these people were present at the consolamentum (although Raymond Bertrand seems to be an amalgamation of Raymond of Péreille, and Bertrand of Le Congoust): but they did not do the consoling. If, however, another word is used – like 'factum haereticum' above, or 'reddidit se haereticum' – then what is happening appears much more clearly in the introduction. Here there is a marked difference between the depositions of Ferrier and his associates, who use 'consolari' frequently, and those of Bernard of Caux and John of Saint-Pierre, who prefer 'haereticare'. Here, from their register, is the introduction to the deposition of another youthful 'perfectus' – where the writer of the introduction seems to have understood much better:

> Deposition de Mafredus de Poalhac, chevalier, contenant qu'Arnaud Arufat et Guillaume Salamo l'avoient rendu heretique a la age de 14 ans.[38]

> dixit quod Arnaldus Arrufat et Willelmus Salamo, hæretici, et Arcurandus Ros de Viridifolio, hæreticaverunt ipsum qui loquitur, sanum et incolumen sed iuvenem quatuordecim annorum, apud Viridefolium.[39]

It is only the large FFF volume that gives rise to these confusions. Bernard of Caux and John of Saint-Pierre use 'haereticare', and the two later groups of inquisitors from the 1270s and 1280s also prefer this word. Ferrier's use of a word which seems to be taken from what the heretics themselves call this ritual does not catch on.

'Consolamentum' is not the only word that causes problems for the writers of the introductions. The word for 'heretic' was another. It had been used in two language fields in the thirteenth century. In inquisition texts it meant a full heretic in a sect; someone who had undergone the 'consolamentum' was a 'haeretica' or 'haereticus'. Within the Church's discursive texts and canon law it covered two categories, heretics and their believers. The dictum 'someone who believes in heretics is to be adjudged a heretic' (credens hereticis judicatur ut hereticus) needs to be thought of like simple arithmetic: 'heretics + believers in heretics = heretics'. The churchmen who used this vocabulary thought simultaneously of the two categories (heretics and their

---

[37] 'that Alzieu of Massabrac, suffering from an illness of which he died, was visited and consoled by Raymond Bertrand, Bernard and Galhard of Le Congoust, by Bernard Bataille of Ventenac, and by Raymond of Salles of Lordat, knights, and by many other knights and ladies named here': Doat 24, fol. 39r.

[38] 'The deposition of Matfre of Paulhac, knight, containing that Arnold Arrufat and William Salamo had made him a heretic at the age of fourteen years': Doat 22, fol. 58r.

[39] '[He] said that Arnold Arrufat and William Salamo, heretics, and Arcurand Ros of Verfeil, hereticated the speaker, hale and hearty but a youth of fourteen years, at Verfeil': Doat 22, fol. 58v.

believers) and the semantic basket holding both as people to be regarded as heretics. Here is an example from Doat 21, fol. 34r: 'Dominus archiepiscopus Narbonensis ... interrogatus an suprascripti nobiles sint hæreticorum publici defensores, et an sint publice de hæresi infamati, et an a catholicis hæretici reputentur' (The lord Archbishop of Narbonne ... [was] asked whether the nobles named above are public defenders of heretics, and whether they are publicly defamed with heresy, and whether they are considered as heretics by Catholics). The archbishop is asked if all the Niort family are considered to be heretics, and the archbishop answers yes, then going on to specify that the mother is 'hæretica perfecta, et vestita' (a fully-fledged and vested heretic), and the sons 'credentes sunt, fautores et receptatores hæreticorum' (are believers and supporters and receivers of heretics).

Some of the introductions seem to suggest the predominance of the wider idea of 'heretic', covering all believers and supporters. Here, for example, a knight, out hunting, comes across some 'hæretici' preaching to lay supporters:

> Item dicit quod dum ipse testis, quadam die, esset venatum, casu fortuito invenit in dicto nemore ... Arnaudum Hugonem et socios eius, hæreticos; et prædicabant ibi dicti hæretici. Quorum prædicationi interfuerunt Petrus Bernard et Assaut de Baure, milites ...[40]

But in the introduction, the listeners are also heretics:

> qu'un jour, estant a la chasse, il racontra, dans le bois de Las Sausieiras, Arnaud Hugon, qui y preschoit a plusieurs heretiques, et entre autres a Pierre Bernardi et a Assaut de Baure, chevaliers.[41]

This wider and less specialised understanding of 'heretic' would be consistent with a heresy such as Protestantism, where there is much less distinction between grades of believers. The scribes are not grasping the range and subtle distinctions exemplified above in the questions put to the archbishop of Narbonne.

It is interesting to compare these introductions to a document edited in 1856 by Alexandre Germain, an Inventory from the Dominican convent of Montpellier of manuscripts from the Dominican house of Carcassonne which had been taken there, including FFF.[42] The hand is seventeenth century,

---

[40] 'Item, he says that while the same witness, one day, was out hunting, he found by chance in the said wood ... Arnold Hugh and his companion, heretics; and the said heretics were preaching there. Present at their preaching were: Peter Bernard and Assaut of Lavaur, knights': Doat 23, fol. 78r.

[41] 'that one day, when he was hunting, he met, in the wood of Las Sausieiras, Arnold Hugh, who was preaching there to several heretics, and among others to Peter Bernard and to Assaut of Lavaur, knights': Doat 23, fol. 75v.

[42] A. Germain, 'Inventaire inédit concernant les archives de l'inquisition de Carcassonne', *Mémoires de la Société archéologique de Montpellier* 4 (1855), 287–308

The seventeenth-century introductions to medieval inquisition records

according to Germain (although Dossat suggests that it might be early eighteenth century) and while it may be a copy of an earlier document, any original can date from no earlier than 1552. The manuscripts inventoried are mostly concerned with heresy, and date from various periods. This inventory thus gives us a chance to see how a Dominican of not very dissimilar date to our introductions characterises heresy.

It would seem that this inventory, though inclined to go into more detail, takes a very similar line to the Doat introductions. A typical example would be this: '**1310**: Autre rouleau parchemin, contenant la recepte ou estat des biens confisqués a des heretiques albigeois, assis a la ville ou teroir d'Alby, relevant la directe du roy et de l'evesque'. The word 'Albigeois' is very occasionally used, as here, but the manuscript descriptions mostly describe heretics by their beliefs and actions, rather than labelling them – understandable, as many kinds of heretical and unorthodox behaviour are covered. Like the Doat introductions, these summaries seem quite clearly to be based on a close translation from the Latin.

But when it comes to heretical worship, these Dominicans have the same problems of understanding as the writer or writers of the Doat introductions. A detailed description of a *consolamentum* allows it to be correctly identified as the ceremony that makes one a heretic:

> **1258 jusques a 1284**: Autre Registre, contenant auditions 1° de ceus qui s'estoint faits heretiques en la maniere suivante, scavoir: Estant interogez par les heretiques, ils promettoint qu'ils ne mangeroint plus ny chair ny oefs ny fromage, ny ce qui provenoit de la chair, mais seulement huile et poisson et fruits; et apres d'autres promesses lesdits heretiques imposoint les mains et un livre sur la teste desdits apostats, et lisoint en priant Dieu a genoux; 2° des tesmoins contre ceux qui avoint adoré et suivi les heretiques, et auditions d'iceux.[43]

However, the word itself leads to the same confusions as it does in Doat. This example is perhaps ambiguous:

> **1244**: Un livre en parchemin, sans couverture, contenant depositions contre les heretiques qui alloint en divers lieus des diocezes de Carcassonne et Narbonne et dans les maisons des malades, pour les consoler et les obliger

---

(pp. 295–308). I would like to thank Pete Biller for drawing my attention to this document.

[43] '**1258 until 1284**: Another register, containing the hearings: firstly, of those who became heretics in the following manner, that is, being questioned by the heretics, they promised that they would no longer eat flesh or eggs or cheese, or anything that came from the flesh, but only oil and fish and fruits, and after other promises the said heretics placed their hands and a book on the heads of the said apostate, and read, praying to God on their knees; secondly, of witnesses against those who had adored and followed the heretics, and their hearings'.

a se faire heretiques; et ainsy disoint ils se soumettre a Dieu et a l'Evangile, ce que lesdits malades faisoint, et se mettoint de leur secte.[44]

But this one clearly understands 'consolation' as comfort given to the sick – 'beaucoup de consolation' makes no sense in any other context:

> **1241 et 1252**: Un livre en parchemin, contenant depositions contre pleusieurs heretiques, et adveus de pleusieurs persones de divers dioceses de la seneschaussée de Carcassonne, comm'ils avoint mangé avec les heretiques, en avoint receu beaucoup de consolation dans leurs infirmités, receu la benediction et la paix, et qui s'en allant coucher priont Dieu qu'il leur permit de mourir entre les mains des bons hommes.[45]

This manuscript would suggest a similar state of knowledge of heresy to that found in the introductions to the documents in the Doat volumes. Labels such as 'Albigeois' and 'Vaudois' are known, but Cabanès and Aurieres, and any others who may have written introductions the 'tiltres particuliers' seem to be influenced less by any pre-existing idea of heresy than by a close translation of the Latin text – too close sometimes, as misconceptions of what a word like 'consolamentum' means can lead them into error. The roughly contemporary Dominican manuscript from Montpellier suggests that they are not alone in this.

---

[44] '**1244**: A parchment book, without cover, containing depositions against the heretics who went into various places in the dioceses of Carcassonne and Narbonne and into the houses of the sick, to console them and to force them to become heretics; and thus they told them to submit to God and to the gospel, which the said sick people did, and joined their sect'.

[45] '**1241 and 1252**: A parchment book, containing depositions against several heretics, and confessions of several people from different dioceses in the seneschalcy of Carcassonne, how they had eaten with the heretics, had received plenty of consolation from them in their illnesses, received the blessing and the peace, and who in going to bed prayed to God to allow them to die in the hands of the good men'.

12

History in the Dominican Convent in Toulouse in 1666 and 1668: Antonin Réginald and Jean de Doat[1]

Peter Biller

Between 1664 and 1670 Jean de Doat was at work visiting archives in southern France and selecting documents to be transcribed by a team of scribes working under his direction.[2] His commission was from Jean-Baptiste Colbert, and the two aims of copying were the conservation of the rights of the crown and to serve history. Many of the originals are no longer extant. Consequently the copies that were made – which were bound into 258 volumes now kept in the French national library – are of extraordinary interest to historians, as is also the matter of their transmission. How and why were some chosen and others not? Doat's only known writings are his reports on the mission addressed to Colbert's librarian. He listed achievements, criticised his employees and accounted for money. It is only the project-manager's compartment of his mind to which we have direct access.

---

[1] I am grateful to John Arnold, Stuart Carroll, Lucy Sackville and Rob Wyke for their comments, to Patrick Ferté for providing me with a typescript of his account of Antonin Réginald prior to its publication in his history of the University of Toulouse (see n. 3 below) and to Christine Gadrat-Ouerfelli for making available to me her work on the Dominican enquiry of 1694 (see n. 10 below).

[2] H. Omont, 'La collection Doat à la Bibliothèque Nationale. Documents sur les recherches de Doat dans les archives du sud-ouest de la France de 1663 à 1670', *Bibliothèque de l'École des Chartes* 77 (1916), 286–336, also published separately, paginated 1–51 (Paris, 1917); L. Kolmer, 'Colbert und die Entstehung der Collection Doat', *Francia* 7 (1979), 463–89; *Inquisitors and Heretics in Thirteenth-Century Languedoc. Edition and Translation of Toulouse Inquisition Depositions, 1273–1282*, ed. P. Biller, C. Bruschi and S. Sneddon, Studies in the History of Christian Traditions 147 (Leiden and Boston, 2011), pp. 20–6; J. Soll, *The Information Master: Jean-Baptiste Colbert's Secret State Information System* (Ann Arbor, 2009), p. 104; L. Albaret, 'La collection Doat, une collection moderne, témoignage de l'histore religieuse méridionale des XIIIe et XIVe siècles', in *Historiens modernes et Moyen Âge méridional*, ed. M. Fournié, D.-O. Hurel and D. Le Blevec, Cahiers de Fanjeaux 49 (Toulouse, 2014), pp. 57–93.

Peter Biller

This has dictated the indirect approach adopted in this chapter, which provides a close-up picture of just one visit made by Doat, to the Dominican convent in Toulouse in November 1668. It sketches the setting: the timing, the appearance and character of the convent at the time and what might have struck him about the place and the people in it.[3]

i. The medieval archive

Raymond Gros of Toulouse turned up one spring morning in 1236 at the Dominican convent in Toulouse. He had been a full heretic (*hereticus perfectus*) for about twenty-two years, and now turned into a super-grass. He had so many beans to spill that the inquisitors authorised local chaplains to work alongside Dominican and Franciscan friars receiving his confession, writing it down over many days. The text was still there among the records of the Toulouse inquisitors in the early 1300s. The Dominican who saw it then, Bernard Gui, was a man inclined to laconic understatement. He just said it was big.[4]

This is the story of these records in a nutshell. The early friars breathed the air of Toulouse: a city of notaries, authenticated documents and record-keeping. They were part of this culture and did likewise: wrote things, got them witnessed and kept them in an ever-growing archive.[5] Around 1300, then, Gui had at his disposal a treasure house and in his dual capacity of inquisitor and historian he ransacked it. But he is the last person we can name

---

[3] This exercise in micro-history is not a contribution to broader analyses of counter-reformation historiography or the religious role of Toulouse. For an up-to-date short account of Toulouse in this period, see the the chapters by P.-J. Souriac in *Histoire de Toulouse et de la metropole*, ed. J.-M. Olivier and R. Pech (Toulouse, 2019), pp. 295–386; bibliography, 767–71. On Catholic Toulouse as a bastion of orthodoxy, see E. Martinazzo, *Toulouse au Grand Siècle: Le rayonnement de la Réforme catholique (1590–1710)* (Rennes, 2015) and B. B. Diefendorf, *Planting the Cross. Catholic Reform and Renewal in Sixteenth- and Seventeenth-Century France* (Oxford, 2019). On its university, see *Histoire de l'Université de Toulouse*, ed. C. Barrera and P. Ferté, 3 vols. (Portet-sur-Garonne, 2019–20), vol. 2, P. Ferté, *L'époque moderne, xvie-xviiie siècle*. On historical writing in Toulouse, the succinct panorama in *Histoire de Toulouse*, ed. Olivier and Pech, pp. 298–300, is valuable, and much is caught in the net of *Historiens modernes et Moyen Âge méridional*, ed. Fournié et al.

[4] Guillaume Pelhisson, *Chronique (1229–1244)*, ed. J. Duvernoy (Paris, 1994), pp. 92–7; transl., W.L. Wakefield, *Heresy, Crusade and Inquisition in Southern France. 1100–1250* (London, 1974), pp. 223–4. The unusual precision of Pelhisson's date, 2 April 1236, indicates that he looked at the depositions. Bernard Gui, *Scripta de Sancto Dominico*, ed. S. Tugwell, Monumenta Ordinis Fratrum Praedicatorum Historica 27 (Rome, 1998), p. 273 ll. 998–1000.

[5] Early losses are also part of the story in more detailed accounts: Y. Dossat, *Les crises de l'inquisition toulousaine au xiiie siècle (1233–1273)* (Bordeaux, 1959), ch. 1; *Inquisitors and Heretics*, ed. Biller, Bruschi and Sneddon, pp. 4–10.

History in the Dominican Convent in Toulouse in 1666 and 1668

who could and did do this. Last, that is, for three and a half centuries, when another Dominican – a historian, not inquisitor – ransacked it again. His name was Antonin Réginald. By this time Raymond Gros's confession had long since gone, like much else. There was pitifully little for Réginald (or Doat) to look at, just a dozen registers – as we shall see in section iii below.

ii. Mid-seventeenth century: the convent

How would the convent have struck visitors in those years?

In 1647 a Breton Dominican described entering the Bourg and catching sight of its 'magnificent church, entirely brick from foundations right up to the rooftop, [and] although built 400 years ago, looking as though it had just come from the hands of the workers'.[6] Beyond lay the convent buildings. We shall look first at the community they contained – its general condition, intellectual life and historical culture – and after that return to what struck visitors' eyes as they walked around inside the establishment. Since the point is to get at the outlook of the Dominicans Doat met and talked to, their accounts of their Order and its mother-convent in Toulouse are taken at face-value in what follows.

The convent had declined into a state of torpor by the mid-sixteenth century. It was sacked by the Huguenots in 1562, and towards the end of the century it was hardly recruiting any novices.[7] Then came radical change. By 1599 it had joined the congregation of reformed observant Dominicans, and between 1599 and 1605 it had the inspirational leadership of its prior, who was the leading figure in the Dominican reform movement: Sébastien Michaëlis (1594–1647).[8] Michaëlis breathed new life into the convent in

---

[6] The description of Jean-Giffre de Rechac (1604–60), quoted by B. Montagnes in his 'Aux Jacobins de Toulouse: l'expérience vécue d'une architecture', *Mémoires de la Société Archéologique du Midi de la France* 51 (1991), 217–22 (219): 'cette magnifique église, toute de brique, depuis les fondements jusqu'au toit, laquelle bien que bâti depuis quatre cent ans, semble sortir des mains des ouvriers'. On the functions of such churches as auditoria and the early Dominican ideal of plainness, see B. Montagnes, 'L'attitude des prêcheurs à l'égard des œuvres d'art', *Cahiers de Fanjeaux* 9 (1974), pp. 87–100. For a broader view of the convent buildings over time, see M. Prin, *L'ensemble conventuel des Jacobins de Toulouse. Son histoire, son architecture, son sauvetage et sa renaissance* (Toulouse, 2007).

[7] On the sacking, ibid., p. 56; Jean-Jacques Percin, *Monumenta Conventus Tolosani* (Toulouse, 1693), pp. 113b no. 2 – 114b no. 8.

[8] B. Montagnes, *Sébastien Michaelis et la réforme d'Occitanie (1594–1647)*, Institutum Historicum FF. Praedicatorum Romae AD S. Sabinae, Dissertationes Historicae 21 (Rome, 1984), with an overview of Michaëlis's life at pp. 254–6; thirteen of Montagnes's articles on the early modern reform are reprinted in his *Les dominicains en France et leurs réformes*, Mémoire dominicaine, special no. 3 (Paris, 2001). See also Diefendorf, *Planting the Cross*, ch. 4.

Peter Biller

Toulouse and many others in Languedoc. There was a return to the primitive austerity of the Order, to fasting and abstinence, and the centrality of prayer and the liturgy. Practicality was shown in the avoidance of extremism, and shrewd opportunism in obtaining regular visits from a local Toulouse Jesuit to instruct the friars in spiritual exercises. Recruitment had gone up sharply in the early 1600s, and the community had come to number about sixty friars. All of this is, of course, conveyed to us by admirers of Michaëlis, such as the historian of the reform movement Jacques Archimbaud, and others friars of the generation after Michaëlis. Though renewal of spiritual fervour may be an intangible idea to many of us, it was real to them, and visitors during these years would sense that the community had a spring in its step.

Spiritual reform was accompanied by intellectual and cultural vigour. The convent's leading role in the university of Toulouse had its symbols. The tolling of its bell called students to their lectures and it kept under safe guard one of the keys to the chest containing the university's charters. Alone in the whole of the Dominican Order, it was the Toulouse convent that was the guardian – since 1369 – of the body of Saint Thomas Aquinas, and it was the leading promoter of Thomism both locally and internationally. It did this through the Dominican who held the chair of theology in Toulouse – in these years one Antonin Réginald – and his work teaching in Toulouse and engaging in heated theological controversy in France, Italy and Spain. We refer readers to the brilliant description provided by Patrick Ferté in his new history of the early modern university of Toulouse,[9] and turn to the area of intellectual life which is of more concern in this chapter: historical research and writing in the convent.

If Dominican reform meant a return by the seventeenth century to the thirteenth, there was something roughly similar here. The mid-thirteenth-century cultivation of Dominican historical writing was now paralleled in the seventeenth century, in Languedoc as a whole but especially in the Toulouse convent. Let us parade some of the historians.[10] Toulouse was where Jacques Archimbaud (c.1584–1667) studied, received his habit from Sébastien Michaëlis (1599) and died. His great work of 1642, probably written in Béziers, was a history of the reform, framed by a providential view of

---

[9] Ferté, L'époque moderne, pp. 63–4; see the index-entry, 'dominicains', ibid., p. 650.

[10] Bernard Montagnes has sketched the historical culture of the southern Dominicans in the seventeenth and early-eighteenth centuries several times: 'Bernard Gui dans l'historiographie Dominicaine', Cahiers de Fanjeaux 16 (1981), 184–203 (187–92); 'L'historiographie de saint Dominique en pays Toulousain de Rechac à Touron (1640–1740)', Cahiers de Fanjeaux 36 (2001), pp. 447–78 (447–54). See also C. Gadrat, 'L'érudition dominicaine au XVIIe siècle et au début du XVIIIe siècle. André de Saint-Géry et l'histoire du couvent de Rodez', Bibliothèque de l'École des Chartes 161 (2003), 645–52; overview, 646–7; C. Gadrat, 'L'enquête de l'ordre dominicain de 1694', in Dom Jean Mabillon, figure majeure de l'Europe des lettres (Paris, 2010), pp. 587–604.

History in the Dominican Convent in Toulouse in 1666 and 1668

the Order's history. God had ordained Dominic to found the order and Michaëlis to renew it.[11] Thomas Souèges (1633–98) professed as a Dominican in Toulouse in 1649, turning quickly to the work that would culminate in his history of the Dominicans, presented in the form of a daily necrology. This was *L'année dominicaine*, whose volumes started appearing in 1678. His own obituary presents the Dominican model of a historian. 'From the earliest years after his profession he took delight in the history of our Order', wrote Jacques Échard in 1721, 'devoting immense labours to illustrating our history'.[12] Jean Benoist (1632–1705) professed in Toulouse in 1650, was an occasional visitor thereafter and returned there to die.[13] His preoccupation was the beliefs and history of the Albigensians and Waldensians, which led to a two-volume work published in 1691. His research led him to inquisition registers in the convents in Carcassonne and Toulouse, and he dug deep, finding in Carcassonne the apocryphon of Bogomil origin, the *Interrogatio Iohannis*, and editing it among his *preuves*.[14] He also found an inquisition register which was in private hands, those of a lawyer and antiquarian in Nîmes, François Graverol. Graverol was a Protestant, and despite the confessional divide, he let Benoist make use of it. Respect and possibly even liking is suggested by a letter in which Graverol wrote that there was no fault to find in Benoist other than his religion.[15]

We shall hold over two other historians, Antonin Réginald and Jean-Jacques Percin, for section iii below. One of them, Percin, conveniently provides a thread that leads outside the convent walls. His life work, *Monumenta Conventus Tolosani* (*Monuments of the Toulouse Convent*), was published in 1693. Its printers, Jean and Guillaume Pech, were located next to the convent. Just as the convent was apart from but also part of the city, so also was its historical culture. Only a few streets and about 500 metres lay between it and the rue Peyras. In the early 1600s a room high up in a house in the rue Peyras constituted the atelier of an important lay historian, as we learn from his

[11] The text was edited by Montagnes, *Sébastien Michaelis*, pp. 53–207; the providential view, ibid., pp. 57–8.

[12] Jacques Quétif and Jacques Échard, *Scriptores Ordinis Prædicatorum*, 2 vols. (Paris, 1719–21), II, 748a: labores immensos in illustranda nostra historia ... a prioribus a professione annis historia ordinis delectatus. See R. Darricau, 'Le P. Souèges, premier auteur de "l'Année dominicaine" (1633–1698)', *Revue de l'Agenais* 101 (1974), 109–21; Montagnes, *Sébastien Michaelis*, p. 11.

[13] Quétif and Échard, *Scriptores*, II, 767a.

[14] Histoire *des Albigeois*, I, 283–96; *Le livre secret des Cathares*. Interrogatio Iohannis. Apocryphe d'origine bogomile, ed. E. Bozóky, Textes Dossiers Documents 2 (Paris, 1980), p. 21; trans. *Heresies of the High Middle Ages*, ed. W. L. Wakefield and A. P. Evans (New York, 1969), pp. 458–65, no. 56b.

[15] Histoire *des Albigeois et des Vaudois ou Barbets*, 2 vols. (Paris, 1691), I, 44–5, 271–3; D. Toti, 'François Graverol e un manoscritto perduto de l'Inquisizione di Tolosa', *Riforma e Movimenti Religiosi* 8 (2020), 215–89 (218–19, 224). See the discussion of Graverol in the introduction above, pp. 30–1.

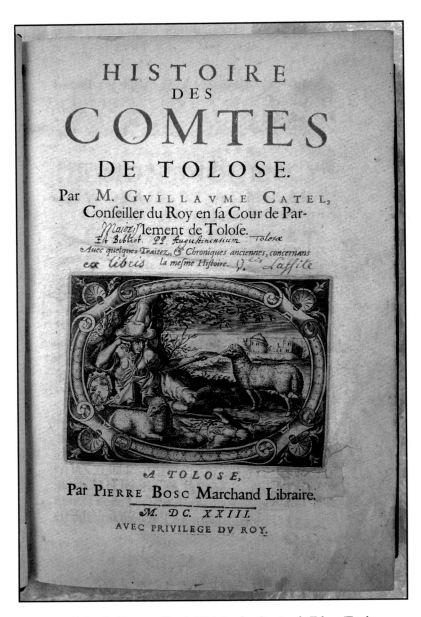

Figure 12.1 Guillaume Catel, *Histoire des Comtes de Tolose* (Toulouse, 1623), title page. Catel's editions in the appendix included Bernard Gui's history of the Counts of Toulouse and William of Puylaurens's Chronicle, the latter based on three manuscripts in Catel's possession. Catel made much use of the library in the Dominican convent in Toulouse. Private collection.

History in the Dominican Convent in Toulouse in 1666 and 1668

will.[16] It was 'mon grand estude', containing printed books, manuscripts, texts, extracts, notes and documents. The Toulouse-born *érudit*, Guillaume Catel, was a Conseiller du Roi at the Court of the Parlement of Toulouse, and it was in this 'large study' that he prepared his *Histoire des Comtes de Tolose*, published in Toulouse in 1623 by the printer and bookseller Pierre Bosc. Catel went to and fro between rue Peyras and the convent. 'I have seen an old Latin chronicle, handwritten, in the library of the friars of St Dominic in Toulouse' (I'ay veu vne ancienne Chronique latine dans la Bibliotheque des Freres de Sainct Dominique de Tolose, escrite à la main), wrote Catel, introducing a passage based on his reading of one of Bernard Gui's works.[17] Later he transcribed a short historical work from the first of the ten volumes of the works of Bernard Gui, which were kept in one of the convent's libraries. This was Gui's *Comites Tolosani*, and Catel provided a careful and complete edition of it.[18]

Catel appended to his account of the friars murdered at Avignonet in 1242 careful transcriptions of the inscriptions on the tombs of the martyrs, and of those in the Franciscan convent Church and the Cathedral of Saint-Etienne, concluding with a description of the tombs of William Arnold and his fellow Dominicans in the chapel of Saint-Hyacinthe in the Church of the Dominican convent.[19] Catel wanted his readers to visualise the tombs. He wrote about marble and gold lettering, and he was helped by the printers who centred the inscriptions on the pages of the *Histoire des Comtes* and set them in large capital letters.

We turn now to what visitors saw. While the shell of the place was ancient, much of its interior was contemporary. Successive priors in recent decades had put a lot of effort into the never-ending task of internal refurbishment of the large complex of ancient convent buildings. The impression given by Percin's reports is that they will have looked spruce: a good background for a spectacular display of modern art.[20] There was a precious and dazzling new mausoleum for Thomas Aquinas, which attracted a pious visit from Anne of Bohemia in 1659. Most recent were the paintings in the refectory and the portraits of famous friars lining the entrance to the main library, commissioned

---

[16] C. Douais, 'Le testament de Guillaume de Catel', *Revue des Pyrenées* 9 (1897), 487–507.

[17] Catel, *Histoire*, p. 358. The work Stephen of Salagnac and Bernard Gui, *De quatuor in quibus Deus prædicatorum Ordinem insignivit*, ed. T. Kaeppeli, Monumenta Ordinis Fratrum Prædicatorum 22 (Rome, 1949), pp. 23 l.21–24 l.19. This was in volume 6 of Gui's works in the convent library (*Monumenta*, p. 70b) and is now Toulouse, Bibliothèque municipale MS 460.

[18] Jean-Jacques Percin, *Monumenta Conventus Tolosani Ordinis FF. Prædicatorum* (Toulouse, 1693; henceforth *Monumenta*), p. 70a no. 7: Primus tomus continet … historiam Comitum Tolosæ; Catel, *Histoire*, appendix, pp. 37–46.

[19] Ibid., *Histoire*, pp. 362–3.

[20] G. Costa, 'Travaux d'art aux Jacobins de Toulouse sous le règne de Louis XIII', *Mémoires de la Société Archéologique du Midi de la France* 67 (2007), 201–29.

by Jean Dominique Rey during his priorate (1657–60).[21] The largest display, however, was on the walls in the chapterhouse. The convent had first hosted representatives of the whole Dominican Order at a general chapter in 1258. In 1627, the year before the seventh such hosting, Gabriel Ranquet (prior 1626–9) had commissioned a vast cycle of images of illustrious friars.[22] Although by 1693, when Percin was writing, they were beginning to show the effects of damp,[23] at the time of Doat's visit they were only forty years old: fresher.

Older histories present Guy François (born Le-Puy-en-Velay before 1578, died Paris 1650) as the painter who executed the cycle in the chapterhouse. The year before (1626) the provincial chapter had been held in Le Puy, the location around this time of Guy's atelier: a plausible moment of contact between patron and painter. The attribution to Guy is significant. In a remarkable monograph written to accompany an exhibition held in Toulouse in 2001–2, the art historian Jean Penent presented painting in Toulouse and Languedoc as being taken over by Caravaggism in the early seventeenth century. In Rome and Bologna Guy had come under the influence of Caravaggio (via his pupil Carlo Sarraceni, 1579–1620) and of Guido Reni. He then led the way, exporting their style of intensely expressive religious art from Italy and introducing it into Languedoc, doing for this region what Georges de La Tour was doing for Lorraine and Zurbaran for Spain. By the mid-1620s Guy was famous and getting many commissions, especially for convent churches and chapter-houses, in Toulouse and elsewhere in Languedoc.[24]

There is now virtually nothing to see on the walls of the chapterhouse in Toulouse. But we can try broadly to envisage the style of their decoration in 1627 by looking at the many paintings by Guy François that do survive. Those he produced for the Dominicans in Le-Puy-en-Velay, for example, include the Polish Dominican St Hyacinthe, whom he had also painted in Toulouse.[25] We are on surer ground with their content, for Percin's little guide *Our Chapterhouse decorated with pictures* details the iconography of the scheme.[26]

---

[21] *Monumenta*, pp. 162a no. 15, 174b no. 54. On Rey, see Montagnes, *Sébastien Michaelis*, p. 259.

[22] On Ranquet, ibid., pp. 258–9; Costa, 'Travaux', 227 n. 150. See the description and photos of the chapter-house in Prin, *L'ensemble conventuel des Jacobins de Toulouse*, pp. 213–21; 218–20 on the 1627 scheme.

[23] *Monumenta*, p. 145b no. 11. Something could still be seen in 1929; Costa, 'Travaux', 225. 227 on the difficulty of identifying painters of such schemes.

[24] J. Penent, *Le temps de caravagisme. La peinture de Toulouse et du Languedoc de 1590 à 1650. Catalogue de l'exposition du Musée Paul-Dupuy de Toulouse* (Paris, 2001). See p. 13 on the vogue for reconstruction, embellishment and iconographic renewal in convents; on Guy's style, p. 71, and the influence of Guido Reni, pp. 85–7; Penent discusses the (probable) attribution to Guy of the Toulouse chapter-house commission, pp. 107–8 and n. 35; Guy's handling of the problem of variety when painting portraits in series, pp. 158–9. Cf., Costa, 'Travaux', 227.

[25] *Monumenta*, p. 147b; Penent, *Le temps de caravagisme*, p. 157, fig. 4.

[26] *Monumenta*, pp. 145a–8b. This is marked off from the preceding text by a bar of

History in the Dominican Convent in Toulouse in 1666 and 1668

Percin indicates eight sections on the walls, and lists the portraits found in each. There are 121 of them. All are Dominicans apart from the pope who confirmed the Order, Honorius III, and the Franciscans who were killed alongside Dominicans at Avignonet in 1242. Percin tells the reader, 'I report the inscriptions from our manuscript', which was presumably the plan from which the artists worked.[27] The wall's sections have varying numbers of portraits: 23, 22, 29, 4, 33, 2 and 8. Only one of these sections is confined to just one category of friars: these are the thirty-three Holy Confessors, who begin with St Thomas Aquinas and are arranged 'above, on the left side of the altar'. While the other sections on the walls do contain short runs of one category of friars – say, a handful of martyrs or inquisitors or Masters-General of the Order, or martyrs or inquisitors – none are entirely only one category.

The idea did not spring from nowhere, for there were broadly similar schemes elsewhere, on walls in Dominican convents and churches and also in books. The genre flourished in particular from the later fifteenth century onwards. Mural paintings and engravings provided elaborate and ambitious representations of the Dominican Order, doing this through the portrayal of large numbers of past friars, sometimes in simple rows, sometimes appended to the many branches of a 'Tree of St Dominic'.[28] Here we do not try to place the Toulouse schema against its analogues and possible iconographic sources. We just note the features that were of distinctively Toulousan significance and in particular those that would have struck observant visitors.

Historical continuity is implied everywhere simply through the chronological range, which runs from the beginnings to the late 1500s.[29] Some portraits underline very early history. A friar who was a companion of St Dominic (Peter Sellan) and the first Dominican to become a bishop (Raymond of Falgar) appear in the first run of portraits, respectively nos. 7 and 6. Inquisitors are scattered throughout. The Toulouse convent itself often features, through brief details about one of its friars. Thus inscriptions date the portraits of two early priors of Toulouse, Colombe and Pons of Saint-Gilles,

---

decorative flourishes crossing the whole page, underneath which runs the title in italicised caps: *CAPITULUM NOSTRUM PICTURIS ORNATUM*. Typographically it is thereby made akin to several other autonomous *opuscula* (little works) printed in the second part of the *Monumenta*.

[27] Ibid., p. 145b no. 11: inscriptiones refero ex nostro manuscripto.

[28] On the tree, see B. Montagnes, 'La lignée toulousaine de saint Dominique', *Cahiers de Fanjeaux* 37 (2002), pp. 238–65 (237–8); B. Montagnes, 'Les inquisiteurs martyrs de la France méridionale', *Praedicatores – Inquisitores. The Dominicans and the Medieval Inquisition. Acts of the 1st International Seminar on the Dominicans and the Inquisition, Rome, 23–25 February 2002*, Institutum Historicum Fratrum Praedicatorum, Dissertationes Historicae 29 (Rome, 2004), pp. 513–38 (514–18), and the illustration from the early sixteenth-century *Triumphus Martyrum*, reproduced opposite p. 513.

[29] The last specified date of death; *Monumenta*, p. 146a.

Peter Biller

by reference to the friars' violent expulsion from the city of Toulouse in 1235, an event long seen in the convent as semi-martyrdom.[30] Actual martyrs begin the portraits in two locations, 'On the right hand side' and again 'Above, on the right hand side of the Altar'. In the first group the topic of 'then and now' is strikingly expressed through the proximity of the martyrs of Avignonet in 1242 to Vincente Valverde, who had been killed by 'Indians' on Puná Island off the coast of Ecuador in 1541, at nos. 3 and 5 respectively. Whereas most images depicted just one friar, the Avignonet picture contained many and the inscription is the longest. This befits the convent's own most important martyrdom and the convent's abiding concern to cast Count Raymond of Toulouse as heretic and blame him for the killing.[31] The convent's friars will have been more aware than most of two figures who were not there, absent because of the cut-off point adopted when the scheme was planned. These were the great Sébastien Michaëlis (ob. 1618) and the martyr Guillaume Courtet (ob. 1627) – the latter an important figure in Réginald's life and outlook, as we shall see in section iii below.

A salutary reminder of the limits of our ability fully to imagine reactions to this cycle comes from one hint that they included mockery. The pictures immediately preceding Avignonet and Puná Island have one very odd feature. No. 1 depicts those called the 'céphalophores' (head-carriers). These were six Dominicans from the convent in Toulouse. After being beheaded by the Albigensians they marched back to the convent – carrying their heads! No. 2 is an image of the inquisitor Francis of Toulouse, martyred in 1260 by heretics who tortured him in ways which combine the sufferings of Christ and St Sebastian: a crown of thorns was put on his head, and his body was

---

[30] Ibid.: Columbus ... Prior Tolosanus erat quando expulsi sunt fratres pro fide Catholica e Tolosa propter inquisitionem (Colombe ... He was the Toulouse Prior when the friars were expelled from Toulouse for the Catholic faith, on account of inquisition). Pontius de S. Ægidio bis fuit Prior Tolosanus. ... 2 vice non diù postquam fratres Ordinis de Tolosa ab hæreticis sunt expulsi (Pons of Saint-Gilles was twice the Toulouse Prior. ... The second time not long after the friars of the Order were expelled from Toulouse by the heretics).

[31] Ibid., p. 146b. F. Guillelmus Arnaldi de Monte Pessulano Inquisitor Tolosanus cum duobus sociis Ordinis, F. Bernardo de Rupeforte, & F. Garcia de Aura, et duobus FF. Minoribus cum allis [sic] Catholicis personis apud Avenionetum diœcesis Tolosanæ, jussu Raymundi Comitis Tolosani hæretici, in vigilia Ascensionis Domini, an. 1242, occiditur (In the year 1242 on the vigil of the Ascension of the Lord the Toulouse Inquisitor William Arnold was killed at Avignonet in the diocese of Toulouse, on the orders of the heretic Count Raymond of Toulouse, together with two companions of the Order, friar Bernard of Roquefort and friar Garcias of Aure, two friars Minor and other Catholic persons). On early modern interest, see Y. Dossat, 'Le massacre d'Avignonet', *Cahiers de Fanjeaux* 6 (1971), pp. 343–59 (at 356–7). Montagnes provides an account of the late medieval and early modern cult in the Toulouse convent in his 'Les inquisiteurs martyrs', pp. 524–7.

History in the Dominican Convent in Toulouse in 1666 and 1668

pierced with arrows.[32] Percin's words take us no further, and we shall never know how the painter responded to the aesthetic opportunities offered by these two scenes.

Just once in *Our Chapterhouse*, Percin is blunt about the gap between his own view and the credulity of others. 'It is believed by some', he writes, commenting on no. 9 in the first sequence, 'that the Toulouse citizen Thomas ... was the half-brother of Peter Sellan: but it is not true'.[33] What then did he think of the head-carriers and Francis the Sebastian-clone? They never appear, of course, in serious documents or serious histories; not in Percin's own voluminous history of his convent. When he does turn to them, briefly, in his *On the Inquisitors ... Killed at Avignonet*, he writes thus: 'One can see their pictures painted in our Chapterhouse. About these [martyrs] I report what I have read, nor do I dwell on pointless criticisms, and I receive in good faith the testimonies of illustrious authors, who I judge to have written nothing uncertain or of dubious credence'. [34] Arch Latin prose conveying a wink?

iii. 1666: Antonin Réginald's *Chronicon Inquisitorum*, the archive and Réginald's work as a research assistant

Réginald now needs introduction. Born in 1606, he joined the Dominican Order in 1624, professing in Avignon.[35] He was a lector there in 1632, but he soon gravitated to Toulouse. A brilliant abstract thinker, he soon became a great luminary of the theology faculty of the University of Toulouse, and found fame throughout the Church as one of the most important exponents of Thomism, a doughty controversialist and a prolific writer. On his death in 1676 the prior of the convent wrote a long obituary which he circulated in a public letter. In this he blamed Réginald's prodigious work-load of lecturing and writing for the eventual breakdown of his health.[36]

---

[32] On the origins and myth of the head-carriers and Francis, see Montagnes, 'La lignée toulousaine de saint Dominique', 239–44; Montagnes, 'Les inquisiteurs martyrs', pp. 527–33.

[33] Percin, *Monumenta*, 145b: a quibusdam (quod tamen verum non est) creditur Fr. Germanus B. Petri Cellani.

[34] Ibid., Part 2, 209b no. 4: imagines videre est pictas in capitulo nostro. De quibus refero quæ legi, nec immoror criticis inutilibus, bonâque fide recipio illustrium autorum de illis testimonia quos certe nihil incertum scripsisse arbitror dubiæque fidei.

[35] *Monumenta*, pp. 169b–73a nos. 26–42; Quétif and Échard, *Scriptores Ordinis Prædicatorum*, II, 661a–3b; M.-M. Gorce, 'Réginald, Antonin', in *Dictionnaire de théologie catholique*, 15 vols. (Paris, 1899–1950), XV.1, 2106–2114; *Histoire de l'Université de Toulouse*, Ferté, *L'époque moderne*, pp. 221, 246–52, 254, 259, 263–4, 266, 572.

[36] *Monumenta*, p. 172b no. 39; Quétif and Échard, *Scriptores*, II, 662a–3b.

Peter Biller

As we survey Réginald's writings, we follow the bibliographies compiled by two fellow Dominicans, one by Percin and another by Échard, published in 1693 and 1721 respectively.[37] Réginald mainly wrote theological treatises, most of which were printed and can still be read. His range also included pious biography and history, and by contrast with his theology the four works in this category are lost or accessible only indirectly. First he wrote a life of the Dominican Guillaume Courtet, with whom he had a personal link. Courtet was the prior in whose hands Réginald had professed when he joined the Order. Courtet went out to Japan as a missionary. In 1637 he was tortured and then beheaded in Nagasaki.[38] Presumably Réginald's Life, which cannot be found, was a piece of advocacy for canonisation – something which did not happen until 1987.

Secondly, there was a two-volume history of the Council of Trent. Anticipated by all, we are told, but it never appeared.

Evidently smaller in scale was the third item. Upon his election on 1 June 1666, the new prior, Louis Achard, 'entrusted to Brother Antonin Réginald the writing of a *Chronicle of Inquisitors*'.[39] Échard wrote that the manuscript was with the friars in the convent in Toulouse. But it has not been seen since.

Fourthly, Réginald did historical work on behalf of a fellow friar. In Percin's words: 'He himself [Réginald] compiled the *Chronicle of Inquisitors*, and many things for the *History of the Three Friars killed at Avignonet in the year 1242*'.[40] The credited author of this *History* was Percin, who did not acknowledge exactly what his research assistant did – *plus ça change*!

The summary so far looks grim for anyone wanting to read Réginald the historian. What is there to read? In fact, there is quite a bit. As we shall see later, we can attribute to him two pieces of precise research in inquisition registers that were used in the *History of the Three Friars killed at Avignonet*. But the big thing is the *Chronicle of Inquisitors*. Percin made many excerpts from it, inserting them into his *Monumenta*. He divided this work into centuries and decades, and he began the interpolations from the *Chronicle* in the decade 1240–50, continuing until his last borrowing, which was in the 1660–70 decade, under the year 1662. He signalled his borrowings, referring to the *Chronicle*, or to Réginald, in phrases such as 'thus far Réginald'. He also placed quotation marks on the left-hand side of the passages in question.

---

[37] *Monumenta*, pp. 169b–70a nos. 26–7; Quétif and Échard, *Scriptores*, II, 552b–3b.

[38] Montagnes, *Sébastien Michaelis*, pp. 216–18, 239–40; B. Montagnes, 'La vocation missionnaire de Guillaume Courtet', *Archivum Fratrum Praedicatorum* 54 (1984), 465–98, reprinted in B. Montagnes, *Les dominicains en France et leurs réformes*, *Mémoire dominicaine*, special no. 3 (Paris, 2001), pp. 221–52.

[39] Is Fratri Antonino Reginaldo commisit scribendum Chronicon Inquisitorum; *Monumenta*, p. 165b no. 22.

[40] Is ipse compilavit Chronicon Inquisitorum & plura pro Historia trium Fratrum Avenionetti occisorum anno, ut retuli, 1242; ibid., p. 170 no. 26.

284

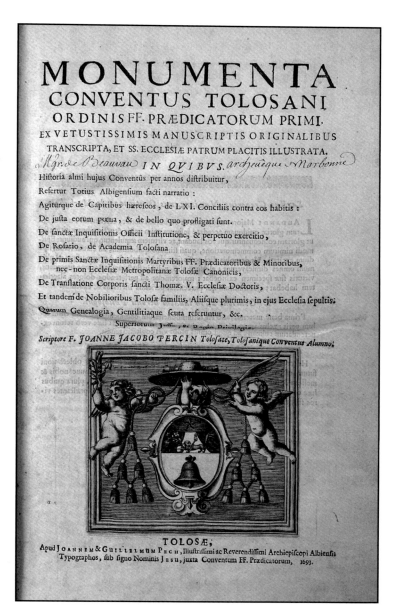

Figure 12.2 Jean-Jacques Percin, *Monumenta Conventus Tolosani* (Toulouse, 1693). Percin's monumental history of the Dominican convent in Toulouse makes him one of the principal figures in the flowering of Dominican historical writing of his times. Percin quickly attracted criticism from fellow Dominicans for his shoddy scholarship. Private collection

Peter Biller

What Percin did was recognised and described precisely by Échard in 1721: he repeatedly worked the *Chronicle* into his *Monumenta*, interpolating passages from Réginald's work into his own.[41] But subsequent historians have not seen this. Buried in Percin's massive *Monuments of the Convent of Toulouse* in this way, the *Chronicle* has not been distinguished from *Monuments*, nor Réginald's voice from Percin's.[42] In order to bring Réginald back into the light, we have provided a transcript and translation of the excerpts in the appendix below, for brevity confining this to 1240–1340.

Readers will see that the text is not unproblematic. Percin was so cavalier in his treatment and quotation of documents, so ready to intrude without saying he was intruding, and so scattergun with his quotation marks that sometimes it can be difficult to determine where one author begins and the other ends.[43] With repeated reading, however, the distinct voices of the two writers emerge. Réginald writes in the third person and calmly sticks to the job; he never cites recent historians on a very early topic. Percin often writes in the first person and comments informally, on occasion very emotionally; and he has a penchant for quoting recent historical writing. The reader alights with relief on the cases where there is no doubt about the border. One of them is comic. Percin quotes Réginald on Bernard Gui's letter of appointment. When concluding the passage copied from Réginald, his acknowledgement that the words were from Reginald was done with sarcastic brevity – 'These words: him' (haec: ille) – and he then goes on to argue that Réginald was wrong.[44] In fact it was Percin who was wrong.

We have not yet formally introduced him.[45] Jean-Jacques Percin (1633–1711) came from a very well-connected noble family, the de Percins

---

[41] Échard's words are few: in suam conv. Tolos. Historiam identidem tamen interpolatum congessit Jacobus Percin citatus (The said Jacques Percin repeatedly worked [the *Chronicle of Inquisitors*], interpolated, into his own history of the convent of Toulouse).

[42] That is, until 2011, when *Inquisitors and Heretics*, ed. Biller, Bruschi and Sneddon, pp. 14–19, made the point.

[43] Percin's misuse of another text is examined by Montagnes in his *Sébastien Michaelis*, pp. 13–14; the comparison is surer because the original is extant.

[44] Appendix, 1306.

[45] In one glowing reference to his episcopal kinsman, Jean-Jacques called him the Carlo Borromeo of this century; *Monumenta*, part 2, p. 97b no. 4. J. Sahuc, *Messire Pierre-Jean-François de Percin de Montgaillard, évêque de Saint-Pons-de-Thomières (1633–1664–1713)* (Paris, 1909), p. 13 n.1, notes Jean-Jacques as a family member but not the precise relationship. Quétif and Échard, *Scriptores*, II, pp. 779b–80a, where spelling of his name as 'Persin' may explain the inaccurate claim by M.-M. Gorce ('Percin, Jean-Jacques', in *Dictionnaire de théologie catholique*, XII.1, 1187) that Échard did not write about him. Most of Bernard Montagnes's accounts of early-modern Dominican historiography contain a few pages on him. Examples include 'Bernard Gui dans l'historiographie Dominicaine', 190–1; *Sébastien Michaelis*, passim; 'L'historiographie de saint Dominique en pays Toulousain', 450–1. See also *L'histoire du catharisme en discussion. Le "concile" de Saint-Félix (1167)*, ed. M. Zerner, Collection du Centre d'Études Médiévales de Nice 3 (Nice, 2001), pp. 23–4.

History in the Dominican Convent in Toulouse in 1666 and 1668

de Montgaillard. A contemporary kinsman of his, Pierre-Jean-François de Percin de Montgaillard, became a bishop at the age of thirty-one. Jean-Jacques was one of the principal figures in the great flowering of Dominican historical writing which we touched on in section ii. His *Monumenta*, published in 1693, was a compendious history of the convent from its foundation to the year of publication. The second and separately paginated part of the published volume contained many undated 'little works' written by Percin, on topics such as the inquisition, the translation of Aquinas's body to the convent, the university of Toulouse and the Avignonet killing. Percin had professed in the Toulouse convent in 1649. Both Percin and Réginald served as priors elsewhere, and we do not have the dates; most priorates were brief. We are limited to this: that between 1649 and 1676 Percin and Réginald's periods of residence in the Toulouse convent will have overlapped intermittently.

We can just about see the existence of the academic story of the two men, but not its details. Percin has been lambasted for the utter shoddiness of his scholarship by fellow Dominican historians over many centuries, from Jacques Échard (1644–1724) to Bernard Montagnes (1924–2018) and the great medieval historian and editor Simon Tugwell. There are only a few words from Percin on his use of Réginald: '*Chronicle of Inquisitors*, which I have used to the *greatest degree* in this *little* enterprise' (Chronicon Inquisitorum, quo *maximè* in hac *Opella* usus sum; my emphasis).[46] The word-play concerned contrasts. Since Percin's 'little' work was in fact huge, how is the reader to understand 'used to the greatest degree'? Percin seems to have been ambivalent about his debt to Réginald, who was the senior of the two men by about twenty-seven years and whose obituaries have nothing but praise for the brilliant thinker, writer and scholar.

Let us now turn to the *Chronicon*. What had Réginald managed to find? Once upon a time the 'house of inquisition' had housed both inquisitors and inquisition records, but no longer. Wherever they were in the convent, Réginald managed to lay hands on about twelve registers. That is the figure we arrive at through listing his references to them, and we are fortunate to have this confirmed by a fellow Dominican, Jean Benoist. As we have noted, Benoist looked at the convent's holdings in relation to the history he published in 1691.[47] The convent, he wrote, had a dozen old inquisition registers. Here they are:[48]

---

[46] *Monumenta*, p. 165b no. 21.
[47] Benoist, *Histoires des Albigeois et des Vaudois*, I, 44, quoted at length in *Inquisitors and Heretics*, ed. Biller, Bruschi and Sneddon, p. 22 n. 68.
[48] Our list runs closely alongside but is not identical to the list in the fundamental account of the Toulouse archive produced by Dossat in his *Crises*, pp. 37–42.

Peter Biller

1. Since Percin started his excerpts in the 1240–50 decade, we can never know whatever may have been in the *Chronicle* from 1230–40. However, for Percin's history of the Avignonet killings, Réginald transcribed two sentences from 'the manuscript Register of Brother Guillaume Arnaud and Brother Étienne, Inquisitors, fol. 3, recto' (Ex Registro mss. F. Guillelmi Arnaldi & F. Stephani fol. 3 pagina prima).[49] This register was one of three dossiers bound together, whose copy occupies BnF Ms Doat 21, fols. 143r–323v, this first dossier in fols. 143r–84v.[50] It contains materials relating to 1235–41.

2. Clearly Réginald had access to the second register in this bundle, whose copy is in Ms Doat 21, fols. 185r–312v.[51] It contains lists of guilty acts committed by people in Quercy, extracted from records of their interrogations by Peter Sellan, and their penances, dated 1241 and 1242.

3(?). Réginald referred to 'Brother Cellan, or Syllan, whose sentences are recorded in an old Register [*r*: beginning] on folio 2', noting that one could gather from these he was inquisitor at least in 1242 and 1243.[52] The phrase 'old Register' sets an amber light flashing, since Réginald was usually more specific than this and we might think this was Percin's sloppy version of Réginald describing the register listed in no. 2 above. Perhaps. A lot would have had to have changed: the form of the inquisition acts in question and the dates.

4. In two of the sentences the inquisitor Ferrier delivered he named a colleague inquisitor: Guillaume Raymond in one from 1243, Peter Durand in another from 1244.[53] Here Réginald made precise use of a register of sentences, bound together with nos. 2–3, whose copy is now Doat 21, fols. 313r–23v.[54]

    Nos. 5–7 concern Bernard de Caux and Jean de Saint-Pierre:

5. Toulouse Bibliothèque municipal MS 609: a copy made in 1260 copy of books 4–5 of depositions made in front of these two inquisitors in 1245–6.[55] We detail at the end of this section Réginald's use of this.

---

[49] *Monumenta*, part 2, pp. 201a–2a.

[50] Dossat, *Crises*, pp. 37–8, no. 1. The copy of the first dossier (Doat 21, fols. 143r–78v) is edited in *The Genesis of Inquisition in Languedoc. Edition and Translation of the Earliest Inquisition Records*, ed. P. Biller, L. J. Sackville and S. Sneddon (forthcoming).

[51] Ibid., p. 38 no. 1. Dossat's 212v should be 312v.

[52] Appendix, 1240–50.

[53] Ibid.

[54] Dossat, *Crises*, p. 38 no. 1; ed. and trans. in *The Genesis of Inquisition in Languedoc*, ed. Biller, Sackville and Sneddon (forthcoming).

[55] Ibid., p. 38 no. 2. The subject of Dossat's *Crises* and M.G. Pegg's *The Corruption of Angels. The Great Inquisition of 1245–1246* (Princeton and Oxford, 2001), and now

History in the Dominican Convent in Toulouse in 1666 and 1668

6. Another register of depositions in front of these two inquisitors, in two groups (1243–4 and 1246–7), was available to Réginald, and a copy is extant in Doat 22, fols. 1r–106r.[56]

7. Réginald looked at the sentences and penances in Bernard and Jean's 'first register', perhaps therefore the first among several registers dedicated to their sentences. The folio numbers of the fragment surviving in Paris fall within the folio numbers of the manuscript Réginald read.[57]

8. 1254: Réginald used Register 4, with the acts of the inquisitors Jean de Saint-Pierre and Renaud de Chartres. Note that Jean de Saint-Pierre was a common name, and this was not the one who had worked with Bernard de Caux.[58]

9. Around 1260: Réginald used Register 2, containing the sentences of Guillaume de Montreveil.[59]

10. Register 6, 1273–82: its copy is Doat 25 in toto and Doat 26, fols. 1–78r.[60]

11. Réginald looked at Bernard Gui's register for 1312.[61]

12. *c.* 1320–1340: Réginald used a register of Pierre Brun containing his sentences.[62]

There was another register, which is no. 12 in Dossat's list. He called it a register of inquisition privileges (1270–1340), and he used part of it in his history of inquisition in Toulouse. Resting upon a mid-fifteenth-century forgery, it was accepted and imported into the *Monumenta* by Percin, who simply said it was from 'our manuscripts' and made no reference to Réginald.[63] The recentness of this manuscript's hand will have been patent, and there is no sign that Réginald had any truck with it.

As the title *Chronicon* suggests, Réginald's aim was modest: establishing the names of inquisitors and a time-line. While some of these registers

---

being edited by Jean-Paul Rehr at Université-Lyon 2. Translations: J.H. Arnold and P. Biller, *Heresy and Inquisition in France, 1200–1300* (Manchester, 2016), pp. 380–440. Réginald's use is detailed below.

[56] Dossat, *Crises*, p. 38 no. 3; Appendix, 1249; ed. and trans. in *The Genesis of Inquisition in Languedoc*, ed. Biller, Sackville and Sneddon (forthcoming).

[57] Dossat, *Crises*, p. 38 no. 4. Appendix, 1249.

[58] Not extant. Appendix, 1254. See Dossat, *Crises*, p. 39 nos. 6–7.

[59] Not extant. Appendix, 1260.

[60] Dossat, *Crises*, p. 39 no. 8; Appendix, 1260, 1276, 1281; ed. and trans., *Inquisitors and Heretics*, ed. Biller, Bruschi and Sneddon.

[61] Not extant. Dossat, *Crises*, p. 39 no. 8 bis; Appendix, 1300–1310.

[62] Appendix, 1330–40.

[63] Appendix, 1270; Dossat, *Crises*, pp. 40 no. 12 and 279 n. 61.

289

gave him only a point or two, Register 6 was a treasure house. This was partly because it covered nine years. But the main thing was the gap in time between it and the earliest registers. The consequence was that the depositions of middle-aged and elderly people in this register sometimes contained the names of earlier inquisitors, in front of whom they had appeared years or even decades before.[64] This treasury of material was right up Réginald's street and he ransacked it. Here and elsewhere he read searchingly and noted carefully. He identified registers by number, and the passage in question by folio number, sometimes indicating recto or verso by 'page 1' or 'page 2'. When we find a slip or omission in these references we should remember that the text we have comes via the slipshod Percin.

The convent had resources other than the registers. In one of its libraries[65] there were ten large volumes containing the works of Bernard Gui. They were well known to Réginald, who incorporated a detailed and precise catalogue in his *Chronicle*. Gui had written a great deal, much of it bearing on the early history of the Order. His account of the foundation of priories included catalogues of the priors, some of whom had periods of inquisition in their careers. Réginald was able to extract dates from these (and also from post-Gui continuations), as well as brief CVs and sometimes what Gui had to say about inquisitors' personal qualities. From Gui's edition of the acts of the provincial chapters and later continuations, Réginald could extract more dated references to inquisitors, and infer their terms of office. One text interpolated into the convent's manuscript of Gui's *Speculum sanctorale* (*Saints' mirror*) was a life of Gui, and this supplied Réginald with data about Gui's post-inquisitorial career.[66]

Réginald's words indicate that Bernard Gui was his hero as both inquisitor and writer, and there is something of Gui in Réginald's sober style. He shows no obvious agenda other than what is implied by steady and precise establishing of the line of Toulouse inquisitors. Part of that was unquestioned attachment to the idea of inquisition as 'righteous persecution',[67] and another part was pride in the leading role played by the locals. In his note on Foulques of Saint-Georges's terms of office there is no mention of the scandals that brought Foulques down, and at the same time no hint of the bizarre attempt

---

[64] See the modern list in *Inquisitors and Heretics*, ed. Biller, Bruschi and Sneddon, pp. 39–40.

[65] M. Morard, 'La bibliothèque evaporée. Livres et manuscrits des dominicains de Toulouse (1216–1840)', in *Entre stabilité et itinérance. Livres et cultures des ordres mendiants, xiiie-xve siècle*, ed. N. Bériou, M. Morard and D. Nebbiai-Dalla Guarda (Turnhout, 2014), pp. 73–128; T. Falmagne, 'Fragments et bibliothèques médiévales à Toulouse: vestiges mineurs, signes de bibliothèques majeures disparues', *Cahiers de Fanjeaux* 51 (2016), pp. 349–413, with a catalogue of fragments surviving from the Toulouse Dominicans, 380–5.

[66] Appendix, 1306, 1312.

[67] C.C. Ames, *Righteous Persecution. Inquisition, Dominicans and Christianity in the Middle Ages* (Philadelphia PA, 2009).

History in the Dominican Convent in Toulouse in 1666 and 1668

of one contemporary Dominican historian to present the criticism Foulques received and his downfall as a kind of martyrdom.[68]

There was one cause for which Réginald was willing to labour in the registers, securing recognition of the martyrdom of those who really had been killed – and bearing in mind his personal attachment to the memory of Guillaume Courtet, we should write 'especially willing'. In the 'many things' (plura) he had compiled for Percin's 'little work' on the Avignonet killing, we can point securely to two. One is the transcription, already mentioned in no. 1 above of two sentences delivered by two of the murdered inquisitors; comparison with the Doat copy of the same text indicates precision.[69] The other concerns a deposition by Guillelma Pelliciera in front of the inquisitor Bernard of Caux in 1246, contained in the register noted in no. 5 above. Her confession included the statement that a man called William had cut out the tongue of one of the inquisitors, William Arnold. The Avignonet tract has this headline event, Pelliciera's name and reference to the register – and Percin's carelessness in copying Réginald was probably responsible for the error in the reference, 'In the 4th Register of Inquisition, folio 8', where 8 should be 85.[70] Dossat carefully compiled a list of the many annotations made to the medieval register in a seventeenth-century hand,[71] recognising that they reflected researches related to a case for canonisation.[72] One of the marginal comments, opposite Ermessendis's deposition, simply said, 'William Arnold's tongue cut out'.[73] The marginalia show that the annotator was a historian of this period at work, ransacking an inquisition register in the Toulouse convent, looking for references to inquisitors and the Avignonet killing, and taking careful notes: Réginald?[74]

---

[68] See Appendix, n. 73.

[69] Percin, *Monumenta*, 201b: Ex Registro mss. F. Guillelmi Arnaldi & F. Stephano Inquisitorum fol. 3 pagina prima.

[70] Percin, *Monumenta*, Part 2, 202b no. 1. In 4. Inquisitionis Registro folio. 8 in depositione Ermisendis Peliceriæ habetur se audivisse plures locatos esse de nece Inquisitorum, quorum, unus nomine Guillelmus dixisse, se cultello linguam F. Guillelmi Arnaldi abscidisse (In Inquisition Register 4, folio 8 [r. 85], it is got from the deposition of Ermessendis Pellicier that she had heard that many had been at the place of the killing of the inquisitors, one of whom, called William, said that he had cut out the tongue of friar William Arnold). T609, 85r: Ermessendis Peliceria ... Dixit etiam quod idem Willelmus dixit quod ipse abscidit linguam fratri Willelmo Arnaldi inquisitori (Ermessendis Pelliceria ... She also said that the same William said that he cut the tongue from the inquisitor friar William Arnold).

[71] *Crises*, pp. 68–9.

[72] *Crises*, pp. 68–9.

[73] In the margin (and noted by Dossat, *Crises*, 69 n. 92): Lingua fratris Guillelmi Arnaldi abscissa. Dossat, *Crises*, 68 and n. 92.

[74] Dossat, Crises, p. 69 n. 92 points to a small number of minor inaccuracies.

Peter Biller

iv. 1668: Jean de Doat's visit

Toulouse had acted as Doat's staging-post and depot. Very large containers of copies made by his team were parcelled up and despatched to Toulouse, and then sent on from there to Paris. But it was only in the fourth year of the project that Doat turned his sights on Toulouse itself. He had got there on Wednesday 4 November 1688 and stayed until Friday 27 November. Colbert's librarian Pierre de Carcavy wrote a memorandum designed to describe Doat's typical procedure.

> While they [the others] worked on copies, he would go with two or three of his men into abbeys or other communities, both ecclesiastical and secular, to choose the acts [deeds *or* documents] he regarded as the best to carry away and have copied in his office. Two of those in his team would look at them and make a summary inventory, and he would mark on this which ones merited and which ones did not merit being copied.[75]

Doat himself described the visit to Toulouse: 'He made a search for documents in the archives of the abbeys of Boulbonne and Grandselve, and of the Daurade, the Carmelites, the Augustinians, the Dominicans, the Inquisition, and the college of the Jesuits… and he had carried to the said town of L'Isle [-en-Albigeois] all the chosen documents and several registers of Inquisition'.[76] The details suggest some deviation from Carcavy's model. Doat's team had an extraordinary amount of inspection and selection to get through in just over three weeks. In the Dominican convent – one among several – just one of the registers (no. 5 in our list) was over 400,000 words long, written over 400 years earlier. How quickly could one of Doat's assistants grasp the essentials of that, before putting it into an inventory for his master's inspection?

There is Doat himself to consider. The director of one of the largest of all seventeenth-century enterprises to preserve documents, partly 'to serve history', must have had some scholarliness of interest and outlook.[77] Doat the scholar is unlikely

---

[75] *Mémoire et calcul* (6 August 1669), ed. Omont, *Doat*, 312–19 (313): Pendant qu'ont travoillent aux copies, il alloit avec trois ou quatre de ses gens dans les abbayes ou autres communautés, tant ecclésiastiques que séculières, choisir les actes qu'il jugeoit les meilleurs pour les porter et les faire coppier dans son bureau. Deux de ceux de sa suitte les voyoient et faisoyent un inventaire sommaire, sur lequel il marquoit ceux qui méritoyent et ceux qui ne méritoyent d'estre coppiez.

[76] 'Les archives des Abbayes de Bourbonne [*r.* Boulbonne] et de Grandselve, de la Daurade, des Carmes et des Augustins, des Jacobins, de l'Inquisition, et du collège des Jésuites … et fit porter en ladite ville de Lille tous les titres choisis et plusieurs registres de l'Inquisition'; J. de Doat, *Mémoire des dépenses* (1 August 1669), ed. Omont, 'Doat', 294–311 (308). Albaret, 'Doat', provides a general account; see ibid., p. 71, on Toulouse.

[77] See Albaret, 'Doat', pp. 61–2, stating that Carcavy must have seen Doat as an able scholar.

History in the Dominican Convent in Toulouse in 1666 and 1668

not to have noticed the Dominican convent's embodiment of four centuries of history, the modern art that expressed its own sense of itself and of Dominican history, and the historical work that was going on in the convent. Doat the busy project-manager is unlikely to have ignored the fact that using an assistant to produce an inventory of the inquisition registers was unnecessary when there was a Dominican there who knew the registers inside out.

He had three manuscripts of inquisition registers carried away. One was the manuscript in which nos. 1, 2 and 4 in our list were bound together, the second was no. 6 and the third no. 10. Let us survey the exclusions and inclusions.

The register based on a fifteenth-century forgery was not chosen. The last register in our list (no. 12) was not chosen. Pierre Brun's period as an inquisitor in the 1320 and 1330s meant dealing only with a few radical Franciscans and Béguins: he had had relatively little to do. Also not chosen was No. 9, the register of Guillaume de Montreveil from around 1260, from a lull relative to the intense activity of 1230s–40s and renewed activity of the 1270s.

At the same time registers of very busy inquisitors were excluded: no. 5, the vast and still extant 1260 copy of the inquisitions of Bernard de Caux and Jean de Saint-Pierre in the Lauragais in 1245–6, and no. 11, the no-longer extant 1312 register of Bernard Gui. Why were these not copied? We have just noted the great length of no. 5 and no. 11 may also have been long. The large undertaking of copying such registers may have given Doat pause for thought. But it was not unimaginable. In Carcassonne he was to order the copying of one inquisition register that contained 240,000 words.[78]

When we turn to what were chosen from the registers in Toulouse, we see several with materials bearing upon topics dear to the friars, and pertinent to Réginald's research for his *Chronicle*. There are the penances imposed by Pierre Sellan, the former wealthy Toulouse citizen who had given the Toulouse Dominicans their first house, and who was one of St Dominic's earliest companions. There are sentences imposed by two of the inquisitors killed at Avignonet, interrogations of members of the consular elite in Toulouse, and materials about a former seneschal of Count Raymond VII of Toulouse, Pierre Grimoardi, as also about the seneschal's circle. One choice, no. 10, was of the register most heavily used in the *Chronicle*.

Of deeper significance, perhaps, is a generic contrast between the three registers that were chosen and two of those that were not chosen, nos. 5 and 11. The inquisition registers we can examine either through medieval or seventeenth-century manuscripts are on a spectrum. In a simplified version of this spectrum, at one end there are copies of interrogations or sentences that are quite close to original registers and contain a large number of these texts, more or less in sequence and unweeded. At the other end there are selections,

---

[78] Copied into MSS Doat 22, fols. 107r–296v, all of 23, and 24, fols. 1r–237v; Dossat, *Crises*, p. 44 no. 1.

anthologies or executive summaries. The fact that Gui's lost register is defined by its year, 1312, indicates it was near the original end of the spectrum. And although no 5 is not a straightforward original – it is a copy and its history includes some re-arrangement – in the larger scheme of things it is also near that end of the spectrum. Modern historians may love large and relatively unprocessed sets of documents. But Doat or Doat and Réginald turned their backs on nos 5 and 11, preferring those registers that were shorter, more processed and more obviously pertinent to particular historical topics.

* * *

Carcavy's culture and outlook made him the one person able to take the larger view, and he did this in a memorandum he wrote at the end of the mission.[79] There was sheer size. Doat, he said, had visited 135 archives in southern France. There could be a utopian result. This was that the copies could form 'a public archive, dependant just on His Majesty, to which all His subjects had access' (un archive public, qui dépendist purement de Sa Majesté et auquel tous ses sujets peussent avoir recours). Carcavy emphasised history. The copies were, he wrote, for the 'illumination of the most interesting parts of our history' (l'eslcaircissement des endroits les plus curieux de nostre histoire), and he went on to provide an Olympian list of the chief topics in French religious and political history. Carcavy chose Doat, and it is possible that his subordinate shared some of this utopian vision.

When Carcavy turned to religious topics his list did include the phrase 'wars with heretics, especially the Albigensians' (des guerres avec les hérétiques, particulièrement avec les Albigeois). But he did not get any nearer to the details of the days Doat spent with the Toulouse Dominicans in November 1668.

[79] Ed. Omont, 'Doat', 325–8.

Appendix

Antonin Réginald, *Chronicon inquisitorum*: edition and translation of excerpts, 1240–1340

The passages are mainly from Jean-Jacques Percin's history of the convent in Toulouse published in *Monumenta Conventus Tolosani Ordinis FF. Prædicatorum* (Toulouse, 1693), with one addition (under 1303) from a little treatise on inquisition written by Percin and published in *Monumenta*, part 2.

In *Monumenta* each page is printed in two columns, and in one of these columns each line contains about six or seven words. The transcriptions given in the left-hand columns below follow the line-lengths of the *Monumenta*, and also its spelling, accents, punctuation – with double quotation marks on the left-hand side of lines – and use of italics. I am grateful to Shelagh Sneddon and Stephen Anderson for comment on the translations.

295

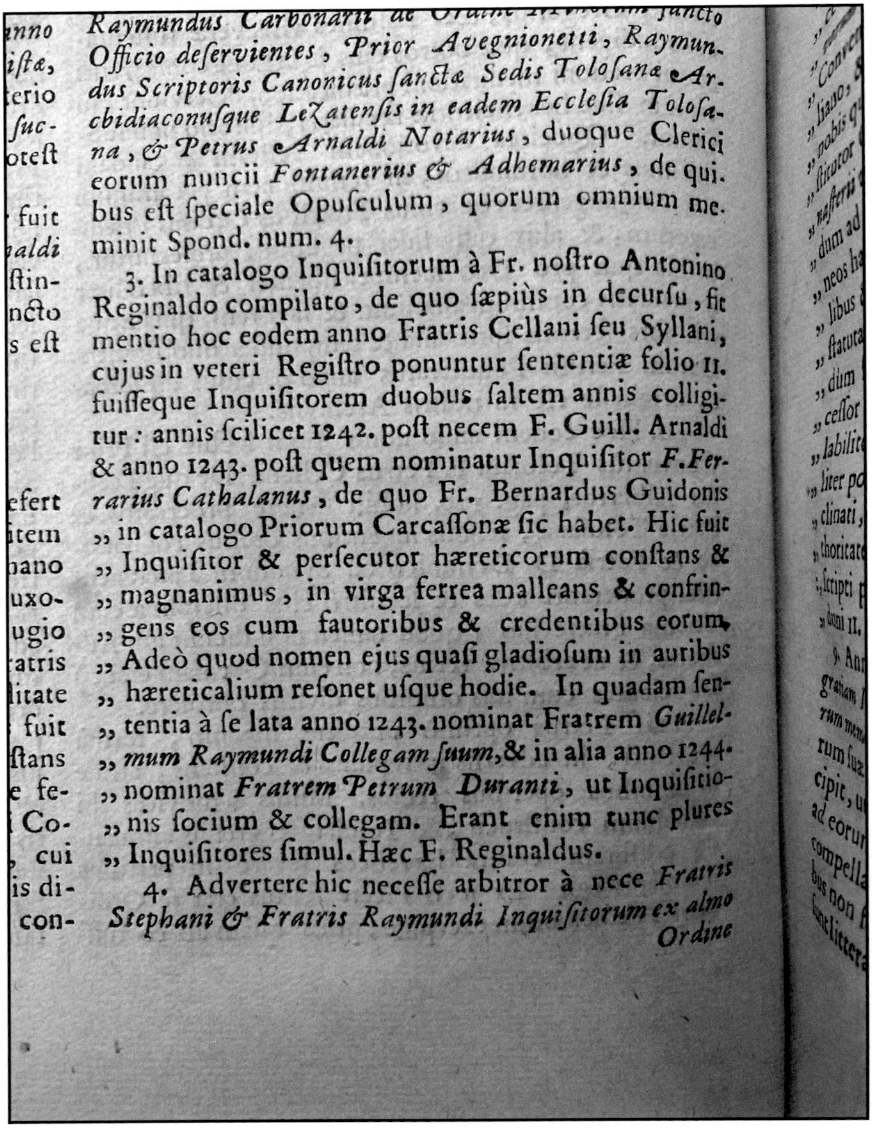

Raymundus Carbonarii de Ordine ... juncto
Officio deſervientes, Prior Avegnionetti, Raymundus Scriptoris Canonicus ſanctæ Sedis Toloſanæ Ar-
chidiaconuſque Lezatenſis in eadem Eccleſia Toloſa-
na, & Petrus Arnaldi Notarius, duoque Clerici
eorum nuncii Fontanerius & Adhemarius, de quibus eſt ſpeciale Opuſculum, quorum omnium me-
minit Spond. num. 4.

3. In catalogo Inquiſitorum à Fr. noſtro Antonino
Reginaldo compilato, de quo ſæpiùs in decurſu, fit
mentio hoc eodem anno Fratris Cellani ſeu Syllani,
cujus in veteri Regiſtro ponuntur ſententiæ folio 11.
fuiſſeque Inquiſitorem duobus ſaltem annis colligitur: annis ſcilicet 1242. poſt necem F. Guill. Arnaldi
& anno 1243. poſt quem nominatur Inquiſitor F. Ferrarius Cathalanus, de quo Fr. Bernardus Guidonis
„ in catalogo Priorum Carcaſſonæ ſic habet. Hic fuit
„ Inquiſitor & perſecutor hæreticorum conſtans &
„ magnanimus, in virga ferrea malleans & confrin-
„ gens eos cum fautoribus & credentibus eorum,
„ Adeò quod nomen ejus quaſi gladioſum in auribus
„ hæreticalium reſonet uſque hodie. In quadam ſen-
„ tentia à ſe lata anno 1243. nominat Fratrem Guillel-
„ mum Raymundi Collegam ſuum, & in alia anno 1244.
„ nominat Fratrem Petrum Duranti, ut Inquiſitio-
„ nis ſocium & collegam. Erant enim tunc plures
„ Inquiſitores ſimul. Hæc F. Reginaldus.

4. Advertere hic neceſſe arbitror à nece Fratris
Stephani & Fratris Raymundi Inquiſitorum ex almo
Ordine

Figure 12.3 Jean-Jacques Percin, *Monumenta Conventus Tolosani* (Toulouse, 1693),
p. 52b. Detail showing Percin's first use of Antonin Réginald's *Chronicon*. Private
collection.

1240–50 no. 3[1]

In catalogo inquisitorum à Fr. Nostro Antonino Reginaldo compilato, de quo saepius in decursu, fit mentio hoc eodem anno Fratris Cellani seu Syllani, cujus in veteri Registro ponuntur sententiæ folio II. fuisseque Inquisitorem duobus saltem annis colligitur: annis scilicet 1242. post necem F. Guill. Arnaldi & anno 1243. post quem nominatur Inquisitor *F. Ferrarius Cathalanus*, de quo Fr. Bernardus Guidonis

In the *Catalogue of Inquisitors*[2] by our Brother Antonin Réginald – from whom more hereafter – there is mention this same year of Brother Cellan, or Syllan,[3] whose sentences are recorded in an old Register [*r*: beginning] on folio 2.[4] And it is gathered from these that he was inquisitor for at least two years: in the years [*r*: year], that is, 1242, after the killing of Brother Guillaume Arnaud,[5] and in the year 1243. After him Brother Ferrier Catalan is named Inquisitor, on whom Brother Bernard Gui has

---

[1] *Monumenta* (Henceforth M), p. 52b no. 3.

[2] Elsewhere *Chronicon or Chronico Inquisitorum*.

[3] J. Feuchter, *Ketzer, Konsuln und Büsser: die städtischen Eliten von Montauban vor dem Inquisitor Petrus Cellani (1236/1241)*, Spätmittelalter, Humanismus, Reformation 40 (Tübingen, 2007), ch. 5; J. Feuchter, 'The first systematic mass inquisition: Peter Sellan in the Quercy, 1234–1236', in *The Origins of Inquisition*, ed. L. J. Sackville (forthcoming)

[4] The form of the documents and their dates suggest this is a lost register, rather than the extant register of guilty acts (*culpae*) and penances in Quercy in 1241–2, ed. J. Duvernoy, *L'inquisition en Quercy. Le registre des penitences de Pierre Cellan 1241–1242* (Castelnaud La Chapelle, 2001) and Feuchter, *Ketzer*, pp. 453–89. On the precise nature of these and the dates 1241–2, ibid., pp. 63–6; on one instance of Sellan's activity as an inquisitor in 1242, p. 306 n. 191; acting as a witness, p. 306.

[5] 28 May 1242: Y. Dossat, 'Le massacre d'Avignonet', *Cahiers de Fanjeaux* 6 (1971), 343–59; on Guillaume as inquisitor, Dossat, *Crises de l'inquisition Toulousaine au XIIIe siècle (1233–1273)* (Bordeaux, 1959) pp. 122–50, 217–22, 224–5.

" in catalogo Priorum Carcassonæ sic habet. Hic fuit
" Inquisitor & persecutor hæreticorum constans &
" magnanimus, in virga ferrea malleans & confrin-
" gens eos cum fautoribus & credentibus eorum.
" Adeò quod nomen ejus quasi gladiosum in auribus
" hæreticalium resonet usque hodie. In quadam sen-
" tentia à se lata anno 1243. nominat Fratrem *Guillel-*
" *mum Raymundi collegam suum*, & in alia anno 1244.
" nominat *Fratrem Petrum Duranti* ut Inquisitio-
" nis socium & collegam. Erant enim tunc plures
" Inquisitores simul. Hæc F. Reginaldus.

it thus, in [his] *Catalogue of the Priors of Carcassonne*.[6] 'He was an Inquisitor and resolute and valiant persecutor of heretics, with an iron rod hammering and beating them together with their supporters and believers, to such an extent that even today his name resonates like a sword in the ears of hereticals'.[7] In a sentence delivered by him in the year 1243, he names Brother Guillaume Raymond his colleague,[8] and in another sentence in the year 1244 he names Brother Pierre Durand as his companion and colleague in inquisition.[9] There were, then, several inquisitors [in office] at the same time. These things: Brother Réginald.

[6] On Ferrier, see W.L. Wakefield, 'Friar Ferrier, Inquisitor', *Heresis* 7 (1986), 35–41.

[7] Bernard Gui, *De fundatione et prioribus conventuum provinciarum Tolosanae et Provincia Ordinis Praedicatorum*, ed. P. A. Amargier, Monumenta Ordinis Fratrum Praedicatorum Historica 24 (Rome, 1961), p. 100. This was in vol. 7 of the convent 's collection of Gui's works; *M*, p. 70b no. 7.

[8] On Guillaume Raymond, see Dossat, pp. 89 n. 2, 150, 153 n. 5, 154, 167–9, 172; L. J. Sackville, 'The *Ordo Processus Narbonensis*: The Earliest Inquisitor's Manual, Lost and Refound', *Aevum* 93 (2019), 363–95. In a sentence of 1244, Ferrier described Guillaume as a former colleague (olim collega); Doat Ms 21, fol. 313r, a copy of a manuscript which was in the Toulouse convent. See the next note.

[9] Ferrier and Pierre Durand are the current joint inquisitors in the sentence of 1244 cited in the previous note, as also in the following sentence of 1244 in the same manuscript, fol. 315r. This supports the possibility that Réginald's 1243 for William Raymond's action with Ferrier rests on lopping one year from 1244 to take account of 'formerly'. On Pierre Durand see Dossat, *Crises*, pp. 153 n. 5, 154, 16 7–9, 172, 199 n. 90; Wakefield, 'Friar Ferrier', 36.

1249 no. 14[10]

" Circà haec tempora ex mss. F. Guidonis erat Inqui-
" sitor Tolos. *F. Bern. de Caucio,* de quo suprà locutus
" sum, persecutor & Malleus haereticorū, vir sanctus &
" Deo plenus. Fuit Fundator Conventûs Aginn. ipsum-
" que locū. suo corpore dedicavit, quod post 28. annos
" & plus, elevatum à terra, & in Ecclesiam, ubi nunc
" jacet, translatum, totum integrum est inventum di-
" vino munere specialis gratiae tanto tempore conser-
" vatum. Dicitur Inquisitor ab anno 1243. usque ad
" 1249. ejusque obitus ponitur anno 1252.. In Regi-
" stris Inquisitionis multa de illo, & de F. Joanne à
" sancto Petro. Nam à primo Registro fol. 45. usque
" ad folium 169. sunt sententiæ & pœnitentiae ab illis
" latae et impositae abjurantibus hæresim, sicut & in

From the manuscripts of Brother Gui:[11] around these times the Toulouse Inquisitor was Brother Bernard de Caux, of whom I spoke above,[12] a persecutor and hammer of heretics, 'a holy man and filled with God. He was the founder of the convent of Agen, and he consecrated that place with his body which – when more than twenty-eight years later it was raised from the earth and translated into the church where it now lies – was found to be entirely intact; by the divine favour of special grace preserved fior such a long time'.[13] He is called 'Inquisitor' from the year 1243 right up to 1249, and his death is placed in the year 1252. There are many things about him and about Brother Jean de Saint-Pierre in registers of inquisition.[14] For, from the first register folio 45 up to folio 169,[15] there are sentences and penances delivered and imposed by them on those abjuring heresy, just as

---

10 *M*, p. 54a no. 14.

11 Meaning, from the ten manuscript volumes of Gui's works held in the convent, described *M*, p. 70a–b no. 7.

12 'of whom I spoke above': an interpolation by Percin, referring to an earlier passage (*M*, p. 53 no. 12) containing the form of a sentence to life imprisonment by Bernard of Caux and Jean of Saint-Pierre, used as the peg for comment on why one should not regard the sentence as too harsh.

13 Gui, *De fundatione*, p. 109. On Bernard: Y. Dossat, 'Une figure d'inquisiteur, Bernard de Caux', *Cahiers de Fanjeaux* 6 (1971), 253–72.

14 Nothing is known about Jean beyond his acting together with Bernard de Caux, and that he was not the same as another inquisitor of the same name from Bordeaux, active 1255–7; Dossat, *Crises*, p. 155, and n. 18 below.

15 Dossat, *Crises*, p. 38 no. 4. A fragment was saved in 1781; C. Douais, *Documents pour servir à l'histoire de l'Inquisition dans le Languedoc* (Paris, 1900), pp. cclii–cclxvi. Currently Paris, Bibliothèque nationale de France, Ms Lat. 9992, fols. 151r–62r; it was edited by Douais, *Documents*, pp. 1–89. Its foliation – CLI–CLXII – falls within the nos. 45–169 of the original seen by Réginald.

" aliis Registris, ubi semper procedit cum fratre Jo-
" anne à Sancto Petro, de quo infrà dicam. Hæc nos-
" ter F. Reginaldus.

in the other Registers,[16] where he [Bernard] always proceeds with Brother Jean de Saint-Pierre, about whom I shall speak below. These things: our Brother Réginald.

1250–60: 1254[17]

Eodem anno *F. Joannes à S. Petro*, de quo
supra, Inquisitionem fecit, & F. Reginaldus Inquisitor
pariter. Primus fuit Prior Burdigalensis & Visitator
nominatus in Capitulo Lemovicensi anno 1233. secun-

In the same year Brother Jean de Saint-Pierre – on whom [see] above – carried out inquisition and likewise the Inquisitor Brother Renaud.[18] The former was prior of Bordeaux and nominated visitor in the chapter of Limoges in the year 1233

[16] Note here that the famous surviving 1260 copy (Toulouse Bibliothèque municipale Ms 609) of interrogations by Bernard de Caux and Jean de Saint-Pierre was of books 4 and 5 of confessions in front of them; Dossat, *Crises*, p. 57. Plural 'Registers' used here leaves open the possibility that others were still extant.

[17] *M*, pp. 54b–55a no. 4; no quotation marks.

[18] In extant records the earliest date of Jean de Saint-Pierre and Renaud de Chartres acting together is 1 July 1255; Toulouse Ms 609, fol. 140v. Describing Jean as prior of Bordeaux, Gui also says that he was Toulouse inquisitor from 1255; *De fundatione*, p. 84. Another ms available to Réginald, Register 6, contained references to the two inquisitors, but without dates; *Inquisitors and Heretics in Thirteenth-Century Languedoc: Edition and Translation of Toulouse Inquisition Depositions, 1273–1282*, ed. P. Biller, C. Bruschi and S. Sneddon, Studies in the History of Christian Traditions 147 (Leiden and Boston, 2011), pp. 364–5, 366–7, 440–1, 724–5, 932–3, 952–3. Dossat noticed that in June 1255 the Toulouse inquisitors were called 'new inquisitors' (novi inquisitores), in an official act; C. de Vic and J.J.Vaissete, *Histoire générale de Languedoc, avec des notes et les pièces justificatives*, ed. A. Molinier and others,3rd edn, 16 vols. (Toulouse, 1872–1905; henceforth HGL), VIII, 1372 no.450 (ii), cited Dossat, *Crises*, p. 185. Dossat, ibid., pp. 190–1, persuasively distinguished two inquisitors called Jean de Saint-Pierre, one active together with Bernard of Caux 1243–9, and another from Bordeaux active together with Renaud de Chartres 1255–7. A third Jean de Saint-Pierre, assigned as a student to Narbonne at the provincial chapter of Castres in 1279 (*Acta Capitulorum Provincialium Ordinis Fratrum Praedicatorum*, ed. C. Douais, 2 vols. (Paris, 1894; henceforth ACP), II, 227 no. 7) underlines the point that it was a common name. On Renaud, see Douais, *Documents*, pp. lxxviii n. 4, clv, clvii, clviii, clxiv, clxvi–clxvii; Dossat, *Crises*, index p. 384; *Inquisitors and Heretics*, ed. Biller, Bruschi and Sneddon, pp. 40, 89, 362, 365 and n. 12, 440–1, 724–5, 932–3, 952–3; *Le livre des sentences de l'inquisiteur Bernard Gui, 1308–1323*, ed. A. Pales-Gobilliard, 2 vols. (Paris, 2002), I, 736–7.

/55a/ dus verò cognominatus de Carnoto. Ambo contrahunt ut Inquisitores cum *civibus Vaurensibus* pro Ecclesia Majori Vaurensi construenda ut habetur in 4. Registro Inquisitorum, in Mss. Guidonis & in Chronico Fratris nostri Antonini Reginaldi, ille actus referetur integrè in opusculo de inquisitione.

1260–70: 1260[21]

" Circà hæc tempora, in Chron. F. Reginaldi,
" *F. Guillelmus Revelli*[22] *Inquisitorem*[23] *agebat.* Fuit bis
" Prior Petragoricensis è cujus Diœcesi oriundus
" erat, & ejus recitantur sententiæ in 2. Registro ter-
" tia parte fol. 60. pag. 2. ubi etiam fit mentio fratris
" Bernardi de Cantio & *F. Guillelmi Arnaldi* pro fi-
" de occisi quondam Inquisitorum, & tandem in 6.

[r: 1253],[19] the latter was surnamed de Chartres. As inquisitors both of them came to an agreement with the citizens of Lavaur, that the major church of Lavaur should be built, as is contained in the Inquisitors' Register [no.] 4, in the manuscripts of Gui, and in the *Chronicle* of our Brother Antonin Réginald. The whole of this act is recorded in *The Little Work on Inquisition*.[20]

Around the same time, in the *Chronicle* of Brother Réginald, Brother Guillaume Reveil [r de Montreveil] was carrying out inquisition. He was twice prior of Périgueux, from which diocese he originated,[24] and his sentences are recorded in Register 2, the third part, folio 60, verso, where there is also mention of the former Inquisitors Brother Bernard de Caux and Brother Guillaume Arnaud, [the latter] killed for the faith.[25] And finally,

[19] The source for this was the acts of the chapter, reported with an error in one digit – 1253 not 1233; *ACP*, II, 57. Gui's edition of these acts was in volume 7 of the convent's collection of his works; *M*, p. 70b no. 7.

[20] Jean-Jacques Percin, *Opusculum de inquisitionis nomine, institutione et exercitio, M*, part 2, p. 97a–b, no. 4; Dossat, *Crises*, p. 185.

[21] *M*, p. 57b no. 3.

[22] *r.* de Monte Revelli.

[23] *r.* inquisitionem.

[24] Derived from Gui, *De fundatione*, p. 92. See on him Dossat, *Crises*, pp. 194 and 318, and *Inquisitors and Heretics*, ed. Biller, Bruschi and Sneddon, pp. 38, 40, 450 and n. 15.

[25] In depositions in front of Guillaume de Montreveil detailing deponents' earlier appearances before Bernard de Caux and Guillaume Arnaud.

" Registro fol. 125. pag. 1. in fine, idem F. Reuvelli
" vocatur quondam Inquisitor.

1260–70: 1260[27]

" Eodem anno Inquisitor Tolosanus fuit post fra-
" trem *Guill. Revelli, F. Stephanus Vastini*, ut con- / 58a /
" stat ex Registro 6. pag. 2.[28] Et fuisse Inquisitorem
" colligitur anno 1273. 1274. 1275. quo anno folio 133.
" pag. 2. fit mentio Fratris *Hugonis de Boniolis, Bo-*
" *niols* in Occitania Dioccesis Uticensis. Vir fuit ma-

in Register 6, folio 125, recto, at the bottom, the same Brother Reveil is called 'the former Inquisitor'.[26]

In the same year the Toulouse Inquisitor after Brother Guillaume Revel was Brother Etienne Gâtine, as is clear from Register 6 [folio and its no.] verso.[29] And it is gathered that he was inquisitor in the year 1273, 1274 [and] 1275.[30] In which year [1275] on folio 135 verso there is mention of Brother Hugues de Boniolis: [that is], Boniol[31] in Occitanie in the diocese of Uzès.

---

26 The only reference in the modern edition of the Doat copy of Register 6 (*Inquisitors and Heretics*, ed. Biller, Bruschi and Sneddon, p. 450) is to 'the aforesaid Guillaume de Reveil, later inquisitor', where 'aforesaid' is puzzling, since the text contains no previous reference: a copyist's mistake? This omitted earlier text is a plausible candidate for the text to which Réginald was referring. See the table of Réginald's references to Register 6 in *Inquisitors and Heretics*, ed. Biller, Bruschi and Sneddon, pp. 18–19.

27 *M*, pp. 57b–8a.

28 Folio no. missing.

29 On Etienne, see Douais, *Documents*, pp. clxix–clxxii, ccxiv; Dossat, *Crises*, pp. 46 no. 6, 154, 178 n. 45, 194–5; *Inquisitors and Heretics*, ed. Biller, Bruschi and Sneddon, pp. 62, 8 0, 257 n. 4, 556 n. 11, 681 n. 9, 784 n. 31, 796 n. 56; the reference to him in the Doat copy of Register 6: ibid., pp. 555–6; *Le livre des sentences*, ed. Pales-Gobilliard, i.206–7, 498–9, 922–3, ii.1104–5.

30 Three consecutive sentences are problematic here: the one containing dates for Etienne de Gâtine, which could not be gathered from Register 6 (or at least its Doat copy); the discussion of Hugues de Boniol, whose career as inquisitor is dealt with again in a later passage; and a plain error about Boniol (see n. 34 below). Our suggestion is that here Percin garbled and interpolated Réginald's text.

31 On Hugues, see Douais, *Documents*, pp. clxxxi, clxxxii; Dossat, *Crises*, pp. 33, 46 no. 7; *Inquisitors and Heretics*, ed. Biller, Bruschi and Sneddon, pp. 48, 51, 60, 76, 82, 557 n. 9, 681 n. 9, 865 n. 14, 920 n. 3; *Le livre des sentences*, ed. Pales-Gobilliard, i.922–3, ii.1104–5, 1106–7. The references to him in the Doat copy of Register 6: ibid., pp. 650–1, 690–1, 696–7, 712–3, 920–1, 930–1. See Boniol, comm. and cant. Bessèges, arrond. Alès, Gard.

" gnæ virtutis & litteraturæ, inquit Chronicon, quem
" fuisse deputatum ad visitandos Conventus Ordinis
" nostri in Scotia lego à Capitulo Generali Barcino-
" nensi 1261. Illi successit in Officio Inquisitoris ex "
" Registro sexto fol. 4. Frater Raymundus seu Ray-
" nulphus de Placiato, pro ut comportum[32] est ex ci-
" tato Registro 6. fol. 4. qui etiam expressè Inquisi-
" tor dicitur anno superiori 1273. & quia Frater *Pon-*
" *tius de Parnaco* Caturcensis vocatur etiam *Inqu-*
" *isitor* citato Registro 6. folio 4. simul exercuisse sanc-
" tum Officium probabile est. Fuit autem F. *Pon-*
" *tius* Prior Perpigniani numeraturque inter Priore

He[33] was a man of great virtue and learning, says the *Chronicle*, who I read was deputed at the chapter-general of Barcelona in 1261 to visit the convents of our Order in Scotland.[34] From Register 6 folio 4: Brother Raymond or Renous de Plassac succeeded him in the office of Inquisitor, as is found in the cited Register 6, folio 4[35] – who is also expressly called Inquisitor in the earlier year 1273 [= earlier than the last year, 1274, listed for Hugues de Boniol]. And because Brother Pons de Parnac of Cahors is also called Inquisitor in the cited Register 6 folio 4, it is probable that they exercised the holy office at the same time.[36] Further, Brother Pons was prior of Perpignan and is numbered among the priors by Brother Bernard Gui,[37] and from that he was

[32] *r.* compertum.

[33] Hugues of Boniol or Etienne Gâtine?

[34] The second part of this sentence seems to be an interpolation by Percin, given the move from 'says the *Chronicle*' in the third person to the first person of 'I read'. The added information is wrong. The modern edition – based on a Bordeaux manuscript, taking the Toulouse manuscript into account – shows that the friar assigned was Etienne de Salagnac, not Hugues de Boniol or Etienne Gâtine; *Acta generalium Ordinis Fratrum Praedicatorum*, vol. 1, *Ab anno 1220 ad annum 1303*, ed. B.M. Reichert, Monumenta Ordinis Frarum Praedicatorum Historica 3 (Rome, 1898), p. 112. The following sentence contained the word Bononiam (Bologna). Rapid reading of the two sentences could have led to Percin thinking the assigned friar's name began with Bon-. The convent's manuscript was bound in volume 6 of Gui's works; *Monumumenta*, p. 70b.

[35] Probably the equivalent of fol. 14r in the Doat copy of Register 6; see *Inquisitors and Heretics*, ed. Biller, Bruschi and Sneddon, pp. 18–19, 204–5. On Renous de Plassac, see ibid., pp. 50–1, and the index-entry (under Ranulph of Plassac) 1041–2; *Le livre des sentences*, ed. Pales-Gobilliard, i.184–5, 746–7.

[36] On Pons, see *Inquisitors and Heretics*, ed. Biller, Bruschi and Sneddon, ch. 2, and the index-entry, p. 1040; *Le livre des sentences*, ed. Pales-Gobilliard, i.184–5, 746–7, 922–3. On the suggestion that he was probably the author of the treatise *Doctrina de modo procedendi contra hereticos*, see J.H. Arnold and P. Biller, *Heresy and Inquisition in France, 1200–1300*, Manchester Medieval Sources (Manchester, 2016), pp. 270–1, transl. ibid., pp. 271–88.

[37] *De fundatione*, p. 256.

" à F. Bernardo Guidonis, indeque assumptus est ad
" Officium *Inquisitoris*, quod solus exercuit anno
" 1275.. & posteà cum dicto *F. Hugone de Boniolis.*
" Hæc citatus F. Reginaldus.

[We attribute the following passage to Percin, who cites a register which seems to be based on a mid-fifteenth-century forgery.]

1270–80: 1270[40]

Ex nostris mss. anno 1270, mense Junio datæ sunt patentes litteræ ab *Alfonso Comite Pictaviensi, & Joanne Comitissa* ejus uxore, filia *Raymundi ultimi Tolosæ Comitis pro Inquisitore Tolosano,* quibus *Inquisitionis* officium confirmant: quæ referuntur in *Registro Inquisitionis,* ubi etiam referuntur littera *Philippi Regis Galliæ 26. Junii anno 1334.* confirmantes *Exercitium & Jurisdictionem Inquisitionis*

taken up to the office of Inquisitor, which he carried out on his own in 1275,[38] and later together with the said Brother Hugues de Boniol.[39]

These things: the cited Brother Réginald.

From our manuscripts.[41] In the month of June in the year 1270 letters patent were given by Alfonse count of Poitiers and his wife countess Jeanne, daughter of Raymond, the last count of Toulouse, on behalf of the Toulouse Inquisitor, with which they confirmed the office of the Inquisition.[42] These are recorded in an Inquisition Register, in which there are also recorded letters of Philip, king of Gaul, 26 June in the year 1334, confirming the exercise and jurisdiction of the Inquisition of Toulouse, folio

---

[38] *Inquisitors and Heretics*, ed. Biller, Bruschi and Sneddon, pp. 690–1, 602–3, 608–11, 614–15.

[39] Ibid., pp. 630–1, 690–1, 696–7.

[40] *M*, p. 60b no. 1.

[41] Dossat, *Crises*, p. 40 no. 12, called it a register of inquisition privileges. He did not notice that all three items in it are reported in the same order, albeit with fewer details, in the *Chronique* of Guillaume de Bardin, written in the mid-fifteenth century and regarded as a forgery; *HGL*, IX, Preuves, 7, 37–8, 43. While including it Percin did not cite Réginald or supply quotation marks.

[42] Set plausibly within a general account of Alphonse and the inquisition by Dossat, *Crises*, p. 279.

Tolosæ. folio 169 & in eodem Registro fol. 210. refertur juramentum *Ludovici de Poitiers* proregis Occitaniæ factum in manibus *Inquisitoris Tolosani* anno 1340. Quod eodem anno referam.

1270–80: 1276[45]

″ Anno 1276. *F. Hugo Amelii de Castro novo*
″ *Arii Prior Tolosæ*, præfuit annis duobus, factus
″ autem est de Priore *Inquisitor* anno 1278. Hic fuit &[46]
″ *F. Guidone* vir justus & rectus, constans & famo-
″ sus, & existens Inquisitor obiit in Conventu Ni-
″ ciensi in itinere Romanæ curiæ constitutus anno
″ 1281. cujus ossa translata sunt de Conventu Niciensi
″ in Tolosanum: quod indicium est magnæ apud
″ Fratres Tolosæ fuisse existimationi sanctitatis. Quod autem spectat ad Inquisitionem, *F. Petrus Arsivi*[47]

169.[43] And in the same Register, folio 210, there is recorded the oath of Louis of Poitiers, viceroy in Occitania, in the hands of the Toulouse Inquisitor, in the year 1340[44] – which I shall report under the same year [in the later entry for 1340].

In the year 1276 Brother Hugues Amiel of Castelnaudary [became] prior of Toulouse, was in charge for two years, and from being prior became Inquisitor in the year 1278. From Brother Gui: 'he was a just, upright, resolute and famous man, and in the year 1281 while still Inquisitor he died in the convent in Nice on a journey to the curia in Rome; his bones were translated from the convent in Nice to the Toulousan [convent]':[48] a mark of the great opinion of his holiness among the brothers of Toulouse. What relates, however, to inquisition – at this time Brother Pierre Arsieu was the Inquisitor;[49] from Brother Gui,

---

[43] See *HGL*, X, Preuves, 37–8, with the date 1334 but not 26 June; compare 1303 below. There is no trace of this in J.-M. Vidal, *Bullaire de l'inquisition française au XIVe siècle et jusqu'à la fin du grande schisme* (Paris, 1913).

[44] Louis, count of Poitiers and Diois (ob. 1345), was named viceroy in Languedoc in December 1340, and visited Toulouse several times; *HGL*, IX, 626–40.

[45] *M*, p. 62b no. 13

[46] *r* ex.

[47] The cessation here of the quotation marks seems to be a mistake, given the final acknowledgement to Réginald.

[48] *De fundatione*, p. 52, slightly adapted. See on him C. Douais, *Les frères prêcheurs en Gascogne au XIIIe et au XIVe siècle. Chapitres, couvents et notices*, 2 vols. (Paris and Auch, 1885), II, 428; Douais, *Douments*, clxxxi–clxxxii; *Inquisitors and Heretics*, ed. Biller, Bruschi and Sneddon, pp. 48–51, 79–82, and index-entry 1022; *Le livre des sentences*, ed. Pales-Gobilliard, i.184–5, 736–7.

[49] On him, see *Inquisitors and Heretics*, ed. Biller, Bruschi and Sneddon, pp. 48–51, and the index-entry, 1029.

fuit hoc tempore *Inquisitor* ex F. Guidonis, qui ipsum etiam numerat inter Priores Carcassonenses, & à castro Malvesii *Mauvesin*, Diœcesis nunc Lumbariensis dicit esse oriundum, factumque asserit *Inquisitorem* die Lunæ post festum S. Jacobi anno 1277. & Tolosæ obiisse anno sequ. 1278. De eo in Registro sexto Inquisitionis folio 148. agitur. Ab anno autem 1278. usque ad 1281. *Inquisitor fuit F. Hugo Amelii*, qui ut jam dicebam, fuit Prior. De eo in Registro Inquisitionis 6. folio 160. & deinde sub finem dicti Registri pluries fit mentio ejus ex F. Reginaldo.

who also counts him among the priors of Carcassonne, and says that he originated in the *castrum* of Malvesie – Mauvesin[50] – now in the diocese of Lombez, and states that he was made Inquisitor on the Monday after the feast of St James in the year 1277 and died in Toulouse in the following year, 1278.[51] On him – he is at issue in the 6th Register of inquisition, folio 148.[52] From the year 1278 right up to 1281 the Inquisitor was Hugues Amiel who, as I have already said, was prior.[53] There is mention many times of him in inquisition register 6 on folio 160 and thereafter up to the end of the said register: from Brother Réginald.

1270–80 (previous date is 1278)[54]

F. Hugo de Boniolis fuit circa hæc tempora *Inquisitor*, ut constat ex Registro 6. in quo de eo fit mentio anno 1275. unà cum *Fratre Pontio de Parnaco* & folio 185. idem *F. Hugo de Boniolis, & F. Hugo Amelii* nominantur *Inquisitores* annis 1278. & 1279.

Around this time Brother Hugues de Boniol was Inquisitor, as is clear from Register 6, in which there is mention of him in the year 1275 together with Brother Pons de Parnac.[55] And on folio 185 the same Hugues de Boniol and Brother Hugues Amiel are named Inquisitors in the years 1278 and 1279.[56]

---

[50] Mauvezin, comm. and cant., arrond.Condom, Gers.

[51] Gui, *De fundatione*, p. 101.

[52] The Doat copy of Register 6 shows him quite often; *Inquisitors and Heretics*, ed. Biller, Bruschi and Sneddon, pp. 688–9, 712–13, 718–19, 722–3, 748–9, 756–7, 762–3, 772–3, 780–1, 8–4–805, 842–3, 846–7, 852–3. See on him Douais, *Documents*, p. clxxxi.

[53] who … prior: probably Percin's interpolation.

[54] *M*, p. 62b n. 13; no quotation marks.

[55] *Inquisitors and Heretics*, ed. Biller, Bruschi and Sneddon, pp. 650–1.

[56] Both named ibid., pp. 688–91, but not acting side by side. Amiel and another inquisitor Peter Arsieu) were acting in place of de Boniol and another (Pons of Parnac).

1280–90: 1281[57]

Anno eodem F. Joannes Galandi fuit Inquisitor ut notatur in 6. Registro, 179. pag. 2.

In the same year Brother Jean Galand was Inquisitor, as is noted in Register 6, [folio] 179, verso.[58]

1280–90: 1284[59] [1284]

" Numeratur inter Inquisitores Tolosae F. Joan-
" nes *Vigorosi de Monte Pessulano* ab anno 1284. us-
" que ad annum 1289. in Chronico F, Reginaldi,
" qui fuit Prior sancti Maximini cum consensu *Caroli* Re.
" gis Siciliae Comitis Provinciae, annis 7. et Prior Pro-
" vincialis Provinciae. Obiit tandem in Montepessu-
" lano Calendis Martii 1304. ab ingressu ordinis anno
" 54. ibi sepultus in Choro Fratrum. His subjungit
" annus dominicanus ...

In the *Chronicle* of Brother Réginald Brother Jean Vigouroux from Montpellier is counted among the Toulouse Inquisitors, from the year 1284 right up to the year 1289,[60] who was the prior of St Maximin, 'with the consent of the king' of Sicily [and] Count of Provence, Charles, 'for seven years' and 'the Prior Provincial of Provence'. Finally 'he died in Montpellier on 1 March 1304, in the fifty-fourth year from his entry into the Order', [and was] 'buried there in the Choir of the brothers'.[61] The *Année Dominicaine* added to these things...[62]

---

57 *M*, p. 62b no. 1; no quotation marks.
58 On Jean Galand, see ibid., pp. 48–9 and n. 60; appearances in Register 6: ibid., pp. 722–3, 838–9, 908–9, 910–11. See Douais, *Documents*, pp. clxxxii–cxc; *Le livre des sentences*, ed. Pales-Gobilliard, i.184–5, 498–9, ii.1106–7; translations of texts concerning him: Arnold and Biller, *Heresy and Inquisition*, pp. 174–81.
59 *M*, p. 63b no. 7.
60 One basis for dates was the Toulouse convent's manuscript of Gui's Acts of the Provincial Councils. Jean is noted as Toulouse inquisitor when acting as a diffinitor for the chapters of Perpignan, 1284, and Avignon, 1288; *ACP*, i.273 n. 2, 282 no. xii; 311 n. 2. On Jean, see Douais, *Frères prêcheurs*, II, 441–2; C. Douais, *Essai sur l'organisation des études dans l'ordre du Frères Prêcheurs au treizième et au quatorzième siècle (1216–1342)* (Paris and Toulouse, 1884), pp. 93–5; Douais, *Documents*, pp. xxx n. 5, clxxxii, clxxxvi, cxcl, ccxxviii n. 2; *Livre des sentences*, ed. Pales-Gobilliard, i.206–207, 266–7, 498–9; D. Toti, 'François Graverol e un manoscritto perduto de ll'Inquisizione di Tolosa', *Riforma e Movimenti Religiosi* 8 (2020), 215–89 (231–2, 254–6).
61 Gui, *De fundatione*, p. 249.
62 Réginald ends and Percin begins to cite from the history, *Annus dominicanus*, compiled by Thomas Souèges OP (1633–98).

1280–90 [preceding numbered sections: no. 5: 1285. no. 6: 'at that time'. no. 7: 1284–9][63]

"Eodem tempore vivebat *Frater Conradus pe-*
"*regrinus Tolosanus* …

    "Huic æqualis fuit *Frater Petrus de Mul-*
"*ceone*, qui Prior fuit Brivensis, & Prior pariter Le-
" movicensis. Hic fuit ex Chro. F. Reginaldi vir Deo
"gratus & hominibus famosus in tota patria, nobi-
"lis genere nobilior virtute humilitatis, super mise-
"os & afflictos gestans viscera pietatis. Fuit etiam
"Prior Monspeliensis & *Inquisitor Tolosanus* paulò
"post natale Domini 1289. posteà Prior Provincialis,
"& obiit tandem in Conventu Montalbanensi non-
"dùm finito Provincialatùs tempore anno 1295. in fe-
"sto sanctæ Marthæ, ubi primò sepultus est, et posteà
"in suum Conventum, Brivensem translatus decreto
"Capituli Provincialis Cathurcensis anno 1298. Quod
"equidem magnam opinionem sanctitatis de eo fuisse
"demonstrat.

[Percin] Living at the same was Brother Conrad Peregrin of Toulouse…[64]

    Contemporary to him was Brother Pierre de Mulceone, who was prior of Brives, and prior also of Limoges. 'He was' – from the *Chronicle* of Brother Réginald – 'a man pleasing to God and men, famous throughout the country, noble by birth but nobler by virtue of humility, opening the bowels of mercy to the wretched and the afflicted'.[65] He was prior of Montpellier and Toulouse Inquisitor shortly after Christmas 1289, later prior Provincial, and, finally, before the period of his provincialate had ended, he died, in the year 1295 on the feast of Saint Martha, [and] in the convent of Montauban, where he was buried first; and later he was translated to his own convent of Brive, by decree of the provincial chapter of Cahors in the year 1298, which certainly shows that there was a high view of his sanctity.[66]

---

63 *M*, p. 63b no. 8.

64 The preceding numbered sections: no. 5: 1285. no. 6: 'at that time'. no. 7: 1284–9. We have not found Conrad Peregrin. A Peregrin of Saint-Gaudens entered the Order in Toulouse and died there in 1286; Douais, *Gascogne*, II, 447.

65 Gui, *De fundatione*, p. 64. The rest of the text is still reliant on Gui, but adapts more freely.

66 On Pierre de Mulceone, see Douais, *Frères prêcheurs*, II, 457; *Livre des sentences*, ed. Pales-Gobilliard, i.180–5, 206–7, 312–13, 314–15, 746–7; Toti, 'François Graverol', 232, 266.

1290–1300: 1292[67]

Anno 1292. F. *Bertrandus de Claro-Monte* re-nunciatur Tolosanus *Inquisitor* ex Lectore Tolosæ & Priore Bergeracensi & Narbonensi. Fuit *Inquisitor* ex Chro. F. *Reginaldi* duobus annis, Prior Provincialis, et Prior Burdigalensis: obiitque in senectute bona in Conventu Bergeracensis, Dominicâ infrà Octavam Omnium Sanctorum anno 1312.

In the year 1292 Brother Bertrand of Clermont is reported as Toulouse Inquisitor, from being [earlier] lector in Toulouse and prior of Bergerac and Narbonne. He was Inquisitor – from the *Chronicle* of Brother Réginald – for two years, prior Provincial and prior of Bordeaux, and died in good old age at the convent of Bergerac, on Sunday within the octave of All Saints, in the year 1312.[68]

1290–1300[69]

F. *Arnaldus de Prato* … / 65a /
"
         … Fuit
"etiam Tolosæ Inquisitor ….
"
         … Fuit Diffinitor in Capitulo Pro-

'Brother Arnaud de Prat … He was also the Toulouse Inquisitor… '. He was diffinitor in the provincial chapter of Perpignan, 1299, together with the Toulouse Inquisitor Bernard [*recte* Bertrand] of Clermont.[70] These things: the manuscripts of Gui.[71]

---

[67] *M*, p. 64b no. 5; no quotation marks.

[68] From Gui, *De fundatione*, pp. 103, 173, but with an error – Gui said that he was Toulouse inquisitor for eight years. If Réginald noted only the first two references to him as inquisitor in the manuscripts of the acts of provincial chapters, in 1293 and 1295, he could have emerged with a small number. But these references continued in the acts of later chapters, 1297, 1299, with 1301 the first chapter where he was not inquisitor; *ACP*, I, 372 n. 3, 394 n. 2, 411 n. 1, 434–5 n. 1 and 442 n. xi, 456–7 n. 1 and 466 no. x. The acts refer to controversial events in Bertrand's career, including his removal from office in 1284 and the composition of a defamatory letter against him in 1285 (*ACP*, I, 280, 290 no. 5), which have not affected Réginald's short account. See further in Gui, *De fundatione*, pp. 67, 77, 87–8, 92, 104, 172, 253; Douais, *Frères prêcheurs*, II, 397–8; Douais, *Documents*, pp. xcvii n. 1, cxxxii n. 3, cxci–cxcvii, ccxlv, ccxci, 322 n. 1; G.W. Davis, *The Inquisition at Albi 1299–1300. Text of Register and Analysis* (New York, 1948), pp. 57, 183, 189, 205, 235, 245; *Le livre des sentences*, ed. Pales-Gobilliard, i.478–9; Toti, 'François Graverol', 232, 270.

[69] *M*, pp. 64b–5a no. 7.

[70] Douais, *Frères prêcheurs*, II, 397–8.

[71] Prat did nothing as an inquisitor, as Réginald will have known through his knowledge of inquisition registers and Gui's picture of Prat as a charming and cultured favourite at the papal court. Apart from his formal title as inquisitor, Prat's career had nothing to contribute

"vinciali Perpigniani 1299. cum Fratre Bernardo de "Claromonte Inquisitore Tolosano. Haec mss. Gui-"donis.

1300–1400, 1300–10: 1301[72]

"... Hoc item anno & sequenti erat Inquisitor "Tolosanus Fr. *Fulco de Sancto Georgio Viennensis.* "qui obiit Carcassone 1307. fuerat Prior Ruthenen-"sis, Carcassonensis & Albiensis. Hoc item anno / 67b / "Albiae condemnati sunt pro crimine haeresis 25. Ca-"tholice fidei desertores. Haec mss.

1301... In this year and the following one the Toulouse Inquisitor was Brother Foulques de Saint-Georges, from Vienne, who died at Carcassonne, 1307. He had been prior of Rodez, Carcassonne and Albi. In this same year twenty-five people at Albi, deserters from the Catholic faith, were condemned on the charge of heresy. These things: the manuscripts [of Gui].[73]

to the *Chronicle.* The part in quotation marks – not transcribed here – was put together entirely from Gui, *De fundatione,* pp. 54 and 158, and the second part from Gui's edition of the acts of the provincial chapters, ACP, I, 434–5 n. 1. See Douais, *Frères prêcheurs,* II, 365; T. Kaeppeli and E. Panella, *Scriptores Ordinis Praedicatorum medii aevi,* 4 vols. (Rome, 1970–93), I, 127–8, nos. 326–8.

72 *M,* p.67a no. 3.
73 On this scandalous inquisitor, see Douais, *Documents,* pp. xcviii, cxcii, ccxii, ccxli; Davis, *Inquisition at Albi,* index-entry 'Foulkes', p. 316; *Processus Bernardi Delitiosi: The Trial of Fr. Bernard Délicieux, 3 September – 8 December 1319,* ed. A. Friedlander, Transactions of the American Philosophical Society 86.1 (Philadelphia, 1996), index-entry, pp. 384–5; *Heresy and Inquisition,* ed. Arnold and Biller, index-entry, p. 513; Toti, 'François Graverol', 233, 273; H. C. Lea, *A History of the Inquisition of the Middle Ages,* 3 vols. (New York, 1887), II, 65, 67, 72, 76–80, 103; A. Friedlander, *The Hammer of Inquisitors. Brother Bernard Délicieux and the Struggle Against the Inquisition in Fourteenth-Century France* (Leiden, Boston and Cologne, 2000), pp. 88–91 and 95–7; Gui's account of Foulques and his successor Guillaume de Morières, in his catalogue of the priors of Albi (*De fundatione,* p. 200), is tight-lipped, not mentioning the scandal. But he does write that Guillaume was made inquisitor while still prior and when he was in Paris, and that Foulques had been released from the office of inquisitor but not – as was usual – at a provincial chapter or by a letter from the provincial prior. An attentive reader would have noticed there was something odd. Réginald used these entries, omitting Foulques's dismissal from office. Very slightly later the first volume of Thomas Souèges's *Année dominicaine* suggests continuing knowledge of opposition to him. It presented the sufferings of 'Faucon de S. George' as inquisitor leading to him dying as a 'sort of martyr' (une espece de martyre'); under the name of Jean-Baptiste Feuillet rather than Souèges, *Annus dominicanus* (Amiens, 1678), p. 702.

In the year 1302. Brother Guillaume de Morières was the Toulouse Inquisitor for three years – he had exercised this office earlier, for he met the supreme pontiff on the business of the faith at Perugia, as the *Chronicle* of Brother Réginald recounts. Finally he died on 4 July 1304.[75] In the same year 1304 Brother Arnaud de Prat was Inquisitor. He was from Condom and lectured in holy scripture in Toulouse and also elsewhere for fifteen years, about which I wrote above.[76]

[Percin] Philip king of Gaul, in letters patent of 26 June 1303, confirmed the exercise and jurisdiction of the Inquisitor, as is

1300–1400, 1300–10: 1301[74]

" Anno 1302. *F. Guill. de Morerris Tol.* fuit Inquisitor "tribus annis, qui priùs hoc officium exercuerat: nam "Perusii pro negotio fidei convenit summum Ponti-"ficem, ut recitat Chronicon F. Reginaldi. Mortuus "tandem est 1304. 4. Nonas Julii. Eodem anno "1304. *F. Arnaldus de Prato* fuit Inquisitor: erat "Condomiensis & Tolosae legerat sacras litteras an-"nis 15. & alibi pariter ferè annis 15. de quo supe-"riùs scripsi.

1300–10: 1303

[Referred to in Percin's *Opusculum* on inquisition.][77]
Philippus Galliæ Rex litteris patentibus 26 Junii anno 1303. confirmat exercitium & jurisdictionem

---

[74] *M*, p. 67b no. 3, continuing straight after the previous passage.
[75] Gui, *De fundatione*, p. 200.
[76] See n. 71 above.
[77] *M*, part 2, p. 101b no. 4.

311

Inquisitoris, ut refertur in Registris Inquisitionis fol. 169. & in chron. Reginaldi eodem anno. Qui subdit. His constat sanctæ Inquisitionis officium continuò perseverasse Tolosæ, & nihil Inquisitoris auctoritati deperdit, cum Tolosæ Comitatus Coronæ Franciæ unitus est. Addam hujus testimonium ex Mss. Carcassonensi.

reported in the Registers of Inquisition, folio 169,[78] and in the Chronicle of Réginald for the same year, who adds that it is clear from these that the office of the holy Inquisition persisted continuously in Toulouse and nothing was lost from the authority of the Inquisitor after the County of Toulouse was united to the Crown of France. [Percin] I shall add evidence of this from a Carcassonne manuscript.

1300–1310: 1306[79]

"Anno eodem 1306. factus est Inquisitor To-
"losanus *F. Bernardus Guidonis* per litteras Provin-
"cialis Franciæ. 17 Calendas Februarii, ex Chron. *F.*
"*Reginaldi:* fuitque Inquisitor usque 1324. quo factus
"est *Episcopus Tudensis,* et paulò post *Lodovensis,*
"cujus habemus Registrum pro 1312. Scripsit tunc
"librum *De Practica Inquisitionis* (qui nobis est

On 16 January in the same year 1306 – from the *Chronicle of* Brother Réginald – Brother Bernard Gui was made Toulouse Inquisitor by a letter of the Provincial of France.[80] And he was Inquisitor right up to 1324 when he became bishop of Tuy, and shortly afterwards of Lodève; we have his Register for 1312. He wrote then the book *On the Practice of Inquisition*[81] – which we have lost, much to our detriment – and many other things, on

---

[78] The date and folio no. indicate that Percin was getting this from the same (apparently forged) text that he used for the passage given above under 1270, while confusing Philip the Fair (1303) with Philip IV of Valois (1334). He follows this with the *Chronicle,* where Réginald seems to have been referring to the confirmation of the Toulouse inquisition – following the removal of Foulques de Saint – Georges and the succession of Guillaume de Morières – in a letter of June 1302; *HGL,* X, Preuves, 385–6 no. viii.

[79] *M,* p. 68b no. 10.

[80] There is modern treatment of most aspects of Gui's life in *Cahiers de Fanjeaux* 16 (1981), devoted to him, and an account of him as historian in A.-M. Lamarrigue, *Bernard Gui (1261–1331). Un historien et sa méthode,* Études d'Histoire Médiévales 5 (Paris, 2000).

[81] *Practica inquisitionis heretice pravitatis,* ed. C. Douais (Paris, 1886); L. Deslisle, *Notice sur les manuscrits de Bernard Gui* (Paris, 1879), pp. 352–62; Kaeppeli and Panella, *Scriptores Ordinis Praedicatorum medii aevi,* II, 222 no. 630, IV, 51.

"deperditus, magno damno) & plura alia de quibus
"infrà. Anno 1318. fuit Lector principalis Capituli san-
"cti Stephani. Hæc ille. Porrò quomodò per litteras Provincialis Franciæ institutus dicatur Inquis-
tor, ignoro, cùm noster Provincialis Inquisitores
institueret in sua Provincia. Error igitur est, & loco
Provincialis Franciæ scribi debet Provincialis Pro-
vinciæ.

which see below.[82] In the year 1318 he was the principal lecturer to the chapter of Saint-Etienne.[83] These things: him [Réginald]. [Percin] However, I do not know how he should be said to have been instituted Inquisitor by a letter from the Provincial of France, since our Provincial would institute Inquisitors in his province. It is an error, therefore, and 'Provincial of Provence' should be written instead of 'Provincial of France'.[84]

1310–20[85]

Anno 1312. *F. Bernardo Guidonis* adjunctus est Inquisitor *F. Gaufridus de Albusiis*, de quibus in citato Registro: nos *F. Bern. Guidonis*, & *F. Gaufridus de Albusiis*, &c.

In the year 1312 Brother Geoffroi d'Ablis was attached to Brother Bernard Gui as Inquisitor – on whom in the cited Register: 'We Brother Bernard Gui and Brother Geoffroi d'Ablis etc'.[86]

[82] Réginald's source for Gui's appointment is Gui's autobiographical note in *De fundatione*, p. 67; other passages on Gui, ibid., pp. 27, 102–3, 114, 146–7, 154, 199, 200, 226. One available source for his episcopal career and the writing of the *Practica* was an anonymous life of Gui, written into the convent's manuscript of his *Speculum Sanctorale*, ed. Philip Labbe, *Nova bibliotheca manuscriptorum librorum*, 2 vols. (Paris, 1657), II, 512–3 and 820; re-edited from a different ms., P. Amargier, 'Éléments pour un portrait de Be rnard Gui', *Cahiers de Fanjeaux* 16 (1981), 19–37 (30–33), where it is tentatively attributed to Gui's nephew Pierre Gui.

[83] Source unknown. In his 'Positions scolaires et fonctions occasionnelles de Bernard Gui', *Cahiers de Fanjeaux* 16 (1981), 55–83 (73–4), M.-H. Vicaire dismissed this as impossible because of Gui's position as procurator of the Dominican Order in Avignon.

[84] Here is an unusually clear boundary between the texts of the two men, underlined by Percin stopping quotation marks at 'haec ille'. Réginald was right, Percin wrong; Vidal, *Bullaire*, p. xxxiii.

[85] *M*, p. 69b no. 2; no quotation marks.

[86] Clearly Réginald's inference, given the earlier reference to the register, in the 1306 account of Gui. On Geoffroi, see *L'inquisiteur Geoffroy d'Ablis et les Cathares du comté de Foix (1308–1309)*, ed. A. Pales-Gobilliard (Paris, 1984), pp. 7–10. Not all their work in 1310 was done jointly. One of Fournier depositions refers to an earlier confession made by the deponent to d'Ablis on his own, in that year; *Le registre*

1310–20[87]

Scripsit autem meritissimus F. Bernardus Guidonis Inquisitor sequentia quæ pretiosè servantur in
nostra Bibliotheca. Elenchum autem opera hujus
dignissimi Inquisitoris subjungo.
… / 70b /
" Obiit tandem meritissimus Inquisitor. & posteà
"Episcopus, ut dixi, Lodovensis dignissimus anno
"1331. sepultusque est in Conventu suo Lemovicensi,
"prout vivens ordinaverat.

The most meritorious Brother Bernard Gui, Inquisitor, wrote
the following, which are preciously preserved in our library. I
provide below a list of the works of this most worthy Inquisitor.
…
… Finally the most meritorious Inquisitor and later, as I said,
most worthy bishop of Lodève died in the year 1331, and was
buried in his convent of Limoges, as he ordained when alive.[88]

1330–40[89]

Frater Petrus Bruni nunciatur Inquisitor in
Chron. F. Reginaldi circà annum 1320. usque
ad 1340. in veteri enim Registro, quod ejus sententias continet, dicit se anno 1324. à longo tempore esse

In the *Chronicle* of Brother Réginald Brother Pierre Brun is
reported as Inquisitor from around the year 1320 until 1340, for
in an old register, which contains his sentences, he says in the
year 1324 that he had been in the office for a long time. Further,

---

d'inquisition de Jacques Fournier évêque de Pamiers (1318–1325), ed. J. Duvernoy, Bibliothèque Méridionale, Third series 41, 3 vols. (Toulouse, 1965), ii.268. They were however, side by side delivering sentences in public in Toulouse on 5 and 10 April 1310, and later on 22 and 23 April 1312 and 6 and 7 March 1316; *Livre des sentences*, ed. Pales-Gobilliard, I, 334–5, 538–9, 546–7, 560–1, 858–9, 866–9, 892–3, 932–3, 952–3. The ever-efficient Gui wrote on the day after d'Ablis's death (11 September 1316) to make provision during the vacancy of inquisition in Carcassonne, in a letter whose expression of emotion about God's taking 'from this world a father and colleague most dear to me' (De hoc mundo karissimum michi patrem et collegam') might have been not only formulaic; *Practica inquisitionis*, ed. Douais, p. 66 no. 46.

[87] *M*, p. 70a–b; the catalogue is accompanied throughout by quotation marks.

[88] The 'ut dixi' in this passage (referring to the Réginald part of the 1306 entry) and the concluding death notice indicate that this long passage is by Réginald. The care, precision and clarity of the bibliography of Gui's works fits, as does also the absence of interruptions. Gui's works were bound in nine volumes, with a tenth one which simply reproduced volume 6.

[89] *M*, p. 71b no. 1; no quotation marks.

the [record of] the chapter of Condom in 1340 has it thus: the diffinitor was Brother Pierre Brun, the Toulouse Inquisitor.[90] [Percin] A letter was given to this most worthy inquisitor by Pope John XXII in the fifteenth year of his pontificate, which I have written out in the *Little Work on Inquisition*.

in officio. In Capitulo verò Condomiensi 1340. sic habetur Definitor fuit *frater Petrus Bruni* Inquisitor Tolosanus. Datæ sunt litteræ illi Inquisitori dignissimo *à Papa Joanne XXII.* anno 15. sui Pontificatûs quas scripsi in Opusculo de Inquisitione.

Toulouse inquisitor in the year 1344 was Brother Pierre Gui, son of the Convent of Limoges and its prior, later primary lecturer in the school of the canons of Saint-Etienne at Toulouse; and he was prior of Périgueux and Carcassonne. While he was [prior] Provincial he had his uncle Bernard Gui's *Lives* [Speculum sanctorale] transcribed.[92]

1340–50: 1344[91]

Inquisitor Tolosanus fuit anno 1344. *F. Petrus Guidonis* filius Conventûs Lemovicensis & Prior, posteà Lector primarius in Schola Canonicorum sancti Stephani Tolosæ, Priorque extitit Petragoricensis & Carcassonensis: qui Vitas à patruo suo F. Bernardo Guidonis conscribi fecit dum esset Provincialis.

---

[90] *M*, p. 71b no. 1. There is a full account in Vidal, *Bullaire*, pp. 97–9; R. Manselli, *Spirituali e Beghini in Provenza* (Rome, 1959), pp. 31, 194, 249, 298–300. Acts of Condom: Douais, *Frères prêcheurs*, II, 244–53; Pierre Brun at 252 no. xv.

[91] *M*, p. 77b no. 7; no quotations marks.

[92] All of this rests on post-Bernard Gui additions in Gui, *De fundatione*, pp. 68–9 and 107, with one exception. This is the fact of him being inquisitor and the date, which probably rest on inference from knowledge that his successor in this office was Jean Dumoulin, who was termed inquisitor in a bull he received in December 1344; Vidal, *Bullaire*, pp. 302–3 no. 195. The sources, style and interest in the detail about copying Bernard Gui's *Vitae* suggest Réginald. However, from this date on the majority of unattributed notices about inquisitors are probably by Percin. On Pierre Gui, inquisitor 1342–4, see Douais, *Frères prêcheurs*, II, 453–4; Vidal, *Bullaire*, pp. xxvii and 282–3 (his nomination) and n. 1 on his career; Kaeppeli and Panella, *Scriptores Ordinis Praedicatorum medii aevi*, III, 229 no. 3238.

[Although Percin continued to make extracts from and to refer to Réginald's *Chronicle*, these occupied a decreasing proportion of the accounts of inquisition that he provided, as he came to rely more upon a mixture of other recent Dominican historians and his own reading of the documents. For the sake of brevity we omit these, providing only Percin's last use of Réginald's work; unusually he gave it the longer title, *Chronicle of Inquisitors*.]

1660–70: 1662[93]

Nimius sum quia nimia mors quæ nobis eripuit F. *Joannem Dominicum Rey Inquisitorem nostrum*; de quo sic Necrologium & Chronicon Inquisitorum. Vir pius & prudens meditationi addictissimus. Prior fuit Montpeliensis anno 12. post Professionem & Ecclesiam nostrum ædificare fecit: in Conventu etiam Sanctæ Mariæ Annunciatæ Parisiis Avenionensis & secundò Tolosæ, semel Vicarius Generalis Congregationis Reformatæ, et postea Provincialis. Quibus hæc addo.

[Percin] I am being excessive [in grief], for excessive is the death which has snatched away from us our Brother Jean Dominique Rey, Inquisitor.[94] On him, the Necrology and the *Chronicle of Inquisitors* thus:
[Necrology] a pious and shrewd man, most given to meditation.
[Réginald]. He was prior of Montpellier in the 12th year after his profession, and he had our [*recte*: their] church built;[95] [prior of] the convent of the Announced Saint Mary [*recte*: Annunciation of Saint Mary] in Paris,[96] [secondly] of Avignon and secondly [*recte*: thirdly] of Toulouse;[97] once Vicar General of the Reformed Congregation,[98] and later Provincial.[99]
[Percin]. To which I add these things.

[93] *M*, p. 164b no. 14.
[94] See the short biography in Montagnes, *Sébastien Michaelis*, p. 259.
[95] From 1624. He built the conventual church of St Matthew at Montpellier.
[96] 1633–5.
[97] 1644–7, second term 1656–8.
[98] 1659–32.
[99] 1658–62.

13

The Roman Inquisition: between reality and myth

Michaela Valente

In early modern Europe, the Holy Office – *inquisitio haereticae pravitatis* (inquisition into heretical wickedness) – stood for a myth in which, as Dostoevsky points out in the Grand Inquisitor episode of The Brothers Karamazov, freedom and fear were two sides of the same coin. In his 1880 novel the great Russian writer describes an encounter between Jesus and the inquisitor in which he draws attention to the great dilemma of liberty and authority. According to the inquisitor, human beings, frightened by the prospect of freedom, prefer to seek refuge in a world in which duties and responsibilities are clearly defined. The kind of freedom Christianity had offered the world is rejected. In this narrative Dostoevsky, with great refinement, lays bare one of the most vital ethical and political questions facing modern culture, the relationship between freedom and power.

The inquisition thus stands for a myth: a mask that can only be lifted away from it with a great deal of care. For it had been crafted and constructed over the course of centuries during which fear, threats and efforts to defend the Holy Office were continuously being deployed by both its critics and supporters. Hostile polemical tracts and apologetic vindications influence our analysis and risk misleading us.

Already at the time of the inquisition's foundation a debate arose over its legitimacy. The existence of heresies had been a constant feature of Christianity but it was not until 1184, with the bull *Ad abolendam*, that pope Lucius III adopted a policy of eliminating heretics outright and summoning the faithful to fight against heresy. But before the birth of the inquisition there had been a long gestation period during which the institution's spiritual and political premises were gradually hammered out.[1] The very idea of an inquisition raises the question of whether faith should be defended and propagated only by means of persuasion or whether coercion is permissible; both positions have a basis in Scripture.[2] Gradually the tribunal came to be presented as

---

[1] See *A Companion to Heresy Inquisitions*, ed. D. S. Prudlo (Leiden, 2019).
[2] For a discussion, see L. Sackville, 'The Church's Institutional Response to Heresy in the 13th Century', ibid., pp. 108–40. See *Compel People to Come In. Violence and*

317

Michaela Valente

'protection of the faith', though in some circles the suspicion circulated that it had been devised for political purposes, especially in the Italian peninsula. This essay examines some important works published in the sixteenth century, and uses them as the basis for a general interpretative approach that will help us to look beyond both the propaganda put out against the Catholic Church and the responses of its apologists. The aim is to deconstruct the image of the Roman Inquisition. Arguments deployed by both sides were closely interwoven, because both the accusation of heresy and the accusation of injustice could be powerful weapons. According to its opponents, the tribunal's activities were based on a very elusive definition of heresy, an increasingly assertive authority and the use of torture to extort confessions: objections that were far removed from the theoretical discussions about rights that would later be recognised and developed. From the other side, however, it was argued that heresy was a threat that needed to be averted.

Scholars today continue to debate reality: the actual role of the Holy Office and its relationship with the pope.[3] Here, however, it is the image of the tribunal of the faith and how it was constructed by promoters and detractors alike that constitute our subject and shape our modus operandi: examining the various forms of both the inquisition's legitimisation and demonisation.[4]

Catholic Conversions in the Non-European World, ed. V. Lavenia, S. Pastore, S. Pavone and C. Petrolini (Rome, 2018).

[3] M. Firpo, *La presa di potere dell'inquisizione romana (1550–1553)* (Rome and Bari, 2014). See *The Inquisition in Early Modern Europe: Studies on Sources and Methods*, ed. G. Henningsen and J. Tedeschi (Dekalb, 1986); J. Tedeschi, *The Prosecution of Heresy. Collected Studies on the Inquisition in Early Modern Europe* (Binghamton, 1991); A. Jacobson Schutte, 'Recent Studies of the Roman Inquisition', in *Politics and Reformations:Communities, Polities, Nations, and Empires: Essays in Honor of Thomas Brady, Jr.*, ed. C. Ocker, M. Printy, P. Starenko and P. Wallace (Leiden, 2007), pp. 91–111; E. Bonora, 'L'archivio dell'Inquisizione e gli studi storici: primi bilanci e prospettive a dieci anni dall'apertura', *Rivista storica italiana* 120 (2008), 968–1002; M. P. Donato, 'Les doutes de l'Inquisiteur. Philosophie naturelle, censure et théologie à l'époque moderne', *Annales.Histoire. Sciences Sociales* 64 (2009), 15–43; my 'Nuove ricerche e interpretazioni sul Sant'Uffizio a più di dieci anni dall'apertura dell'archivio', *Rivista di Storia della Chiesa in Italia*, 2012, no. 2, 569–92; G. Romeo, 'L'Inquisizione romana e l'Italia nei più recenti sviluppi storiografici', *Rivista Storica Italiana* 126 (2014), 186–204.

[4] See G. Romeo, *L'Inquisizione nell'Italia moderna* (Rome and Bari, 2002); A. Del Col, *L'Inquisizione in Italia dal XII al XXI secolo* (Milan, 2006); E. Brambilla, *La giustizia intollerante: Inquisizione e tribunali confessionali in Europa (secoli IV-XVIII)* (Rome, 2006); C. Black, The Italian Inquisition (New Haven and London, 2009) and T. F. Mayer, *The Roman Inquisition. Trying Galileo* (Philadelphia PA, 2015); G. Maifreda, *The Business of the Roman* Inquisition *in the Early Modern Era* (London, 2017); H. Schwedt, *Die römische Inquisition: Kardinäle und Konsultoren 1601 bis 1700* (Freiburg, 2017); *The Roman Inquisition. Centre versus Peripheries*, ed. K. Aron-Beller and C. Black (Leiden, 2018). See also A. Rotondò, *Studi di storia ereticale del Cinquecento*, 2 vols. (Florence, 2008), and *Ripensare la Riforma protestante. Nuove prospettive degli studi italiani*, ed. L. Felici (Turin, 2015).

The Roman Inquisition: between reality and myth

There is no question that, besides being moved by theological concerns and sensitivities stemming from the gospel, those who resisted the inquisition inside the Church were also motivated by the political success of the front that opposed them. While they agreed that heresy needed to be combated and even approved of methods that were justified by the state of emergency, not a few expressed doubts about a procedure that also risked involving innocent parties and warned of the political use that could be made of accusations of heresy; victims were also candidates who had nearly become popes themselves, like Reginald Pole.

In a continuous play of mirrors the defenders emphasised the advantages of the inquisition which protected the true faith and the Church of Rome and prevented the civil wars that were raging and devastating other parts of Europe.[5] From the opposite camp (Erasmus and Erasmians), the legitimacy of a tribunal of the conscience was heavily criticised for its iniquitous procedures and for betraying the message of the Gospels.[6] The two positions gradually hardened and defined themselves in a continuous to and fro of accusation and defence. Some theologians and historians drew attention to the origins of the Inquisition, highlighting its effectiveness against heresy, while others condemned the tribunal as bloody and referred back to the parable of the wheat and the tares and Christ's admonition not to gather up the tares, lest the wheat be uprooted with them (Matthew 13. 34–30).[7]

Ethical and religious themes, legal questions and jurisdictional controversies animated the debate about the Holy Office in the early modern age and the disputes in Europe were coloured by various shades and nuances depending on the political and religious culture in which they arose and developed. In France Henry II tried to establish the inquisition but the *parlement* rose up against him in order to defend its jurisdiction, while in the Netherlands the Inquisition was viewed as a threat.[8] Reactions like these arose out of the images that were being propagated and whatever were the most useful versions were adopted to suit particular political ends. Through some of these works we can get an idea of the intense debate that raged around the Holy Office which,

---

[5] D. Moreno, *La invención de la Inquisición* (Madrid, 2004), p. 175.

[6] See my *Contro l'Inquisizione. Il dibattito europeo secc. XVI-XVIII*, Collana della Società di Studi Valdesi 29 (Turin, 2009); *Tribunal der Barbaren? Deutschland und die Inquisition in der Frühen Neuzeit*, ed. A. Burkardt and G. Schwerhoff (Konstanz, 2012).

[7] R. Bainton, 'The Parable of the Tares as the Proof Text for Religious Liberty to the End of the Sixteenth Century', *Church History* 1 (1932), 67–89. See Y. De Mattos, 'As Notícias recônditas e os escritos contra o Santo Ofício português na época Moderna (1670–1821)', *Topoi*, 20 (2019), 84–110 www.revistatopoi.org

[8] A. Tallon, 'Inquisition romaine et monarchie française au XVIe siècle', in *Inquisition et pouvoir*, ed. G. Audisio (Aix-en-Provence, 2004), pp. 311–24; G. Gielis and V. Soen, 'Inquisitorial Office in the Sixteenth-Century Habsburg Low Countries. A Dynamic Perspective', *Journal of Ecclesiastical History* 66 (2015), 47–66.

Michaela Valente

according to some critics, challenged the Christian message. These debates also involved the very definitions of heresy and heretics.[9]

Further, through these images we can see an institution that operated in different political states, and it had to make some important compromises. In spite of efforts to promote it, attempts to introduce the tribunal led to revolts that were motivated by different reasons, as in Naples in 1547 where the main objection was the defence of jurisdiction, something that was also behind various other anti-inquisition revolts.[10]

When reading these works and examining the different cases, we need to be aware of the degree of manipulation that is hidden between the lines and pay special attention to a text's target audience and its aim.[11]

Obviously, it was the Spanish inquisition in the early sixteenth century that aroused doubts and protests over the legitimacy (as well as duration) of its activities. As early as 1525, before any strong opposition had arisen, Gasparo Contarini, then in Madrid, accused the Spanish inquisition of practising 'terror' and 'tyranny' against the teachings of the Church.[12] It was a view that Contarini did not alter; even many years later, after returning from the failed Diet of Regensburg, he urged great caution about the raging inquisitors and their definitions of heresy.[13] This was one of the most controversial points that would be developed later in anti-inquisitorial polemics: the almost infinite possibility to extend the concept of heresy to cover virtually anything. Reflections on the legitimacy of persecuting heresy, as well as on the definition of heresy itself, were varied, complex and contradictory. But attacks against the inquisition were no longer being made just for the purpose of propaganda. Harsh criticisms and denunciations were raised against the excesses of ecclesiastical jurisdiction and appeals were made to permit dissent over theological questions that were not settled, with special appeals made for Mercy, appeals which were supported by many Catholics. Among them was the General of the Augustinians, Girolamo Seripando, who in 1545

---

[9] John H. Arnold, *Inquisition and Power: Catharism and the Confessing Subject in Medieval Languedoc* (Philadelphia PA, 2001); Christine Caldwell Ames, *Righteous Persecution: Inquisition, Dominicans, and Christianity in the Middle Ages* (Philadelphia PA, 2009); L. Sackville, *Heresy and Heretics in the Thirteenth Century. The Textual Representations*, Heresy and Inquisition in the Middle Ages 4 (York, 2011); *Heresy and Inquisition in France, 1200–1300*, ed. J.H. Arnold and P. Biller, Manchester Medieval Sources Series (Manchester, 2016).

[10] See A. Musi, *L'impero dei vicerè* (Bologna, 2013), pp. 33–7. See V. Lavenia, 'Rivolte', in *Dizionario storico dell'Inquisizione*, ed. A. Prosperi, V. Lavenia e J. Tedeschi, 4 vols. (Pisa, 2010), III, 1329–30.

[11] Sackville, *Heresy and Heretics*, p. 164.

[12] G. Fragnito, *Gasparo Contarini. Un magistrato veneziano al servizio della cristianità* (Florence, 1987), p. 238; E. Gleason, *Gasparo Contarini: Venice, Rome and Reform* (Berkeley, 1993), pp. 35–60.

[13] See *I processi inquisitoriali di Vittore Soranzo*, ed. M. Firpo and S. Pagano (Città del Vaticano, 2004), p. 612.

The Roman Inquisition: between reality and myth

privately expressed the view that the inquisition, after a moderate beginning, had veered into actions that were marked by iniquity:

> Fuit equidem tribunal hoc initio moderatum et mite, quale certe semper fuit Pauli ingenium... inprimis vero Ioannis Petri severitate nulla humanitate aspersa in eam crevit magnitudinem ut nullibi toto terrarum orbe horribilia magis magisque formidolosa iudicia esse existimarentur.

> (In fact, at the beginning this tribunal was cautious and mild, as was certainly the inclination of Paul [Paul III]... however, beginning with Gian Pietro [Carafa]'s harshness – with not a dash of humanity – it grew to such a size that nowhere in the lands of the whole world were there courts reputed to be more horrible or more frightening.)[14]

There is more: Seripando went even further in identifying the person responsible for this extremely dangerous development as Gian Pietro Carafa.[15] This astute observation, made by the General of the Augustinians, stood out from the more commonly proffered explanations, since it was only much later that responsibility came to be attributed to Carafa, who was a supporter of reorganising the Inquisition and of its growing intransigence. In fact, in Europe critics were still blaming the 'first inquisitor' Dominic.[16] According to them the Spanish saint had chosen the path of persecution and abandoned the apostolic method of persuasion.

After Paul III's *Licet ab initio*, we see the emergence of two opposing fronts in official declarations, private letters and diplomatic correspondence. Both of them contributed to the construction of an image of heresy and heretics, deploying the *topoi* that both demonised and legitimised the tribunal.[17] There was however more at stake: the destiny of the Church and the role of the pontiff against the backdrop of the *horrende guerre d'Italia* ('horrendous wars of Italy'),[18] a phrase designating wars sometimes also known as the

---

[14] *Hieronymi Seripandi de Tridentino Concilio Commentarii*, in *Concilium Tridentinum: diariorum, actorum, epistularum, tractatuum nova collectio*, ed. S. Merkle et al., 13 vols. in 20 (Freiburg-im-Breisgau, 1901–2001), II, *Diariorum pars altera*, 405. See A. Prosperi, 'Il grano e la zizzania: l'eresia nella cittadella cristiana', in *L'intolleranza: uguali e diversi nella storia*, ed. P. C. Bori (Bologna, 1986), pp. 51–86 (68, n. 16).

[15] A. Prosperi, *Tribunali della coscienza* (Turin, 1996), p. 168. See S. Seidel Menchi, 'Origine e origini del Santo Uffizio dell'Inquisizione romana (1542–1559)', in *L'Inquisizione. Atti del Simposio Internazionale. Città del Vaticano 29–31 Ottobre 1998*, ed. A. Borromeo, Studi e Testi 417 (Città del Vaticano, 2003), pp. 291–321.

[16] L. Canetti, *L'invenzione della memoria. Il culto e l'immagine di Domenico nella storia dei primi frati Predicatori* (Spoleto, 1996); idem, 'Domenico, santo', in *Dizionario storico dell'Inquisizione*, I, 506–7. See also E. Peters, *Inquisition* (New York, 1988), p. 130.

[17] Sackville, *Heresy and Heretics*, pp. 1–13.

[18] The phrase, often attributed to Machiavelli, is found in a later edition of a work by Paolo Danza, *Libro, o vero Cronica de tutte le guerre de Italia* (Venice, 1522), which was

Michaela Valente

'Great Italian Wars', a scenario that influenced geopolitical and religious balances of power.

The clash between these two ways of conceiving the fight against heresy – either through persuasion or coercion – shows that there was something much more important involved here than the values of faith. It had more to do with power, its expression and its relationship with other institutions. By contrast with Spain, in Italy criticisms of the inquisition were motivated above all by creeping jurisdictional usurpation of the institution, and other considerations did not bear as heavily. In spring 1553 during his famous meeting with Carafa at San Paolo Fuori le Mura (Saint Paul Outside the Walls), after having discussed other more pressing questions, Reginald Pole did not hesitate to openly criticise the methods of the Inquisition, although he agreed with his interlocutor as regards its aims. Carafa, who happened to be in a less than stable situation at the time, but was always adept at camouflaging his intentions, professed to be persuaded by Pole's arguments and promised that he would adopt the path of charity and mercy:[19] a commitment that remained unfulfilled. Nonetheless, the question was never dropped. The inquisition was accused of betraying the message of the Gospels and of acting in a manner that was inappropriate to Church tradition. And gradually the idea gained ground that the intentions behind its actions were more political than religious. Carafa became pope (Paul IV, 1555–9), and in 1557 he is said to have told the Venetian ambassador to Rome, Bernardo Navagero, that he had never thirsted for blood and that he had laboured to fulfil the task given to the Congregation of the Inquisition by Paul III.[20] On this specific occasion he rejected any accusation and stressed the charitable duties of his office. In spite of this, it was Navagero himself who, on 23 October 1557, reported a statement made by the pope that would immortalise him for his stubborn

---

retitled *Guerre horrende de Italia. Tutte le guerre e fatti darme seguiti nella Italia, comenzando dalla venuta di Carlo* ... (Venice, 1524).

[19] 'Vennero dipoi a parlar dell'offitio dell'Inquisizione, nella quale dice il cardinal Polo che non li piace il modo che si tiene se bene consente nel fine, et sopra questo ebbero longo ragionamento; et Napoli consentiva a Polo intanto che, dicendo di voler andare a Napoli a far residentia, non voleva servare il modo che servano li inquisitori a Roma, ma l'altro ch'esso dicea, cioè la via della carità et mansuetudine fino ad un certo termine...' (They started to talk about the Inquisition. Pole argued he approved its purpose, but not approve the methods. They debated a lot about this assessment, and then Carafa agreed with Pole, and promised that once he was in Naples he would abandon the inquisitorial methods adopted in Rome and would act differently, that is using, up to a certain point following the path of charity and mercy); *Monumenti di varia letteratura tratti dai manoscritti di monsignor Lodovico Beccadelli*, ed. G. Morandi, 3 vols. (Bologna, 1797–1804), I.ii, 351. See Firpo, *La presa di potere*, pp. 151–2.

[20] Prosperi, *Tribunali della coscienza*, p. 146 n. 26; D. Santarelli, *La corrispondenza di Bernardo Navagero, ambasciatore veneziano a Roma (1555–1558)* (Rome, 2011), pp. 237–8.

The Roman Inquisition: between reality and myth

consistency and loyalty to his own office. Carafa declared that he would be ready to send even his own father to the stake: 'If our father were a heretic, we would carry the bundles of sticks to burn him'.[21]

This line of iron intransigence is entirely in keeping with views he had expressed earlier on the topic of heresy in his 1532 memorandum *De lutheranorum haeresi reprimenda et ecclesia reformanda ad Clementem VII* (*To Clement VII on the need to repress the heresy of the Lutherans and to reform the Church*),[22] in which he adopted the ideas of Girolamo Aleandro on the historical evidence that 'the great heresies are never extinguished unless with blood' (Si trova per le istorie che le grandi eresie mai non si estinguono se non col sangue).[23] Against heresy it was necessary to build a 'tower fortified by the holy faith and by Your Holiness'.[24]

In private documents indignation with the inquisition on the part of the elites and members of the clergy left traces that were often not publicly visible, while popular reaction may be gauged from the *pasquinate* (satires) that expressed the mood of those who had no voice.[25] In one of these the pope 'volea con crudel inquisitione/ e con ferro e con foco esser temuto' (wanted to be feared by means of cruel inquisition, iron and fire).[26] Clearly, instilling fear was still an instrument in the exercise of control. As is well known, when Carafa died on 18 August 1559 the Roman populace reacted with a degree of violence that went far beyond its usual displays during a vacancy of the Holy See. The people rose up as if they had been liberated after a period

---

[21] Navagero, 28 October 1557, cited by B. Croce, *Un calvinista italiano. Il marchese di Vico, Galeazzo Caracciolo* (Bari, 1933), pp. 34–5. Cf. P. Simoncelli, *Il caso Reginald Pole. Eresia e santità nelle polemiche religiose del Cinquecento* (Rome, 1977), p. 166; M. Firpo, with D. Marcatto), *Il processo inquisitoriale del Cardinal Giovanni Morone. Edizione critica*, 6 vols. (Rome, 1981–95), II, 35; M. Firpo, *Vittore Soranzo vescovo ed eretico. Riforma della Chiesa e Inquisizione nell'Italia del Cinquecento* (Rome and Bari, 2006), pp. 494–5. See A. Aubert, *Paolo IV. Politica, Inquisizione e storiografia*, 2nd edn (Florence, 1999); A. Vanni, *'Fare diligente inquisitione'. Gian Pietro Carafa e le origini dei chierici regolari teatini* (Rome, 2010); idem, 'La carriera di Paolo IV, tra inquisizione e ordini religiosi', *Tiempos Modernos*, 37 (2018/2) http://www.tiemposmodernos.org/tm3/index.php/tm/article/download/5078/804

[22] *Concilium Tridentinum. Diariorum, actorum, epistularum, tractatuum*, XII.i, 67–77.

[23] Aleandro, 14 November 1531, in C. Cantù, *Gli eretici d'Italia* 3 vols. (Turin, 1864–6), I, 371.

[24] *Concilium Tridentinum. Diariorum, actorum, epistularum, tractatuum*, XII.i, 76.

[25] *Ex Marmore: Pasquini, Pasquinisti, Pasquinate nell'Europa moderna*, ed. C. Damianaki, P. Procaccioli and A. Romano (Rome, 2006); *Pasquin, Lord of Satire, and his Disciples in Sixteenth-Century Struggles for Religious and Political Reform*, ed. C. Damianaki and A. Romano (Rome, 2014).

[26] F. Gori, 'Papa Paolo IV ed i Carafa suoi nipoti giudicati con nuovi documenti', *Archivio Storico, Artistico, Archeologico e Letterario della Città e Provincia di Roma* 2 (1877), 180, and O. Niccoli, *Rinascimento anticlericale. Infamia, propaganda e satira in Italia tra Quattro e Cinquecento* (Rome and Bari, 2005), pp. 128–36. See M. Pattenden, *Pius IV and the Fall of the Carafa. Nepotism and Papal Authority in Counter-Reformation Rome* (Oxford, 2013).

of oppression,[27] storming the palace of the Inquisition in order to destroy the documents housed there and decapitating the statue of the pope. In his *Diario* Seripando also mentioned the disturbances (referring to the 'turmoil directed against the Inquisition and the statue', 'tumultus in inquisitionem et statuam')[28] and various other accounts condemned the people for their ignorance and violence, characterising their actions as loathsome.[29] There is almost a note of relish in the words used by Carnesecchi when writing to Giulia Gonzaga on September 2 1559. 'Vostra Signoria harà inteso come la Santa Inquisitione è morta di quella morte istessa di che era solita dare morire li altri, cioè di foco', a sign that 'alla divina clementia non piaccia che quel ufficio si esserciti (...) con tanta austerità et rigore' ('Your Lordship has heard that the Holy Inquisition has died from the same kind of death it used to inflict on others, that is, by fire', a sign that 'that Divine Mercy does not wish this office to be carried out ... with such rigour and severity').[30] These sincere criticisms of the Inquisition's methods are not surprising and they were probably shared by many others. Similar voices of dissent began to emerge from within the Church, though, as Gianni Romeo has observed, the importance of these should not be overemphasised since there were also many others who encouraged and supported the strategy of the Holy Office, including the Jesuits.[31] This was a battle that was fought inside and outside the Church, among the hierarchies, in society, in the Italian peninsula and elsewhere with motivations that differed widely, though each of them contributed to the constructing of the myth. In one of his pamphlets the exile Pier Paolo Vergerio, the first archbishop of Capodistria, inveighed against the inquisitors as part of his propaganda campaign, accusing them of being afraid that their real political and non-ethical religious motives would be revealed.[32] It was in order to reply to accusations like this that a legitimising

---

[27] J. Hunt, *The Vacant See in Early Modern Rome. A Social History of the Papal Interregnum* (Leiden, 2016), pp. 188–9. See I. Fosi, *La giustizia del papa. Sudditi e tribunali nello Stato Pontificio in età moderna,* (Rome and Bari, 2007).

[28] H. Seripando, *Diarium de vita sua (1513–1562),* ed. D. Gutiérrez, *Analecta Augustiniana* 26 (1963), 129.

[29] E. Bonora, *Giudicare i vescovi. La definizione dei poteri nella Chiesa tridentina* (Rome and Bari, 2007), pp. 155–64. See P. Forbes, *A full view of the public transactions in the reign of Q. Elizabeth, or a Particular account of all the memorable affairs of that queen in a series of letters and other papers of State, written by herself and her principal Ministers, and by the foreign Princes and Ministers with whom they had negotiations,* 2 vols. (London, 1740–1), I, 234.

[30] I processi inquisitoriali di Pietro Carnesecchi (1557–1567), ed. M. Firpo and D. Marcatto, 3 vols. (Città del Vaticano, 1998–2000), II, 689. See P. Simoncelli, 'Inquisizione romana e Riforma in Italia', *Rivista Storica Italiana* 100 (1988), 5–125 (71, n. 203). In addition, *Concilium Tridentinum,*II *Diariorum pars altera,* 515 and 606–7.

[31] G. Romeo, 'Note sull'Inquisizione romana tra il 1557 e il 1561', *Rivista di Storia e Letteratura Religiosa* 36 (2000), 115–41 (139–41). Cf. P. Scaramella, 'I primi gesuiti e l'Inquisizione romana', *Rivista Storica Italiana* 117 (2005), 135–57.

[32] *A gl'inquisitori che sono per l'Italia. Del catalogo di libri eretici stampato in Roma*

The Roman Inquisition: between reality and myth

self-representation of the Holy Office and its activities began to spread. In Italy inquisitors and many ecclesiastics crafted an image of the inquisition that came with clear outlines and almost no shadows, while those writing on the other side of the Alps, who were engaged with altogether different interlocutors, had to marshal their own detailed arguments. A significant example of this is the jurist Conradus Brunus (Konrad Braun), who in his *De haereticis* found it necessary to start by clarifying the definition of heresy and heretics, illustrating the evils they provoked, and discussing the problem of responsibilities and jurisdictions. It is only after all of this, in Book IV, that he deals at last with the question of the inquisition and comes out with this declaration. 'Iusti esse debent Inquisitores haereticae pravitatis, qui officium inquisitionis ad Dei gloriam, et augmentum fidei Catholicae (...) exercere debent' (The Inquisitors of heretical wickedness, who have the duty of carrying out the office of inquisition to the glory of God and for the augmentation of the Catholic faith, ought to be just).[33] He goes further. In prescribing punishment, the inquisitor performs the office of a physician, shepherd and gardener, for he is healing the Church by excising the rotten part, initially applying the treatment with gentleness and later with severity, with the special aim of preventing the contagion from spreading.[34] These were words that served to construct a positive image of an institution and they were intended to win it acceptance as well as to rebut earlier negative propaganda. Remarkable stories and works like these were deployed to illustrate and reinforce the invective against the persecuting Church or, conversely, to emphasise the need to wage war on heresy as the Scriptures enjoin.

In its early years the Roman Inquisition presented itself as a reply, a reaction and a remedy to the spreading infection of heresy, intervening wherever the contagion threatened to spread the most rapidly, which meant inside the religious orders. Later a change occurred. Shortly after the outbreak of civil war in France, the inquisitor Umberto Locati argued cogently in his *Italia travagliata* (*Troubled Italy*) that the aristocracy in Italy had not opposed the introduction of the inquisition, as they were persuaded of its usefulness, given the dramatic rise of heresy in France:

> Essendo in Francia cresciuto il fatto dell'heresia, i principali si risolvettono molto bene a pensare di mettere impedimento a tale contagione: vedendo i popoli erano sedotti et messi in arme sotto pretesto di Religione: et poi per questo mezo alcuni potenti aspiravano ad occupare quel Reame. Per tanto i grandi de Italia temendo à se stessi, furono costretti, quel che prima negato avevano, proferire il lor favore al S. Officio dell'Inquisitione di eresia.

---

nell'Anno presente ... (s.l,1559), fol. 27v.

[33] Conradus Brunus (Konrad Braun), *Libri sex de* haereticis in genere (Mainz, 1549), p. 225.

[34] Ibid., p. 261.

Michaela Valente

(Heresy having arisen in France, the princes were right in their resolution to stem that contagion: seeing that the people had been seduced and taken up arms under the pretext of Religion, several powerful figures, aspired to use them as means for taking possession of that kingdom. Thus, the nobles in Italy fearing for themselves, were forced to favour what they had previously rejected and support the Holy Office of the Inquisition).[35]

What Locati failed to mention in his analysis was that, though the Italian aristocracy may have been well disposed to the tribunal, they were also convinced that they were immune from it. Many aristocrats deceived themselves into thinking they were at no risk themselves of falling into the Inquisition's net and later they watched helplessly as their illusions faded along with hopes that Carafa's death would put an end to the Inquisition.[36] Their growing realisation gradually turned into full awareness of the Inquisition's invasiveness and the powerful expression in the political arena. The jurisdiction of the State (and thus, the aristocrats' room for manoeuvre) was being eroded by the presence of the Holy Office, a fact which, as we have seen, led to uprisings, revolts and attacks on the Inquisition's local headquarters which involved the burning of documents and caused other damage.[37]

In this sense, the cases of Gianfrancesco Alois and Giovanni Grimani provide a telling indication of the kind of encroachment that was going on – where the Holy Office could not punish for heresy, it could still throw a spanner into the works of a *cursus honorum* (the successive stages of someone's career).[38] The rage of Giovanni Grimani, patriarch of Aquileia, who was forced to renounce the cardinalate, was explosive. Within a place where he was safe from unpleasant consequences he gave vent, not hesitating to describe the inquisitors as 'diavoli vestiti di negro che stanno per rovinare le anime et fare disperare' (devils dressed in black who are intent on ruining souls and making them despair) and to identify as the main purpose of the Holy Office its wish to confiscate property.[39] This was

---

[35] U. Locati, *Italia travagliata* (Venice, 1576), p. 218. Cf. A. Prosperi, 'L'Inquisizione nella storia: i caratteri originali di una controversia secolare', in his *L'Inquisizione romana. Studi e ricerche* (Rome, 2003), pp. 69–96 (72). See also S. Ditchfield, 'Umberto Locati L. O.P. (1503–1587): inquisitore, vescovo e storico', *Bollettino Storico Piacentino* 84 (1989), 205–21; E. Valeri, 'L'"Italia travagliata" dell'inquisitore Umberto Locati (1503–1587)', in '*Nunc alia tempora, alii mores'. Storici e storia in età postridentina*, ed. M. Firpo (Florence, 2005), pp. 311–34. Cf. *L'Italia dell'inquisitore. Storia e geografia dell'Italia del Cinquecento nella Descrittione di Leandro Alberti*, ed. M. Donattini (Bologna, 2007).

[36] S. Peyronel Rambaldi, *Speranze e crisi nel Cinquecento modenese: tensioni religiose e vita cittadina ai tempi di Giovanni Morone* (Milan, 1977), passim.

[37] Simoncelli, *Il caso Reginald Pole*, p. 153.

[38] P. Scaramella, 'Inquisizione, eresia e poteri feudali nel Viceregno napoletano alla metà del Cinquecento', in *Per il Cinquecento religioso italiano. Clero, cultura, società*, ed. M. Sangalli (Rome, 2003), pp. 512–21.

[39] M. Firpo, 'Le ambiguità della porpora e i "diavoli" del Sant'Ufficio. Identità e storia

The Roman Inquisition: between reality and myth

not enough. Grimani decided to leave a record of the evil he had suffered at the hands of the Inquisition through the frescoes of his palace in which the episode is depicted.[40]

The persistent murmuring of disquiet among this elite was accompanied by criticism from the humanists, ranging from Erasmus, who had been the first to question the usefulness of theological disputes, to Agrippa, who denounced the ulterior motives of the inquisitors, those 'sanguisitibundi vultures' (bloodsucking vultures). The murmurings and criticism finally culminated in a series of pamphlets and works, one of which is the *Modus solennis et autenticus, ad inquirendum et inveniendum et convincendum Lutheranos*. (*The Solemn and Authentic Mode of Enquiring into, Finding and Convicting Lutherans*).[41] This short work, published in 1553, was incorrectly attributed to the Master of the Sacred Palace, Silvestro Mazzolini, also called Prierate. But it is clear that the real author was Girolamo Massari, who also wrote the *Eusebius captivus* (*Eusebius a prisoner*). It is a spoof, a parody of inquisitorial manuals. In the form of a manual to be used to flush out Lutherans, the exile Massari offers up a satire in the manner of Lucian, accompanied by Erasmian doctrinal considerations, designed to mock the Inquisitorial method as well as to expose its utter wickedness. Sarcastically, Massari shows that the inquisitor's skill lies in persuading the heretic to confess, regardless: his real aim is to obtain a victory and not to ascertain the truth. Some years later, Justus Velsius also condemned the Inquisition and appealed to the secular authorities to defend its subjects (*Apologia contra haereticae pravitatis appellatos inquisitores* [*Apologia against those called inquisitors of heretical depravity*], 1556). These remarkable pamphlets intensified the level of invective against the persecuting Church by appealing to the right to dissent. As Marie von Lüneberg has recently shown, in those years in the Holy Roman Empire, the image of the Inquisition was mainly constructed through attention to its victims, to those who later ended up as martyrs.[42]

From the Catholic side, Girolamo Muzio's *Historia sacra* (*Sacred History*) (1570) argues in rather shrill tones that the Lutheran enemy was by far the most pernicious and that for this reason it required and justified various forms of counter-measures.

---

nei ritratti di Giovanni Grimani', *Rivista Storica Italiana* 117 (2005), 826–71 (852).

[40] Ibid., pp. 863–71. See Andrea Del Col, 'Le vicende inquisitoriali di Giovanni Grimani, patriarca di Aquileia, e la sua lettera sulla doppia predestinazione', *Metodi e ricerche* 27 (2008), 81–100, and G. Paolin, 'Grimani, Giovanni', in *Dizionario storico dell'Inquisizione*, II, 735–8.

[41] It was published in Basle in 1553. Part of the joke was the pretence on the title page that it was printed in Rome. On Massari, see A. Olivieri, 'Massari, Girolamo', in *Dizionario Biografico degli Italiani* LXXI (2008); http://www.treccani.it/enciclopedia/girolamo-massari_(Dizionario-Biografico)/.

[42] Marie von Lüneburg, 'Die Inquisition im Medium deutschsprachiger Flugschriften: „Das ist die antichristliche pepstische und kayserliche und teuffellische Tyranney', in *Tribunal der Barbaren?*, pp. 71–100.

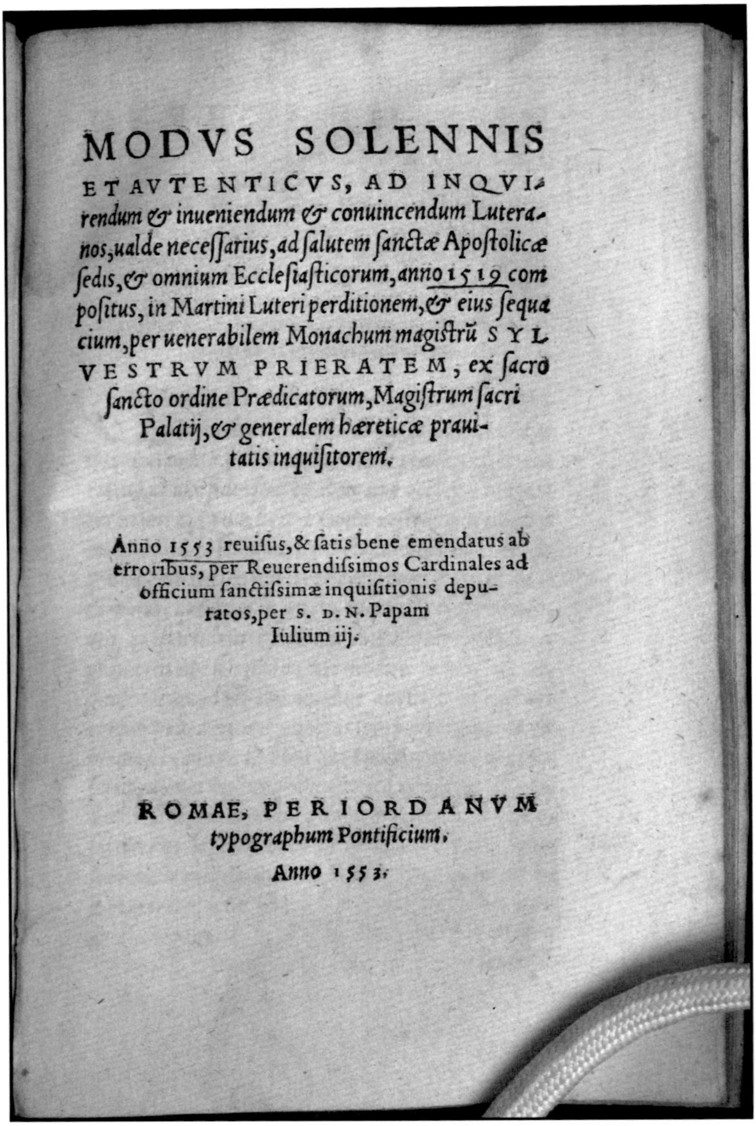

MODVS SOLENNIS

ET AVTENTICVS, AD INQVI-
rendum *&* inueniendum *&* conuincendum Lutera-
nos, ualde neceffarius, ad falutem fanctæ Apoftolicæ
fedis, *&* omnium Ecclefiafticorum, anno 1519 com
pofitus, in Martini Luteri perditionem, *&* eius fequa
cium, per uenerabilem Monachum magiftrū S Y L
VESTRVM PRIERATEM, ex facrô
fancto ordine Prædicatorum, Magiftrum facri
Palatij, *&* generalem hæreticæ praui-
tatis inquifitorem.

Anno 1553 reuifus, & fatis bene emendatus ab
erroribus, per Reuerendifsimos Cardinales ad
officium fanctifsimæ inquifitionis depu-
tatos, per S. D. N. Papam
Iulium iij.

ROMAE, PER IORDANVM
typographum Pontificium,

Anno 1553.

Figure 13.1   Silvestro Mazzolini, *Modus solennis et autenticus, ad inquirendum et inveniendum et convincendum Lutheranos* (Rome, 1553), title page. York Minster Library IX.K.24(2). This was a parody of an inquisitor's manual of procedure, and in reality it was written by Girolamo Massari and printed in Basle. The word 'authentic' in the title should have alerted readers to the possibility that this was a spoof. Reproduced by permission of the Chapter of York.

The Roman Inquisition: between reality and myth

Though the Inquisition had been victorious on every front in the Italian peninsula, the battle to affirm the legitimacy and the vital necessity of its activities continued. This period saw, on the one hand, the publication of manuals for inquisitors like that of Nicholas Eymeric, edited by Francisco Peña, and on the other Tommaso Garzoni's *Piazza universale* (1587). Garzoni was still emphasising the continuities in the struggle against heresy between the medieval and early modern ages, and in Discourse LXIII of the *Piazza universale* (*Universal town-square*), entitled *Degli eretici, e degli inquisitori*, he attacks all those who prevent the Holy Office from acting against the spread of heresy and against the 'superbia asinesca di questi arcibuffoni' (the asinine pride of these archclowns). Garzoni recalls how the Church Fathers (Augustine and Tertullian) were personally engaged in the fight against heresy, called the faithful to arms, an exhortation which could not be disregarded.[43]

The image of the Holy Office was also forged by propaganda: there were reports of many events that led to various claims that the Antichrist was not only present in Italy.[44] Among the cases that raised the most interest and dismay in England and in Europe was that of Francesco Spiera. In 1548 the Paduan professor recanted under the pressure of inquisitorial proceedings and returned to the Catholic fold, later on succumbing to despair at having betrayed his conscience and dying of a broken heart.[45] Another interesting story was that of Fanino Fanini. It was recounted by Giulio da Milano and was later included in his *Esortazione al martirio* (*Exhortation to martyrdom*) (1552) for the purpose of condemning any form of Nicodemism (public dissimulation of one's beliefs). Giulio urged martyrdom instead.[46] Through cases such as these, the image of the inquisition as 'the Tribunal of Antichrist' spread even further in Europe,

---

[43] T. Garzoni, *Piazza universale di tutte le professioni del mondo*, ed. G. B. Bronzini (Firenze, 1996), pp. 647–55.

[44] L. Felici, 'Il papa diavolo. Il paradigma dell'anticristo nella pubblicistica europea del Cinquecento', in *La papauté à la Renaissance*, ed. F. Alazard and F. La Brasca (Paris, 2007), pp. 533–69.

[45] See M. McDonald, 'The Fearefull Estate of Francis Spira: Narrative, Identity, and Emotion in Early Modern England', *Journal of British Studies* 31 (1992), 32–61; M. A. Overell, 'The Exploitation of Francesco Spiera', *The Sixteenth Century Journal* 26 (1995), 619–37; A. Prosperi, *L'eresia del Libro grande. Storia di Giorgio Siculo e della sua setta* (Milan, 2000), passim; S. Cavazza, 'Una vicenda europea: Vergerio e il caso Spiera, 1548–1549', in *La fede degli italiani. Per Adriano Prosperi*, ed. G. Dall'Olio, A. Malena and P. Scaramella (Pisa, 2011), pp. 41–51.

[46] See L. Felici, 'Fanino, Fanini', in *Dizionario biografico degli italiani* XLIV (1994), 589–92; http://www.treccani.it/enciclopedia/fanino-fanini_(Dizionario-Biografico)/; M. Albertoni, 'L'eredità di Fanino Fanini. Integrazioni e nuovi argomenti su eresia e inquisizione a Faenza', *Rivista di Storia e Letteratura Religiosa* 53 (2017), 269–93. On Nicodemism, see A. Overell, *Italian Reform and English Reformations, c. 1535 – c. 1585* (Aldershot, 2008) – see the index-entry; J. J. Martin, 'Nicodemismo', in *Dizionario storico dell'inquisizione*, II, 1115–16 and now A. Overell, *Nicodemites: Faith and Concealment Between Italy and Tudor England* (Leiden, 2018).

Michaela Valente

alongside various heresiologies and martyrologies. The persecution of the true Church and the appearance of Protestant martyrs were phenomena that contributed to raising Protestant self-consciousness while the Inquisition represented the persecution perpetrated by the Catholic Church.

Already in the early years of the Elizabethan age, John Foxe, mindful of the excesses of Marian persecution, portrayed the martyrs in his work as models of moderation and endurance, in stark contrast to the unbridled fury of the Inquisition which was an illegitimate persecution. In this way Foxe sought to reply to the accusation of religious extremism that Catholic propaganda had raised against the reformers. Later, a significant and potent example of the battle of images was Richard Verstegan's *Theatrum Crudelitatum haereticorum nostri temporis* (*Theatre of Cruelties of Heretics of Our Time*, Antwerp, 1587), recounting the executions of Catholics in England.

The inquisitor of Sicily, Luis Paramo, seems to have been almost completely unaware of the polemics and criticisms levelled against the Holy Office, and in the section of his historical work that is most widely read and quoted he offered up again the view that the Inquisition had its origins in the expulsion from the Garden of Eden. The *De origine et progressu Officii Sanctae Inquisitionis eiusque dignitate et utilitate* (*The Origin and Progress of the Office of Holy Inquisition and its Dignity and Utility*) is a veritable mine of images that both apologists and critics would later freely draw on.[47] By contrast, in his *Catholicæ institutiones...quicquid ad præcavendas et extirpandas hæreses necessarium est* (*Catholic Institutions ... Whatever is necessary to Prevent and Extirpate Heresies*, Valladolid, 1552), Diego de Simancas stressed the classical roots of the inquisition, quoting – and stretching his interpretation of – an excerpt from Cicero's *De Legibus* (*On Laws*). As Kimberly Lynn has pointed out, for Simancas, 'although heresy violated divine law, the post of inquisitor was clearly a human office. For Paramo, inquisitors held a place in the apostolic succession'.[48] Simancas's historical reconstruction then becomes a legitimisation: he stresses the vital necessity of the inquisition as a remedy for a faith that is becoming weaker; he depicts the Inquisition as something that glorifies the Church; and he points to it as an instrument for both religion and secular society in their hostility to heresy. Whether the Inquisition's origins were biblical or classical, the desire to legitimise appears clear and it was also perhaps a response to the many criticisms and protests that arose during the sixteenth century against the inquisition's activities and against the very existence of the tribunal in Spain.[49] Following in their footsteps was Eliseo

---

[47] It was published in Madrid in 1598. See K. Lynn, 'Was Adam the First Heretic? Diego de Simancas, Luis de Paramo, and the Origins of Inquisitorial Practice', *Archiv für Reformationsgeschichte* 97 (2006), 184–210. See M. Rivero Rodríguez, 'Paramo, Luis', in *Dizionario Storico dell'Inquisizione*, III, 1170–1.

[48] Lynn, 'Was Adam the First Heretic?', 199.

[49] See S. Pastore, *Il vangelo e la spada. L'Inquisizione di Castiglia e i suoi critici (1460–1598)*

The Roman Inquisition: between reality and myth

Masini. In his *Sacro Arsenale* Masini describes the inquisitor's role as a celestial task and sets it in an ancient tradition, going back to Christ and his apostles.[50]

The need to go back to the origins, to establish the continuity of the Office and to emphasise its legitimacy crops up in all the procedural manuals and histories of the tribunal.[51] Debate about the Inquisition in the sixteenth century was still characterised by the opposition between the image of the true Church of Christ and that of the Antichrist as well as by reformed propaganda that stigmatised the inquisitors' abuses and depicted them as greedy, ambitious, ignorant and merciless. At the same time a critical front was growing that viewed the Holy Office as intransigent and heedless of the Christian tradition of mercy and persuasion, and here the argument of the abundance of divine mercy was also deployed. Ranged against this and opposing it was the Holy Office's representation of itself, in which one card that as played was the divine legitimacy of the Office, alongside assertion of the Church's mission as teacher. Both were responses to arguments against the coercion of consciences based on interpretations of the parable of the tares and wheat and patristic literature – themes and texts around which debate in Europe would continue to revolve for centuries to come. In the course of the century the image of the Roman tribunal had evolved, and through these changes thinking had emerged that would lead to a rejection of every type of persecution. Simultaneously, though still only in embryonic form, we begin to see the first expressions of a hardening of political and jurisdictional attitudes towards the Inquisition, something which would have considerable later development.

During the seventeenth century we begin to see the publication of works that also looked at the Inquisition from a historical perspective in France and in England. In Europe polemical writing against the Inquisition was strongly characterised by anti-Roman and, anti-Catholic motifs. 'Antichristian principles', 'Hellish plots' and 'bloody and abominable tribunal' were just a few of the recurrent phrases, and it was made into a symbol of persecution, almost as if it had been emptied of its religious character: a 'Monster of Persecution'.[52] Polemical writing against the Inquisition, which had initially been religiously motivated and later engaged in legal arguments, ultimately came to focus on political, ethical and philosophical issues. In spite of this transformation, interest in the Inquisition did not decline. In the second half of the eighteenth century several Inquisitorial tribunals closed, while the Inquisition

---

(Rome, 2003); V. Lavenia, *L'infamia e il perdono. Tributi, pene e confessione nella teologia morale della prima età moderna* (Bologna, 2004); K. Lynn, *Between Court and Confessional: The Politics of Spanish Inquisitors* (New York, 2013).

[50] *Sacro Arsenale overo practica dell'Officio della S. Inquisitione* (*Holy Arsenal, or Practice of the Office of Holy Inquisition*) (Genoa, 1621). Masini was a Dominican from Bologna who became an inquisitor and died in 1627.

[51] Prosperi, *Inquisizione romana*, pp. 70–5.

[52] *La polemica europea sull'Inquisizione*, ed. U. Baldini (Rome, 2015).

itself continued to fascinate during the nineteenth and twentieth centuries. Its central themes were taken up again in the Gothic novel and in the political debate that led to the emancipation of the Catholics in 1829 in England, and contributed to its demonisation during the Risorgimento in Italy.[53]

If we compare the evolution of the Holy Office's image in Europe with the Roman inquisitors' self-representation, we see how the defenders of the faith allowed little space for new arguments: for the most important questions remained those of procedural legitimacy and compatibility with the message of the Gospels. Here we select just two instances of this self-representation. This is how Michele Ghislieri (later Pius V) showed his awareness that his role as inquisitor made him hateful in the eyes of the world.

> Attendiamo pur a servir al Signor Iddio in questo Santo Officio non stimando calunnie perché conviene presupponer chi entra in questo Officio di farsi odioso al mondo; ma tanto quanto il mondo ne ha in odio tanto il Signor Iddio harà risguardo de noi et saremo da lui amati.

> (In this Holy Office, we think only of serving the Lord God, paying no attention to attacks on our character. For anyone who takes on the Office needs to realise that he will make himself hateful to the world. However, the more the world hates us, the more the Lord God will hold us in esteem, and the more we shall be loved by Him).[54]

Some years later, a famous preacher, Francesco Panigarola, following others, claimed for the tribunal the merit of saving Italy from the wars of religion.[55]

Over the years the inquisitors transmitted an image of themselves that answered the needs for legitimacy and the exceptional nature of the office with which they were entrusted. With its contradictory legacy, the Roman Inquisition attracts little sympathy. Its picture is the product of a continuous game of mirrors reflecting legitimising images and distorted representations, and in this picture politically motivated condemnations predominate over ethical concerns. In the sixteenth century there surfaced, especially in the writings of Castellione, Ochino, Curione and Aconcio, the idea that coercion *per se* should be rejected and that consciences should never be forced from whatever side, as may be seen in the case of Michael Servetus. Nevertheless, the polemics against the tribunal had been triggered and their concentration was on abuses and on the demonisation of practices (from torture to inquisitorial secrecy) that could be a cover for any kind of wish for revenge and that had nothing to do with the

---

[53] V. Sciuti Russi, *Inquisizione spagnola e riformismo borbonico fra Sette e Ottocento. Il dibattito europeo sulla soppressione del 'terrible monstre'* (Florence, 2009).

[54] Michele Ghislieri to the Inquisitor of Genova, Girolamo Franchi, 28 May 1556; Prosperi, *Tribunali della coscienza*, p. 148.

[55] F. Panigarola, *Lettioni sopra dogmi ..Nelle quali da lui dette Caluiniche; come si confonda la maggior parte della dottrina di Gio. Calvino, e con che ordine si faccia, doppo la lettera si dimostrerà* (Venice, 1584), fol. 325v.

The Roman Inquisition: between reality and myth

faith. From the other side, efforts to legitimise the tribunal quoted Scripture, the Inquisition was defined as holy and its origins were traced back to Adam and Eve. As a result of this clash an enduring myth was created, one that was used politically by both supporters and detractors alike, with different aims and raising questions that still need to be addressed critically.

Index

Abbey of St Théodard   74, 80, 87–90, 103, 104
Aconcio, Jacopo   332
Ad abolendam   317
Ad nostrum   see under Council of Vienne
Adelaide, beguine   120, 125, 126, 127, 128, 129, 130–1, 132
Adhémar of Chabannes, OSB   245
Agenais   *see under* France
Agrippa, Heinrich Cornelius   327
Aimery of Collet, named by deponent   262
Aimery, Raymond, named by deponent   266–7
Aix   230
Albaret, Laurent   257
Albi   79, 256, 310
Albigensian Crusade   24, 26, 45, 50, 79, 80, 88, 103, 247, 248, 249, 251, 253
Albigensians, *see* 'Cathars'
Albigeois   *see under* France
Aldric, son of Raymond Saix, deponent   260
Aleandro, Girolamo   323
Allix, Peter   31, 32 fig. 0.7, 33 fig. 0.8
Alois, Gianfrancesco   326
Alphonse Jourdain, count of Toulouse   80
Alphonse of Poitiers, count of Toulouse   72, 79, 86, 94, 95, 304
Alzieu of Massabrac, named by deponent   268
Amaury, Arnaud   42
Amiel, Peter, archbishop of Narbonne   270
Anabaptists   246
Andreas of Regensburg   225
Anne of Bohemia   279
Anne, beguine   121
Anti–heretical crusade in Germany   61, 63, 65
Anti–heretical preaching   37, 51
Antichrist   237, 239, 240, 241, 252–3, 329, 331
Antoine de Bourbon   248
Antwerp   251

Apeczko of Ząbkowice (Frankenstein), judge   115
Apocalypticism   240, 246, 252
Aquinas, Thomas, OP   113, 140, 154, 179, 276, 279, 281, 283, 287
Archimbaud, Jacques, OP   276
Arians   250
Ariberti, Peter, notary   92, 99
Aristotle   191, 193
Arles   230
Armenian Christians   15, 135–56
Arnalda, wife of Pons Grimoard   100
Arnaud Faure of Laurac, named by deponent   268
Arnaude de Lamothe de Montauban, deponent   260, 266–7
Arnold of Prat, OP, inquisitor   309, 311
Arnold of Protzan   112
Arnold Roger of Mirepoix, deponent   261
Arnold, John H.   16, 148, 170
Arnold, rector of Świdnica leper house   128
Arnold, William, OP, inquisitor   82, 83, 279, 288, 291, 297, 301
Arsieu, Pierre, OP, inquisitor   305
Articuli Waldensium   159, 161, 223
Athanasius   154
Augsburg   167
Augustine   29, 44, 135, 138, 139, 146
Augustinians   292, 321
Aurieres, Doat scribe   259, 272
Austria   17, 163, 214, 219, 220, 226, 231, 233
Avignon   316
  papal court   15–16, 135–56, 230, 236
Avignonet massacre   266, 279, 281–3, 284, 287, 288, 291, 293

bad fruit   48–9
Baldwin, John   9
Bale, John   10, 26, 242
Barbanson, demon   206
Barber, Malcolm   263
Barcelona   303
Baronio, Cesare (Baronius)   21
Barrabas, demon   205

Index

Barthelemy Cerdani of Pennautier,
deponent 265–6
Basil, Greek patriarch 154
Beggiami, Vito, OP, inquisitor 200
Beguines and Beghards 12, 13, 110–34,
161, 221
Béguins 139
Bellarmine, Robert, SJ, cardinal 252
Benedict of Alignan, OP, bishop of
Marseille 15, 16, 135–56, esp.
148–50
Benoist, Jean, OP 30–1, 277, 287
Berengar, archbishop of Narbonne 47
Bergerac 309
Berlin 218, 223, 233, 235
Bernabé, Boris 76
Bernard of Caux, OP, inquisitor 10,
11, 73, 90, 97–8, 99, 101, 103, 104,
256, 261, 263, 269, 288–9, 291,
293, 299–300, 301 *see also* John of
Saint–Pierre
Bernard of Clairvaux, OCist 44, 243
Bernard of Gaus, inquisition scribe 92,
95
Bernard of La Garrigue, deponent 265
Bernard of Ladinhac, inquisition
scribe 92, 98, 99, 101
Bernard Oth of Niort, enquiry into him
and his family 260, 270
Bersuire, Pierre, OSB 139
Bertrand of Clermont, OP,
inquisitor 309
Beyer, Hartmann, superintendent of
Frankfurt am Main 217
Beza, Theodore 250
Béziers 276
Biller, Peter 27, 28, 159, 161
Bird, Jessalynn 8
Bishops 10, 12, 39–40, 46, 55, 58, 60, 61,
67, 69, 96, 98, 100, 111, 221, 230, 236,
243, 256, 260, 270
Blanche of Castille 247, 248
Blind Anne, beguine 123, 130, 133
Bodecker, Stephen, bishop of
Brandenburg 161
Bogomils 277
Bohemia 158–9, 215, 226, 231, 232–3,
241
Bolko III, duke of Legnica and
Brzeg 113
Bollbuck, Harald 19, 25–6

Bonivarda, Caterina, tried as a
witch 200, 201
Bordeaux 300, 309
Borjos, Doat scribe 259
Borst, Arno 16
Bosc, Pierre 279
Bosnia 10, 67
Bossuet, Jacques-Bénigne, bishop of
Meaux 20, 22 fig. 0.5, 23 fig. 06, 31,
183 fig. 7.1, 239, 253
Bourges *see* Pragmatic Sanction
Brabant 37, 122
Brandenburg 233
Brenz, Johannes 241
Brown, Peter 195
Brun, Pierre, OP, inquisitor 289, 293,
314
Brunus, Conradus 325
Brzeg (Brieg), Dominican convent 113
Bueno, Irene 15–16

Cabanès, Doat scribe 259
Cabrières 241
Caesarius of Heisterbach, OCist 40, 43,
44, 48, 53
Cahors 303
Calvin, John 252
Calvinism 241, 243, 246, 252, 253
Cambiaire, John, named by
deponent 268
Cameron, Euan 241
Canon law 10, 38, 58, 71, 72–109, 103,
138, 142, 143, 156, 221, 269
Canterbury 214
Capel, Bernard, vicar of the count of
Toulouse 89
Capellario, Giovanni, accused of
heresy 66
Capetians 79, 94, 105
Capot, Gratien 256–7
Carafa, Gian Pietro (Pope Paul IV) 28,
322–3, 326
Caravaggio 280
Carcassonne 100, 255, 256, 266, 270,
271, 277, 293, 310, 315
Cardenal, Peire, troubadour 45
Carion, John 240, 246
Carmelites 292
Carnesecchi, Pietro 324
Castellio, Sebastian 332
cat, witchy black 205

336

Index

Catalogus Testium Veritatis *see under*
  Flacius Illyricus, Matthias
Catel, Guillaume   278 fig. 12.1, 279
Cathars   7, 11, 14, 22 fig. 0.5, 26–7, 30,
  31–2, 39, 43, 103, 107 n. 153, 109, 145,
  224, 238–54, 252, 257, 263, 264, 277,
  294
Catherine of Leipzig, beguine   120, 127,
  128, 129, 130
cattle/livestock victims   200, 201, 207
Celestines   158, 179, 223
céphalophores (head carriers)   282
Cerda, Arnald, inquisition scribe   92 n.
  84, 99
Charles IV, emperor, king of
  Bohemia   236
Charles IX, king of France   247, 248
Charles of Anjou   307
Charles V, emperor   155
Charles, cardinal of Lorraine   247
Chassanion, Jean   27, 251–2
chastity   161, 165–6, 168, 215
Chronicle of Ursberg   225
Church Fathers   226, 244–5
Cicero   330
Cistercians   39, 41, 42, 46, 53
Civil law   76
Clement VI, pope   137, 140, 146
Colbert, Jean–Baptiste   27, 255, 273, 294
Cologne   121 (Beguine house), 223
Colombe, OP, prior of Toulouse   281
Comestor, Peter   42, 49
Concordat of Bologna   243
Condom   311, 315
confession, false   197–8
confession   12, 52
confessional historiography   21, 24,
  26–7, 29
confessors' handbooks   53
confraternities   249
Conrad of Marburg   58, 60, 61–4
Conspiracy of Amboise of March   247
Constantine, emperor   211
  donation of 185–6
construction of heresy   6, 14–15, 57–71,
  110–34, 170, 178, 251
consuls   85, 105
Contarini, Gasparo, cardinal   320
copyists   255–72, 292
Council of Basel   225
Council of Béziers 1246   100
Council of Constance   240

Council of Lyon, 1st   148
Council of Narbonne 1227   37
Council of Narbonne 1243/4   223, 230
  n. 73
Council of St–Félix   253
Council of Tarragona 1242   52
Council of Toulouse 1229   37
Council of Trent   155, 156, 284
Council of Vienne   12, 111, 117–18, 121,
  128, 131, 134
  Cum de quibusdam mulieribus   111, 112,
  116, 117, 121, 132
  Ad nostrum   12, 111, 116, 117, 125, 128,
  131, 132
Counter-Reformation   136, 252
Courson, Robert, legate and cardinal   37
Courtet, Guillaume   282, 284, 291
Crespin, Jean   214, 243
Cromwell, Oliver   24
Cum de quibusdam mulieribus   *see under*
  Council of Vienne
Cum dormirent homines   *see under*
  Zwicker
Cunegund of Ziębice, beguine   128, 129
Curione, Celio Secondo   332
Cyril, Greek patriarch   154

d'Abbeville, Jean Halgrin, cardinal   8,
  24, 37–56
Daniel of Tabriz   147
Dauphiné   19
David, Catherine, tried as a
  witch   203–4
de Allo, Ansaldo, accused of heresy   66
de Baulmes, Jordana, tried as a
  witch   203
de Belleforest, François   250–1
de Capdoill, Pons, troubadour   45
de Carcavy, Pierre, Colbert's
  secretary   28, 292, 294
de Castro, Alfonso   155
de Coradis, Bagarotus   75 fig. 3.1, 76,
  102 fig. 3.2a, 105–6, 108
de Ericinio, Adalbert Ranconis   236
de Guinis /de Cumis, Guido   78
de la Posca, Bartholomew   86, 90
de la Roche–Chandieu, Antoine   250
de la Tour, Georges   280
de la Vacquerie, Jean   246
de Lusignan, Hughes   247
de Mariana, Juan, SJ   24
de Mouchy, Antoine   245

337

Index

de Rada, Rodrigo Jimenez 38
de Rechac, Jean–Giffre, OP 275 n. 6
de Saint–Quentin, Huon 45
de Simancas, Diego 330
de Vio Cajetan, cardinal Thomas, OP, master general 211
De vita et actibus 18, 166 *see also* Waldensians
De vita et conversatione 18, 157–77, esp. 173–7 (ed and tr)
de Vitry, Jacques, cardinal, bishop of Acre 37–56
de' Medici, Catherine 247–8, 249
Délicieux, Bernard, OFM 310 n. 73
della Mirandola, Giovanni Pico 212
demons 63, 64, 199–200, 201, 202, 204, 208
des Gallars, Nicolas 245, 250
devil 19, 45, 49, 61, 138, 167, 182, 185, 195, 197, 199, 201, 205, 213, 264, 326
diabolical agents 48, 138
diabolism 19, 195, 196, 206, 207, 208
Dias, wife of Pons of Saint–Germier, deponent 260
Diet of Regensburg 320
Diplovatatius, Thomas 74
Directorium inquisitorum *see under* Eymerich
disease 61, 62, 69, 138, 325
disputation 55–6, 179, 327
disputational literature 53, 148, 180
divination 143
Doat collection 2, 6, 24–25, 27, 100–1, 255–72
Doat, Jean de 27–8, 255–72, 273–94 esp. 292–4
doctrine of grace 211, 213, 237
Dominic of Caleruega 226, 277, 281, 321
Dominicans 8, 10, 13, 28, 47 n. 24, 53, 54, 63, 65, 68, 70, 73, 112, 114, 121, 122 n. 58, 128, 166, 224, 249, 256, 261, 270–1, 273–94
Donation of Constantine 185, 186
Dondaine, Antoine, OP 13
Dostoevsky, Fyodor, *The Brothers Karamazov*, story of the grand inquisitor 317
du Cange, Charles du Fresne 20
du Tillet, Jean 247, 249
du Val, Antoine 246
du Voisin de la Popelinières, Lancelot 251

dualism 139
Durand of Huesca, Waldensian, Poor Catholic 14
Durand, Pierre, OP, inquisitor 261, 288, 298
Durand, Pierre, royal judge 205

Eastern Christianity 15, 135–56
Échard, Jacques, OP 277, 284, 286, 287
Eden 330, 333
Edict of Amboise 248
Edict of Moulins 249
Edict of Nantes, revocation of 31, 239
Edicts of Pacification 247, 248
eels, salted 265
Elijah 186–7
Elizabeth of Strzegom, beguine 124, 128, 129
Elizabeth of Ząbkowice, beguine 129
Else of Meersburg, tried as a witch 202
Engilbert, Bernard, named by deponent 262
England 82 n. 37, 197, 214, 241, 243, 246, 248, 331
Epiphanes, Antiochus 244
Erasmus, Desiderius 245, 246, 319, 327
Erfurt, Beguine house 121
Espaze, Martiale, tried as a witch 201
Estates General 247
Eudes de Sully, bishop of Paris 39, 47
Eymerich, Nicholas, OP, inquisitor 15–16, 20, 135–56 esp. 150–56, 216–18, 222, 329
   Directorium inquisitorum 15, 20 n. 53, 135, 140, 148, 150–56, 216–18, 222

false knowledge/truth 2, 59, 70, 132, 133–4, 214, 236
false prophets 41, 48–9, 54, 244
false witches 64
fama/reputation 40, 55, 205, 207
Fanini, Fanino 329
Ferrier, OP, inquisitor 100–1, 255, 261, 266–9, 288, 297–8, *see also* Raymond, William; Pierre Durand
Ferté, Patrick 276
Feuchter, Jörg 11–12, 27
Filioque 141, 145, 154
Finas, wife of Isarn of Tauriac, deponent 260
Flacius Illyricus, Matthias 19, 21, 25, 30, 210 fig. 9.1, 211–37, 241, 242

Index

Catalogus Testium Veritatis 25, 26, 214, 220, 226, 227 fig. 9.3, 24
Consultation on Writing Accurate Church History 215–6
flagellants 222, 230
Flanders 37, 68, 122
Foix 260
Folcaut, Peter Raymond, judge, recipient of penance for heresy 86, 90
Fontana, Guglielmo, accused of heresy 66
Foulques of Saint–Georges, OP, inquisitor 290–1, 310
Foulques, Gui (Pope Clement IV) 223
Fournier, Jacques, OCist, bishop of Pamiers, inquisitor 16
Fourth Lateran Council 9, 15, 37, 47, 93, 148
Foxe, John 26, 214, 242, 250, 330
Foxes 52, 54–5
France 10, 26, 197, 215, 231, 243, 312, 313, 331
  Agenais 79, 97, 98, 99, 104
  Albigeois 11, 78–80, 85–6, 105, 292
  Languedoc 2, 12, 14, 94, 108, 252, 255
  Lauragais 10, 73, 91, 101, 255–72, 293
  Northern France 37, 68, 214
  Quercy 11, 79, 80, 82, 83, 86, 97, 98, 99, 100, 101, 104, 288
  Southern France 14, 27–8, 37, 72–109, 201, 203–6, 226, 230, 241, 246, 248, 270–94, 295–316
Francis II, king of France 247
Francis of Arquata 221–2
Francis of Assisi 226
Francis of Toulouse, OP, imaginary inquisitor 282
Franciscans 18, 53, 119, 128, 137, 143, 155, 159, 203–5, 279, 281
Franco–Habsburg War 247
François, Guy 280
François, second Duke of Guise 247, 249
Frank, consul of Montauban, inquisition notary 87, 89, 99, 101, 104
Frankfurt 215
Fraticelli 245
Frederick II, emperor 61, 65, 231
French Reformed Church 250, 251
French Revolution 253
French Wars of Religion 238–54, 325
Fresapa, Peter, notary 92, 94–5
frescoes 29, 280–8, 327

Fulk of Marseilles, bishop of Toulouse 8, 9, 41, 45, 50, 53
Fulk of Neuilly 55

Galand, John, OP, inquisitor 256, 265, 307
Gallus of Jindřichův Hradec, OP, inquisitor 166
Gałuska, Tomasz 110 n. 1, 118
Gappit, Perrissone, tried for witchcraft 199
García, Diego 47
Garcias, Peter 100, 258
Garzoni, Tommaso 329
Gâtine, Etienne, OP, inquisitor 302
Gay, Jean 248, 249
Geneva Bible 252
Geneva 243
Geoffroi d'Ablis, OP, inquisitor 313
George of Poděbrad, king of Bohemia 115
Georgian Christians 15, 135–56
Germain, Alexandre 270–1
Germany 10, 12, 14, 17, 53, 60, 61–5, 114, 116, 120, 133, 157, 158–9, 163, 164, 197, 211, 212, 213, 215, 218, 219, 223, 225, 226
  Rhineland 63, 120, 122, 163, 215
Gerson, Jean 224
Gertrude of Mościsko, beguine 129
Gertrude of Oleśnica, beguine 123
Gertrude of Świdnica, beguine 123, 130, 132, 133–4
Geza, beguine 123
Ghislieri, Michele (Pope Pius V) 332
Giovanni d'Andrea 74
Giulio da Milano 329
Gnesio–Lutherans 246
Gonzaga, Giulia 324
Goulard, Simon 240, 243, 246, 253
Gouron, André 77
Gratian 138, 142, 143, 144, 226
Graverol, François 30–1, 33 fig. 0.8, 277
Greece 137
Gregorio da Romania, papal chaplain 65–6
Gregory IX, pope front cover, 8, 9, 10, 29, 38, 43, 46, 47, 50, 53, 57–71
  Vox in Rama 61–3
Gregory VII, pope 240
Gretser, Jakob, SJ 23 fig. 0.6, 24, 25, 183 fig. 7.1, 184 fig. 7.2, 224–5

Index

Grimani, Giovanni, patriarch of
  Aquileia 326
Grimoard, Pons, seneschal of
  Quercy 83, 100, 101, 104, 293
Grundmann, Herbert 12, 116, 117
Grünsleder, Ulrich 225
Gudulchi, John 221–2
Gui, Bernard, OP, inquisitor, bishop of
  Tuy, bishop of Lodève 1, 2, 5 fig.
  0.3, 18, 20, 30, 164, 223, 234, 274,
  276 n. 10, 278 fig. 12.1, 286, 289, 290,
  293–4, 295–316
  Practica inquisitionis 223, 234, 312
Gui, Pierre, OP, inquisitor 315
Guibert of Nogent, OSB, abbot of
  Nogent 245
Guilabert of Castres, mentioned by
  deponent 262
Guilabert of Saint-Michel,
  deponent 258
Guillem, bishop of Vic 38, 42

Hagen, Mattheus 221, 235
Haupt, Herman 163
Hedwig of Wrocław, beguine 114, 125,
  127, 128, 129, 130–1
Heilwig of Prague, beguine 120, 123
Heinrich-Julius, duke of
  Braunschweig–Wolfenbüttel 220
Henry II, king of France 247, 319
Henry IV, emperor 240
Henry of Wierzbna, bishop of
  Wrocław 112, 128
Henry VII, emperor 61
Henry, third Duke of Guise 249
heresiography 135–56
Heresy of the Free Spirit 12, 13, 110–34
heresy
  definitions 65, 81 and nn. 33–4,
  135–56 esp. 141–5, 192, 193
  doctrine 12, 14, 26, 31, 51–2,
  110,116–17, 128, 131–2, 134–6,
  138–9, 157, 162, 165–6, 169, 174–5,
  176–7,178, 185–7, 190–2, 219, 226,
  234, 241–2, 245, 264
  heretical learning/ignorance 149,
  167–8, 170, 190, 192
  heretical lifestyle/mores 116, 130,
  133, 163, 165–7, 174–5, 239, 263
  heretical sacraments 38–9, 165–7, 169,
  176–7, 234, 244, 263, 265, 266, 267–9,
  271–2

see also Arians, Bogomils, Cathars,
  Luciferans, Manicheans, Montanists,
  Nestorians, Pelagians, Pseudo–
  Apostles, Waldensians
Hildesheim 60, 61
Holinka, Rudolph 163
Honorius III, pope 38, 40, 41, 43, 46,
  281
Hotman, François 247
Hugh of Boniol, OP, inquisitor 302–4,
  306
Hugh, consul of Montauban 87
Hughes Amiel of Castelnaudary, OP,
  inquisitor 305–6
Huguenots 275
Humbert of Romans, OP, master
  general 37–56
Hungary 17, 67, 233
Hus, Jan 155, 212, 232, 237, 240
Hussites 22 fig. 0.5, 212, 221, 224, 233,
  235, 237, 263
Huter, Elizabeth, tried for heresy 168
Huter, Konrad, tried for heresy 168
Hyacinthe of Poland, OP 280

idolatry 143
Iliana, beguine 128, 129
Inghirami, Tommaso 29
Ingolstadt 24
Innocent III, pope 40, 41, 43, 46, 80
Innocent VII, pope 221–2
Inquisition
  administration 69, 90, 91–4, 9, 98,
  99, 101, 104, 113, 114, 124, 233 n. 93,
  245, 260
  Dominican 1, 13, 15, 41, 91, 94, 104,
  110–34, 111, 131, 135, 166, 200, 202,
  242, 255–72, 274, 295–316 *see also*
  Bernard of Caux, Ferrier, John of
  Saint–Pierre, Toulouse 609
  episcopal 37, 38, 111, 137
  Franciscan 111, 137, 203–5, 274, 282
  n. 31
  handbooks 13 and n. 35, 25, 39, 71,
  158, 160, 211–37 esp. 220–5, 327, 328
  fig. 13.1, 13.1, 329
  heretical texts 158, 164, 167, 169, 170
  informant 274
  inquisition records 12, 13, 18–19, 114,
  129, 130, 131, 132, 133, 198, 211–37
  esp. 220–5, 255–72, 273–316
  inquisition, Roman 29, 154, 317–33

Index

inquisition, Spanish 38, 154, 320, 330
interrogation 7, 114, 124, 128–34, 159, 198, 203, 204, 206, 207, 219, 271
myth 28, 317–33
period of grace 83
sentences/penances 90, 92, 105, 107 n. 153, 130
torture 198, 199, 203, 205, 207, 332
Interim of Augsburg 246
Interrogatio Iohannis 277
Investiture Contest 240
Isarn of Tauriac, deponent and named by deponent 260, 263
Isidore of Seville, bishop of Seville 139, 146
Italy 10, 14, 65, 77, 103, 137, 138, 197, 200, 202, 215, 226, 226, 231, 241, 245, 318, 322, 325, 332
iurisperiti 90, 230 and n. 73

Jacobites 15, 135–56
Jaime I, king of Aragon 38
Jeanne, countess of Toulouse 304
Jerome 143
Jerusalem 187, 212, 244
Jesuits 21, 224, 252, 276, 292, 324
Jews 15, 105, 135, 139, 148, 182, 185, 199, 244
Joachim of Fiore, OCist 139
Johann Friedrich, elector Saxony 212
John of La Rochelle, OFM 40
John of Saint–Gaudens, scribe 92 n. 84
John of Saint–Pierre, of Bordeaux, OP, inquisitor 289
John of Saint–Pierre, OP, inquisitor 10, 11, 73, 90, 95 n. 102, 97–8, 99, 101, 103, 104, 256, 261, 263, 269, 288–9, 293, 299–300, *see also* Bernard of Caux
John of Schwenkenfeld 13, 110–34
History of the killing of brother John of Schwenkenfeld 114
John the Baptist 43, 44
John XXII, pope 111, 137, 140, 315
Jonquier, Antoine, witch's accomplice 207
Jordan, son of Raymond of Péreille, deponent 258
Julien, Paulette, tried as a witch 206, 207
Julius II, pope 29
Jurieu, Pierre 31, 33 fig. 0.8

Kantzow, Thomas 232
Kerkow 223
Kieckhefer, Richard 13, 19
Koudelka, Vladimír, OP 116
Kraków 115
Kras, Paweł 13

La Charité–sur–Loire 10
laity 48, 56
Landi, Guglielmo 66
Langton, Stephen, archbishop of Canterbury 43, 46, 47, 49
Languedoc *see under* France
Lateran *see* Third and Fourth councils
Lauragais *see under* France
Lavaur 301
Lavenia, Vicenzo 155
le Bougre, Robert, OP, inquisitor 10, 53, 58, 67–70, 242
Lecoy de la Marche, Albert 41
Leff, Gordon 13, 117
legates 40, 42, 43, 260
Leipzig 121 (Beguine house), 219, 240
lepers 51–2, 128, 187, 199
Lerner, Robert 13, 19, 117, 126
letters 9, 10, 13, 41, 57–71, 219
Levant 15, 139
Liber electorum 17 see also Waldensians
Liber extra 29
Liber fugitivus 72–109, esp. 74–7, 105–9 *see also* Nepos; de Coradis
liberty 317
Librarius, Henricus, deponent 166
Limborch, Philip van 1–2, 3 fig. 0.1, 4 fig. 0.2, 5 fig. 0.3, 20
Limoges 300, 308, 315
Livonia 232
local agents 10, 85, 57–71, 105, 197
Locati, Umberto, OP 325–6
Locke, John 1–2, 3 fig. 0.1, 4 fig. 0.2, 5 fig. 0.3, 188
Lodève 312, 314
Lollards 243
Lombard, Peter, bishop of Paris 46, 226
Lombardy 14, 15, 226, 231
Lotter, Melchior 219
Louis IX, king of France 79, 247
Louis of Poitiers, viceroy 305
Louis, prince of Condé 247, 248
Lubéron 241
Lubusz (Lebus) 110–34
Lucas, bishop of Tuy 9, 24, 38, 50

341

Index

Luciferans   10, 63
Lucius III, pope, *Ad abolendam*   317
Lucius III, pope   317
Ludgard of Leipzig, beguine   121, 128, 129
Lull, Ramon   150
Luther, Martin, OSA   211, 212, 226, 235, 236, 237, 240, 253 *see also* Lutheranism
Lutheranism   211–12, 216, 226, 234, 236–7, 237, 240–3, 246, 323, 327 *see also* Luther, Martin
Lynn, Kimberley   330

Madrid   320
Magdeburg Centuries   241
Magdeburg   213
Mainz   60, 61
Majorca   137
Malvesie   306
Manicheans   43, 107, 145, 243–6, 250, 251–3, 263
Manselli, Raoul   18
Margaret of Środa Śląska, beguine   129
Margaret the Embroideress, beguine   120, 126, 128, 129, 131, 132
Margareta, niece of Konrad Huter   168
Marie d'Oignies, beguine   50
Maronites   146
Maroux, Jean   224
Marsilius of Padua   16, 137, 138
Martin the demon   200
Martinus of Prague, inquisitor   159, 160, 163, 164, 168, 170
Masini, Eliseo   330–1
Massari, Girolamo   327
   spoof inquisitors' handbook   327, 328 fig. 13.1
Mazzolini, Silvestro (also Prierate)   327
Meijers, Edward M.   77
Melancthon, Philip   212, 213, 235, 237, 240, 241
mendicants   39, 40, 42, 46, 53, 58, 69, 111, 123, 128, 240, 252, 255–72, 274
Mérindol   241
Michaëlis, Sébastien, OP, prior provincial of Occitanie   275, 276–7, 282
Michelet, Jules   253
Moneta of Cremona, OP   15, 17, 180
moniales capuciatae   118–21 *see also* Beguines
Monophysitism   145

Montagnes, Bernard, OP   287
Montanists   245
Montauban   11, 80–7, 88, 248, 250, 251, 308
Montpellier   270, 307, 308, 316
Moritz of Saxony, elector   212
Morlana, Arnaud, named by deponent   265
Morland, Samuel   24
Moses   44
Motossa, Giovanna, tried as a witch   200, 201
Müntzer, Thomas   246
Murano, Giovanna   72
Muslims   43, 135, 148
Muzio, Girolamo   327

Na Bareges, deponent   262
Nanker, bishop of Kraków, bishop of Wrocław   112, 114–15, 128
Nantes   *see* Edict
Narbonne   100, 226, 230, 270, 309
Navagero, Bernardo, Venetian ambassador   322
Nazianzus, Gregory of   154
necromancy   199
Nepos of Montauban   11, 12, 72–109
Nestorians   146, 148
Nice   305
Nicholas *de Pencwynsdorph*, notary   113, 114–15, 131, 132
Nickson, M. A. E.   1
Nicodemism   329
notaries   92, 95, 113, 114, 130, 131, 168, 255–72, 274 *see also* Inquisition: administration
Nubian Christians   135–56
Nuremburg   220
Nysa (Neisse)   110

Ochino, Bernardino   332
Odelind of Pyrzyce   121
Odo of Châteauroux, cardinal   40, 43, 53
Odo of Cheriton   43
Olbrechts–Tyteca, Lucie   191
Olivi, Peter of John, OFM   137, 139
Order of the Brothers of the Common Life   217
Orléans   248
Otho de Baretges   100, 101
Otto, bishop of Würzburg   222
Oybin, Celestine convent   160

342

Index

paganism 143, 182, 185
Panigarola, Francesco 332
Paolino of Venice, OFM 139
Papal primacy 138, 143–4, 146
Paramo, Luis, inquisitor 330
Paris, Matthew, OSB 10, 242
Paris 214, 244, 316
parish priests 12, 39, 42, 50, 57–71, 96, 123, 191, 203
Parlements 248, 248, 249, 279
Parmeggiani, Riccardo 11
Passau Anonymous 24, 183 fig. 7.1, 233
  see also Pseudo–Reinerius
Passau 219, 224
Paul II, pope 115
Paul III, pope 321
Paul, apostle 48
Peace of Paris 1229 79, 82 n. 38
Peirona of Claustre, deponent 262
Peirona, sister of Arnaude de Lamothe 267
Pelagians 145
Pelagius, Alvarus, OFM, papal penitentiary, bishop of Coron, bishop of Sylves 15, 16, 135–56, esp. 135–48
Pelhisson, William, OP, assistant inquisitor 83
Pelliciera, Guillelma, deponent 291
Peña, Francisco 153 fig. 5.3, 154–5, 329
Penent, Jean 280
Percin, Jean-Jacques, OP 30, 277, 279–80, 281, 283, 284–90, 291, 295–316
Peregrin, Conrad, OP 308
Perelman, Chaïm 191
Périgueux 301, 315
Perpignan 303, 309
Perrin, Jean–Paul 252
persuasion 178–94
Perugia 311
Peter IV, king of Aragon 150
Peter of Albalat, archbishop of Tarragona 9, 38, 39, 47, 52
Peter of Collemieu, papal legate, cardinal 230
Peter of Laurac, named by deponent 258
Peter of les Vaux-de-Cernay, OCist 26, 249, 251, 263
Peter of Montbiza, inquisition scribe 92

Peter of Mulceone, OP, inquisitor 308
Peter of Pillichsdorf 183 fig. 7.1, 184 fig. 7.2
Peter of Pulkau 224
Peter of Saint–Michel, deponent 268
Peter the Chanter 46, 49
Peter the Venerable, OSB 180
Peters, Edward 28
Peucer, Gaspard 240
Philiberti, John, Waldensian follower 164
Philip the Chancellor 40, 43, 46, 53, 54, 55
Philip VI, king of France 304, 311
Philippists 246
Piccolomini, Aeneas Silvius (Pope Pius II) 115, 225
Piedmont 19, 241
Pierre d'Aulnay, OP, inquisitor 202
pirates 51
Pius II, pope *see* Piccolomini
Poland 110–34, 215, 231 n. 77, 233, 280
Pole, Reginald, cardinal, archbishop of Canterbury 319, 322
polemic 7, 13, 135–56, 135, 161, 167, 170, 180, 239, 248–9, 317, 320, 331–2
Polkowski, Ignacy 115
Polonus, Peregrinus, inquisitor 113
Pomerania 232–3
Pons of Parnac, OP, inquisitor 256, 303, 306
Pons of Saint-Gilles, OP, inquisitor, prior of Toulouse 281
Poor of Lyon *see* Waldensians
popular belief/culture 19, 195–208
Portugal 137
poverty, false 51, 160, 169, 235 n. 104
poverty/asceticism/apostolicity 39, 43, 50, 53, 56, 117 n. 34, 120, 123–5, 133, 157, 165, 186, 243, 244
Poznański, Adam 17–18, 110 n. 1, 118
Practica inquisitionis see under Gui, Bernard
Pradoune, Frénouze, tried and burned as a witch 206
Pragmatic Sanction of Bourges 243
Prague 114, 115 n. 19, 164, 222, 235, 236
preachers' handbooks 53
prison 2, 205
Probi homines 85, 86
Processus Petri see under Zwicker
Protestants 16, 19, 24, 30, 263, 270, 330

343

Index

Pseudo-Apostles 139, 14
Pseudo-Reinerius 1 n. 1, , 183 fig. 7.1,
 224, 233 *see also* Passau Anonymous
purgatory 145, 170, 215

Quantin, Jean–Louis 20–1 n. 56
Quercy *see under* France
Quicquat, Catherine, tried as a
 witch 202–3

Raban, bishop of Speyer 222
Rabaud, Camille 239, 253
Rabus, Ludwig 214
Racaut, Luc 8, 10, 26–7
Ranquet, Gabriel, OP, prior of
 Toulouse 280
Ranulph of Plassac, OP, inquisitor 256
Raphael Sanzio 29
Ratgeb, Heinrich 225
Raymond Gros of Toulouse, converted
 heretic, informer 274–5
Raymond of Falgar, OP, bishop of
 Toulouse 281
Raymond of Peñafort, OP, master
 general 9, 29, 38, 39, 42, 43, 47, 50,
 52, 53
Raymond of Péreille, deponent 258
Raymond VI, count of Toulouse 104
Raymond VII, count of Toulouse 88, 98
 n. 113, 282, 293, 304
Raymond, William, OP, inquisitor 288,
 298
reform 9, 37, 39, 44, 45–7
Reformation 211, 212, 214, 236, 243, 245,
 248, 251–2
Refutatio errorum see under Zwicker
Regensburg 168, 215
Reginald of Chartres, OP, inquisitor 95
 n. 102, 289, 300
Réginald, Antonin, OP 28, 273–94 esp.
 283–94, 295–316
Rehr, Jean–Paul 10, 96
Reni, Guido 280
reptiles, poisonous 69
Reuchlin, Johannes 212
Rey, Jean Dominique, OP, prior of
 Toulouse 280, 316
Rhineland *see under* Germany
Ricart, Doat scribe 259
Richer of Senones, OSB 12
Risorgimento 332
Robert of Sorbonne 40

Rodez 310
Rodrigo, archbishop of Toledo 47
Roger of Latour of Laurac, named by
 deponent 268
Roland of Cremona, OP, inquisitor 65
Rome, papacy 29, 41, 141, 243, 319
Rome 29, 38, 39, 305, 323
Romea, Gianni 324
Rostock 231–2
Rotier, Esprit, OP, inquisitor 249
Rouergue 79
Rucherath, Johannes 225
rue St Jacques, affair of 26, 244, 245,
 247, 250, 251
Rutze, Nikolaus 231, –2

Sacraments 12, 26, 111, 117, 128, 142,
 146, 149, 187, 190, 211, 216, 234, 237
Sala, Alessandro 9–10
Saracens 146, 154
Sarraceni, Carlo 280
satire 29, 327–8
Saxony 213, 233
Schammonis, Henry 128
Schiesserin, Else, hellraiser 201, 202
schismatics 143, 144, 146
Schmalkaldic war 212
Schmidt, Charles 161, 163, 173
Schoenvelt, Henry, inquisitor 222, 230
Schopenhauer, Artur 188
Schwenkenfeld 112
Scotland 303
Scoto, Thomas 138
secret gatherings 232, 245, 251 *see also*
 sexual depravity
secular arm 179, 206, 223
Sellan, Peter, OP, inquisitor 81–2, 86, 97
 n. 111, 104, 281, 283, 288, 293, 297
Seripando, Girolamo, OSA, General of
 the Augustinians 320–1, 324
sermons/preaching 37–56
Servetus, Michael 246, 332
sexual depravity 43, 117, 168, 233 n. 89,
 243, 245, 246, 251
Sicilian Vespers 253
Sicily 330
Silesia 158–9
Simon V de Montfort 8, 41, 45, 80, 249
Sinhon, Monnet, tried as a
 witch 203–4
Sneddon, Shelagh 27–8, 173, 295
Sorbin, Arnaud 249, 251

Index

sorcery 19, 195, 201, 203, 204
Spain 8, 14, 37–56, 137, 138, 150, 155
Speyer 235
Spiera, Francesco 329
St Bartholomew's Day Massacre 250, 253
St Sernin, Toulouse 91, 104
Stapleton, Thomas 242
Stedinger 62–4
Stephen of Bourbon, OP 41, 53
Stephen of St–Thibéry, OFM, inquisitor 288
Stephen Roger of Roumens, deponent 258
stereotype 7, 10, 17, 18–19, 54, 55, 64, 71, 178, 192, 237
Steyr 220
Stieffel, Michael 219
Strasbourg 117
Struss, Kuningund Snr, deponent 166–7
Styria 220
summae auctoritatum 14
Swarczmann, Peter, OFM, lector 128
Świdnica 13, 110–134
    Dominican convent of Holy Cross 112
Switzerland 197, 199, 202, 203, 233, 243
Sylvester I, pope 182
Synod of La Rochelle 251
Szczecin (Stettin) 17, 25, 110–34, 168, 223
Szymański, Jarosław 118

Targueira, Bernarda, deponent 262
Tartars 154
taxation 87
Templars 89
Terreni, Guido, OCarm, bishop of Mallorca, bishop of Elna, prior general 15, 16, 135–56, esp. 135–48
Tertullian 29, 245
theology 16, 112, 140, 143, 148, 156, 190, 195, 212–3, 231, 246, 276, 283
Third Lateran Council 93
Tholosan, Claude 206
Thomas of Cantimpré, OP 53
Thuringia 223, 230, 233
Toti, Daniel 30 n. 30
Totting, Heinrich 235
Toulmin, Stephen 191
Toulouse MS 609 10 n. 22, 90, 91, 92,

93, 95, 96, 97 n. 111, 98, 100, 101, 288, 300 n.16
Toulouse 1, 30, 78, 79, 80, 86, 97, 98, 101, 104, 248, 249, 255–72, 273–94, 295, 305, 308
Tours 248
Trencavel, Raymond–Roger, viscount of Béziers and Albi 79
Tugwell, Simon, OP 287
Turks 154
Turnau, Peter, Hussite 235
Tuy 312

Udenheim 235
Udilind's Daughters 121–2 *see also* Beguines
Ulanowski, Bolesław 115, 117
universal compilations 16, 139
university learning 46, 96, 72–109, 86, 90, 103, 112, 129, 130–1, 134, 137, 179, 194, 195–208, 231, 235
University of Bologna 86, 103, 137
University of Montpellier 78, 103, 106 n. 136
University of Padua 329
University of Paris 8, 9, 16, 37, 38, 39, 41, 42, 46, 49–50, 53–6, 137
University of Prague 235
University of Rostock 231–2
University of Toulouse 37, 86, 276, 283, 287
University of Vienna 236
University of Wittenberg 212
Ussher, James, archbishop of Armagh 24
Uzès 302

Valdes 226, 233 n. 93
Valente, Michaela 28–9
Välimäki, Reima 17, 18, 26
Valverde, Vincent 282
van Haemstede, Adrian Cornelis 214
Velsus, Justus 327
Vener, Job 219
Venice 215
Vergerio, Pier Paolo, bishop of Capodistria 324
Verstegan, Richard 330
viaticum/ritual murder 245, 251
Vienna 214, 216, 219, 233
Vienne 310
Vignier, Nicolas 252

345

Index

Vigouroux, Jean, OP, inquisitor   307
Villemur   267
Virgin Mary   44, 127, 129, 182, 189, 264
Vision of Isaiah   30
Voigt, Jörg   118
von Amsdorf, Nicolaus   212
von der Hardt, Hermann   220
von Drändorf, Johann, Hussite   235
von Kremsier, Milič   235
von Langenstein, Heinrich   236
von Lübeck, Johann   232
von Lüneberg, Marie   327
von Nidbruck, Caspar   214, 216–19
von Wesel, Johann   212
Vox in Rama   see under Gregory IX

Wakefield, Walter L.   14, 91
Waldensians   11, 14, 15, 17–18, 19–20, 22
   fig. 0.5, 23 fig. 0.6, 25–6, 80, 103, 111,
   139, 157–77, 179, 190, 215, 216–7, 219,
   224, 225, 228 fig. 9.4, 231, 232, 233–4,
   237, 240–1, 242, 250, 252–3, 263, 277
Waldner, Wolfgang   220
Werner, Ernst   159, 163
Wesenbec, Peter   251
William Faure of Pechermier,
   deponent   260, 262
William Mate of Carcassonne, named by
   deponent   265
William of Auvergne, bishop of
   Paris   15
William of Malavielle, OFM,
   inquisitor   203, 206
William of Marnhac, deponent   31, 33
   fig. 0.8

William of Montreveil, OP,
   inquisitor   293, 301–2
William of Morières, OP, inquisitor   310
   n. 73, 311
William of Ockham, OFM   16, 137
William of Puylaurens, rector of
   Puylarens   263, 278 fig. 12.1
Wismar   232
witchcraft   195–208
Witches' Sabbath   195, 196, 199, 201,
   203, 207
witnesses   12, 72–109, 110
Wittenberg   212, 237
wolves   41, 42, 45, 48–50, 53–5, 192, 193,
   202
Worms   235
Wouters, Cornelius   217
Wrocław (Breslau)   110, 111, 115, 128
Wyclif, John   155
Wycliffites   22 fig. 0.5, 221
Wyrozumski, Jerzy   116

York, University of   2

Zerner, Monique   238
Zgorzelec (Görlitz), Franciscans   159
Zwicker, Peter, OCelest, Provincial of
   the Celestines in Germany   17–18,
   20, 24, 25, 157–77, 178–94, 219, 223,
   224, 234
   Cum dormirent homines   17, 158,
   178–94
   Processus Petri   158, 160, 165
   Refutatio errorum   17, 163
   see De vita et conversatione
Zwinglians   246

HERESY AND INQUISITION IN THE MIDDLE AGES

I   *Heresy and Heretics in the Thirteenth Century: The Textual Representations,* L. J. Sackville (2011)

II   *Heresy, Crusade and Inquisition in Medieval Quercy,* Claire Taylor (2011)

III   *Heresy, Inquisition and Life Cycle in Medieval Languedoc,* Chris Sparks (2014)

IV   *Cathars in Question,* ed. Antonio Sennis (2016)

V   *Late Medieval Heresy: New Perspectives, Studies in Honor of Robert E. Lerner,* ed. Michael D. Bailey and Sean L. Field (2018)

VI   *Heresy in Late Medieval Germany: The Inquisitor Petrus Zwicker and the Waldensians,* Reima Välimäki (2019)

VII   *Inquisition in the Fourteenth Century: The Manuals of Bernard Gui and Nicholas Eymerich,* Derek Hill (2019)

VIII   *Inquisition and its Organisation in Italy, 1250–1350,* Jill Moore (2019)

IX   *Herbert Grundmann (1902–1970): Essays on Heresy, Inquisition, and Literacy,* ed. Jennifer Kolpacoff Deane, trans. Simon Rowan (2019)

X   *Inquisition and Knowledge, 1200–1700,* ed. Peter Biller and L J Sackville (2022)

XI   *The Beguines of Medieval Świdnica: The Interrogation of the "Daughters of Odelindis" in 1332,* Tomasz Gałuszka and Paweł Kras (2023)

Details of other York Medieval Press volumes are available from Boydell & Brewer Ltd.

Printed in the United States
by Baker & Taylor Publisher Services